Advanced Digital Preservation

David Giaretta

Advanced Digital Preservation

Springer

David Giaretta
STFC and Alliance for Permanent Access
Yetminster, Dorset
United Kingdom
david@giaretta.org

Further Project Information and Open Source Software under:
http://www.casparpreserves.eu
http://developers.casparpreserves.eu
http://www.alliancepermanentaccess.org

ISBN 978-3-642-16808-6 e-ISBN 978-3-642-16809-3
DOI 10.1007/978-3-642-16809-3
Springer Heidelberg Dordrecht London New York

Library of Congress Control Number: 2011921005

ACM Codes H.3, K.4, K.6

Cover design: deblik, Berlin

Printed on acid-free paper

Springer is part of Springer Science+Business Media (www.springer.com)

"How to preserve all kinds of digital objects"

and

"OAIS: what it means and how to use it"

and

"The CASPAR book"

and

"Everything you wanted to know about digital preservation but were afraid to ask"

Preface

There has been a growing recognition of the need to address the fragility of the digital information that is deluging all aspects of our lives, whether in business, scientific, administrative, imaginative or cultural activities.

Society's growing dependence on the digital for its smooth operation as it becomes an information society provides the real urgency for addressing this issue. This case has been made very well in the large number of books and articles already published on the topic of digital preservation and therefore this case will not be expanded upon in this book.

Since there are many books about digital preservation why is there a need for yet one more?

At the time of writing the books and articles on digital preservation, for the most part, focus on consideration of documents, images and web pages; things which are normally just displayed by software for a human to view or listen to (or perhaps smell, taste or touch). We will refer to these as things which are *rendered*.

Yet there are clearly many more types of digital objects on which our lives depend and which may need to be preserved, such as databases, scientific data and software itself. These are things which are not simply rendered – they are processed and used in many different ways.

It should become clear to the reader that the tools and techniques used for preserving rendered objects are inadequate for all these other types of digital objects and we need to set our sights higher and wider. This book provides the concepts, techniques and tools which are needed.

Of course it is easy to make claims about digital preservation techniques – and there are many such claims! Therefore it is important that evidence is provided to support any such claims, which we do for our claims by using accelerated lifetime scenarios about the important changes which will challenge us. We use as examples a variety of digital objects from many sources and show tools and techniques by which they may be preserved.

1 Who Should Read This Book and Why?

This book is aimed at those who have problems in preserving digitally encoded information that they need to solve, especially where it goes beyond simply preserving rendered objects. The PARSE.Insight survey [1] suggests that while all researchers have documents and images, about half have non-rendered digital holdings such as raw data, scientific/statistical data, databases and software, therefore this book should be of wide interest.

It should also be essential reading for those who wish to audit their own archives, perhaps in advance of an independent audit, about how well they are doing in the preservation of the digitally encoded information which has been entrusted to them.

Researchers in digital preservation theory and developers of tools and techniques should also find valuable information here. Developers in the area of e-Science (also known as Cyberinfrastructure) may also gain a number of useful insights.

Some of the material in this book may be found to be too technical by some readers. For those readers we suggest that they skim over such material in order to at least be aware of the issues. This will allow them to advise more technical implementers who will certainly need such details.

To further help readers, the book is supported by other resources, including many hours of videos and presentations from the CASPAR project [2], which provides ❍ an elevator pitch for digital preservation, ❍ examples of digital preservation from several repositories, ❍ detailed lectures by the contributors to this book on many of the issues described here and ❍ lectures about, and video captures of, many of the software components. The open source software and further documentation is also available.

2 Structure of This Book

Part I of the book provides the concepts and theoretical basis that are needed, introducing, as examples along the way, digital objects from many sources. Since much of this book is based on the work of the CASPAR project, the examples will be derived from many disciplines including science, cultural heritage and contemporary performing arts.

The approach we take throughout is one of asking the questions which we believe a reasonably intelligent person may ask, and then providing answers to them. Sometimes, when there are some subtle but important points, we guide the reader towards the appropriate questions. As noted above, this will lead us into a number of technical issues which will not be to the taste of all readers but all topics are necessary for at least some readers.

Part II of the book shows practical examples of preserving a variety of specific objects and gives details of a range of tools and techniques. One obvious question, which an intelligent (but sceptical) reader may ask is "these tools and techniques may do something but why should I believe that they help to preserve things?"

After all, the only real way would be to live a long time and check the supposedly preserved objects in the future. However that is not very practical, and perhaps more importantly it does not help one to decide now whether to follow the ways proposed in this book. Choosing the wrong way could have a disastrous effect on what one intends to leave for future generations!

We provide what we believe is strong evidence that what is proposed **does** actually work for a wide variety of digital objects from many disciplines, through a number of accelerated lifetime scenarios, validated by members of the appropriate communities.

Part III provides answers to the questions about how to ensure that resources devoted to preserve digital objects are not wasted, showing a number of ways in which effort can be shared. In addition this part provides guidance on how to evaluate whether a particular repository (perhaps your own) is doing a good job, and where it might be improved. This part also describes the thinking behind the work carried out to produce the ISO standards on which the international audit and certification process can be based.

Throughout the book we indicate points where experience shows there is a danger of misunderstanding by the symbol

3 Preservation and Curation

This book is about digital preservation but there is another term which is being used, namely digital curation. The UK Digital Curation Centre [3] used to define this in the following way: "*Digital curation is maintaining and adding value to a trusted body of digital information for current and future use; specifically, we mean the active management and appraisal of data over the life-cycle of scholarly and scientific materials*". This definition has been changed more recently to *"Digital curation involves maintaining, preserving and adding value to digital research data throughout its lifecycle"*. Sometimes the phrase "digital curation and preservation" is also used.

We prefer the term preservation in this book since we do not wish to restrict our consideration to "scholarly and scientific materials" nor "research data", because we wish to ensure we can apply our techniques to all kinds of digital objects including, for example, commercial and legal material. Nor do we wish to restrict ourselves to only a "trusted body of digital information" – since one might wish to preserve falsified data for example as evidence for legal proceedings. Moreover as we will see, our definition of preservation requires that if we are to preserve digitally encoded information we must ensure it remains understandable and usable. In other words preservation is the *sine qua non* of curation. For example it is possible to manage and publish digitally encoded information without regard to future use; on the other hand if one wishes to ensure future as well as current use, one must understand the requirements for preservation.

4 OAIS Definitions

OAIS [4] plays a central role in this book. Many definitions, and some descriptive text, are taken from the updated OAIS; these are shown as ***bold italics***.

5 Acknowledgements

This book would not have been written without the work carried out by the many members of the CASPAR [2], DCC [3] and PARSE.Insight [1] projects, as well as the members of CCSDS [5] and others who have worked on developing OAIS [3] and the standards for certification of digital repositories [6], all of whom must be thanked for their efforts.

A fuller list of contributors may be found in "Contributors" at the end of the book.

Finally the editor and main author of this book would like to thank his family, in particular his wife Krystina and daughter Zoe, for their support and help in preparing this book for publication.

Contents

List of Figures

Chapter 1
Introduction

This chapter provides a quick view of why digital preservation is important – and why it is difficult to do.

There is a need to be able to preserve the understandability and usability of the information encoded in digital objects. Because of this focus on information we shall often refer to digitally encoded information where we wish to stress the information aspects.

However the basic techniques of digital preservation, discussed in many books on this subject, for example [7–12], focus, by analogy with traditional paper-based libraries and archives, on preserving the media or bit sequences and preserving the ability to render documents and images.

This book addresses what might be termed the more advanced issues of digital preservation, beyond keeping the bits and the ability to render, bringing into play concepts of understandability, usability, knowledge and interoperability. In addition it is recognised that there are rights associated with digital objects; there is concern about how one can judge the authenticity of digital objects; there is uncertainty about how digital objects may be identified and located in the future.

In responding to each of these concerns the likelihood is that additional digital artefacts will be created (such as the specification of the digital rights) – which themselves need to be preserved so they can be used in future when they are needed!

Thus we argue that one must be able to preserve many additional different digital objects if one wishes to really preserve any particular single digital object.

Part I of this book provides the theoretical basis for preservation.

In **Part II** we provide evidence from a variety of sources using many types of data from many disciplines, and show many tools which provide reasonable implementations of the techniques described here. These examples and much of the work described in this book are derived from the CASPAR project [2].

Part III addresses the important questions of how to keep costs under control and how to make sure money is not wasted by preparing one's archive for independent evaluation.

D. Giaretta, *Advanced Digital Preservation*, DOI 10.1007/978-3-642-16809-3_1,

1.1 What's So Special About Digital Things?

One might say that digital objects give rise to special concerns because the '1's and '0's which make up binary things are difficult to see. "*Hold on!*" you might say, "*in the case of CD-ROMs one can, with a microscope, see the pits in the surface*". Well that may be true, but those little pits on the disk are not the bits.

To get to the bits one needs to unravel the various levels of bit-stuffing, the error correction codes and logical addressing. These things are handled by the electronics of the CD-ROM reader or of the computer hard disk, where one would be looking at magnetic domains rather than pits, and they expose a relatively simple electronic interface that talks to the rest of the computer systems in terms of bits. Such electronic interfaces illustrate a type of virtualisation which is widely used to allow equipment from many manufacturers to be used in computers. However the underlying technology of such disks changes relatively quickly and so do the interfaces, as a result one cannot usually use an old type of disk in a new computer. This applies both to the well known example of floppy disks, CD-ROMs and to internal spinning hard disks.

"*Alright*" you may say, "*I know a better, simpler way, which has been proven to hold information for hundreds of years. How about simply writing my '1's and '0's on paper? Of course we could use the right acid-free paper! Or if one wanted something for thousands of years we could take a leaf from the Ancient Egyptians and carve the '1's and '0's on stone. Or to bring that up to date I know that people in the nuclear industry are trying out writing very tiny characters on Silicon Carbide sheets.*" [13].

Those techniques would get around some problems, although one might only want to use them for really, really, really important digital objects since they sound as if they could be very expensive. Therefore they are not solutions for the family photographs although they may be very good for simple text documents (although in that case one might as well simply print the characters out rather than the '1's and '0's). However there are some more fundamental problems with these approaches. For example they are not even the solution for things like spreadsheet where one needs to know what the columns and cells mean. Similarly scientific data, as we will see, needs a great deal of additional information in order to be usable.

1.1.1 Threats to Digital Objects of Importance to You

Take a moment to think about the digital objects which affect your life. These days at home we have family photographs and videos, letters, emails, bank records, software licences, identity certificates, spreadsheets of budgets and plans, encrypted private data and also zip files containing some or all of these things. One might have more complex things such as Word documents with linked-in spreadsheets or databases. Widening the picture now to one's work and leisure the list might include games, architectural plans, home finances, engineering designs, and scientific data from many sources, models and analysis results.

Many will already have had the experience of finding a digital object (let's say for simplicity that this is a file) for which one no longer remembers the details or for which one no longer has the software one used to use. In the case of images or documents there is, at the moment, a reasonable chance of finding some way of viewing them, and that may be perfectly adequate, although one might for example want to know who the people in a photograph are, or what language the book is written in and what the words mean. This would be equivalent to storing a book or photograph on a shelf and then picking it up after many years and still being able to view the symbols or images on the page as before, although the reader may not be able to understand the meaning of those symbols.

On the other hand many may also have had the experience of finding a spreadsheet, still being able to view all the numbers, text and formulae, and yet be unable to remember what the various formulae, cells and columns mean. Thus despite knowing the format of the file and having the appropriate software, the information is essentially lost!

Looking yet further afield, consider the digital record of a cultural heritage site such as the Taj Mahal measured 10 years ago.

In order to know whether or not visitors have damaged this heritage site one would need to compare those measurements with current day measurements – which may have been captured with different instruments or stored in a different way. Thus one needs to be able to combine data of various types in order to get an answer. Based on the comparison one may decide that urgent remedial work is needed and that site visitor numbers should be restricted. However before expending valuable resources on this there must be confidence that the old data has not been altered, and that it is indeed what it is claimed to be.

Other complications may arise. For example many digital objects cannot, or at least should not, be freely distributed. Even photographs taken for some purpose which has some passers-by in the scene perhaps should not be used without the permission of those passers-by – but that may depend upon the different legal systems of the country in which the photograph was taken, the country where the photograph is held and the country in which it is being distributed. As time passes, legal systems change. Is it possible to determine the legal position easily?

Thinking about another everyday problem – many Web links no longer work. This will probably get worse over time, yet Web links are often used as an intrinsic part of virtual collections of things. How will we cope with being unable to locate what we need, after even a quite short time?

Of course we may deposit our valuable digital objects in what we consider a safe place. But how do we know that it is indeed safe and can counter the threats noted above. Indeed what happens when that organisation which provides the "safe" place loses its funding or is taken-over and changes its name and function, or simply goes out of business? As a case in point the domain name "casparpreserves.eu", within which the CASPAR web site belongs, is owned by the editor of this book; what will happen to that domain name in 50 year's time when the DNS registration charge is no longer being paid?

Increasingly one finds research papers, for example in on-line journals, which have links to the data on which the research is based. In such a case some or all of the above issues may threaten their survival.

Another peculiarity of digital data is that it is easy to copy and to change. Therefore how can one know whether any digital object we have is what it is claimed to be – how can we trust it?

A related question is – how was a particular digital object made? A digital object is produced by some process – usually some computer application with certain inputs. In fact it could have been the product of a multitude of processes, each with a multitude of input data. How can we tell what these processes and inputs were, and whether these processes and inputs were what we believe them to have been? Or alternatively perhaps we want to produce something similar, but using a slightly changed process – for example because the calibration of an instrument has changed – how can this be done?

To answer these kinds of questions for a physical object, such as a velum parchment or a painting one can do physical tests to give information about age, chemical composition or surface contaminants. While none of these provide conclusive answers to the questions, because one needs documentation about, for example, the chain of ownership of paintings, but at least such physical measurements provide a reality check. None of these techniques are available for digital objects. Of course these techniques can be applied to the physical carriers of the bits, but those bits can usually be changed without detection. One can think of technologies – for example the carvings on stone – where it might be easy to detect changes in the bits by changes in the physical medium, but even if no changes are detected one is still not certain about whether it is what is claimed..

One often hears or reads that the solution to all these issues is "**metadata**" i.e. data about data. There is some truth in that but one needs to ask some pertinent questions not the least of which are "what types of 'metadata'?" and "how much 'metadata'?" For example it is clear that by "metadata" many people simple refer to ways of classifying or finding something – which is not enough for preservation. Without being able to answer these questions one might as well simply say we need "extra stuff".

Much of the rest of this book is about the multitude types of "metadata" that is needed.

We will put the word in italics and quotes when we use it – "metadata" – to remind the reader to be careful to think about what the word means in its particular context.

Much of the rest of this book aims at answering those two questions, namely:

- what types of "metadata" are needed?

and

- how much of each of those types of "metadata" is needed?

The answers will be based on the approach provided by the Open Archival Information System (OAIS) Reference Model, also known as ISO 14721 [1], an international standard which is used as the basis of much, perhaps most, of the work in this area. Indeed it has been said [14] that it is "*now adopted as the 'de facto' standard for building digital archives*".

This book aims to lead the reader into the more advanced topics which need to be addressed to find solutions to the threats to our digital belongings, and more.

1.2 Terminology

Throughout this book we use the term "archive" to mean, following OAIS [1], the organization, consisting of people and systems, responsible for digital preservation (this is not the full OAIS definition – more on this later). Occasionally the term "repository" or phrase "digital repository" is used to convey the same concept where it fits with other usage.

1.3 Summary

Our society increasingly depends upon our continuing ability to access, understand and use digitally encoded information. This chapter should have provided the 10,000 ft view of the issues which the rest of the book aims to map out the solutions for in detail.

Chapter 2
The Really Foolproof Solution for Digital Preservation

Please turn over

D. Giaretta, *Advanced Digital Preservation*, DOI 10.1007/978-3-642-16809-3_2,

MONEY

. . ..enough of it, and for an indefinite period.

If this cannot be guaranteed then the rest of this book will be essential for you.

If on the other hand you are in the fortunate position of having unlimited resources then this book will still be of use because it addresses many of the techniques which will be of use.

Part I
Theory – The Concepts and Techniques Which Are Essential for Preserving Digitally Encoded Information

Chapter 3
Introduction to OAIS Concepts and Terminology

If language is not correct, then what is said is not what is meant; if what is said is not what is meant, then what must be done remains undone; if this remains undone, morals and art will deteriorate; if justice goes astray, the people will stand about in helpless confusion. Hence there must be no arbitrariness in what is said. This matters above everything.

(Confucius)

This chapter aims to provide the basic ideas and concepts needed to build the rest of this book on. We do this by jumping in feet first, based on the terminology from the OAIS Reference Model. We need to do this in order to be able to talk clearly about digital preservation, because we want to say what we mean.

Another way of looking at this is to realise that different people have slightly different definitions in mind, depending upon their backgrounds, for many common terms. If we are not careful we will talk at cross-purposes because of these differences. In order to avoid this we need clear definitions.

The next few sections discuss some of the basic OAIS definitions and concepts.

3.1 Preserve What, for How Long and for Whom?

The "O" in OAIS stands for "Open" but refers to the open way the standard was developed rather than anything to do with open-access. Indeed the OAIS Reference Model can apply to any type of archive whether open access, closed, restricted, "dark" or proprietary.

OAIS takes a very general definition of its prime concern which, as the "I" in OAIS suggests, is information:

Information: ***Any type of knowledge that can be exchanged. In an exchange, it is represented by data.*** An example is a string of bits (the data) accompanied by a

D. Giaretta, *Advanced Digital Preservation*, DOI 10.1007/978-3-642-16809-3_3,

description of how to interpret the string of bits as numbers representing temperature observations measured in degrees Celsius.

Note that Knowledge is not defined in OAIS.

The accompanying definition of data is equally broad:

Data: ***A reinterpretable representation of information in a formalized manner suitable for communication, interpretation, or processing.*** Examples of data include a sequence of bits, a table of numbers, the characters on a page, the recording of sounds made by a person speaking, or a moon rock specimen.

And in the case of things digital:

Digital Object: ***An object composed of a set of bit sequences***.

Note that this does not mean we are restricted to a single file. The definition includes multiple, perhaps distributed, files, or indeed a set of network messages.

The restriction to "bits" i.e. consisting of "1" and "0", means that if we move to trinary (i.e. "0", "1" and "2") instead of binary then we would have to change this definition, but it would not affect the concept – however it would change the tools we could use.

One might wonder why data includes physical objects such as a "moon rock specimen". The answer should become clear later but in essence the answer is that to provide a logically complete solution to digital preservation one needs, eventually, to jump outside the digital, if only, for example, to read the label on the disk.

As to the question of length of time we need to be concerned about, OAIS provides the following pair of definitions (the text in bold italics below is taken from OAIS):

Long Term: ***A period of time long enough for there to be concern about the impacts of changing technologies, including support for new media and data formats, and of a changing Designated Community, on the information being held in an OAIS. This period extends into the indefinite future.***

Long Term Preservation: ***The act of maintaining information, Independently Understandable by a Designated Community, and with evidence supporting its Authenticity, over the Long Term.***

In other words we are not only talking about decades into the future but, as is a common experience, we need to be concerned with the rapid change of hardware and software, the cycle time of which may be just a few years. Of course even if an archive is not itself looking after the digital objects over the long term, even by that definition, the intention may be for another archive to take over later. In this case the first archive needs to capture all the "metadata" needed so that it can hand these on also.

Three key concepts are embedded in the above definition namely:

Authenticity: ***The degree to which a person (or system) may regard an object as what it is purported to be. The degree of Authenticity is judged on the basis of evidence.***

There will be much more to say about authenticity in Chap. 13, where the whole chapter is devoted to it.

Independently Understandable: ***A characteristic of information that is sufficiently complete to allow it to be interpreted, understood and used by the Designated Community without having to resort to special resources not widely available, including named individuals.***

By being able to "understand" a piece of information is meant that one can do something useful with it; it is not intended to mean that one understands all of its ramifications.

For example in a criminal investigation of a murder one may have a database with digitally encoded times of telephone calls; here we would be satisfied if we could say "the telephone call was made at 12:05 pm on 1st January 2009, UK time", but to then understand that this implied that the person who made the call was the murderer is beyond what OAIS means by being able to "understand" the data.

Now we approach one element of what that the "preservation" part of "digital preservation" means. To require that things are able to be "interpreted, understood and used" is to make some very powerful demands. It not only includes playing a digital recording so it can be heard, or rendering an image or a document so that it can be seen; it also includes being able to understand what the columns in the spreadsheet we mention earlier means, or what the numbers in a piece of scientific data mean; this is needed in order to actually understand and in particular **use** the data, for example using it in some analysis programme, combining it with other data in order to derive new scientific insights. The "Independently" part is to exclude the easy but unreliable option of being able to simply ask the person who created the digital object; unreliable not because the creator may be a liar but rather because the creator may be, and in the very long term certainly will be, deceased!

Finally, we have the other key concept of "Designated Community".

Designated Community: ***An identified group of potential Consumers who should be able to understand a particular set of information. The Designated Community may be composed of multiple user communities. A Designated Community is defined by the archive and this definition may change over time.***

Why is this a key concept? To answer that question we need to ask another fundamental question, namely "How can we tell whether a digital object has been successfully preserved?" – a question which can be asked repeatedly as time passes.

Clearly we can do the simple things like checking whether the bit sequences are unchanged over time, using one or more standard techniques such as digital digests [15]. However just having the bits is not enough. The demand for the ability for the object to be "interpreted, understood and used" is broader than that – and of course it can be tested.

But surely there is another qualification, for is it sensible to demand that *anyone* can "interpret, understand and use" the digital object – say a 4 year old child?

Clearly we need to be more specific. But how can such a group be specified, and indeed who should choose? This seems a daunting task – who could possibly be in a position to do that?

The answer that OAIS provides is a subtle one. The people who can should be able to "interpret, understand and use" the digital object, and whom we can use to test the success or otherwise of the "preservation", are defined by the people who are doing the preservation.

The advantage of this definition is that it leads to something that can be tested. So if an archive claims "we are preserving this digital object for astronomers" we can then call in an astronomer to test that claim.

The disadvantage is that the preserver could choose a definition which makes life easy for him/her – what is to stop that? The answer is that there is nothing to prevent that but who would rely on such an archive?

As long as the archive's definition is made clear then the person depositing the digital objects can decide whether this is acceptable. The success or failure of the archive in terms of digital objects being deposited will be determined by the market. Thus in order to succeed the archive will have to define its Designated Community(ies) appropriately.

Different archives, holding the same digital object may define their Designated Communities as being different. This will have implications for the amount and type of "metadata" which is needed by each archive.

As we will discuss later on, we need to be able to be a more specific, and we will see, in Chap. 7, how this can be done.

3.2 What "Metadata", How Much "Metadata"?

One fundamental question to ask is "What 'metadata' do we need?" The problem with "metadata" is that it is so broad that people tend to have their own limited view. OAIS provides a more detailed breakdown. The first three broad categories are to do with (1) understandability, (2) origins, context and restrictions and (3) the way in which the data and "metadata" are grouped together.

The reason for this separation is that given some digitally encoded information one can reasonably ask whether it is usable, which is dealt with by (1). This is a separate question to the one about where this digital object came from, dealt with by (2). Since there are many ways of associating these things it seems reasonable to want to separate consider (3) separately.

It could be argued that to understand a piece of data one needs to know its context. However the discussion about "Independently Understandable" in the previous section points out that OAIS does not require understanding of all the ramifications so this separation of context from understandability is reasonable, although it does not mean that all context is excluded from understandability since a piece of "metadata" may have several roles.

The packaging is something which is separate from the content. The next few sub-sections briefly introduce these different categories; they will each be discussed in much greater detail in separate chapters.

3.2.1 Understandability (Representation Information)

One type of "metadata" we can immediately identify is that which we need to "interpret, understand and use" the digitally encoded information. OAIS defines this as:

Representation Information: ***The information that maps a Data Object into more meaningful concepts.*** An example of Representation Information for a bit sequence which makes up a FITS file might consist of the FITS standard which defines the format plus a dictionary which defines the meaning of keywords in the file which are not part of the standard.

Figure 3.1 indicates that the Representation Information is used to interpret the Data Object in order to produce the Information Object – something which one can then understand and use.

The OAIS definition of **Information Object** is: ***A Data Object together with its Representation Information.*** This is a very broad definition.

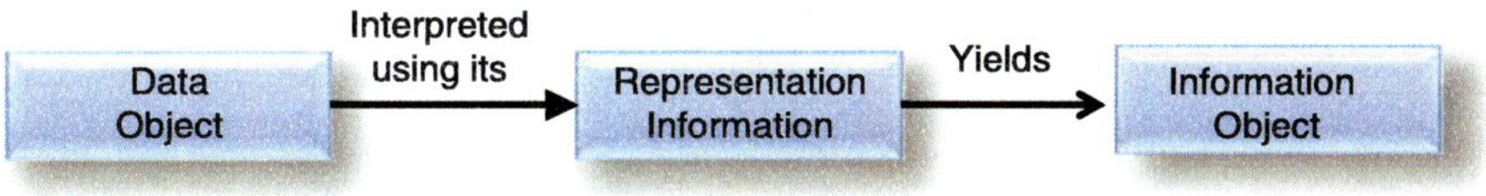

Fig. 3.1 Representation information

The definition of Information Object may seem a little circular. However its purpose is not to define something specific, for example in a computer programme. Instead it really only provides a simple term for something which we can apply to many different things in people's heads. The key idea is that it is something that allows us to talk about what knowledge is being exchanged.

When we are referring to something specifically targeted for preservation the term **Content Information** is used. This is ***a set of information that is the original target of preservation or that includes part or all of that information. It is an Information Object composed of its Content Data Object and its Representation Information.***

In a little bit more detail, recognising that the Data Object could be either digital or physical, one can draw Fig. 3.2, which is a simple UML [257] diagram.

This diagram is a way of showing that

- an Information Object is made up of a Data Object and Representation Information
- a Data Object can be either a Physical Object or a Digital Object. An example of the former is a piece of paper or a rock sample.
- a Digital Object is made up of one or more Bits

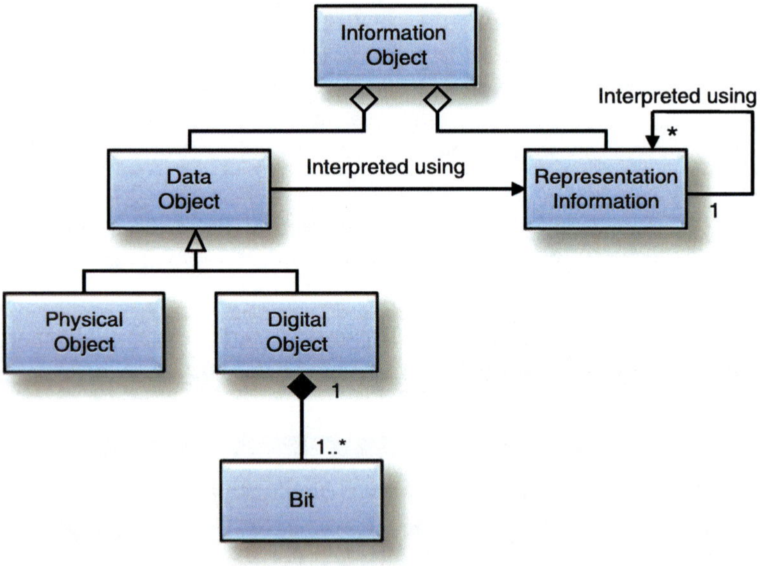

Fig. 3.2 OAIS information model

Note that this does not mean we are restricted to a single file. The definition includes multiple, perhaps distributed, files, or indeed a set of network messages.

- a Data Object is interpreted using Representation Information

It is important to realise that Representation Information can be anything from a scribbled handwritten note, needing a human to read it, to a complex machine readable formal description.

- Representation Information is itself interpreted using further Representation Information

Figure 3.3 denotes that Representation Information may usefully be subcategorised into several different types, namely Structure, Semantic and (the imaginatively named) Other Representation Information. This breakdown is useful because Structure Representation Information is often referred to as "format"; Semantic Representation Information covers things such as ontologies and data dictionaries; Other Representation Information is a catch-all for anything and everything else.

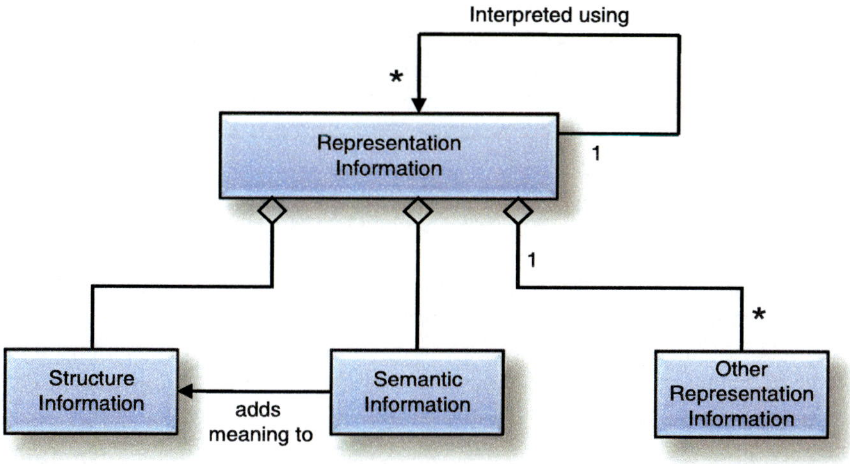

Fig. 3.3 Representation information object

One useful way to understand why this breakdown may be useful is to consider a number of different variations.

For example two copies of a simple message (i.e. a piece of information) may be contained in two text files (i.e. in the same format), but in one case the message is written in English and in the other case it is in French (needing different dictionaries).

Similarly one can have the English text both in a PDF and a Word file – two different formats but needing the same dictionary.

In general breaking things down into smaller pieces means that one is not forced to treat objects as a sticky mess. Instead one can deal with each (smaller) part separately and usually more easily.

When this is coupled with the fact that Representation Information is an Information Object that may have its own Data Object and other Representation Information associated with understanding that Data Object, as shown in a compact form by the *interpreted using* association, the resulting set of objects can be referred to as a Representation Network. Detailed examples will be provided in Part II.

In the extreme, the recursion of the Representation Information will ultimately stop at a physical object such as a printed document (ISO standard, informal standard, notes, publications etc). This allows us to make a connection to the non-digital world. However use of things like paper documentation would tend to prevent "automated use" and "interoperability", and also complete resolution of the complete Representation Network, discussed further below, to this level would be an almost impossible task. Therefore we would prefer to stop earlier, and this will be discussed next.

As the final part of this rush through the OAIS concepts we turn to something a little different in order to answer the question *"How much 'metadata'?"*

A piece of Representation Information is just another piece of Information – hence the name Representation Information rather than Representation Data. In order for there to be enough Representation Information it has to be understandable and usable by the Designated Community – in order to be used to understand the original data object. However what if this is not the case?

The Representation Information may be encoded as a physical object such as a paper document, or it may be a digital object. In the latter case we can simply provide Representation Information for that digital object. If the Designated Community still cannot understand and use the original data, we can repeat the process. Clearly this provides us with a way to answer the "How much" question: we provide a network of Representation Information until we have enough for the Designated Community to understand the Data Object. OAIS defines:

Representation Network: ***The set of Representation Information that fully describes the meaning of a Data Object. Representation Information in digital forms needs additional Representation Information so its digital forms can be understood over the Long Term.***

To complete the picture we can then see a way to define the Designated Community, namely we define them by what they know, by what OAIS terms their Knowledge Base:

Knowledge Base: ***A set of information, incorporated by a person or system that allows that person or system to understand received information.***

All these terms will be discussed at much greater length in Chap. 6.

3.2.2 Origins, Context and Restrictions (Preservation Description Information)

OAIS defines a group of types of "metadata", under the name of Preservation Description Information (PDI), which are to do, broadly, with knowing what and where the digital object came from.

The idea is that one needs to name a way to identify the digital object; to know how and by whom and why the digital object is what it is; to know the broader context within which it exists; to be sure that the digital object has not been changed and finally, to know what rights are attached to it (see Fig. 3.4).

The following sections provide the OAIS definitions with a little additional explanation; further details are provided in Chap. 10.

3.2.2.1 Reference Information

Reference Information: ***The information that is used as an identifier for the Content Information. It also includes identifiers that allow outside systems to refer unambiguously to a particular Content Information***. An example of Reference Information is an ISBN. Clearly what are often called persistent identifiers, which we discuss further in Sect. 10.3.2, provide a form of Reference Information.

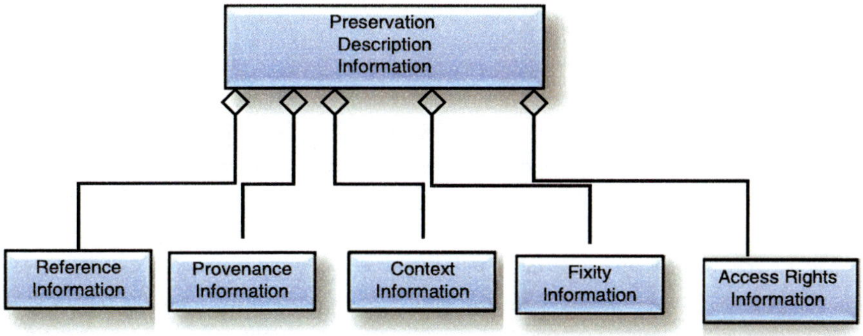

Fig. 3.4 Preservation description information

3.2.2.2 Provenance Information

Provenance Information: ***The information that documents the history of the Content Information. This information tells the origin or source of the Content Information, any changes that may have taken place since it was originated, and who has had custody of it since it was originated. The archive is responsible for creating and preserving Provenance Information from the point of Ingest; however, earlier Provenance Information should be provided by the Producer. Provenance Information adds to the evidence to support Authenticity.***

Provenance may reasonably be divided into what we might term Technical Provenance – things that, for example, are recorded fairly automatically by software. This must be supplemented by Non-technical Provenance, by which we mean, for example, the information about the people who are in charge of the Content Information – the people who could perhaps fake the other PDI. In other words in order to judge whether we can trust the multitude of information that surrounds the Content Information, we must be able to judge whether we trust the people who were responsible for collecting it, and who may perhaps have been able to fake it. This will be discussed in more detail in Sect. 13.

3.2.2.3 Context Information

Content Information: ***The information that documents the relationships of the Content Information to its environment. This includes why the Content Information was created and how it relates to other Content Information objects.***

It is worth noting here that many traditional archivists would say that "context" is all important and trumps all other considerations [16]. OAIS defines "context" in a rather more limited way, but on the other hands provides a greater level of granularity with which to work, although does point out that Provenance, for example, is a type of Context.

3.2.2.4 Fixity Information

Fixity Information: ***The information which documents the mechanisms that ensure that the Content Information object has not been altered in an undocumented manner.*** An example is a Cyclical Redundancy Check (CRC) code for a file.

Digests [15] are often used for this purpose, relying on the fact that a short bit sequence can be created, using one of several algorithms, from a larger binary object which it represents, essentially uniquely. By this we mean that it is, practically speaking, impossible to design a different file with a matching digest. This means that if we can keep the (short) digest safely then we can use it to check whether a copy of a (perhaps very large) digital object is what we think it is. This can be done by recomputed the digest, using the same algorithm, using the digital object which we wish to check. If the digest matches the original one we carefully kept then we can be reasonably sure that the digital object does indeed have the same bit sequence as the original.

3.2.2.5 Access Rights Information

Access Rights Information: ***The information that identifies the access restrictions pertaining to the Content Information, including the legal framework, licensing terms, and access control. It contains the access and distribution conditions stated within the Submission Agreement, related to both preservation (by the OAIS) and final usage (by the Consumer). It also includes the specifications for the application of rights enforcement measures.***

Access rights and digital rights are discussed further in Sects. 10.6 and 17.7. Examples of PDI from different disciplines are given in Table 3.1.

3.2.3 Linking Data and "Metadata" (Packaging)

The idea behind packaging is that the one must somehow be able to bind the various digital objects together. Remember also that Content Information is the combination of Data Object plus Representation Information, and PDI has its various components. Fig. 3.5 shows the other conceptual components of a package.

The package does not need to be a single file – it is very important to understand this. It could be, but it does not have to be. The package is a logical construction, in other words one needs to be able to have something which leads one to the other pieces, by one means or another. About the package itself one needs to be able to identify it i.e. is it a file, a collection of files, a sequence of bytes on a tape? The information which provides this is the Packaging Information.

Packaging Information: ***The information that is used to bind and identify the components of an Information Package.*** For example, it may be the ISO 9660 volume and directory information used on a CD-ROM to provide the content of several files containing Content Information and Preservation Description Information. For a ZIP file it would be the information that the package is the file which probably has a name ending in ".zip".

In addition the package contains something and the Package Description provides the description of what this is; it is something that can be used to search for this particular package.

Table 3.1 Examples of PDI

Content information type	Reference	Provenance	Context	Fixity	Access rights
Space science data	• Object identifier • Journal reference • Mission, instrument, title, attribute set	• Instrument description • Principal investigator • Processing history • Storage and handling history • Sensor description • Instrument • Instrument mode • Decommutation map • Software interface specification • Information property description	• Calibration history • Related data sets • Mission • Funding history	• CRC • Checksum • Reed-Solomon coding	• Identification of the properly authorized Designated community (access control) • Permission grants for preservation and for distribution • Pointers to fixity and provenance information (e.g., digital signatures, and rights holders)

Digital library collections	• Bibliographic description
	• Persistent identifier
		• For scanned collections:
		  • "metadata" about the digitization process
		  • pointer to master version
		• For born-digital publications:
		  • pointer to the digital original
		• "Metadata" about the preservation process:
		  • pointers to earlier versions of the collection item
		• change history
		• Information property description
			• Pointers to related documents in original environment at the time of publication	• Digital signature
				• Checksum
				• Authenticity indicator
					• Legal framework(s)
					• Licensing offers
					• Specifications for rights enforcement measures applied at dissemination time
					• Permission grants for preservation and for distribution
					• Information about watermarking applied at submission and preservation time
					• Pointers to fixity and provenance information (e.g., digital signatures, and rights holders)

Table 3.1 (continued)

Content information type	Reference	Provenance	Context	Fixity	Access rights
Software package	• Name • Author/ originator • Version number • Serial number	• Revision history • Registration • Copyright • Information property description	• Help file • User guide • Related software • Language	• Certificate • Checksum • Encryption • CRC	• Designated community • Legal framework(s) • Licensing offers • Specifications for rights enforcement measures applied at dissemination time • Pointers to fixity and provenance information (e.g., digital signatures, and rights holders)

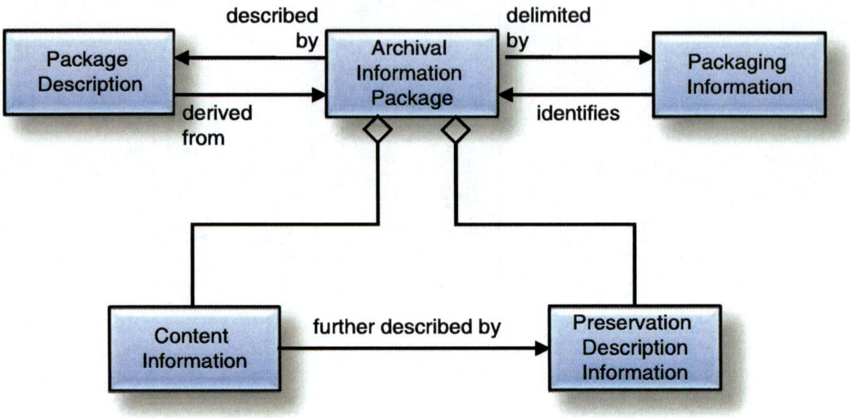

Fig. 3.5 Information package contents

It may perhaps have been noticed that the various additional concepts we have identified are called "Information". In most cases these will be digitally encoded. This leads us to a fundamentally important point.

3.3 Recursion – A Pervasive Concept

Those with a mathematical background will recognise some of this as a type of recursion. It comes up time and again in preservation. By this we mean that ideas which appear at one level of granularity re-appear when we take a finer grained view, within the detailed breakdown of those or other ideas. As is well known in mathematics, it is important to understand where the recursion ends otherwise it becomes impossible to produce practical results. For example the factorial function is defined as $n! = n*((n-1)!)$ i.e. $6! = 6*(5!) = 6*5*(4!) = \ldots$ This stops when we get to 0! because we define 0! as equal to 1.

It is worth making some remarks about this concept here.

Representation Information (RepInfo for short) – remember it is Representation Information rather than Representation Data – is encoded as data (which could be called representation data but in fact OAIS does not use that terminology) which itself needs its own Representation Information. The recursion stops at the Knowledge Base of the Designated Community.

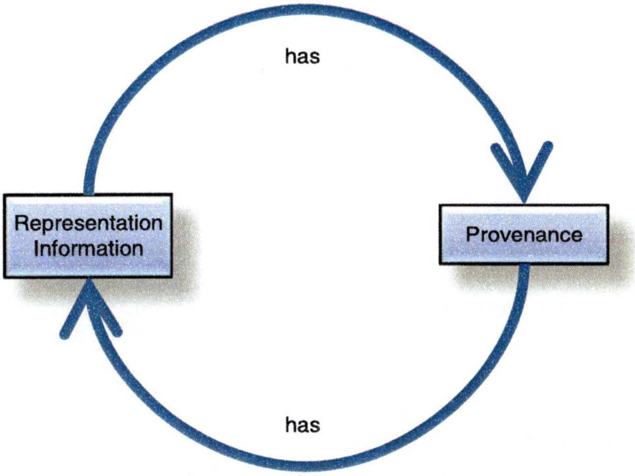

Fig. 3.6 Recursion – Representation information and provenance

Any piece of "metadata", such as Provenance (to be discussed in detail later), will itself be encoded as a Data Object, which needs Representation Information. Representation Information as a digital object will also need its own Provenance, as illustrated in Fig. 3.6.

The recursion in this case might end with Provenance being a simple text file (or piece of paper) in plain English (assuming the Designated Community can read English) so the Representation Information is quite simple and hence the Representation Information Network terminates.

A formal way of showing this in OAIS is by showing that many of the concepts that are used are Information Objects as shown in Fig. 3.7.

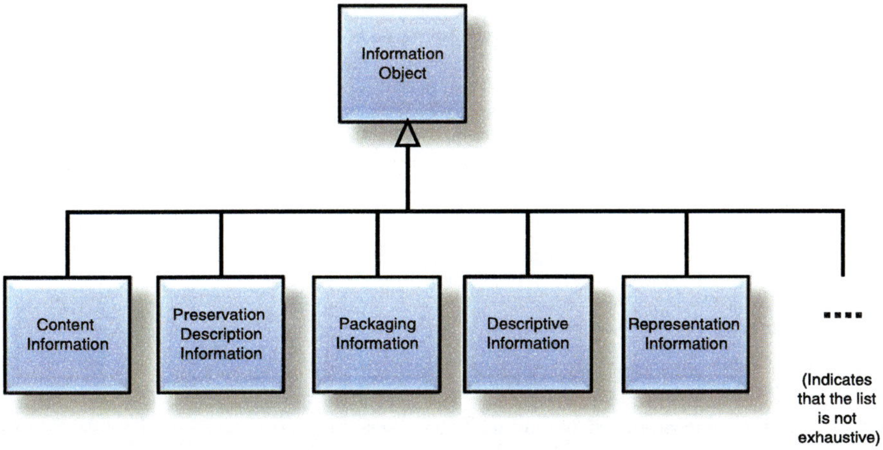

Fig. 3.7 Sub-types of information object

Components of a preservation infrastructure themselves need to be preservable – for example a Registry (see Sect. 16.2.1.1) which supports OAIS-type archives must itself be an OAIS-type archive in that it must be relied upon to preserve its (Representation) Information objects over the long term.

3.4 Disincentives Against Digital Preservation

It is important to realise that although many of those reading this book will regard preserving our digital heritage as self-evident, nevertheless this is not universal opinion.

As time passes more and more digitally encoded information is accumulated. It is therefore possible that the costs increase over time, yet experience tells us that the budget available for a preservation organisation usually does not. Figure 3.8 might therefore be projected to be the case.

If this is the projection then no responsible body would find it acceptable; a decision would have to be taken not to preserve everything – or perhaps not to preserve anything. The focus here is on how we could try to control the costs so that either the graph of preservation costs is level rather than increasing, or is increasing only slowly so that the crossing-point is acceptably far into the future.

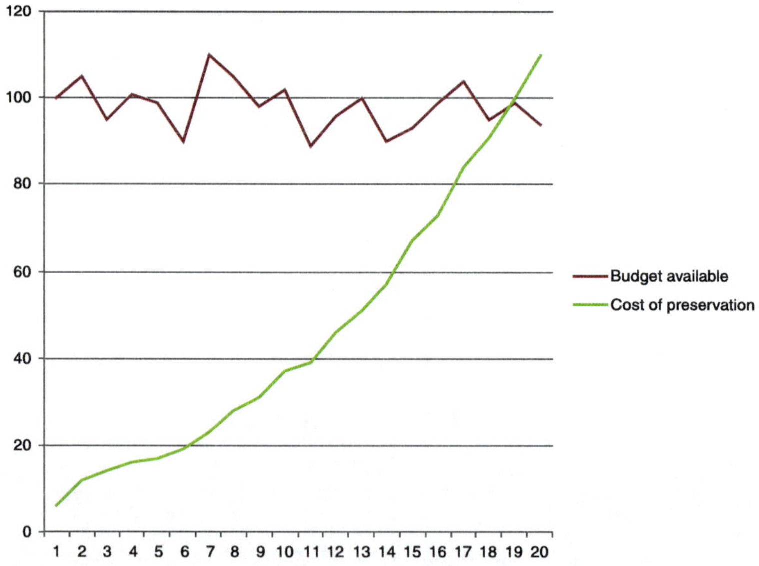

Fig. 3.8 Money disincentives – if the annual cost of preservation of the accumulated data increases over time

3.4.1 Cost/Benefit Modelling

It is very hard to model the costs of digital preservation [17], and even more difficult to evaluate possible benefits. However it is worth discussing at least some of the costs at this point to illustrate the point.

One of the simplest costs which one may try to estimate is that of storage. The argument sometimes used is that the cost of a unit of storage reduces by 50% each technology cycle (say 3 years). Suppose that the initial cost is £X. If at each cycle one buys new hardware then one spends $X/2 in 3 year's time, £X/4 after a further 3 years, and so on. Therefore one would spend

$$\pounds X + \pounds X/2 + \pounds X/4 + \pounds X/8 + \ldots\ldots = \pounds 2X \text{ in total}$$

Thus one can argue that the hardware cost is at least controlled.

However each 3 years the amount of data may easily have increased by, say, a factor of 8, thus the cost keeping all the data would be:

$$\begin{array}{cccccccc} X & + & X/2 & + & X/4 & +\ldots & = & 2^*X \\ & & 8^*X/2 & + & 8^*X/4 & +\ldots & & 8^*X \\ & & & & 64^*X/4 & +\ldots & & 32^*X \end{array}$$

Thus one can see that there is a real danger that the growth of data volumes may easily swamp the cost savings introduced by new technologies. Moreover the cost of personnel, and, more importantly, the cost of preserving the information rather than simply keeping the bits, has been left out of the calculations.

More complex modelling is available based on cost data from real, anonymised, archives [18]. However the cost models which are available omit the cost of maintaining understandability, which could be labour intensive.

The Blue Ribbon Task Force on Sustainable Preservation and Access [19] has looked at the broader view and identifies the fact that one can effectively purchase "future options" without making an indefinite committment.

3.4.2 Future Generations

Although preserving our digital heritage for future generations is a laudable ambition, it must be admitted that those future generations have two great weaknesses (1) they do not (yet) have a vote and (2) they do not (yet) pay taxes! As a result other priorities can overwhelm our ambitions, no matter how laudable.

Clearly one cannot preserve everything and there are always more or less formal mechanisms to choose what to keep and what to leave to decay (or leave for someone else to preserve); it may be that the availability of funding determines what stays and what goes and, in the long term, if money runs out then the whole of the collection could die.

The ways of deciding what should be preserved is not part of this book in part because there are too many variations depending on particular circumstances. However there are a number of generally applicable techniques discussed in Chap. 14 concerning preservation objectives and building a business case for preserving digital assets.

3.5 Summary

In this chapter we have very briefly introduced the key concepts about digital preservation that will stand the reader in good stead throughout the rest of the book.

Chapter 4
Types of Digital Objects

There are more things in heaven and earth, Horatio, than are dreamt of in your philosophy.

***(William Shakespeare**, "Hamlet")*

There are many types of digital objects which we may come across and we need to recognise the extent of their diversity otherwise we will aim too low when we design our tools and techniques for digital preservation.

It is impossible to give an exhaustive list of types of digital objects, yet it is useful to remind ourselves of at least some of the great variety that we must be able to deal with. By ***types*** we mean not just different formats, but rather different classifications.

One reason for being interested in the variety of types is that unless one is aware of the distinctions it is very easy to assume that everything is the same and the same tools can be used. For example if one normally deals with the preservation of documents, for example Word or PDF, then one might assume that all digitally encoded information can be preserved using the same tools. Unfortunately this is not true, as we will see. The next sections present a brief overview of some of the distinctions which can be made, without any claim of being exhaustive.

4.1 Simple vs. Composite

One way to classify digital objects is by whether they normally are treated as a whole – for example an image such as Fig. 4.1 – or whether they are normally treated as a collection of simpler parts, for example a FITS file which has several images and tables, as in Fig. 4.2. The latter we will call Composite Objects (or sometime Complex Objects).

It is important to make this distinction because if we can break the preservation challenge of a composite object into smaller components then it will make the preservation task easier. On the other hand if we treat the composite object as if it were a simple one then we could run into a great deal of trouble in future.

D. Giaretta, *Advanced Digital Preservation*, DOI 10.1007/978-3-642-16809-3_4,

Fig. 4.1 A simple image – "face.jpg"

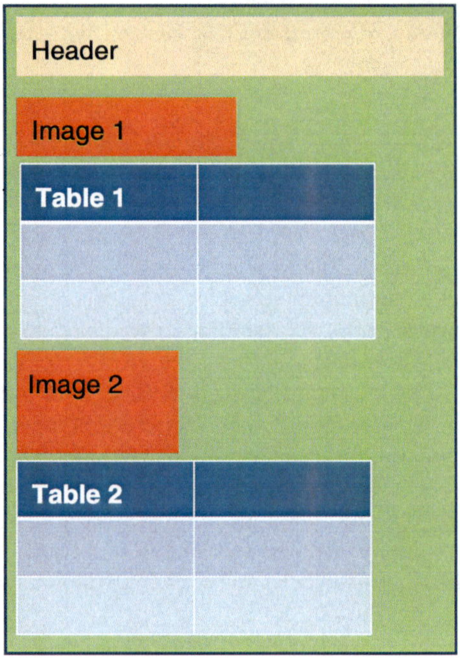

Fig. 4.2 FITS file as a composite object

However it is never completely clear cut – because whether a digital object is simple or composite often depends upon the eye of the beholder. Nevertheless this is a useful distinction to draw.

A Word document may normally be treated a simple object. In actual fact it is, internally, very complex, containing information about styles and page layout etc. However one normally disregards this because the software we use deals with the Word file as a whole. On the other hand some Word files have embedded spreadsheets and drawing objects which can be edited separately; in this case one might often treat such an object as a collection of parts.

The FITS file (Fig. 4.2) is a whole digital object but the analysis is normally done on a component by component basis. In other words Image 1 is displayed and processed, and then the same thing, or something different, is done with Image 2.

A particular format may allow many possibilities, and such formats may evolve and increase in complexity over time [20]. The original FITS format allowed only simple images; the current definition allows much greater complexity – but can still contain a single image if that is what is wanted. Thus we need to be concerned with the particular digital object, not the format, when we look at whether it is simple or composite.

Further details for FITS are given in Sect. 7.3.2.1.

In some ways one can regard a composite object as a container of simpler things, as with the Word example above, and may be represented in general as in Fig. 4.3.

Fig. 4.3 Composite object as a container

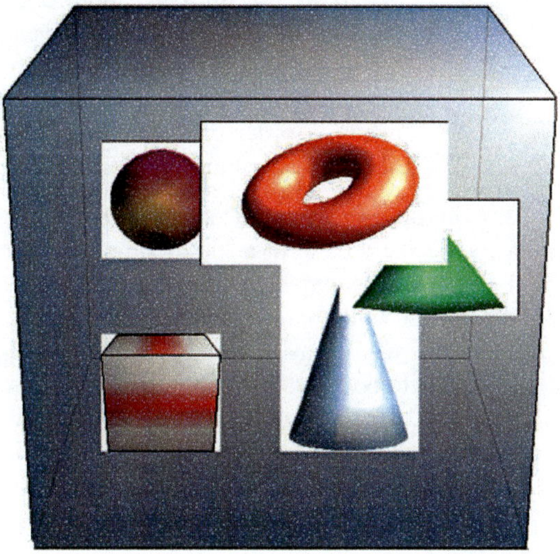

4.2 Rendered vs. Non-rendered

Another way to divide the digital world is as follows.

There are digital objects which are usually processed by some software to produce a rendering which is presented to a human user who can then interpret what he/she sees/hears/feels/tastes, and this is normally regarded as adequate. This can include documents, pictures, videos and sounds. These we will refer to as Rendered Digital Objects.

On the other hand one can have a digital object for which it is not enough to simply render it but for which one needs to know what the contents mean in order to be able to further process it.

It is useful to make this distinction because it is easy to think that every digital object is simply rendered; that every digital object need only be displayed.

Indeed one could argue that the ultimate user of a digital object is a human who needs to see or hear (or perhaps in future to feel, taste or smell) the result. For example even a FITS image is (often) displayed.

However displaying a FITS image is rarely the ultimate aim. Instead an astronomer might want to make measurements which require an understanding of the units and coordinate systems. He/she might also reasonably want to combine this piece of data with another. In other words what is wanted is to do more than render it in one particular way; instead there is an enormous variety of ways users may want to deal with the object.

When we are thinking about digital preservation one must look to the future – not in order to guess what it may to be but rather to recognise that it may be different from today. Therefore we need to identify what someone – at least the Designated Community – needs in order to understand and use a non-rendered object digital object in any number of different ways.

For example consider two text files. In one case one can have some English text, say a recipe for a cake in a file "recipe.txt" (see Fig. 4.4). Using a Windows PC the file is easily readable because the ".txt" part of the name lets the machine try an application which can display an ASCII encoded file – which is what this is. Normally one would say that no special knowledge is needed to understand this – it simply needs to be read.

However there is a requirement to be able to read English and also to know what the various measures are (for example what size is "a cup"?) and also to know what the ingredients are (for example what is "lemon zest"?); without such knowledge the recipe is neither understandable nor usable.

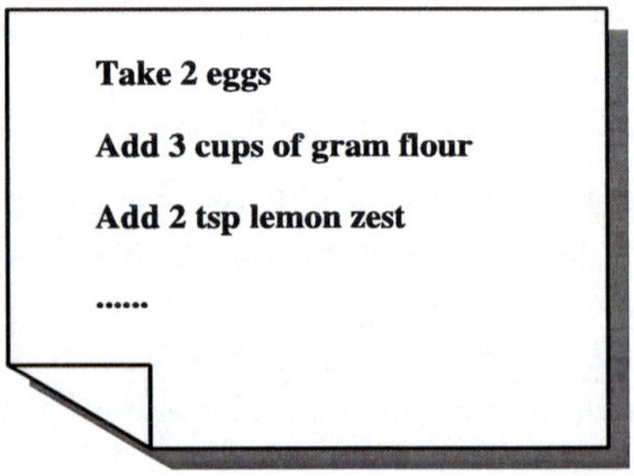

Fig. 4.4 Text file "recipe.txt"

Consider now another text file ("table.txt") which, as a simple ".txt" file is easily readable on a PC – again the ".txt" usually lets us guess, correctly in this case, that this is an ASCII encoded file.

In this case we are more obviously in some trouble because although we can see something which we can reasonably assume are numbers, we do not know what the numbers mean.

If we are told that the numbers under the headings "X", "Y" and "Z" provide us with the sides of a rectangular cuboid, then we can calculate the volume of that shape using the formula "X*Y*Z" for each row, namely 14.742. 31.8 and 114.034.

On the other hand we might be told that "X" is the longitude on Earth, "Y" the latitude, both measured in degrees and "Z" is the concentration of a certain chemical in parts per billion.

We see that the format alone is insufficient; one needs to know what the contents (e.g. the numbers) mean.

By Non-Rendered Digital Object we mean things which, like table.txt, are not simply rendered but rather are to be processed to produce any number of possible outputs. For example table.txt could be plotted, displayed as a pie-chart or histogram. Alternatively the information in the columns of table.txt could be used to calculate the density of chlorophyll in the Amazon rain forest (if that is the sort of information there is in table.txt).

As another example one can take a digital object from the GOME instrument [21], which might be as shown in Figs. 4.5, 4.6, and 4.7.

```
0010100100100010100001010100101010l
010011100100100101010101010010101
0010010011101010101010101010010l010
01010101010100101010101010100l0l010
010101010101010101010010101010100
0101010100101010100101010100101010l
0101010010101001010101010010101010l
```

Fig. 4.5 GOME data – binary

latitude	longitude	Ozone	Time
132	50	34.9	12/03/1999
178	50	45	12/03/1999
190	50	78	12/03/1999

Fig. 4.6 GOME data – as numbers/characters

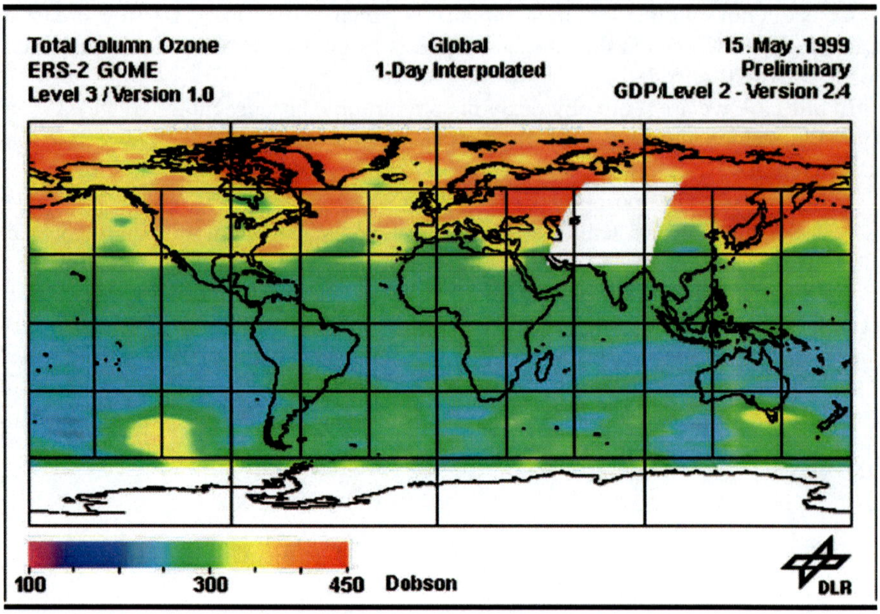

Fig. 4.7 GOME data – processed to show ozone data with particular projection

We can also have two files of the same format, say a sound file such as MP3, the first of which ("music.mpg") is indeed something that can be used to play music, but a second, also an MP3 file ("config.mpg"), which contains numbers which are configuration parameters for setting up some software. If we click on the first on a home computer then it will play some music because the ".mpg" causes the computer try to use a music application. Clicking on the second will cause the computer to try to use that same application but it may produce only a brief grating sound, or perhaps nothing audible at all.

The important points are that we currently rely on many clues, such as having a file ending ".txt" or ".mpg" which many computers use to choose an application for displaying or playing the file. On the other hand, even now these clues are insufficient, as with "table.txt" (Fig. 4.8).

Of course computers are not intelligent – in fact they have been instructed which applications to use for which file extensions, for example Notepad for files with

X	Y	Z
1.3,	2.7,	4.2
2.4,	5.3,	2.5
7.4,	2.3,	6.7

Fig. 4.8 Text file "table.txt"

names ending in ".txt". Sometimes this does not do what is expected, as with "config.mpg". In other cases we can do something with the file but not very much, as with "table.txt".

Some others mentioned in the introduction, such as family photographs ("face.jpg", Fig. 4.1) are very similar in that what one expects is to display or play contents of the file and then it is up to the viewer, or listener, to understand it. Of course one is not listening to the bits – what we mean is that there is an application which is used to convert the bits to an image or a sound. The application may also allow one to zoom in to part of an image or search for a piece of text or copy a piece of music and insert it in a separate file. But even without these extra functions, one can make use of the file, by which we mean we can look at or hear the output of the application and we would be quite happy if that was all we could do.

These type of files – let's use the term ***Digital Object*** as a more general term instead of "file"- we will refer to as ***Rendered Digital Objects***. For these types of objects it is (currently) normally regarded as sufficient if in future one can simply display it if it is an image or movie, or play it if it is a sound.

These are the types of digital objects which one commonly deals with in everyday life, documents, images, web pages etc. There are many books which talk about the preservation of these kinds of objects:

- word processor documents
- financial files
- spreadsheets
- databases of various sorts
- .....

Throughout this book we will also look at examples from a variety of disciplines including science, cultural heritage and contemporary performing arts.

Science

- Observations of the Earth from space, including multi-spectral images, synthetic aperture radar images
- Measurements of the atmosphere, chemical or electrical composition
- Software for processing raw date to data which is scientifically useful

Cultural Heritage

- Laser scans of buildings and artefacts
- Plans of buildings
- 3-D virtual reality models

Performing Arts

- "patch" file for processing what the performer plays
- configuration file which map video capture of movement to musical performance.

All the above are just some of the example of "non-rendered" data which are of importance to society.

4.3 Static vs. Dynamic

Digital objects do (usually) need software and hardware to extract information from the bits – as discussed in Sect. 1.1. Static objects are ones which, unless they are transformed, are unchanged as bit sequences. These we will refer to as **Static Digital Objects**.

On the other hand we can think about database files which naturally change over time as entries are changed. Alternatively we can consider a whole collection of files as the data object. Such a collection might change as additional files are added to the collection over time. Such digital objects we will refer to as **Dynamic Digital Objects**.

Of course at any particular time the Dynamic Digital Object is a particular Static Digital Object which we may preserve. On the other hand it may be of interest, in the case of a Dynamic Digital Object, to know what the state of the object was at any particular time. In fact some would argue that most datasets change over time and the state at each particular moment in time may be important. This is an important area requiring further research; however from the point of view in this book it may be useful to break the issue into separate parts. At each moment in time we could, in principle, take a snapshot and store it. That snapshot has its associated Representation Network. Efficient storage of a series of snapshots may lead one to store differences or include time tags in the data. Additional Representation Information would be needed which describes how to get to a particular time's snapshot from the efficiently encoded version.

4.4 Active vs. Passive

One other useful distinction is between what may be called active and passive digital objects.

By **Passive Digital Object** we mean something with which things are done, for example used by other applications (software) to do something. For example a document file is used by a word processing programme to print the document or display it on the screen, or an astronomical image in a FITS file would be used by astronomical analysis software to do scientific research. Such digital objects are often referred to as "data" but since the term Data Object is already used by OAIS we prefer the term Passive Digital Object.

An **Active Digital Object** on the other hand does something. For example the word processing application or the astronomical analysis software mentioned in the previous paragraph might be the digital objects to be preserved.

Once again there will always be fuzzy boundaries, so one could consider an Access[TM] database as a Passive Digital Object – used by the Access software – but it could easily itself contain software (for example some form of BASIC) which would mean that it could be considered to be an Active Digital Object.

4.5 Multiple-Classifications

The classifications are not mutually exclusive, and in fact one can think of a simple-rendered-static-passive object – the image "face.jpg" is an example of this. One can also have a composite-non-rendered-dynamic-active object such as a database with built in queries into which new rows are being inserted. The Word.exe executable file may be thought of as a composite-non-rendered-static-active object.

Figure 4.9 shows a representation of multiple classifications – although we are limited to drawing in 3-dimensions!

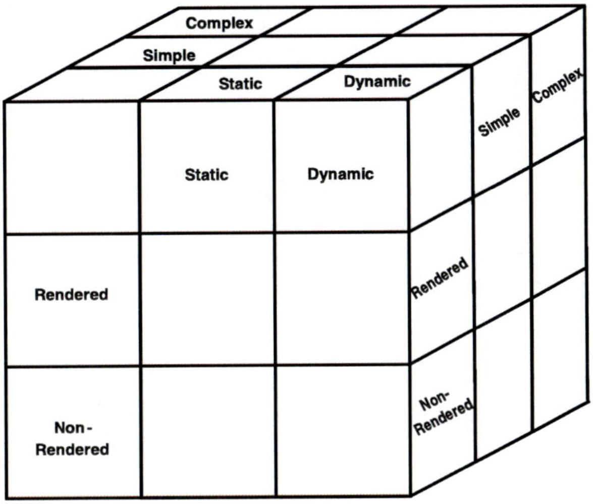

Fig. 4.9 Types of digital objects

4.6 Summary

The purpose of this chapter has been to provide a partial view of the variety of types of digital objects which exist "in the wild" and which one might be required to preserve. The reason has been to ensure that the reader can at least recognise the possibilities when confronted with the challenge of preserving a digital object. Later chapters will discuss preservation techniques for some of this multitude of possibilities.

Chapter 5
Threats to Digital Preservation and Possible Solutions

Keep constantly in mind in how many things you yourself have witnessed changes already. The universe is change, life is understanding.

(Marcus Aurelius)

We indicated in the Introduction some of the things we need to be worried about. In this chapter we look at these in more detail, supported by information about what others worry about.

There are some obvious threats to the preservation of digitally encoded information. One is what one might call "bit rot" i.e. the deterioration in our ability to read the bits in which the information is encoded. While this is fundamental, nevertheless there are an increasing number of ways to overcome this problem, the simplest of which is replication of the bits i.e. making multiple copies.

One way to think about this is to consider what one might be able to rely on in the long term.

Within a single organisation, with a continuous supply of adequate funding, the job of digital preservation is at least feasible. However no-one can be sure of continued funding, and examples of such continued, and generous, funding are hard if not impossible to find. Instead the preservation of any piece of digitally encoded information almost certainly will rely being passed from one organisation to another. Thus it depends on a chain of preservation which is only as strong as its weakest link.

In the following sub-sections we discuss some of the major potential points of failure in these chains and some of the ways in which these points might be addressed. Subsequent sections provide more details of the concepts needed to support these solutions.

D. Giaretta, *Advanced Digital Preservation*, DOI 10.1007/978-3-642-16809-3_5,

Potential points of failure	Potential solutions
Failure of any chain of preservation may be imagined as involving changes in, or non-maintainability of, essential hardware, software or support environment. Additionally the human methodology established for preservation may not be followed (sudden changes of a whole team of people, etc.)	One of the recognised techniques of isolating dependencies on hardware, software and environment is virtualisation. By this is meant the technique of identifying important, abstract, interfaces/processes which can be implemented on top of concrete implementations which are available at any particular time in the future
OAIS stresses the importance of taking into account the changes in the knowledge base of the designated community. This may not be done adequately	Changes in Knowledge Base can only be truly solved by the community itself, but procedures can be proposed which help to ensure that gaps in understandability are at least recognised and the information requested from the community before it is entirely lost
Additionally one may have a loss in the chain of evidence and lack of certainty of provenance or authenticity	Provenance and authenticity is, in part at least, dependent on social and information policy concerns, process documentation, and other aspects which cannot have a purely technical solution. However some tools can be made available to ameliorate the risks of security breaches. Systems security and data integrity are only two aspects of provenance and authenticity, and we should be careful not to assume that tools for these problems will provide solutions to larger problems
Encodings used to establish lack of tampering and currently considered unbreakable, may eventually be broken using increasingly powerful processors or sophistication of attack	Constant vigilance about security of encodings and a preparedness to apply more secure encoding
The custodian of the data, an organisation or project, no matter how well established, may, at some point in the future, cease to exist	Custodianship should always be regarded as a temporary trust and techniques are needed to allow a smooth handing over of holdings from one link in the chain of preservation to the next
Even if the organisation exists, the mechanisms to identify the location of data, for example a DNS entry pointing to a host machine, may no longer be resolvable	The provision of a definitive system of persistent actionable identifiers which spreads the risk of the deterioration of identifier systems must be proposed
Mandating the continued use of specific systems or formats is one possible way to try to ensure preservation. For example we might try to mandate all images to be JPEG, all documents to be PDF/A, and all science data to be kept as XML files, or demand that a specific ontology be adopted. Even if we were to be successful for a limited time, the one thing we can be sure of is that things would change and the mandates would fail	Given the constantly changing world we need a system which does not force a specific way of doing things but instead we should be able to allow anything to be accommodated. For example we cannot mandate a particular way of producing representation information or provenance. While it might have some advantages in terms of interoperability in the short term, in the long term we would be locked into a dead-end. However this should not prevent us from advising on best practise

5.1 What Can Be Relied on in the Long-Term?

While we cannot provide rigorous proofs, it is worth, at this point, listing those things which we might credibly argue would be available in the long term, in order to clarify the basis of our approach. We should be able to trace back our preservation plans to these assumptions. Were we able to undertake a rigorous mathematical proof these would form the basis of the axioms for our "theorems".

- Words on paper (or Silicon Carbide sheets) that people can read; ISO standards are an example of this. Over the long term there may be an issue of language and character shape.

  Carvings in stone and books have proven track records of preserving information over hundreds of years.

- The information such as some fundamental Representation Information which is collected.

  A somewhat recursive assumption, however it is difficult to make progress without it. This Representation Information includes both digital as well as physical (e.g. books) objects.

- Some kind of remote access

  Network access is the natural assumption but in principle other methods of obtaining information from a given address/location would suffice, for example fax or horse-back rider.

- Some kind of computers

  Perhaps not strictly necessary but this seems a sensible assumption given the amount of calculation needed to do some of the most trivial operations, such as displaying anything beyond simple ASCII text, or extracting information from large datasets.

- People? Organisations?

  Clearly neither the originators of the digital objects nor the initial host organisations can be relied on to continue to exist. However if no people and no organisations exist at all then perhaps digital preservation becomes a moot topic.

- Identifiers?

  Some kind of identifier system is needed, as discussed in Sect. 10.3.2, will be needed, but clearly we cannot assume that any given URL, for example, will remain valid.

With these in mind we are almost ready to move on to some general considerations about future-proofing digitally encoded information.

5.2 What Others Think About Major Threats to Digital Preservation

A major survey carried out by the PARSE.Insight project [1], with several thousand responses from around the world, across disciplines and across stakeholders, has shown that the majority of researchers thought that there were a number of threats to the preservation of digital objects which were either very important or important.

There are a number of general threats as shown in Fig. 5.1.

It is interesting to see that human error, natural disasters and political instability are included in the list, in addition to concerns about funding and continuity.

There were also some more specific threats which are summarised in Table 5.1. These were regarded by a clear majority across disciplines, countries and roles as either "important" or "very important".

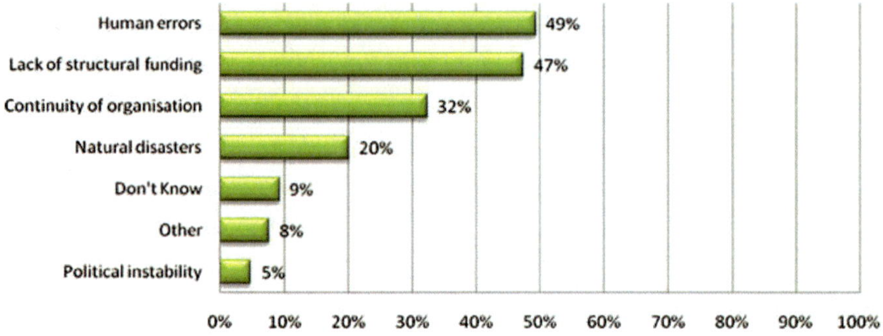

Fig. 5.1 General threats to digital preservation, $n = 1{,}190$

Table 5.1 Threats to digital preservation

Outline threat	Examples
Users may be unable to understand or use the data e.g. the semantics, format, processes or algorithms involved	Things which used to be tacit knowledge are no longer known. For example particular terminology may fall out of use; whole languages may die; paradigms of ways to analyse problems may disappear
Non-maintainability of essential hardware, software or support environment may make the information inaccessible	Hardware on which one currently depends, for example on Intel x86 CPUs, or tape readers, or whole operating systems which software relies, on may no longer function through lack of support. Open source software may be available but its developers may drift away

Table 5.1 (continued)

Outline threat	Examples
The chain of evidence may be lost and there may be lack of certainty of provenance or authenticity	Someone may claim that a digital object is something of significance, for example a diary of a famous person or a piece of missing scientific data, but one may have doubts about its origin and whether it has been surreptitiously altered
Access and use restrictions may make it difficult to reuse data, or alternatively may not be respected in future	A piece of software may refuse to work after a certain date because of a time limit on the licence; it may not be possible to back up a digital object because it would not be legal; your own data, which you had submitted to a repository, may be used without your permission even though you explicitly stated that it should be kept for 30 years without anyone else accessing it
Loss of ability to identify the location of data	An XML schema may reference other schema, but the location suggested for that other schema cannot be found A Web page contains a link to an image but the URL does not work – in fact the DNS may say there is no such address registered
The current custodian of the data, whether an organisation or project, may cease to exist at some point in the future	The organisation that is charged with looking after the digital object may lose its funding
The ones we trust to look after the digital holdings may let us down	The people we entrust with our digital objects may make preservation decisions which in the long run mean that the digital objects are not usable

5.3 Summary

In order to preserve digitally encoded information we must have some understanding of the types of threats that must be guarded against. This chapter should have provided the reader with requisite background knowledge to be aware of the wide variety of threats which must be countered.

Chapter 6
OAIS in More Depth

Do not hover always on the surface of things, nor take up suddenly, with mere appearances; but penetrate into the depth of matters, as far as your time and circumstances allow, especially in those things which relate to your profession.

(Isaac Watts)

Some of the OAIS concepts were introduced in Chap. 3. This chapter delves more deeply into these concepts and the models which OAIS defines. It also explains the hows and whys of OAIS conformance.

A number of OAIS [4] concepts were introduced in Chap. 3. In this chapter we delve somewhat deeper.

The OAIS standard (ISO 14721) serves several different purposes. Its fundamental purpose is to provide concepts that can guide digital preservation. Using these concepts a number of conformance requirements, including mandatory responsibilities, are then described. However another set of related concepts are defined in OAIS which, although not essential for preserving digitally encoded information, may nevertheless be extremely useful to facilitate clear discussion by providing a common terminology.

It is essential to distinguish the concepts which provide useful terminology from those needed for conformance.

An OAIS is ***an archive, consisting of an organization, which may be part of a larger organization, of people and systems that has accepted the responsibility to preserve information and make it available for a Designated Community***. It meets a set of responsibilities as defined in the standard, and this allows an OAIS archive to be distinguished from other uses of the term “archive”.

D. Giaretta, *Advanced Digital Preservation*, DOI 10.1007/978-3-642-16809-3_6,

The term “Open” in OAIS is used to imply that the standard, as well as future related standards, are developed in open forums, and it does not mean that it only applies to open access archives.

The information being maintained has been deemed to need Long Term Preservation, even if the OAIS itself is not permanent. Long Term is long enough to be concerned with the impacts of changing technologies, including support for new media and data formats, or with a changing user community. Long Term may extend indefinitely. In the reference model there is a particular focus on digital information, both as the primary forms of information held and as supporting information for both digitally and physically archived materials. Therefore, the model accommodates information that is inherently non-digital (e.g., a physical sample), but the modelling and preservation of such information is not addressed in detail. The OAIS reference model says it:

- provides a framework for the understanding and increased awareness of archival concepts needed for Long Term digital information preservation and access;
- provides the concepts needed by non-archival organizations to be effective participants in the preservation process;
- provides a framework, including terminology and concepts, for describing and comparing architectures and operations of existing and future archives;
- provides a framework for describing and comparing different Long Term Preservation strategies and techniques;
- provides a basis for comparing the data models of digital information preserved by archives and for discussing how data models and the underlying information may change over time;
- provides a framework that may be expanded by other efforts to cover Long Term Preservation of information that is NOT in digital form (e.g., physical media and physical samples);
- expands consensus on the elements and processes for Long Term digital information preservation and access, and promotes a larger market which vendors can support;
- guides the identification and production of OAIS-related standards.

The reference model addresses a full range of archival information preservation functions including ingest, archival storage, data management, access, and dissemination. It also addresses the migration of digital information to new media and forms, the data models used to represent the information, the role of software in information preservation, and the exchange of digital information among archives. It identifies both internal and external interfaces to the archive functions, and it identifies a number of high-level services at these interfaces. It provides various illustrative examples and some "best practice" recommendations. It defines a minimal set of responsibilities for an archive to be called an OAIS, and it also defines a maximal archive to provide a broad set of useful terms and concepts.

6.1 OAIS Conformance

It is important to remember that, as noted in the introduction, OAIS serves many functions, and two of these functions can cause some confusion when people consider conformance to OAIS.

The terminology introduced is designed to be widely applicable. Therefore just about any archive can describe its functions in OAIS terms, and this leads to claims of OAIS conformance. However this is not true conformance, it is merely verifying that OAIS terminology is indeed widely applicable. OAIS itself defines what conformance involves as follows:

- A conforming OAIS archive implementation shall support the model of information (essentially what is described in Sect. 3.2 and expanded upon in Sect. 6.3 of this book). The OAIS Reference Model does not define or require any particular method of implementation of these concepts.
- A conforming OAIS archive shall fulfil the responsibilities listed in Sect. 6.2 of this book.

A conformant OAIS archive may provide additional services to users that are beyond those required of an OAIS.

It can also provide services to users who are not part of the Designated Community.

It has been said, perhaps half in jest, that a chicken with its head cut off is conformant with OAIS. While it may be possible to use OAIS terminology to describe such a fowl, nevertheless it should be clear that since, for example, it is doubtful that it supports the OAIS information model, and hence it cannot be conformant to OAIS.

Digital archives sometimes claim to be conformant with OAIS when in fact what they mean is that they can use OAIS terminology to describe their functions. It cannot be stressed enough that this is not actually conformance; it just means that OAIS terminology is very useful.

The details of how digital repositories can be assessed in practice will be discussed in Chap. 25, although OAIS conformance is a necessary but not sufficient condition there because OAIS does not cover aspects such as financial stability.

6.2 OAIS Mandatory Responsibilities

The mandatory responsibilities which an OAIS must fulfil are discussed within the standard itself – we use here the text from the updated version of OAIS. The following attempts to provide the whys and hows of these responsibilities:

> Negotiate for and accept appropriate information from information Producers.

WHY: The reason for this requirement is that many times in the past digital objects have essentially been dumped on an archive with little or no documentation about it, making them practically impossible to preserve. In order to help prevent this the archive should make an agreement with the Producer for the hand over not just of the digital objects but also the Representation Information and Preservation Description Information (see Chap. 10), which includes, amongst other things, Provenance Information.

HOW: OAIS does not give a model for such an agreement, but the follow-on standards PAIMAS [22] and PAIS [23] provide some guidelines.

> Obtain sufficient control of the information provided to the level needed to ensure Long Term Preservation.

WHY: The issue here is that the archive needs physical as well as legal control over the information. The need for physical control is fairly obvious, for example to ensure that the bits are safe. Legal control is required because copyright and other legal restrictions, which may be different from one country to the next and may change over time, could otherwise limit [24] the copying and migrations (see Chap. 12) that the archive almost certainly will have to perform. While the lack of such legal control might not stop the archive performing such copying, nevertheless there is a risk that subsequent legal action may force the archive to stop and delete such copies or face financial penalties which could, at the extreme, cause the archive to cease operations.

HOW: The most obvious way of taking physical control would involve the archive taking a copy of the digital objects and keep them in its own storage. Legal and contractual control would require appropriate licences and/or right transfers from the owners of those rights. Further information about Digital Rights Management is provided in Sect. 10.6.

> Determine, either by itself or in conjunction with other parties, which communities should become the Designated Community and, therefore, should be able to understand the information provided, thereby defining its Knowledge Base.

WHY: As discussed earlier, it is essential for the archive to define the Designated Community for a data set in order for preservation to be tested. The definition of the Designated Community allows the archive to be clear about how much Representation Information is needed.

HOW: The Designated Community for a piece of digitally encoded information is not set in stone – it is a decision for the archive (possibly after consulting other stakeholders). It may reasonably be asked "What's to stop the archive making its life easy by defining the Designated Community which is easiest for it to satisfy?" It could for example just say "The Designated Community is that set of people who understand these bits". The answer to the question may be understood by asking oneself the following: "Would I trust my digital objects to an archive which adopts such a definition of Designated Community?" It is to be hoped that it would be fairly self-evident that the use of such a definition would lead to a rapidly diminishing set of people who could understand the digital objects and therefore the archive could not really be said to be doing a good job. Therefore depositors will, if they know that the archive uses such a definition, will not wish to entrust their valuable digital objects to such an archive. Thus it is the "market" which keeps the archive honest. As will be clear when we discuss audit and certification, this definition(s) the archive adopts have to be made available. The question then arises from the point of view of the archive:" How should I define a Designated Community?" OAIS provides no explicit guidance on this point but this is discussed in much more detail in Chap. 8.

> Ensure that the information to be preserved is Independently Understandable to the Designated Community. In particular, the Designated Community should be able to understand the information without needing special resources such as the assistance of the experts who produced the information.

WHY: As discussed earlier the "Independently Understandable" aspect is to make it clear that a member of the Designated Community cannot simply pick up the phone and ask one of the people who created the digital objects for help. This is a practical consideration because such a phone call may be possible when the data is deposited, but certainly will not be possible in 200 (or even 20) year's time. This is not a one-off responsibility. It is one which must continue into the future as the Knowledge Base of the Designated Community changes.

HOW: The archive must have adequate Representation Information in order to satisfy this responsibility. This means that it must be able to create, or have access to, Representation Information, and it must be able to determine how much is needed. These key requirements require the kinds of tools which are discussed in subsequent chapters; Chap. 7 describes many techniques for creating Representation Information and describes where each technique is applicable. Chapter 23 describes the ways in which Representation Information may be shared, in order to avoid unnecessary duplication of effort across large numbers of archives, and instead to share the burden. These techniques also help over the long term, as the Knowledge Base of the Designated Community changes. Chapter 16 covers the tools developed by CASPAR to detect gaps in the Representation Information as the Knowledge Base changes, and techniques for filling those gaps. These tools will be discussed in Sect. 17.4.

Follow documented policies and procedures which ensure that the information is preserved against all reasonable contingencies, including the demise of the archive, ensuring that it is never deleted unless allowed as part of an approved strategy. There should be no ad-hoc deletions,

WHY: This responsibility states the fairly obvious point that the archive should look after the information in the basic ways e.g. against floods and theft. The demise of the archive deserves special consideration. Although many archives act as it they will always exist with adequate funding, this particular responsibility points out that such an assumption must be questioned. In addition of course the archive should not be able to delete its holdings on a whim. Many might take the view that deletions should never be allowed, however others insist that deletions are a natural stage in the life of the data. The wording of this responsibility allows the archive to make such deletions but only under (its own) strictly defined circumstances.

HOW: Backup policies and security procedures should take care of the "reasonably contingencies" as long as they are adequate. While it is not possible to guard against the demise of the archive, for example if funding dries-up, nevertheless it is possible to make plans to safeguard the digital objects by making agreements with other archives. Such agreements would provide a commitment by the second archive to take over the preservation of the digital objects. Of course since one cannot be sure which other archives will continue to exist, an archive may make agreements with several other archives, and perhaps different archives may agree to take different subsets of the holdings.

Make the preserved information available to the Designated Community and enable the information to be disseminated as copies of, or as traceable to, the original submitted Data Objects with evidence supporting its Authenticity.

WHY: There are two parts to this responsibility. The first is that the digitally encoded information has to be made available, at least to the Designated Community. The second part contains a new requirement which is introduced here because we are talking not about understandability, which many other responsibilities cover, but about access. The key question concerns how a user can have confidence that the digital object which the archive provides to him/her is authentic i.e. what it is claimed to be. Chapters 10 and 13 contain a detailed discussion of Authenticity. The phrase "copies of, or as traceable to" means that the archive may keep the original bits and send a copy to the user, or it may have performed various operations such as sending only a sub-set of the original or carried out preservation activities, such as transformation, which change the bit sequences, but will have to maintain appropriate evidence.

HOW: The way in which digital objects are made available to any users are many and varied. In fact access is the user-facing part of the archive where it can make its mark and an immediate impression on users and potential users. OAIS has very little to say about the types of access which may be provided, nor does this book have much to say about it beyond some points about Finding Aids in Chap. 17. On the other hand Authenticity is the subject of Chap. 13 which also contains many examples of the types of evidence which may be provided by the archive and a number of tools which might be useful; it also provides ways of dealing with the "as copies of, or as traceable to" requirement.

Dark Archives are those which hold digital objects but do not make them accessible – at least not for some period or until some pre-determined trigger. These archives can still be preserving the understandability and usability of the digital objects for a Designated Community but do not, during that "dark" period, allow even the Designated Community to access them. During that "dark" period it would not be possible, without special access being granted, to verify the preservation of those digital objects.

6.3 OAIS Information Model

For convenience, the following repeats some of the material from Chap. 3, with some additional explanations and examples.

6.3.1 OAIS: Representation Network

A basic concept of the OAIS Reference Model (ISO 14721) is that of information being a combination of data and Representation Information as shown in Fig. 6.1.

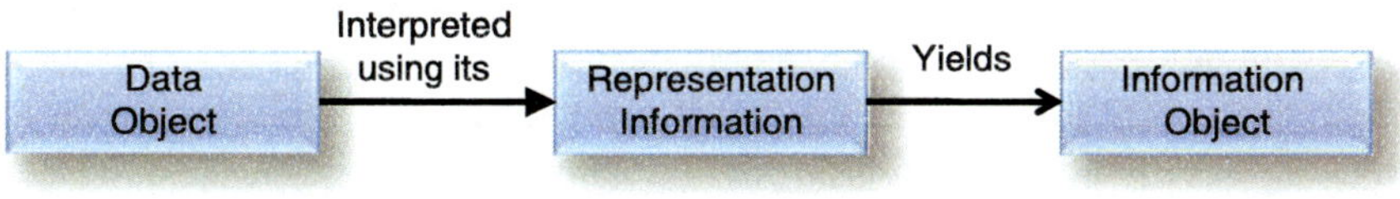

Fig. 6.1 Representation information

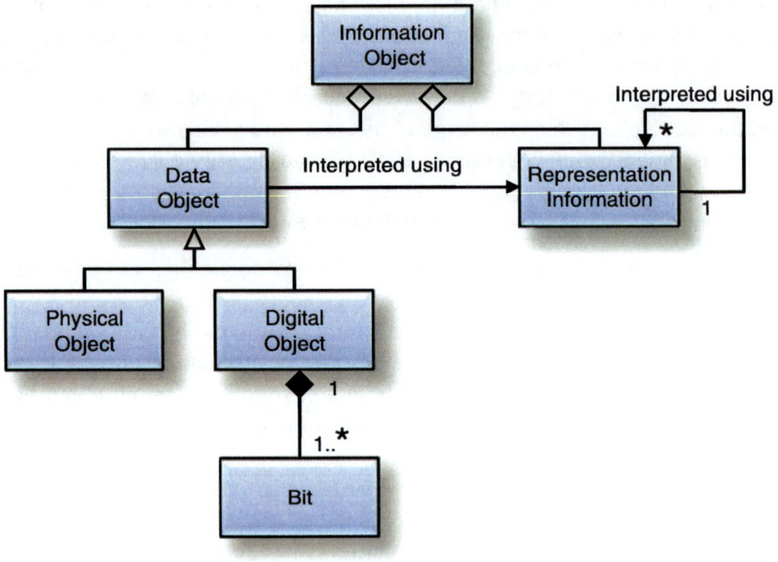

Fig. 6.2 OAIS information model

The UML diagram in Fig. 6.2 illustrates this concept. The Information Object is composed of a Data Object that is either physical or digital, and the Representation Information that allows for the full interpretation of the data into meaningful information. This model is valid for all the types of information in an OAIS.

This UML diagram means that

- an Information Object is made up of a Data Object and Representation Information
- A Data Object can be either a Physical Object or a Digital Object. An example of the former is a piece of paper or a rock sample.
- A Digital Object is made up of one or more Bits.
- A Data Object is interpreted using Representation Information
- Representation Information is itself interpreted using further Representation Information

This figure shows that Representation Information may contain references to other Representation Information. When this is coupled with the fact that Representation Information is an Information Object that may have its own Digital Object and other Representation Information associated with understanding each Digital Object, as shown in a compact form by the interpreted using association, the resulting set of objects can be referred to as a Representation Network.

Representation Information Object shows more details and in particular breaks out the semantic and structural information as well as recognising that there may be Other representation information such as software illustrated in Fig. 6.3.

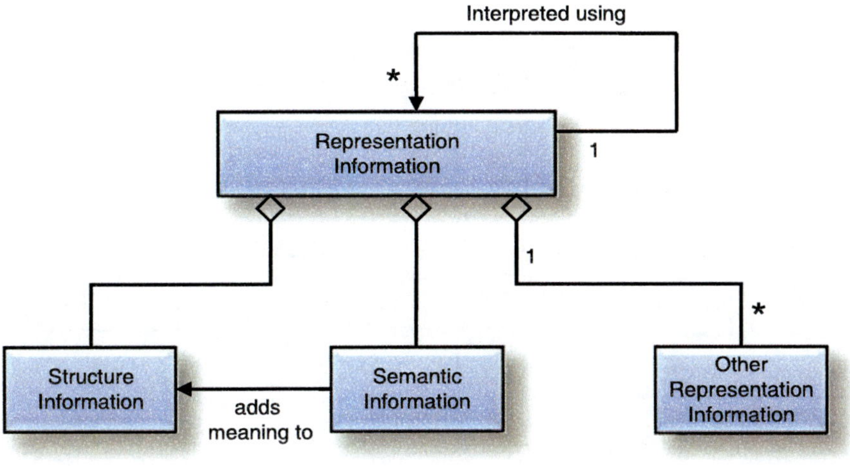

Fig. 6.3 Representation information object

The recursion of the Representation Information will ultimately stop at a physical object such as a printed document (ISO standard, informal standard, notes, publications etc) but use of things like paper documentation would tend to prevent "automated use" and "interoperability", and also complete resolution of the complete Representation Network to this level would be an almost impossible task. Therefore we would prefer to stop earlier. In particular we can stop for a particular Designated Community when the Representation Information can be understood with that Designated Community's Knowledge Base.

For example a science file in FITS format would be easily understood and used by someone who knew how to handle this format – someone whose Knowledge Base includes FITS – for example an astronomer who has some appropriate software (although see [25]). Someone whose Knowledge Base does not include FITS would need additional Representation Information, for example would have to be provided with some software or the written FITS standard, as illustrated in Fig. 6.4.

This means that for a FITS file to be understood, assuming for the moment we choose our Designated Community such that its members are ignorant of these pieces of information:

- one needs the FITS standards which specify the mandatory keywords and structures. Let's assume these are provided in the form of PDF files. In order to understand these one needs
- the PDF standard – perhaps as a simple ASCII text file. But in order to use the PDF file containing the FITS standard one would probably need some software. One could either write some afresh or one may prefer to use
- PDF software e.g. the Acrobat reader.
- however instead of reading the FITS standard one may want to use some FITS software. If this is Java software then one would need

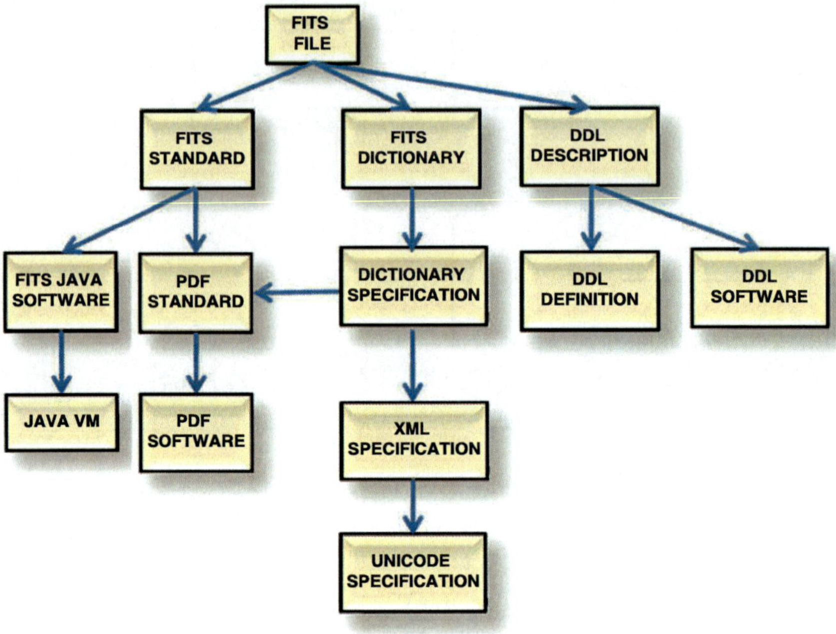

Fig. 6.4 Representation network for a FITS file

- a Java Virtual Machine – let's assume our Designated Community has such a thing.
- As an alternative to using the FITS software or working through the FITS standards and then constructing appropriate software, there may also be a formal definition of the structure using some Data Description Language (DDL), which itself has a specification, and associated software which can use the data description to extract data from the FITS file.

However even with all these things we would find that the FITS standards or the FITS software only really tells us about a few dozen of the keywords in the FITS file; FITS files often have hundreds of keywords in the headers. In order to understand these one would need:

- the keyword dictionary. If this were in some formal structure such as DEDSL (see Sect. 7.5.1), one would need
- the dictionary specification – the specification may be in a PDF which we discussed before (by the way this shows that in general we are dealing with graphs i.e. the connections can form loops, rather than trees, where there are no loops). But the dictionary itself may be expressed in XML, in which case we may need
- a specification of XML. The binary encoding of XML uses Unicode therefore one would also need
- the Unicode specification

If we had a different definition for our Designated Community, for example a current day professional astronomer, then such a person would not need to be provided with all such Representation Information. However in the future, say 30 years ahead, then a professional astronomer may not be familiar with, for the sake of example let's say, XML. This may be a reasonable possibility when one considers that XML did not exist 30 years ago, and it might not be in use in 30 year's time. Therefore one must be able to supply that piece of Representation Information at that future time.

The end of the recursion we link to the Knowledge Base of the Designated Community. However the CEDARS [26] project referred to *Gödel ends*. They argued by analogy with Gödel's Theorem, which states "any logical system has to be incomplete", that "representation nets must have ends corresponding to formats that are understood without recourse to information in the archive, e.g. plain text using the ASCII character set, the Posix API.". The difference is that although the analogy is quite nice, it is hard to see where the net ends without using the concept of a Designated Community. It would mean that the repository is not testable because one does not know who to use as a test subject (a 3-year old? a bushman?).

Moreover a problem with Representation Information is that the amount needed for a particular object could be vast and impractical to do anything with in reality. It is for that reason that the concept of the Designated Community is so important. It allows us to limit the Representation Information required to be captured at any one time, and allows the judgement of how much to be testable.

6.3.2 Preservation Issues

Given a file or a stream of bits how does one know what Representation Information is needed? This question applies to Representation Information itself as well as to the digital objects we are primarily interested in preserving and using; how does one know, for example, if this thing is, for example, in FITS format?

1. Someone may simply know what it is and how to deal with it i.e. the bits are within the Knowledge Base
2. One may have a pointer to the appropriate Representation Information.
3. One may be able to recognise the format by looking for various types of patterns, for example the UNIX file command does this.
4. One may feed the bits into all available interpreters to see which ones accept the data as valid
5. Other means.

Of the above, if (1) does not apply then only (2) is reliable because (3) and (4) rely on some form of pattern recognition and there is no guarantee that any pattern is unique. Even if the File Format is unique (perhaps discoverable using the UNIX ***file*** command) the possible associated semantics will almost certainly not be guessable with any real certainty.

However if neither (1) nor (2) are available then one of the other methods must be used, as would be the case for data rescue (in the sense of data inherited without adequate "metadata".

6.3.3 *Representation Information vs. Format*

To simply give the format of a piece of digital information is inadequate to communicate information, as a simple counter-example shows. Suppose that someone gives you a piece of digital data and tell you that it is MS Word version 6 format. This enables you to find the right software to display the contents. However when you do that you see the following text:

sfqsftfoubujpo jogpsnbujpo svmft

To understand what this means, one must be supplied with the additional information that a simple alphabetic substitution cipher (a→b, b→c etc) with spaces unchanged, has been used.

With that additional information we can find out that the message is:

representation information rules

One should be suspicious of any discussion of digital preservation which talks only about formats, with no mention of semantics or other types of Representation Information.

6.3.4 *Information Packaging*

Another part of the OAIS Information Model is related to packaging. The reason this is important is because the digital data is almost never "naked". In other words it might be a file in a file system and that may seem "naked" but in fact the computer operating system has to be able to recognise it as a file and hence it cannot be completely "naked". This is even more evident when one is transferring data from one place to another.

OAIS Packaging Information is that information which

> ***either actually or logically, binds or relates the components of the package into an identifiable entity on specific media. For example, if the Content Information and PDI are identified as being the content of specific files on a CD-ROM, then the Packaging Information may include the ISO 9660 volume/file structure on the CD-ROM. These choices are the subject of local archive definitions or conventions. The Packaging Information does not necessarily need to be preserved by an OAIS since it does not contribute to the Content Information or the PDI. However, there are cases where the OAIS may be required to reproduce the original submission exactly. In this case the Content Information is defined to include all the bits submitted.***
>
> ***The OAIS should also avoid holding PDI or Content Information only in the naming conventions of directory or file name structures. These structures are most likely to be used as Packaging Information. Packaging Information is not preserved by Migration. Any information saved in file names or directory structures may be lost when the Packaging Information is altered. The subject of Packaging Information is an important consideration to the Migration of Information within an OAIS to newer media.***

The contents of a general Information Package is illustrated in Figs. 6.5 and 6.6.

This general Information Package has

- Zero or only one piece of Content Information
- Zero, one or multiple pieces of PDI
- Exactly one piece of Packaging Information
- Zero, one or multiple pieces of Packaging Description i.e. there could be many possible ways to describe the package

The minimal package therefore is empty except for some packaging information, which might not seem very useful but the definition is at least extremely flexible.

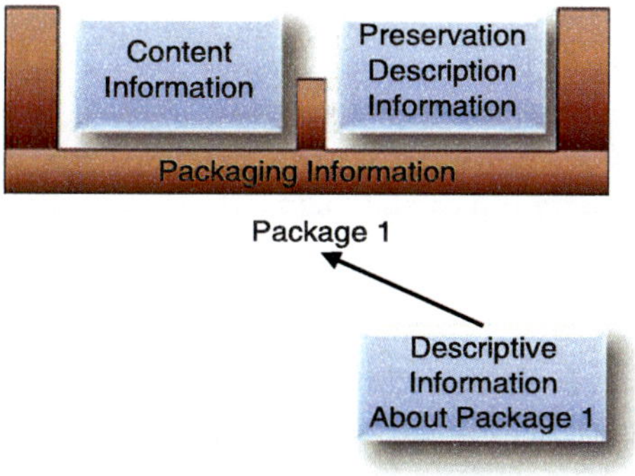

Fig. 6.5 Packaging concepts

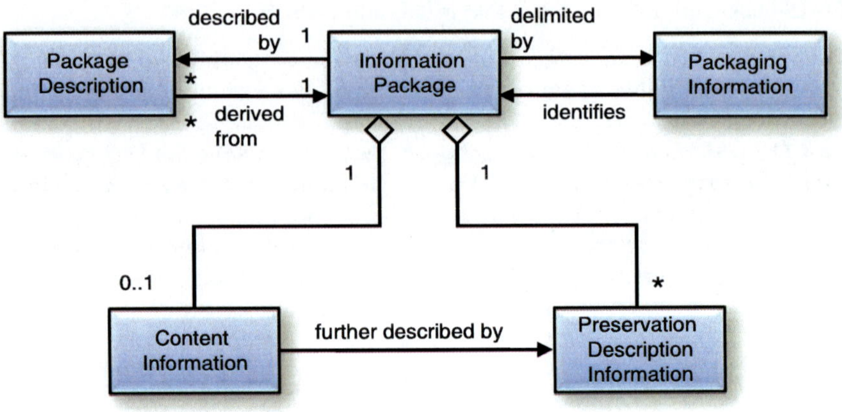

Fig. 6.6 Information package contents

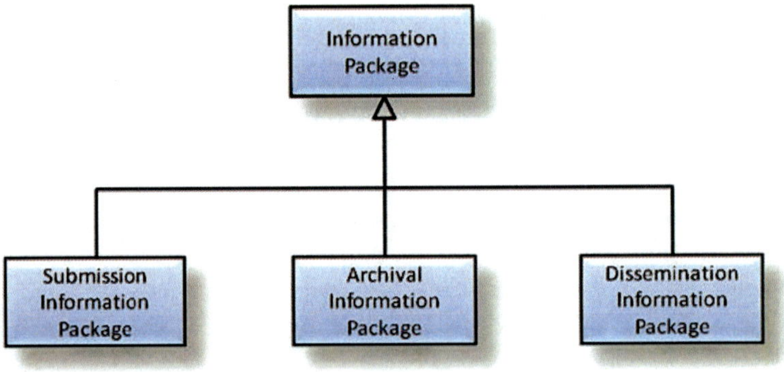

Fig. 6.7 Information package taxonomy

OAIS further introduced a taxonomy of Information Packages, as shown in Fig. 6.7. This shows the Dissemination Information Package (DIP), which is sent to Consumers, the Submission Information Package (SIP), which the archive receives from the Producer, and the Archival Information Package (AIP) which is discussed in detail below. The roles of these Information Packages are shown in Fig. 6.8. Note that the contents of the SIP and DIP can be almost anything – for this reason OAIS says very little about them.

6.3.5 Archival Information Package

Of these types of Information Packages the only one which OAIS describes in detail is the Archival Information Package (AIP), which is conceptually vital for

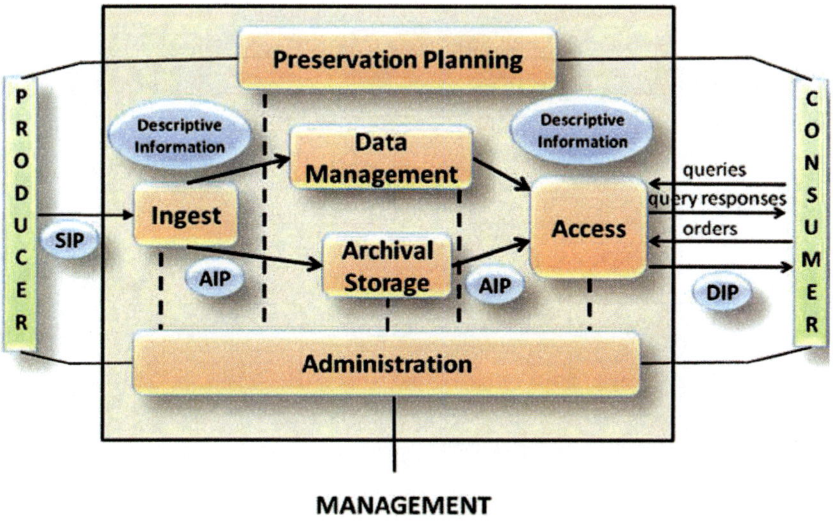

Fig. 6.8 OAIS functional model

the preservation of a digital object. According to OAIS the ***AIP is defined to provide a concise way of referring to a set of information that has, in principle, all the qualities needed for permanent, or indefinite, Long Term Preservation of a designated Information Object.***

It is important to realise that the AIP is a logical construct i.e. it does not have to be a single file.

The AIP is shown in Fig. 6.9. Note that this means that, unlike the general Information Package, the AIP must have exactly one piece of Content Information and one piece of PDI.

Remember that a single Information Object (i.e. Content Information or PDI) could consist of many separate digital objects.

The full AIP is illustrated in Fig. 6.10.

There are very many ways of packaging information, both physically as well as logically. As we will see, we must provide at least one packaging implementation which can be used in the Testbeds in Part II. It should also be possible to provide

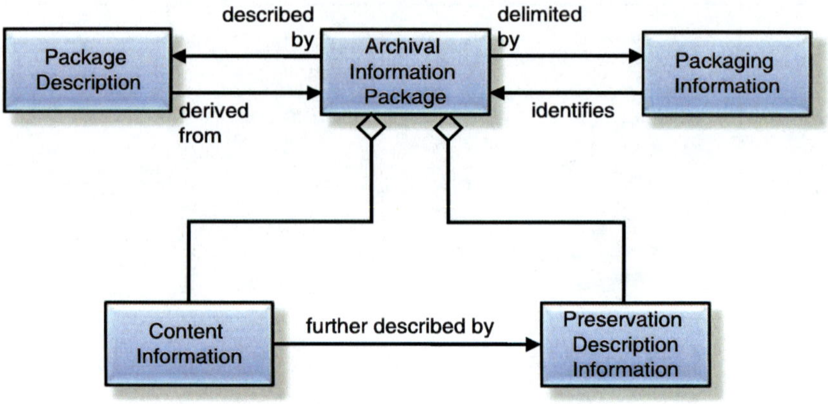

Fig. 6.9 Archival information package summary

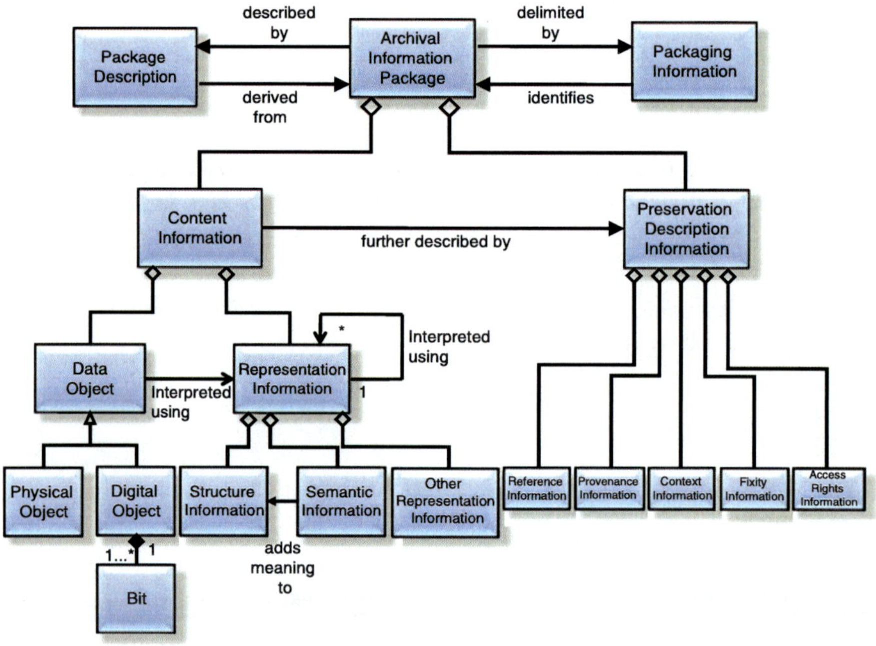

Fig. 6.10 Archival information package (AIP)

some level of Virtualisation (see Sect. 7.8) – possibly related to the "tree" structure of a simple or complex object. In addition there will have to be some aspects of the "on-demand" object, for example where a sub-component in the package has to be uncompressed in order to produce the next level of unpacking which is needed.

6.4 OAIS Functional Model

The Functional Model is what one often sees in expositions or training sessions about OAIS. However, although this provides some important vocabulary, and provides a good checklist if one is creating an archive, it is not relevant to OAIS compliance.

6.4.1 OAIS Functional Entities

The role provided by each of the entities in Fig. 6.8 is described briefly by OAIS as follows:

The ***Ingest*** entity provides the services and functions to accept Submission Information Packages (SIPs) from Producers (or from internal elements under Administration control) and prepare the contents for storage and management within the archive. Ingest functions include receiving SIPs, performing quality assurance on SIPs, generating an Archival Information Package (AIP) which complies with the archive's data formatting and documentation standards, extracting Descriptive Information from the AIPs for inclusion in the archive database, and coordinating updates to Archival Storage and Data Management.

The ***Archival Storage*** entity provides the services and functions for the storage, maintenance and retrieval of AIPs. Archival Storage functions include receiving AIPs from Ingest and adding them to permanent storage, managing the storage hierarchy, refreshing the media on which archive holdings are stored, performing routine and special error checking, providing disaster recovery capabilities, and providing AIPs to Access to fulfil orders.

The ***Data Management*** entity provides the services and functions for populating, maintaining, and accessing both Descriptive Information which identifies and documents archive holdings and administrative data used to manage the archive. Data Management functions include administering the archive database functions (maintaining schema and view definitions, and referential integrity), performing database updates (loading new descriptive information or archive administrative data), performing queries on the data management data to generate query responses, and producing reports from these query responses.

The ***Administration*** entity provides the services and functions for the overall operation of the archive system. Administration functions include soliciting and negotiating submission agreements with Producers, auditing submissions to ensure that they meet archive standards, and maintaining configuration management of system hardware and software. It also provides system engineering functions to monitor and improve archive operations, and to inventory, report on, and migrate/update the contents of the archive. It is also responsible for establishing and maintaining archive standards and policies, providing customer support, and activating stored requests.

The ***Preservation Planning*** entity provides the services and functions for monitoring the environment of the OAIS, providing recommendations and preservation plans to ensure that the information stored in the OAIS remains accessible to, and understandable by, the Designated Community over the Long Term, even if the original computing environment becomes obsolete. Preservation Planning functions include evaluating the contents of the archive and periodically recommending archival information updates, recommending the migration of current archive holdings, developing recommendations for archive standards and policies, providing periodic risk analysis reports, and monitoring changes in the technology environment and in the Designated Community's service requirements and Knowledge Base. Preservation Planning also designs Information Package templates and provides design assistance and review to specialize these templates into SIPs and AIPs for specific submissions. Preservation Planning also develops detailed Migration plans, software prototypes and test plans to enable implementation of Administration migration goals.

The ***Access*** entity provides the services and functions that support Consumers in determining the existence, description, location and availability of information stored in the OAIS, and allowing Consumers to request and receive information products. Access functions include communicating with Consumers to receive requests, applying controls to limit access to specially protected information, coordinating the execution of requests to successful completion, generating responses (Dissemination Information Packages, query responses, reports) and delivering the responses to Consumers.

In addition to the entities described above, there are various ***Common Services*** assumed to be available. These services are considered to constitute another functional entity in this model. This entity is so pervasive that, for clarity, it is not shown in Fig. 6.8.

Many archives have mapped themselves to the OAIS Functional Model; see for example the BADC archive [27].

It has been said that almost anything could be mapped to the Functional Model. For example a simple network switch has

- a Producer – the one who generates the network packets
- Ingest – which accepts the packet
- a Consumer, to whom the network packets are sent which it receives from Access
- an Administration which determines which packet goes to which consumer
- Archival Storage – for the few nano-seconds for which the packet is to be held
- Data Management which looks after the network packet
- Preservation Planning is, in this case, essentially nothing

In this way we can describe a network switch using OAIS terminology. However it does not mean that the switch does anything useful when it comes to digital preservation.

On the other hand the terminology is extremely useful when intercomparing different archives, especially those which have a different disciplinary background and hence a different vocabulary.

6.5 Information Flows and Layering

OAIS describes a number of logical flows of information within a repository. This book will not discuss these flows. Instead we introduce a different view which will help us later on in the discussions.

It is useful to think in general what happens when one archives digital objects, as illustrated in Fig. 6.11

The idea behind this diagram is that in order to preserve a digital object one needs to capture, during the ingest process (starting at the upper left of the figure and following the curved arrow, a number of aspects about it in order that one can satisfy the concerns raised in Chap. 1. For example one needs to know about the access rights associated with it; one needs to capture aspects of the high level knowledge associated with it; one needs to understand how to extract numbers and other data elements from the bits, and so forth.

This is presented as layers because one can imagine changing the lower layers without affecting the layers above. For example the High Level Knowledge to be captured may change depending upon the Designated Community; such a change would not affect the Access Control information. Also the Access Control information is likely to be applicable to many different Information Objects. Similarly the information may be encoded in different ways, which would alter the bit-level descriptions, but the High Level Knowledge would be unaffected, thus the latter could apply to many of the former.

It is useful to think about these kinds of variations in order to identify commonalities and differences.

We will return to these considerations later, in Part II.

6.6 Issues Not Covered in Detail by OAIS

As noted at the start of this section OAIS does not address all issues to do with digital preservation. Some of these topics fall outside the remit of the OAIS standard; some of these were left for follow-on standards, while still others were thought to be too specialised or too immature to be amenable to this type of standardisation.

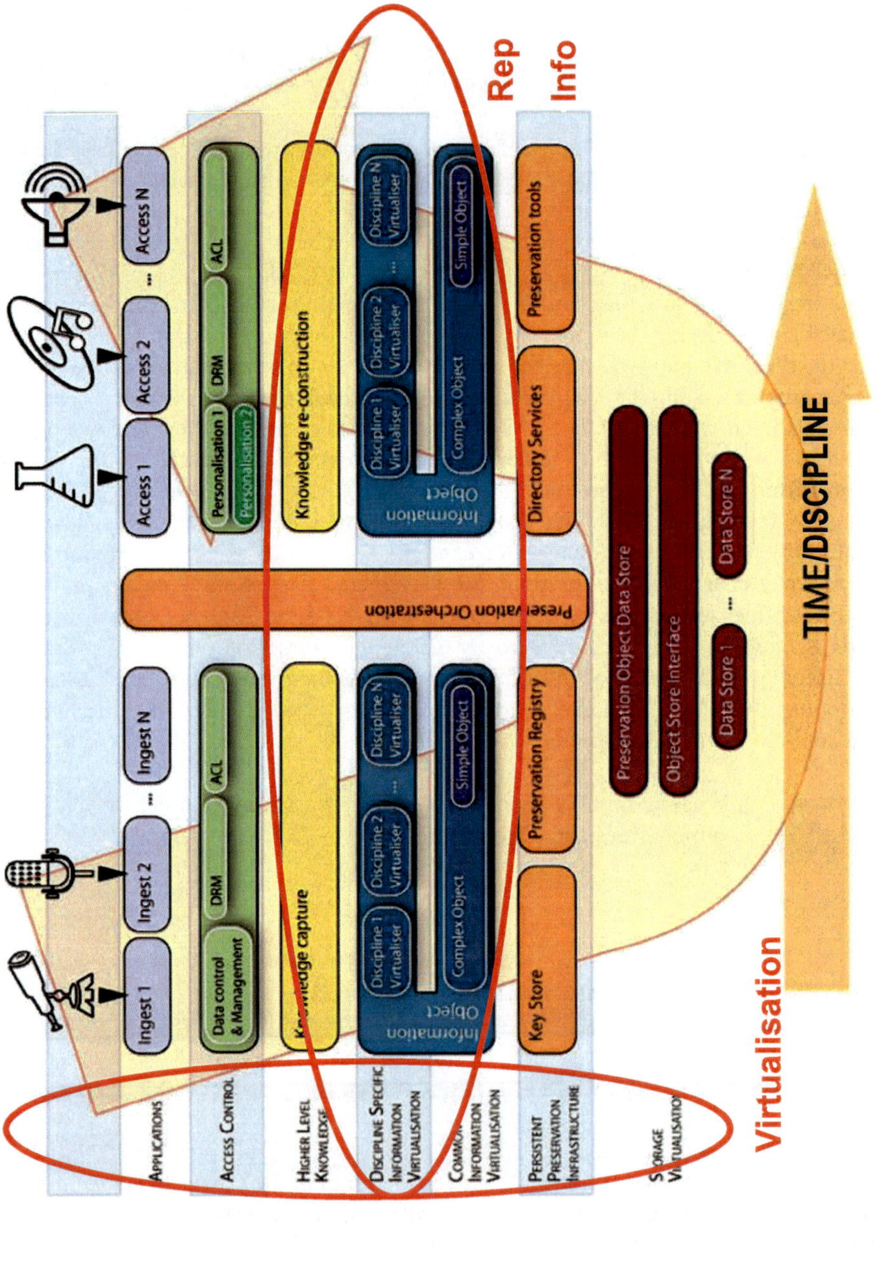

Fig. 6.11 Information flow architecture

The former category includes:

- standard(s) for the interfaces between OAIS type archives;
- standard(s) for the submission (ingest) methodology used by an archive;
- standard(s) for the submission (ingest) of digital data sources to the archive;
- standard(s) for the delivery of digital sources from the archive;
- standard(s) for the submission of digital "metadata", about digital or physical data sources, to the archive;
- standard(s) for the identification of digital sources within the archive;
- protocol standard(s) to search and retrieve "metadata" information about digital and physical data sources;
- standard(s) for media access allowing replacement of media management systems without having to rewrite the media;
- standard(s) for specific physical media;
- standard(s) for the migration of information across media and formats;
- standard(s) for recommended archival practices;
- standard(s) for accreditation of archives.

The latter category, namely those too archive/domain specific for OAIS-type standardisation includes:

- appraisal process for information to be archived
- access methods and Finding Aids
- details of Data Management

6.7 Summary

Working through this chapter, the reader should have gained a greater understanding of the OAIS Reference Model, in particular an appreciation of why it is the way it is. The reader should also have a clear understanding of which parts of the model must be followed for conformance and which parts are there simply to provide common terminology.

Chapter 7
Understanding a Digital Object: Basic Representation Information

Co-author Stephen Rankin

Representation of the world, like the world itself, is the work of men; they describe it from their own point of view, which they confuse with the absolute truth.

(Simone de Beauvoir)

This chapter describes some of the basic techniques for creating Representation Information and how these techniques can be applied to a variety of digital objects.

7.1 Levels of Application of Representation Information Concept

OAIS is not a design; its lack of specificity gives it wide applicability and great strength but it also forces implementers to make choices, among which is the level of application of the OAIS concepts. In this chapter we look particularly at Representation Information.

7.1.1 OAIS as a Checklist

OAIS "***provides a framework, including terminology and concepts, for describing and comparing architectures and operations of existing and future archives***."

The simplest way of applying OAIS is as a checklist. In particular, instead of "*Do we have enough 'metadata'?*", the question becomes "*Do we have Representation Information? Do we have Representation Information for that piece of Representation Information? Do we have Preservation Description Information (PDI)? Do we have Packaging Information?*" and so on.

Similarly one can ask whether the various processes and functions defined in OAIS can be identified in an existing or planned archive.

D. Giaretta, *Advanced Digital Preservation*, DOI 10.1007/978-3-642-16809-3_7,

7.1.2 Preservation Without Automation

Going beyond a simple checklist one can use OAIS as the framework for, for example, Representation Information. Here we must simply ensure that there is adequate Representation Information for the Designated Community. Other users may or may not be able to understand the data content.

Any piece of that Representation Information could itself be as "opaque" as any other piece of data. OAIS requires that each piece of Representation Information has its own Representation Information – with the recursion stopping, as discussed in Sect. 8, where it meets, in a sense which needs to be properly defined, the Knowledge Base of the Designated Community – which itself needs to be adequately defined.

However even the Designated Community may need to put in a considerable effort, for example to read documentation and create specialised software at each level of the recursion, in order to understand and use the content.

The point is that without the Representation Information this would very likely be impossible; application of digital forensics or guesswork may be allow something to be done, but one would not be certain.

Example: The Representation Information could be in the form of a detailed document describing, in simple text and diagrams, how the information is encoded. The text description would have to be read by a human and presumably software would have to be written – possibly requiring significant effort. The IETF Request for Comments (RFC) system (http://www.ietf.org/rfc.html) is an example of this use of simple text files to describe all the major systems in the Internet.

7.1.3 Preservation with Automation and Interoperability

The next level is to try to ensure that the use of the Representation Information is as easy and automated as possible, and is widely usable beyond the Designated Community. This demands increasing automation in the access, interpretation and use of Representation Information, and also the provision of more clues to users from different disciplines.

For the latter one can begin by offering some common views on data – for example allowing easier use in generic applications – by means of virtualisation. An example of this would be where the information is essentially an image. This fact could be made explicit in the Representation Information so that an application would know that it makes sense to handle the data as a 2-dimensional image. In particular the data can be displayed; it has a size specified as a number of rows and columns. Further discussion is provided in Sect. 7.8.

This type of virtualisation is common in many other, non-preservation related, areas. It is the basis on which computer operating systems can work, surviving many generations of changes in component technologies, on a variety of hardware. For example, the operations which a disk drive must perform can be specified and used throughout the rest of the operating system, but the specifics of how that is implemented are isolated within a driver library and drive electronics. The underlying idea here is, in software terms, to define a set of interfaces which can be implemented on top of a variety of specific instances which will change over time.

7.2 Overview of Techniques for Describing Digital Objects

The OAIS Reference Model standard has a great deal to say about Information Modelling in general terms and a number of these ideas are used in this section.

Figure 7.1 shows Representation Information can contain Structure Semantic and Other Information. In the following sub-sections we describe some of the basic techniques for each of these types and then give some examples of applying these to the various classifications of digital objects presented in Chap. 4.

It is important to note that the classification indicated in Fig. 7.1 does not require that the various pieces are separate digital objects, or separate digital files. For example a single document could provide all these types of Representation Information, possibly heavily intertwined.

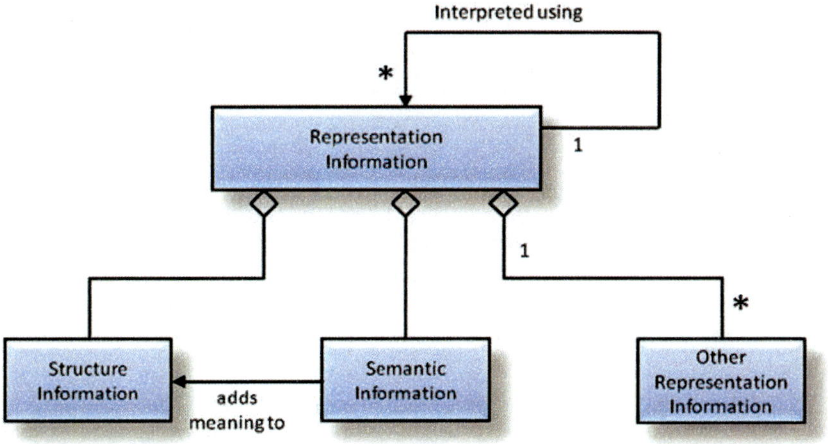

Fig. 7.1 Representation information object

There will be a great deal more said about Semantics in Chap. 8, making links to the Designated Community.

As pointed out in Sect. 7.1, Representation Information can simply be a handwritten note or a text document which provides, in sufficient human-readable detail, enough information for someone to write special software to access the information – for example by rendering the image or extracting the numbers a digital object contains. Providing Representation Information in this way, as has been pointed out, makes automated use rather difficult at present (at least until there are computers which can understand the written word as well as a human can). Therefore we focus in these sections on more formal methods of description.

To define what we might call "good" RepInfo is somewhat difficult to quantify and depends on many factors, three of which are:

- what does a piece of RepInfo allow someone to do with the data - what is it used for? Alternatively, what does one expect people to do with the data, and what information about the data will enable them to do it?
- how long into the future does one expect the data and RepInfo to be used?
- who is supposed to be using the RepInfo and data, and what is their expected background knowledge?

Of course one is not expected to foresee the future. Instead one defines the Designated Community and then one sees what Representation Information is needed now. As time goes by, more Representation Information will be needed.

However there are good reasons for going a little further, namely to collect as much Representation Information as possible (within reason):

- having machine processable Representation Information facilitates interoperability
- the longer one waits to collect Representation Information the more difficult it may be, because the experts who used to know the details may have retired
- it may be of use to other repositories which have a different definition of its Designated Community.

For example, in Sect. 7.3, we talk about Structure RepInfo. In doing so we try to provide an abstract description of what should be contained within it.

In most cases some of the information highlighted in Sect. 7.3.1 can be omitted. If you assume, for example, that current and future users of it know that the data uses IEEE floating point values, then there is no need to include that information. It is really up to you do decide if the RepInfo is adequate for your users now and in the future.

The detailed definitions of RepInfo given here also provide the reader the knowledge required to evaluate existing RepInfo. For example, if there is existing document on Structure RepInfo for some data, then does it contain the types of information described in Sect. 7.3.1? If not, then the reader may have to consider whether or not the existing Structure RepInfo is adequate for current and future use.

Inevitably there can never be an absolutely complete set of definitions for RepInfo about data in general. This is simply due to the fact that data is so varied and complex.

Here we provide further details of the basic techniques. Most of these characteristic have been gained by studying many data sets and formal data description languages.

Once the abstract notions about a particular type of RepInfo have been described, then existing tools and standards are described that may help you in creating RepInfo if you discover that your existing RepInfo is inadequate for your purposes (or non-existent). Most of these tools do not attempt to create a perfect collection of RepInfo, and we will try to highlight what they can and cannot describe. Most of the tools generate RepInfo in accordance to some formal standard and format. As noted several times above, this has advantages that when the RepInfo comes to be used; it allows the data to be used much more easily than if one just had the traditional "informal" documentation.

The OAIS layered information model (Fig. 7.2) gives a high level view which is quite useful at this point.

This model is in an appendix of the OAIS Reference Model and as such is not part of that standard. However it contains a number of useful ideas, including:

- The Media Layer simply models the fact that the bit strings are stored on physical or communications media as magnetic domains or as voltages. The function of this layer is to convert that bit representation to the bit representation that can be used in higher level (i.e., 1 and 0). This layer has as single interface, which

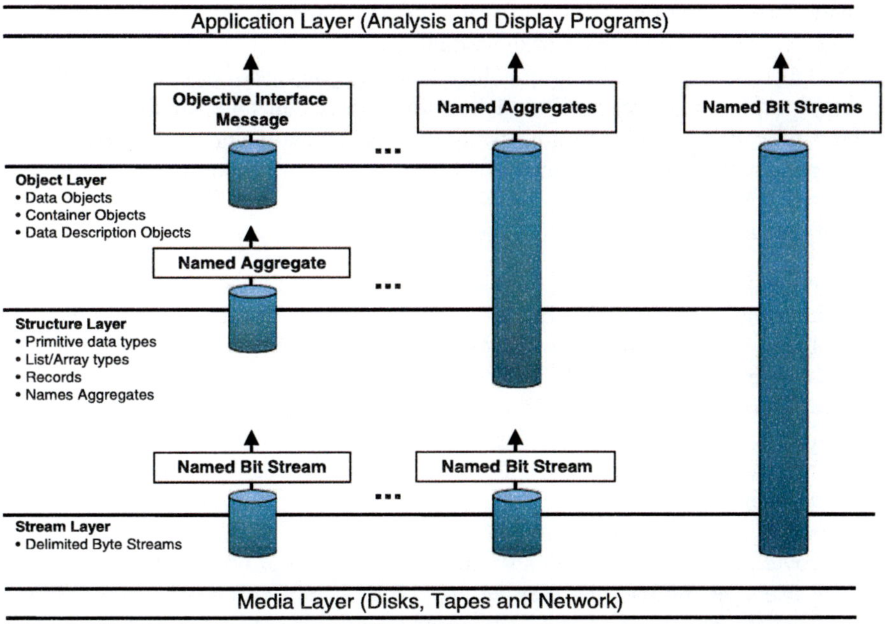

Fig. 7.2 OAIS layered information model

enable higher layers to specify the location and size of the bitstream of interest and receive the bits as a string of 1 and 0 bits. In modern computing systems device drivers and chips built into the physical storage interface provide much of this functionality.

- The Stream Layer hides the unique characteristics of the transport medium by stripping any artefacts of the storage or transmission process (such as packet formats, block sizes, inter-record gaps, and error-correction codes) and provides the higher levels with a consistent view of data that is independent of its medium. The interface between the Stream Layer and higher layers allows the higher layers to request Data Blocks by name and receive a bit/byte string representing those Data Blocks. The term "name" here means any unique key for locating the data stream of interest. Examples include path names for files or message identifiers for telecommunication messages. In modern computing systems, operating system file systems often provide this layer of functionality.
- The Structure Layer converts the bit/byte streams from the Stream Layer interface into addressable structures of primitive data types that can be recognized and operated on by computer processors and operating systems. For any implementation, the structure layer defines the primitive data types and aggregations that are recognized. This usually means at least characters and integer and real numbers. The aggregation types typically supported include a record (i.e., a structure that can hold more than one data type) and an array (where each element consists of the same data type). Issues relating to the representation of primitive data types are resolved in this layer. The interface from the Structure Layer to higher levels allows the higher levels to request labelled aggregations of primitive data types and receive them in a structured form that may be internally addressable. In modern computing systems programming language compilers and interpreters generally provides this layer of functionality.
- The Object Layer, which converts the labelled aggregates of primitive data types into information, represented as objects that are recognizable and meaningful in the application domain. In the scientific domain, this includes objects such as images, spectra, and histograms. The object layer adds semantic meaning to the data treated by the lower layers of the model. Some specific functions of this layer include the following:

  - define data types based on information content rather than on the representation of those data at the structure layer. For example, many different kinds of objects – images, maps, and tables – can be implemented at the structure level using arrays or records. Within the object layer, images, maps, and tables are recognized and treated as distinct types of information.
  - present applications with a consistent interface to similar kinds of information objects, regardless of their underlying representations. The interface defines the operations that can be performed on the object, the inputs required for each operation and the output data types from each.
  - provide a mechanism to identify the characteristics of objects that are visible to users, operations that may be applied to an object, and the relationships between objects. The Interface between the Object Layer and the Application

Layer allows the higher levels to specify the operation that is to be applied to an object, the parameters needed for that operation and the form in which results of the operations will be returned. One special interface allows the user to discover the semantics of the objects, such as operations available and relationships to other objects. In modern computing systems subroutine libraries or object repositories and interfaces supply this functionality.

- The Application Layer contains customized programs to analyze the Data Objects and present the analysis or the data object in a form that a Data Consumer can understand. In modern computing systems application programs supply this functionality.

7.3 Structure Representation Information

OAIS has the following to say about Structure Representation Information (SI):

Structure Information: The information that imparts meaning about how other information is organized. For example, it maps bit streams to common computer types such as characters, numbers, and pixels and aggregations of those types such as character strings and arrays.

The Digital Object, as shown in* Fig. 7.3, *is itself composed of one or more bit sequences. The purpose of the Representation Information object is to convert the bit sequences into more meaningful information. It does this by describing the format, or data structure concepts, which are to be applied to the bit sequences and that in turn result in more meaningful values such as characters, numbers, pixels, arrays, tables, etc. These common computer data types, aggregations of these data types, and mapping rules which map from the underlying data types to the higher level concepts needed to understand the Digital Object are referred to as the Structure Information of the Representation Information object. These structures are commonly identified by name or by relative position within the associated bit sequences. The Structure Information is often referred to as the 'format' of the digital object.

We have seen the following figure several times before, but this time we will move from the very abstract view to the concrete.

An obvious example of Structure RepInfo is a document or standard that describes how to "read and write" a file format.

Structure RepInfo can be broken down into levels, the first level being the structure of the bits and how they map to data values. This involves the exact specification of how the bits contain the information of a data value and involves the definition of several generic properties. This bit structure will be referred to as the Physical Data Structure, and often is dictated by the computing hardware on which the data was created and the programming languages used to write the data. Data values are then

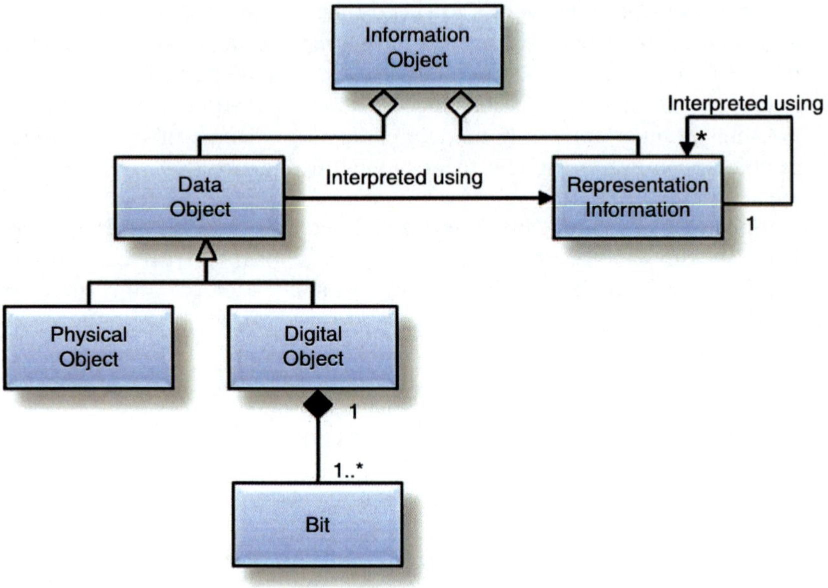

Fig. 7.3 Information object

grouped together in some form of order (that may or may not have meaning) this will be described as the Logical Data Structure.

7.3.1 Physical Data Structure

7.3.1.1 The Bits

All digital data is composed of bits, which are simply zeros or ones. Their exact physical representation is unimportant here, but can be the state of a magnetic domain on a magnetic computer storage device (hard disk for example), a voltage spike in a wire etc., although as pointed out in Sect. 1.1 there is usually not a one-to-one mapping between, for example, the magnetic domains or voltage spikes, and bits. Digital data is just a sequence of bits, which, if the structure of those bits is undefined, is meaningless to hardware, software or human beings. Bits are usually grouped together to encode and represent some form of data value. Here we will use the term "Primitive Data Types" (PDT) as the description of the structure of the bits and "Data Value" (DV) as an instance of a given PDT in the data. The exact nature of the structure of the different PDTs will be discussed in the following sections, but for now we can summarise the PDTs in a simple diagram, see Fig. 7.4.

As we can see from Fig. 7.4 there are (at least) ten PDTs. All other PDTs can that can be found in digital data can be derived from these types (subclasses of Integer,

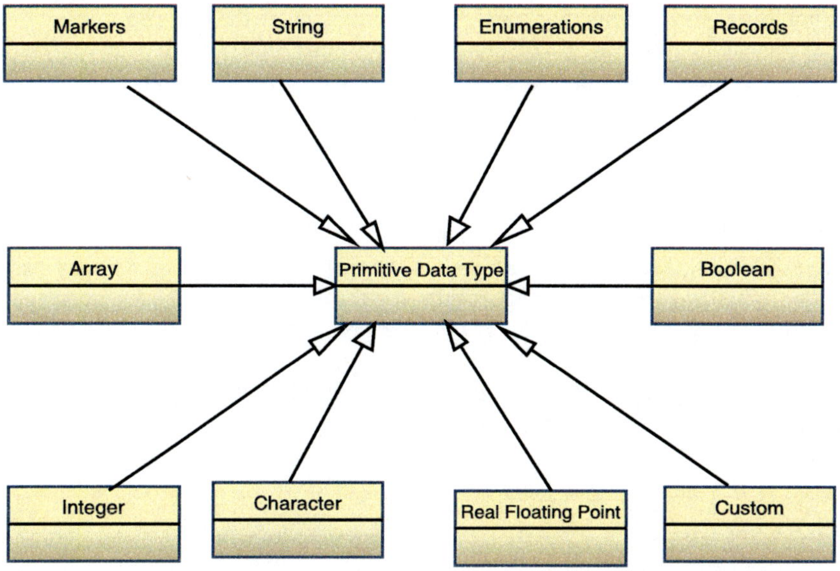

Fig. 7.4 The primitive data types

Character, String, Boolean, Real Floating Point, Enumeration, Marker, Record or Custom). These will each be described in more detail below.

One other important organisational view of data is viewing the data as sequences of octets (eight bit bytes – bytes have varied in bit size through the history of computing but currently eight bits is the norm). Typically PDTs are composed of one or more octets and the order in which the octets are read is important. This ordering of the octets is usually called byte-order and is a fundamental property of the PDT. There are two types of byte-order in common use (although others types do exist), big-endian and little-endian. Figure 7.5 shows a PDT instances that has four octets.

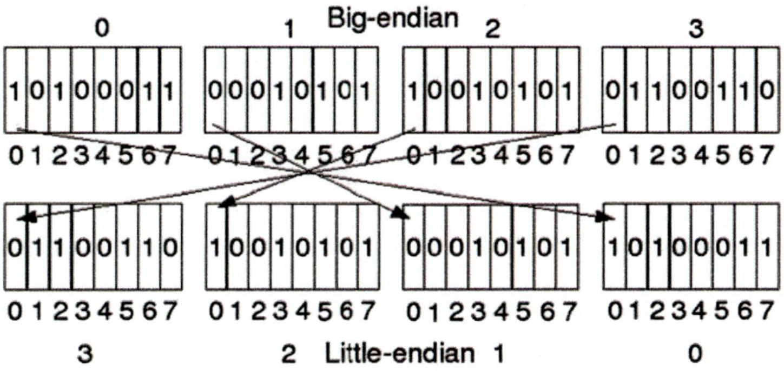

Fig. 7.5 Octet (byte) ordering and swapping

First the octets are arranged in big-endian format where the most significant octet is the 0 octet which is read first on big-endian systems. Bit 0 of the 0 octet represents the decimal integer value $2^{31} = 2{,}147{,}483{,}648$ and is the most significant bit. Bit 7 of octet number 3 represents the decimal integer value $2^0 = 1$ and is the least significant (in terms of its contribution to the decimal integer value). With little-endian the least significant octet is read first and the most significant octet is read last.

Every hardware computer system manipulates PDTs in one or more of the endian formats. Reading little-endian data on a system that is big-endian without swapping the octets will give incorrect results for the DVs, and hence its importance as a fundamental property of the PDTs. Swapping the octets is a simple procedure of reordering the octets, in this case converting from big-endian to little-endian would involve moving octet 3 to appear first (reading left to right) then octet 2, octet one and finally octet zero. Note that it is not simply reversing the order of the bits!

7.3.1.2 Characters

Characters are digital representations of the basic symbols in human written language. Typically they do not correspond to the glyph of a written character (such as an alphabetic character) but rather are a code (code point) which can be used to associate with the corresponding glyph (character encoding) or some other representation.

One of the most common character encodings is ASCII [28]. ASCII is represented as seven bits making 128 possible character encodings. Not all the ASCII characters are printable; some represent control symbols such as Tab or Carriage Return which are used for formatting text. ASCII was extended to use octets with the development of ISO/IEC 8859 giving a wider set (255) character encodings. ISO/IEC 8859 [29] is split over 15 parts where the first part is ISO/IEC 8859-1 is the Latin alphabet no. 1. Each part encodes for a different set of characters and so a given encoding value (158 say) can correspond to different characters depending on what part is used. Typically a file containing text encoded with say ISO/IEC 8859-1 would not be interpreted correctly if decoded with ISO/IEC 8859-2, even though they are both text files with eight bit characters. The encoding standard used for a text file is thus very important representation information.

Recently a new set of standards have been developed to represent character encodings, these new standards are called Unicode [30]. Unicode comes with several character encodings, for example UTF-8, UTF-16 and UTF-32. UTF-8 is intended to be backwards compatible with ASCII, in that it needs one octet to encode the first 128 ASCII characters.

Unicode supports far more characters than just ASCII, it in fact tries to encode the characters of all languages in common use (Basic Multilingual Plane) and even historical languages such as Egyptian Hieroglyphs. This means that it requires more than one octet to encode one character. UTF-8 actually allows a sequence of up to four octets to represent one character which turns out to be quite a complex encoding mechanism (described in the Unicode standard). UTF-16 contains two octets where the byte-order is significant. The byte order of text encoded in UTF-16 is usually indicated by a Byte Order Mark (BOM) at the start of the text. This BOM is the byte sequence FEFF (hexadecimal notation) when the text is encoded in big-endian byte-order or FFFE when the text is encoded in little-endian byte-order. FEFF also represents the "zero-width no-break space" character, i.e. a character that does not display anything or have any other effect and FFFE is guaranteed not to represent any character.

One can conclude that a character is a sequence of bits (bit pattern) that can, when encountered in data, be represented in a more meaningful form such as a glyph or some other representation such as a decimal value etc. This implies that a character type could in fact be more formally described by representing the whole character set as an enumeration. The exact nature of the decoding from code to its representation is data or even domain specific.

7.3.1.3 Integers

Integers come in a variety of flavours where the number of bits composing the integer varies or the range of the numbers the integer can represent varies. Typically there are 8, 16, 32, 64 and 128 or more bits in integer types. In Fig. 7.5, the big-endian 4 octet integer (32 bits) can be read as an unsigned integer with values ranging from 0 to 4,294,967,295. The exact value of the big-endian integer in Fig. 7.5 is 2,736,100,710, but if it was read as little-endian without swapping the octets then the value would read 1,721,046,435, but if swapped first one would still get the correct value of 2,736,100,710.

Integers can also be signed. Usually the most significant bit is the sign bit (but can be located elsewhere in the octets), zero for positive and one for negative. The rest of the bits are used to represent the decimal values of the number.

In Fig. 7.5 the big-endian value as a signed integer is -1,558,866,586. We must of course state how we calculated the decimal values of the integer. In the above signed integer example we have actually used two's complement interpretation of the bits. In two's complement the most significant bit is the sign bit and the other bits are all inverted (zero goes to one, one goes to zero) and then one is added, this gives the binary representation that can be read in the normal way. There are other ways of interpreting integers, such as sign-and-magnitude, one's complement etc. This method of interpretation is a fundamental property of digital integers.

Integers then have three properties, the octet (byte) order, the location of the sign bit and finally the way in which the bits should be interpreted (two's complement etc). Integers can also be restricted in data value, i.e., they can have a minimum, maximum (or both) or fixed value. For example, the EISCAT Matlab 4 format [31] has several possible record structures (matrices) and an integer value is used to identify each type of matrix. The integer value has a fixed number of values; each value represents a different type of matrix.

7.3.1.4 Real Floating Point Numbers

Floating point numbers draw their notation from the fact that the decimal point can vary in position, i.e. 1.24567 and 149.243. Their notation is usually the along the same lines as the scientific notion for real numbers e.g.,

$$1.49243 \times 10^{-3}$$

where there is a base (b) (which in this case it is base 10), an exponent (e) (which in this case is –3) and a significand (mantissa) which is the significant digits 149,243 having a precision of 6 digits. The decimal point is assumed to be directly after the leftmost digit when reading left to right. But in data and in computer systems the representation of floating point numbers is binary, for example, $1.010\text{x}2^{1011}$. Here the base is $b = 2$ and the exponent value has a binary representation along with the significand. Usually the number is normalised in that the decimal point is assumed to be directly after the left most non-zero digit reading left to right, as this digit is then guaranteed to be 1. This digit can then be ignored and the significand reduced to 010 (this is what is actually stored in the data). This normalisation is just a way of making the best use of the bits available where there are a finite number of bits representing the floating point value and thus increasing the precision. For example a 24 bit significand can be represented with 23 bits.

The significand as with integer values can be interpreted as a two's compliment number, one's compliment number or some other interpretation scheme. The exponent is also usually subject to some interpretation scheme to get a signed integer value, typically this is a bias scheme where the number is first treated as an unsigned integer and then some bias is deducted from it. So for an 8 bit exponent with a value $10001101 = 141$ and a bias (c) of –127 the exponent would be $141–127 = –113$. Also there will be a sign bit (d) to apply to the final number where a 0 may represent a positive number and a 1 a negative number.

Sometimes some bit patterns in the exponent and the significand are reserves to represent floating point exceptions. Exceptions can occur during floating point calculations such as dividing by zero, calculations that would yield an imaginary number or calculations resulting in a number too large or small to be represented in the finite range of the floating point type. Most systems of representing floating point types explicitly state what the bit patterns are reserved for these exceptions.

The exact location of the bits that correspond to the significand, exponent and sign bit also needs to be known. Fig. 7.6 shows an IEEE 754 [32] 32 bit big-endian and little-endian floating point value (same value). The first bit of the big-endian representation is the sign bit then it is followed by the exponent (8 bits) and finally

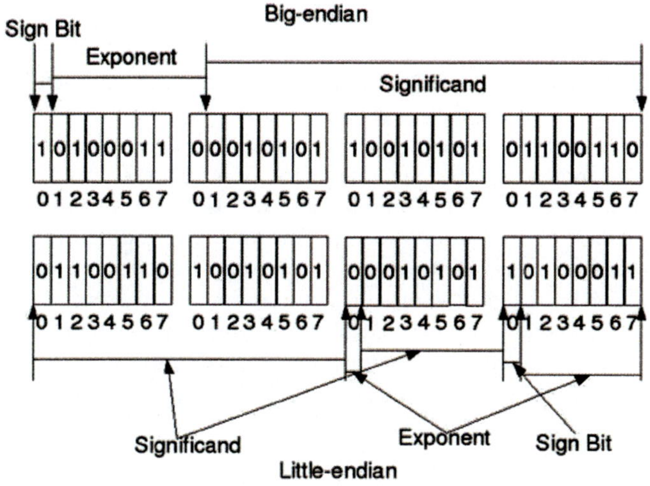

Fig. 7.6 An IEEE 754 floating point value in big-endian and little-endian format

the 23 bit normalised significand, which when interpreted, should have an a additional bit set to 1 added to the left most position making it 24 bits. When the octets are swapped, the location of the sign, exponent and the significand change considerably and hence either the octet order or the specific locations of the bits must be specified.

A formula can be written for representing the exact nature of the interpretation of the floating point value. The formula for IEEE 754 floating point numbers is:

erhf

In Fig. 7.6 the value of the floating point value is calculated by adding a bit to the left most side of the significand (1.00101011001010101100110) and then converting it directly to its decimal value (IEEE 754 uses Sign and Magnitude as the interpretation scheme for the significand) which gives 1.168621778.

The exponent is also treated as an unsigned integer and converted directly to its decimal value which gives 70. The bias is –127 so the actual exponent is 70 –127 = –57. The sign bit is 1 which indicates a negative number.

Using the formula one has $-1.168621778 \times 2^{-57} = -8.108942535 \times 10^{-18}$.

As already mentioned there are bit patterns reserved for exception values. For IEEE 754 32 bit floating point values when a number is too large to be expressed in the 32 bit range then the sign bit is set to 0 the exponent to 11111111 and the bits in the significand are all set to zero. This bit pattern would appear in stored binary data and so are important RepInfo for interpreting data files that use IEEE 754 32 bit floating point values.

The IEEE 754 standard is good RepInfo for data files that contain IEEE 754 floating point values and it should be expected that Structure RepInfo describing data should give the type of floating point values being used, i.e. via a reference to the IEEE 754 standard or other documentation describing the bit structure of the values if they are not IEEE 754. Not all data uses IEEE 754 floating point values. For example data produced from VAX systems have a very different floating point format. A list of floating point formats and their respective structure can be found in the CCSDS green book [33], though it is not a comprehensive list.

Floating point values can also, like integer values, be restricted. They can be specified to have maximum or minimum value (or both), and fixed values.

7.3.1.5 Markers

In some instances it may be necessary to terminate a sequence of DVs in a data file with a marker. This allows the number DVs to be variable. The marker could be a DV of any of the PDT that has a size greater than zero and can be made unique (a value that other DVs are guaranteed not to take), such PDT are usually Integer, Real Floating Point, Character, or String. An important marker is the End of File (EOF) marker. Although there is no specific value held in data representing the EOF, the operating system usually provides some indication to software that the EOF has been reached. This can be used by some data reading software to find the end of a particular structure. For example, one may need to keep reading DVs from a file until the EOF has been reached.

7.3.1.6 Enumerations

Enumerations are essentially a Lookup Table, or Hash Table. It consists, conceptually, of two columns of values where each column has values of a single PDT type. The first column is referred to as the "keys" while the second column is referred to as the "values". When a data structure in the data file is indicated to contain values that are to be "looked up" (enumeration type) the enumeration is used to find the correct value by reading the DV from the file and then finding the corresponding value in the enumeration. So here the DVs in the data file are "keys" and its corresponding values in the enumeration are the "values".

Enumerations can be used where data has only a fixed number of values, say ten names of people in a family (Strings). The names can then be represented as 8 bit integer values (for example 1 to 10 in decimal notation). Here the 8 bit value would be stored in the data, and when reading the data the enumeration would be used to "look up" the name as a string. This results in a reduction of the number of octets used in the data as a name as a string will be composed of a number of 8 bit characters, but the stored data is only one 8 bit integer.

7.3.1.7 Records

Records are purely logical containers and do not have a specific size. More shall be said about records later when talking about such logical structures.

7.3.1.8 Arrays

Arrays are simply sequences of DVs that can have one or more dimensions (a one dimensional array is just an ordered list of values). The dimensions of an array are important properties and may be static (for example defined externally in the RepInfo) or dynamic. If the dimensions are dynamic then there will be a DV in the data file that will give the value of the dimension(s), i.e. an integer or a numerical expression to calculate the dimensions from one or more DVs. Restrictions may also exist on the dimensions, i.e. the maximum or minimum and also if there are only fixed dimensions allowed (for example, fixed dimensions of 1, 3, 6 and 10).

Another important property of arrays is the ordering of the values, which allows one to calculate where in the data file a particular indexed value is to be found. Figure 7.7 shows a two dimensional array which can be stored in the data in one of two ways - the first index "i" varies fastest in the data file followed by the second index "j" (row order) and then the case is shown where the second index "j" varies fastest in the data file followed by the first index "i" (column order). These two methods of storing arrays are the most common, but any ordering may be used. For example, the FORTRAN [34] programming language stores arrays of data with the "i" index varying fastest while the C programming language stores arrays of data with the "j" index varying fastest.

i,j	i=1	i=2	i=3	i=4	i=5	i=6	i=7
j=1	1,1	2,1	3,1	4,1	5,1	6,1	7,1
j=2	1,2	2,2	3,2	4,2	5,2	6,2	7,2
j=3	1,3	2,3	3,3	4,3	5,3	6,3	7,3
j=4	1,4	2,4	3,4	4,4	5,4	6,4	7,4
j=5	1,5	2,5	3,5	4,5	5,5	6,5	7,5
j=6	1,6	2,6	3,6	4,6	5,6	6,6	7,6
j=7	1,7	2,7	3,7	4,7	5,7	6,7	7,7

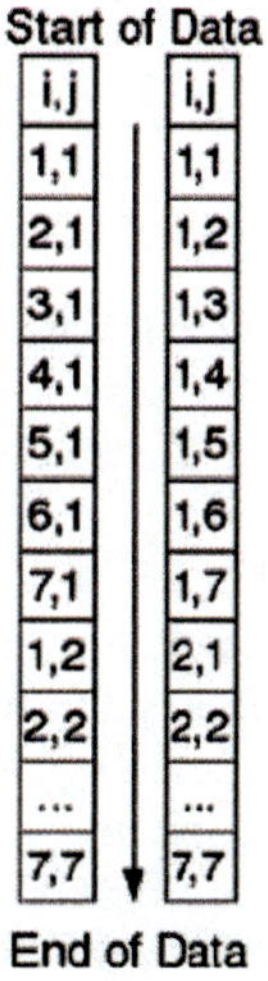

Fig. 7.7 Array ordering in data

7.3.1.9 Strings

Strings are simply one dimensional array of characters. They can be mixed with other PDTs in binary data or they can exist on their own, usually in text files. The most important basic characteristic is that of the character PDT used in the string (ASCII [28], UTF-8 [35] etc).

Strings can be structured or unstructured. When a string is unstructured there are only two additional properties that characterise the string structure. The first is the length in characters of the string and the second is the range of allowed characters ("A"–"Z" say) that can appear in the string, though this is optional.

When a string is structured it means that is contains a known set of sub-strings each of which may or may not contain a limited set of characters. The most common way of defining the structure of stings is using a variant of the Backus Naur Form (BNF) [36]. Extended *Backus Naur Form* (EBNF) – ISO-14977 [37] is a standardised version of BNF.

Most text file formats, for example XML [38], use their own definitions of BNF. BNF is used as a guide to producing parsers for a text file format, BNF is not machine processable and has not been used to automatically generate code for parsers. Usually a parser generator library is used to map the BNF/EBNF grammar to the source code which involves hand-crafting code using the grammar as a guide. Tools such as Yet Another Compiler Compiler (Yacc) [39] and the Java Compiler Compiler (JavaCC) [40] can help in creating the parser. They are called compiler compilers because they are used extensively in generating compliers for programming languages. The source files for programming languages are usually text files where the allowed syntax (string structures) are defined in some form of BNF, see for example the C language standard [41].

BNF is not the only way of defining the structure of a string. Regular expressions can also be used. Regular expressions can be thought of in terms of pattern matching where a given regular expression matches a particular string structure. For example, the regular expression

'structure' |'semantics'

matches the string 'structure' OR 'semantics' where the "|" symbol stands for OR. One advantage of regular expressions over BNF is that the regular expression can be use directly with software APIs that handle them. The Perl language [42] for example has its own regular expression library that takes a specific form of regular expression, applies this to a string and outputs the locations in the string of the matching cases. Other languages such as Java also have their own built-in regular expression libraries. The main disadvantage of regular expression is the variability of their syntax (usually not the same for all libraries the support them). The Portable Operating System Interface (POSIX) [43] does define a standard regular expression syntax which is implemented on many UNIX systems. Another disadvantage is that the expressions themselves can increase considerably in complexity as the string structure complexity increases making them very difficult to understand and interpret.

The two main reasons (there are others) that languages such as BNF and regular expressions are required become obvious when the task of storing data in text files is considered. Data values in text files, such as a floating point values, can exist as a variable length strings (variable number of characters/precision) and they can be separated by delimiters and variable numbers of white spaces (spaces, tabs etc). Defining the exact location and size (in terms of the number bits) of a given floating point value in text data is usually not possible. In contrast, for non-text data files, the exact size in bits and the location (typically measured as an offset in bits from the start of the file or the last occurring value) of the data value is usually known (or can be calculated) exactly, see the discussion of logical structure below for details. So for strings and text data a mechanism for specifying that a data value can contain a variable number of characters and is separated by zero or more white spaces and a delimiter becomes necessary, hence the need for BNF and regular expressions, which allow such statements to be made formally.

Strings and text data cannot normally be treated in the same way as other binary data, even though at their lowest level they are indeed bit sequences (just a sequence of characters of a given character set). Strings and text data are some of the most complex forms of data to describe structurally. Research into formal grammars and languages is still ongoing and is far too complex a topic to be described in detail here. But needless to say when looking for structure RepInfo for string and text data some formal grammar should be sought. In the case of very simple text data it may be sufficient to have a document describing the string structure.

The length of a string may also be dynamic, and may be given by the value of another DV in the data file, it may also be calculated via an expression using one or more DVs in the data file.

7.3.1.10 Boolean

Boolean data values are a binary data type in that they represent true or false only. Boolean data values can have many different representations in data. The simplest is to have a single bit which can be either zero or one. But also a string could be used such as "true" or "false", or an integer (of any bit size) could also be used as long as the values of the integer that represent true and false are specified. This makes the Boolean data type potentially a derived data type, but with restrictions on the values of the data type it is derived from.

7.3.1.11 Custom

Some data can take advantage of the fact that software languages allow the manipulation of data values at the bit level. In some data formats, particularly older data formats, bit packing was the norm due to memory and storage space constraints. For example, it is perfectly possible to create a four bit integer with sixteen possible values. Then eight of these four bit integers could be packed into a standard 32 bit integer. The alternative would be to have eight 8 or 16 bit integers (depending on what the programming language natively supported). The fact remains that a set of bits can be used to represent any information.

7.3.2 Logical Structure Information

Strings and text files have been discussed above and their structure can, in the case of structured strings, be broken down into sub-structures (sub-strings). Similarly any binary file can be broken down into sub-structures ending in individual DVs of a given PDT. We will now concentrate on the logical structure of binary files. But binary (non-text) files can also contain strings which are usually a fixed number of characters of a given character set. These strings may also have structure which can be further described by a BNF type description or regular expressions.

We can view binary data as just a stream of DVs of a given PDT. But this simple view is not usually helpful as it does not allow us to locate DVs that may be of particular interest, nor does it allow us to logically group together DVs that belong together such as, for example, a column of data values from table of data. With binary data DVs or groups of DVs can usually be located exactly if the logical structure is known in advance. The next sections show the common methods used in binary data that facilitate the logical structuring of DVs.

7.3.2.1 Location of Data Values

Numerous data file formats use offsets to locate DVs or sub-structures in binary data. For example, TIFF [44] image files contain an octet (byte) offset of the first Image File Directory (IFD) sub-structure, where in IFD contains information about an image and further offsets to the image data. The offset in this case is a 32 bit integer which gives the number of octets from the beginning of the file. Offsets are usually expressed in data as integers but the actual value may correspond to the number of bits, octets or some other multiplier to calculate the location exactly. Offsets may also be calculated from one or more DVs in the data, which requires the expression for the calculation to be stated in the structure RepInfo. In NetCDF [45] the location of the DVs for a given variable (collection of DVs) are calculated from a few DVs in the file, i.e. the initial offset of the variable in octets from the start of a file, the size in bits of the DVs and the dimensions of the variable (one, two or three dimensional array etc.)

Markers may also be used to locate DVs or sub-structures and to also indicate the type of sub-structure. The FITS file format [46] uses markers to indicate the type of a given sub-structure. For example a FITS file can contain several types of data structure (as described in Sect. 4.1) such as table data, image data etc. Each of these sub-structures is indicated with a marker, in the case of table data the marker is an ASCII string with the value “TABLE”. The end of the data sub-structure corresponding to the table data is also marked with the ASCII string value "END". Note, the table or image data values themselves are in fact stored in binary (i.e. non-text) format where additional "header" information is contained in fixed width ASCII strings.

7.3.2.2 Data Hierarchies

It is common to think of the structure of a data file as a tree of DVs and sub-structures. XML is a classic example of storing data in a tree like structure where an element may contain other child elements and they too may have children, and so on – see Fig. 7.8. Viewing data in such a way gives logical view of the data as a

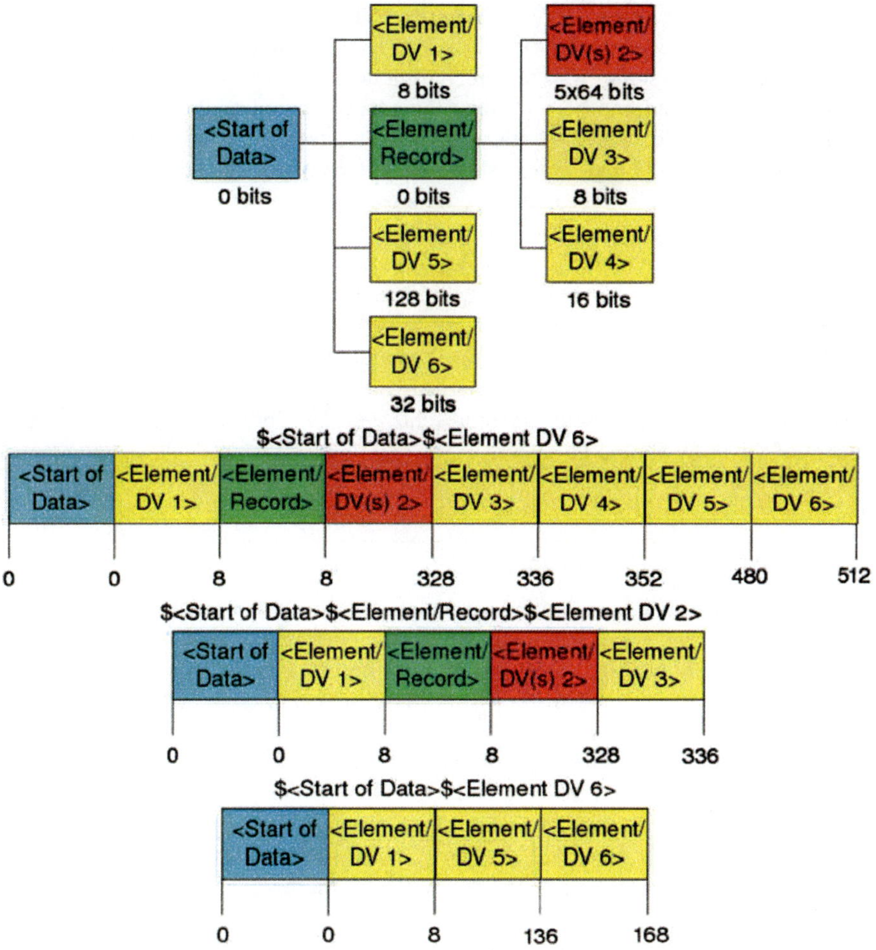

Fig. 7.8 Data hierarchies

hierarchy. More importantly, it also gives one a way of calculating the locations of DVs and sub-structures and a way of referencing them.

DVs in a binary data file are in a sequence (one after the other), but the intended structure is usually a logical tree. Figure 7.8 shows a tree structure of several DVs, here only the size in bits of the DVs is important but for clarity sake we have indicated that the element is the start of the data file (at 0 bits and zero size and can also be considered as a record), boxes marked "<Element DV n>" are individual values, those marked "<Element Records>" are containers or records (zero size) and those marked "<Element DV(s) n>" are arrays of values.

One can think of walking through the tree starting at the location <Start of Data> and then going directly to <Element Record> and then to <Element DV 3>. Using this information it is possible to provide a simple statement (path statement) that represents this walk-through by separating each element name with a $ sign, so for this example (Example 1 in Fig. 7.8) the path statement would be $<Start of Data>$<Element Record>$<Element DV 3>. Given the tree structure and the path statement you can reference a data element uniquely.

This path statement can be related to the exact location of the DV in the data file. To do this we first have to realise that elements in the same column in the tree (vertically aligned) that appear above the element we are trying to locate are located directly before it in the data file (as long as they are part of the same record). In this case <Element DV(s) 2> is in the same column and record in the tree as <Element DV 3> but it above it and so appears before it in the data file. <Element DV(s) 2> is actually an array of values and so there are in fact five 64-bit DVs before it.

Adding a predicate to the path statement can allow the selection of an individual element of the array, for example, $<Start of Data>$<Element Record>$<Element DV(s) 2>{2}, where the predicate represented as {2} indicated that the second element of the array should be selected.

7.3.2.3 Conditional Data Values

Elements or records in the logical structure may be conditional, which means that they may or may not exist, depending on the result of a logical expression (true if it exists or false if it does not exist). There may also be a choice of elements or records in the data from a list, where only one of the choices exists in the data.

A logical expression may consist of one or more DVs combined using the logical operators AND, OR, NOT etc. Typically the DVs in the expressions are either a Boolean PDT or and integer data type that is restricted to have the values 0 or 1, they could also be the string "true" or "false". The result of evaluating the expression will either be true or false (0 or 1) and will indicate whether the value exists (true) or not (false). The expressions are dynamic as they contain DVs, so one data file may contain a given element or record but another may not depending on the DV in the specific data file.

Another type of logical expression could be the identification of an element with a specific DV. For example, in the FITS format there are several different structures where each is identified by a keyword (String), so here an expression must exist that compares the value of the string against a lists of possible values. If it matches one then the appropriate structure is selected. Integer values are another possible DV that can be used for selecting structures.

7.3.3 Summary of Some Requirements for Structure Representation Information

From the above we can summarise the some of the important characteristics (properties) of data that form Structure RepInfo. It will be shown later that some existing formal languages capture some of these properties allowing one to form detailed and accurate Structure RepInfo that can be validated against the data and used in an automated way.

1. Physical Structure Information
    1. Endienness of the data (big-endian or little endian).
    2. Character type
        1. endienness.
        2. character set used.
        3. size in octets/bits.
    3. Integers
        1. endienness.
        2. size in octets/bits.
        3. signed/unsigned.
        4. location of signed bit.
        5. interpretation method - two's compliment etc.
        6. restriction on maximum and minimum size.
        7. fixed number of values.
    4. Real floating point numbers
        1. endienness.
        2. location and structure of the significand bits.
        3. location and structure of the exponent bits.
        4. normalised.
        5. interpretation method of significand - two's compliment etc.
        6. bias scheme for exponent.
        7. reserve values/exceptions.
        8. location of signed bit.
        9. formula for interpreting the number.
        10. restriction on maximum and minimum size.
        11. fixed values.

5. Arrays
    1. number of dimensions if static.
    2. calculation of Number of dimensions if dynamic.
    3. number of values in each dimension if static.
    4. calculation of number of values in each dimensions if dynamic.
    5. ordering of the arrays (row order or column order).
    6. data type (integer, real etc).
    7. restriction on maximum and minimum number of dimensions.
    8. fixed number of values the dimensions of the array can take.
    9. restriction on maximum and minimum number of values in a dimension.
    10. fixed number for size of the dimensions of the array.
    11. restriction on maximum and minimum values the values of the array can take.
    12. markers indicating the end of a dimension or an array.
6. Strings
    1. character set used.
    2. size in octets/bits of each character.
    3. structured or unstructured.
    4. if structured then a description of the structure such as BNF etc.
    5. the length in characters of the string.
    6. expression for calculating the length of the string.
    7. allowed characters in the string.
    8. fixed values of strings.
7. Boolean
    1. data type used to represent Boolean value.
    2. values of data type that represent true/false.
8. Markers
    1. data type.
    2. values of the marker.
9. Records
    1. existence expression
    2. child elements and their order
    3. parent element
10. Enumerations
    1. data types of enumeration.
    2. number of enumeration values.
    3. the enumeration table.

2. Logical Data Structure
    1. elements and their names.
    2. element PDT.
    3. path statements with predicates for accessing array elements.
    4. calculation for offsets from other DVs.
    5. offset values.

6. calculation of existence of elements or records from other DVs in a logical expression.
7. comparison expressions, i.e. string comparisons etc.
8. existence values.
9. choice statements of elements or records.

7.3.4 Formal Structure Description Languages

In this section we look at a number of formal languages which support automation.

These formal languages are rather powerful but not really applicable to digital objects such as Word files.

Each method has its own strengths.

7.3.4.1 East

The EAST (**E**nhanced **A**da **S**ubse**T**) language [47] is a CCSDS and ISO standard language used to create descriptions of data, called Data Description Records (DDRs). Such DDRs aim to ensure a complete and exact understanding of the structure of the data and allow the data values to be extracted and used in an automated fashion. This means that a software tool should be able to analyze a DDR and interpret the format of the associated data. This allows the software to extract values from the data on any host machine (i.e., on a different machine from the one that produced the data).

EAST is fully capable of describing the physical structure of integer, real floating point and enumerations. It does not support boolean data types. The exception bit patterns of real floating point values are not supported. The byte-order for the data can be specified globally for the digital object, but not for individual DVs. Characters are restricted to 8 bit and the code points are specified in the EAST specification. String made up of 8 bit characters are allowed with a fixed length. The appropriate restrictions and facets for strings are supported. The lack of ability to define dynamic offsets for the logical structure is the main restriction; file formats such as TIFF cannot be described with EAST. No path language is specified in the EAST standard.

EAST has a comprehensive set of tools (see [47] and [48]).

The EAST standard gives the following examples.

A communications packet format is illustrated in Fig. 7.9

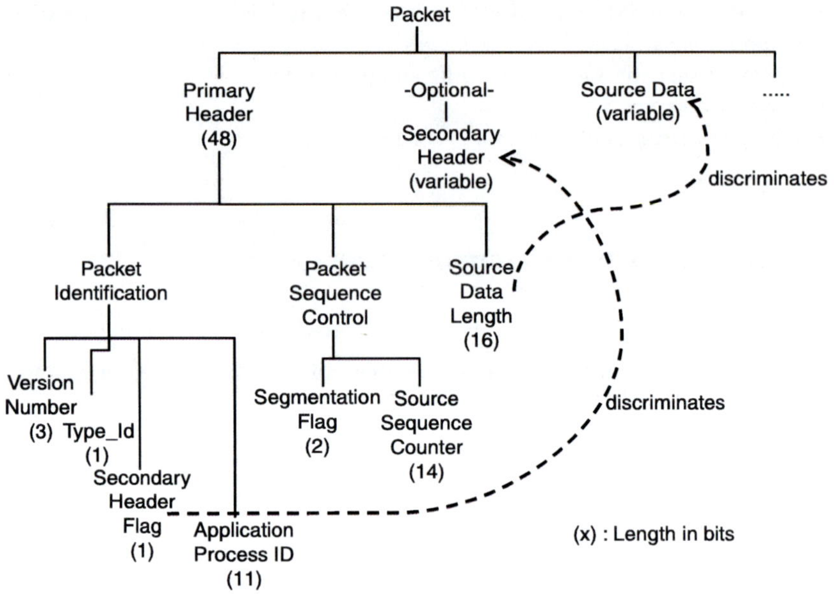

Fig. 7.9 Discriminants in a packet format

This has the EAST description shown in Fig. 7.10.

EAST is used extensively in operational archives, most notably in the CDPP [49] and other archives using the SITOOLS software [34]. Data deposited in CDPP must have an EAST description and this allows automated processing including subsetting and transformations. For the latter one needs EAST descriptions of the two formats and a mapping between the data elements of each.

7.3.4.2 DRB

The Data Request Broker [50] DRB API® is an Open Source Java application programming interface for reading, writing and processing heterogeneous data.

DRB API® is a software abstraction layer that helps developers in programming applications independently from the way data are encoded within files. Indeed, DRB API® is based on a unified data model that makes the handling of supported data formats much easier. A number of implementations for particular cases are shown in Fig. 7.11.

Of particular interest is the SDF implementation which allows one to describe a binary data file. The description is placed as an XML annotation element within an XML Schema.

DRB-SDF is based on XML Schema [51] and XQuery [52] and uses some additional non-standard extensions to deal with binary data. The main restriction is that the physical structure of data types cannot be defined explicitly as can be done

```
-- basic data types used in the first branch
type VERSION is (VERSION_1, VERSION_2);

type PACKET_TYPE is (TELEMETRY , TELECOMMAND);

type PRESENCE_FLAG is (ABSENT , PRESENT);

type PROCESS_IDENTIFICATION is (WORKING , IDLE);

-- structuring type for the Packet Identification
type PACKET_IDENTIFICATION_TYPE is record
      VERSION_NUMBER: VERSION;
      TYPE_ID: PACKET_TYPE;
      SECONDARY_HEADER_FLAG: PRESENCE_FLAG;
      APPLICATION_PROCESS_ID: PROCESS_IDENTIFICATION;
end record;

-- basic data types used in the second branch
type STATUS is (CONTINUATION_SEGMENT,
           FIRST_SEGMENT, LAST_SEGMENT, UNSEGMENTED_PACKET);

type COUNTER is range 0 .. 16383;

-- structuring type for the Packet Sequence Control
type PACKET_SEQUENCE_CONTROL_TYPE is record
      SEGMENTATION_FLAG: STATUS;
      SOURCE_SEQUENCE_COUNT: COUNTER;
end record;

-- basic data types used in the other branches
type NUMBER is range 0 .. 65535;

type OCTET is range 0 .. 255;

-- structuring types
type DATA_ARRAY is array (NUMBER range <>) of OCTET;
type SECONDARY_HEADER_TYPE is array (1 .. 4) of OCTET;

type PRIMARY_HEADER_TYPE is record
  PACKET_IDENTIFICATION: PACKET_IDENTIFICATION_TYPE;
  PACKET_SEQUENCE_CONTROL: PACKET_SEQUENCE_CONTROL_TYPE;
  SOURCE_DATA_LENGTH: NUMBER;
end record;

type PACKET_FORMAT_TYPE(
      VIRTUAL_SECONDARY_HEADER_FLAG: PRESENCE_FLAG := PRESEN;
      -- point to the secondary header flag located in the first branch
      VIRTUAL_SOURCE_DATA_LENGTH: NUMBER := 256)
      -- point to the source data length located in the third branch
is record
      PRIMARY_HEADER: PRIMARY_HEADER_TYPE;
      case VIRTUAL_SECONDARY_HEADER_FLAG is
        when ABSENT =>
SOURCE_DATA_0: DATA_ARRAY (1 .. VIRTUAL_SOURCE_DATA_LENGTH);
        when PRESENT =>
             SECONDARY_HEADER: SECONDARY_HEADER_TYPE;
SOURCE_DATA_1: DATA_ARRAY (1 .. VIRTUAL_SOURCE_DATA_LENGTH);
      end case;
end record;
```

Fig. 7.10 Logical description of the packet format

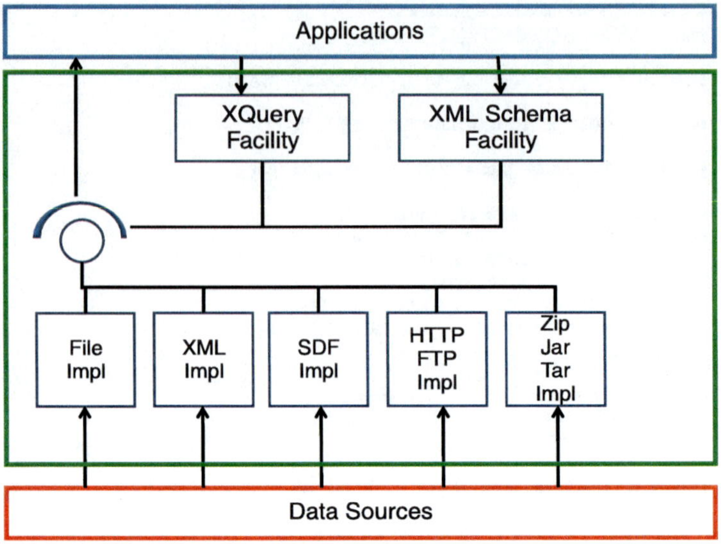

Fig. 7.11 DRB interfaces

with EAST. Byte-order can be specified for each DV, but the interpretation scheme for integers is restricted to two's compliment and real floating point data types are assumed to be IEEE 754.

XPath [53] can be used as a path language, and the XQuery API is also implemented for more complex data queries. Using XQuery complicates the language, potentially making the descriptions difficult to understand and software difficult to maintain or re-implement in the long-term.

The library supplied allows the application to extract and use individual data elements, as allowed by the DRB data model.

The integration with XML allows one to use the other XML related tools as illustrated in Fig. 7.12.

7.3.4.3 DFDL

Data Format Description Language (DFDL) is being developed by the DFDL Working Group [34] as a tool for describing mappings between data in formatted files (text as well as binary) and a corresponding XML representation for use within the GRID. A DFDL specification takes the form of an XML Schema with "application annotations" that make the correspondence between file characters (or bytes or even bits) and XML data values precise. It appears that there is significant overlap between DFDL and DRB.

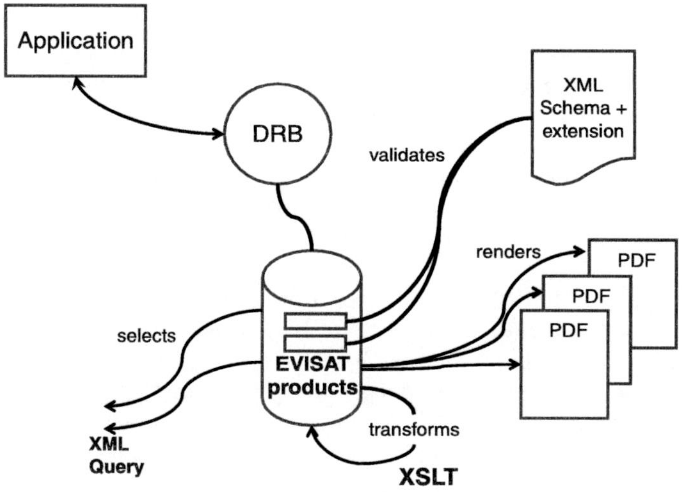

Fig. 7.12 Example of DRB usage

7.3.5 Benefits of Formal Structure Representation Information (FSRI)

There are a number of benefits of having a formal description for the structure RepInfo, these are:

1. Machine readability of the FSRI, allowing analysis and processing.
2. Common format for FSRI that can apply to many data formats giving a common (single) software interface to the data.
3. Higher probability of future re-use due to having a single software interface.
4. Easy validation of the data against the FSRI and also easy validation of the FSRI against its formal grammar.
5. Ensures that all the relevant properties of the structure have been captured.

Machine readability of the FSRI is important as information about the structure can be easily parsed making the implementation of data access routines that use them easier to programme. This has the added benefit of a reduction in cost of producing software implementations now and in the future. Being able to process the FSRI also gives rise to the possibility for automating some aspects of data interoperability. For example, PDT of DVs and sub-structures such as arrays and records can be automatically discovered and compared between FSRIs which can allow the automatic mapping and conversion between different data formats.

Software can be produced that takes the FSRI and the data and produces a common software interface to the DVs and sub-structures. In effect one has a single software interface that reads the DVs from many data files with different structures (formats). Having many FSRIs for many different data formats (XML Schema for example) increases the likelihood that an implementation will exist in the future, or if one does not exist, then the likelihood and motivation to produce one will be increased. Basically this is due to the value and amount of data that has been described (consider the vast number of XML schemas that exist for XML data). Currently though, binary data is not usually accompanied with FSRI, and their structure is usually described in a human readable document. But the relatively recent development of formal languages to describe binary data structures may change this if they are adopted more widely. Such an adoption would be highly beneficial for data preservation.

The current set of FSRIs are themselves formally described, for example, EAST and DRB are both described with a form of BNF as they are structured text based formats. This allows an instance of the FSRIs to be validated to ensure its structure and content follow the formal grammar. Having FSRI for data also allows one to automatically check that the data is written exactly in accordance with the FSRI, i.e. each instance of the data has the correct structure. This ability is important for data preservation for the following reasons:

- it can be used to check the valid creation of a data structure.
- it can be used to periodically check the data structure for errors or corruption (also useful in authenticity to check for deliberate structure tampering).
- It can be used to identify a data file accurately – it is accurate because knowledge about the whole data structure is used as opposed to simple file format signatures.

Properties that the FSRI highlights guide a person in capturing the relevant structure information that is required to read the DVs. Having a well thought out FSRI which ensures that all the relevant structure information is captured is possibly the most important thing for the preservation of data. The current set of FSRIs are good but still incomplete. They either restrict the types of logical data structure that can be described or fail to provide sufficient generality to describe the physical data structure (or both). EAST for example has most of the properties defined to provide an adequate description of the physical structure, but is quite restrictive in the logical structures it can describe. But if one can describe a data file format with EAST then it will provided a good basis for a complete FSRI for that data in terms of providing all the information required for long-term preservation of the structure.

7.4 Format Identification

Even if one cannot create a formal description, there are a number of tools to at least identify the structure (format). Some of these are described below.

The simplest method is to look at the file name extension and make an educated guess. For example "file.txt" is probably a text file, probably ASCII encoded.

PRONOM [54] would suggest such a file is a Plain Text File, although clearly this provides just a suggestion for the file type since a file is easily renamed.

The MIME-type [55] is a more positive declaration of the file type in internet messaging.

Many binary (i.e. non-text) file start with a bit sequence which can be used to suggest the file type, often known as "magic" numbers [56]. Some amusing examples are:

- Compiled Java class files (bytecode) start with the hexadecimal code CAFEBABE.
- Old MS-DOS .exe files and the newer Microsoft Windows PE (Portable Executable) .exe files start with the ASCII string "MZ" (4D 5A), the initials of the designer of the file format, Mark Zbikowski.
- The Berkeley Fast File System superblock format is identified as either 19 54 01 19 or 01 19 54 depending on version; both represent the birthday of the author, Marshall Kirk McKusick.
- 8BADF00D is used by Apple as the exception code in iPhone crash reports when an application has taken too long to launch or terminate.

The magic number is again not definitive since it would be possible for a particular short pattern to be present by co-incidence.

Well known to Unix/Linux users, but not to Windows users, the *file* command is used to determine the file type of digital objects using more sophisticated algorithms. The file command uses the "magic" database [57] which allows it to identify many thousands of file types. A summary of file identification techniques is available [58]. Tools such as DROID [59] and JHOVE [60] provide file type identification, albeit for a more limited number of file types (a few hundred at the time of writing), but they do provide additional Provenance for these formats.

7.5 Semantic Representation Information

Semantic (Representation) Information supplements Structure (Representation) Information by adding meaning to the data elements which the latter allows one to extract. Chapter 8 provides a much extended view of semantics but here it is worth providing a few basic techniques.

7.5.1 Simple Semantics

Data Dictionaries provide the fairly simple definitions. A fairly self-explanatory example using the CCSDS/ISO Data Entity Dictionary Specification Language (DEDSL) [61] is:

NAME	LATITUDE_MODEL
ALIAS	('LAT', 'Used by the historical projects EARTH_PLANET')
CLASS	MODEL
DEFINITION	'Latitudes north of the equator shall be designated by the use of the plus (+) sign, while latitudes south of the equator shall be designated by the use of the minus sign (-). The equator shall be designated by the use of the plus sign (+).'
SHORT_DEFINITION	'Latitude'
UNITS	Deg
SPECIFIC_INSTANCE	(+00.000, 'Equator')
DATA_TYPE	REAL
RANGE	(-90.00, +90.00)

NAME	DATA_2
CLASS	DATA_FIELD
DEFINITION	'It represents an image taken from spacecraft W2'
SHORT_DEFINITION	'Spacecraft W2 Image'
COMMENT	'The image is an array of W_IMAGE_SIZE items called DATA_2_PIXEL'
COMPONENT	DATA_2_PIXEL (1 .. W_IMAGE_SIZE)
KEYWORD	'IMAGE'
DATA_TYPE	COMPOSITE

This can be supplemented by the following, which defines the pixels within the image.

NAME	DATA_2_PIXEL
CLASS	DATA_FIELD
DEFINITION	'It represents a pixel belonging to the image taken from spacecraft W2'
SHORT_DEFINITION	'Spacecraft W2 Image pixel'
DATA_TYPE	INTEGER
RANGE	(0 , 255)

The DEDSL approach allows one to inherit definitions from a "community dictionary" and override or add additional entities.

The mandatory attributes are indicated in bold characters below, while the optional and conditional attributes are in italic characters:

Attribute_Name	Attribute_definition
NAME	The value of this attribute may be used to link a collection of attributes with an equivalent identifier in, or associated with, the data entity. The value of this attribute may also be used by the software developer to name corresponding variables in software code or designate a field to be searched for locating particular data entities. The **name** shall be unique within a Data Entity Dictionary.
ALIAS	Single- or multi-word designation that differs from the given name, but represents the same data entity concept, followed by the context in which this name is applied. The value of this attribute provides an alternative designation of the data entity that may be required for the purpose of compatibility with historical data or data deriving from different sources. For example, different sources may produce data including the same entities, but giving them different names. Through the use of this attribute it will be possible to define the semantic information only once. Along with the alternative designation, this attribute value shall provide a description of the context of when the alternative designation is used. The value of the alternative designation can also be searched when a designation used in a corresponding syntax description is not found within the **name** values.
CLASS	The value of this attribute makes a clear statement of what kind of entity is defined by the current entity definition. This definition can be a model definition, a data field definition, or a constant definition.
DEFINITION	Statement that expresses the essential nature of a data entity and permits its differentiation from all the other data entities. This attribute is intended for human readership and therefore any information that will increase the understanding of the identified data entity should be included. It is intended that the value of this attribute can be of significant length and hence provide a description of the data entity as complete as possible. The value of this attribute can be used as a field to be searched for locating particular data entities.
SHORT_DEFINITION	Statement that expresses the essential nature of a data entity in a shorter and more concise manner than the statement of the mandatory attribute: **definition**. This attribute provides a summary of the more detailed information provided by the **definition** attribute. The value of this attribute can be used as a field to be searched for locating particular data entities. It is also intended to be used for display purposes by automated software, where the complete definition value would be too long to be presented in a convenient manner to users.
COMMENT	Associated information about a data entity. It enables to add information which does not correspond to definition information.
UNITS	Attribute that specifies the scientific units that should be associated with the value of the data entity so as to make the value meaningful to applications.

Attribute_Name	Attribute_definition
SPECIFIC_INSTANCE	Attribute that provides a real-world meaning for a specific instance (a value) of the data entity being described. The reason for providing this information is so that the user can see that there is some specific meaning associated with a particular value instance that indicates something more than just the abstract value. For example, the fact that 0° latitude is the equator could be defined. This means that the value of this attribute must provide both an instance of the entity value and a definition of its specific meaning.
INHERITS_FROM	Gives the name of a model or data field from which the current entity description inherits attributes. This name must be the value of the **name** attribute found in the referred entity description. Referencing this data entity description means that all the values of its attributes having their **attribute_inheritance** set to **inheritable** apply to the current description.
COMPONENT	Name of a component, followed by the number of times it occurs in the composite data entity. The number of times is specified by a range.
KEYWORD	A significant word used for retrieving data entities
RELATION	This attribute is to be used to express a relationship between two entity definitions when this relation cannot be expressed using a precise standard relational attribute. In that case the relationship is user-defined and expressed using free text.
DATA_TYPE	It specifies the type of the data entity values. This attribute shall have one of the following values: **Enumerated**, **Text**, **Real**, **Integer**, **Composite**.
ENUMERATION_VALUES	The set of permitted values of the **enumerated** data entity.
ENUMERATION_MEANING	Enables to give a meaning to each value given by the attribute enumeration_values.
ENUMERATION_CONVENTION	Gives guidance on the correspondence between the **enumeration_values** and the numeric or textual values found within the products.
RANGE	The minimum bound and the maximum bound of an **Integer** or **Real** data entity
TEXT_SIZE	The limitation on the size of the values of a Text data entity. This attribute specifies the minimum and the maximum number of characters the text may contain. If the minimum and the maximum are equal, then this implies that the exact size of the text is known.
CASE_SENSITIVITY	The value of this attribute specifies the case sensitivity for the Identifiers used as values for the attributes of the current entity. When used in a data entity, the value of the attribute overrides the value specified at the dictionary level.
LANGUAGE	Main natural language that is valid for any value of type TEXT given to the attributes of the current entity. When used in a data entity, the value of the attribute overrides the value specified for the dictionary entity.
CONSTANT_VALUE	The value of this attribute is the value given to a constant (entity whose **class** attribute is set to **constant**).

In addition to these standard attributes a user can define his/her own extra attributes. Each new attribute has a number of descriptors. The obligation column indicates whether a descriptor is mandatory (M), conditional (C), optional (O) or defaulted (D).

Descriptor of attribute	Obligation
ATTRIBUTE_NAME	M
ATTRIBUTE_DEFINITION	M
ATTRIBUTE_OBLIGATION	M
ATTRIBUTE_CONDITION	C
ATTRIBUTE_MAXIMUM_OCCURRENCE	M
ATTRIBUTE_VALUE_TYPE	M
ATTRIBUTE_MAXIMUM_SIZE	O
ATTRIBUTE_ENUMERATION_VALUES	C
ATTRIBUTE_COMMENT	O
ATTRIBUTE_INHERITANCE	D
ATTRIBUTE_DEFAULT_VALUE	C
ATTRIBUTE_VALUE_EXAMPLE	O
ATTRIBUTE_SCOPE	D

The standard defines, for each of the standard attributes, all the above descriptors.

Particular encodings are defined, the one of most interest being perhaps the XML encoding [62].

Related, broader, capabilities are provided by the multi-part standard ISO/IEC 11179 [63] which is under development to represent this kind of information in a "metadata" registry.

7.5.1.1 Complex Semantics

In simple semantics we have the ability to provide limited meaning about a data entity, with some very limited relationship information. For example the RELATIONSHIP attribute of DEDSL is defined as "used to express a relationship between two entity definitions when this relation cannot be expressed using a precise standard relational attribute. In that case the relationship is user-defined and expressed using free text". More formal specifications of relationships, and more complex relationships, are provided in tools such as those based RDF and OWL. Chapter 8 provides further information about these aspects.

7.6 Other Representation Information

"Other" Representation Information is a catch-all term for Representation Information which cannot be classified as Structure or Semantics. The following sub-sections discuss a number of possible types of "Other" Representation Information.

Software clearly is needed for the use of most digital objects, and is therefore Representation Information and in particular "Other" Representation Information because it is not obvious how it might be classified as Structure or Semantic Representation Information.

One suggested partial classification [64] of OTHER Representation Information is

- AccessSoftware
- Algorithms
- CommonFileTypes
- ComputerHardware
  - BIOS
  - CPU
  - Graphics
  - HardDiskController
  - Interfaces
  - Network
- Media
- Physical
- ProcessingSoftware
- RepresentationRenderingSoftware
- Software
  - Binary
  - Data
  - Documentation
  - SourceCode

7.6.1 Processing Software

Emulation is discussed in Sect. 7.9

7.7 Application to Types of Digital Objects

In this sub-section we discuss the application of the above techniques to the classifications of digital objects described in Chap. 4.

7.7.1 Simple

An example of a simple digital object is the JPEG image shown in Fig. 4.1 ("face.jpg") which is described in the JPEG standard [65].

A FITS file containing a single astronomical image could be considered Simple, and its Representation Information is the FITS specifications [46] with the Representation Network shown in Fig. 6.4.

7.7.2 Composite

Composite digital objects are all those which are not Simple, which of course covers a very large number of possibilities.

A FITS file such as that illustrated in Fig. 4.2 has the same Representation Information Network as for the Simple example above. Each of the components would also be (essentially) a Simple FITS file. What would be missing is the explanation of the relationship between the various components. That information would have to be in an additional piece of Representation Information, for example a simple text document or perhaps a more formal description using RDF.

7.7.2.1 NetCDF – Data Request Broker (DRB) Description

Network Common Data Format (NetCDF) [45] is a binary file format and data container used extensively within the scientific community. The full DRB description is an XML schema (Fig. 7.13) consisting of XML schema elements with the addition of extra SDF tags to describe the underlying data structures whether BINARY or ASCII. For example the magic complex type, the first shown in the format diagram, consists of a sequence of two elements CDF and VERSION_BYTE respectively and can be expressed by the following code.

```
<xs:element name="magic">
 <xs:complexType>
  <xs:sequence>
   <xs:element name="CDF">
        <xs:annotation>
         <xs:appinfo>
               <sdf:block>
                    <sdf:length unit="byte">3</sdf:length>
                    <sdf:encoding>ASCII</sdf:encoding>
               </sdf:block>
         </xs:appinfo>
        </xs:annotation>
        <xs:simpleType>
              <xs:restriction base="xs:string"/>
        </xs:simpleType>
   </xs:element>
   <xs:element name="VERSION_BYTE" type="xs:unsignedByte">
        <xs:annotation>
         <xs:appinfo>
```

```
                <sdf:block>
                        <sdf:encoding>BINARY</sdf:encoding>
                </sdf:block>
          </xs:appinfo>
         </xs:annotation>
    </xs:element>
   </xs:sequence>
  </xs:complexType>
 </xs:element>
```

Here the CDF element, the first item of interest in the file, is binary information and represented as a 3 byte character string, the VERSION_BYTE is described as simply being one unsigned Byte. Part of the more complete XML schema structure of the NetCDF file is shown below however the complete description is quite lengthy and so not shown.

Using the DRB engine http://www.gael.fr/drb/features.html open source software created by Gael, it is possible to use the XML Schema description as an interface to the underlying data. The software supports access and querying of the described data using the XQuery XML accessor language. For example to access the CDF and the VERSION_BYTE one could have a query like the following

```
<magic id="{/netcdf/header/magic/CDF}"
version="{/netcdf/header/magic/version_byte}"/>
```

More complex queries have been created to access the data sets contained within the file.

There is also BNF format description located in the unicar website for NetCDF http://www.unidata.ucar.edu/software/netcdf/docs/netcdf/Classic-Format-Spec.html#Classic-Format-Spec however this is purely for documentation and cannot be used as an interface to the underlying data.

7.7.3 Rendered

The image described in Sect. 7.7.1 is a rendered object.

Other rendered objects are, for example, Web pages. Here the Representation Information would include the HTML standard [66]. We may have this standard in the form of a PDF, written in English, thus the Representation Network would include descriptions of these, or specify them as part of the Designated Community's Knowledge Base.

7.7.4 Non-rendered

Digital Objects which are not normally rendered would by definition be non-rendered, but as noted the boundary is not always clear-cut. As discussed in Sect. 4.2

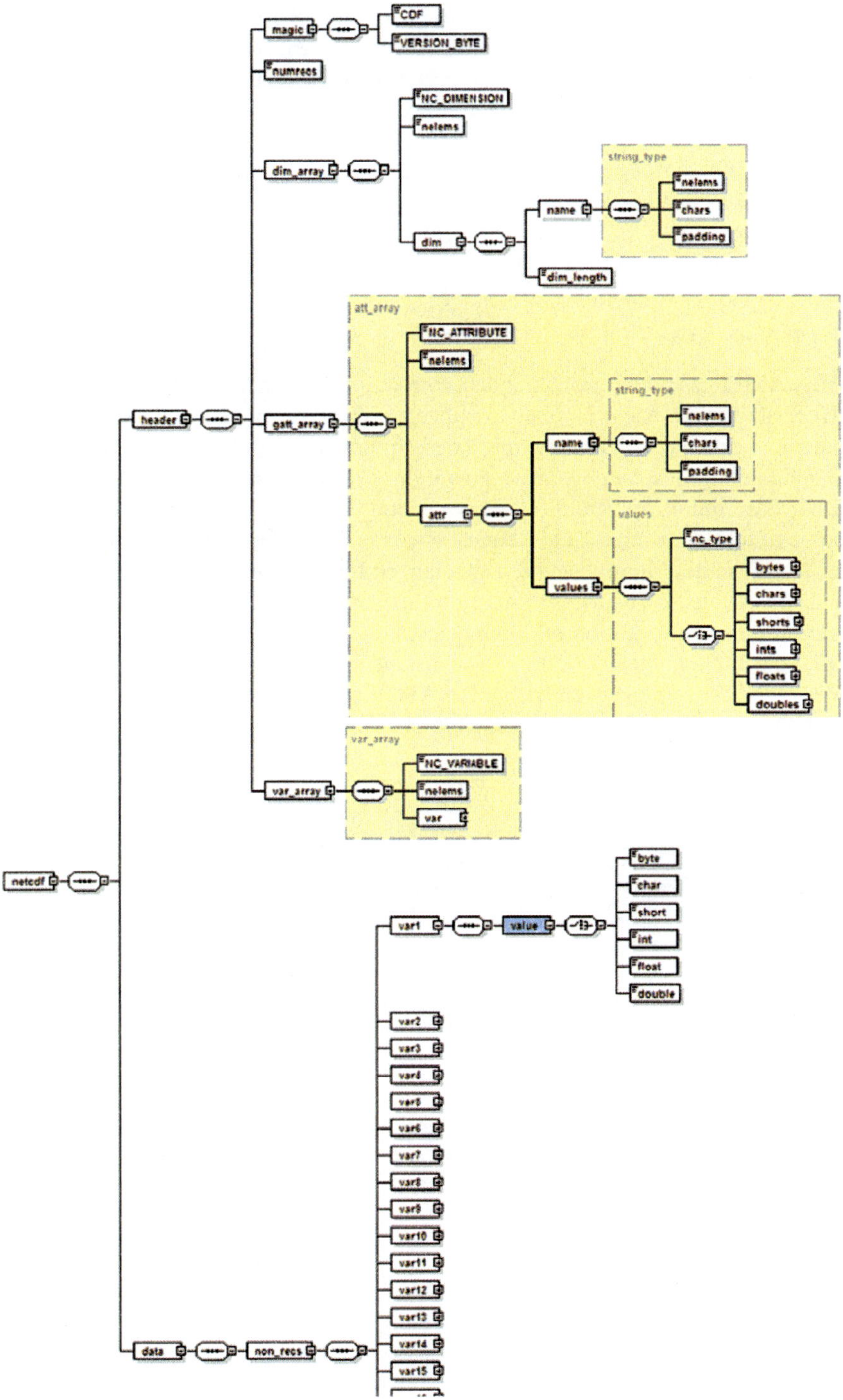

Fig. 7.13 Schema for NetCDF

digital objects, or something derived from them, are eventually rendered but the point is that there are an infinite number of different ways of processing, most of which have not been invented yet, and most of which will involve being combined with data which has not been collected yet. Therefore the Representation Information we need is that which will allow us to extract the individual pieces of information such as numbers or characters, as described in Sect. 7.3, together with their associated Semantic information as described in Sect. 7.5.

The following is an example of such a digital object and its Representation Information.

7.7.4.1 Nasa Ames

NASA AMES is another scientific data format for data exchange, the overall NASA AMES file format has a number of subtypes, each having differing structures for header and data records, for example a description of the NASA AMES versions can be found at http://espoarchive.nasa.gov/archive/docs/formatspec.txt which includes a BNF description of Version 2. This version 2 format is an ASCII file and can also be described using a Data Request Broker (DRB) description, partly shown in Fig. 7.14. The description has been specialized for the scientific application of storing data collected by the Mesosphere-Stratosphere-Troposphere (MST) Radar. The description has the addition of domain specific parameter semantics detailed in the XML schema documentation tags. For instance the TropopauseAltitude parameter is described as an integer represented in ASCII with a description of the parameter. The XML schema declaration is shown as:

```
<xs:element name="TropopauseAltitude" type="xs:int">
 <xs:annotation>
  <xs:documentation xml:lang="en">
     (m) This is the altitude of the (static stability)
tropopause, in metres above mean sea level,
  </xs:documentation>
 <xs:appinfo>
  <sdf:block>
  <sdf:encoding>ASCII</sdf:encoding>
  </sdf:block>
 </xs:appinfo>
</xs:annotation>
</xs:element>
```

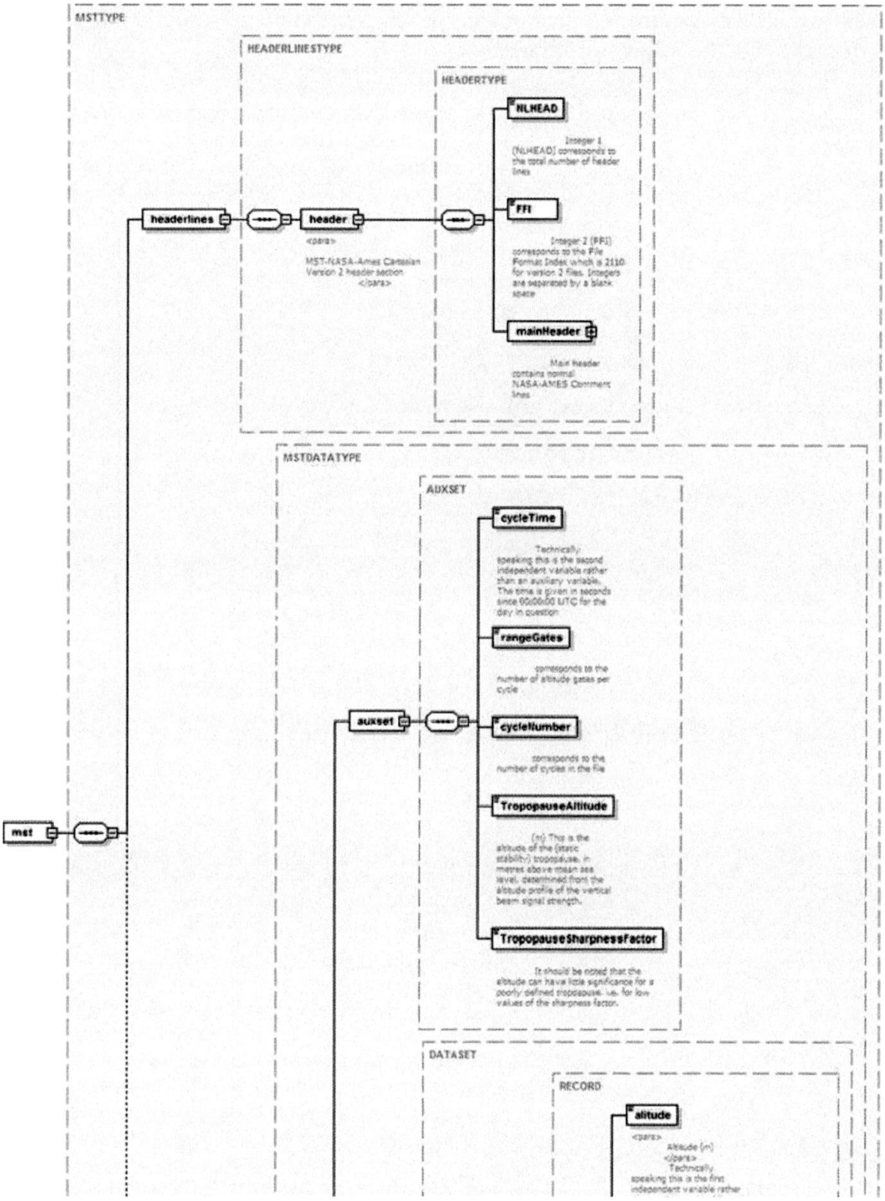

Fig. 7.14 Schema for MST data

The complete MST NASA AMES schema is too lengthy to display in this document but part of is it is shown below:

Again it is possible to access and query the stored data through the description using Xquery, which can facilitate automated processing. For example it is possible to extract all the documentation from any XML schema document and this can be performed with the following Xquery:

```
declare variable dataDescription external;

declare function local:output($element,$counter)
{
    <documentation
    nodeType="{node-name($element)}"
    type="{data($element/@type)}"
    name="{data($element/@name)}"
    >{data($element/annotation/documentation/)}
    </documentation>
};

declare function local:walk($node,$counter)
{
 for $element in $node
  where node-name($element)="element" or node-name
($element)="complexType" or node-name($element)="schema"
  return
    local:output($element,$counter)
};

declare function local:process-node($element,$counter)
{
  for $subElement in $element where $counter < 3
   return
   if(node-name($subElement)="element" or node-
name($subElement)="complexType" or node-
name($subElement)="schema") then
   <node nodeType="{node-name($subElement)}">
   {
    local:walk($subElement,$counter+1)
   }
```

```
   <child>
   {
    local:process-node($subElement/*,$counter+1)
   }
   </child>
  </node>
 else if(node-name($subElement)="sequence") then
 local:walk($subElement/*,$counter+1)
 else
 ()
};
let $element := ""

let $xsd := doc($dataDescription)/schema
let $queryFile :=xs:string("xsd-doc2.xql")
return
<demo>
  <doc schema="{$dataDescription/schema/annotation/
documentation}" query="{$queryFile}"> </doc>
{
   local:process-node($xsd,0)
}
</demo>
```

For example in applying the above to a NASA AMES MST XML schema this would pull out the following documentation (only part of the result is shown):

```
<demo>
<doc schema="../drb_mst_09/MST-NASA-Ames_2110_
Cartesian_Version_2.xsd" query="xsd-doc2.xql"/>
<node>
...
<child>
```

```
<documentation nodeType="element" type="xs:token"
name="ONAME">a character string specifying the name(s)
of the originator(s) of the exchange file, last name
first. On one line and not exceeding
132 characters.</documentation>

<documentation nodeType="element" type="xs:token"
name="ORG">character string specifying the organization
or affiliation of the originator of the exchange file.
Can include address, phone number, email address, etc.
On one line and not exceeding 132 characters.
</documentation>

</child>

....

</node>

</demo>
```

7.7.5 Static

Static Digital Objects are those which should not change and so all the above examples, the JPEG file, the NetCDF file etc fall into this category.

7.7.6 Non-static

Many, some would say most, datasets change over time and the state at each particular moment in any time may be important. This is an important area requiring further research, however from the point of view of this document it may be useful to break the issue into separate parts:

- at each moment in time we could, in principle, take a snapshot and store it. That snapshot would have its associated Representation Network.
- efficient storage of a series of snapshots may lead one to store differences or include time tags in the data (see for example [67]). Additional Representation Information would be needed which describes how to get to a particular time's snapshot from the efficiently encoded version.

Common ways of preserving such differences for text files such as computer source code, use the diff [24] format to store the changes between one version and the next. Thus the original plus the incremental diff files would be stored and to reproduce the file at any particular point the appropriate diffs would be applied. Regarding the collection of the initial plus the diffs as the digital object being preserved, the Representation Information needed to construct the object at any point is therefore the definition of the diff format plus the naming convention which specifies the order in which the diffs are applied.

Another trivial example would be where essentially the only change allowed is to append additional material to the end of the digital object. The recording of Provenance is often an example of this. One common way of recording when the addition was made, and of delimiting the addition, is to add a time-tag. The Representation Information needed here, in addition to that needed to understand the material itself, is the description of the meaning of the time tag – what format, what timezone, does it tag the material which comes after it or before it?

7.7.7 Active

7.7.7.1 Actions and Processes

Some information has, as an integral part of its content, an implicit or explicit process associated with it. This could be argued to be a type of semantics, however it is probably sufficiently different to need special classification. Examples of this include databases or other time dependent or reactive systems such as Neural Nets.

The process may be implicitly encoded in the data, for example with the scheme for encoding time dependence in XML data as noted above. Alternatively the process may be held in the Representation Information - possibly as software. Amongst many other possibilities under this topic, Software and Software Emulation are among the most interesting [68]. Emulation is discussed in more detail in Sect. 7.9.

However an important limitation is that one is "stuck in time" in that one can do what was done before but one cannot immediately use the digital object in new ways and with other tools, for example newer analysis packages.

For other processes and activities text documentation, including source code, can, and is, created. In general such things are difficult to describe in ways which support automation. However these things are outside the remit of this book and will not be described further here.

7.7.8 Passive

The other digital objects described above, apart from those explicitly marked as "active" are "passive".

7.8 Virtualisation

Virtualisation is a term used in many areas. The common theme of all virtualisation technologies is the hiding of technical detail, through encapsulation. Virtualisation creates external interfaces that hide an underlying implementation. The benefits for preservation arise from the hiding of the specific, changing, technologies from the higher level applications which use them.

The Warwick Workshop [69] noted that Virtualisation is an underlying theme, with a layering model illustrated in Fig. 7.15.

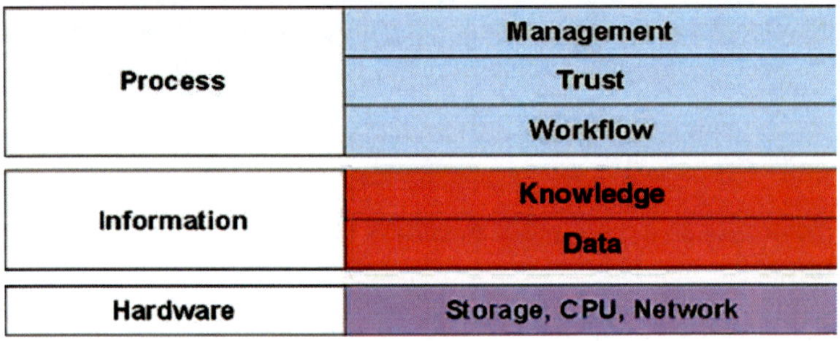

Fig. 7.15 Virtualisation layering model

7.8.1 Advantages of Virtualisation

Virtualisation is not a magic bullet. It cannot be expected to be applied everywhere, and even where it can be applied the interfaces can themselves become obsolete and will eventually have to be re-engineered/re-virtualised, nevertheless we believe that it is a valuable concept. This is a point which will be examined in more detail in Chap. 8; the aim is to identify aspects of the digital object which, we guess, will probably be used in future systems.

This is because, for example, in re-using a digital object in the future the application software will be different from current software; we cannot claim to know what that software will be. How can we try to make it easier for those in the future to re-use current data?

The answer proposed here is that if we treat a digital object, for example, as an image then it is at least likely that future users will find it useful to treat that object as an image - of course they may not but then we cannot help them so readily. If they do want to treat the object as an image then we can help them by providing a description of the digital object which tells them how to extract the required information from the bits.

For a 2-dimensional image one needs the image size (rows, columns) and the pixel values. Therefore if we can tell future users:

Take these bits in order to know the number of rows. These other bits tell you the number of columns; then for each pixel, here is a way to get the pixel value,

then that would make it easier for them to create software to deal with the image. The same argument applies to the different types of virtualised objects which we discuss below.

Each of these types of virtualisation will have its own Representation Information which we may call "virtualisation information"; this Representation Information will of course need its own Representation Information.

The Wikipedia entry provides an extensive list of types of virtualisation, and distinguishes between

- Platform virtualisation, which involves the simulation of virtual machines.
- Resource virtualisation, which involves the simulation of combined, fragmented, or simplified resources.

Figure 6.11 indicates in somewhat more detail than Fig. 7.15 a number of layers in which we expect to use Virtualisation including:

- Digital Object Storage virtualisation – discussed in Sect. 16.2.2.
- Common information virtualisation
- Discipline specific information virtualisation
- Higher level knowledge
- Access control
- Processes

Of course even the Persistent Preservation Infrastructure has to be virtualised.

Each of these is discussed in more detail in Chaps. 16 and 17, introducing the various concepts in a logical manner. For simplicity, these discussions do not follow the layering schemes in Fig. 6.11 or Fig. 7.15 because there are a number of recursive concepts which can be explained more clearly in this way..

7.8.2 Common Information Virtualisation

The Common Information Virtualisation envisaged in CASPAR tries to extract those properties of an Information Object which are widely applicable.

7.8.2.1 Simple Objects

There are several types of relatively simple objects which appear again and again in scientific data, including images, trees, tables and documents. The benefit of this type of virtualisation is that for each of them one can rely upon a certain – admittedly simple – behaviours. Despite this simplicity they are powerful and are the basis of many familiar software applications.

In software terms these virtualisations would be regarded as data types which have an associated API. The specialisations would each support the parent API but add new methods or interfaces. This is a common approach in Object Oriented programming and some references to existing software libraries are provided where appropriate.

Many of these software libraries provide a great deal of functionality built on top of a small core set of interfaces which must be implemented for any new implementation. The analysis which has developed these core interfaces are a great benefit. It is this core set of interfaces which were of particular interest in CASPAR because the other capabilities can be built on top of them. Identifying this small core set of functions means that if we can indicate how to implement these for a piece of data then, right now, we can use rich sets of software applications, and in the future we have the core capabilities which stand a good chance of being implemented in future software systems.

We focus here on reading the data rather than the ability to write it, since we want to be able to deal with data which already exists, having been written by some other means.

7.8.2.1.1 Images

In common usage, an image or picture is an artefact that reproduces the likeness of some subject, say a physical object or a person. An image may be thought of as a digital object which may be displayed as a rectangular 2-dimensional array in which all the picture elements (pixels) have the same data type, and normally any two neighbouring pixels have some type of mathematical or physical relationship e.g. they help to make up a part of a picture. All 2-dimensional images have a number of common features, including

- Size
- number of rows and
- number of columns i.e. all rows have the same number of pixels, making a rectangular array
- Pixel type – same for all pixels
- Attributes (name-value pairs)

The digital encoding of the image may not be a simple rectangular array of numbers – there may be compression for example. Such encodings are not of concern in this virtualisation. The same image may have many different digital encodings, each of which needs some appropriate Structural Representation Information. The Java2D and the java.awt.Image provide sets of interfaces with a very rich set of capabilities for manipulating graphics and images. The java.awt.Image [70] has a core set of methods which match the above list, namely getHeight, getWidth, getSource and getProperty. Put into a wider context one can view images as a special case of 2-dimensional arrays of data, where for each new type one would support a new capability as illustrated in Fig. 7.16.

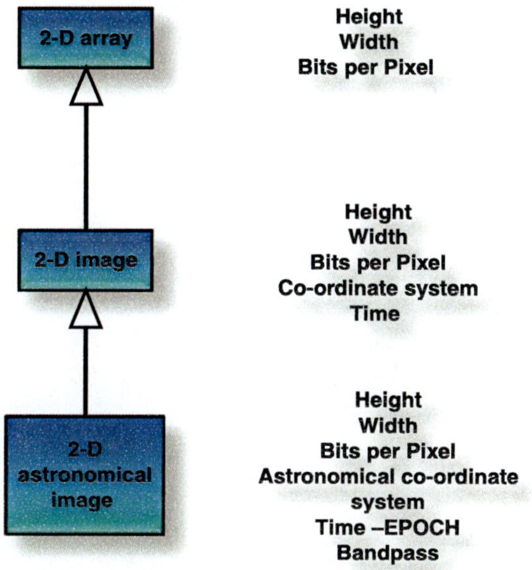

Fig. 7.16 Image data hierarchy

Thus a 2-dimensional array is the most general; this can be specialised into a 2-dimanesional image with, for example, additional methods to get co-ordinate systems and the time the image was created. For the even more specialised astronomical image one would add, for example the spectral bandpass of the instrument with which the image was created.

7.8.2.1.2 Tables

A table consists of an ordered arrangement of rows and columns. This is a simplified description of the most basic kind of table. Certain considerations follow from this simplified description:

- the term row has several common synonyms (e.g., record, k-tuple, n-tuple, vector);
- the term column has several common synonyms (e.g., field, parameter, property, attribute);
- column is usually identified by a name;
- column name can consist of a word, phrase or a numerical index;

A hierarchy of table models is shown in Fig. 7.17

The elements of a table may be grouped, segmented, or arranged in many different ways, and even nested recursively. Additionally, a table may include "metadata" such as annotations, header, footer or other ancillary features.

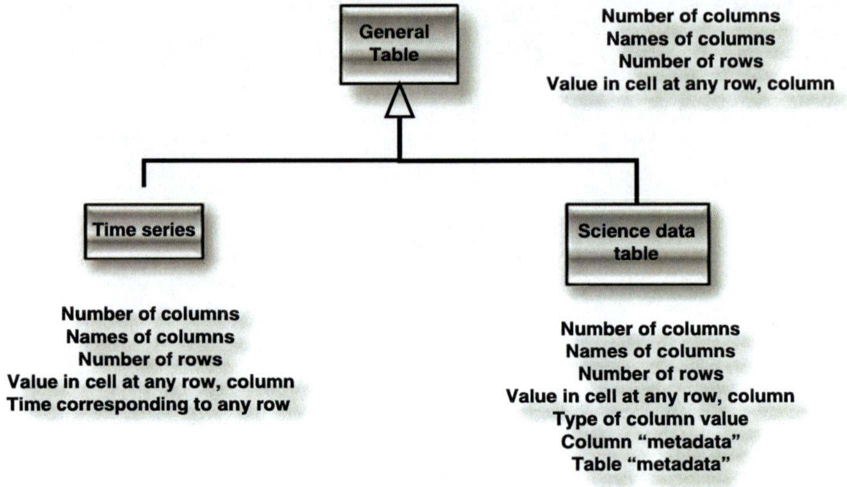

Fig. 7.17 Table hierarchy

Tables can be viewed as columns of information – each column has the same type – as illustrated in Fig. 7.18 which comes from the Starlink Tables Infrastructure Library (STIL) table interface. This is rather rich in functionality and which is itself built on top of the Java TableModel [71] interface. The latter has a core set of methods, namely

- get the number of columns (getColumnCount)
- get the column names (getColumnName)
- get the number of rows (getRowCount)
- get the value at a particular cell (getValueAt)

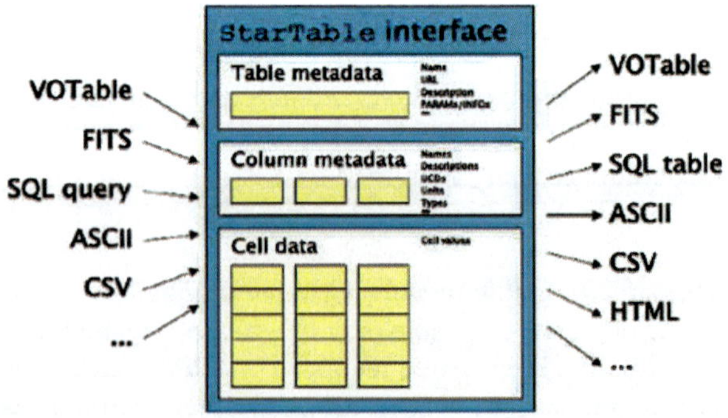

Fig. 7.18 Example Table interface

An extension which is used in astronomical applications is shown in Fig. 7.18 and further documentation is available from the TOPCAT web site [72]. This application illustrates the power of virtualisation. Tables can be read in the form of FITS tables, CSV files [73], VOTable [74]; the software allows each of these formats of data can be used in what may be called a generic application of considerable power, illustrated in Fig. 7.19.

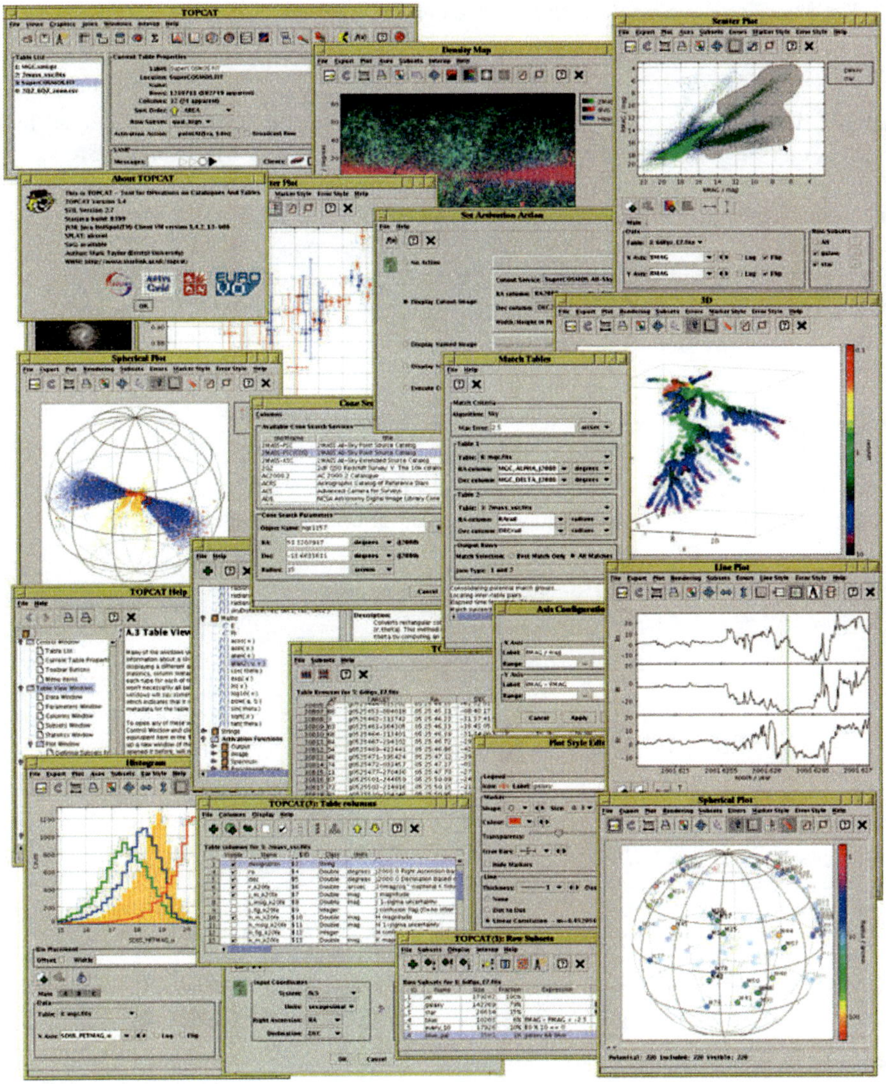

Fig. 7.19 Illustration of TOPCAT capabilities – from TOPCAT web site

7.8.2.1.3 Trees

In computer terms a tree is a data structure that emulates a tree structure with a set of linked nodes, each of which has a single parent node – except the (single) root node – and there are no closed "loop" structures (i.e. it is acyclic). A node with no children is a "leaf" node. This type of structure is illustrated in Fig. 7.20, and it appears in many areas including XML structures. A variety of tree structures can be created by associating different properties with the nodes.

The Java TreeModel interface [75] is an example of this.

7.8.2.1.4 Documents

Simple documents, i.e. something with text and images that can be displayed to a user, can also be virtualised; an example of this is the Multivalent Browser [76], which defines common access methods to documents in a number of formats including scanned paper, HTML, UNIX manual pages, TeX, DVI and PDF. The Multivalent browser central data structure is the document tree – a specialised version of the tree structure described in Sect. 5.2.1.1.3. Another, simpler, document model is provided by the W3C's Document Object Model (DOM) [77] and the Java implementation [78].

7.8.3 Composite Objects

The concept Composite Object is a catch-all term which covers a variety of structured (tree-like) objects, which may contain other complex and simple objects. The

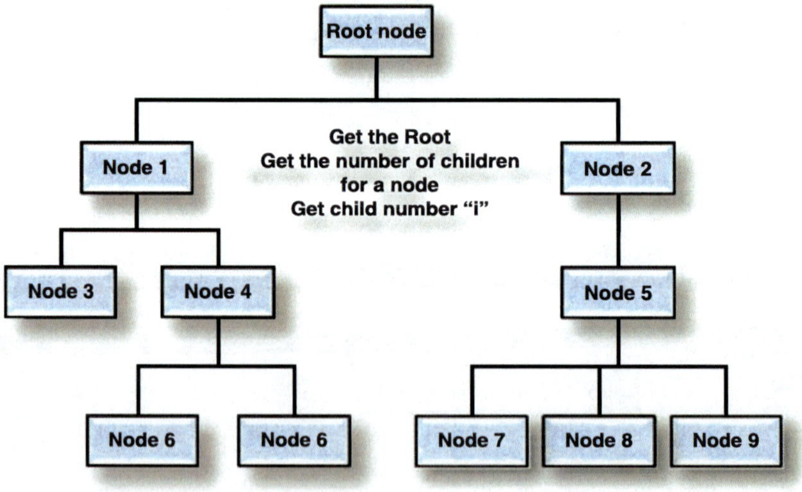

Fig. 7.20 Tree structure

boundary between Simple Objects and Composite Objects is not sharp. For example a Tree-type object where the leave nodes are not primitive types may be considered a Composite Object; the Multivalent Browser document model may be rather complex. Nevertheless it is worth maintaining the distinction between

> Simple Objects, where we have some chance of being able to do something sensible with the information content using widely applicable, reasonably standard, interfaces – display, search, process etc.

and

> Composite Objects, which are likely to require a number of additional steps to unpack the individual Simple Objects – however the difficulty is then that the relationship between those Simple Objects has to be defined elsewhere. Usually creators of Composite Objects embed the knowledge of those relationships within associated software. These relationships may be captured using Knowledge Management techniques.

7.8.3.1 On-demand Objects

In the process of managing objects and creating, for example, DIPs, there is a need to create objects "on-the-fly". One can in fact regard on-demand as the norm, depending on the level of detail at which one looks at the systems; there are many processes hidden from view in the various hardware and software systems.

Of more immediate interest are processes and workflows which act on the data objects to produce some desired output. There are a variety of workflow description languages and types of process. The virtualisation required here is an abstract layer which can accommodate several different underlying workflow systems. This level of abstraction is outside the scope of this book and will not be covered here.

7.8.4 Discipline Specific Information Virtualisation

As noted above, each of the common virtualisations in the previous section is useful because one can rely on some (simple) specific behaviour from each type. Although simple, the behaviours can be combined to produce quite complex results. However different disciplines can produce a number of specialised types of, for example, images. By this is meant that a number of additional, specialised, behaviours become available for each specialised type. Expanding in Fig. 7.16, Fig. 7.21 shows some further examples of specialisations of image types. The Astronomical image will add the functionality of, for example, a World Coordinate System i.e. the Right Ascension/Declination of object at the centre of the image, and the direction and angular size on the sky of each pixel in the image. The set of FITS image standards provide the basis of this type of additional functionality. Astronomical images can

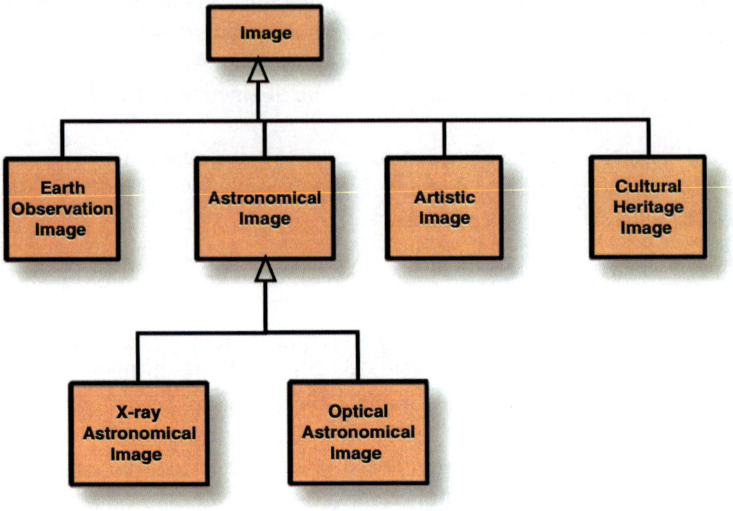

Fig. 7.21 Image specialisations

in turn be specialised further so that, for example, an X-Ray image can add the functionality of providing the energy of each X-ray photon collected by the observing instrument.

Each increasingly specialised sub-area will produce increasingly specialised aspects for their, in this case, images. Each specialisation will introduce additional functionality.

7.8.5 Higher Level Knowledge Virtualisation

Knowledge Management covers a very large number of concepts. We do not go into these here but instead note that there are multiple encodings available. Some of these are discussed in the next chapter.

7.8.6 Access Control/Trust Virtualisation

As with Knowledge Management there are several approaches and implementations. A virtualisation effort which CASPAR has undertaken is to try to identify a relatively simple interface which can be implemented on top of several of these existing systems. Access Control, Trust and Digital Rights Management are related concepts, although they cover, in general, distinct functions and different domains. For example, Access Control can be distinguished from DRM mainly by the following aspects:

- **Functional**: Access Control focuses only on the enforcement of authorization policies, while DRM covers several aspects related to the management of authorization policies
- **Policy domain**: The Access Control authorization policies lose their semantics and validity once the digital objects leave the information system, while the digital rights have system independent semantics and legal validity
- **Enforcement extent**: DRM focuses on persistent protection of rights, as it remains in force wherever the content goes, while a digital content that is protected by an information system's Access Control mechanism loses its protection once it leaves the system

Keeping the above characteristics in mind, it can be recognized that both Access Control and Digital Rights Management are needed to govern the access administration of OAIS archive holdings. Moreover, both aspects are subjected to changes over time, which need proper attention in order to preserve the access policies that protect the digital holdings.

The interface would have to cover, amongst other things:

1. DRM policy creation
2. Recognition of rights
3. Assertion of rights
4. Expression of rights
5. DRM policy projection
6. Dissemination of rights
7. Exposure of rights
8. Enforcement of rights
9. DRM security and cryptography
10. Access Control technologies

Access Control policies are defined and are valid within the archival information system.

There may be access restrictions on Content Information that are of different natures: copyright protection, privacy law, as well as further Producer's instructions. The Producer might wish to allow access only under the condition that some administrative policies are respected (e.g. defining a group of authorized Consumers, or specifying minimum requirements to be met by enforcement measures).

In the long term, the "maintenance" of all such information within the archive (and between archives) becomes "preservation of administrative information". In fact, the administrative aspects related to the content access may be subject to some modifications in the long term due to legislative changes, technology evolution, and events that influence the semantics of access policies.

In the updated OAIS the administrative information is held as part of the Preservation Description Information (PDI), as "Access Rights Information" information. It identifies the access restrictions pertaining to the Content Information, in particular to the Data Object, including the legal framework, licensing terms, privacy protection, and agreed Producer's instructions about access control. It contains the access and distribution conditions stated within the Submission Agreement, related to preservation (by the OAIS), dissemination (by the OAIS or the Consumer) and final usage (Designated Community). It includes the specifications for the application of technological measures for rights enforcement.

7.8.7 Digital Object Storage Virtualisation

Storage Virtualisation refers to the process of abstracting logical storage from physical storage. This will be addressed in more detail in Part II, but for completeness we include a brief overview here. It aims to provide the ability to access data without knowing the details of the storage hardware and access software or its location. This isolation from the particular details facilitates preservation by allowing systems to survive changing hardware and software technologies. Significant work on this has been carried out in many areas, particularly the various Data Grid related projects.

The Warwick Workshop [69] foresaw the need to address the following:

- development and standardisation of interfaces to allow "pluggable" storage hardware systems.
- standardisation of archive storage API i.e. standardised storage virtualisation
- development of languages to describe data policy demands and processes, together with associated support systems
- development of collection oriented description and transfer techniques
- development of workflow systems and process definition and control

In more detail, one can, following Moore, identify a number of areas requiring work to support virtualisation, the most basic being:

- creation of infrastructure-independent naming convention
- mapping of administrative attributes onto the logical file name such as the physical location of the file and the name of the file on that particular storage system.
- Association of the location of copies (replicas) with the logical name.
- mapping access controls onto the logical name, then when we move the file the access controls do not change.
- map descriptive attributes onto the logical name, and discover files without knowing their name or location.
- characterization of management policies independently of the implementation needs to cover:
- validation policies
- lifetime policies
- access policies

- federation policies
- presentation policies
- consistency policies

in order to manage ownership of records independently of storage systems one needs details of the Data collection

- at each remote storage system, an account ID is created under which the preservation environment stores files
- management of roles for permitted operations
- management of authentication of users
- management of authorization

in order to manage the execution of preservation processes across distributed resources on further needs:

- management of execution state
- management of relationships between jobs
- management of interactions with remote schedulers

7.9 Emulation

Emulation may be defined as "*the ability of a computer program or electronic device to imitate another program or device*" [79]. This is a type of virtualisation but thinking more generally one can regard the information one needs to do this as a type of "Other Representation Information" because such information (including the emulators discussed below) may be needed to understand and, more importantly, to use the digital object of interest.

There are many reasons for wanting to do this in digital preservation, and several ways of approaching it. One significant classification of these approaches is whether the emulation is aimed at one particular programme or device, or whether one aims at providing functionality which can support very many programmes or devices. Section 12.2.2.1 discusses the former; an example of the latter is where it may be sensible to provide the Designated Community with the look and feel of (formerly) widely used proprietary Access software. In this case, if the OAIS has all the necessary compiled applications and associated libraries but is unable to obtain the source code, or has the source code but lacks the ability to create the required application for example because of unavailability of a compiler, necessary libraries or operating environment, it may find it necessary to investigate use of an emulation approach.

The disadvantage of emulation is that one tends to be stuck with the applications that used to be available; one tends to be cut off from the more modern applications, including one's favourite software. The ability to combine data from different eras and areas is thereby severely curtailed. However this may not matter if one simply needs to render a digital object, for example display or print a document or image.

We discuss in what follows emulation of the underlying hardware or software. One advantage of hardware emulation is that once a hardware platform is emulated successfully all operating systems and applications that ran on the original platform can be run without modification on the new platform. However, the level of emulation is relevant (for example whether it goes down to the level of duplicating the timing of CPU instruction execution). Moreover, this does not take into account dependencies on input/output devices.

Emulation has been used successfully when a very popular operating system is to be run on a hardware system for which it was not designed, such as running a version of Windows™ on a SUN™ machine. However, even in this case, when strong market forces encourage this approach, not all applications will necessarily run correctly or perform adequately under the emulated environment. For example, it may not be possible to fully simulate all of the old hardware dependencies and timings, because of the constraints of the new hardware environment. Further, when the application presents information to a human interface, determining that some new device is still presenting the information correctly is problematical and suggests the need, as noted previously, to have made a separate recording of the information presentation to use for validation.

Once emulation has been adopted, the resulting system is particularly vulnerable to previously unknown software errors that may seriously jeopardize continued information access. Given these constraints, the technical and economic hurdles to hardware emulation appear substantial except where the emulation is of a rendering process, such as displaying an image of a document page or playing a sound within a single system.

There have been investigations of alternative emulation approaches, such as the development of a virtual machine architecture or emulation at the operating system level. These approaches solve some of the issues of hardware emulation, but introduce new concerns. In addition, the current emulation research efforts involve a centralized architecture with control over all peripherals. The level of complexity of the interfaces and interactions with a ubiquitous distributed computing environment (i.e., WWW and JAVA or more general client-server architectures) with heterogeneous clients may introduce requirements that go beyond the scope of current emulation efforts.

In the following sections we provide a more detailed discussion of the current state of the art.

7.9.1 Overview of Emulation

An emulator in this context refers to software or hardware that runs binary software (including operating systems) on a system for which it was not compiled. For example, the SIMH [80] emulator runs old VAX operating systems and software on newer PC ×86 hardware. The system on which the emulator runs is usually referred

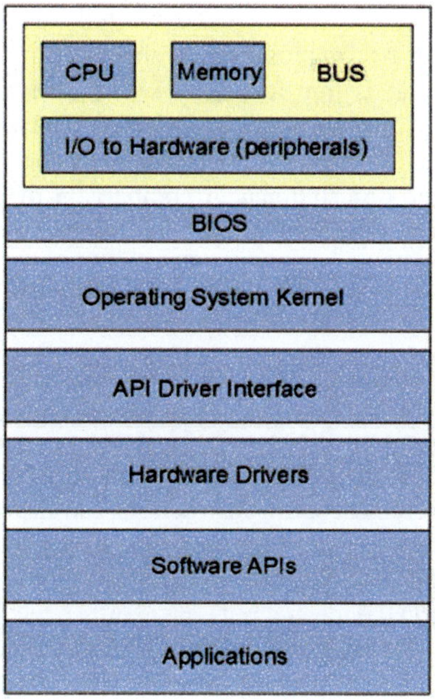

Fig. 7.22 Simple layered model of a computer system

to as the host system, and the system being emulated is referred to as the target system. Emulators can emulate a whole computer hardware system (see Fig. 7.22 for a simple model of a computer system) including CPU and peripheral hardware (graphics, disk etc). This means that they can run operating systems and software that used to run on the target system on any newer hardware even if the instruction set of the new system is different.

The concept of emulation for running old software on newer systems has been around for nearly as long as the modern digital computer. The IBM 709 computer system build in 1958 contained hardware that emulated the older legacy IBM 704 system built in 1954 and enabled it to run software from the old 704 system [81].

The main purpose of Emulation techniques has been to run older, legacy, software on new hardware. Usually this has been to extend the life of software and systems such that the transition to newer systems can be done at a more leisurely and cost effective pace. During this time, new software can be written as a replacement and also data can be migrated. Another factor that makes emulation useful is it gives time to train people to use the newer systems and software. Usually emulation is only a short term, stop gap, solution when moving to a new hardware/software system. Only recently has emulation been suggested [82] as a long-term preservation strategy for software.

It has been proposed for the preservation of digitally encoded documents by preserving the ability to render those digital objects, ignoring the semantics of the encoded object. Later we will discuss the issues and benefits of emulation as a long-term preservation strategy.

It is not intended here to give a detailed description of how emulators work or how to write an emulator. But some simplified technical details of emulation and computer systems (mostly terminology) must be described, as it then allows the description and comparison of current emulator software solutions and their features, particularly with reference to their suitability to long-term preservation.

7.9.2 A Simple Model of a Modern Computer System

Central Processing Unit (CPU) decodes and executes the instructions of the Software APIs and Applications. Typically this involves executing numeric, logical and control instructions (an instruction set) which take data from memory and outputs the result back to memory. The control instructions may also be executed by I/O devices, i.e. the CPU just forwards the instructions and data to the appropriate I/O device and puts the results back into memory or storage.

Memory simply stores instructions and data in a logical sequential map so they can be accessed by the CPU and I/O devices. Memory can be non-volatile (content is kept when power is switched off) or volatile (content is lost when power is switched off).

The Bus connects everything together thus providing the communication between the different components of the system (CPU, Memory, I/O devices). Typically within the computer the Bus resides on the motherboard (which holds the CPU, Memory and I/O interfaces) and is controlled by the CPU and other control logic.

Basic Input/Output System (BIOS) is the first code run by a computer when it is powered on. It is stored in Read Only Memory (ROM) memory which is persistent when the power is switched off. It initialises the peripheral hardware attached to the system (such as the hard disk and graphics card) and then boots (runs) the operating system which then takes control of the system and peripherals.

The (Input/Output) I/O takes the form of several interfaces that allow peripheral hardware attached to the system (such as the hard disk and graphics card, printer etc). Common I/O interfaces are Universal Serial Bus (USB), Parallel, Serial, Graphical and Network interfaces.

The system software consists of the Operating System, API Driver Interface, Hardware Drivers, Software APIs and Applications. They are all built for a specific instruction set. This mean that they will run only on a system with a particular CPU type that executes that particular instruction set. By "built" we mean that source code for the software (usually text files with statements that relate to a specific programming language such as C or C++) are converted (compiled) to binary application files that contain data and instructions that are read sequentially by the hardware (loaded into and read from memory) and executed by the CPU and peripheral hardware.

To run software built for one instruction set on a hardware system with a different instruction set means that the software needs to be converted to contain instruction for the new hardware (instruction sets, and hence binary application files, are not usually compatible between different hardware systems). This conversion is usually what is meant by emulation, and there are a variety of methods for doing this conversion (types of emulation).

7.9.3 Types of Emulation

Emulation comes in several forms. These relate to the level of detail and accuracy to which the emulator software reproduces the functionality and behaviour of the original computer hardware system (and some peripheral hardware) [83]. The basic forms of Emulation we shall discuss are, Hardware Simulation, Instruction Emulation, Virtualisation, Binary Translation, and Virtual Machines.

The aim of Hardware Simulation (and confusingly sometimes also referred to as just emulation) is to reproduce the behaviour of the computer hardware system and peripheral hardware perfectly. This is achieved by using mathematical and empirical models of the components of the computer system (electronic and mechanical engineering simulation). Inevitably such an approach is difficult to accomplish and also produces emulators that run very slowly.

A typical application of these emulators is to test the behaviour of real hardware, i.e. as a diagnostic tool, and also as a design tool for creating the electronics for computer hardware [84, 85]. Hardware simulation is very little used in terms of emulation for running software, but does provide a specification for the functions and behaviour of hardware that potentially could be used as a source of information in the future for writing other forms of emulators. Problematically, such information about the design of the hardware is not usually available from the companies producing the hardware.

Characterising some aspects of the behaviour of the hardware can be done, and proves to be useful, even if the full simulation is unavailable. The reproduction of the accuracy of the output of a given CPU instruction can easily be defined (and usually is in the specification of the CPU instruction set [86]). Also the time the instructions take to execute can be measured. These two characteristics can be used when producing Instruction Emulators that faithfully reproduce the "feel" of the original system when software executes as well as producing accurate results from execution of the instructions. The down side of this reproduction of timing and accuracy is usually a significant loss in speed of the emulator (all instructions have accurate timing relative to one another but are scaled relative to the original system).

Instruction Emulation is one of the most common forms of emulation. This involves the instructions for the CPU and other hardware being emulated in software such that binary software (including operating systems) will run on systems with different instruction sets without the need for the source code to be recompiled (but little or no guarantee is given to timing and accuracy of the execution of the instructions).

Instruction emulation is achieved by mapping the operation codes (Op Codes), which are the part of the instruction set that specifies the operation to be performed, from the instruction set to a set of functions in software. Typically software instruction emulators are written in C or C++ to maximise speed. For example, the instruction for adding two 32 bit floating point numbers together on an Intel 32 bit i386 CPU takes two 32 bit floating point numbers and returns another 32 bit floating point number as the result; the addition is done in a very few machine cycles using the built-in hardware on the chip . It is relatively easy to emulate this by writing a software function in, say, the C language, that takes the two 32 bit floating point numbers and adds them together; however running this simple function takes many machine cycles.

The simplest form of an emulated CPU is a software program loop that reads the instructions (Op Codes) from memory (also emulated) and matches it to the relevant function that implements that Op Code.

Other peripheral hardware needs to be emulated too, this is done in a similar way to the CPU, as each piece of hardware will have an "instruction set" where the appropriate instructions from the software are passed to the hardware to be "executed". For example, graphics cards can perform a number of (usually mathematical/geometrical) operations on image data before it is displayed. Once the emulation code has been written, then any compiler for the language that the emulator is written in can be used to transform the emulation software code to the instruction set of a new computer hardware system.

The performance of running software on an instruction emulator is in the order of 5–500 times slower than running it on the original hardware, depending on the techniques used to write the emulator and the accuracy and timing required. Assuming that computing performance continues to roughly double every 2 years then an instruction emulator will run software at the speed it ran on the original hardware in about 4–18 years.

Most instruction emulators are modular in nature, that is, they have separate software code for each of the components of a computer system (CPU, Memory, BIOS etc). This means that, for example, CPUs can be interchanged providing an emulator that can run a variety of operating systems and software from built for many different systems with different instruction sets. Typically in modern desktop systems it is only the CPU instruction set that differs, most of the other hardware is similar and can be interchanged between the different systems. The emulator called QEMU [22] takes advantage of this and emulates a variety of different computer systems such as SPARC, Intel x86 etc (QEMU will be discussed later).

Virtualisation is a form of emulation where all the hardware is emulated except the CPU. This means a virtualiser can only run on systems with one specific type of CPU. It means one can run a variety of different operating systems and software as long as they are built for the CPU that the virtualiser runs on. Typical examples of virtualiser software are VMware [87] and Xen [88].

Binary translation is a form of emulation where a binary software application (not operating systems) is translated from one instruction set to another. In this case one ends up with a new piece of software that can run on a different system with a different instruction sets. Software applications are rarely self contained and typically rely on one or more other pieces of software (software libraries etc). In this case not only does the software application need to be translated but also its dependencies may need translating too (if they do not already exist on the new system at the appropriate version). If the operating system of the new target system is different too, then the binary file format that the software instructions are contained in will also need to be translated. For example, Windows software executable binary files have a different format to that of executable binary files on a Linux system.

Virtual Machines (VMs) take a slightly different approach to running software on a variety of different computer systems. They define a hardware independent instruction set (Bytecode) which is compiled (often dynamically) to the instruction set of the host system. The software that does the compilation is called a Virtual Machine (VM), The VM must be re-written for, or ported to, the host system. On top of these VMs usually sits a unique programming language (unique to that VM) which when compiled is compiled to the VMs bytecode. This bytecode can then be executed with the VM, i.e. it is dynamically compiled to the hardware instruction set of the host system.

One problem with VMs is that they usually do not emulate hardware systems other than the CPU. Instead they provide a set of functions/method (software libraries) in the programming language unique to that VM that interface and expose the functionality of the hardware systems (graphics, disc I/O etc) to applications written in the VMs unique programming language. These software libraries are then implemented via some other programming language (usually C or C++) and compiled for the host system. This mean that whenever one needs to run a VM and its software libraries on a new system (to run programs written in the VMs unique programming language) one has to re-implement the VM and libraries or port the existing one to the new system. This is potentially problematic in that the behaviour of the VM and the associated software libraries needs to be reproduced accurately on the new system; if it is not reproduced accurately, then it may lead to the failure of applications to run on the new VM or for them to behave in an undesirable way. Examples of VMs and porting problems will be given later.

7.9.4 Emulation and Digital Preservation

Emulation has difficulties but also a number of advantages, especially related to digital objects which are difficult to describe in detail, for example Word files. A piece of Representation Information for a Word file is likely to be the WINWORD.EXE programme. The Representation Information for WINWORD.EXE could well be an emulator; indeed it may be the only practical way of using the Word executable digital object. Emulation therefore has an important role to play, certainly for some types of digital objects.

7.9.4.1 OAIS and Emulation as a Preservation Strategy

OAIS does describe instruction emulation as possible method of preserving Access Software (AS). In OAIS, AS refers to software that reads, processes and renders data that is being preserved for a given designated community. It sees the preservation of AS as necessary when the look (rendering) and feel of the software in important to the reuse and understanding of the data being preserved and also when inadequate Representation Information is available that would allow the reproduction of the software's capabilities. For example when software provides a unique plotting method for data (rendering) or a unique and complex algorithm for processing the data before it is rendered. Here, rendering could be a visual, audio or even a physical rendering (plotting for example) of data.

When we talk about the "feel" of software we usually refer to the timing to which things happen within the software. For example, the movement of a character in a computer game may be required to happen in a smooth and uniform way for the game to be played properly. Timing is usually related to the timing of the execution of the instructions of the computers instruction set (they are executed at the appropriate time and for the right duration relative to the other instructions). An example of where timing could prove to be a problem is in the playing of video and audio data. If the instructions used by the software playing the audio or video are not executed at the appropriate time then the audio or video could slow down or speed up causing an unusual reproduction. Similarly, if some instructions took too long to execute relative to the other instruction then a similar effect would be observed. This is not the necessarily the same as the emulator simply running slowly so that the whole recording is played in "slow motion"; lack of synchronisation may also arise.

OAIS also states that the reimplementation of the functionality of software and software APIs is an emulation technique. If adequate information is available about the software, algorithms and rendering methods it uses, then software can simply be re-implemented in the future. But OAIS points out that even then problems may arise as documentation of the APIs may still not be enough to reproduce the behaviour of the old software. This is because one can never be sure that the new implementation behaves like the original unless the software has been tested and its behaviour and output compared against the old software. This problem can be overcome by recording any input and the corresponding output from the original software and using it as test and comparison against the output of the new software ensuring that the new implementation is correct.

7.9.4.2 Preserving Software with an Emulator

An important aspect of preserving software and data with an emulator is simply testing to see if the emulator runs the software correctly (assuming that we are keeping both the software and the emulator together for preservation). The software may run slowly on the emulator, but as long as the look, feel, and accuracy is preserved then this is one test we can do to ensure the software's correct and "trustworthy" preservation using emulation as a preservation strategy. In this case, the relative execution speed (instruction timing and duration problems as mentioned previously) need only be considered when considering the feel, as it is assumed that the emulator will run the software at the original speed in the future when hardware systems are faster.

When preserving emulation software though, we must also consider that it will be more than likely preserved as source code. Preserving the binary form of an emulator would then mean that it itself would have to be run on an emulator in the future. This could potentially cause problems as the speed of execution of the software being preserved would be slowed by a factor of the product of the speed reduction of the two emulators. So if both emulators ran software 500 times slower, then the software being preserved would run 25,000 times slower than it did on the original hardware. Given that the speed of hardware roughly doubles every 2 years this would mean the software would only run at its original speed on hardware 28–30 years in the future. Carrying on running emulators in emulators means that the time before the software runs at the original speed can increase dramatically. Preserving the binary form of the emulator is therefore probably not a really practical solution, although in principle it serves its purpose.

Preserving the source of the emulator for the long-term also has its problems. In the first instance the source code would have to be recompiled for the new hardware system. Any software source code being transferred to a new system usually invokes software porting problems. Porting software usually means it has to be modified before it will compile and run correctly; this takes time and effort. Even if one ports the software and gets it to compile, one is still left with the same problem as discussed above when software is re-implemented, namely that that the software has to be tested and compared to the original to ensure that it is behaving and running correctly. To do this, the tests, test data and the corresponding test outputs from the original emulator also have to be preserved along with the emulator itself.

Another potential problem also arises in the very long-term when preserving source code for the emulator. The source code will be written in one or more programming languages which will need complier software to produce machine code so that it can be run. In the future there is no guarantee that the required compilers will exist on any future computer systems, which could potentially render the emulator code useless. The source code for the emulator may still be of some use though, but only as "documentation" that may guide someone willing to attempt to re-implement the emulator in a new programming language. It would be much better in this case to have sufficient documentation about the old hardware so as to capture enough information as to make the reimplementation possible. Such documentation would include information about the CPUs instruction set [86], and information about the peripheral hardware functionality and supported instructions.

One question remains about instruction emulators, and that is, why is it not better to just preserve the source code for the software that needs to be preserved and then port it to future systems? The main argument for this is that an emulator will allow many different applications to be run, and thus the effort in porting or re-implementing an emulator is far less that that required to port or to re-implement a lot of different software applications. But preserving the source for the applications is still a good idea as it gives another option if no emulator for the binary form of the software has been ported or documented. The other argument is that not all software has the source available, i.e. propriety applications where only the binary is available. In this case the only option if one needs to preserve the software is to run it under an emulation environment.

7.9.4.3 Emulation, Recursion and the UVC

One can look at emulation from the point of view of recursion. One uses an emulator to preserve software; the emulator is itself a piece of software – which needs to be preserved, for example as the underlying hardware or operating systems change. Some testbed examples are given in Sect. 20.5.

One way to halt the recursion is to jump out and instead of preserving the "current" emulator one simply replaces it – one could look at this as a type of transformation but that seems a little odd.

The source code of many emulators is available and so one can use a less drastic alternative and make appropriate changes to the source code of the emulator being used so that it works with the new hardware. This can work with a number of the emulators discussed in the next section.

If the software one wishes to preserve is written in Java, then the challenge becomes how to preserve the Java Virtual Machine (JVM); this is discussed in some more detail in the next section.

It may be possible to develop a Universal Virtual Computer (UVC) [89]. However, recognising that one of the prime desirable features of a UVC is that it is well defined and can be implemented on numerous architectures, it may be possible to use something already in place, namely the JAVA Virtual Machine [90]. However it is argued [91] that since the JVM has to be very efficient, because it needs to run current applications at an acceptable speed, there are various constraints such as fixed numbers of registers and pre-defined byte-size. The UVC on the other hand can afford to run very slowly now, instead relying on future processors which should be very much faster, as a result it can afford to be free of some of these constraints.

A "proof-of-concept" implementation of the UVC is available [92] – interestingly that UVC is implemented in Java.

The only advantage for the UVC is if its architecture remains fixed for all time, then at least some base software libraries written for it would continue to run. But as soon software starts to require other software dependencies and specific versions, then specifying those dependencies becomes a problem for the UVC just as it does for any other system. Software maintenance is also a problem, in the future one may need a lot of representation information to understand and use some software source code or a binary.

Perhaps the biggest hurdle for the UVC is the need to write applications for the UVC to deal with a variety of digital encoded information. However in principle this effort can be widely shared for Rendered Digital Objects such as images, for example JPEG and GIF, and documents such as PDF. Dealing with Non-rendered Digital Objects could be rather more challenging.

7.9.5 Examples of Current Emulators and Virtual Machines

7.9.5.1 QEMU

QEMU [93] is a multi system emulator that emulates all aspects of a modern computer system, including networking. It purports to be fast, in that emulation speeds are in the order of 5–10 times slower than the original hardware (depending on the instruction being executed). The following CPUs are emulated:

- PC (x86 or x86_64 processor)
- ISA PC (old style PC without PCI bus)
- PREP (PowerPC processor)
- G3 Beige PowerMac (PowerPC processor)
- Mac99 PowerMac (PowerPC processor, in progress)
- Sun4m/Sun4c/Sun4d (32-bit Sparc processor)
- Sun4u/Sun4v (64-bit Sparc processor, in progress)
- Malta board (32-bit and 64-bit MIPS processors)
- MIPS Magnum (64-bit MIPS processor)
- ARM Integrator/CP (ARM)
- ARM Versatile baseboard (ARM)
- ARM RealView Emulation baseboard (ARM)
- Spitz, Akita, Borzoi, Terrier and Tosa PDAs (PXA270 processor)
- Luminary Micro LM3S811EVB (ARM Cortex-M3)
- Luminary Micro LM3S6965EVB (ARM Cortex-M3)
- Freescale MCF5208EVB (ColdFire V2).
- Arnewsh MCF5206 evaluation board (ColdFire V2).
- Palm Tungsten|E PDA (OMAP310 processor)
- N800 and N810 tablets (OMAP2420 processor)
- MusicPal (MV88W8618 ARM processor)
- Gumstix "Connex" and "Verdex" motherboards (PXA255/270).
- Siemens SX1 smartphone (OMAP310 processor)

QEMU is quite capable of running modern complex operating systems including Microsoft Windows XP (see Fig. 7.23) as well as complex applications such as Microsoft Word. 3D graphic programs would be problematic as it does not emulate 3D rendering graphics hardware. Many devices can be attached as it emulates USB, Serial and Parallel interfaces as well as networking.

The source for QEMU is freely available under LGPL and BSD licences, and extensive documentation exists on how QEMU works and how to port it to new host systems. QEMU is geared towards speed over accuracy.

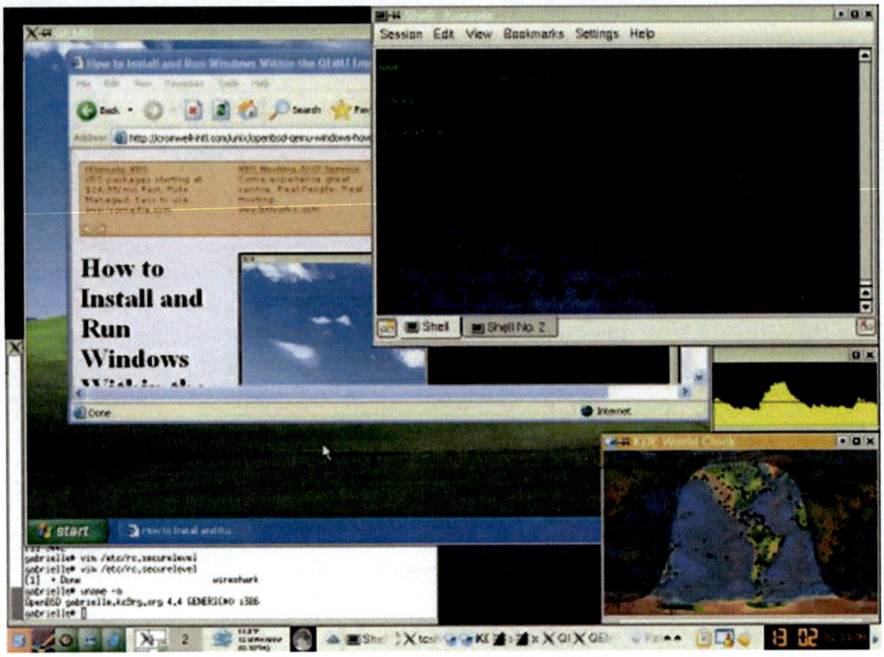

Fig. 7.23 QEMU emulator running

7.9.5.2 SIMH

SIMH is an emulator for old computer systems, and is part of the Computer History Simulation Project [80] (note here simulation is used to refer to instruction emulation rather that true hardware simulation).

SIMH implements instruction emulators for:

- Data General Nova, Eclipse
- Digital Equipment Corporation PDP-1, PDP-4, PDP-7, PDP-8, PDP-9, PDP-10, PDP-11, PDP-15, VAX
- GRI Corporation GRI-909, GRI-99
- IBM 1401, 1620, 1130, 7090/7094, System 3
- Interdata (Perkin-Elmer) 16b and 32b systems
- Hewlett-Packard 2114, 2115, 2116, 2100, 21MX, 1000
- Honeywell H316/H516
- MITS Altair 8800, with both 8080 and Z80
- Royal-Mcbee LGP-30, LGP-21
- Scientific Data Systems SDS 940

One of the most important systems it emulates is VAX, and it can run OpenVMS operating system. The Computer History Simulation Project also collects old operating systems and software that ran on these old systems as well as important documentation about the system hardware.

7.9.5.3 BOCHS

BOCHS [94] is an instruction emulator for 386, 486, Pentium/PentiumII/PentiumIII/Pentium4 or x86-64 CPUs with full system emulation support. It is intended for emulation accuracy and so does not run particularly fast. It is capable of running Windows 95/98/NT/2000/XP and Vista (see Fig. 7.24), all Linux flavours, all BSD flavours, and more and any application that runs under them. It is highly portable, and runs on a wide variety of host systems and operating systems.

7.9.5.4 JPC

JPC [95] is a pure Java emulation of x86 PC hardware in software. Given that it is pure Java, then it will run on any system that has the SUNs Java Virtual Machine ported to it. It claims to be fast but there is no mention of accuracy or timing.

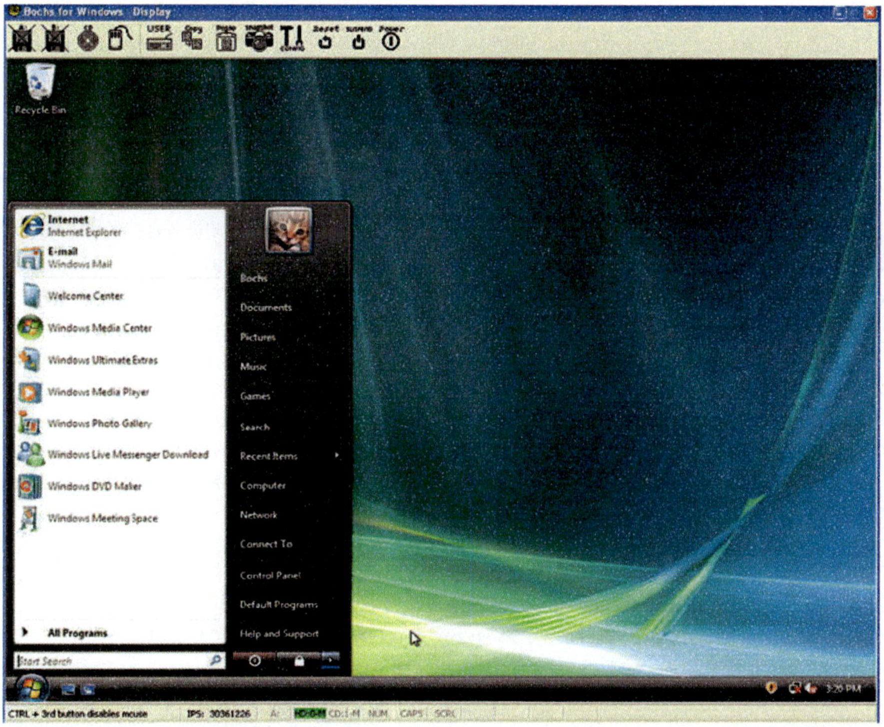

Fig. 7.24 BOCHS emulator running

Currently it will only run a few operating systems such as DOS, some simple Linux distributions and Windows 3.0. One advantage of JPC is its use over the network and through browsers. Because it runs on the SUN JVM it inherits a number of security features that allow software running under it to be executed relatively securely. JPCs memory and CPU emulation are used in the Dioscuri emulator (see below).

7.9.5.5 Dioscuri

Dioscuri [96] is an emulation technology that was designed for digital preservation in mind. The main focus is to make the emulator modular such that various components can be substituted, i.e. substitute the emulation of one CPU for another emulated CPU. The other feature is that the emulator sits on top of a Universal Virtual Machine, and in this case that machine is Java. So in this case the CPU etc of the target system will be implemented in Java. But here we have to remember that Java is not just the virtual machine but a set of software libraries too that are implemented for the host system directly. This implies that they will require porting to any new host system in the future.

Dioscuri does provided a "metadata" specification of the emulator [97, 98] which can be associated with the software being preserved to provide a set of dependences (CPU type, Graphics type and resolution) required to run the software. It also provides a Java API that serves as high-level abstraction of a computer system, i.e. it allows the creation of hardware modules such as the CPU etc. Currently the capabilities of Dioscuri are similar to JPC as it uses the JPC CPU and memory emulation.

7.9.5.6 Java

Java was developed by SUN initially to work on embedded devices but it soon became popular on desktop and server system. It consists of a Java Virtual Machine (JVM) specification [99] which provides a hardware and operating system independent instruction set. It also provides a specification for a high level object orientated programming language called Java [100]. The Java compiler, unlike other native compilers, compiles Java source code to Java bytecode which can then be executed on the JVM. The JVM acts as a dynamic compiler and compiles the bytecode to the native instruction set of the hardware. The JVM itself is implemented in C and compiled using a native compiler to binary software. This means that the JVM has to be ported to any new hardware/operating system environment. The JVM does not itself act as a full system emulator, other hardware functions such as graphics and I/O are provided through specified Java APIs [101]. Some of the Java API is implemented in C and compiled using a native compiler, and hence, like the JVM, they need porting to new hardware/operating systems. Together, the JVM, Java Programming language and the Java API (Java platform) provide all the necessary components to develop complex graphical applications.

Java applications are portable in a sense that they will run on a system to which the Java platform has been ported. If there is no Java platform for a system then

Java applications will not run on that system. Currently many popular systems have a Java platform, but in the future this may or may not be the case.

Porting Java to a new platform implies a significant amount of effort but also some quality issues. SUN make most of the source for Java publically available (some parts of the implementation include propriety code), but one cannot simply port it to a new system and call it Java. Java is a brand name and to call a port *Java* it has to pass a fixed number of tests (Java Compatibility Kit – JCK), these tests are available from SUN [102] and ensure that the port will enable any Java application to run without problems. Using Java as a means of providing an abstract computer model for preserving software inevitably means that any future implementation or port has to pass the test given by SUN to ensure that the applications being preserved will run correctly. The tests are not free to use (only to view) and a license to use them is currently about $50 K (2004), however a specific license [103] allows one to run the JCK in the OpenJDK [104] context, that is for any GPL implementation deriving substantially from OpenJDK.

7.9.5.7 Common Language Infrastructure (CLI) and Mono/.Net

The CLI [105] is a similar technology to Java in that it includes a VM that runs a set of bytecodes rather that the hardware system's native instructions. The VM dynamically compiles the bytecodes to the hardware system's native instructions. The CLI is an ISO standard developed by Microsoft and others and forms part of the .NET infrastructure on which newer Windows software is built (although .NET contains more components than just the CLI). One of the most significant aspects of the CLI is that it provides an interface (Common Language Interface) so that it simplifies the process of interfacing programming languages. In fact many programming languages have been interfaced to the CLI such as C#, Visual Basic .NET, C++ (managed) amongst others [106]. Having many languages that can be compiled to the CLI bytecode opens up the possibility of porting existing software to the CLI with reduced effort and cost. As this ported software would be running under a standardized system (the CLI) then we have the relevant documentation to re-implement such a system in the future if required, or if an implementation exists, a computer preservation environment for all software that has been ported to the CLI.

Mono [107] is an open source implementation of the CLI, so it has already been proven that the CLI can be re-implemented successfully. The full source of an implementation is available so that it can be kept and freely ported to new systems in the future.

7.10 Summary

This chapter should have given the reader an appreciation of the types of Representation Information may be necessary, from the "bits" up.

For those used to dealing with data at least some of this will be familiar.

To those with no familiarity with data and programming it may come as a surprise that there are more than just formats defined by document processing software such as Word or PDF. Nevertheless it is worth remembering that the digital objects we deal with, even documents are likely to become increasingly complex and at least some awareness of the full range of Representation Information will be essential.

Chapter 8
Preservation of Intelligibility of Digital Objects

Co-authors Yannis Tzitzikas, Yannis Marketakis, and Vassilis Christophides

Apathy can be overcome by enthusiasm, and enthusiasm can only be aroused by two things: first, an ideal, with takes the imagination by storm, and second, a definite intelligible plan for carrying that ideal into practice.

(Arnold J. Toynbee)

This whole chapter is rather technical and may be omitted by those without a technical background.

8.1 On Digital Objects and Dependencies

We live in a digital world. Everyone nowadays works and communicates using computers. We communicate digitally using e-mails and voice platforms, watch photographs in digital form, use computers for complex computations and experiments. Moreover information that previously existed in analogue form (i.e. in paper) is now digitized. The amount of digital objects that libraries and archives maintain constantly increases. It is therefore urgent to ensure that these digital objects will remain functional, usable and intelligible in the future. But what should we preserve and how? To address this question we first summarise the discussion in previous Chapters about what a digital object is.

A Digital object is an object composed of a set of bit sequences. At the bit stream layer there is no qualitative difference between digital objects. However in upper layers we can identify several types of digital objects. They can be classified to simple or composite, static or dynamic, rendered or non-rendered etc. Since we are interested in preserving the intelligibility of digital objects we introduce two other broad categories based on the different interpretations of their content: exchange objects and computational objects.

D. Giaretta, *Advanced Digital Preservation*, DOI 10.1007/978-3-642-16809-3_8,

Exchange objects encode knowledge about something in a data structure that allows their exchangeability – hence they are essentially encoded Information Objects i.e. Data Objects. Examples of Information Objects include documents, data-products, images and ontologies. The content of exchange objects can often be described straightforwardly in non digital form. For example, for a reader's eyes the contents of a digital document as rendered in a computer screen are the same as the contents of a printout of that document.

Exchange objects are absolutely useless if we cannot understand their content. To understand them we may need extra information (Representation Information) which can be expressed using other information objects. For example, to understand the concepts of an ontology A we have to know the concepts defined in each ontology B that it is used by A. As another example consider scientific data products. Such products are usually aggregations of other (even heterogeneous) primitive data. The provenance information of these data products can be preserved using scientific workflows [108].

The key advantage of scientific workflows is that they record data (and process) dependencies during workflow runs. For example, Fig. 8.1 shows a workflow that generates two data products. The rectangles denote data while the edges capture derivations and thus express the dependability of the final products from the initial and intermediate results. Capturing such dependencies is important for the understandability, reproducibility and validity of the final data products.

Exchange objects are typically organized as files (or collections of files). It is often not possible (and more often not convenient) to identify the contents of a file if we do not have the software that was used to create it. Indeed exchange objects use complex structures to encode information and embed extra information that is meaningful only to the software application that created them. For example a MS-Word document embeds special formatting information about the layout, the structure, the fonts etc. This information is not identifiable from another text editor, i.e. Notepad. As a result exchange objects often become dependent on software.

In what follows we look at dependencies using software as the exemplar although there are many other possible dependencies.

Therefore it is useful to define Computational objects which are actually sets of instructions for a computer – a type of Representation Information. These objects use computational resources to do various tasks. Typical examples of computational objects are software applications.

Software applications in turn typically use computational resources to perform a task. For example a Java program that performs complex mathematic calculations does not explicitly define the memory addresses that will keep the numbers. Instead it exploits the functionalities provided by other programs (or libraries) that handle such issues. Furthermore, software reusability allows one to reuse a software program and exploit its functionalities. Although software re-use is becoming a common practice, this policy results to dependencies between software components. These dependencies are interpreted as the reliance of a software component on others to support a specific functionality. In other words a software application

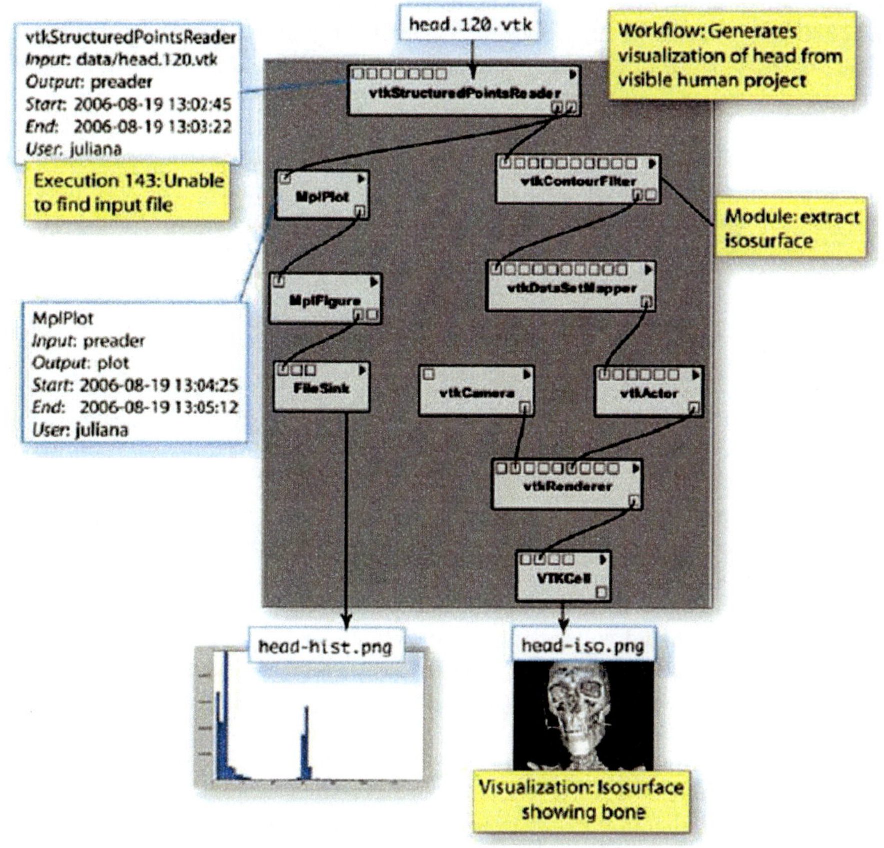

Fig. 8.1 The generation of two data products as a workflow

cannot even function if the applications it depends on are not available, e.g. we cannot run the above Java program if we haven't installed a Java Virtual Machine.

This has been discussed in general terms in previous chapters. Here we wish to go into more detail, particularly about software dependencies because these are, as has been explained, important in their own right, and they provide clear illustrations of dependencies.

It is becoming clear that many, perhaps most, digital objects are actually complex data structures that either contain information about something or use computational resources to do various tasks. These objects depend on a plethora of other resources whose record is of great importance for the preservation of their intelligibility. Additionally, these dependencies can have several different interpretations. In [108, 109] dependencies between information objects are exploited for ensuring consistency and validity. Figure 8.1 illustrates dependencies over the data products of a scientific workflow and such dependencies, apart from being useful for understanding and validating the data, can also allow or aid the reproduction of the final data products. [110] proposes an extended framework for file systems that allows users to define dependency links between files where the semantics of these links are defined by users through key-value pairs. Finally, many dependency management approaches for software components [111–115] have been described in the literature. The interpretation of software dependencies varies and concerns the installation or de-installation safety, the ability to perform a task, the selection of the most appropriate component, or the consequences of a component's service call to other components.

8.1.1 OAIS – Preserving the Understandability

As outlined in Chap. 3, ***Data Objects*** are considered in OAIS to be either physical objects (objects with physically observable properties) or digital objects. Every Data Object along with some extra information about the object forms an ***Information Object***. Following OAIS, information is defined as any piece of knowledge that is exchangeable and can be expressed by some type of data. For example the information in a Greek novel is expressed as the characters that are combined to create the text. The information in a digital text file is expressed by the bits it contains which, when they are combined with extra information that interprets them (i.e. mapping tables and rules), will convert them to more meaningful representations (i.e. characters). This extra information that maps a Data Object into more meaningful concepts is called Representation Information (RI). It is a responsibility of an OAIS to find (or create new) software conforming to the given Representation Information for this information object.

We note that the notion of interpretation as stated by OAIS is more restricted than the general notion of dependency. Dependencies can be exploited for capturing the required information for digital objects not only in terms of their intelligibility, but also in terms of validity, reproducibility or functionality (if it is a software application).

8.2 A Formal Model for the Intelligibility of Digital Objects

8.2.1 A Core Model for Digital Objects and Dependencies

We introduce here a core model for the intelligibility of digital objects based on dependencies. The model has two basic notions: Module and Dependency. As we described in Sect. 8.1, digital objects depend on a plethora of other resources. Recall that these resources can be described as objects containing information or using other resources. We use the general notion of module to model these resources (in our examples either exchange or computational objects). There is no standard way to define a module, so we can have modules of various levels of abstraction, e.g.

a module can be a collection of documents, or alternatively every document in the collection can be considered as a module.

In order to ensure the intelligibility of digital objects first we have to identify which are the permissible actions with these objects. This is important because of the heterogeneity of digital objects and the information they convey. For example considering a Java source code file `HelloWorld.java`, some indicative actions we can perform with it are to compile it and read it. To this end we introduce the notion of tasks. A task is any action that can be performed with modules. Once we have identified the tasks, it is important, for the preservation of intelligibility, to preserve how these tasks are performed. The reliance of a module on others for the performability of a task is captured using dependencies between modules. For example for compiling the previous file we can define that it depends on the availability of a java compiler and on all other classes and libraries it requires. Therefore a rich dependency graph is created over the set of modules.

In what follows we use the following notations; we define $\mathcal{T}$ as the set of all modules and the binary relation > on $\mathcal{T}$ is used for representing dependencies. A relationship

$$\boxed{t > t' \ (t, t' \in \mathcal{T})}$$

means that module t depends on module t'.

The interpretations of modules and dependencies are very general in order to capture a plethora of cases. Specifying dependencies through tasks leads to dependencies with different interpretations. To distinguish the various interpretations we introduce dependency types and we require every dependency to be assigned at least one type that denotes the objective (assumed task) of that dependency. For example the dependencies illustrated at Fig. 8.2 (Sect. 8.1) are the dependencies of a software application required for running that application. We can assign to such dependencies a type such as `_run`.

We can then organize dependency types hierarchically to enable deductions of the form "*if we can do task A then certainly we can do task B*". For example if we can edit a file then we can read it.

If D denotes the set of all dependency types, and types $d, d' \in D$, we shall use $d \rhd d'$ to denote that d is a subtype of d', e.g. `_edit` $\rhd$ `_read`.

Analogously, and for specializing the very general notion of module to more refined categories, module types are introduced. For example, the source code of a program in java could be defined as a module of type `SoftwareSourceCode`. Since every source code contains text, `SoftwareSourceCode` can be defined as a subtype of `TextFile`. For this reason module types can be organized hierarchically. If C is the set of all modules and $c, c' \in C$ then $c \rhd c'$ denotes that c is a subtype of c'.

Since the number of dependency types may increase, it is beneficial to organize them following an object-oriented approach. Specifically we can specify the domain and range of a dependency type to be particular module types. For example the

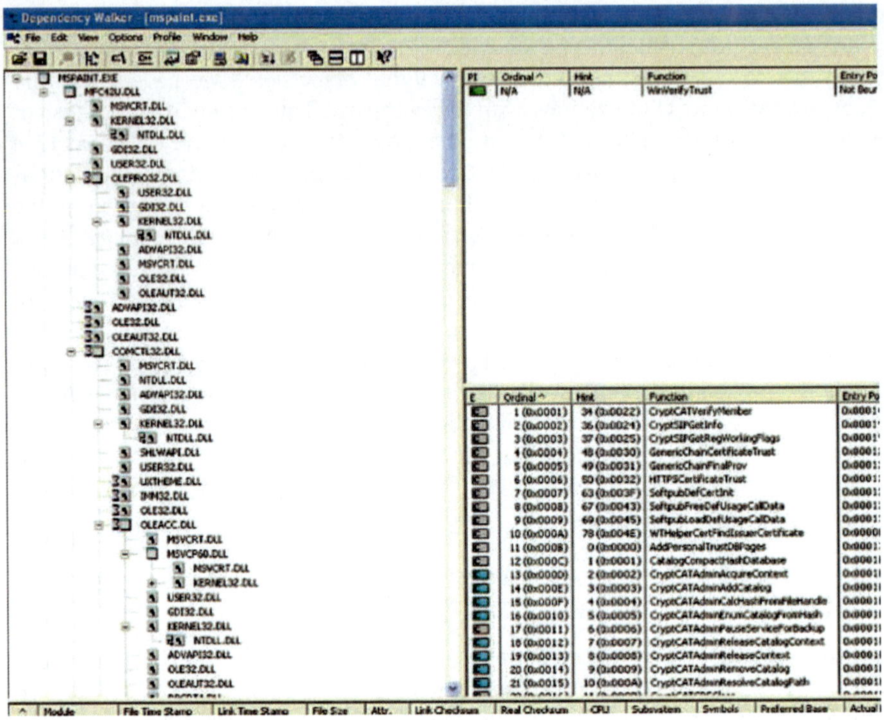

Fig. 8.2 The dependencies of mspaint software application

domain of the dependency type `_compile` must be a module denoting source code files while the range must be a compiler. This case is shown in Fig. 8.3 where thick arrows are used to denote subtype relationships.

This model can host dependencies of various interpretations. For instance, the workflow presented at Fig. 8.1 expresses the derivation of data products from other data products and such derivation histories are important for understanding, validating and reproducing the final products.

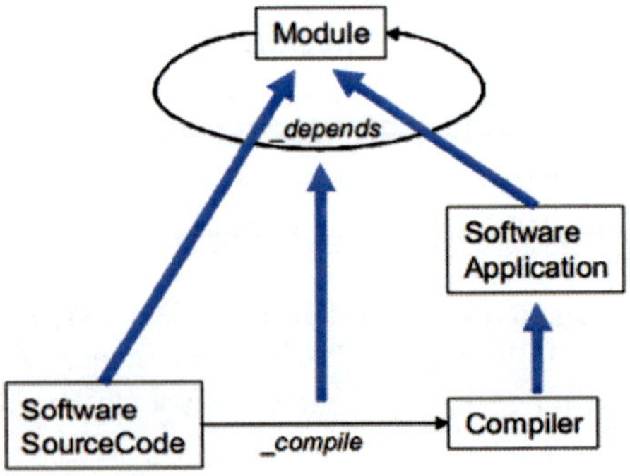

Fig. 8.3 Restricting the domain and range of dependencies

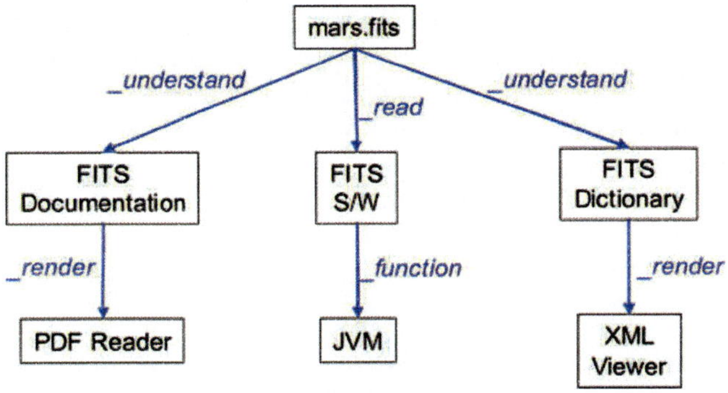

Fig. 8.4 Modelling the dependencies of a FITS file

According to the model, data are modelled as modules, while derivation edges are modelled as dependencies (important for the aforementioned tasks). Similarly, this model allows a straightforward modelling of an OAIS Representation Network (Fig. 6.4), since the notion *interpretedUsing* can be considered as a specialized form of dependency. In addition, a module can have several dependencies of different types. For example, Fig. 8.4 illustrates the dependencies of a file in `FITS` format where boxes denote modules and arrows denote dependencies of different types (the starting module depends on the ending module; the label denotes the type of the dependency. The file `mars.fits` can be read with an appropriate application which is modelled with the `FITS S/W` module. This in turn requires the availability of Java Virtual Machine in order to function. If our aim is to understand the concepts of the file then we must have available the `FITS` Documentation and the `FITS` Dictionary. These files are in PDF and XML format and therefore require, for example, the existence of the appropriate application that renders their contents. Such a dependency graph provides a richer view of an OAIS Representation Network (recall Sect. 6.3.1), since it allows the definition of dependencies of various interpretations.

8.2.1.1 Conjunctive Versus Disjunctive Dependencies

Usually there are more than one ways to perform a task. For example for reading the file `HelloWorld.java` a text editor is required, say `NotePad`. However we can read this file using other text editors, e.g. `VI`. Therefore, and for the task of readability, we could say that `HelloWorld.java` depends on `NotePad` OR `VI`.

However, the dependencies considered so far are interpreted conjunctively, so it is not possible to capture the above scenario. The disjunctive nature of dependencies was first approached at [116] using the concept of generalized module (which is a set of modules interpreted disjunctively) but the management of such modules was rather complex.

A clearer model, based on Horn Rules, which also allows the defining the properties (e.g. transitivity) of dependencies straightforwardly, was presented in [117].

Hereafter we will focus on that model. Consider a user's system containing the files `HelloWorld.java`, `HelloWorld.cc` and the software components `javac`, `NotePad`, `VI` and `JVM`, and suppose that we want to preserve the ability to edit, read, compile and run these files. We will model these modules and their dependencies using facts and rules. The digital files are modelled using facts while rules are employed to represent tasks and dependencies. Moreover rules are used for defining module and dependency type hierarchies (i.e. `JavaSourceCode` ⊳ `TextFile`, `_edit` ⊳ `_read`). Below we provide the set of facts and rules that hold for the above example in a human readable form.

1. `HelloWorld.java` is a `JavaSourceFile`
2. `HelloWorld.cc` is a `C++SourceFile`
3. `NotePad` is a `TextEditor`
4. `VI` is a `TextEditor`
5. `javac` is a `JavaCompiler`
6. `JVM` is a `JavaVirtualMachine`
7. Every `JavaSourceFile` is also a `TextFile`
8. Every `C++SourceFile` is also a `TextFile`
9. A `TextFile` is Editable if there is a `TextEditor`
10. A `JavaSourceFile` is `JavaCompilable` if there is a `JavaCompiler`
11. A `C++SourceFile` is `C++Compilable` if there is a `C++Compiler`
12. A file is Readable if it is Editable
13. A file is Compilable if it is JavaCompilable
14. A file is Compilable if it is C++Compilable

Lines 1–6 are facts describing the digital objects while lines 7–14 are rules denoting various tasks and how they can be carried out. In particular, rules 7 and 8 define a hierarchy of module types (`JavaSourceFile` ⊳ `TextFile` and `C++SourceFile` ⊳ `TextFile`), while rules 12–14 define a hierarchy of tasks (`Editable` ⊳ `Readable`, `JavaCompilable` ⊳ `Compilable` and `C++Compilable` ⊳ `Compilable`). Finally, rules 9–11 express which are the tasks that can be performed and which the dependencies of these tasks are (i.e. the readability of a `TextFile` depends on the availability of a `TextEditor`).

Using such facts and rules we model the modules and their dependencies based on the tasks that can be performed. For example in order to determine the compilability of `HelloWorld.java` we must use the rules 1,5,10,13. In order to read the content of the same files we must use the rules 1,3,7,9,12. Alternatively (since there are 2 text editors) we can perform the same task using the rules 1,4,7,9,12.

Using the terminology and syntax of Datalog [118] below we define in more detail the modules and dependencies of this example.

Modules – Module Type Hierarchies

Modules are expressed as facts. Since we allow a very general interpretation of what a module can be, there is no distinction between exchange objects and software components. We define all these objects as modules of an appropriate type. For example the digital objects of the previous example are defined as:

```
JavaSourceFile('HelloWorld.java').
C++SourceFile('HelloWorld.cc').
TextEditor('NotePad').
TextEditor('VI').
JavaCompiler('javac').
JavaVirtualMachine('JVM').
```

A Module can be classified to one or more modules types. Additionally these types can be organized hierarchically. Such taxonomies can be represented with appropriate rules. For example the source files for Java and C++ are also TextFiles, so we use the following rules:

```
TextFile(X) :- JavaSourceFile(X).
TextFile(X) :- C++SourceFile(X).
```

We can also capture several features of digital objects using predicates (not necessarily unary), i.e.

```
ReadOnly('HelloWorld.java').
LastModifDate('HelloWorld.java','2009-10-18').
```

Tasks – Dependencies – Dependency Type Hierarchies

Tasks and their dependencies are modelled using rules. For every task we use two predicates; one (which is usually unary) to denote the task and another one (of arity equal or greater than 2) for denoting its dependencies. Consider the following example:

```
IsEditable(X) :- Editable(X,Y).
Editable(X,Y) :- TextFile(X), TextEditor(Y).
```

The first rule denotes that an object X is editable if there is any Y such that X is editable by Y. The second rule defines a dependency between two modules specifically it defines that every TextFile depends on a TextEditor for editing its contents. Notice that if there are more than one text editors available (as here) then the above dependency is interpreted disjunctively (i.e. every TextFile depends on any of the two TextEditors). Relations of higher arity can be employed according to the requirements e.g.

```
IsRunnable(X) :- Runnable(X,Y,Z).
Runnable(X,Y,Z) :- JavaSourceFile(X),
                   Compilable(X,Y),
                   JavaVirtualMachine(Z).
```

Furthermore we can organize dependency types hierarchically using rules. As already stated, the motivation is to enable deductions of the form "*if we can do task A then we can do task B*". For example suppose that we want to express that if we can edit a file then certainly we can read it. This can be expressed with the rule: `Read(X) :- Edit(X)`. Alternatively, or complementarily we can express such deductions at the dependency level:

```
Readable(X,Y) :- Editable(X,Y).
```

Finally we can express the properties of dependencies (e.g. transitivity) using rules. For example if the following two facts hold:

```
Runnable('HelloWorld.class','JavaVirtualMachine').
Runnable('JavaVirtualMachine', 'Windows').
```

then we might want to infer that the HelloWorld.class is also runnable under Windows. This kind of inference (transitivity) can be expressed using the rule:

```
Runnable(X,Z) :- Runnable(X,Y), Runnable(Y,Z).
```

Other properties (i.e. symmetry) that dependencies may have can be defined analogously.

8.2.1.2 Synopsis

Summarising, we have described a method for modelling digital objects and their dependencies.

- A Module can be any digital object (i.e. a document, a software application etc.) and may have one or more module types.
- The reliance of a module on others for the performability of a task is modelled using typed dependencies between modules.

Therefore the performability of a task determines which the dependencies are. In some cases a module may require all the modules it depends on, while in other cases only some of these modules may be sufficient. In the first case dependencies have conjunctive semantics and the task can be performed only if all the dependencies are available, while in the second case they have disjunctive semantics and the task can be performed in more than one ways (a text file can be read using `NotePad` OR `VI`).

8.2.2 Formalizing Designated Community Knowledge

So far dependencies have been recognized as the key notion for preserving the intelligibility of digital objects. However since nothing is self-explaining we may result in long chain of dependent modules. So an important question which arises is: how many dependencies do we need to record? OAIS address this issue by exploiting the knowledge assumed to be known by a community. According to OAIS a person, a system or a community of users can be said to have a *Knowledge Base* which allows them to understand received information. For example, a person whose Knowledge Base includes the Greek language will be able to understand a Greek text. We can use a similar approach to limit the long chain of dependencies that have to be recorded.

A Designated Community is an identified group of users (or systems) that is able to understand a particular set of information, and a DC Knowledge is the information that is assumed to be known by the members of that community. OAIS only makes implicit assumptions about the community Knowledge Base. However here we can make these assumptions *explicit* by assigning to the users of a community the modules that are assumed to be known from them. To this end we introduce the notion of DC Profiles.

Definition 1 If u is a DC (Designated Community), its profile, denoted by $T(u)$, is the set of modules assumed to be known from that community.

As an example, Fig. 8.5 shows the dependency graph for two digital objects, the first being a document in PDF format (`handbook.pdf`) and the second a file in FITS format (`mars.fits`). Moreover two DC profiles over these modules are defined. The first (the upper oval) is a DC profile for the community of astronomers and contains the modules $T(u_1)$= {`FITS Documentation`, `FITS S/W`, `FITS Dictionary`} and the other (lower oval) is defined for the community of ordinary users and contains the modules $T(u_2)$= {`PDF Reader`, `XML Viewer`}. This means that every astronomer (every user having DC profile u_1) understands the module `FITS S/W`, in the sense that he/she knows how to use this software application.

We can assume that the graph formed by the modules and the dependencies is global in the sense that it contains all the modules that have been recorded, and we can assume that the dependencies of a module are always the same

Axiom 1 Modules and their dependencies form a dependency graph $\mathcal{G} = (\mathcal{T}, >)$. Every module in the graph has a unique identifier and its dependencies are always the same.

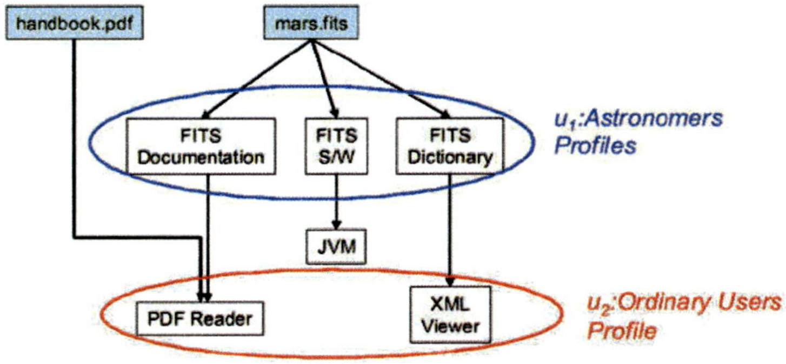

Fig. 8.5 DC profiles example

Definition 1. implies that if the users of a community know a set of modules they also know how to perform tasks on them. However the performability of tasks is represented with dependencies. According to Axiom 1 the dependencies of a module are always the same. So the knowledge of a module from a user implies, through the dependency graph, the knowledge of its dependencies as well, and therefore the knowledge of performing various tasks with the module.

In our example this means that since astronomers know the module `FITS S/W`, they know how to run this application, so they know the dependency `FITS S/W > JVM`. So if we want to find all the modules that are understandable from the users of a DC profile, we must resolve all the direct and indirect dependencies of their known modules (*T(u)*). For example the modules that are understandable from astronomers are {`FITS Documentation, FITS S/W, FITS Dictionary, PDF Reader, JVM, XML Viewer`}, however their DC profile is a subset of the above modules.

This approach allows us to reduce the size of DC profiles by keeping only the maximal modules (maximal with respect to the dependency relation) of every DC profile. Therefore we can remove from the DC profile modules whose knowledge is implied from the knowledge of an "upper" module and the dependency graph. For example if the astronomers profile contained also the module `JVM` then we could safely remove it since its knowledge from astronomers is guaranteed from the knowledge of `FITS S/W`.

We will discuss the consequences of not making the assumption expressed in Axiom 1, later in Sect. 8.2.5.

8.2.3 Intelligibility-Related Preservation Services

8.2.3.1 Deciding Intelligibility

Consider two users u_1, u_2 who want to render (play) the music encoded in an mp3 file. The user u_1 successfully renders the file while u_2 does not recognize it and requests its direct dependencies. Suppose that the dependency that has been recorded is that the mp3 file depends (regarding renderability) on the availability of an mp3-compliant player, say `Winamp`. The user is informed about this dependency and installs the application. However he claims that the file still cannot be rendered. This happens because the application in turn has some other dependencies which are not available to the user, i.e. `Winamp > Lame_mp3`. After the installation of this dependency, user u_2 is able to render the file. This is an example where the ability to perform a task depends not only on its direct dependencies but also on its indirect dependencies.

This means that to decide the performability of a task on a module by a user, we have to find all the necessary modules by traversing the dependency graph and then to compare them with the modules of the DC profile of the user. However the disjunctive nature of dependencies complicates this task. Disjunctive dependencies express different ways to perform a task. This is translated in several paths at the dependency graph, and we must find at least one such path that is intelligible by the user. The problem becomes more complicated due to the properties (e.g. transitivity) that dependencies may have (which can be specified using rules as described in Sect. 8.2.1.1). On the other hand, if all dependencies are conjunctive, then the required modules obtained from the dependency graph are unique.

Below we describe methods for deciding the intelligibility of an object for two settings; the first allows only conjunctive dependencies, while the second permits also disjunctive dependencies.

Conjunctive Dependencies

If dependencies are interpreted conjunctively the module requires the existence of all its dependencies for the performability of a task. To this end we must resolve all the dependencies transitively, since a module t will depend on t', this in turn will depend on t'' etc. Consequently we introduce the notions of required modules and closure.

- The set of modules that a module t requires in order to be intelligible is the set $Nr^{+}(t) = \{t' t >^{+} t'\}$
- The closure of a module t, is the set of the required modules plus module t. $Nr^{*}(t) = \{t\} \cup Nr^{+}(t)$

The notation $>^{+}$ is used to denote that we resolve dependencies transitively. This means that to retrieve the set Nr^{+}(t) we must traverse the dependency graph starting from module t and recording every module we encounter. For example the set Nr^{+}(mars.fits) in Fig. 8.5 will contain the modules {`FITS Documentation`, `FITS S/W`, `FITS Dictionary`, `PDF Reader`, `JVM`, `XML Viewer`}. This is the full set of modules that are required for making the module `mars.fits` intelligible.

In order to decide the intelligibility of a module t with respect to the DC profile of a user u we must examine if the user of that profile knows the modules that are needed for the intelligibility of t.

Definition 2 A module t is intelligible by a user u, having DC profile $T(u)$ iff its required modules are intelligible from the user, formally $Nr^{+}(t) \subseteq Nr^{*}(T(u))$

Recall that according to Axiom 1 the users having profile $T(u)$, will understand the modules contained in the profile, as well as all their required modules. In other words they can understand the set Nr^{*}(T(u)).

For example the module `mars.fits` is intelligible by astronomers (users having the profile u_1) since they already understand all the modules that are required for making `mars.fits` intelligible, i.e. we have:

$$\mathrm{Nr}^{+}(\texttt{mars.fits}) \subseteq \mathrm{Nr}^{*}(\mathrm{T}(\mathrm{u}_1)) .$$

However

$$\mathrm{Nr}^{+}(\texttt{mars.fits}) \not\subset \mathrm{Nr}^{*}\,(\mathrm{T}\,(\mathrm{u}_2))\,.$$

Disjunctive Dependencies

The previous approach will give incorrect results if we have disjunctive dependencies. For example, consider the dependencies shown in Fig. 8.6 and suppose that all of them are disjunctive. This means that o depends on either t_1, or t_2. In this case we have two possible sets for $Nr^{+}(o)$; $Nr^{+}(o)=\{t_1, t_3\}$ and $Nr^{+}(o)=\{t_2, t_4\}$.

For capturing disjunctive dependencies we use the rule-based framework described at Sect. 8.2.1.1. Figure 8.7 shows the logical architecture of a system

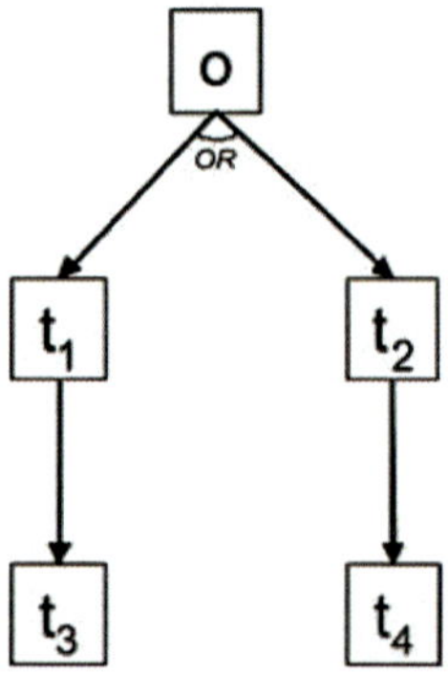

Fig. 8.6 The disjunctive dependencies of a digital object o

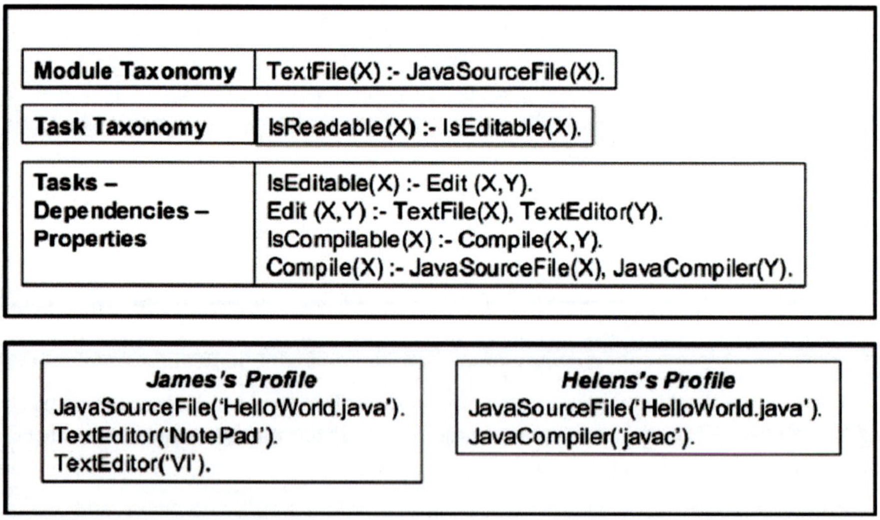

Fig. 8.7 A partitioning of facts and rules

based on facts and rules. The boxes of the upper layer contain information available for all users regarding tasks, dependencies and taxonomies of tasks/ modules. The lower layer contains the modules that are available to each user. Every box corresponds to a user, e.g. *James* has a file `HelloWorld.java` in his laptop and has installed the applications `Notepad` and `VI`. If a user wants to perform a task with a module then he can use the facts of her box and also exploit the rules from the boxes of the upper layer.

In general, the problem of deciding the intelligibility of a module relies on Datalog query answering over the set of modules that are available to the user. More specifically we send a Datalog query regarding the task we want to perform with a module and check if the answer of the query contains that module. If the module is not in the answer then the task cannot be performed and some additional modules are required. For example in order to check the editability of `HelloWorld.java` by *James* we can send the Datalog query `IsEditable(X)` using only the facts of his profile. The answer will contain the above module meaning that *James* can successfully perform that task. In fact he can edit it using any of the two different text editors that are available to him. Now suppose that we want to check whether he can compile this file. This requires answering the query `IsCompilable(X)`. The answer of this query is empty since *James* does not have a compiler for performing the task. Similarly *Helen* can only compile `HelloWorld.java` and not edit it.

8.2.3.2 Discovering Intelligibility Gaps

If a module is not intelligible from the users of a DC profile, we have an Intelligibility Gap and we have to provide the extra modules required. In particular, the intelligibility gap will contain only those modules that are required for the user to understand the module. This policy enables the selection of only the missing modules instead of the selecting all required modules and hence avoiding redundancies. However the disjunctive nature of dependencies makes the computation of intelligibility gap complicated. For this reason we again distinguish the case of conjunctive from the case of disjunctive dependencies.

Conjunctive Dependencies

If the dependencies have conjunctive semantics then a task can be performed only if all its required modules are available. If any of these modules is missing then the module is not intelligible from the user. So if a module t is not intelligible by a user u, then intelligibility gap is defined as follows:

Definition 3 The intelligibility gap between a module t and a user u with DC profile $T(u)$ is defined as the smallest set of extra modules that are required to make it intelligible. For conjunctive dependencies it holds:

$$Gap\,(t,u) = Nr^{+}\,(t)\,\backslash Nr^{*}\,(T\,(u))$$

For example in Fig. 8.5 the module `mars.fits` is not intelligible from ordinary users (users with DC profile u_2). Therefore its intelligibility gap will be:

$$Gap(\texttt{mars.fits}, u_2) = \{\texttt{FITS Documentation}, \texttt{FITS SW}, \texttt{FITS Dictionary}, \texttt{JVM}\}.$$

Notice that the modules that are already known from u_2 (`PDF Reader`, `XML Viewer`) are not included in the gap.

Clearly, if a module is already intelligible from a user, the intelligibility gap will be empty i.e.

$$Gap(\texttt{mars.fits}, u_1) = \emptyset.$$

Consider the file `HelloWorld.java`, shown in Fig. 8.8. This file depends on the modules `javac` and `Notepad` representing the tasks of compiling and editing it correspondingly. Furthermore a DC profile u is specified containing the module Notepad. Suppose that a user, having DC Profile u, wants to edit the file `HelloWorld.java`. The editability of this file requires only the module `Notepad`. However if the user requests for the intelligibility gap ($Gap($`HelloWorld.java`$,u)$) it will contain the module `javac` even if it is not required for the editability of the module. This motivates the need for type-restricted gaps which are described below.

In general, to compute type-restricted gaps we have to traverse the dependencies of a specific type. However since dependency types are organized hierarchically, we must also include all the subtypes of the given type. Furthermore, the user might request the dependencies for the performability of more than one task, by issuing several dependency types.

Given a set of dependency types W, we define:

$$t >_W t' \text{ iff } (a)\ t > t' \text{ and } (b)\ types\left(t > t'\right) \cap W^* \neq \emptyset$$

where $types(t>t')$ is used to denote the types of the given dependency and W* is the set of all possible subtypes of the given set of types, i.e. $W^* = \bigcup_{d \in W} \left(\{d\} \cup \left\{d' | d \rhd d'\right\}\right)$. This means that $t >_W t'$ holds if $t > t'$ holds and at least one of the types of $t > t'$ belong to W or to a subtype of a type in W. Note that a dependency might be used for the performability of more than one tasks (and therefore it

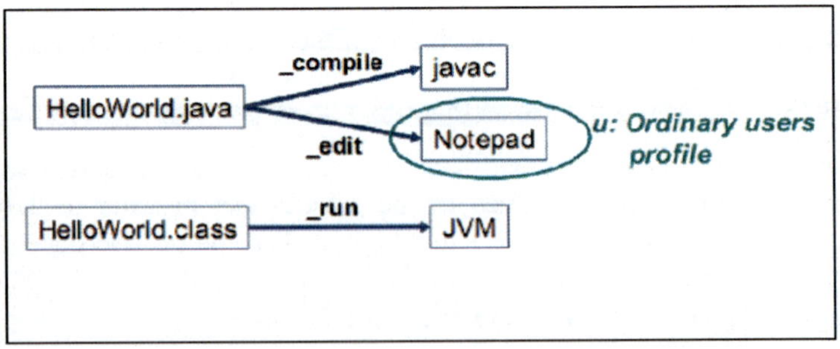

Fig. 8.8 Dependency types and intelligibility gap

can be associated with more than one types). Now the intelligibility gap between a module t and a user u with respect to a set of dependency types W is defined as:

$$Gap\,(t, u, W) = \left\{t' | t >^{+}_{W} t'\right\} \setminus Nr^{*}\,(T\,(u))$$

Note that since we want to perform all tasks in W, we must get all the dependencies that are due to any of these tasks, which is actually the union of all the dependencies for every task denoted in W. In our example we have:

Gap(`HelloWorld.java`, *u*, {_edit})= Ø

Gap(`HelloWorld.java`, *u*, {_compile})= {`javac`}

Gap(`HelloWorld.java`, *u*, {_edit, _compile})={`javac`}

Disjunctive Dependencies

If the dependencies are interpreted disjunctively and a task cannot be carried out, there can be more than one ways to compute the intelligibility gap. To this end we must find the possible "explanations" (the possible modules) whose availability would entail a consequence (the performability of the task). For example assume that *James*, from Fig. 8.7, wants to compile the file HelloWorld.java. Since he cannot compile it, he would like to know what he should do. What we have to do in this case is to find and deliver to him the possible facts that would allow him to perform the task.

In order to find the possible explanations of a consequence we can use *abduction* [119–121]. *Abductive reasoning* allows inferring an atom as an explanation of a given consequence. There are several models and formalizations of abduction. Below we describe how the intelligibility gap can be computed using logic-based abduction.

Logic-based abduction can be described as follows: Given a logical theory T formalizing a particular application domain, a set M of predicates describing some manifestations (observations or symptoms), and a set H of predicates containing possible individual hypotheses, find an explanation for M, that is, a suitable set $S \subseteq H$ such that $S \cup T$ is consistent and logically entails M.

Consider for example that *James* (from Fig. 8.7) wants to compile the file `HelloWorld.java`. He cannot compile it and therefore he wants to find the possible ways of compiling it. In this case the set T would contain all the tasks and their dependencies, as well as the taxonomies of modules and tasks (the upper part of Fig. 8.7). The set M would contain the task that cannot be performed (i.e. the fact `IsCompilable(HelloWorld.java)`). Finally the set H would contain all existing modules that are possible explanations for the performability of the task (i.e. all modules in the lower part of Fig. 8.7). Then `JavaCompiler('javac')` will be an abductive explanation, denoting the adequacy of this module for the compilability of the file. If there are more than one possible explanations (e.g. if there are several java compilers), logic-based abduction would return all of them. However, one can define criteria for picking one explanation as "the best explanation" rather than returning all of them.

8.2.3.3 Profile-Aware packages

The availability of dependencies and community profiles allows deriving *packages*, either for archiving or for dissemination, that are *profile-aware*. For instance OAIS [122] distinguishes packages to AIPs (Archival Information Packages), which are Information Packages consisting of Content Information and the associated Preservation Description Information (PDI) and DIPs (Dissemination Information Packages), that are derived from one or more AIPs as a response to a request of an OAIS.

The availability of explicitly stated dependencies and community profiles, enables the derivation of packages that contain exactly those dependencies that are needed so that the packages are intelligible by a particular DC profile and are redundancy-free. For example in Fig. 8.5 if we want to preserve the file Mars.fits for astronomers (users with DC profile u_1) then we do not have to record any dependencies since the file is already intelligible by that community. If on the other hand we want to preserve this module for the community of ordinary users (users with DC profile u_2), then we must also record the modules that are required for this community in order to understand the module.

Definition 4 The *(dissemination or archiving) package* of a module *t* with respect to a user or community *u*, denoted by, *Pack(t, u)*, is defined as: *Pack(t, u) = (t, Gap(t, u))*

Figure 8.9 shows the dependencies of a digital object o_1 and three DC profiles. The dependencies in the example are conjunctive. The packages for each different DC profile are shown below:

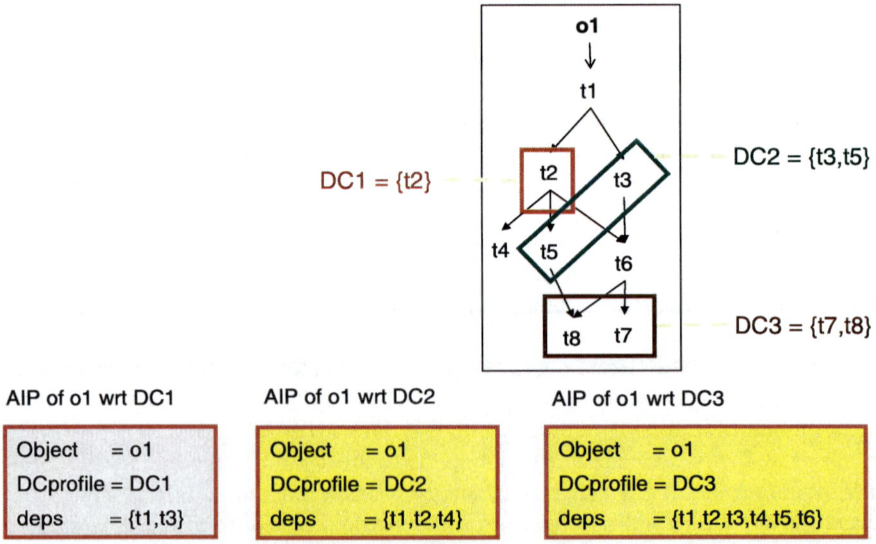

Fig. 8.9 Exploiting DC Profiles for defining the "right" AIPs

$Pack(o_1, DC_1) = (o_1, \{t_1, t_3\})$

$Pack(o_1, DC_2) = (o_1, \{t_1, t_2, t_4\})$

$Pack(o_1, DC_3) = (o_1, \{t_1, t_2, t_3, t_4, t_5, t_6\})$

We have to note at this point that there is not any qualitative difference between DIPs and AIPs from our perspective. The only difference is that AIPs are formed with respect to the profile decided for the archive, which we can reasonably assume that it is usually richer than user profiles. For example in Fig. 8.9 three different AIPs for module o_1 are shown for three different DC Profiles. The DIPs of module o_1 for the profiles DC_1, DC_2 and DC_3 are actually the corresponding AIPs without the line that indicates the profile of each package.

We should also note that community knowledge evolves and consequently DC profiles may evolve over time. In that case we can reconstruct the AIPs according to the latest DC profiles. Such an example is illustrated in Fig. 8.10. The left part of the figure shows a DC profile over a dependency graph and at the right part it is a newer, enriched version of the profile. As a consequence the new AIP will be smaller than the original version.

8.2.3.4 Dependency Management and Ingestion Quality Control

The notion intelligibility gap allows for a reduction in the amount of dependencies that have to be archived/delivered on the basis DC profiles. Another aspect of the problem concerns the ingestion of information. Specifically, one question which arises is whether we could provide a mechanism (during ingestion or curation) for identifying the *Representation Information* that is required or missing. This requirement can be tackled in several ways:

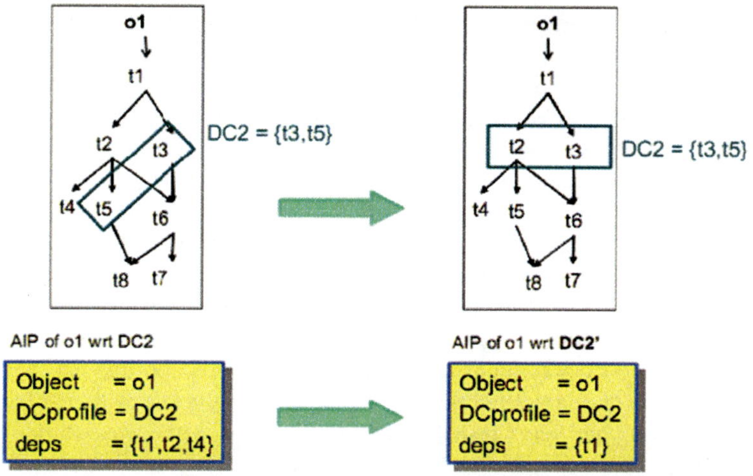

Fig. 8.10 Revising AIPs after DC profile changes

(a) we require each module to be classified (directly or indirectly) to a particular class, so we define certain facets and require classification with respect to these (furthermore some of the attributes of these classes could be mandatory),
(b) we define some dependency types as mandatory and provide notification services returning all those objects which do not have any dependency of that type,
(c) we require that the dependencies of the objects should (directly or indirectly) point to one of several certain profiles.

Below we elaborate on policy (c).

Definition 5 A module t is *related* with a profile u, denoted by $t \mapsto u$, if $Nr^*(t) \cap Nr^*(T(u)) \neq \emptyset$

This means that the direct/indirect dependencies of a module t lead to one or more elements of the profile u. At the application level, for each object t we can show all *related* and *unrelated* profiles, defined as:

$$RelProf(t) = \{u \in U | t \mapsto u\} \text{ and}$$

$$UnRelProf(t) = \{u \in U | t \textit{ not} \mapsto u\} \text{ respectively.}$$

Note that *Gap(t, u)* is empty if either t does not have any recorded dependency or if t has dependencies but they are known by the profile u. The computation of the related profiles allows the curators to distinguish these two cases ($RelProf(t) = \emptyset$ in the first and $RelProf(t) \neq \emptyset$ in the second).

If $u \in RelProf(t)$ then this is just an indication that t has been described with respect to profile u, but it does not guarantee that its description is complete with respect to that profile.

If dependencies are interpreted disjunctively, to identify if a module is related with a profile we can compute the intelligibility gap with respect to that profile and with respect to an empty profile (a profile that contains no facts at all). Since dependencies are disjunctive there might exist more than one intelligibility gaps, so let *gap1* and *gap2* be the union of all possible intelligibility gaps or each case. If the two sets contain the same modules (the same facts) then the module is not be related with that profile. If *gap1* is a subset of *gap2*, this means that the profile contains some facts that are used to decide the intelligibility of the module and therefore the module is related with that profile.

As an example, Fig. 8.11 shows the disjunctive dependencies of a digital video file regarding reproduction. Suppose that we want to find if that module is related with the profile u which contains the module WindowsOS. To this end we must compute the union of all intelligibility gaps with respect to u and with respect to an empty profile, *gap1* and *gap2* respectively. Since there are two ways to reproduce (i.e. render or play) the file, there will be two intelligibility gaps whose unions will contain:

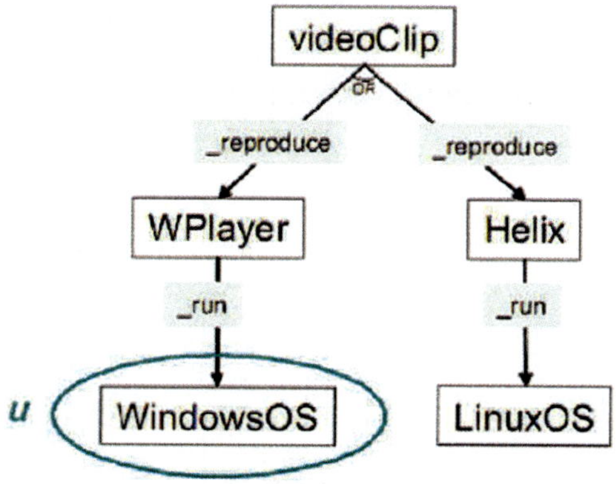

Fig. 8.11 Identifying related profiles when dependencies are disjunctive

AllGaps1={`{WPlayer}, {Helix, LinuxOS}`},
so *gap1*=`{WPlayer, Helix, LinuxOS}`
AllGaps1={`{WPlayer}, {Helix, LinuxOS}`},
so *gap2*=`{WPlayer, WindowsOS,Helix, LinuxOS}`
Since *gap1*$\subset$ *gap2* it follows that `videoClip` $\mapsto$ *u*.

8.2.4 Methodology for Exploiting Intelligibility-Related Services

Below we describe a set of activities that could be followed by one organization (or digital archivist\curator) for advancing its archive with intelligibility-related services. Figure 8.12 shows an activity diagram describing the procedure that could be followed. In brief the activities concern the identification of tasks, the capturing of dependencies of digital objects, the description of community knowledge, the exploitation of intelligibility-related services, the evaluation of the services and the curation of the repository if needed. Additionally we provide an example clarifying how an archivist can preserve a set of 2D and 3D images for the communities of DigitalImaging and Ordinary users.

Act. 1 **Identification of tasks.** The identification of the tasks whose performance should be preserved with the modules of an archive is very important since these tasks will determine the dependencies types. In our example, the most usual task for digital images is to render them on screen. Since there are two different types of images we can specialize this task to *2Drendering* and *3Drendering*.

Act. 2 **Model tasks as dependencies.** The identified tasks from the previous activity can be modelled using dependency types. If there are tasks that can be organized hierarchically, this should be reflected to the definition of the corresponding dependency types. In our example, we can define the dependency types *render*, *render2D*, and *render3D*, and we can define two

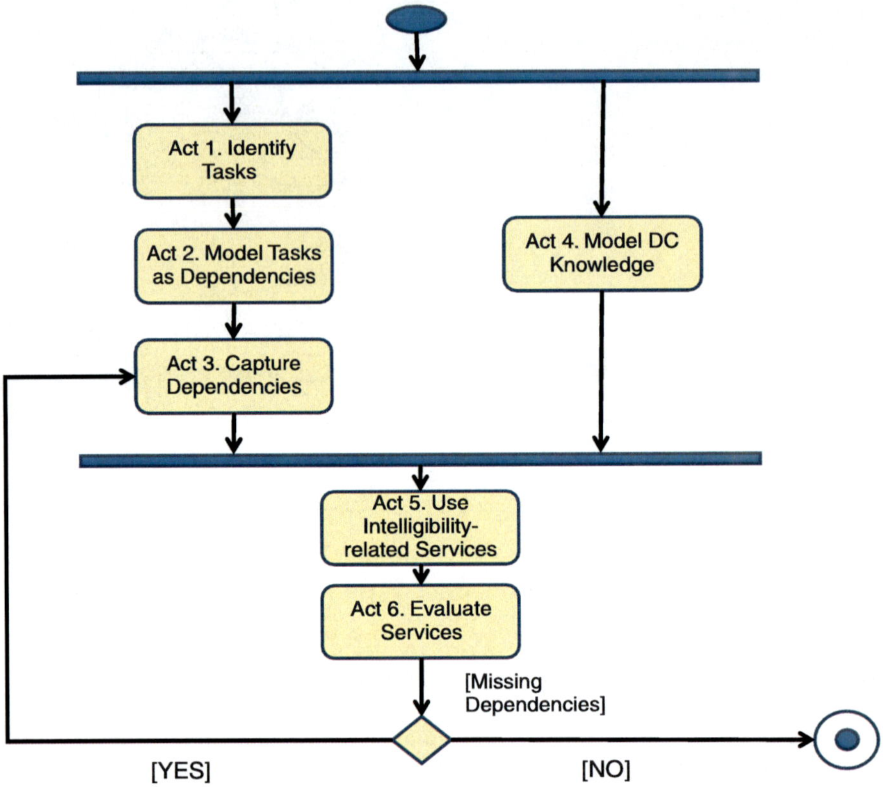

Fig. 8.12 Methodological steps for exploiting intelligibility-related services

subtype relationships, i.e. *render2D*⊳*render* and *render3D*⊳*render*. We can also define hierarchies of modules e.g. 2DImage ⊳ Image.

Act. 3 **Capture the dependencies of digital objects.** This can be done manually, automatically or semi-automatically. Tools like PreScan [123] can aid this task. For example if we want to render a 2D image then we must have an Image Viewer and if we want to render a 3D image we must have the 3D Studio application. In our example we can have dependencies of the form

$$landscape.jpeg >_{render2D} ImageViewer,$$

$$illusion.3ds >_{remder3D} 3D\_Studio \text{ etc.}$$

Act. 4 **Modelling community knowledge.** This activity enables the selection of those modules that are assumed to be known from the designated communities of users. In our example suppose we want to define two profiles; A DigitalImaging profile containing the modules {`Image Viewer`, `3D Studio`}, and an Ordinary profile containing the module {`Image Viewer`}. The former is a profile referring to users that are familiar with digital imaging technologies and the later for ordinary users. We should note at this point that Act. 3 and Act. 4 can be performed in any order or in parallel. For example, performing Act. 4 before Act. 3 allows one to reduce the dependencies that have to be captured, e.g. we will not have to analyze the dependencies of `Image Viewer` because that module is already known from both profiles.

Act. 5 **Exploit the intelligibility-related services according to the needs.** We can answer questions of the form: *which modules are going to be affected if we remove the* `3D Studio` *from our system*? The answer to this question is the set $\{t|t > 3D\ Studio\}$. As another example, we can answer questions of the form: *which are the missing modules, if an ordinary user u wants to render the 3D image* `Illusion.3ds`? In general such services can be exploited for identifying risks, for packaging, and they could be articulated with monitoring and notification services.

Act. 6 **Evaluate the services in real tasks and curate accordingly the repository.** For instance, in case the model fails, i.e. in case the gap is empty but the consumer is unable to understand the delivered module (unable to perform a task), this is due to dependencies which have not been recorded. For example assume that an ordinary user wants to render a 3D image. To this end we deliver to him the intelligibility gap which contains only the module `3D Studio`. However the user claims that the image cannot be rendered. This may happen because there is an additional dependency that has not been recorded, e.g. the fact that the `matlib` library is required to render a 3D model correctly. A corrective action would be to add this dependency (using the corresponding activity, Act. 3). In general, empirical testing is a useful guide for defining and enriching the graph of dependencies

8.2.5 Relaxing Community Knowledge Assumptions

DC profiles are defined as sets of modules that are assumed to be known from the users of a Designated Community. According to Axiom 1 the users of a profile will also understand the dependencies of a module and therefore they will be able to perform all tasks that can be performed. However users may know how to perform certain tasks with a module rather than performing all of them. For example take the case of Java class files. Many users that are familiar with Java class files know how to run them (they know the module denoting the Java class files and they understand its dependencies regarding its runability, i.e. the module JVM), but many of them do not know how to decompile them.

In order to capture such cases, we must define DC profiles without making any assumptions about the knowledge they convey (as implied from Axiom 1). No assumptions about the modules of a profile means that the only modules that are understandable from the user u of the profile are those in the set $T(u)$. Additionally the only tasks that can be performed are those whose modules and

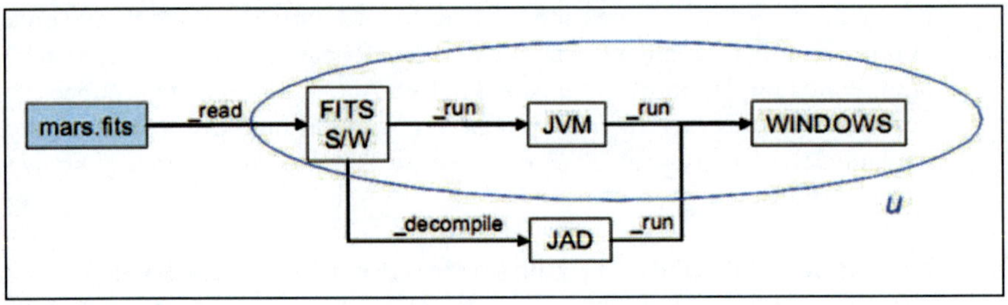

Fig. 8.13 Modelling DC profiles without making any assumptions

their dependencies exist in the DC profile. For example Fig. 8.13 shows some of the dependencies of a file in FITS format. The users of profile *u* know how to run the module `FITS S/W` since all the modules it requires exist in *T(u)*. However they cannot decompile it, even if they know the module `FITS S/W`, since we cannot make the assumption that a user *u* will also understand `JAD` and its dependencies.

This scenario requires changing the definitions of some intelligibility-related because the set of modules understandable by a user *u* is its profile *T(u)*, and not Nr^*(T(u)). Intelligibility checking and gap computation are now defined as:

Deciding Intelligibility: True if $Nr^+(t) \rhd T(u)$

Intelligibility Gap: $Nr^+(t) \setminus T(u)$

Another consequence is that we cannot reduce the size of DC profiles by keeping only the maximal elements since no assumptions about the knowledge are permitted.

In the case where dependencies are disjunctive, we do not make any assumptions about the knowledge that is assumed to be known, since the properties of the various tasks and their dependencies are expressed explicitly. In this case the performability of a task is modelled using two intentional predicates. The first is used for denoting the task i.e.

```
IsEditable(X) :- Editable(X,Y).
```

and the second for denoting which are the dependencies of this task i.e.

```
Editable(X,Y) :- TextFile(X), TextEditor(Y).
```

DC profiles contain the modules that are available to the users (i.e. `TextEditor('NotePad')`.). To examine if a task can be performed with a module we rely on specific module types as they have been recorded in the dependencies of the task, i.e. in order to read a TextFile X, Y must be a TextEditor.

However users may know how to perform such a task without necessarily classifying their modules to certain module types or they can perform it in a different way than the one that is recorded at the type layer. Such dependencies can be captured by enriching DC profiles with extensional predicates (again with arity greater than 2) that can express the knowledge of a user to perform a task in a particular way, and associating these predicates with the predicates that concern the performability of the task. For example for the task of editing a file we will define three predicates:

```
IsEditable(X)  :- Editable(X,Y).
Editable(X,Y)  :- TextFile(X), TextEditor(Y).
Editable(X,Y)  :- EditableBy(X,Y).
```

The predicates IsEditable and Editable are intentional while the predicate EditableBy is extensional. This means that a user who can edit a text file with a module which is not classified as a TextEditor, and wants to define this explicitly, he could use the following fact in his profile `EditableBy('Readme.txt', 'myProgr.exe')`.

8.3 Modelling and Implementation Frameworks

8.3.1 Modelling Conjunctive Dependencies Using Semantic Web Languages

Semantic web languages can be exploited for the creation of a standard format for input, output and exchange of information regarding modules, dependencies and DC profiles. To this end an ontology has been created (expressed in RDFS). Figure 8.14 sketches the backbone of this ontology. We shall hereafter refer to this ontology with the name COD (Core Ontology for representing Dependencies). This ontology contains only the notion of DC Profile and Module and consists of only two RDF Classes and five RDF Properties (it does not define any module or dependency type). It can be used as a standard format for representing and exchanging information regarding modules, dependencies and DC profiles. Moreover it can guide the specification of the message types between the software components of a preservation information system.

The adoption of Semantic Web languages also allows the specialization of COD ontology according to the needs. Suppose for example we want to preserve the tasks

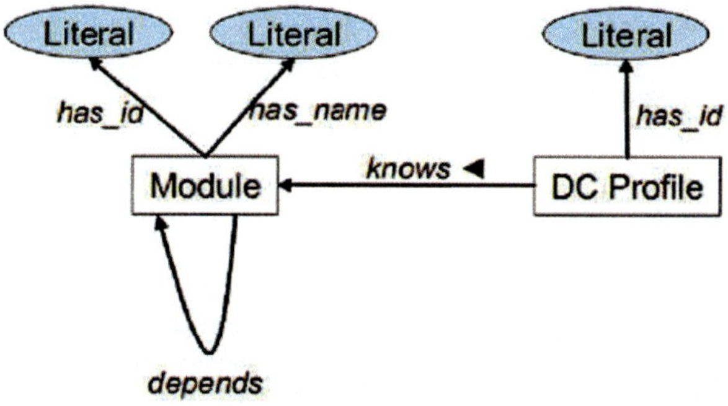

Fig. 8.14 The core ontology for representing dependencies (COD)

that can be performed with the objects of Fig. 8.8, specifically `_edit`, `_compile`, `_run`. These tasks are represented as dependency types, or in other words as special forms of dependencies. To this end we propose specializing the dependency relation, by exploiting "subPropertyOf" of RDF/S. This approach is beneficial since: (a) a digital preservation system whose intelligibility services are based on COD will continue to function properly, even if its data layer instantiates specializations of COD and (b) the set of tasks that can be performed cannot be assumed a priori, so the ability to extend COD with more dependency types offers extra flexibility.

Additionally COD could be related with other ontologies that may have narrower, wider, overlapping or orthogonal scope. For example someone could define that the dependency relation of COD corresponds to a certain relationship, or path of relationships, over an existing conceptual model (or ontology). For example the data dependencies that are used to capture the derivation of a data product in order to preserve its understandability, could be modelled according to OPM ontology [124] using *wasDerivedFrom* relationships, or according to the CIDOC CRM Ontology [125] using paths of the form:

S22 was derivative created by → C3 Formal Derivation → *S21 used as derivation source*

The adoption of an additional ontology allows capturing "metadata" that cannot be captured only with COD. For example, assume that we want to use COD for expressing dependencies but we also want to capture provenance information according to CIDOC CRM Digital ontology. To gain this functionality we should merge appropriately these ontologies.

For instance if we want every Module to be considered as a C1 Digital Object, then we would define that Module is a `subClassOf` C1 Digital Object. Alternatively one could define every instance of Module also as an instance of C1 Digital Object. The ability of multiple classification and inheritance of Semantic Web languages gives this flexibility. The upper part of Fig. 8.15 shows a portion of the merged ontologies. Rectangles with labels C1 etc represent classes according to CIDOC CRM Digital ontology and those without such labels describe classes from COD ontology. Thick arrows represent `subclassOf` relationships between classes and simple labelled arrows represent properties. The lower part of the figure demonstrates how information about the dependencies and the provenance of digital files can be described. Notice that the modules `HelloWorld.java` and `javac` are connected in two ways: (a) through the *_compile* dependency, (b) through the "provenance path":

Module("`HelloWorld.java`") → *S21 was derivation source for* → C3 Formal Derivation ("`Compilation`") → *P16 used specific object* → Module("javac").[1] Note that an implementation policy could be to represent

[1]The property *S21 was derivation source for* that is used in the "provenance path" is a reverse property of the property S21 used as derivation source that is shown in Fig. 8.15 These properties have the same interpretation but inverse domain and range.

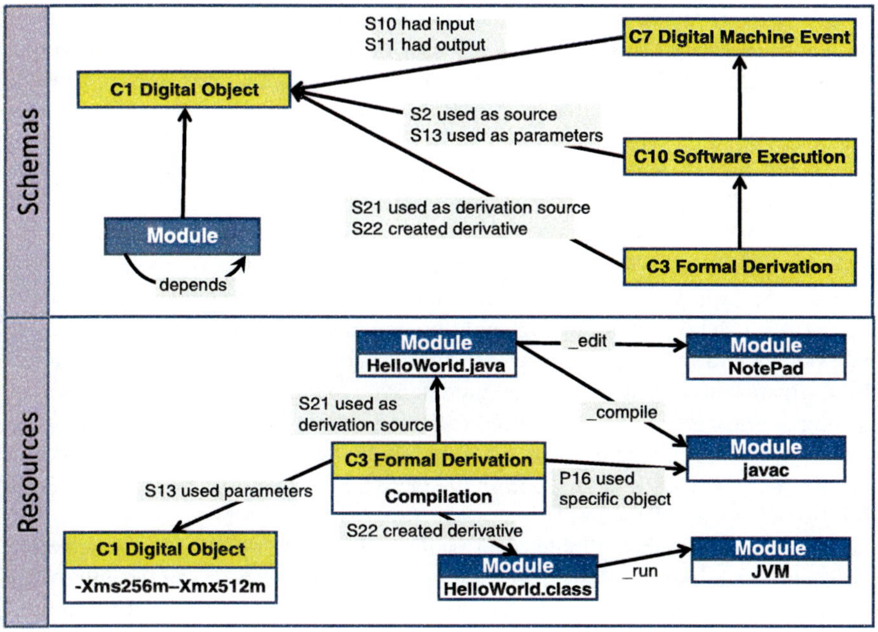

Fig. 8.15 Extending COD for capturing provenance

explicitly only (b), while (a) could be deduced by an appropriate query. Furthermore the derivation history of modules (i.e. HelloWorld.class was derived from `HelloWorld.java` using the module javac with specific parameters etc.) can be retrieved by querying the instances appropriately.

8.3.2 Implementation Approaches for Disjunctive Dependencies

The model based on disjunctive dependencies is founded on Horn rules. Therefore we could use a rule language for implementing it. Below we describe three implementations approaches; over Prolog, over SWRL, and over a DBMS that supports recursion.

Prolog is a declarative logic programming language, where a program is a set of Horn clauses describing the data and the relations between them. The proposed approach can be straightforwardly expressed in Prolog. Furthermore, and regarding abduction, there are several approaches that either extend Prolog [126] or augment it [127].

The Semantic Web Rule Language (SWRL) [128] is a combination of OWL DL and OWL Lite [129] with the Unary/Binary Datalog RuleML.[2] SWRL provides

[2] http://ruleml.org

the ability to write Horn-like rules expressed in terms of OWL concepts to infer new knowledge from existing OWL KB. For instance, each type predicate can be expressed as a class. Each profile can be expressed as an OWL class whose instances are the modules available to that profile (we exploit the multiple classification of SW languages). Module type hierarchies can be expressed through *subclassOf* relationships between the corresponding classes. All rules regarding performability and the hierarchical organization of tasks can be expressed as SWRL rules.

In a DBMS-approach all facts can be stored in a relational database, while *Recursive SQL* can be used for expressing the rules. Specifically, each type predicate can be expressed as a relational table with tuples the modules of that type. Each profile can be expressed as an additional relational table, whose tuples will be the modules known by that profile. All rules regarding task performability, hierarchical organisation of tasks, and the module type hierarchies, can be expressed as Datalog queries. Recursion is required for being able to express the properties (e.g. transitivity) of dependencies. Note that there are many commercial SQL servers that support the SQL:1999 syntax regarding recursive SQL (e.g. Microsoft SQL Server 2005, Oracle 9i, and IBM DB2).

The following table (Table 8.1) summarises the various implementation approaches and describes how the elements of the model can be implemented. The table does not contain any information about the Prolog approach since the terminology we used for founding the model (Sect. 8.2.1.1) is the same with that of Prolog.

Table 8.1 Implementation approaches for disjunctive dependencies

What	DB approach	Semantic web approach
Module type predicates	Relational table	Class
Facts regarding modules (and their types)	Tuples	class instances
DC profile	Relational table	Class
DC profile contents	Tuples	class instances
Task predicates	IDB predicates	predicates appearing in rules
Task type hierarchy	Datalog rules, or *isa* if an ORDBMS is used	*subclassOf*
Task performability	Datalog queries (recursive SQL)	Rules

8.4 Summary

Although this Chapter is heavy going and the theory is not yet complete, it is worth knowing that there is a theoretical basis for techniques to deal with Knowledge Bases. Of particular importance is that some automation is possible in identifying and fillings gaps in knowledge dependencies.

Chapter 9
Understandability and Usability of Data

I hear and I forget. I see and I remember. I do and I understand.

(Confucius)

Ensuring that digitally encoded information remains usable and understandable over time is, together with authenticity, at the heart of digital preservation. The previous chapter discussed some of the formal aspects of intelligibility. This chapter discusses the complementary issue of usability of the data.

Usable means "*capable of use*" (OED), "*available or convenient for use*" (www.dictionary.com).

In design, usability is the study of the ease with which people can employ a particular tool or other human-made object in order to achieve a particular goal. In human – computer interaction and computer science, usability studies the elegance and clarity with which the interaction with a computer program or a web site is designed (Wikipedia).

Here, by usable we mean that someone is able to do something sensible with the information it contains. We recognise that this might not be easy – but at least it should be possible to carry out.

One could of course use a digital object simply by printing out its constituent sequences of "1"'s and "0"'s on paper and using this to decorate one's home. However it seems reasonable to suppose that this has little to do with the information content in the digital object – unless of course that is what it was designed for. For example the Arecibo message [130] was designed to be understood by extra-terrestrials. This consisted of a sequence of 1,679 bits, which if displayed as 73 rows by 23 columns looks like Fig. 9.1 (the shading has been added on the right to make the different parts of the image clearer).

The idea is that even with no shared cultural or linguistic roots one can rely on basic counting, an awareness of prime numbers, elements, chemistry and physics – which any being able to receive the message might reasonably be expected to possess.

It is not clear how many human recipients could decipher the message without help!

D. Giaretta, *Advanced Digital Preservation*, DOI 10.1007/978-3-642-16809-3_9,

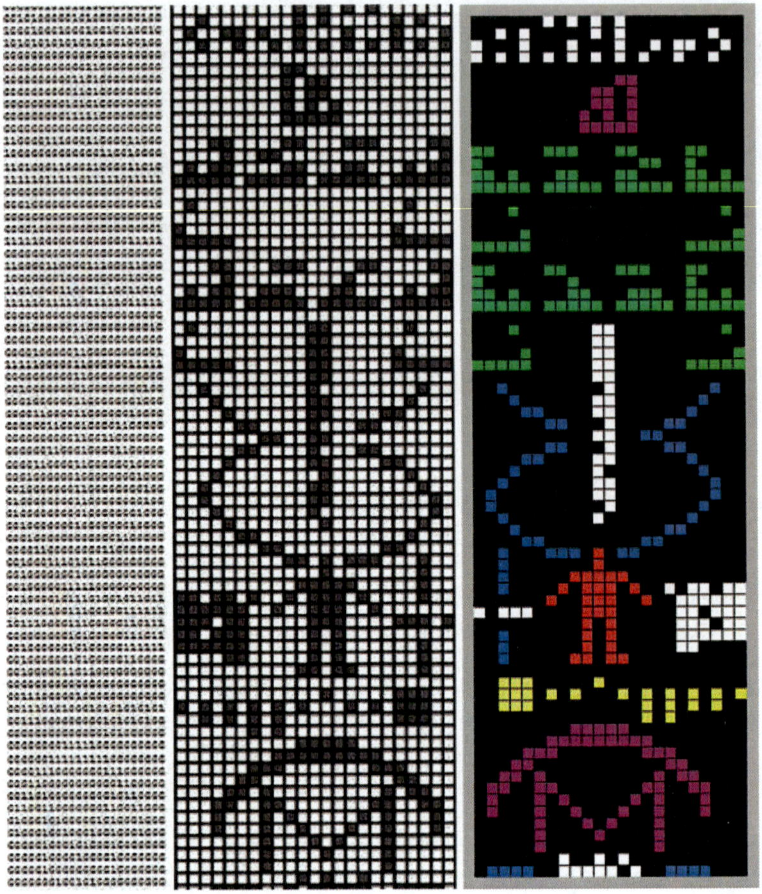

Fig. 9.1 Arecibo message as 1's and 0's (*left*) and as pixels – both *black* and *white* (*centre*) and with shading added (*right*)

9.1 Re-Use of Digital Objects – Interoperability and Preservation

One of the interesting, and indeed useful benefits of following OAIS and judging digital preservation in terms of usability and understandability is that resources which are needed for preservation also produce immediate benefits in terms of wider, contemporary, use of the digital objects.

We justify this claim by noting that if one is familiar with a particular piece of digitally encoded information then, apart from keeping the bits, one needs nothing else. Representation Information – beyond that held in one's mind – is needed only where information is unfamiliar in some sense. This unfamiliarity can arise from the passage of time – in which case we are in the realm of digital preservation. Alternatively unfamiliarity can arise from distance in discipline or experience – which can apply no matter what the difference in time – and is necessary for usability by a wider community.

This is a very important consideration which should help to justify the expenditure of those resources in preservation.

9.1.1 Relationship Between Preservation and (Re-)Use

Preservation of digitally encoded information requires that it continues to be usable and understandable by a Designated Community. This has been extensively discussed in the previous chapters. A Designated Community is defined by the repository (see Sect. 6.2) and this definition is vital for the testability of the effectiveness of the preservation activities of the archive. However the point to realise is that the Representation Information Network can (perhaps easily) be extended to that needed by another Designated Community – or perhaps more precisely, to match the Knowledge Base of some other user community, for immediate use.

In other words although the digitally encoded information is not guaranteed by the repository to remain usable by these other users, by making the Representation Information required to fill the knowledge gap explicit, this is much more likely to be the case. Moreover the types of Registry/Repository(ies) of Representation Information which are described in this book will make it much easier to share the Representation Information required. The repository holding the data does not itself have to fill the gap; it needs to make it clear what the end points of the Representation Information Network it can provide are.

This is not to say that everything becomes trivial. It is instructive to look at a number of possibilities. One can first consider a single data object – which may of course consist of several bit sequences (for example several files). After this the implications for combining digitally encoded information may be analysed.

9.1.2 Digital Object Used By Itself

A digital object may be used by itself, for example a user may simply want to find a particular fact from a dataset. For the sake of concreteness let us say that (s)he wants to determine the photon counts at a certain position in the sky from data captured by a particular astronomical instrument, and that data is held in a FITS file. Other examples could include determining the character or the font used at a particular position, say "the 25th character of the second paragraph of page 51", in a document. These are in many ways the simplest pieces of information which one might wish to extract from a digital object. However if one can do this then one can build up to the extraction of more complex pieces of information, using the concepts of virtualisation discussed in Sect. 7.8.

The Representation Information Network (RIN) (Fig. 9.2 – an annotated version of Fig. 6.4) indicates that a Java application is available to extract the numbers from

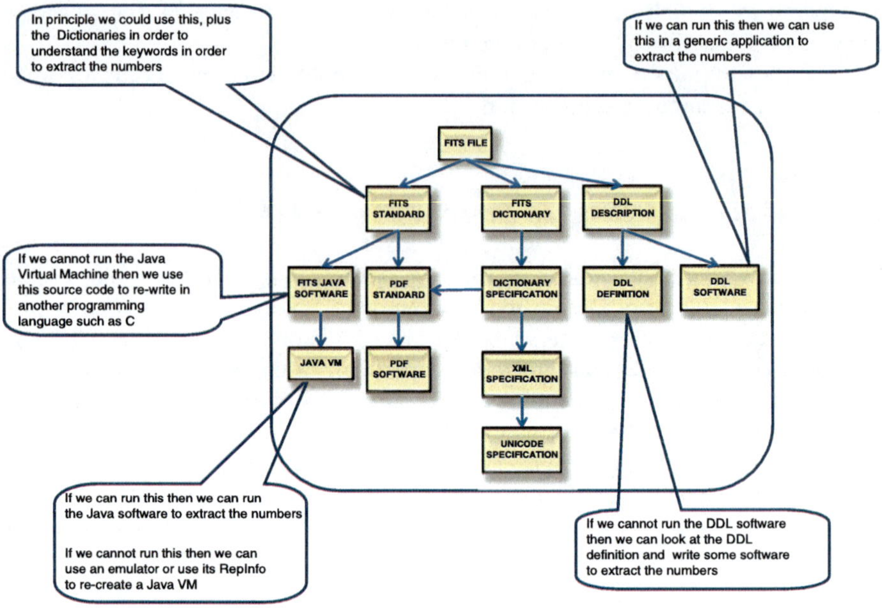

Fig. 9.2 Using the representation information network in the extraction of information from digitally encoded information (FITS file)

the data. Of course this RIN will also let us know which version of Java is needed and so forth. If the user can run the Java application then it is a simple matter to extract the number.

Other options include:

A. if (s)he does not have the correct version of Java at hand then (s)he at least has the option of trying to obtain it from another Registry/Repository – because (s)he knows what is needed.
   a. An important variant of this is the use of emulators, described in Sect. 7.9.

B. if the Java application cannot be run then it might be possible to take the Java source code, if available, and convert it to some programming language, say the C programming language, from which one can create an appropriate application.

C. if neither (A) nor (B) are possible, then a data description language (DDL) such as EAST or DRB, together with the associated data dictionary, may be used. Again there are a number of possibilities.
   a. The easiest is that a generic application such as the one described in Sect. 7.3.5 can use the data description to extract the information needed.
   b. Otherwise one might have to read the DDL description, together with the definition of that DDL, and the associated Data Dictionary or other piece of

Semantic Representation Information, and then write an appropriate application. This would no doubt be harder, but at least one would not have to guess at what information the digital object holds.

Some of these options are trivial – which would be very convenient for the user. However if a trivial option is not available then at least the other options are possible – the information can be extracted with considerable certainty and used for other purposes.

9.2 Use of Existing Software

Option (A) above is an example of using existing software – albeit probably old software. A more interesting example is the case where one wants to use information from this digital object with one's current favourite software. This may be because of the additional functionality which that favourite software provides. The additional functionality could include being able to combine that data with other data more easily. Again one can imagine that this other software may be associated with (e.g. in the Representation Information Network of) other archived data or it may be more modern software – the argument applies equally.

Once again one can imagine several ways of doing this and these are described next.

9.2.1 Migration/Transformation

Migration – or more precisely Transformation (using OAIS terminology) – involves changing the bit sequences from the original to something else. Following the recent revision of OAIS one can recognise that if this transformation is reversible then one can be confident that no information has been lost. On the other hand non-reversible transformations probably have lost information and someone must take responsibility to confirm that the transformation adequately maintains the "important" information. This is discussed in much more detail in Sect. 13.6.

For those with an eye for recursion, the ways in which the transformation could be carried out are special cases of this sub-section, namely using a single digital object. For example one can use existing software, the subject of this sub-section, if there is software which can take in the original bit sequences in order to perform the transformation.

One could alternatively use a data description language (DDL) description to extract values from the original and write them out as the new bit sequences. This could be done using generic applications as illustrated in Fig. 9.3 or else could be hand-crafted.

The transformation chosen will of course be one which produces something which can be used by the software which has been chosen to deal with the

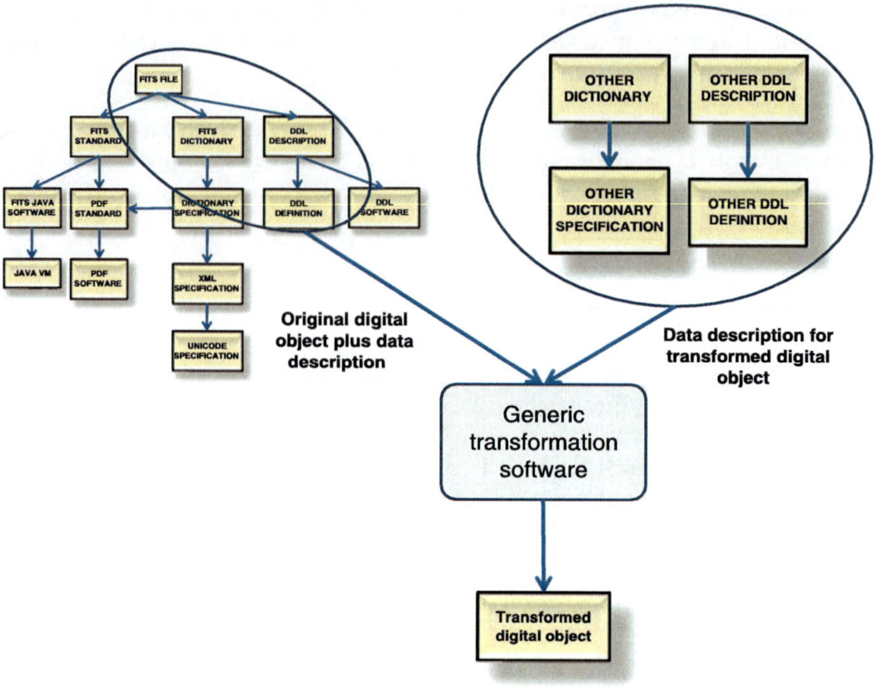

Fig. 9.3 Using a generic application to transform from one encoding to another

information in the digitally encoded information. Authenticity evidence should of course be provided by someone, providing values and other information about selected Transformational Information Properties (also known as *Significant Properties*), as discussed in Sect. 13.6.

9.2.2 Interfacing

A related but alternative way of using the digital object in one's preferred software is to use or create an appropriate programming interface. Whether or not this is possible depends upon the flexibility of that preferred software – for example whether or not it is possible to use plug-ins.

Instead of transforming the digital object as a whole one essentially does it on the fly, treating only the piece that is needed. The advantage is that one might be dealing with an object of many gigabytes, perhaps, in the case of scientific information, many terabytes (1 terabyte = 1,024 gigabytes) or even more. If one is only interested in a small part of the information then transforming the whole digital object may be a waste of effort. Being able to transform only the part that is needed can be a great saving in computation time and temporary disk storage in such circumstances.

If a large number of such objects are to be dealt with, the cumulative savings could offset the effort needed to create the programming interface.

With luck this may be done automatically; the alternative is to do it manually.

9.2.2.1 Manual Interfaces

The manual option may be described using the data shown in Sect. 19 as an example. That data is essentially tabular. The EAST description allows one to extract individual values. It is in principle fairly easy to implement the following Java methods:

- public int getRowCount();
- public int getColumnCount();
- public Object getValueAt(int row, int column);

in order to extend the AbstractTableModel class [71].

If this is done then many Java applications are available to manipulate or display the data (see Sect. 7.8.2.1.2).

9.2.2.2 Automated

The automated option is the most convenient but is not often available. Essentially the manual steps above are carried out automatically. Whether or not this is possible depends, for example, on the amount and type of Representation Information available and the tools which can use them.

9.3 Creation of New Software

Entirely new software may be needed in order to adequately deal with the digitally encoded information. Techniques described in the previous sections to extract information from the digital object are applicable here. The difference is that one needs to design and implement the rest of the application, rather than having one already available. Of course what the software does is dependent on one's imagination and the requirements.

9.4 Without Software

Software is not always needed, as illustrated by the data at the start of this section, where one can imagine drawing each of the pixels by hand on squared graph paper. Pencil and paper may be all that is needed – clearly this would only be practical for small amounts of data.

9.5 Software as the Digital Object Being Preserved

When software itself is the digital object being preserved all the above applies. However there are some additional considerations because to do some of what is described in the previous sections could be very complex. This is because the software which "uses" a software digital object is an operating system or virtual machine.

The options discussed above become:

A. If (s)he does not have the correct version of operating at hand then (s)he at least has the option of trying to obtain it from a Registry/Repository of Representation Information – because (s)he knows what is needed.
   a. An important variant of this is the use of operating systems running in emulators, described in Sect. 7.9.

B. If the application cannot be run then it might be possible to take the source code, if available, and port it to an available operating system or convert it to another programming language.

The remaining option, of using a data description language, is not an easy one. An example of this could be a Java application, where we could argue that Java byte code is well described; this would require a re-implement a Java Virtual machine – quite a daunting task.

The testbed example in Sect. 19 provides further examples of using the Representation Information Network for software.

9.6 Digital Archaeology, Digital Forensics and Re-Use

The above starts from the assumption that Representation Information is available, as should be the case where digitally encoded information is being adequately preserved.

There are times when one is not in such a fortunate position, for example where one finds some digital data but does not know much about it. In such a case one may be able to find the format (i.e. the appropriate Structure Representation Information), as discussed in Sect. 7.4. What will be much more difficult to do is to find the semantics associated with it. For example one may be able to discover that a file is a PDF. This allows one to render the contents of the file. This does not mean that one understands or can use the information it contains – for example the rendered text might contain a string of "1"s and "0"s, as described at the start of this chapter, or it might be in some unknown language.

In some cases this has not been an insuperable problem – an analogy may be drawn with the interpretation of cuneiform – but this can take a considerable amount of time and effort. Therefore this is a method of last resort.

9.7 Multiple Objects

Dealing with multiple pieces of digitally encoded information introduces more complexity but the essential concepts have been coved therefore no more will be said.

9.8 Summary

Although not providing all the details, it is hoped that this chapter will have provided the reader with an understanding of how digital objects may be used and re-used over the long-term. Examples of some of these are provided in Part II. It may not be a trivial process but, if the right Representation Information has been collected then at least it should be possible. It should also be clear that the formal description techniques offer the possibility of making re-use easier for the future users.

Chapter 10
In Addition to Understanding It – What Is It?: Preservation Description Information

10.1 Introduction

Preservation Description Information, as defined by OAIS as being made up of several types of Information (Fig. 10.1): Fixity, Reference, Context Provenance and Access Rights, will be detailed below. Note that Access Rights Information was not in the original version of OAIS but was added in the first update.

Many aspects are very likely to be discipline independent, for example Fixity, Reference and some aspects of Provenance. It is also likely that at least some aspects of Provenance will be discipline dependent, as will be Context information.

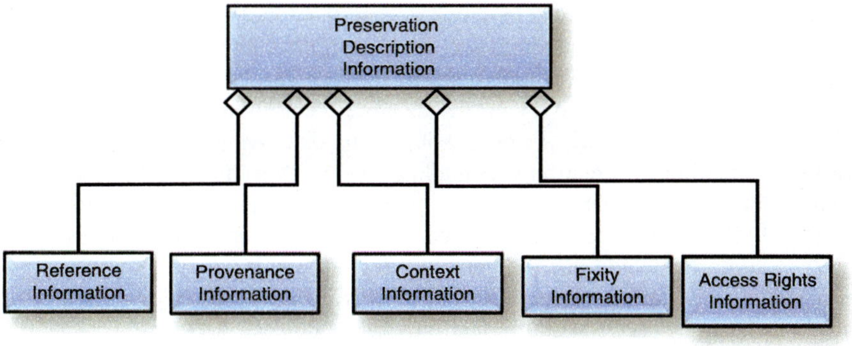

Fig. 10.1 Types of preservation description information

10.2 Fixity Information

OAIS defines Fixity Information as the:

information which documents the authentication mechanisms and provides authentication keys to ensure that the Content Information object has not been

D. Giaretta, *Advanced Digital Preservation*, DOI 10.1007/978-3-642-16809-3_10,

altered in an undocumented manner. An example is a Cyclical Redundancy Check (CRC) code for a file.

This information provides the Data Integrity checks or Validation/Verification keys used to ensure that the particular Content Information object has not been altered in an undocumented manner. Fixity Information includes special encoding and error detection schemes that are specific to instances of Content Objects. Fixity Information does not include the integrity preserving mechanisms provided by the OAIS underlying services, error protection supplied by the media and device drivers used by Archival Storage. The Fixity Information may specify minimum quality of service requirements for these mechanisms.

Fixity is relevant within the repository or in the transfer phase, but cannot be itself the guarantee for long-term integrity, because of the problem of obsolescence. There are a large number of object digest/hash/checksum algorithms, such as CRC-32, MD5, RIPEMD-160, SHA and HAVAL, some of which are, at the moment, secure in the sense that it is almost impossible for changes in the digital object to fail to be detected – at least as long as the original digest itself is kept secure. However in the future processing power, of individual processors and of collections of processors, will increase and algorithms may become "crackable". Warning of the vulnerability of any particular type of digest algorithm would be another function of the Orchestration manager (detailed in Sect. 17.5).

Since Fixity is concerned with whether or not the bit sequences of the digital object have been changed, having nothing to do with the meaning of those bits, it is reasonable to say that the way in which we create or check Fixity Information is independent of the discipline from which the information comes.

In a broad sense the tools for fixity used by the repositories (and by the creator of the Digital Object) have to be documented. More precisely the Fixity Information will be encoded in some way as a digital object and that digital object must have its own Representation Information which allows one to understand and use it. It will also have Provenance associated with it. This is another example of recursion.

The CASPAR Key Store concept – which could be simply be a Registry-type entity – could provide additional security for the digests. It may be possible to use one object digest as an identifier to be sent to the Key Store which returns the other digest which can be used to confirm the fixity of the object.

More sophisticated techniques have been proposed using a publicly available digests of digests [131].

10.3 Reference Information

OAIS defines Reference Information as the information which:

> ***identifies, and if necessary describes, one or more mechanisms used to provide assigned identifiers for the Content Information. It also provides those identifiers that allow outside systems to refer, unambiguously, to this***

particular Content Information. Examples of these systems include taxonomic systems, reference systems and registration systems. In the OAIS Reference Model most if not all of this information is replicated in Package Descriptions, which enable Consumers to access Content Information of interest.

The identifiers must be persistent and are referred to here as Persistent Identifiers, and are unique in that an identifier should be usable to locate the specific digital object with which it is associated, or an identical copy of that object.

We discuss first name spaces in general and then persistent identifiers in particular. This rather extensive discussion is a little out of place here but because PIDs are not discussed in the implementation section this seemed the best location.

10.3.1 Name Spaces

There are many names spaces in the preservation environment covering, for example, names for files, users, storage systems and management rules. Each of these may change over time as information is handed over in the chain of preservation, or as any single archive evolves. These name spaces, and their associated Access Controls and Representation Information must themselves be managed.

10.3.2 Persistent Identifiers

Persistent Identifiers (PIDs) have been the cause of much debate, and there are many proposed systems [132], including ARK [133], N2T [134], PURL [135], Handle [137] and DOI [138]. To produce general purpose Persistent Identifiers, which could be used to point to any and all objects, is well known to be challenging, the difficulty being social rather than technological. On the other hand, given the increasing number of such systems, one might be led to think that at least some are technological solutions in search of a problem. Indeed it sometimes seems that conferences and discussions of PIDs are dominated by those offering solutions rather than by those defining the problem.

A more limited type of Persistent Identifier is the Curation Persistent Identifier (CPID) which was introduced in Sect. 7.1.3 as pointing to Representation Information.

It is relatively easy to generate a unique identifier by having a hierarchical namespace,

$$x.y.z$$

each segment or namespace (i.e. each of x, y, z) forms a hierarchy of naming authorities, and where necessary to generate unique strings some algorithm such as that used by the UUID [138] is used. A UUID is a Universal Unique IDentifier which is a 128 bit number which can be assigned to any object and which is guaranteed to be unique. The mechanism used to guarantee uniqueness is through combinations of hardware addresses, time stamps and random seeds.

The difficulty task is to make the link between the identifier (as a character string) to the object to which it points. In particular the bootstrap procedure must be in place, in other words given a string – how does one know what to do with it – where does one start?

The steps involved would be

1. given "x.y.z" one somehow knows (i.e. the bootstrap step) that one uses some service "X" with which one can find out what "x" means i.e. tells one where to go to look up some service ("Y") associated with "x". "X" will be referred to here as the bootstrap resolver service
2. using service "Y" we then find out something about "y" - in particular some service "Z"
3. using service "Z" we then find out something about "z" - in particular some service "T" which will point, at last, to the object wanted. This will be referred to here as the terminal resolver service

We presumably can say have some control about the last service "T". On the other hand we may have no control over the others in the hierarchy.

Thus we have the issues of:

1. the bootstrap into the name resolution system
2. the persistence of each of the name resolvers

We look at these issues in a little bit more detail, and use our old friend ***recursion***.

Figure 10.2 indicates a PID "*ABC:xyz/abc/def/xxx*" (here we use "/" as the namespace separator rather than ".")

This PID is a String embedded in some Digital Object; it requires some Representation Information to allow it to be understood and used. This Representation Information tells one that one should use a particular root names resolver. This then unpacks the next part of the PID and so on until one gets to the correct repository.

Thinking about this from a more abstract point of view one can say:

- name resolvers contain digital information – the association between a String and a pointer to the next name resolver
- this information must be preserved if we are to have persistence

Therefore each name resolver should be regarded as an archive - an OAIS – illustrated in Fig. 10.3. This allows us to apply all the OAIS concepts to them, including audit and certification, which would require, for example, that each has handover plans.

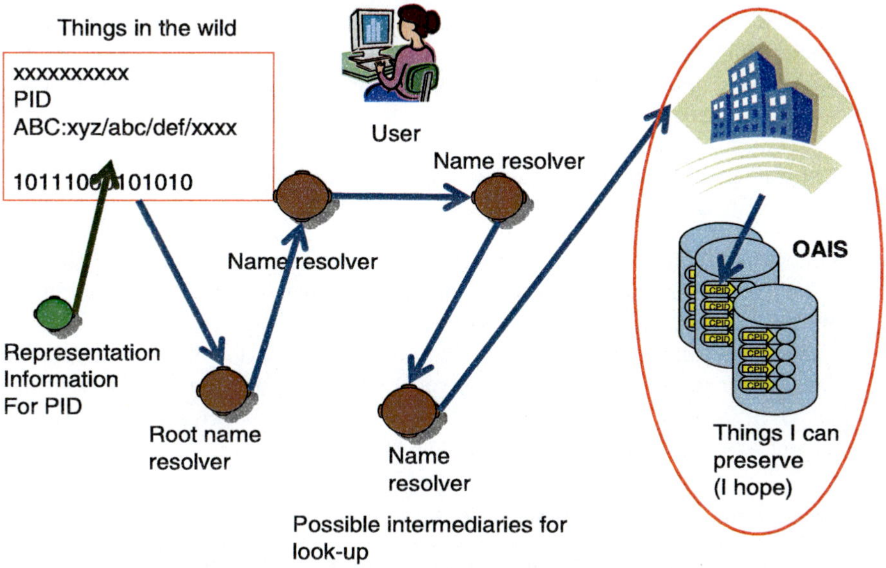

Fig. 10.2 PID name resolution

10.3.2.1 Persistence of Persistent Identifier Name Resolver Information

In many ways name resolution is fairly simple. What is more difficult is the persistence. As with all OAIS, funding plays an important role, as do policies, plans and

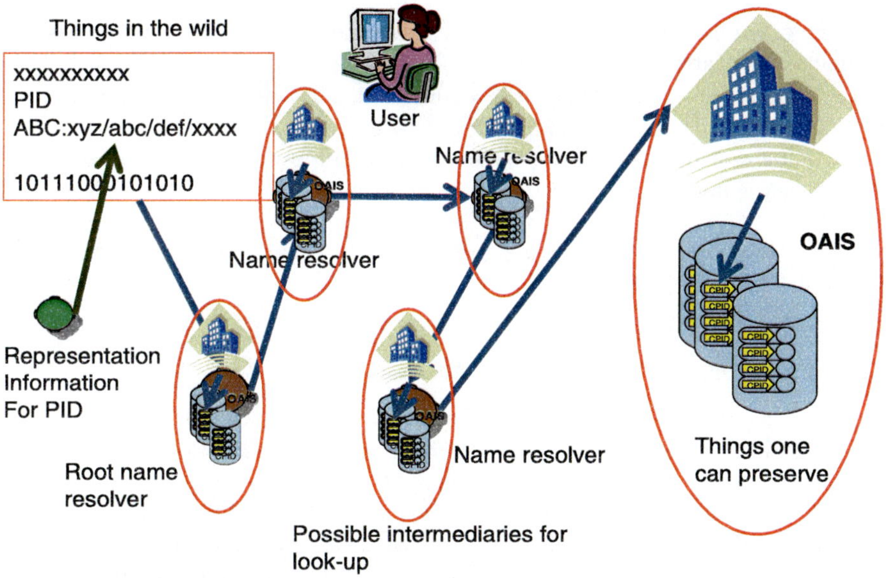

Fig. 10.3 PID name resolvers as OAIS repositories

systems. The discussions earlier in the book about digital preservation all apply to PID name resolvers.

However a number of additional factors come into play more immediately, namely that things which are pointed to do move. One can imagine a number of general scenarios based on the movement of digital objects – which may be either something in a name resolver or something in a "normal" repository. As will be argued below, it is important to distinguish between:

- whether the whole collection of information moves and the repository (which may be a name server) ceases to exist, or alternatively only part of those holdings move and the repository continues to exist.
- whether or not the repository knows who is pointing to it – this is particularly important for intermediate name resolvers. The basic function of such a name resolver is to point forwards to the next in the chain; backward pointers, i.e. knowing who is pointing to you, are not so common.

With these in mind we can imagine various scenarios:

1. A particular piece of information (or collection of information) moves but the repository/name resolver continues to exist.
   a. If the repository has "backward pointers" then special arrangements could be made with its predecessor in the look-up chain – for example "instead of pointing to me, look over there when you get certain lookup names"
   b. If there are no backward pointers then the repository itself can act as a name resolver for that piece of information and when that piece of information is sought it redirects to the new location.

2. A repository/name resolver ceases to exist and its entire holding moves to another repository/name resolver.
   a. If the repository has "backward pointers" then the repository should inform the ones pointing to it and let them know the new location
   b. If there are no backward pointers then the repository must hand over its location information, for example its DNS entry, to its chosen successor.

Following these one can ensure that the PID name resolution continues to work despite these kinds of changes.

10.3.2.2 Alternative: Application of DNS Concepts

The DNS is very familiar to users of the internet and allows users to connect to billions of internet nodes. An important concept it employs is that of "Time-To-Live" (TTL) which is a hint to the name resolver about how long the lookup entry is going to be valid for. Beyond this time the name resolver could, for example, seek to verify whether or not the lookup entry remains valid. If an internet node ceases to exist then, without any further action, after the TTL time, the DNS will cease to point to the old address.

If one were to use this idea then one could allow repositories to die without notifying anyone. However that is not good for persistence. Moreover of another repository advertised itself as a replacement for the dead repository then there would be concerns about the provenance and authenticity of the holdings.

10.3.2.3 Root Name Resolver

The root name resolver needs some special consideration because it is the thing to which users' applications point and so resolving its location will be integrated into huge numbers of those applications. Its persistence is therefore of particular importance.

The funding of that root name resolver could be guaranteed, for example by some kind of international investment which yields guaranteed continued funding – perhaps not guaranteed forever but certainly much longer than typical funding cycles.

This is analogous to the non-digital preservation – cryonics – where there are commercial companies which offer to freeze a person's head when they die. The supply of liquid nitrogen is paid for by the interest on a lump sum of several tens of thousands of dollars paid before death.

10.3.2.4 Practical Considerations

While the previous sections described a single PID system, there are already many "Persistent" ID systems in use and it is probably impractical to get everyone to change what they have in use. One could minimise disruption by, for example, adopting the most popular PID system to minimise confusion but one would need to check whether the most popular system can satisfy the full set of requirements – whatever they are.

It might be possible for the root name resolver to deal with the multitude of PID systems in order to provide a more homogeneous PID system but this would require careful analysis.

Another possibility would be to make the PID string more flexible in order to use several PID systems simultaneously. The concept introduced here follows the adage "do not put all one's eggs in one basket". Conceptually one needs to allow multiple name resolution mechanisms in the hope that at least one survives, in order to get to the host (or hosts) which hold the digital object. An XML encoding may look something like:

```
<pid>
   <value>xxxxxxxxxxx
      <nameresolver type=n1>http://x.y.z</nameresolver>
      <nameresolver type=n2>DOI:123456</nameresolver>
      <nameresolver type=n3>urn::xx::dd</nameresolver>
   </value>
</pid>
```

Nevertheless it seems clear that there is no solely technological solution; instead the more important aspects are sociological and financial. For example the Handle system provides the name resolution for several persistent identifier systems such as DOI [137], which act essentially as look-up tables. However registration requires an annual subscription fee and the question arises as to what happens if the fee is not paid.

Two reasons for a Web page to become inaccessible are that the page is not available on the machine (or the machine is no longer working) or the DNS entry no longer exists – because the registration renewal fee has not been paid. It is well known that most web pages' addresses (URLs) cannot be relied on in the long term. But one can then ask whether there is a real difference between something like the Handle System and URLs. One answer might be that a Handle or DOI lookup will continue even if payment is not made; however this may cause problems with the business case of these systems in the long term!

We argue here that the only realistic way for any system to be persistent is for the sociological and financial support to be adequately guaranteed, for example by being funded by national or international funders such as NSF or the EU. The technical implementation is less important.

10.4 Context Information

This information

> ***documents the relationships of the Content Information to its environment. This includes why the Content Information was created and how it relates to other Content Information objects existing elsewhere.***

May archivists would regard context as the sine qua non of preservation. One danger is that context becomes as difficult to pin down in meaning as "metadata". For this reason OAIS defines the more precise concepts of Representation Information, and the other components of PDI and Packaging, and then has context as a general catch-all. Context does cover an extremely broad range of topics and it is difficult to define a precise boundary. In fact Provenance Information, described next, can be viewed as a special type of Context Information.

10.5 Provenance Information

This information

> ***documents the history of the Content Information. This tells the origin or source of the Content Information, any changes that may have taken place since it was originated, and who has had custody of it since it was originated. This gives future users some assurance as to the likely reliability of the Content Information.***

There are a wide variety of approaches to describing, modelling and tracking provenance; a full survey is beyond the scope of this document. Related work includes (amongst many others) the Open Provenance Model [124], CIDOC-CRM, PREMIS [139] and the Chimera Virtual Data Language (VDL) [140]. Some projects have focused on formal computer languages for representing the origins and source of scientific and declarative data; VDL falls in this category, as do Semantic Web systems such as W3C's SPARQL which have explicit fine-grained support for representing the source of pieces of information, and characteristics of that source. Others emphasise an analysis of common concepts (often expressed in some formal ontology language) that capture important aspects relating to Time, Event and Process.

Another consideration is the sharability of Provenance [141], in that given a digital object with a certain Provenance there are a number of directly related objects, which share the Provenance of that object, including:

- a copy of the object – which will have identical Provenance plus an additional event, namely the copy process which created it
- an object derived from the original object – plus perhaps several others. In this case the Provenance of the new object inherits Provenance from its "parents", and has a new event, namely the process by which it was created.

An important question which needs to be tackled is the extent to which we could or should avoid duplications of the Provenance entries. It is worth noting that this question comes to the fore with digital, as opposed to physical, objects.

Finally it is worth remembering that over time the Provenance Information is added to, for example with each copy or change of curatorship. Each time the person or system responsible will use the current system for recording provenance. This each object will inevitably have a collection of heterogeneous entries. Each entry will (one way or another) have to have its own Representation Information. All this of course complicated the sharability mentioned above. Virtualisation is likely to play an important role here since each entry in the provenance will have to do a certain job in recording time, event and process.

In summary, Provenance Information is bound to be difficult to deal with but is nevertheless absolutely critical to digital preservation. This sub-section has at least pointed out some of the challenges and options for their solution.

10.6 Access Rights Management

When one hears about Digital Rights, one will probably think about restrictions and payment of fees that one must respect if one wants to download and enjoy one's favourite song or read some parts of the intriguing e-book about digital preservation found on Internet. That's true, but Digital Rights exist and have a legal validity even if one is not forced to respect the conditions. So, which are the issues that Digital Rights pose on the long-term preservation?

If one is preserving "in-house" all the pictures one has taken since one first bought a digital camera, then one will have no problem. But if one needs to curate of some artistic, cultural or scientific material that was not produced by oneself, then the Law imposes limitations on the use, distribution and any kind of exploitation of that material.

One might think "*Fine, I know already what I'm allowed to do! Why should I further care about rights*?" The reason is that things will change: new Laws will come into force, the Copyright will at a given time expire or the heirs of the original right holder could give up the exploitation rights and put the work one is preserving into the Public Domain. All these things have an impact on what anybody is allowed to do.

And is there anything else to care of, except Copyright? Yes, there is Protection of Minors, Right to Privacy, Trademarks, Patents, etc., and they all share the same aim: they protect people from potential damages due to incorrect use of the material being held! One should be aware of that.

The main questions one has to ask oneself are:

- do the activities related to digital preservation violate any of the above rights?
- are there some limits in copying, transforming and distributing the digital holdings?
- is the object of preservation some personal material or is it intended for a wider public?

Future consumers will have to respect to the same limitations, and they should also be informed about the special permissions that the Laws grant them or that the rights holder was willing to grant. In other words access conditions depend both on legislation and on conditions defined within licenses and both must be preserved over time and be kept updated.

10.6.1 Limitations and Rights to Perform Digital Preservation

Preserving a digital work in the long-term requires that a number of actions are undertaken, including copying, reproducing, making available and transforming its binary representation.

These actions might infringe existing Copyright: for instance, if one wanted to transform a digital object from an obsolete format to a most recent one, and so would risk altering the original creation in a way that the rights holder might not agree with.

To ascertain that no such exclusive rights are violated, a preservation institution has the following main options (which are all, within the conditions defined, in line with the OAIS mandatory responsibilities):

- to become the owner of the digital material and to obtain the exclusive rights from the creators (excluded the non-transferrable moral rights);

- to preserve only material that is in Public Domain (e.g. where Copyright is expired or the author has released the work into Public Domain);
- to carry out preservation in accordance with the conditions defined by the Law (e.g. in some countries there are Copyright Exceptions which grant to some kind of institutions the permissions to perform digital preservation)
- to obtain from the right holders, by means of a license, the permissions to carry out the necessary preservation activities.

Many countries have defined exceptions in their Copyright Laws to facilitate libraries, archives and other institutions to carry out digital preservation. However, until a legal reform is carried out, it is good practice to get the required authorization from the right holders through rights transfer contracts or licenses, and not to rely solely on the existing jurisdiction to ensure a comprehensive preservation of copyrighted materials.

10.6.2 Preserving Limitations and Rights over Time

At some time in the short- or long-term, somebody will desire or need to access one of the preserved archive holdings. Protection of Minors and Privacy Laws regulate the use of particular types of data. However, the most complex limitations come from Intellectual Property Rights (IPRs): Copyright, Related Rights and Industrial Property Rights, such as Trademarks, Industrial Design and Patents.

Dealing with IPR-protected material poses risks, because it could conflict with the normal exploitation of the work or prejudice the legitimate interests of the rights holders. Therefore, the preservation institution should reduce the risk taken by future consumers, and try to arrange things so that those consumers are able lawfully to exploit the materials.

We will see that it is not enough just to identify and store the details on who holds some Copyright and the licenses that are attached to the content; it is necessary to preserve also other kinds of information, to monitor the changes in the legislation and to be continuously updated about the ownership of rights. If the consumer was authorized to exploit a piece of content in the way (s)he intends, (s)he should have the ability to show the appropriate authorization.

Since the revision of the OAIS Reference Model a specific section of the Preservation Description Information (PDI) has been defined to address authorization in the long-term, namely Access Rights. This information is specified in part by the right holders within the Submission Agreement. For example, it could contain the license to carry out preservation activities, licenses offered to interested consumers and the right holders' requirements about rights enforcement measures. But this PDI section could even include the special authorizations that are granted by the Law. In short, OAIS Access Rights include everything related to the terms and conditions for preservation, distribution and usage of the Content Information.

There are two kinds of access rights to be considered. On the one hand there are the exclusive ownership rights that are typically held by the owners of the works, and on the other hand there are the non-exclusive permissions that are granted to other persons. In order to be able to correctly preserve all the existing rights – exclusive ownership rights and non-exclusive permissions – the following information is required:

- Ownership of rights
- Licences
- Rights-relevant Provenance information
- Post-publication events
- Laws

Each of these is discussed in turn below.

10.6.2.1 Ownership of Rights

Ownership rights can be derived from the application of the Law to provenance and to post-publication events. Thus one could just preserve the latter and "calculate" the existing rights only when the legitimacy of some intended action must be controlled.

In practice however it is useful to have the ownership rights already processed and stored in explicit form, for instance for statistical purposes and for searching and browsing the preserved material. This requires that adequate mechanisms are put in place for notification about changes in the Law and on some other relevant events in the history of a work, because these could imply some change in the status of rights.

10.6.2.2 Licenses

When a right holder is willing to grant some specific permission to other people to exploit his/her creation, (s)he can do this through a licence. Licences contain the terms and conditions under which the use of the creation is permitted.

Preserving licences over time gives the future consumer a better chance to exploit an intellectual work.

10.6.2.3 Rights-Relevant Provenance Information

This information includes the main source of information from which the existing exclusive rights can be derived by applying the Law. In the simplest case it corresponds to the creation history, saying who the creators are, when and in which country the creation was made public for the first time, and the particular contribution of each creator.

However, the continuously changing legislation poses a challenging issue, namely that it is impossible to predict which information might be relevant.

Consider for example that France has, at a certain point, extended the Copyright duration with provision of five and nine years respectively for works created in the years of the First and the Second World War, and it has added further 30 years if the author "died for France". This means that the publication year is not sufficient to derive the rights, as it is necessary also to trace if an author died during active service!

This kind of information is absolutely crucial to correctly identify all the existing ownership rights, their duration and the jurisdiction under which they are valid.

10.6.2.4 Post-publication Events

This information concerns events that have an impact on ownership rights and on permissions, but which cannot be considered as part of the creation history. It includes:

- Death of a creator: the date of death influences the duration of the ownership rights; the identities of the heirs are crucial if particular authorizations need to be negotiated
- Release in Public Domain: the right holders might decide to give up all rights even before the legal expiration date
- Transfer of Rights: the right holders might transfer some or all of their exclusive rights to someone else.

If this kind of information is preserved and kept updated, it should be possible to exploit the IPR-protected material in the near and the far future.

10.6.2.5 Laws

Tracking laws is crucial for the correct preservation of rights: changes must be immediately recognized, because they might strengthen or reduce the legal restrictions for some materials.

Laws need not to be preserved themselves, but an archive should be able to recognize and to handle the changes. This is true not only for Intellectual Property Rights, but also for Right to Privacy and Protection of Minors.

10.6.3 Rights Enforcement Technologies

Technological solutions like encryption, digital signatures, watermarking, fingerprinting and machine-understandable licenses could be applied to enforced access rights. Thus, the right holders and content providers could ask the preservation institution to make the deposited material available only under some restrictions and to enforce them with proper security measures.

Each OAIS archive is free in implementing rights enforcement in whatever way it chooses. The only necessary restriction is to not introduce potential future barriers to the access by altering the raw Content Data Object, as it is stored within the Archival Information Package (AIP); alterations due to encryption and watermarking of the raw data objects should only be applied when the content is finally presented to the user and in the construction of the Dissemination Information Packages (DIPs).

Further information is available in Sects. 16.2.4 and 17.8.

10.7 Summary

Preservation Description Information as defined by OAIS covers many topics, each of which deserve treatment at greater depth. This chapter should have provided the reader with enough information to understand the relationship of the various topics and be able to judge the adequacy of various solutions.

Chapter 11
Linking Data and "Metadata": Packaging

11.1 Information Packaging Overview

OAIS describes packaging at a high level, as outlined in Sect. 6.3.4, where it is stressed that the package is a logical structure, i.e. does not have to be a single file. Despite stressing the logical structure, it can be useful to package digital objects – let's say files – together in a single file, for example a ZIP [142] file. However if one simply did that then there would be no indication of the relationship between the files, so there must be some mechanism for specifying the relationship. In any practical system one needs to encode the links somehow.

If it is not practical to put everything into a single file then an alternative would be to point to one or more of the digital objects using some kind of identifier system. As in the single file case, one would need to specify the relationships somehow.

There are many ways of implementing this kind of packaging and each has its own mechanism for specifying such relationships. Regarding the package as a digital object, another way of thinking about this is that one needs the appropriate Representation Information in order to use the package – however it seems useful to have some special terminology in this case.

One can imagine that these mechanisms for specifying the relationships between the components of the package could include:

- Naming conventions for the components
- Reliance on specific software to extract the components
- Indirection, for example by means of an XML schema which provides the semantics to distinguish different components. Of course the schema would need its own Representation Information, and in particular the semantics associated with the element names.
- General relationship techniques such as RDF – again there would need to be additional Representation Information meaning of the tags would have to be specified separately.

There are a number of techniques which have been proposed including

IMS content packaging [143], SOAP [144], METS [145] and XFDU [146].

D. Giaretta, *Advanced Digital Preservation*, DOI 10.1007/978-3-642-16809-3_11,

Of these only XFDU has close connections to OAIS and in particular full support for all types of Representation Information. Therefore we use XFDU in our examples, but this should not be taken to mean this is the only way.

OAIS describes several package variants, but only the Archival Information Package (AIP) has mandatory contents and we look in detail at the AIP next.

11.2 Archival Information Packaging

The AIP is a critical element in OAIS. There is a distinction which is made between an Archival Information Unit (AIU) and an Archival Information Collection (AIC), both of which are special types of AIPs (Fig. 11.1).

There is an analogy here with what were termed in Sect. 4.1 Simple Objects and Composite Objects.

OAIS defines:

- **Archival Information Collection (AIC):** ***An Archival Information Package whose Content Information is an aggregation of other Archival Information Packages.***
- **Archival Information Unit (AIU):** ***An Archival Information Package where the archive chooses not to break down the Content Information into other Archival Information Packages. An AIU can consist of multiple digital objects (e.g., multiple files).***

This shows that an AIC is a Composite Object, and the AIU could in some ways be described as a Simple Object – although clearly it has components.

For further details of the useful terminology associated with AICs the reader should consult OAIS.

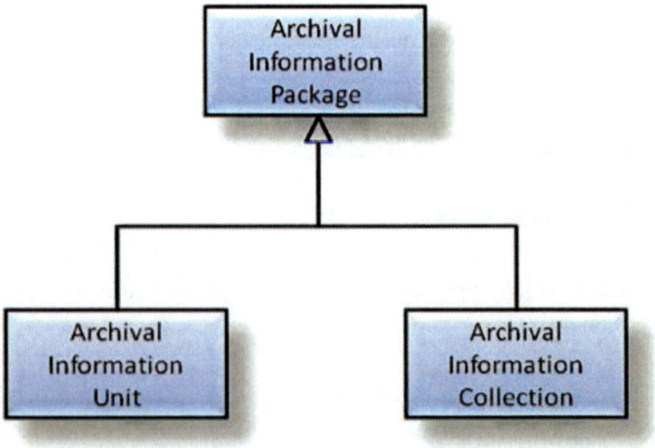

Fig. 11.1 Specialisations of AIP

11.3 XFDU

Much of the packaging described in Part II uses the XFDU and, although this is not the only possible packaging technique, so it is convenient to provide a little more detail here.

XFDU has been standardized and well-documented by CCSDS with the idea of supporting OAIS terminology from its conception. One key feature is the flexibility it allows in terms of which things are pointed to and which are physically inside the XFDU encoding.

It has been used in an operational environment by The European Space Agency (ESA) in the form of the Standard Archive Format for Europe (SAFE) [147], a packaging format fully-compatible with XFDU. Developing XFDU solutions can be facilitated through existing open-source Java toolkits and APIs, which have been created by ESA and NASA, allowing the construction, editing and analysis of standardized XFDU Information Packages.

The Manifest document shown in Fig. 11.2 contains the information about the relationships between the information that is packaged together. XFDU uses an XML schema to describe this manifest file which is split into five sections. The packageHeader documents information about the package itself, its versioning, its position in a sequence or volume, and PDI about it existence.

The dataObjectSection and metadataSection are used to relate the digital information to be preserved to its RepInfo or PDI, respectively. Both data objects and "metadata" objects can be either connected by reference or encoded within the manifest itself (Fig. 11.3). Each object is assigned an XML identifier, which is used to link objects between the two sections. Objects in both sections can be given built-in classifications or associated with user-defined classification schemes.

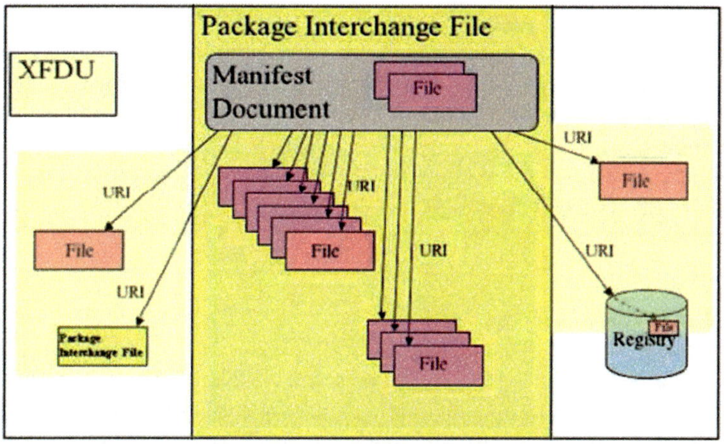

Fig. 11.2 Conceptual view of an XFDU

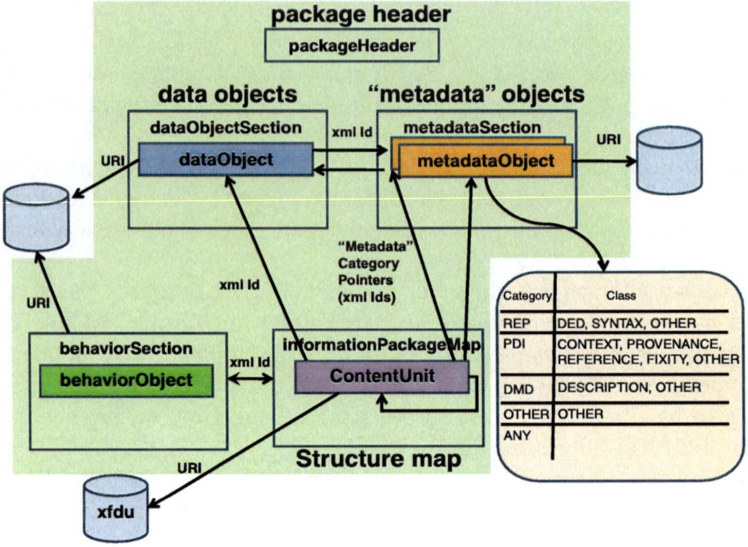

Fig. 11.3 XFDU manifest logical view

The informationPackageMap records information about content units, which are used to associate data in the dataObjectSection to "metadata" in the metadataSection. The association is done via XML identifiers, and maps to the OAIS concept of Content Information Object, the combination of a digital object and its RepInfo.

A diagram of the full XML schema of the XFDU is shown in Fig. 11.4. This schema keeps AIPs consistent and standard while allowing a flexible and adaptable implementation. By extending the XFDU schema to provide domain specific AIPs it is possible to allow the inclusion of additional information while maintaining the standardization and consistency that are two of the main advantages of using XFDU for preservation. ESA has demonstrated this by extending the XFDU schema into SAFE, which includes spacecraft mission-specific information embedded in the XFDU manifest.

A toolkit for creating and reading XFDUs is available from the XFDU web site [148] and GAEL XFDU web site [149].

11.3.1 XFDU and TDO

Because both embody packaging techniques, the XFDU structure does implement many, perhaps all, of the concepts of the Trustworthy Digital Object (TDO) [8]. However the latter seems to rely on emulation (see Sect. 7.9) and in particular the UVC (see Sect. 7.9.4.3) as its ultimate preservation technique.

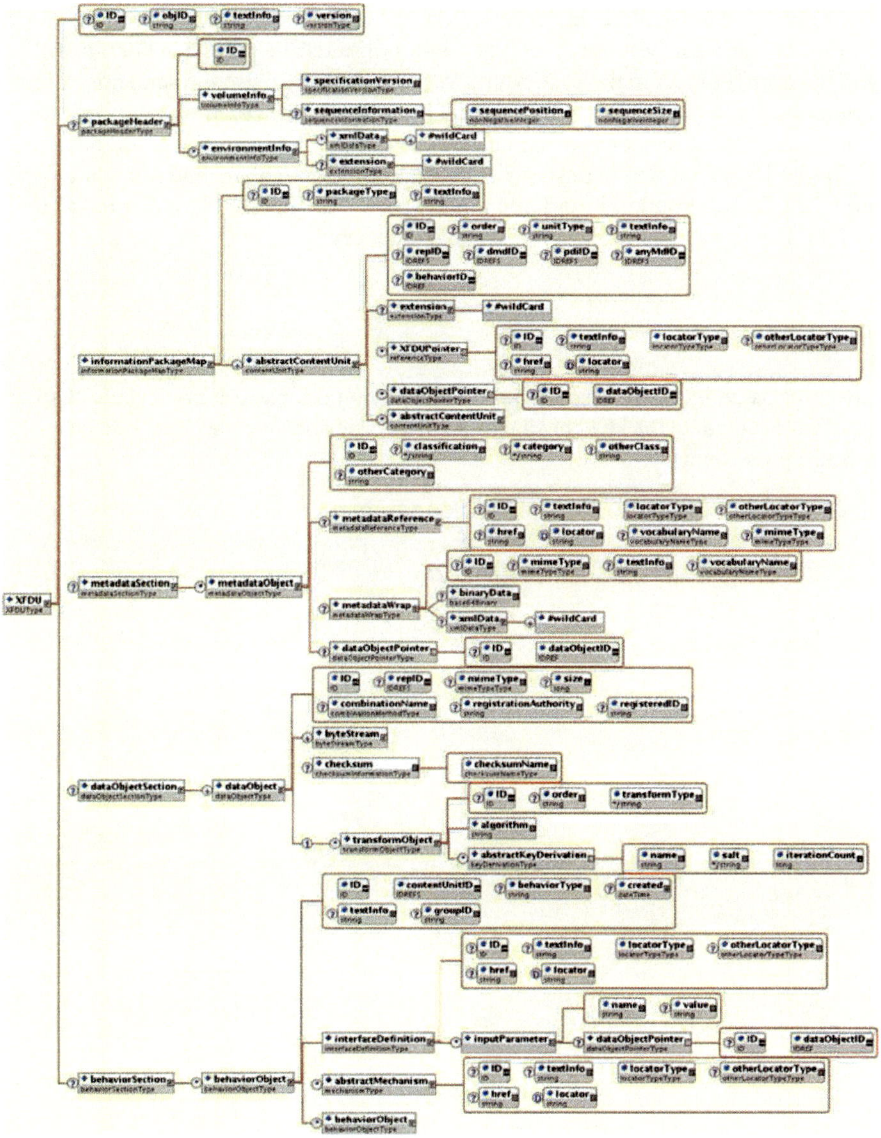

Fig. 11.4 Full XFDU schema diagram

Emulation has its place in preservation but as we point out in Sect. 7.9, this is limiting not least because in essence one is limited to what has been possible with the digital object in the past. Moreover especially because the semantics of the digital object are not made explicit in the TDO, even if one could link the emulation to modern applications, one would be limited with what new things could be done.

The XFDU is not tied in any way to emulation, although an emulator can be one part of the Representation Information in the package. Therefore it is fair to say that the XFDU is a superset of the TDO technical concept.

11.4 Summary

Packaging is an important requirement with many possible solutions. This chapter has tried to elucidate the key considerations and describe in some detail one possible packaging mechanism.

Chapter 12
Basic Preservation Strategies

Strategy without tactics is the slowest route to victory. Tactics without strategy is the noise before defeat.

(Sun Tzu)

There are a number of basic preservation strategies upon which one can build more complex strategies. These are the ones which are described explicitly or implicitly by OAIS, based around ensuring that the digital object will be usable and understandable to the Designated Community. Of course one also has to maintain the trail of information to support evidence of authenticity *and other PDI.*

Many publications on digital preservation say that the available strategies may be summed up in the phrase "emulate or migrate". We show here that this is inadequate.

OAIS discusses some important aspects of information preservation as follows.

The fast-changing nature of the computer industry and the ephemeral nature of electronic data storage media are at odds with the key purpose of an OAIS: to preserve information over a long period of time. No matter how well an OAIS maintains its current holdings, it will eventually need to migrate much of its holdings to different media (which may or may not involve changing the bit sequences) and/or to a different hardware or software environment to keep them accessible. Today's digital data storage media can typically be kept at most a few decades before the probability of irreversible loss of data becomes too high to ignore. Further, the rapid pace of technology evolution makes many systems much less cost-effective after only a few years. In addition to the technology changes there will be changes to the Knowledge Base of the Designated Community which will affect the Representation Information needed.

There are a number of fundamental approaches to information preservation. In the first the Content Data Object remains in its original form, and access and use is achieved by providing adequate descriptions of the digital encoding with Structure and Semantic Representation Information; in some cases the original access and use mechanisms are adequate, in which case software emulation (using Other Representation Information) may be useful, although this tends to limit the ways

D. Giaretta, *Advanced Digital Preservation*, DOI 10.1007/978-3-642-16809-3_12,

in which the Content Data Object may be used. One advantage of leaving the bit sequences unchanged is that evidence of Authenticity is more easily sustained.

Alternatively the object may be changed into one that can be processed with contemporary access and use mechanisms. This is referred to in OAIS as a Transformation, a type of Migration, which is discussed below. There are implications for Authenticity which are discussed in Chap. 13, particularly Sect. 13.6.2.

The following matrix shows the various combinations of these alternatives.

	Content data object unchanged	Content data object changed
Access service unchanged	If using the original software executable: emulation If using the original source code: rebuild executable	Re-implement access service
Access service changed	Implement new access services based on the representation information describing original content data object	Implement new access services based on the representation describing the new content data object

12.1 Description – Adding Representation Information

As should be clear from the discussion in earlier chapters it is necessary to maintain the Representation Network so that it is adequate for a member of the Designated Community to continue to understand and use the digital object. However things change over time and so the Representation Network must be altered appropriately.

In order to do this the techniques extensively discussed in Chap. 8 to identify any potential gaps in the Representation Network can be used. Practical ways of doing this are described in detail in Chap. 16 and illustrated in Part II.

This approach allows the greatest flexibility because one has the ability to discover entirely new ways of looking at the digital objects, however whilst it can be the most rewarding, it can also be the most difficult.

12.2 Maintaining Access

An alternative to using description is to maintain the "current" ways of accessing the digital object, and OAIS discusses several ways of doing this. One can think of this in terms of interfaces, either programmatic or user interfaces. In addition hardware emulation can be viewed as doing essentially the same thing but this deserves the more extensive discussion given in Sect. 7.9, although another type of emulation is described below.

12.2.1 Access and Use Services

OAIS discusses maintaining the Dissemination API in order to continue to support applications which the Designated Community uses to access and use the digital object. This is closely related to the ideas of virtualisation discussed in Sect. 7.8.

The virtualisation approach has the advantage that it facilitates the ability of the Designated Community to be able to use their favourite applications to access and use the digital object. This can be consistent with maintaining the Dissemination API by means of appropriate software wrappers. A number of options are discussed in some detail in Chap. 9.

12.2.2 Access Software Look and Feel

This option focuses on the assumption that the Designated Community wishes to maintain the original "look and feel" of the Content Information of a set of AIUs as presented by a specified application or set of applications. Discussion of hardware emulation, which provides the ultimate maintenance of look and feel is provided in Sect. 7.9. Conceptually, the OAIS provides (i.e. makes available/points to) a software environment that allows the Consumer to view the AIUs Content Information through the application's transformation and presentation capabilities. For example, there may be a desire to use a particular application that extracts data from an ISO 9660 CD-ROM and presents it as a multi-spectral image. This application runs under a particular operating system, requires a set of control information and use of a CD-ROM reading device, and presents the information to driver software for a particular display device. In some cases this application may be so pervasive that all members of the Designated Community have access to the environment and the OAIS merely designates the Content Data Object to be the bit string used by the application. Alternatively, an OAIS may supply (as Representation Information) such an environment, including the Access Software application, when the environment is less readily available. However, as the OAIS and/or the Designated Community moves to new computing environments, at some point the application will cease to function or will function incorrectly. At such a point Transformation will become an attractive option.

12.2.2.1 Emulation of Look and Feel the Hard Way

It is worth discussing in a little more detail another way of maintaining look and feel when, for example the compiled version of the application or libraries it depends upon, are not available, nor is the source code. The term emulation may be applied to this technique since emulation may be defined as "*the ability of a computer program or electronic device to imitate another program or device*" [79].

The OAIS may, despite the drawbacks, consider emulation for the access application in the following way. If the application provides a well-known set of operations and a well-defined API for access, the API could be adequately documented and tested to attempt an emulation of that application. However, if the consumer interface is primarily one of display or other devices which affect human senses (e.g., sound), this reverse engineering becomes nearly impossible, because it may not be obvious when the application runs but does not function correctly for all possible inputs. To guarantee the discovery of all such situations, it would be necessary to record the Access Software's correctly functioning output, and preserve this alongside the emulation. The behaviour would need to be checked with the results obtained after from the emulation. This may be quite difficult if the application has many different modes of operation. Further, if the application's output is primarily sent to a display device, recording this stream does not guarantee that the display looks the same in the new environment and therefore the combination of application and environment may no longer be giving completely correct information to the Consumer.

Maintaining a consistent look and feel may require, as a starting point, capturing that look and feel with a separate recording to use as validation information. In general, it may be difficult if not impossible to formally describe the look and feel. However, a number of Transformational Information Properties may essentially define criteria against which preservation may be tested; validation against these Information Properties would be a necessary, although not always sufficient, condition for testing the adequacy of the preservation activity.

12.3 Migration/Transformation

At some point it may be decided that maintaining the original medium or the Representation Network for a digital object is not practical for cost reasons, or does not meet requirements for some other reason. Therefore the digitally encoded information must be encoded in some other way, either the same bit sequences on new media or else changed bit sequences.

It is possible to identify four primary digital Migration types. The primary types, ordered by increasing risk of information loss, are:

1. Operations which do not change the bit sequences
   - **Refreshment***: A Digital Migration where a media instance, holding one or more AIPs or parts of AIPs, is replaced by a media instance of the same type by copying the bits on the medium used to hold AIPs and to manage and access the medium. As a result, the existing Archival Storage mapping infrastructure, without alteration, is able to continue to locate and access the AIP.*
     - As discussed at the start of the book many processes go on to translate from magnetic domains (for a magnetic disk) to bits. This bit copy may not be a physical copy.
   - **Replication***: A Digital Migration where there is no change to the Packaging Information, the Content Information and the PDI. The bits used to convey these information objects are preserved in the transfer to the same or new*

media-type instance. Refreshment is also a Replication, but Replication may require changes to the Archival Storage mapping infrastructure.

2. Operations which change the bit sequences
   - **Repackaging:** ***A Digital Migration where there is some change in the bits of the Packaging Information.***
   - **Transformation:** ***A Digital Migration where there is some change in the Content Information or PDI bits while attempting to preserve the full information content.*** This deserves some extended discussion, which follows.

12.3.1 Transformation

Transformation implies a change in the bit sequence of either the Content Information or the PDI.

In many discussions of digital preservation the term Migration is used when in fact what is meant is specifically Transformation because the aim in those discussions is to change the digital encoding of the information.

Given a certain piece of information there could be many different ways of encoding it digitally. For example an image could be encoded as a TIFF file or a JPEG; a document could be held as Word or PDF; a table containing scientific data could be held as a FITS table or as a CSV (comma-separated values) file. Each of these alternatives would need it their own, different, Representation Network.

However some Transformations make more sense than others. This will commonly be regarded as changing from one data format to another, but one must also think about the associated *semantics*. Some formats have little or no room for the semantics. Another consideration is the number and types of applications commonly associated with the various formats.

For example an image could be regarded as a table where each of the cells contains a number. However it would not make good sense to encode the image as a CSV file because of the loss of semantics involved. Moreover the applications (e.g. spreadsheet programmes) normally used to deal with a CVS file do not normally display the data as one would expect an image to be displayed.

With regard to the semantics, one can supplement the capabilities of a particular format with something else e.g. the CSV file could have an associated text file to supply the missing semantic information, such as the meanings of the columns, which would otherwise be missing. In this case one would need the Representation Information for (1) the CSV file (2) the text file and (3) the relationship between them. While this is possible, the more attractive option would be to choose a new format which can itself handle the required semantics, with available applications that supply the required functionality, at least as well as the original format. Therefore given a piece of digitally encoded information that one needs to preserve, the transformation which one should reasonably apply is not arbitrary.

There are deep reasons for making a careful choice and documenting that choice appropriately. This is discussed in detail in Sect. 13.6.

However there are a number of useful points which should be made here. For example one can think of the ideal Transformation in which the new digital object has the same information as the original. If this is the case then it should be possible to confirm this by means of another Transformation back to the original bit sequence. If one can find this pair of Transformations then one can define (following the revised version of OAIS):

> **Reversible Transformation***: A Transformation in which the new representation defines a set (or a subset) of resulting entities that are equivalent to the resulting entities defined by the original representation. This means that there is a one-to-one mapping back to the original representation and its set of base entities*.

On the other hand if one looks at the other transformations mentioned above, for example from FITS to CSV, then one would, without additional information, e.g. the supplementary text file mentioned above, lose information and therefore not be able to make the reverse transformation.

It is therefore reasonable to define:

> **Non-Reversible Transformation***: A Transformation which cannot be guaranteed to be a Reversible Transformation*.

An important point to note is that the definition of *non-reversible* is drawn as broadly as possible. For example one does not need to have to prove there is no backward transformation, only that one cannot *guarantee* that such a transformation can be constructed.

We will come back to these definitions in Chap. 13 where they play an important role in considerations of Authenticity.

12.4 Summary

This chapter has raced through a number of the basic preservation strategies and techniques; it should be clear that each technique has its own strengths and weaknesses, and one must be careful to recognise these. The reader must be careful not to be misled by the amount of material on emulation here; this was a useful location for this material. Other preservation techniques are discussed in much more detail throughout this book. Other chapters are devoted to descriptive Representation Information and also to Transformations.

In Part II we provide examples of many of these techniques with evidence to support their efficacy when applied appropriately.

Chapter 13
Authenticity

authenticity (plural authenticities)

1. *The quality of being genuine or not corrupted from the original.*
   I hereby certify that this is an authentic copy.
2. *Truthfulness of origins, attributions, commitments, sincerity, and intentions.*
   The painting was not authentic after all; it was just a copy.
3. *(obsolete) The quality of being authentic (of established authority).*
   (Wiktionary definition *from* http://en.wiktionary.org/wiki/authenticity *downloaded 14 Aug 2010)*

Authenticity is a fundamental issue for the long-term preservation of digital objects: the relevance of authenticity as a preliminary and central requirement has been investigated by many international projects. Some focused on long-term preservation of authentic digital records in the e-government environment, and in scientific and cultural domains.

Much has been written about Authenticity. However in order to create tools which can be relied upon and which are practical we must achieve the following:

- *build on the excellent work which has already been carried out*
  - *previous work has for the most part focussed on what we have referred to as Rendered Digital Objects therefore we must ensure that we can deal with the variety of other types of objects as discussed in Chap. 4*
- *convert these rather abstract ideas into something which is widely applicable but also practical and implementable*
- *show some practical examples, from real archives, using a practical tool.*

Therefore this chapter first discusses the previous work on Authenticity, including the definitions from OAIS, and introduces a number of basic concepts. From these concepts we build up a conceptual model. The concept of Significant

D. Giaretta, *Advanced Digital Preservation*, DOI 10.1007/978-3-642-16809-3_13,

Properties has been much discussed, especially with respect to Rendered Digital Objects. We show how this can be extended to Non-rendered Digital Objects, and how it fits into the work on Authenticity. Finally we apply these concepts and models to a number of digital objects from real archives, using a tool based on the conceptual model.

13.1 Background to Authenticity

Authenticity is a key concept in digital preservation, and some would argue that is it the pre-eminent concept, in that unless one can show that the data object is, in some provable sense, what was originally deposited, then one cannot prove that digital preservation has been successful.

On the other hand OAIS defines preservation in terms of understandability and usability as well as authenticity; it therefore provides a view in which Representation Information and Authenticity are equal partners.

It is worth noting the distinction made by InterPARES [150], although specifically referring to *records*, between verification and maintenance of authenticity. Some would argue that everything is a *record* but this point will not be discussed here.

Verification of authenticity is "the act or process of establishing a correspondence between known facts about the record and the various contexts in which it has been created and maintained, and the proposed fact of the record's authenticity" [151].

Maintenance of authenticity is related to records which "have been presumed or verified authentic in the appraisal process, and have been transferred from the creator to the preserver".

This book focuses on both the maintenance of authenticity i.e. providing a continuing chain of evidence about the custodianship and treatment of the information as well as the verification of authenticity in so far as a Consumer must be able to make that judgement.

13.1.1 Links to Previous Literature

A separate position paper [24] reviews the InterPARES authenticity work in more detail; the main conclusions from that paper are included in this book. However it is worth mentioning two concepts which are regarded in the literature as crucial, namely integrity and identity of digital resources; authenticity is regarded as being established by assessing the integrity and the identity of the resource.

The integrity of a resource refers to its wholeness. A resource has integrity when it is complete and uncorrupted in all its essential respects. These essential respects will be discussed in much greater detail in the Sect. 13.6.

The identity of a resource, from this point of view, has a very wide meaning, beyond its unique designation and/or identification. Identity refers to the whole of the characteristics of a resource that uniquely identify it and distinguish it from any other resource. In addition to its internal conceptual structure, it refers to its general context (e.g., legal, technological). From this point of view, identity is strongly related to PDI: Context, Provenance, Fixity, Reference and Access Rights Information, as defined in OAIS, help to understand the environment of a resource.

This information has to be gathered, maintained, and interpreted together – as far as possible – as a set of relationships defining the resource itself: a resource is not an isolated entity with defined borders and autonomous life, it is not just a single object; a resource is an object in the context, it is both the object itself and the relationships that provide complete meaning to it. These relationships change over time, so we need not only to understand them and make them explicit but also to document them to have a complete history of the resource: we cannot omit it without also losing a bit of the identity of the resource, with consequences on its authenticity.

13.2 OAIS Definition of Authenticity

It must be admitted that in the original version of OAIS authenticity was not dealt with very well; however the OAIS update has significantly improved the situation and we use the definitions from that update.

OAIS defines **Authenticity** as:

the degree to which a person (or system) may regard an object as what it is purported to be. The degree of Authenticity is judged on the basis of evidence.

We have the associated definition:

Provenance Information is the information that documents the history of the Content Information. This information tells the origin or source of the Content Information, any changes that may have taken place since it was originated, and who has had custody of it since it was originated. The archive is responsible

for creating and preserving Provenance Information from the point of Ingest, however earlier Provenance Information should be provided by the Producer. Provenance Information adds to the evidence to support Authenticity.

The concept of authenticity as defined by OAIS requires a detailed analysis on the basis of the rich literature in the sector and of the main outputs of research projects like InterPARES, as mentioned in the CASPAR position paper [24].

There are some basic assumptions to be considered before entering into a detailed analysis. First of all, authenticity cannot be evaluated by means of a boolean flag telling us whether a document is authentic or not. In other words there are degrees of confidence about the authenticity of the digital resources: certainty about authenticity is a goal, but one which is unlikely to be fully met.

In the case of physical objects such as a parchment, one can look at physical composition, confirm the age with carbon dating, and compare to similar documents. The identity and integrity concepts can fairly obviously be applied to such physical objects which cannot be readily copied of changed without leaving some trace. What is so different with digital objects? What process of evaluation and what sort of tools must be developed?

One fundamental issue arises from the basic points about why digital objects are different, namely that one cannot really ensure the ability to maintain the original bits or even to provide methods for easily evaluating whether they are the original. At the very least one has to copy the bits from one medium to another. How can we be sure that the copy was done correctly? Here we want to guard against both accidental changes as well as changes made on purpose, perhaps for nefarious purposes.

Other issues arise from the basic preservation strategies described in Chap. 12. Adding Representation Information, maintaining access and emulation do not require any changes to the bit sequences of the digital object, nor do the types of migration described as refreshment of replication. Repackaging requires changes in the packaging but not of the digital object of interest. In all these cases we can use, for example, digests as the evidence about the lack of change in the bit sequences.

Only the Transformation preservation technique (Sect. 12.3.1) implies a change in the digital object and therefore the use of digests will not apply. As an example of Transformation, consider a WordStar version of a document which may be converted into Word 2007 format in order to ensure that this (Rendered) Digital Object can continue to be rendered. Is it an authentic version (whatever that means in this context)? We will return to this a little later in Sect. 13.6.

Looking in more detail at the use of digests, one compares the digest of the original to the copy and then one can be fairly, but not completely, certain things are as they should be. It would be alright if one has access to the original and could calculate the digest oneself, but this is rarely the case. So where does the digest come from, and how can we be sure it is indeed the digest i.e. that it is what it purports to be? This sounds like a familiar question – we have come round in a circle! This is of course another example of recursion which we discussed in Sect. 3.3.

So how does this help us with the Authenticity of digital objects? It seems that the key points are that

- we need various types of evidence. The questions then become:
  - what evidence must be collected – are there procedures to follow?
  - from whom?, and
  - how are we going to be sure the evidence has not been altered?
- we need to be able to trace the evidence back to someone. The follow-on questions are then:
  - can we identify the person?
  - can we be sure that that person supplied the evidence?
  - how can we be sure that the person identified is the person claimed, and that this information has not been altered?
  - is the person trustable?
- we need to have a view on how this evidence can be evaluated

These ideas have clear links to the OAIS definitions which will be expanded below.

As was mentioned, we focus on the maintenance of (evidence about) authenticity. Defining and assessing authenticity in the repository (or more formally – in the custodial environment) – on which we focus here – are complex tasks and imply a number of theoretical and operational/technical activities. These include a clear definition of roles involved, coherent development of recommendations and policies for building trusted repositories, and precise identification of each component of the custodial function.

Thus it is crucial to define the key conceptual elements that provide the foundation for such a complex framework. Specifically we need to define how, and on what basis authenticity has to be managed in the digital preservation processes in order to ensure the trustworthiness of digital objects. In order to do this we need a more formal model about authenticity.

The authenticity of digital resources is threatened whenever they are exchanged between users, systems or applications, or any time technological obsolescence requires an updating or replacing of the hardware or software used to store, process, or communicate them. Therefore, the preserver's inference of the authenticity of digital resources must be supported by evidence provided in association with the resources through its documentation (recursion again!), by tracing the history of its various migration and treatments, which have occurred over time. Evidence is also needed to prove that the digital resources have been maintained using technologies and administrative procedures that either guarantee their continuing identity and integrity or at least minimize risks of change from the time the resources were first set aside to the point at which they are subsequently accessed.

Let's go back a step and see what we can learn from a more familiar case. How do you prove that you are who you say you are? For people with whom you grew up there is probably no problem – they have seen you every day from a small baby to a grown up and know you are the same person (ignoring any philosophical digressions) despite all the changes that have happened to you physically. To prove who you are when you enter a new country you would present your passport – why is that accepted? It is a physical object (a little booklet) that can be examined and checked against some known standard document. But why is that accepted? The assumption is that it is backed by your government, but how does the government which issued it know that the person represented there is in fact you? In the UK, and perhaps elsewhere, one has to fill in a form and provide a photograph, both of which are signed by someone known, and probably trusted, in the community such as a doctor or local politician. How does the state know that that person is indeed who he/she is indeed the person who claims to be that doctor or local politician? There may be other information that the government has to cross check, but it could just rely on going back to the community and check – because they are known in the community in some way.

So how does this help us with the Authenticity of digital objects? It seems that a key point is that we need to be able to trace back to someone who is, in some way, trusted. Also there is some type of evidence collected. The questions then become: what evidence must be collected, from whom, and how are we going to be sure the evidence itself is true? These ideas will be expanded below.

13.3 Elements of the Authenticity Conceptual Model

There are technical parts of the evidence where there is a need for guidance as to what needs to be captured, as well as some non-technical aspects of evidence such as who is trustworthy. What follows is a formalism which helps to capture such evidence in such a way that makes it easier to make judgements about Authenticity. We do this by defining, at a high level, building blocks we call Authenticity Steps, which are combined into Authenticity Protocols. These are described next.

13.3.1 Authenticity Protocol (AP)

The protection of authenticity and its assessment is a process. In order to manage this process, we need to define the procedures to be followed to assess the authenticity of specific type of objects.

We call one of these procedures an Authenticity Protocol (abbreviated as AP). An AP is a set of interrelated steps, each of one we will refer to as an Authenticity Step (abbreviated as AS). An AP is applied to an Object Type, i.e. to a class of objects with uniform features for the application of an AP. Any AP may be recursively used in the design of other APs, as expressed in a general workflow relation. Every AS models a part of an AP that can be executed independently, and constitutes a significant phase of the AP from the authenticity assessment point of view. The relationships amongst the steps of an AP establish the order in which the steps must be executed in the context of an execution of the protocol. To model these relationships we can use any workflow model. We do not enter into the details of this modelling here, and simply denote as Workflow the set of required relationships. The model introduced so far can be expressed in UML notation as shown in Fig. 13.1.

One would expect these protocols to be written by appropriate experts or curators. Moreover there may be several possible APs associated with any particular

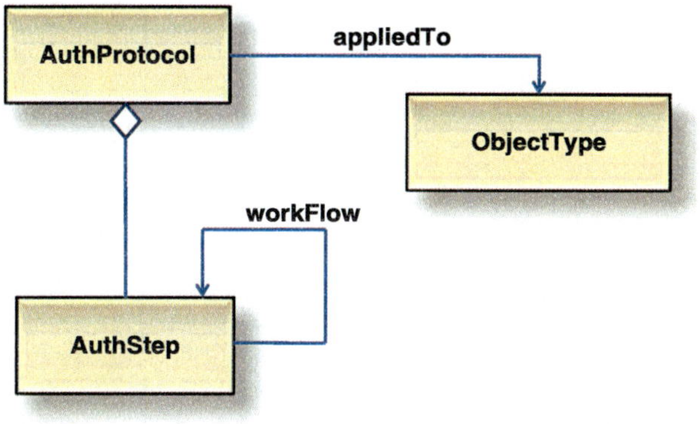

Fig. 13.1 Authenticity protocol applied to object types

object type. It may be best to regard APs as advice/guidance, unless of course there are legal requirements or community standards.

13.3.2 Authenticity Step (AS)

An AS is performed by an Actor, which can act either in an automatic (hardware, software) or in a manual (person, organization) way (Fig. 13.2):

There can be several types of ASs. Following OAIS, we distinguish ASs based on the kind of Preservation Description Information required to carry out the AS.

Consequently, we have five types of steps (Fig. 13.3):

- Reference Step
- Provenance Step
- Fixity Step
- Context Step
- Access Rights Step

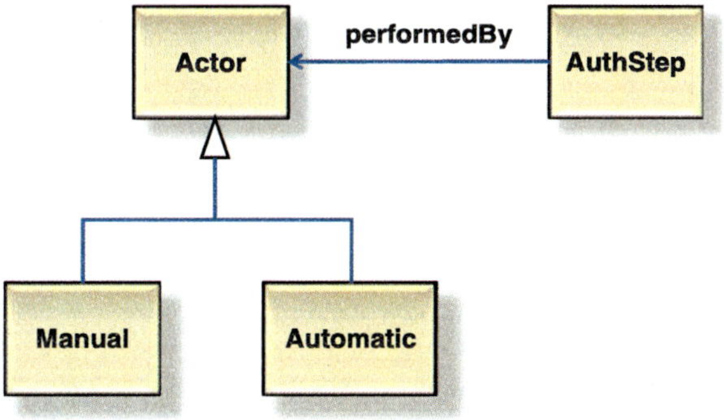

Fig. 13.2 Authenticity step performed by actor

Fig. 13.3 Types of authenticity step

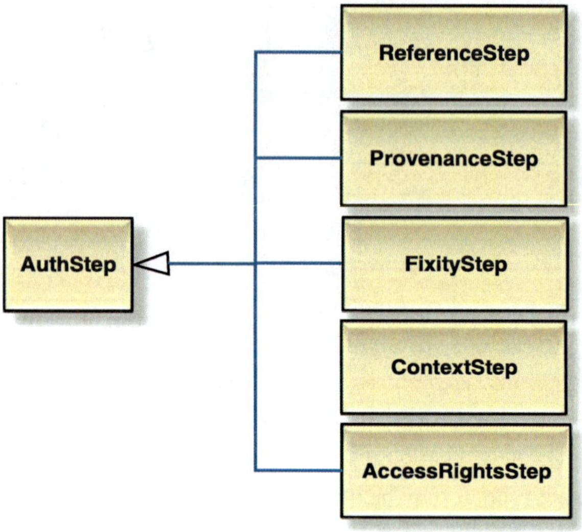

Since an AS involves a decision followed by an action, it is expected that it contains at least information about:

- the criteria that must be satisfied in taking the decision
- good practices or methodologies that must be followed
- the actors who are entitled to take the decision.

Detailed examples are given in Sect. 13.7.6.

Moreover an AS is defined (possibly) following Recommendations and is disseminated as established by a Dissemination Policy (Fig. 13.4):

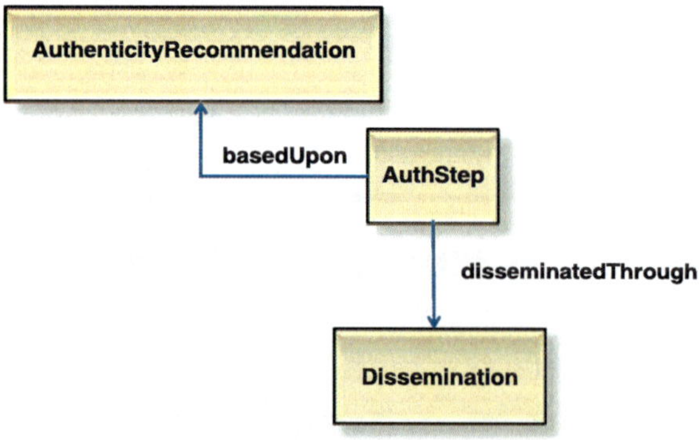

Fig. 13.4 Authenticity step

All the above may be regarded as plans which guide a curator in collecting appropriate evidence. The next group of diagrams show what should happen when the evidence is collected and made available so that people can evaluate it.

13.3.3 Authenticity Protocol Execution (APE)

APs are executed by an actor on objects of the type or types for which they were designed, in the context of Authenticity Execution Sessions. The execution of an AP is modelled as an Authenticity Protocol Execution (APE for short). An APE is related to an AP via the *IsExecutionOf* association and consists of a number of execution steps (Authenticity Step Executions, ASEs for short). Every ASE, in turn, is related to the AS via an association analogous to the *IsExecutionOf* association, and contains the information about the execution, including:

- the actor who carried out the execution
- the information which was used
- the time, place, and context of execution
- possibly the outcome of the execution.

Not every step necessarily implies a decision (in other words the decision is null), some steps simply imply collecting information related to a specific aspect of the object, e.g. title, extent, dates, and we are only interested into declaring the step has been done, without any form of evaluation. From a modelling point of view, we could classify steps as decisional (and the outcome is the decision) and non-decisional ones (having a different kind of outcome as an attribute, e.g. "step done" or "step not completed for such and such reason").

Different types of ASEs have different structures and the outcomes of the executions must be documented to gather information related to specific aspects of the object, e.g. title, extent, dates and transformations. An Authenticity Protocol Report simply documents that the step has been done and collects all the values associated with the data elements analysed in a specific ASE.

The Authenticity Protocol Report provides a complete set of information upon which an entitled actor (human or application) can build a judgment regarding the authenticity of the resource, bearing in mind issues of both its identity and integrity.

13.3.4 Authenticity Step Execution (ASE) and Authenticity Protocol History

Different types of ASEs will have different structures. Additionally, an ASE may contain a dissemination action. Moreover, we are dealing with preservation and so we also want our model to be able to cope with the evolution of both APs and their executions over time. The evolution of an AP may concern the addition, removal or modification of one of the steps making up the AP. In any case, both the old and the new step should be retained, for documentation purposes. When an AS of an AP is changed, all the executions of the AP which include an ASE related to the changed

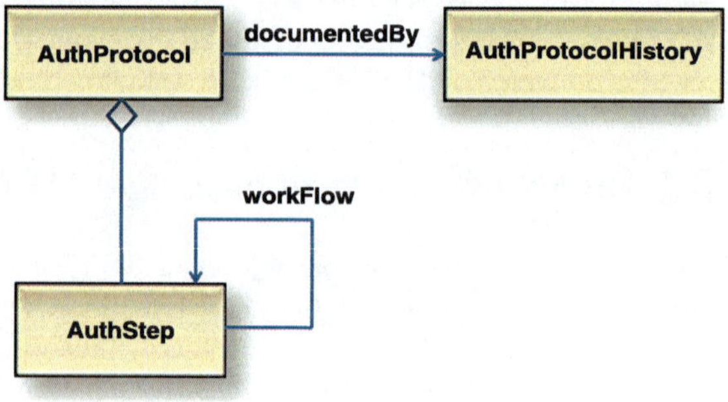

Fig. 13.5 Authenticity protocol history

step, must be revised and possibly a new execution required for the new (modified) step. In this case also, the old and the new ASEs must be retained.

Authenticity should be monitored continuously so that any time a resource is somehow changed or a relationship is modifies, an Authenticity Protocol can be activated and executed in order to verify the permanence of the resource's relevant features that guarantee its authenticity. Any event impacting on a resource should trigger the execution of an appropriate protocol. For this reason the Authenticity Protocol Execution is triggered by an Event Occurrence, i.e., the instantiation of an Event Type that identifies any act and/or fact related to a specific Authenticity Protocol.

The authenticity of a resource is strongly related to the criteria and procedures adopted to analyse and evaluate it: the evolution of the Authenticity Protocols over time should be documented – via the *Documented By* relation – in an Authenticity Protocol History (Fig. 13.5).

13.3.5 Preservation of Evidence

The evidence which is collected itself must be preserved, and evidence for its own authenticity must be collected. We will look at the use of digests of the evidence about a digital object as used by one possible tool, but in trying to use that evidence when making a judgement of the authenticity of that object, all of the considerations of preservation apply. In particular, transformation and/or virtualisation of the evidence are likely to be needed, for example when combining the evidence made over a considerable period of time using a variety of tools and techniques. This is another very clear example of the recursion which was discussed in Sect. 3.3.

13.4 Overall Authenticity Model

Putting all these ideas together the overall model is shown in Fig. 13.6.

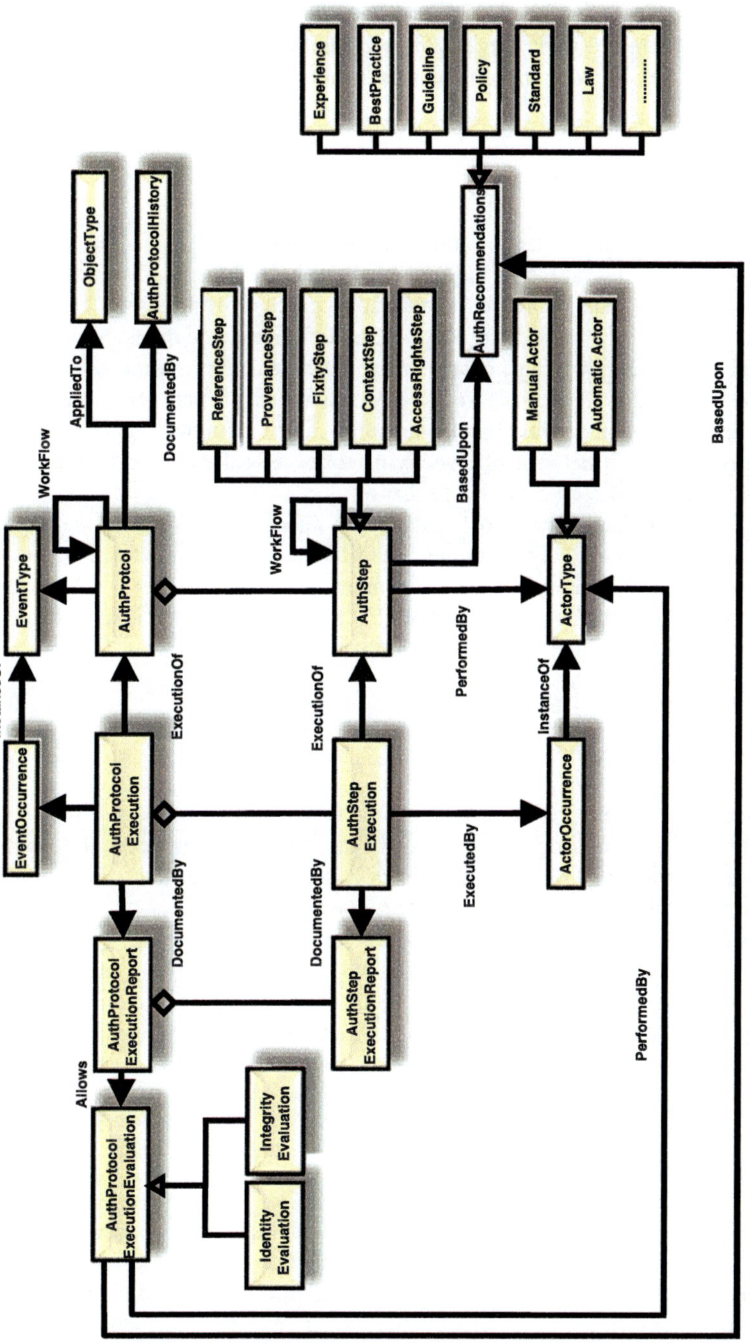

Fig. 13.6 Authenticity Model

13.5 Authenticity Evidence

As noted above there are several types of evidence namely technical evidence and non-technical evidence. We give some examples of each type next.

13.5.1 Technical Evidence

Each AS contain several possible technical points. An obvious one is that related to Fixity, for example checksums or digests, used to check that the bit sequences are unchanged. Of course each of these, regarded as a piece of information, will need it own Representation Information, for example to define how the digest has been calculated. The digest value will also have its own evidence of Authenticity since, as we noted at the start of this Chapter, if we have doubts about that value then we will not trust what any checks on digital object against the digest value will also be in doubt.

A related step could be someone verifying that a re-calculated digest confirms the previous value, and recording that fact.

A related but different piece of evidence is needed if, for some reason, the sequence has to be changed. This might arise if it is decided that the format in which a document or dataset is held is no longer supportable. A new digest will have to be calculated of course. But how do we know that the new document is an acceptable replacement for the previous one? This is discussed in Sect. 13.6.

13.5.2 Non-technical Evidence

Non-technical evidence is, for example, the reputation and trustability of the people who recorded the evidence, or the reputation of the tools which are used, for example to calculate the digests. This type of evidence is likely to be much more elusive than the technical evidence, especially in an open world. In other words if we are dealing with a limited community, for example state archives or within a scientific discipline, personal reputations are likely to be well established, at least within a limited timeframe. However we cannot make that assumption, as we must deal with potentially a broader set of custodians, and a broader set of tools being used. Thus the non-technical evidence is likely to be very difficult to collect and evaluate.

13.6 Significant Properties

Transformations are an important preservation technique but, as we have seen, mean that the techniques such as digests cannot be used. The underlying question is whether or not a particular transformed digital object can be said to have the same level of authenticity as the object which underwent the transformation. As we will see in this Section, what have been termed "significant properties" provide a solution, although the concept has been used in the literature somewhat differently.

Thus we need to review the previous literature and then explain the approach taken in this book.

13.6.1 The Role of "Significant Properties"

The notion of Significant Properties has emerged as a key concept in preservation within the library community but has not been a concept that is much used in the context of the preservation of research data that is not normally viewed as a document. A number of definitions of Significant Properties have been proposed.

The CEDARS project [152] defined Significant Properties as

those characteristics [technical, intellectual, and aesthetic] agreed by the archive or by the collection manager to be the most important features to preserve over time.

Sergeant [153] on the other hand proposed that

Significant Properties are those attributes of an object that constitute the complete (for the intended Consumer) intellectual content of that object

However the example given of Significant Properties for an e-thesis of

- the complete text, including divisions into Chapters and Sections
- the layout and style – particular fonts and spacing are essential
- Diagrams
- (perhaps web adverts are not Significant for our e-journals).

does seem more oriented to the rendering of the document in print or on screen, rather than its intended intellectual content. These could be consistent if the Designated Community were defined to have the appropriate knowledge base to understand the rendering. However there would be problems if the knowledge base of the Designated Community changes, for example if the language of the designated community changes from, say, English to Chinese. There must be underlying Representation Information that supports the expression, or value, of the significant properties listed for the e-thesis information object.

The OCLC/RLG Working Group on Preservation "Metadata" [154] proposed the definition:

Properties of the Content Data Object's rendered content which must be preserved or maintained during successive cycles of the preservation process

Hedstrom and Lee [155] defined Significant Properties as

those properties of digital objects that affect their quality, usability, rendering, and behaviour.

In that paper they have a number of links to the OAIS Reference Model, for example

> ***whether or not colour, for example, is a significant property of the given digital object or collection will depend on the extent to which colour features affect the quality and usability of the preserved object for a designated community,***

and

> ***decisions about which Significant Properties to maintain will depend on institutional priorities, anticipated use, knowledge of the designated community, the types of materials involved, and the financial and technical resources available to the repository***

Within the InSPECT project, Wilson [156] defines Significant Properties in a similar fashion as

> ***the characteristics of digital objects that must be preserved over time in order to ensure the continued accessibility, usability and meaning of the objects.***

He categorises these Significant Properties into Content, Context, Appearance, Structure, and Behaviour. Knight [90] built on Wilson's work and proposed a framework of description for Significant Properties which includes identifier, function, level of significance, optionally the designated community, and optionally notes of any property constraints.

That project applied this to a number of digital object types (structured documents, raster images, audio files, email messages). Four further studies considered significant properties of vector images [157], moving images [158], software [159], and learning objects [160]. It is notable that each of these studies took a different view on what constituted a significant property. Again, here we have notions of significant property which cover some aspects of meaning (content and behaviour), although it is not clear how these are to be supported.

Thus it can be seen that there has been no general agreement on the definition of what a significant property is, what its primary role is, or how they should be categorised, recorded and tested. Moreover it has not been clear how to apply any of the proposals to Non-Rendered digital objects (see Sect. 4.2).

13.6.1.1 Limitations of Significant Properties

Clearly the usages of Significant Properties focus on those aspects of digital objects which can be evaluated in some way and checked as to whether they have been preserved. However the meaning associated with a value of the Significant Property is nowhere defined. Thus it is assumed that the value of a Significant Property will be understood by the curator and Designated Community. Therefore it must also be the case that the Significant Properties, while useful, do not strictly contribute to understandability of the Information Object. For example a Significant Property might be that a text character must be red, however the meaning (significance) of that "redness", i.e. why is it red and what is the importance of its redness to its intended audience, is not defined. Therefore this must already be part of the intended audience's (i.e., designated community) knowledge base or be defined elsewhere within the Information Object.

OAIS, as described earlier, proposes that to ensure preservation, one must have enough Representation Information to allow the defined Designated Community to understand the information, given that Designated Community's knowledge base. This must include, for example, information used to expresses value of a Significant Property. This is consistent with the comment *"As with file formats, the Representation Information for a digital object should allow the recreation of all the significant properties of the original digital object"* from the PARADIGM project [161].

It should be noted that even those studies of Significant Properties which include Designated Community only have it as an optional item and for example [162] states *"By leaving the Designated Community value blank, the archive declares that the property is, as far as they are aware, important for all user communities"*. Thus the stress in this usage is on "importance". It leaves open the issue as to whether the value of that Significant Property is understandable to that very broad Designated Community.

Comparing the various definitions only [156] includes "meaning" in its definition, and therefore seems somewhat out of step with the other definitions; [153] includes what might be interpreted as a more ambitious phrase "*complete (for the intended Consumer) intellectual content*"; [156] *is the only one to include "accessibility*". Both [155] and [156] include "usability" in their definitions which is plausible but hard to see, for example, with "redness". The terms "appearance" and "experienced" is used in [163 while [155] includes "rendering" and "behaviour"; [154] refers to "rendered content" and, as noted above, the example in [153] makes it fairly clear that the rendering is the main concern.

With such a diversity of definitions and a seeming clash with the OAIS definition of preservation, what is the real purpose of Significant Properties? In order to explore this, we first discuss a number of important related concepts which are identified within OAIS.

13.6.2 Authenticity and Significant Properties

Given that to be able to judge authenticity requires evidence, we note that some of this evidence is technical, for example Fixity, and some of the many types of Provenance are non-technical in the sense that they tell one how trustworthy an individual is or was regarded to be. As noted above, if the bit sequences are unchanged then there are well established mechanisms for checking this although, of course, issues arise over the long term as to, for example, the security of any particular message digest algorithm.

If however the bit sequences of the digital object are changed then these mechanisms are ineffective. For example a Word file may be converted to a PDF; in that case the bit sequences will have been changed extensively. In such cases the curator presumably would have satisfied himself or herself that the object as transformed had not lost required information content and therefore was still being adequately preserved. Therefore the curator would see the new object has continuing to maintain authenticity.

This may have been done by, for example, checking that the words agreed between the Word file and the PDF file; that the rendering of the pages was reasonably consistent between the two versions; that text which had been emphasised in the Word version by highlighting or by changing colour, was also a emphasized in some appropriate way in the PDF version.

It will be recognised that for the Word to PDF conversion the curator checked and documented various properties that are often called out as Significant Properties.

Thus we argue that the function of Significant Properties, consistent with Wilson in [156], is the identification of "*those characteristics [technical, intellectual, and aesthetic] agreed by the archive or by the collection manager to be the most important features to preserve over time*".

Wilson presents a related argument in [164]. Also Rothenberg and Bikson [163] suggest, with respect to authenticity criteria: "*the intent of these criteria is to ensure that preserved records retain their original behavior, appearance, content, structure, and context, for all relevant intents and purposes*" which echoes Significant Properties.

However the important point to note is that their real importance is that Significant Properties provide some of the evidence about the Authenticity of the digital objects after Transformation (a point emphasized by Wilson), and are selected by the curator, who may or may not take the Designated Community into account, and moreover different curators may make different choices. Wilson considers the notion of Performance as a test of the authenticity of preservation with respect to significant properties. This is an important feature, which as we shall see, can be transferred into a science data context.

13.6.3 Significant Properties and Data

Scientific data has yet to be dealt with in studies of Significant Properties. However some clarification may be gained by considering another Transformation, this time of a FITS file converted to a CDF file. Again the bit sequences will have been changed extensively. In such a case it could be asked how a curator could have satisfied himself or herself that the object as transformed had not lost required information content and therefore was still being adequately preserved. If (s)he could do this then the curator would see the new object as having continued to maintain authenticity.

The FITS file might contain an image; the CDF file should therefore contain a similar image. However just comparing the two images rendered on screens would be inadequate for scientific purposes. Instead the curator would need to be satisfied, for example, that the data values of the pixel elements were identical in the two images at corresponding points; that the co-ordinates associated with each pixel in the two images were identical, for example the same latitude and longitude; that the units associated with the numerical values were the same in both images.

Science data is largely numerical or documentary. In a transformation the way in which the numbers are encoded may change, for example from an IEEE real to a scaled integer. In such a case a number in the old and the new formats should be the same to within rounding errors or predefined accuracy. Additionally co-ordinate system transformations may also require changes to the numerical values, which however should be reversible. Thus the validity of the transformation in preserving these significant data values is testable.

Alternatively the curator might simply document the fact that the trusted application, which was widely believed to maintain these numerical values, had been used in the transformation and thus implicitly those important values would automatically be the same in the two versions. In that case details of the tool would need to be available and the adequacy of its preservation of significant values can be evaluated. Thus in these two cases, we can identify how the Performance of the transformed format can be evaluated to test the Authenticity of preservation.

By analogy one can see that (some) Significant Properties of the data in this case are the pixel data values, units and the co-ordinate values. However of course this would not provide enough information to use the image. For example - what frequencies of light were collected? what was the instrument response? when was the data collected? All these, and more, would be needed to understand and use that data and, unless very specific (restricted) definitions of the Designated Community were used, which included this knowledge, all would therefore be required to be described in appropriate Representation Information.

13.6.4 Significant Properties and Representation Information

Rendered objects such as JPEG images or audio files tend to be accompanied only by structural information; in the OAIS terms this is equivalent to stating that the knowledge base of the designated community includes whatever is needed to interpret the contents of the JPEG image or audio file; as this can be anything, the Designated Community is not explicitly defined. This is analogous to normal library practice where the onus is on the reader to understand the printed document.

Scientific Data on the other hand tend to be numerical; even in the simplest case, where the numbers are encoded in a document as text, although it may be acceptable to assume that for an implicit Designated Community with a general knowledge of standard Arabic numerals in decimal notation, they will be able to understand that the sequence of characters "1" "2" means twelve. However it is not reasonable to assume that the implicit Designated Community will understand what the twelve signifies, for example 12°C or 12 m or 12 apples (or even eighteen in hexadecimal). In order to fill in this missing information some Semantic Representation Information must be provided.

The normal library practice of ignoring, by default, Semantic Representation Information, has allowed Significant Properties, as usually considered without attention to meaning of their values, to appear to play a more general role in preservation, to the detriment of the full use of the Representation Information concept. It is only when looking at a broader class of digital objects, including scientific data and software, and a broader definition of preservation, that their true role may be seen.

For any Significant Property some aspect of the information object has been encoded in a way which is described by Representation Information (often structural). However to be useful to the designated community the meaning associated with this property's value must also be available in their knowledge base. If the knowledge base changes then appropriate additions should be made in the information object's Representation Information to again ensure understandability by the designated community.

On the other hand the Representation Information of an information object by itself does not provide much direct guidance as to what Transformation to apply. The transformation will usually alter the digital object and certainly new Representation Information must be provided.

Clearly one could check that any new digital structure provided the capabilities needed to support the semantics of the information object. However Significant Properties provide a much simpler, albeit incomplete, way of choosing an appropriate transformation, consistent with their use in a number of testbeds [165]. In addition Significant Properties do provide hints on how the Designated Community has been defined (implicitly or explicitly) and the types of Representation Information which must be present. In these ways the use of Significant Properties could supplement the role of Representation Information.

13.6.4.1 Relationship to OAIS Concepts

In the updated version of OAIS the term Significant Properties is not explicitly defined because it was felt that this would simply add to the already extensive and inconsistent list of definitions for this term. Instead a number of inter-linked definitions are provided, which are introduced here with some explanatory text.

The Significant Properties concept, however loosely defined, leads one to think that there are "Insignificant Properties" i.e. properties which can be ignored from the preservation point of view. Therefore OAIS introduced the concept of an Information Property and its associated Information Property Description:

Information Property: ***That part of the Content Informationas described by the Information Property Description. The detailed expression, or value, of that part of the information content is conveyed by the appropriate parts of the Content Data Objectand its Representation Information.***

and

Information Property Description: ***The description of the Information Property. It is a description of a part of the information content of a Content Informationobject that is highlighted for a particular purpose.***

Having these definitions one can then go on to define the concept which the discussion earlier in this Chapter suggests, namely something which comes into play when digital objects are transformed:

Transformational Information Property: ***An Information Property whose preservation is regarded as being necessary but not sufficient to verify that the Non-Reversible Transformationhas adequately preserved information content. This could be important as contributing to evidenceabout Authenticity. Such Information Properties will need to be associated with specific Representation Information, including Semantic Information, to denote how they are encoded and what they mean. (Note that the term 'significant property', which has various definitions in the literature, is sometimes used in a way that is consistent with it being a Transformational Information Property).***

Note that if the Transformation were reversible then it is reasonable to take it that no information is lost. It is for this reason that the above definition focuses on non-reversible transformations. For completeness the definitions of the reversible and non-reversible transformations are as follows:

Reversible Transformation: ***A Transformation in which the new representation defines a set (or a subset) of resulting entities that are equivalent to the resulting entities defined by the original representation. This means that there is a one-to-one mapping back to the original representation and its set of base entities.***

Non-Reversible Transformation: ***A Transformation which cannot be guaranteed to be a Reversible Transformation.***

The important point is that the definition of non-reversible is drawn as broadly as possible.

Having this theoretical underpinning, we can now describe a tool which brings together the ideas about authenticity and significant properties, showing some real examples.

13.7 Prototype Authenticity Evidence Capture Tool

In order to delve into the practicalities we now describe in some detail an Authenticity Management tool created in the CASPAR project. This should make clear some of the design considerations needed to be taken into account when one deals with evidence about authenticity, where one must also be concerned about the authenticity of that evidence (recursion again!). It also allows us to describe in more detail the practical examples in Sect. 13.7.6.

This tool imports an XML formatted set of Authenticity Protocols (AP), an AP defining a set of procedures that should be undertaken by the capturer. Each AP is made up of Authenticity Steps (AS). An Authenticity Step will define specific PDI information required for capturing and imposing questions on the capturer, for instance by asking what standards or methodologies have been followed and detailing other criteria that must be satisfied. Each step is executed by an actor, usually a human but some steps maybe automated by software plug-ins, for example these may read information from file headers or work out fixity information. After each protocol instance is signed off as finalised, the results are compiled into the Authenticity Protocol Execution Report which will be used to make the informed judgment as to the authenticity of the digital asset. The report is exportable in a suitable digital format allowing it to be attached to an Archival Information Package (AIP), thus allowing it to be stored directly or referenced by the asset itself. When the AIP and the digital asset it preserves is moved, processed or transformed, the Authenticity Report can be updated and maintained, keeping the provenance of the digital information relevant throughout its lifecycle.

13.7.1 Digests

In order to verify that the collected evidence is itself trustworthy it is important to detect any forgery and whether or not the evidence has been tampered with. In order to allow this to be determined by a consumer, a digital digest can be used to digital sign the evidence. To create a digest, a cryptographic hash function (commonly built into many programming languages) is applied to the captured evidence, returning a (cryptographic) hash value, such that an accidental or intentional change to the data will change the hash value. To investigate if there has been some change, the hash value can be recalculated and compared the original. The Hash value itself is known simply as a digest and should have been created in such a way that it would be computationally impracticable to find a message from a given digest, impracticable to modify a message without changing its digest and impracticable to find two different messages with the given digest. The tool creates a digest of every captured item of information along with the timestamp of its capture, when the complete capture is signed-off – with a digital signature, a new digest of the complete Authenticity Protocol Execution Report is created and thus available for a fixity comparison.

13.7.2 The Authenticity Management Tool

As has been noted, the Authenticity Management Tool is based upon the Authenticity Model, facilitating the capture of all relevant Preservation Description Information (PDI) deemed necessary for the a member of the designated community to make an informed judgment as to the trustworthiness of a preserved digital asset. The tool may be used by data producers, administrators and analysts with responsibility for creating and managing data as part of a project's preservation strategy. The results of the tool, the Authenticity Execution Report will be used by those who need to evaluate the authenticity of the digital information.

Such a tool could be used throughout the life of the digital asset, importing new Protocols and Steps as use of the data changes and evolves or new events are deemed to be important. For example in the creation of data by a scientific instrument, the project scientist may define Authenticity Protocols to be followed on initial first level data processing, then when the data is archived for the long term a new set of Protocols may be applied by that archive, allowing the archive administrators to capture information about format migration or encryption.

In addition to capturing all necessary evidence, the tool can provide the following benefits to a project:

- basing the tool on the Authenticity Model will provide a standard process and terminology which can be shared and understood between communities
- defining the protocols helps to document the preservation actions and the key events taking place in the preservation system
- providing a customisable and flexible mechanism for project preservation staff to formally define what are the important characteristics about their own data that need capturing

13.7.3 Tool Requirements

Determined from examining user requirements for scientific case studies, the following requirements were gathered for the CASPAR Authenticity management tool:

- The tool will focus on capturing information in textual form, making the capture process as fast and user friendly as possible
- The tool must be customisable, Authenticity Protocols and Steps will be encoded in XML conforming to an XML schema and imported into the tool, these will capture non generic, project specific information
- Some Authenticity Steps and the information they capture will be generic and therefore standard to the tool
- Some information capture would be automated through the use of pre-existing archival software or from new plug-in tools, for instance a plug-in may read file format descriptions to pull relevant information from file headers
- An Authenticity Execution Report must be compiled from the results of information capture, this should be exportable in various formats such as RDF or XML for inclusion into an AIP
- The tool must provide a mechanism for local information storage either using a database or file system in order to allow a user to save their current progress and come back to the information capture at a later time.
- The tool may make suggestions as to what information should be captured by an Authenticity Protocol
- The tool must collect provenance information about who is doing the capture, for example name, organisation, time and date
- The tool will digitally sign the captured evidence through a digest to provide an indication whether the information has been modified or corrupted.
- The tool will provide a visually indication of what information has been captured, what is missing and provide metrics informing to what degree the capture process has met the requirements outlined in the protocol document.

13.7.4 Practical Details

The prototype authenticity management tool is an online web tool, accessed from a web browser, there are no requirements for special browser plug-ins. The tool provides an Authenticity Administrator and an Authenticity Capture Sections to the tool accessed through high level menus. The Administrator area allows the setting up of an Authenticity project and the importing of Authenticity protocols. The Authenticity capture area allows the capture of authenticity information and the sign-off of the protocol as complete.

13.7.5 The XML Schema

Capturing and recording the complex protocol information is done by creating an XML document conforming to the protocol XML schema showing in Fig. 13.7. The XML schema defines exactly what is in the XML protocol document. Each protocol document applies to one project, at the top level the schema describes some reference information about the project, the name of the project, a description, the project domain.

The schema then defines a header Section which is aimed at recording key context information such as an overall description of the protocols and their purpose, the author or the protocols document, its creation date and a reference or identifier to the project the protocols are associated with.

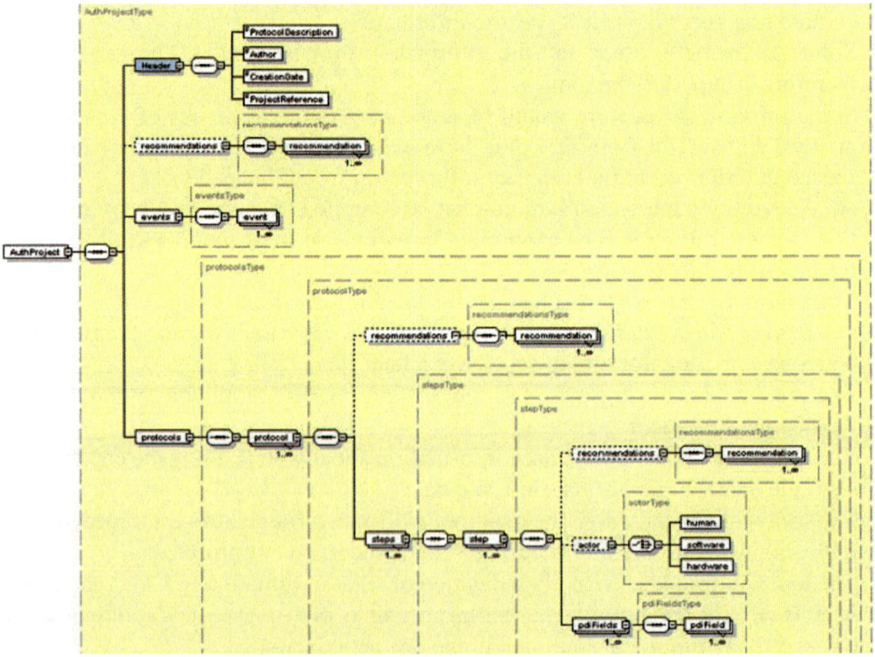

Fig. 13.7 XML schema for authenticity protocols

Following this there is a Section for recommendations, detailing overall standards or procedures which should be followed. Then there is a Section detailing each key event that triggers the capture of evidence about the event, specifically one needs to at least name the event, provide a description, a description of information on what triggers the event and an order identifier, so it is possible to specify the order of events in a sequence. Following that is the protocols Section; there is a sequence of protocols for each event; a protocol has a description, its own recommendations and a sequence of steps.

Internally each step can have its own recommendations, a sequence of actual PDI data fields to capture and details the type of actor performing the PDI evidence capture. Additionally a PDI data field can be given an importance rating depending on how critical the protocol document creator feels the field is to capture. It is also possible to specify that additional documents or files are required.

The following few images give a view of a prototype tool which guides a curator through the process of capturing evidence and then allowing a user to display the evidence.

Capturing PDI

The capture screen (Fig. 13.8) details the step to execute, with the project owners recommendations. The capture is made in a text box, the capturer can rate their

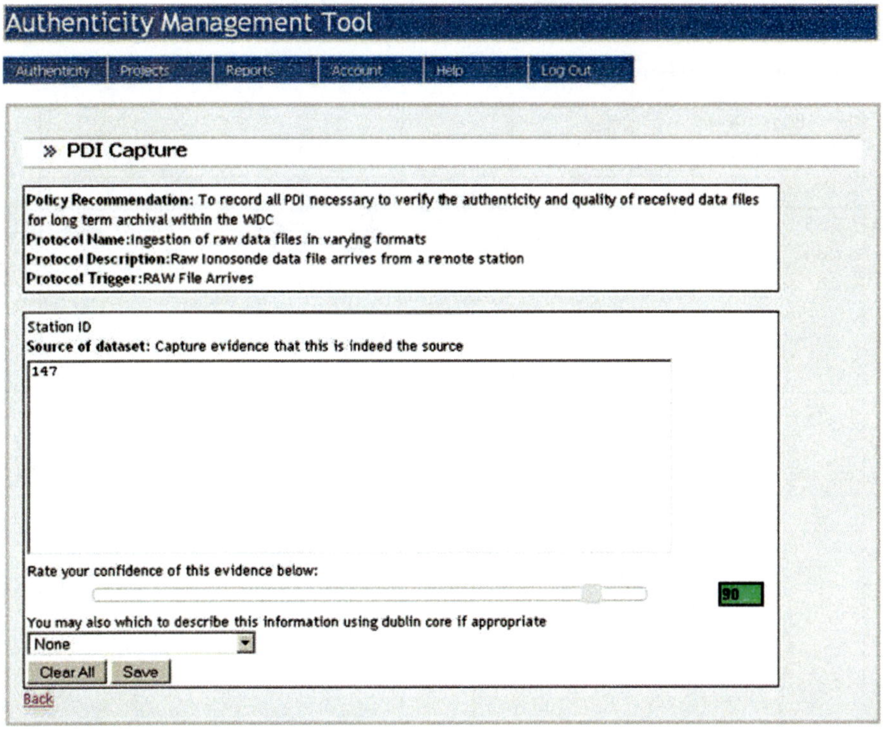

Fig. 13.8 Authenticity management tool

confidence in the evidence and optionally select Dublin Core terminology to associate with the evidence if appropriate. Clicking the 'save' button will store the result and provide the option to continuing with another PDI field.

Browsing Results

Browsing the information capture provides a quick indication of what evidence has been captured and what is missing. When browsing the authenticity catalogue users can choose a project, followed by an instance. The user will be able to access a breakdown of Event, Steps and PDI fields which captured results.

Moving the mouse pointer over a capture result will pop up the capturer's information and a timestamp (Fig. 13.9).

Authenticity Metric Display

To try and display an indication of the authenticity graphically, a bar chart of confidence against importance is shown for each capture field (Fig. 13.10). This gives

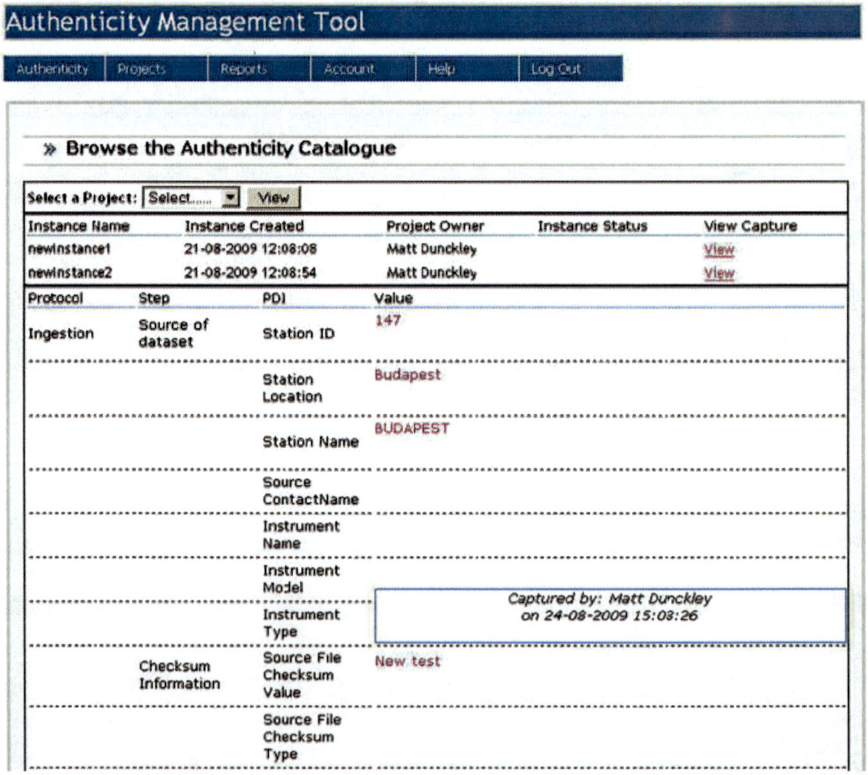

Fig. 13.9 Authenticity Tool browser

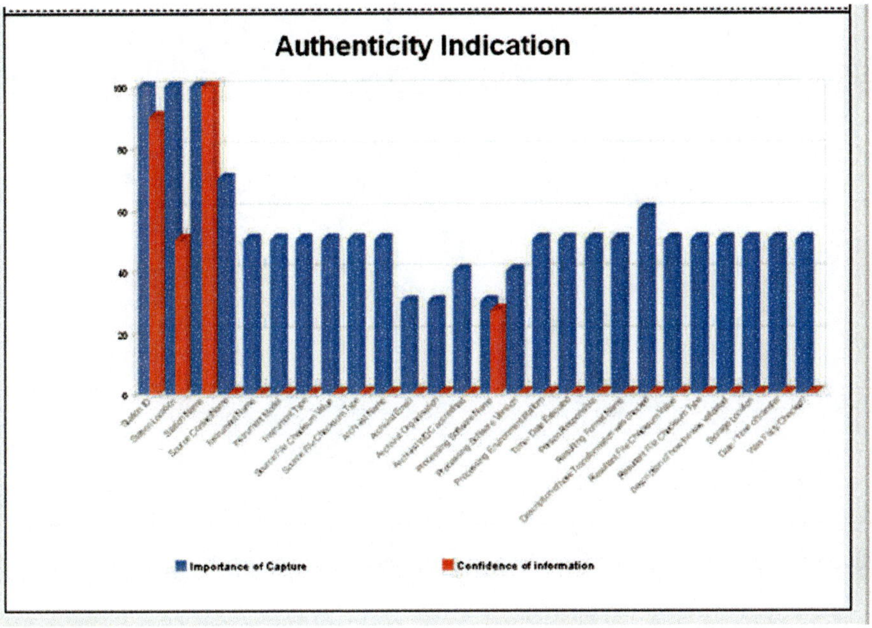

Fig. 13.10 Authenticity Tool-summary

a quick and clear indication of what evidence is missing and an indication of the strength of the captured evidence against what was expected.

13.7.6 Applying the Tool to Scientific Data Case Studies

13.7.6.1 Case Study 1 Ionosonde Raw Data Archival

This case study is based on World Data Centre (WDC) archived data held at Rutherford Appleton Laboratory, STFC and focuses on the long term archival of Ionosonde scientific research data.

The World Data Centre (WDC), established by the United States, Europe, Russia, and Japan, now includes 52 Centres in 12 countries shown in Fig. 13.11. Its holdings include a wide range of solar, geophysical, environmental, and human-related data. The WDC for Solar-Terrestrial Physics based at the Rutherford Appleton laboratory holds Ionospheric data comprising vertical soundings from over 300 stations, mostly from 1957 onwards, though some stations have data going back to the 1930s.

Ionospheric research is performed using Ionosonde radar instruments, these "Vertical Incidence" radars measure the time of flight of a radio signal swept through a range of frequencies (1–30 MHz) and reflected from the ionised layers of the upper atmosphere (90–800 km) as an "ionogram". The measurements are analysed to give

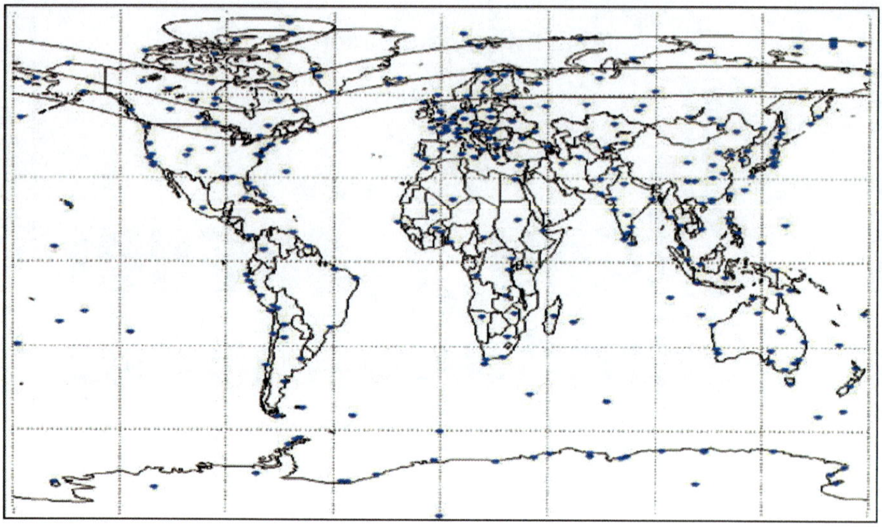

Fig. 13.11 Worldwide distribution of ionosonde stations

the variation of electron density with height up to the peak of the ionosphere. Such electron-density profiles provide most of the Information required for studies of the ionosphere and its effect on radio communications.

The WDC receives data from the many Ionosonde stations around the world through a variety of means including ftp, email, CD-ROM. Data is provided in a number of formats: raw data, URSI (simple hourly resolution) and IIWG (more complex, time varying) standard formats as well as station specific "bulletins". The WDC stored data in digital formats comprises 2.9 GB of data in IIWG format and 70 GB of Multi-Maximum Method (MMM) formatted data, SAO, ART files from Lowell digisondes. The WDC also holds about 40,000 rolls of 16/35 mm film ionograms and ~10,000 monthly bulletins of scaled ionospheric data. Some of this data is already in digital from, but much, particularly the ionogram images, are yet to be digitised.

Some Ionosonde stations provide a small set of standard parameters in a station specific "bulletin" format which is similar to the paper bulletins traditionally produced from the 1950 s onwards. The WDC has some bespoke, configurable software to extract the data from these bulletins and convert it to IIWG format, this kind of raw data forms the basis of this case study.

13.7.6.1.1 Determining What Needs to Be Captured

This case study will briefly discuss how the Authenticity Management tool can be used to capture prominent PDI about the WDC's process of ingestion and archival, resulting in the creation of an Authenticity Execution Report for the raw Ionosonde data which has been received. The resultant Authenticity Execution Report would be a useful guide to a data user wishing to determine the authenticity of these data files.

In order for the Authenticity Protocol designer to model what PDI needs to be captured and also for a future data user to establish if all the evidence is available, the Authenticity Protocol should include a qualifying statement of intent, decided as the first step and forming part of the Authenticity Recommendations. For each AP there also needs to be Authenticity Steps stating clearly and unambiguously the criteria that the intended captured evidence must support. Only when this is decided can the scope of the capture be decided and the correct PDI necessary to support this claim be determined. To design the WDC Authenticity Protocols, it is important to identify the major event types that occur between the data arriving and its final storage. These event types map to the APs.

If the WDC set the initial criteria *"to record PDI necessary to verify the authenticity and quality of received data files for long term archival within the WDC"* then the appropriate event types that occur in the system up to and including the point of long term storage within the archival ingestion system can be identified. In this scenario there are three event types which can occur between ingestion and archival of the incoming Ionosonde data files. The occurrence of these event types will trigger the execution of the following APs:

- Ingestion of raw data files in varying formats
- Transformation of received data files into IIWG format
- Final validation and archival of IIWG file within WDC

Each AP should have an Authenticity Step stating the criteria against which these steps are measured, for example:

1. Ingestion of raw data files in varying formats – *"In order for this digital data to be accepted as Ionosonde data of sufficient quality the reliability of its source must be verified and recorded by a WDC accredited archivist"*
2. Transformation of received data files into IIWG format – *"For the received data file to be deemed as sufficient quality to support data analysis it must have been successfully transformed into standard IIWG data format, the use of processing software must be recorded"*
3. Final validation and archival of IIWG file within WDC – *"Successful validation of the IIWG structure and syntax must be achieved and recorded before long term archival can take place"*

At this point it is possible to identify the necessary steps for each protocol, these are shown in Table 13.1.

The Authenticity Steps for each protocol can now be completed with the specific PDI fields necessary for modelling the capture of the appropriate evidence. The complete list of PDI fields is considerable and is not included here.

The completed steps with PDI fields are then encoded into the XML schema and imported into the tool. The authenticity steps can then be followed through the tool with all captured information being used to create the digest for export.

Table 13.1 Steps for each event

Protocol/event	Step to record	Explanation
Ingestion of raw data files in varying formats	Source of dataset	Capture evidence that this is indeed the source
	Checksum information	Capture checksum information about the received data file
	Archivist name and details	Record the identity and capture credentials of the archivist
Transformation of received data files into IIWG format	Format transformation	Capture details of the transformation, the software used, the environment and who performed it
	Detail transformational information properties	Capture details of transformational information properties checked, how was the transformation validated
Final validation and archival of IIWG file within WDC	Details of validation process	Capture details of the validation process performed, how was the file validated
	Details of transfer to storage	Capture details about the transfer of IIWG to storage

13.7.6.2 Case Study 2 EISCAT Recording the Processing Chain

The European Incoherent Scatter (EISCAT) association was founded in 1975 by the research councils of Norway, Sweden, Finland, France, Germany and the United Kingdom to build and operate a research radar system in the auroral regions of Scandinavia; Japan joined the association in 1996. The technique measures the scattering of high power radio waves at UHF and VHF frequencies by the ionosphere. The returned signal allows routine measurement of Electron Density, Ion Velocity and Electron and Ion temperatures from about 80 km to over 1,000 km with height resolution down to a few hundred meters. The incoherent scatter technique provides the widest ranging measurements of the ionosphere over an extensive height range. The mainland UHF system is unique in the world having the ability to produce true three dimensional velocity data and to make observations of non-maxwellian plasma effects.

The raw data from the radar is both large and almost impossible to understand without the comprehensive analysis system but it has been noted that the analysed results lack a clear audit trail to ensure their veracity, this case study aims to address this issue by partly recording the processing and audit chain. The raw and processed data from the receivers are initially stored by the archive held at Kiruna, Sweden.

This data, for the UK and common programmes, is downloaded to the STFC archive from the Kiruna web server and stored in a directory structure having one top-level directory per year with file names consisting of the experiment name performed and a timestamp.

As stated, this case study aims to capture processing information about the integration analysis performed, how it was done, whether a filter was used to detect anomalies, the integration strategy, the analysis strategy and detail the software used. It is also important to capture human information about who performed the analysis, when, where and provide a trail of the origin of analysed files. Capturing the necessary PDI fields for the EISCAT data follows the same process as for the WDC case study. Through a thorough examination and discussion with the EISCAT archivist stationed at STFC, four key events were identified.

13.7.6.2.1 The Events and the Capture Criteria

1. **Receive and ingest raw data from the Kiruna archive** – *"In order for this digital data to be accepted as EISCAT data of sufficient quality the reliability of its source must be verified and the format of the received data must be recorded"*
2. **Perform data storage** – *"The storage of data in a directory name matching <experiment_name>@<site>/yyyymmdd_hh will be checked and verified for consistency"*

Table 13.2 Events for each step – EISCAT example

Protocol/event	Step to record	Explanation
Receive and ingest raw data from the Kiruna archive	Source of dataset	Capture evidence that this is indeed the source
	Checksum information	Record checksum information about received files
	Archivist name and details	Capture credentials of archivist
Perform data storage	Directory structure	Capture details of the directory structure
	Matlab file name convention	Record consistency with the file-naming convention
Check file contents for consistency	Detail file parameters	Capture details of the required file parameters
	Compare with observation details	Data parameters should be consistent with the observation, the date, the site and the experiment name
Perform integration and analysis	Data integration	Detail the integration performed
	Data analysis strategy	Detail the analysis strategy used

3. **Check file contents for consistency** – *"Archivist will check the file contents for the required parameters and consistency with the date of observation, if the data is part of a sequence of files then check the sequence is consistent"*
4. **Perform integration and analysis** – *"It should be possible to perform integration and analysis on the data and the analysis strategy is appropriate and recorded."*

At this point it is possible to identify the necessary steps for each protocol; these are shown in Table 13.2.

The Authenticity Steps for each protocol can now be completed with the specific PDI fields necessary for modelling the capture of the appropriate evidence. The complete list of PDI fields is considerable and is not included in this document.

13.8 Summary

This Chapter should have provided the reader with a good understanding of the issues surrounding Authenticity. It is a complex and often misunderstood topic and therefore we have provided some fairly detailed examples.

Chapter 14
Advanced Preservation Analysis

Co-author Esther Conway

So far we have used the OAIS terminology for digital preservation. Now we turn to a complementary way of looking at it. We can say that the challenge of digital preservation of scientific data lies in the need to preserve not only the dataset itself but also the ability it has to deliver knowledge to a future user community. This entails allowing future users to reanalyze the data within new contexts. Thus, in order to carry out meaningful preservation we need to ensure that future users are equipped with the necessary information to re-use the data.

Note that it would be foolish to even try to anticipate all possible uses for a piece of data; instead we can try to at least enable future users to understand the data well enough to do what current data users are able to do. Further uses are then only limited by the imagination and ability of those future users – they will not be held back by our lack of preparation.

In this chapter we discuss in some detail the creation of "research assets" for current and future users.

The Digital Curation Centre SCARP [166] and CASPAR [2] projects have a strong focus on the preservation and curation requirements for scientific data sets. These projects engaged with a number of archives based at the STFC [167] Rutherford Appleton Laboratory. In particular extensive analysis was carried out to consider the preservation requirements of the British Atmospheric Data Centre [168], the World Data Centre [169] and the European Incoherent Scatter Scientific Association (EISCAT) [170]. During these studies it became clear that there was a need for a consistent preservation analysis methodology.

There are currently a number of tools available which have focus on digital preservation requirements. Drambora [171] provides audit/risk assessment and PLATTER [172] provides planning on the repository level but they do not provide an adequate analysis methodology for data set specific requirements. The Planets [173] planning tool Plato [174] deals with objects within a collection on an individual basis but does not examine the inclusion of additional digital information objects and how they interact to permit the meaningful re-use of data.

We describe next a new approach to preservation analysis which has been developed.

D. Giaretta, *Advanced Digital Preservation*, DOI 10.1007/978-3-642-16809-3_14,

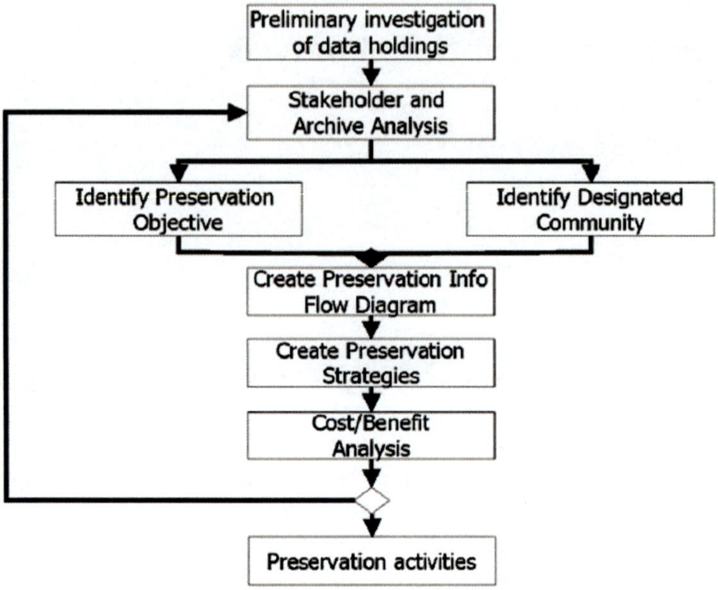

Fig. 14.1 Preservation analysis workflow

The methodology seeks to incorporate a number of analysis techniques, tools and methods into an overall process capable of producing an actionable preservation plan for scientific data archives. Figure 14.1 illustrates the stages of this methodology. In the rest of this section we discuss the stages in detail, illustrated with examples of work with the scientific archives.

14.1 Preliminary Investigation of Data Holdings

The first step is to undertake a preliminary investigation of the data holdings of the target archive. The CASPAR project developed a questionnaire [175] containing key questions which allowed what we might call the preservation analyst to initiate discussion with the archive. It critically allows the analyst to:

- understand the information extracted by users from data
- identify Preservation Description and Representation information
- develop a clearer understanding of the data and what is necessary for is effective re-use
- understand relationships between data files and what constitutes a digital object within the archive

While it is appreciated that this questionnaire is not an exhaustive list of questions which one may need to ask about a preservation target, it still provides sufficient information to commence the analysis process. The full questionnaire and results from the Ionosonde WDC holdings [176] can be obtained from the CASPAR website.

14.2 Stakeholder and Archive Analysis

After carrying out the questionnaire process for each archive it is necessary to carry out a stakeholder analysis for these archives. This is because:

- stakeholders may hold different views of the knowledge a data set was capable of providing an end user
- stakeholders can identify different end users whose skill sets and knowledge base vary
- stakeholders may have produced or be custodians of information vital for re-use of data

14.2.1 Stakeholder Categories

The stakeholder analysis classifies stakeholders into a number of categories each with their own concerns. From experience with a number of datasets the following categories of stakeholder are felt to be most useful.

Every digital archive will have some form of funding body associated with it which provides the resources to collect and maintain the data. During its lifetime, the custody of a data set may pass through several bodies generating rich documentation which explains the scientific purpose of the dataset and how it has evolved over time. These documents can take the form of experimental proposals which will explain the original intent of the experiment/observation, institutional reports which state the intent of maintaining supply of the data to a scientific community, and reports which record scientific output.

Scientific organizations such as university departments or national and international institutes and laboratories are frequently associated with datasets. They tend to work within a particular branch of science and can provide a great deal of detailed information on how a dataset can fulfil that particular area of scientific potential, providing for example software, support materials and field specific bibliographies.

Every dataset will have an individual scientist, or group of scientists responsible for its production. In addition to the scientific intent recorded in an experimental proposal, they may have made observations at the time of the data production which could can enhance use of the data or produce new avenues of investigation. Theses could be associations of events with other phenomena for example lighting strikes with the ionization of a region of the atmosphere or identification of recurrent patterns which would merit further investigation.

Scientists in the Community are the most diverse and distributed. While they tend to be most difficult to assess this is nonetheless an important activity as they may generate and possess a great deal of information critical to data reuse.

The data archivist is the group or individual who is the current custodian of the data. The extent to which they have interacted with other stakeholder groups and extracted knowledge requirement with its associated information will be highly dependent on the resources available to, and the motivations, background and personal bias of, the individual archivist.

14.2.2 Archive Evolution and Management

In addition to identifying the stakeholders from the different categories it is also beneficial to understand how an archive has evolved and been managed. This can used to illuminate the different uses of data over time and the production of associated Representation Information. For example the following kinds of factors have influenced the use and re-use of data over time:

- birth and development of a science
- events which influence data use such as the second world war or global warming
- development of countries technologies and the emergence of global networks
- publication of journals technical manuals, interpretative handbooks, conference proceeding, minutes of user group meetings, software etc.
- emergence of branches of science and associated organisations
- stewardship of data and the influence of different custodians

This is not an exhaustive list as many factors influencing data re-use are domain specific as is the categorization of the stakeholders. Naturally most of these can only be expected to be dealt with in the most cursory way in any practical study nevertheless even this can be extremely important in understanding the situation. As after this evaluation one should be in position to scope what types of reuse may be realistically achieved.

As examples, we compare two archives which were examined as part of the SCARP project, namely the archive of a single site wind profiling instrument based in Wales and that of a global network of ionosondes which create ionization profiles of the atmosphere.

The Mesosphere Troposphere Stratosphere (MST) [177] data set is extremely well documented and well managed. Access to the data is restricted, with end users required to report back on how they have used the data. The Archivist is the key manager of these data for a number of reasons

- he is the project scientist involved in production of the data
- he is a field expert and practising scientist in close contact with relevant scientific organisations
- he provides support, runs and keeps records of user group meetings.

When we consider these factors we can see that it is reasonable to try to capture information from current users which facilitate the re-use of data by future scientists. This is possible because of the archivist's domain knowledge and close connection to users.

By contrast the ionosonde data archivist, whilst being a skilled individual with some domain knowledge, does not have the same strong connection with current users. The data currently comes from 252 geographically diverse locations and current users are simply required to provide an e-mail address to gain access. As a result it would be completely impractical to capture user generated information even if it might facilitate re-use.

The added value of information from end users or the impact of the absence of such information must be considered in determining the value of the research asset to be created. If creation of such asset is deemed viable an archive may then begin to form preservation objectives and define user communities based on the information in scope.

14.3 Defining a Preservation Objective

The analysis carried out up to this point may present one with a natural, easily defined, preservation objective or alternatively there may be a greater number of options which overlap and are more difficult to define. It is important to note that this type of analysis cannot advise one as to which preservation option to choose but merely clarifies the available options. Preservation objectives should be:

- specific, well defined and clear to anyone with a basic knowledge of the domain
- actionable – the objective should be currently achievable.
- measurable – it is critical to be able to know when the objective has been attained in order to assess if any preservation strategy developed is adequate.
- realistic based on findings from the previous stages of analysis

We shall now take an example preservation objective from the MST data. We set the preservation objective as follows.

> *A user from a future designated community should be able to extract a specific set of 11 parameters from data files for a given time and altitude. These include typical measurements such as vertical wind shear and tropopause sharpness. We would also want the data user to be able to correctly interpret the scientific parameter definitions and to be able access and read the following materials:*
>
> - *scientific output resulting from use of the data set*
> - *the MST international workshop conference proceedings*
> - *the MST user group meeting minutes*

This objective has the desired qualities of being specific, actionable, measureable and realistic. While it could be tempting to try and specify a replication of current use this may not be advisable. If we had set the preservation objective as the being the ability to study gravity waves or ozone layering occurring in the atmosphere above the MST site we would rapidly discover that this is too vague an objective. This opens too many avenues of investigation when determining the skill and knowledge base needed to correctly interpret or analyze the data for these purposes. The unfortunate consequence would have been a time consuming analysis process and a lack of certainty that this objective had been achieved for future users.

14.4 Defining a Designated User Community

The Designated Community is defined in OAIS [1] as "***An identified group of potential Consumers who should be able to understand a particular set of information. The Designated Community may be composed of multiple user communities. A Designated Community is defined by the archive and this definition may change over time***".

An archive defines the Designated Community for which it is guaranteeing to preserve some digitally encoded information and must therefore create Archival Information Packages (AIP) with appropriate Representation Information.

The Designated Community will possess skills and a knowledge base which allows them to successfully interact with a set of information stored within an AIP in order to extract required knowledge or recreate the required performance or behaviour. The analysis of Chap. 8 provides a way of defining this more specifically. In common with the preservation objective the analysis up to this point may present one with a range of community groups which the archive may chose serve.

The definition of the skill set is vital as it limits the amount of information which must necessarily be (logically) contained within an AIP in order to satisfy a preservation objective. In order to do this the definition of the Designated Community must be:

- clear, with sufficient detail to permit meaningful decisions to made regarding information requirements for effective re-use of the data.
- realistic and stable in so far as there is reasonable confidence in the persistence of the knowledge base and skill set.

While the need to define the Designated Community is universal, the nature of a knowledge and skill set will tend to be domain specific. The following are typical examples from atmospheric science:

- ability of a community to successfully operate software i.e. knowledge of correct syntax to input commands into a UNIX command line.
- ability to utilize correct analysis techniques with data to remove background noise or identify specific phenomena

- comprehension of community vocabularies
- appreciation of different scientific techniques employed during the production of data, their limitations and comparative success rates for picking up desired phenomena.
- knowledge of atmospheric events or processes which may be affecting the atmospheric state being measured within a data set.

It is the appraisal of this knowledge base as permanent attributes of the Designated Community which will determine whether it is necessary to preserve this information by inclusion in an AIP.

If we take an example from the ionospheric data set we can see how the Designated Community determines what needs to be included within an AIP. The figure below is take from an html page which contains a structural description of ionospheric parameters which have been encoded within IIWG formatted files.

Upon inspection we can see that the current structural description contains FORTRAN notation (Fig. 14.2). If knowledge of FORTRAN is not deemed to be a permanent stable attribute of the community this information must then be included directly within the AIP. This ensures the structural description can be interpreted correctly in the future.

Record #	Format	Description
1	A30	Station Name
1	A5	Station code
1	I4	Meridian time used by station
1	F5.1	Latitude N
1	F5.1	Longitude E
1	A10	Scaling type: Manual/ Automatic
1	A10	Data editings: Edited/ Non-edited/ Mixed
1	A30	Ionosonde system time
2, 3	30I4*	Year
		Month
		Number of days in the month, M
		Number of characteristics
		Total number of measurements
		Number of measurements for each of the M days, NM
4, i	12A10*	List of characteristics
i+1, j	12A10*	Dimensions
j+1, k	60A2*	List of corresponding URSI codes
k+1, l	20(3I2)*	The NM sample times HHMMSS for each of the M days
l+1, m	24(I3, A2)*	The N1 values of characteristic 1 for day 1
.....	...	... repeated for each of the M days
m+1	24(I3, A2)	Hourly medians for characteristic 1
m+2	24(I3, A2)	The counts for the hourly medians, Range
m+3	24(I3, A2)	Upper quartile

Fig. 14.2 Structural description information

14.5 Preservation Information Flows

Once the objective and community have been identified and described an analyst should be in position to determine the information required to achieve an objective for this community. An analyst proceeds by identifying risks which are to be addressed by preservation action. We advocate the creation of an OAIS preservation information flow diagram at this juncture.

An OAIS preservation information flow diagram is graphical representation and analysis tool which is a hybrid of an information flow diagram and the OAIS information model. It provides a convenient format to facilitate group discussions over preservation plans and strategies. A preservation information flow diagram created for the MST data is shown in Fig. 14.3.

The OAIS reference model specifies that within an archival system, a data item has a number of different information items associated with it, each performing a different role in the preservation process. The preservation objective for a designated community is satisfied when each item of the OAIS information model has been adequately populated with sufficient information. The information model provides a checklist which ensures that the preservation objective can be met. All information objects must be mapped to at least one of the element of the OAIS information model.

In addition to information objects and the standard OAIS information model the diagram contains a number of other components which we will now examine in turn.

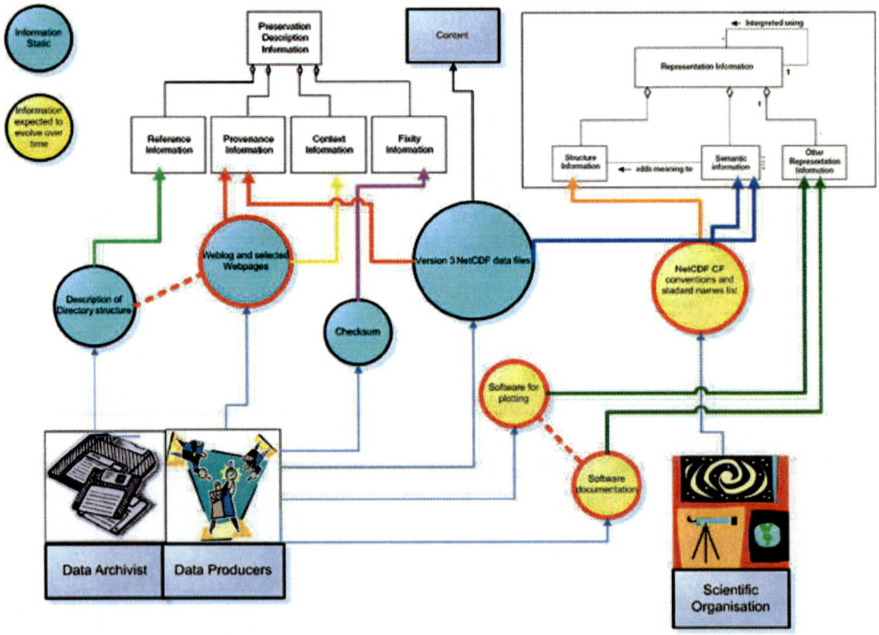

Fig. 14.3 OAIS information flow diagram for the MST data set

14.5.1 *Information Objects*

An information object is a piece of information suitable for deposit within an AIP as it currently exists. An information object must have the following attributes

- Name
- Description of information contained by entity which is vital for the preservation objective e.g. a piece of software contains structural information and algorithms for the processing of data within its code
- Description of format i.e. website, PDF, database or software
- Assessment of preservation risks and dependencies

Notation used

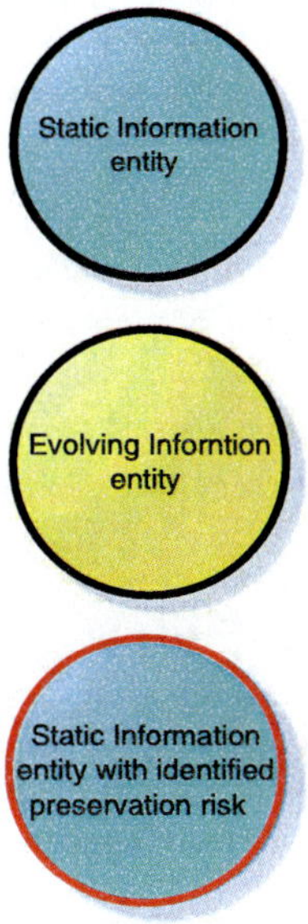

Fig. 14.4 Notation for preservation information flow diagram – information objects

14.5.2 *Stakeholder Entities*

A stakeholder entity is the named custodian of the required Information entity

Notation used

Fig. 14.5 Notation for preservation information flow diagram – stakeholder entities

14.5.3 Supply Relationship

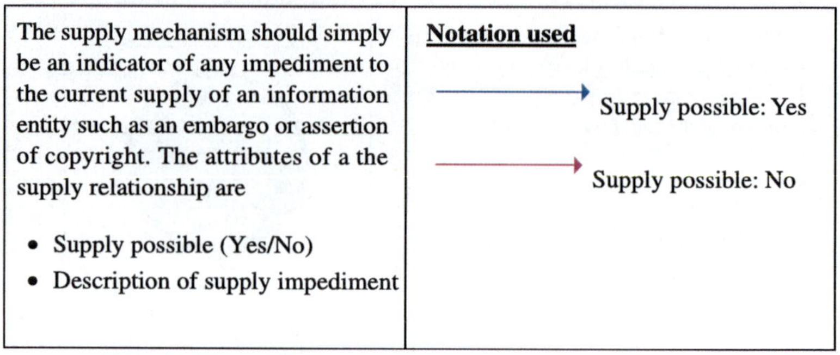

Fig. 14.6 Notation for preservation information flow diagram – supply relationships

14.5.4 Supply Process

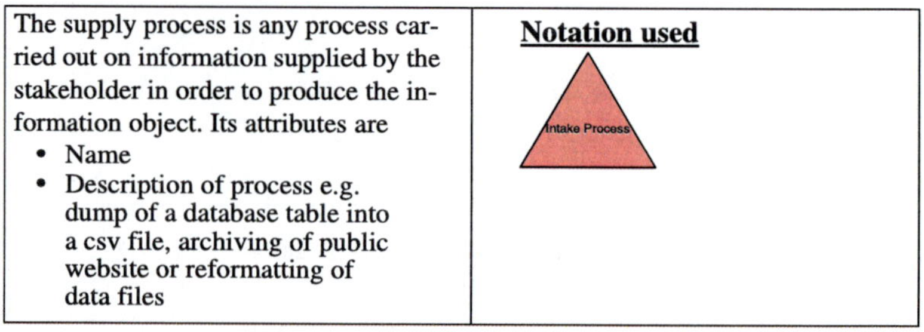

Fig. 14.7 Notation for preservation information flow diagram – supply process

14.5.5 Packaging Relationship

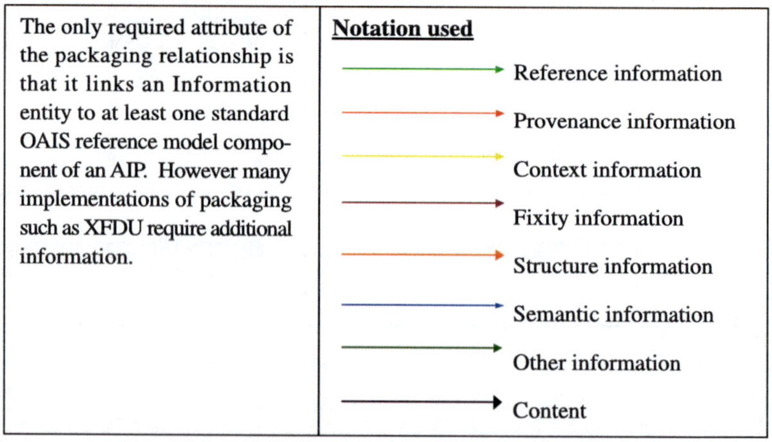

Fig. 14.8 Notation for preservation information flow diagram – packaging relationship

14.5.5.1 Information Object Dependency Relationships

The information object dependency relationship connects two information objects. If preservation action is carried out on one object the impact on another object with a dependency. For example if a piece of software is identified to be at preservation riskand deconstructed to a structural format and analysis algorithm descriptions, the software user manual will be flagged upby the dependency relationship and maybe removed on the basis that this information is now irrelevant.	**Notation used**

Fig. 14.9 Notation for preservation information flow diagram – dependency relationships

14.6 Preservation Strategy Topics

Once the Information flow diagram has been created an archive must identify suitable preservation strategies in the following areas.

14.6.1 Strategies in Response to a Supply Impediment

Where there is an impediment to the supply of a required information object, a strategy must be developed. One may be able to overcome the impediment immediately or alternatively develop a mechanism that effectively references the external information object in tandem with a mechanism for monitoring the situation (preservation orchestration).

The international workshop on MST radar is held about every 2–3 years, and is a major event gathering together experts from all over the world, engaged in research and development of radar techniques to study the mesosphere, stratosphere and troposphere (MST). It is attended by young scientists, research students and new entrants to the field to facilitate close interactions with the experts on all technical and scientific aspects of MST radar techniques. It is this aspect which makes the proceedings an ideal resource to support future users who are new to the field.

Permanent access to these proceedings is at risk with supply impeded by the distribution and failure to deposit proceedings in a single accessible institution. The MST 10 proceedings are available for download from the internet and from the British Library. Proceedings 3, 5–10 are also available from the British Library, meeting 4 is only available from the Library of Congress. Unfortunately the proceedings from meetings 1 and 2 have not been deposited in either institution.

A number of strategies present themselves. Copies of proceedings 1, 2 and 4 could be obtained from the still active community, digitised and incorporated into the AIP. The proceedings which are currently held by the British Library can be obtained, digitised and incorporated into the AIP. Alternatively bibliographic records which include the British Library as a location can be obtained and incorporated into the AIP as a reference. This is a satisfactory approach as there is a high to degree of confidence in the permanence of the holdings and the user communities' ability to access them.

14.6.2 Strategies in Response to an Identified Information Preservation Risk

Information objects must be inspected on a case by case for their individual preservation risk based on dependencies which will be affected by the passage of time. Different strategies which effectively obviate these risks should be developed and evaluated.

If we take another example from the MST data archives where an information object, the GNU plot software analysis programs is deemed to be at risk. This software extracts parameters and plots Cartesian product of wind profiles from NetCDF data files.

Preservation risks have arisen due to the following user skill requirements and technical dependencies.

- The software requires a UNIX or Linux distribution the user community may lose access to or the ability to operate these systems.
- A future user may lose the ability to install different libraries and essential software packages python, the with python-dev module, *numpy* array package or *pycdf*
- GNU plot may no longer be installed
- The community may lose the technical ability to set environmental variables or run required python scripts through a UNIX command line
- The GNU plot template file to format plot output may no longer be accessible.

A number of preservation strategies now present themselves,

One solution is preserving the software through emulation, using for example Dioscuri [178] which should be capable of running operating systems such as Linux Ubuntu, which should satisfy platform dependencies. With the capture of specified software packages/libraries and the provision of all necessary user instructions this is a potentially a viable strategy for these stand-alone applications.

It is additionally possible to convert NetCDF files to another compatible format such as NASA AMES [179]. The conversion can be achieved using community developed software and the scripting language Python. This is a compatible "self describing" ASCII format, information would still be accessible and easily understood as long as ASCII encoded text can still be read (and assuming the Representation Information is available). There would however be some reluctance to do this now as NASA AMES files are not as easily manipulated making it more cumbersome to analyse data in the desired manner.

Preservation by addition of Representation Information is an alternate strategy. Capturing NetCDF documentation and libraries from Unidata [180] means that if future user community still have skills in FORTRAN, C, C++ or Java they will be able to easily write software to access the required parameters.

14.6.3 Secondary Responses to a Preservation Strategy

Where a dependency between information objects has been identified a secondary preservation strategy may need to be developed for the associated object.

14.7 Preservation Plans

As multiple strategies can be developed a number of competing preservation plans are available. A preservation plan should consist of:

- a set of information objects
- a set of supply relationships
- a set of preservation strategies

Each plan will allow an archive to carry out a series of clear preservation actions in order to create an AIP. The archive should then be in a position to take a number of plans to the cost/benefit/risk analysis stage where they can be evaluated and a preferred option chosen.

14.8 Cost/Benefit/Risk Analysis

The final stage of the workflow is where plan options can then be assessed according to

- Costs to the archive directly as well as the resources knowledge and time of archive staff
- Benefits to future users which ease and facilitate re-use of data
- Risks – what are the risks inherent the preservation strategies and are they acceptable to the archive.
- Options – if the answers to be above are not entirely clear then what options should be kept open so that decisions can be made in future.

While it is recognised that it is not possible to assess these in a quantitative way, nevertheless it should be possible to get enough of an evaluation, supported by evidence, to allow decision makers to make an informed judgement. Once this analysis is complete the optimal plan can be selected and progressed to preservation action. If no plans are deemed suitable then the process must begin again with an adjustment to the preservation objective and/or the designated community to be served.

14.9 Preservation Analysis Summary

We believe that this approach, although further development and documentation is needed, is successful at delivering preservation analysis which permits planning at the data set level. Most importantly it allows an archive to establish a process which is comprehensive and aware of all elements required for the re-use of data in the long term.

14.10 Preservation Analysis and Representation Information in More Detail

Following on from the previous section we now look in more detail at the Preservation Analysis step, bringing OAIS concepts in more fully. In order to make it easier to read we repeat some of the material from previous sections.

There is the initial need [181] to perform the following activities:

- understand the information extracted by users from data
- identify Preservation Description and Representation information
- develop a clearer understanding of the data and what is necessary for is effective re-use
- understand the relationships between data files and what constitutes a digital object within the archive

The Representation Information Network will contain all the information needed to satisfy a stated preservation objective, therefore to determine the scope of the network there is a need to have a preservation objective in mind when beginning a preservation plan; the preservation objective should have the following attributes:

- Specific, well defined and clear to anyone with a basic knowledge of the domain
- Actionable, the objective should be currently achievable.
- Measurable, it is critical to be able to know when the objective has been attained or has failed in order to assess if any preservation strategy developed is adequate.
- Realistic and economically feasible based on findings from the previous stages of analysis

The resulting network for an objective will be aimed at implementing a preservation solution for the Designated Community; therefore it is important that the Designated Community is well defined. The Designated Community will possess the skills and knowledge base which allows them to successfully interact with the preserved data in order to extract the required knowledge or recreate a required performance or behaviour.

In common with the preservation objective the analysis up to this point may present one with a range of community groups which the archive may chose to serve. The definition of the skill set is vital as it limits the amount of information which must necessarily be contained within an Archival Information Package (AIP) in order to satisfy a preservation objective. In order to do this the definition of the Designated Community must be:

- clear, with sufficient detail to permit meaningful decisions to be made regarding information requirements for effective re-use of the data.
- realistic and stable in so far as there is reasonable confidence in the persistence of the knowledge base and skill set.

In finding a workable solution for a data set there will possibly be competing strategies available, each with their own associated costs and risks. The size and complexity of the networks for the competing strategies may differ. The costs associated with any RepInfo Network solution should be analysed according to:

- costs to the archive, directly as well as the resources, knowledge and time of archive staff to implement a new network or possibly extend and reuse an existing network.
- benefits to future users, which ease and facilitate re-use of data – there maybe questions of how many data sets a network solution might cover or apply to?
- risks – what are the risks inherent in the preservation strategies and are they acceptable to the archive? What are the points of failure in the network? Are there multiple paths in the network which would allow a consumer to use and understand the data if one of the other paths fails? If for instance we lose some part of the network through the understood threats to digital information, is it possible to recover the information using another network path? This allows us to illustrate some issues raised in Chap. 8.

The first phase of the analysis process described above is the focus of the next section of this chapter and it is vital that the modelling is performed to identify the complexity, scope, risks and overall cost of the resulting preservation network. Once this analysis is complete the optimal plan can be selected and progressed to preservation action. If no plans are deemed suitable then the process must begin again with an adjustment to the preservation objective and/or the Designated Community to be served. Once a preservation network model is deemed realistic and workable it can be implemented as a Representation Information Network (RIN).

14.11 Network Modelling Approach

Through the work at STFC and the CASPAR project, there has been an effort to utilise RIN enabled Archival Information Packages (AIPs).

By modelling the network it is possible to expose the risks, dependencies and tolerances within an Archival Information Package (AIP) allowing for the automation of event driven or periodic review of archival holdings by knowledge management technologies. By clearly defining all important relationships we can also facilitate the identification of reusable solutions which can be deposited within

Registry/Repositories, thus sharing preservation efforts within and across communities. We outline the modelling process briefly here. The process used within the CASPAR project is described in more detail elsewhere [182].

The approach to preservation network modelling is based upon the idea of making logical statements about what is known about the preservation resources available, consisting of digital objects and the relationships between them.

The objects are uniquely identifiable digital entities capable of independent existence which possess the following attributes:

- Information – exposed through preservation analysis, this is the information required to satisfy the preservation objective for the designated community
- Location – information required by the consumer to locate and retrieve the digital object.
- Status – describing the form of a digital object, such as version, variant, instance and dependencies.
- Risks – detail the inherent risks and threats to the digital information. These may include for example the interpretability of the information, technical dependencies, loss of skills over time by the designated community.
- Termination – the scope of the network up to the point at which no additional information is required by the Designated Community to achieve the preservation objective.

The relationships are modelled to capture an idea of how the information will be utilized to achieve the preservation objective within the Designated Community. Therefore it is important to model:

- Function – a digital object being modelled will be used to perform a specific function or action, producing a preservation outcome, for example representing the physical binary data as textual information understood by a human.
- Tolerance – not every object having a function is critical for the fulfilment of the preservation objective, some objects maybe included to enhance the quality of the solution or facilitate the preservation solution.
- Quality Assurance – the reliability of the object to perform the specified function to a sufficient quality may be recorded for the relationship.
- Alternate and Composite relationships – The case may exist where multiple relationships within the network must function concurrently for a preservation objective to be fulfilled or it may be that only one of many needs to function. In Chap. 8 this was terms conjunctive and disjunctive dependencies.

If we take the following example from [183], the preservation objective was set as follows:

> A user from a future designated community should be able to extract a specific set of parameters from data files for a given time and altitude.

These include typical measurements such as vertical wind shear and tropopause sharpness. In addition we would want the data user to be able to correctly interpret the scientific parameter definitions and to be able access and read the following materials.

1. Scientific output resulting from use of the data set
2. The MST international workshop conference proceedings
3. The MST user group meeting minutes

The resultant preservation action produced a collection of digital objects and relationships described by the diagram below.

In Fig. 14.10, we can see that the preserved data object (the MST Cartesian data file stored in the NetCDF format) has first level dependencies on Representation Information, each of these items is linked to their own Representation Information. The diamond icon represents a choice of options (disjunctive dependencies), the circle represents a composite group (conjunctive dependencies) of items.

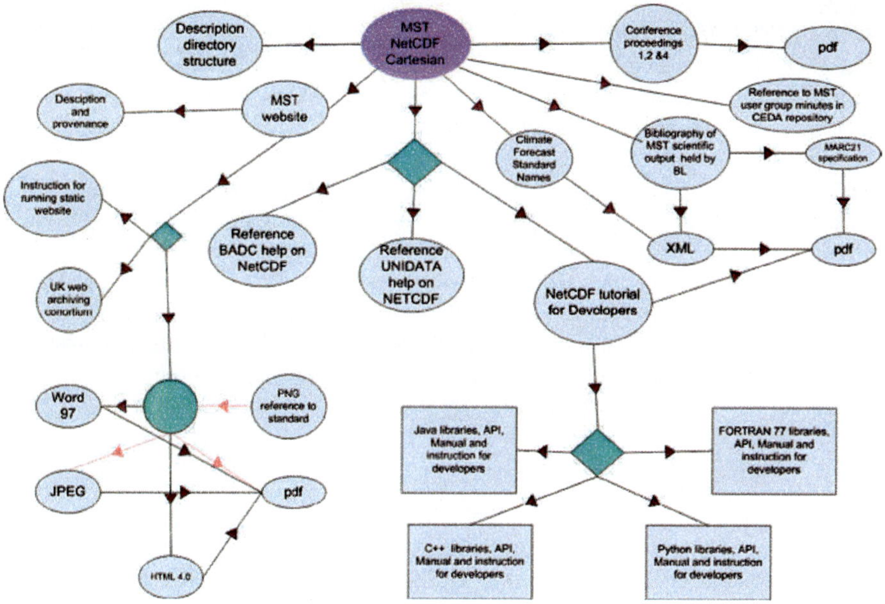

Fig. 14.10 Preservation network model for MST data

14.11.1 *Stability and Review*

The preservation network model describes a preservation solution whereby a number of digital object interact to fulfil a preservation objective for a Designated Community. The preservation solution consists of a number of digital objects and sources of information which will have been subjected to preservation action such as format conversion or the addition of Representation Information. A future user may be required to interact with a number of unfamiliar digital objects in order to achieve meaningful reuse of data. As a result an archivist will be confronted with the task of designing an information network which a future data user can navigate and effectively engage with.

These solutions are also not permanent but have dependencies and associated risks. These must be monitored and managed by an archive as the realization of these risks may result in a critical failure to the point where the network can no longer fulfil the defined objective.

Realization of risk leads to the three different types of failure:

- partial,
- within tolerance
- critical

14.11.2 Partial Failure

The preservation network model below gives an example of a partial failure scenario. We can imagine a scenario in the future where, following a periodic holdings review it is discovered that the British Atmospheric Data Centre and UNIDATA have withdrawn support for the NetCDF file format, the Designated Community has also lost the skill to write programs in C++, FORTRAN 77 and Python. As the community can still write a program to extract the required parameters the preservation objective can still be met. However withdrawal of the British Atmospheric Data support for the NetCDF format may prove to be an appropriate juncture to covert the file to a different format. Figure 14.11 shows that even if the paths with dashed arrows fail, there is still a reliable route through the preservation network model allowing a recovery of the preservation objective.

14.11.2.1 Failure Within Tolerances

The preservation network model section below gives an example scenario of failure within tolerances. The Ionospheric monitoring group website contain vital provenance and context information relating to Ionosonde raw output files that are the target of current preservation efforts. For instance Fig. 14.12 highlights that in this scenario, the loss of being able to render or access the jpeg images from the website could be tolerated as they do not contain any critical information and hence will not put achieving the preservation objective in jeopardy.

14.11.3 Critical Failure

The preservation network model section shown below in Fig. 14.13 gives an example of critical failure. In this scenario failure of the community's ability to read

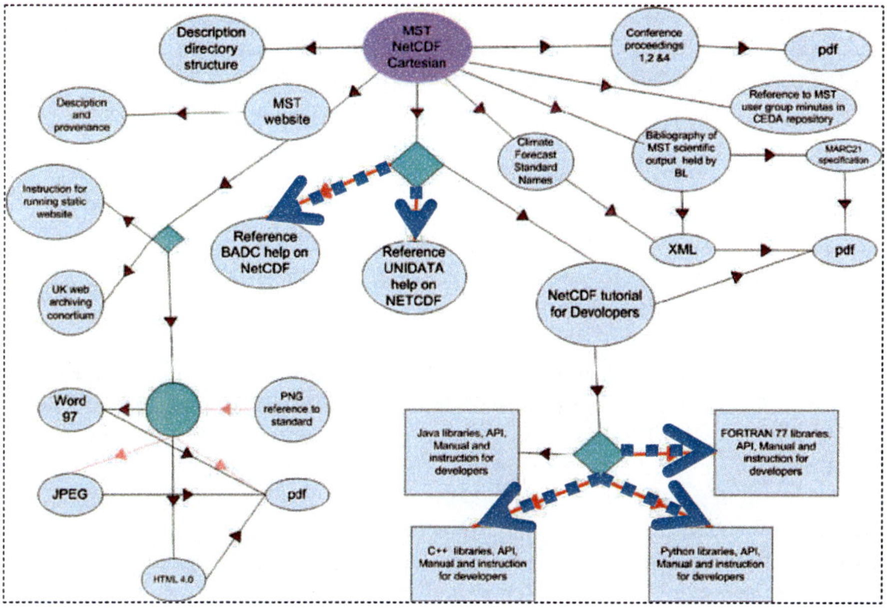

Fig. 14.11 Partial failure of MST data solution

Fig. 14.12 Failure of within tolerances for Ionospheric monitoring group website solution

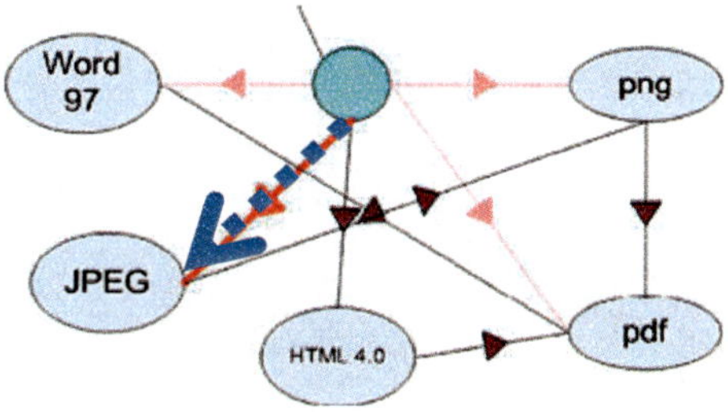

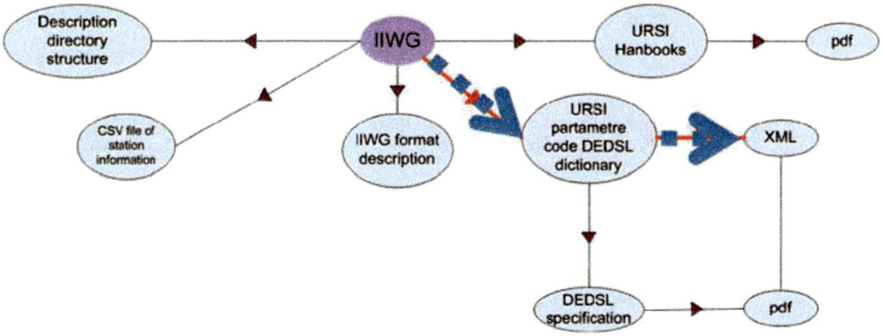

Fig. 14.13 Critical failure for Ionospheric data preservation solution

XML documents would prevent them from reading the Data Entity Description Specification Language (DEDSL) dictionary which allows users to correctly interpret the parameter codes and therefore the contents of the data file causing critical failure of the solution and the preservation objective. In other words, if the network paths shown as dashed fail there may be no way to understand the data in the file.

14.11.4 Re-usable Solutions and Registry Repositories of Representation Information

If we look at the network section above in Fig. 14.14, the objects and relationships described allow a user to extract the desired parameters from NetCDF formatted files. There are eight different strategies a user can employ all of which must fail before there is a critical failure of the solution. As this section of the network has a specific well defined function which is to allow a user to extract parameters from NetCDF formatted files, the solution can be deposited within a Registry/Repository of Representation Information. It can then be reused as part of wider solution for different atmospheric data sets which utilize the format. In this way the effort put in to creating and maintaining the RIN can cover a very great number of data objects.

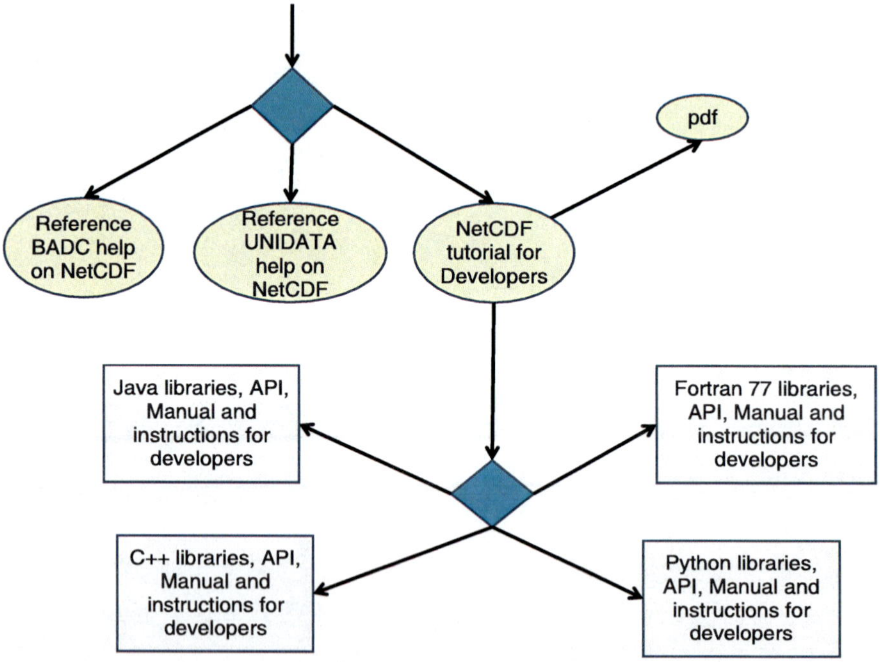

Fig. 14.14 Preservation network model of a NetCDF reusable solution

A further validation of the approach took place within a preservation exercise for Solar-Terrestrial Physics data. This study considered raw data which could be analysed to extract an Ionogram – a graph showing ionization layers in the atmosphere. Currently scientists use a software product called SAO Explorer to extract Ionograms from the data. This software was archived in accordance with the methodology described in [184]. The archived software could with confidence be integrated into a larger OAIS compliant solution for the preservation of Multi-Maximum Method (MMM) data files. This preservation objective permits the long term study of specified atmospheric phenomena from this geographic location. The archived SAO Explorer solution could also then be deposited in the DCC/CASPAR Registry Repository of Representation Information (RORRI), discussed in more detail in Part II, thereby providing a solution shown in Fig. 14.15 which can be re-used by hundreds of ionosphere monitoring station which are active globally.

We believe that the preservation network modelling process described supports and facilitates the long term preservation of scientific data by providing a sharable, stable and organized structure for digital objects and their associated requirements. This approach permits the management of risk and promotes the reuse of solutions allowing the cost of digital preservation to be shared across communities.

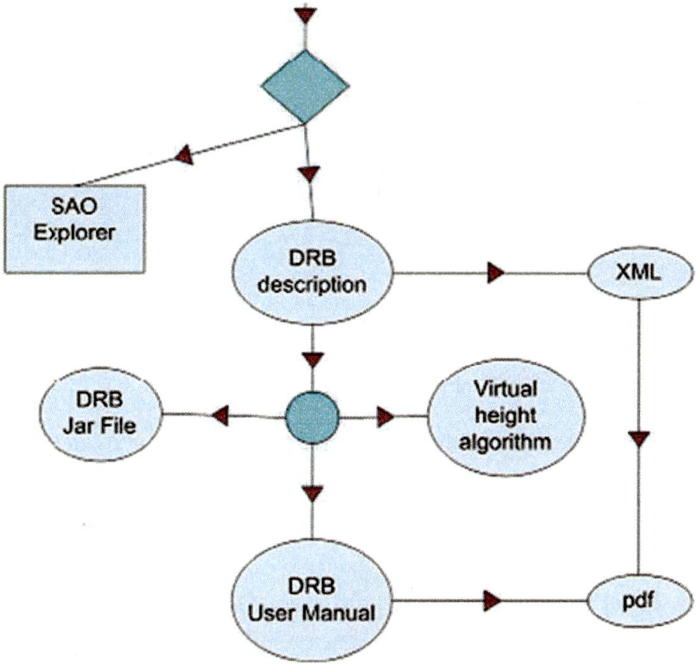

Fig. 14.15 Preservation network model of a MMM file – reusable solution

14.11.5 Example Modelling Case Studies

In this report we detail the application of network modelling of two further preservation scenarios for atmospheric science data held by the STFCs World Data Centre.

14.11.5.1 IIWG – Ionosonde Parameter Extraction

The first scenario is concerned with supporting and integrating a solution into the existing preservation practices of the World Data Centre, which means creating a consistent global record from 252 stations by extracting a standardised set of parameters from the Ionograms produced around the world. The stated preservation objective is that:

> *a user from a future designated community should be able to semantically understand the following fourteen standard Ionospheric parameters from the data for a given station and time. They should also be able to structurally understand the values that these parameters represent.* Fmin, *foE' h_E,foes h_Es,* type of *Es, fbEs, foF*1, *M(*3000*)F*1, *h_F, h_F*2, *foF*2, *fx* , *M(*3000*)F*2.

The network modelling process has provided the RepInfo network of information objects and their relationships shown in Fig. 14.16.

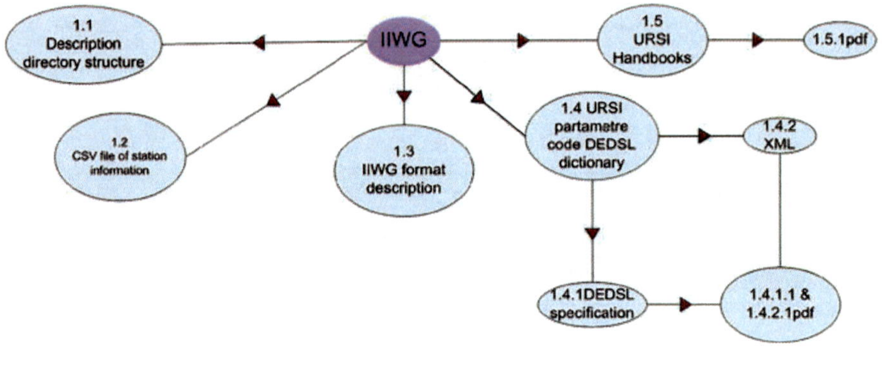

Fig. 14.16 Network model for understanding the IIWG file parameters

The information objects and their relationships found in the model are detailed below:

- 1.1 A very simple description of the IIWG directory structure
- 1.2 A CSV dump of parameter values from the PostgreSQL database, this was validated by comparing the content of file to output from the current system http://www.ukssdc.ac.uk/gbdc/station-list.html. Original content collected and validated by the archivist for World Data Centre (for solar terrestrial physics) based at RAL.
- 1.3 The original IIWG format description which can be found at http://www.ukssdc.ac.uk/wdcc1/ionosondes/iiwg_format.html, this was not deemed as an

appropriate long term solution for the designated user community as it contains FORTRAN notation and is written in a way that would be difficult to reinterpret. The description was written in a more verbose format and validated by the archive manager at STFC.

- 1.4 The parameter code definitions were prepared via community consultation by the international scientific organisation known as The International Union of Radio Science (URSI http://ursi-test.intec.ugent.be/). URSI is a non-governmental and non-profit organisation under the International Council for Science, it has responsibility for stimulating and co-ordinating, on an international basis, studies, research, applications, scientific exchange, and communication in the fields of radio science to represent radio science to the general public, and to public and private organisations.
- 1.4.1 The DEDSL standard is a CCSDS blue book recommendation
- 1.4.1.1 & 1.4.2.1 PDF description is an ISO standard
- 1.4.2 XML specification is a W3C and ISO standard
- 1.5 The URSI handbooks have been developed by URSI. The quality of content has been validated by members of the atmospheric science team at STFC. One of the team is a technician who has had over 25 years experience of manually scaling ionograms at the Rutherford Appleton Laboratory having been initially trained in the task using these resources. Another is trained physicist and part of the Ionospheric Monitoring Group at the Rutherford Appleton Laboratory
- 1.5.1 PDF description is an ISO standard

Now the scope and complexity of the network has been identified and validated by scientists who understand the data. Risk and cost benefit analysis can now be carried out to further determine if implementing this solution is realistically possible. Without undertaking this analysis stage for the IIWG data set any subsequent preservation analysis and strategy would be difficult.

14.11.5.2 Preservation of Raw Ionosonde (MMM Formatted) Data Files

The second preservation scenario for the World Data Centres Ionosonde data files can only be carried out for 7 European stations but would allow a consistent Ionogram record for the Chilton site which dates back to the 1920 s. The preservation objective is for

> *a user of a future designated community to be able reproduce an Ionogram from the raw MMM formatted data files.*

To do this they will also need to have access to the Ionospheric Monitoring group's website, the URSI handbooks of interpretation and Lowell technical documentation, all containing vital semantic and structural representation information for this preservation objective. Being able to preserve the Ionogram record is significant as it is a very rich source of information, able to covey the state of the atmosphere when correctly interpreted. The network model for this solution is shown below in Fig. 14.17.

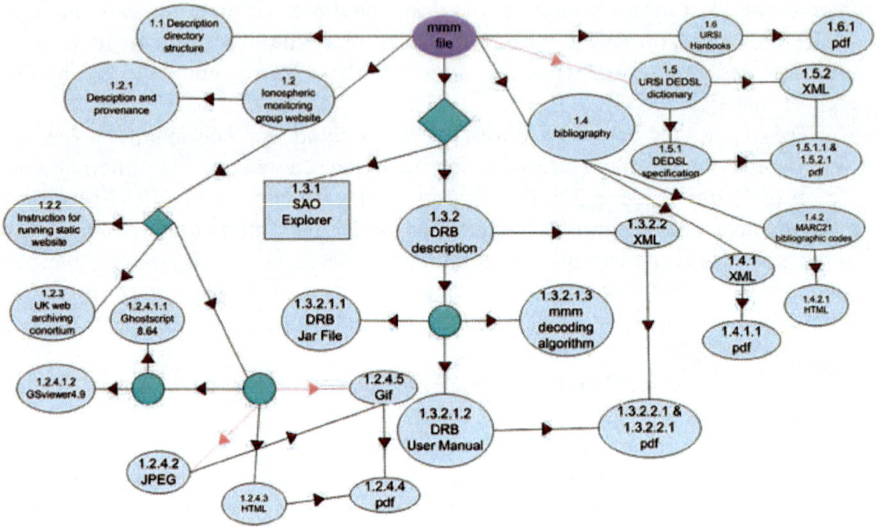

Fig. 14.17 The network model for ensuring access and understandability to raw Ionosonde data files

The information objects and their relationships found in the model are detailed below:

- 1.1 A description of the WDCs MMM Directory Structure with file naming conventions
- 1.2 The website content supplied validated and managed by the Ionospheric monitoring group, the information is subject to community and user scrutiny
- 1.2.1 MST website provenance validated by the website creator and manager at STFC
- 1.2.2 Instructions for accessing the static website – this was tested locally with the group user, the website can be unzipped and accessed with a web browser and Ghostscript viewer installed on a machine running a Windows 32-bit operating system
- 1.2.3 Reference Information. The risk that this reference needs to be monitored is accepted.
- 1.2.4 Composite strategy elements of MST website have been scrutinised by the research team. It was established that the website contained postscript, jpeg, gif and html files formats and use of these file types was stable in the user community. RepInfo for these file types can also be added to the AIP so the file type could easily be understood and monitored.
- 1.2.4.1.1 Ghostscript software tested by Brian McIlwrath, developer of RORRI Representation Information Registry
- 1.2.4.1.2 Ghostscript viewer software
- 1.2.3.4.2 Reference to British and ISO standards on JPEG
- 1.2.3.4.3 W3C validated specification HTML

- 1.2.3.4.4 Reference to ISO standard on PDF
- 1.2.3.4.5 Reference to ISO standard on GIF
- 1.3.1 SAO Explorer
- 1.3.2 The structural DRB description of the MMM file was created and tested by members of the CASPAR project.
- 1.3.2.1.2 DRB software engine JAVA application was validated by members of the CASPAR project
- 1.3.2.1.2 DRB user manual published by GAEL the application developers
- 1.3.2.1.3 Digisonde 256 data decoding: 16 channel ionograms written by Terence Bullett 1, Ivan Galkin 2, David Kitrosser. 1– Air Force Research Laboratory, Space Vehicles Division. Hanscom AFB, MA2– University of Massachusetts Lowell Center for Atmospheric Research, Lowell. MA
- 1.3.2.2 W3C standard for XML
- 1.3.2.2.1 ISO standard for PDF
- 1.4 Bibliography supplied by Chris Davis, Ionosonde scientist
- 1.4.1 W3C standard for XML
- 1.4.1.1 ISO standard for PDF
- 1.4.2 MARC 21 codes from the Library of congress
- 1.4.2.1 W3C standard for html
- 1.5 The parameter code definitions were prepared by URSI http://ursi-test.intec.ugent.be/.
- 1.5.1 The DEDSL standard is a CCSDS blue book recommendation
- 1.5.1.1 & 1.5.2.1 PDF description is an ISO standard
- 1.5.2 XML specification is a W3C and ISO standard
- 1.6 The URSI handbooks have again been developed by URSI. The quality of content has been validated by members of the Ionospheric Monitoring Group at the Rutherford Appleton Laboratory STFC.
- 1.6.1 PDF description is an ISO standard

14.11.6 Implementing the Network Models

The following section describes how the CASPAR project and STFC has implemented RepInfo networks to support their preservation activities. The STFC has implemented RepInfo networks utilizing the DCC/CASPAR Registry Repository of Representation Information (RRORI), details of which are provided in Sect. 17.2

The Registry/Repository allows the centralised and persistent storage and retrieval of OAIS Representation Information (RepInfo) (including its Preservation Description Information). The RepInfo Registry/Repository structures this Representation Information into the network of dependencies required to fully describe the meaning and format of the preserved Digital Data Object associated with it, thus providing through the network all the information needed to understand and use the digital asset for the long term.

The registry also contains maintenance tools for user interaction allowing for

- Manual RepInfo ingest
- Creation and maintenance of the XML structures (RepInfoLabels) which connect related RepInfo in the Registry into an OAIS network (using the predefined categories Semantic, Structure and Other)

Registry component has the following responsibilities:

- ingest RepInfo into Registry–with appropriate name, description and classification
- extract RepInfo from Registry reliably.
- search Registry for RepInfo matching appropriate (wild carded) criteria (a combination of name, description or classification)
- keep a full audit trail providing PDI generation

In addition there is a development Java API allowing software developers to work with and develop applications around any implementation of RORRI.

However the networks of information stored by RORRI must be connected and associated to the data they describe. This packaging is described in Chap. 11, with an implementation described in Sect. 17.10.

Keeping all these supporting "metadata" organised and bound to the original digital asset raises complex problems, as follows:

- What "metadata" should go into an AIP?
- How can "metadata" be kept up to date within an AIP?
- How can the relationships between information objects be expressed?
- How can remote "metadata" be adequately referenced?
- How can the re-use of "metadata" be facilitated?

The concept of Information Packaging addresses these problems. Requirements gathering and a detailed study of the current state of the art technology had shown that in addition to these points there was a need for the STFC packaging implementation to provide benefits such as:

- facilitating information transfer and archival by providing a mechanism to bind a Digital Asset together with all of the information needed to ensure its long term usability and understandability in a standard transferable unit
- allowing detailed specification of information structures and the relationships between information objects
- providing support for post ingestion processing such as data analysis, information reuse and format migration and transformation
- providing packages which are platform independent to facilitate electronic transfer between often remote heterogeneous data systems
- providing packages that are self describing, containing all the information necessary to allow the extraction or discovery of component information objects
- providing packages that described themselves using a standard syntax or language which could be validated by a document model

- having an ability formally to specify the complex relationships between Information Objects which can be queried and examined
- having a package syntax that may provide support for preservation concepts and terminology
- facilitating the re-use of existing RepInfo

The Packaging software component developed through the CASPAR project is a Java API defining a set of interfaces based around the OAIS Reference Model. The packaging component implements the NASA produced XFDU toolkit, providing functionality to construct, manipulate and validate XFDU packages.

Loosely coupled with RORRI, the Packaging component API can interrogate the registry to retrieve information held about a piece of RepInfo. The API can also support operations to send and retrieve a Package to storage.

For convenience we repeat a little of the material about packaging which appeared in earlier chapters, but here we supply some more practical examples.

The XFDU format is focused around the idea of having a "table of contents" called a package *manifest*. The manifest is an XML document that is stored within the AIP and contains all the valuable information about the digital assets the AIP stores. The manifest logically or physically associates the asset with its RepInfo and PDI and can detail the complex relationships between these Information Objects using user defined or pre-defined classifications.

Given that the manifest is XML based, it is platform independent, and can be moved and easily exchanged and read between heterogeneous data systems. Information can be added to the manifest to support archival curation services such as providing information for finding aids for package discovery, digital rights management, format migration and transformation, data analysis and data validation.

14.11.7 Three Approaches to Packaging

A digital asset in an XFDU thus requires an XML manifest and RepInfo to be properly preserved. As stated earlier there are three approaches that could be taken to AIP implementation:

1. **Complete separation:** store the manifest independently of the both data asset and the RIN. In this situation the manifest references, through URI and Curation Persistent Identifiers (CPIDs), to the digital asset and information stored in RORRI respectively. The benefit of this approach is that previously archived data does not have to be moved or modified in order to include an identifier to externally referenced representation information, as the manifest would therefore act as a bridge between the data and the RepInfo as shown in Fig. 14.18. The RIN could be separately managed and maintained to change and evolve with the needs of the community.

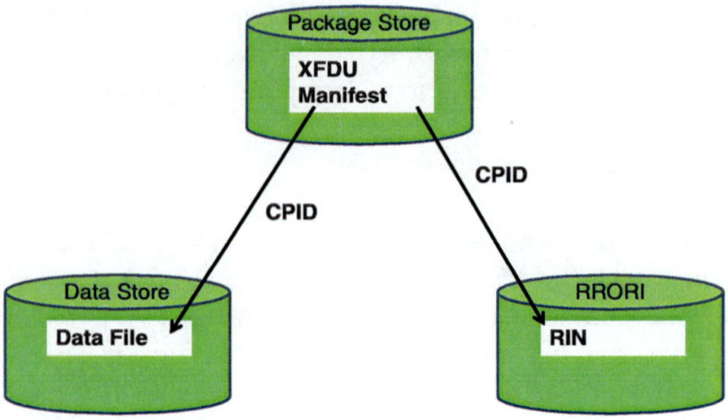

Fig. 14.18 Complete separation

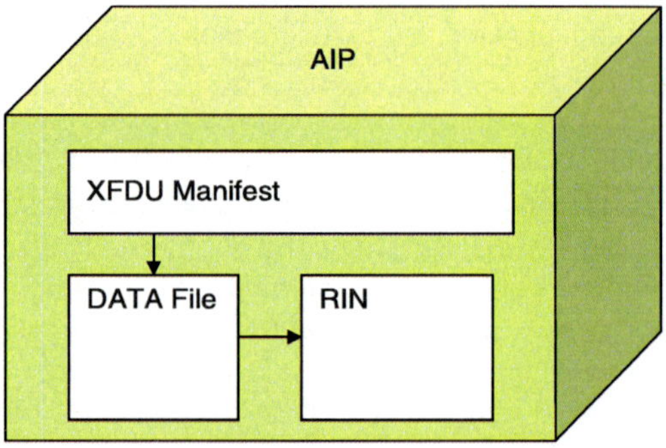

Fig. 14.19 All in one packaging – AIP as ZIP or TAR file

2. **All-in-one approach:** shown in Fig. 14.19, is to archive a more standalone AIP, containing a digital asset together with all of the RepInfo deemed necessary by the designated community at the time embedded within the same container (e.g., a ZIP or TAR file). The advantage of this solution is that all the information objects are kept together and hence immediately available, this approach removes reliance on a remote registry which may or may not be accessible long term. The producer would need to make a decision as to what level the embedded RepInfo dependencies should terminate at, in order to satisfy the community needs. This scenario presents the lowest preservation risk however could prove to be a cumbersome and impractical solution in situations which involve large data holdings or extensive RINs.
3. **Representation Information Network (RIN):** The RIN solution is to archive the digital asset with the XFDU manifest referencing an external RIN held within a registry like RORRI via CPIDs. This scenario is illustrated in Fig. 14.20. The main advantage is to store the asset independently of its community built RIN, which is itself separately and securely managed and maintained remotely from the digital data itself. Giving the advantage of RepInfo reuse, the network may be applied to multiple data sets within the holdings of many archives. This solution

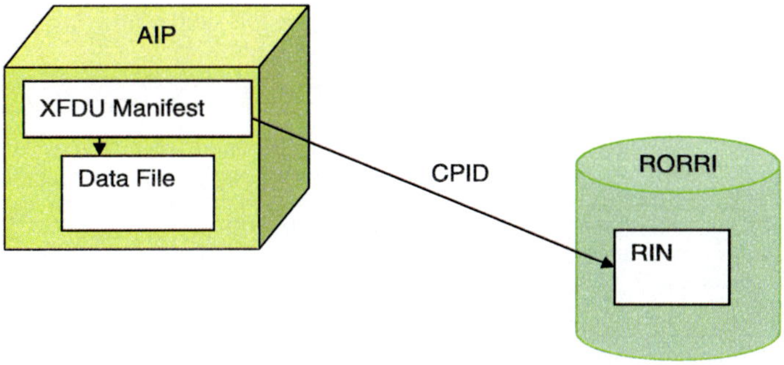

Fig. 14.20 Using a remotely stored RIN

introduces the risk of possible loss of access to the RIN network but reduces the amount of storage space and hence the cost of archiving large data sets. The RIN can much more easily change and evolve in line with the community as its knowledge changes.

An intermediate case would be to keep a local cache of the Registry/Repository's RIN, updated periodically. This would remove the risk of loss of access to the RRORI.

Of course a combination of the described implementations maybe required based on the level or risk in the network model and the perceived degree to which the designated community might change. As this section is focused on the idea of RIN resource reuse, the following details the building and implementation of RIN enabled packaging solutions.

14.11.8 Using CPIDs to Reference a RIN from an AIP

Persistent Identifiers have been discussed in Sect. 10.3.2; here we look at a practical example, although the persistence of this particular implementation cannot be guaranteed.

When a RIN is referenced from an AIP, the RIN becomes, logically, a part of that AIP, therefore it is important to discuss how this might be implemented. Because each piece of RepInfo has its own RepInfo, one need only point using CPIDs to the immediate dependencies and the whole RIN can be accessed.

The mechanism to connect the XFDU packages built by CASPAR and their data assets to the RIN in RORRI uses the attributes of the XFDU metadataReference type. For instance in the example below we have a "metadata" object categorised and classified using OAIS terminology as semantic RepInfo, the reference is to a RepInfo object stored within RORRI identified by a URI, the location type has been listed as CPID and the XML identifier is set to the CPID value. At the point of package construction, the CASPAR packaging component, given the data and a CPID, can pull extra information from RORRI such as textual descriptions of the RepInfo and these can be inserted into the XFDU manifest.

```
<metadataObject category="REP"classification="SEMANTIC" ID="REP_OTHER01">
<metadataReference otherLocatorType="CPID" locatorType="OTHER"
href="http://registry.dcc.ac.uk/omar/registry/http?interface=QueryManager&amp;method=getR
epositoryItem&amp;param-id=urn:uuid:fe5b94c3-070c-4a9e-af7a-b355aa6b37b8"
textInfo="Semantic description Climate Forecast standard Names XML description" ID="cpid-
fe5b94c3-070c-4a9e-af7a-b355aa6b37b8"/>
</metadataObject>
```

Fig. 14.21 Example of addition to XFDU manifest

This method provides an entry point into the RIN, a first level dependency. Using the CASPAR Packaging subsystem, if required it is possible to download all further necessary RepInfo in the network for addition into an AIP.

14.11.9 Packaging Guidelines

From the experience gained and lessons learnt from the work undertaken through the CASPAR project and the STFC we define 10 steps which we feel will facilitate the preservation of digital assets using information packaging. These are as follows:

1. Understand the complexities of the digital asset to be preserved, what is it used for currently? Why is it important?
2. Understand the Designated Community, what are their needs, what skills do they currently use to get value from the asset
3. Perform preservation analysis in order to full understand and realise the risks and threats to the digital asset
4. Clearly state the preservation objectives for the digital asset based on risks and costs involved – remember that depositors should also have some input into this
5. Use preservation network modelling to determine the scope and complexity of the RepInfo and PDI required for the digital asset to ensure its long term understandability. Structural and Semantic RepInfo are both essential to ensure the long term understandability of the asset
6. Be aware of, or discover, existing sources of RepInfo such as RORRI which may provide the reuse of an available RIN for the digitally encoded object in question.
7. Determine whether it is appropriate to embed the RepInfo directly with the asset inside the package ("all-in-one"), reference a remotely stored RIN, or use a combination.
8. If packages are to be ingested by an archive it may be necessary to formulate an agreement between the producer and archive stating the specifics of what needs

to be archived, the size of packages, what validation will be performed when packages are received and how often packages will be sent.

9. Use a standardised and well documented packaging format (for example XFDU) that fits the preservation objectives and provides the mechanism to form the relationships between the digital asset and the RIN determined in points 5, 6 and 7.
10. Associate AIPs with resolvable identifiers and descriptive information which can be used to later find and retrieve them

14.11.10 Example MST Implemented Network

The MST scenario described earlier in this document has been implemented using the RORRI and XFDU information packaging software components. Using the above method, the packaging software component has been used to create AIPs which reference the external RIN held within RORRI. The Packaging Builder software and visualiser is a Java application allowing the creation and visualization of network enabled AIPs. The following application screen shot in Fig. 14.22, shows an AIP with a partially expanded network.

We can see the preserved data object represented as the grey square, its RIN connections are also clearly shown. In this implementation the first level dependencies are stored directly within the AIP denoted by triangles, subsequent dependency levels are stored in the RIN held within RORRI denoted by circles. The first level packaged items are as follows:

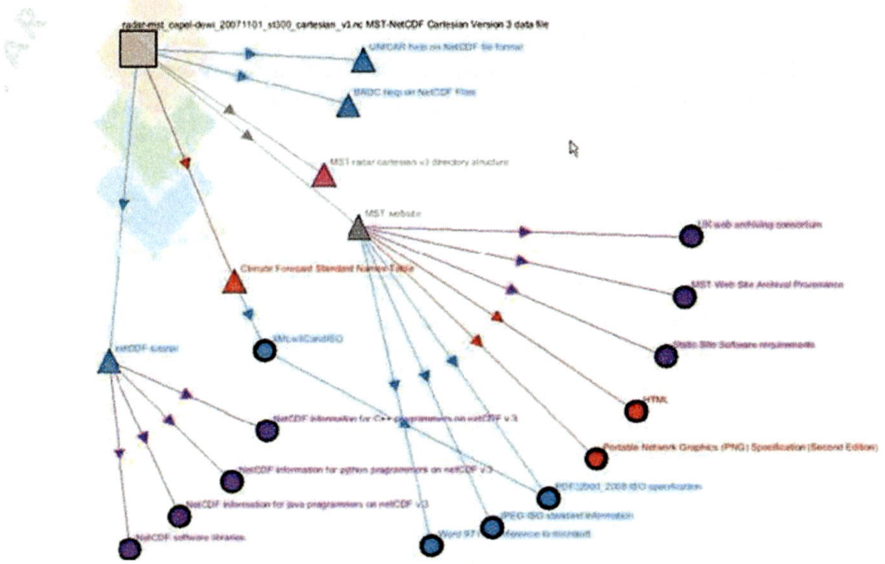

Fig. 14.22 MST network visualized with the packaging builder

- UNICAR help for NetCDF file format, a set of software libraries to support the creation and access of NetCDF files
- BADC help for NetCDF files, information compiled by the BADC about its NetCDF holdings
- MST radar directory structure, a description of the directory structure and file naming conventions of NetCDF files held by the BADC
- MST website, the MST project website, archived into a zip file
- Climate Forecast standard names list, a description of the climate forecast standard parameters found within the NetCDF MST data files
- NetCDF tutorial for developers, a collection of software libraries for working with the NetCDF file formats in various computer languages like Java and C++

Second level dependencies can be expanded out and downloaded from the registry. The second level dependencies act as RepInfo for the 1st level dependencies and so on as the network is traversed. The Representation Information network shown is an implementation of the MST modelled network described earlier in this document.

14.12 Summary

This chapter has explained the concept of the Representation Information Network using a number of preservation and curation scenarios based around scientific data sets held in archives by the Science and Technology Facilities Council (STFC). It has described an approach to planning and producing a strategy for developing a preservation solution and detailed a preservation network modelling process allowing one to determine the scope and complexity of the Representation Information Network and allowing one to further facilitate cost benefit analysis on implementing a preservation solution. We believe that the preservation network modelling process described supports and facilitates the long term preservation of scientific data by providing a sharable, stable and organized structure for digital objects and their associated requirements. This approach permits the management of risk and promotes the reuse of solutions allowing the cost of digital preservation to be shared across communities.

Further to this we have discussed an implementation of a preservation network model using a combination of Information Packaging and Representation Information registry applications to connect the preserved data to its RIN.

Part II
Practice – Use and Validation of the Tools and Techniques that Can Be Used for Preserving Digitally Encoded Information

Chapter 15
Testing Claims About Digital Preservation

In this part of the book we show a number of real examples of digital preservation activities; these have been chosen to illustrate a number of scenarios and preservation strategies using a great variety of types of data, from the simplest to highly complex.

15.1 "Accelerated Lifetime" Testing of Digital Preservation Techniques

In order to understand what and how claims about digital preservation should be tested, we need to understand what things can change over time and what we might expect to be able to rely on. Then we can simulate the passage of time, at an accelerated rate. Some of this duplicates, for convenience, some of the text from Chap. 5.

15.1.1 What Can Change?

We can consider some of the things can change over time and hence against which an archive must safeguard the digitally encoded information.

15.1.1.1 Hardware and Software Changes

Use of many digital objects relies on specific software and hardware, for example applications which run on specific versions of Microsoft Windows which in turn runs on Intel processors. Experience shows that while it may be possible to keep hardware and software available for some time after it has become obsolete, it is not a practical proposition into the indefinite future, however there are several projects and proposals which aim to emulate hardware systems and hence run software systems.

D. Giaretta, *Advanced Digital Preservation*, DOI 10.1007/978-3-642-16809-3_15,

15.1.1.2 Environment Changes

These include changes to licences or copyright and changes to organisations, affecting the usability of digital objects. External information, ranging from the DNS to XML DTDs and Schema, vital to the use and understandability, may also become unavailable.

15.1.1.3 Termination of the Archive

Without permanent funding, any archive will, at some time, end. It is therefore possible for the bits, i.e. the binary objects, to be lost, and much else besides, including the knowledge of the curators about the information encoded in those bits. Experience shows that much essential knowledge, such as the linkage between holdings, operation of specialised hardware and software and links of data files to events recorded in system logs, is held by such curators (in their heads) but not written down or encoded for exchange or preservation. Bearing these things in mind it is clear that any repository must be prepared to hand over its holding – together with all these tacit pieces of information – to its successor(s).

Other, major, threats include financial, political or environmental (such as floods or earthquakes) upheaval.

15.1.1.4 Changes in What People Know

As described earlier the Knowledge Base of the Designated Community determines the amount of Representation Information which must be available. This Knowledge Base changes over time as terminology, tools and theories change.

15.1.2 What can be Relied on in the Long Term?

While we cannot provide rigorous proofs, it is worth, at this point, listing those things which we might credibly argue would be available in the long term, in order to clarify the basis of our approach. We should be able to trace back our preservation plans to these assumptions. Were we able to undertake a rigorous mathematical proof these would form the basis of the axioms for our "theorems".

- Words on paper (or titanium sheets) that people can read; ISO standards kept in national libraries are an example of this. Over the long term there may be an issue of language and character shape.

  Carvings in stone and books have proven track records of preserving information over hundreds of years.
- The information such as Representation Information which is collected.

  A somewhat recursive assumption, however it is difficult to make progress without it. This Representation Information includes both digital as well as physical (e.g. books) objects.
- Some kind of remote access

Network access is the natural assumption but in principle other methods of obtaining information from a given address/location would suffice, for example fax or horse-back rider.

- Some kind of computers

  Perhaps not strictly necessary but this seems a sensible assumption given the amount of calculation needed to do some of the most trivial operations, such as displaying anything beyond simple ASCII text, or extracting information from large datasets.
- People? Organisations?

  Clearly neither the originators of the digital objects nor the initial host organisations can be relied on to continue to exist. However if no people and no organisations exist at all then perhaps digital preservation becomes a moot topic.
- Identifiers?

  Some kind of identifier system is needed, but clearly we cannot assume that any given URL, for example, will remain valid.

15.2 Summary

This short chapter provides a very brief introduction to what we need to think about when we are planning to preserve digitally encoded information. Later chapters discuss these topics in much more detail.

Chapter 16
Tools for Countering the Threats to Digital Preservation

We begin with a brief recap of the points made in Chap. 5 about the broad threats to the preservation of our digitally encoded information. Then a number of components, both infrastructure and domain dependent, are discussed and the CASPAR implementations of these are introduced. Subsequent chapters build up the details of the infrastructure and tools which indicate how these solutions could be implemented and for which strong prototypes exist at the time of writing.

The major threats and their solutions are as follows:

Threat	Requirements for solution
Users may be unable to understand or use the data e.g. the semantics, format, processes or algorithms involved	Ability to create and maintain adequate Representation Information
Non-maintainability of essential hardware, software or support environment may make the information inaccessible	Ability to share information about the availability of hardware and software and their replacements/substitutes
The chain of evidence may be lost and there may be lack of certainty of provenance or authenticity	Ability to bring together evidence from diverse sources about the authenticity of a digital object
Access and use restrictions may make it difficult to reuse data, or alternatively may not be respected in future	Ability to deal with digital rights correctly in a changing and evolving environment. Preservation-friendly rights or appropriate transfer of rights is necessary
Loss of ability to identify the location of data	An ID resolver system which is really persistent
The current custodian of the data, whether an organisation or project, may cease to exist at some point in the future	Brokering of organisations to hold data and the ability to package together the information needed to transfer information between organisations ready for long term preservation
The ones we trust to look after the digital holdings may let us down	Certification process so that one can have confidence about whom to trust to preserve data holdings over the long term

D. Giaretta, *Advanced Digital Preservation*, DOI 10.1007/978-3-642-16809-3_16,

16.1 Key Preservation Components and Infrastructure

When thinking about what tools and services are needed to help us with preservation, we should consider how to deal with all the types of digital objects discussed in Chap. 4, without having to tailor software for each. Identifying commonalities allows us to share the cost of such tools and services – remember one of the key disincentives is cost.

One way of doing this is to distinguish between those things which can be used for many different types of digitally encoded information and those things which are closely tied to the specific type of digital object. The former we shall refer to as domain independent while the latter we will refer to as domain dependent. We use the term "domain" (or sometimes "discipline") because it is then easier to map to the real world, instead of having to think about different digital object types. Each domain will tend to use many different digital object types, and there will be overlaps although often with a different focus, nevertheless people tend to think about their own domain of work rather than their digital object types.

Since one tends to refer to tools which can be used for many different kinds of things as infrastructure we shall often use the term "domain independent infrastructure" or simply "infrastructure".

To make the distinction we can examine the issues from several angles, making use of the diagrams we have discussed earlier.

Figure 16.1, which was briefly introduced in Sect. 6.5, and the associated table, pick out the main components, following the lifecycle of a piece of digitally encoded

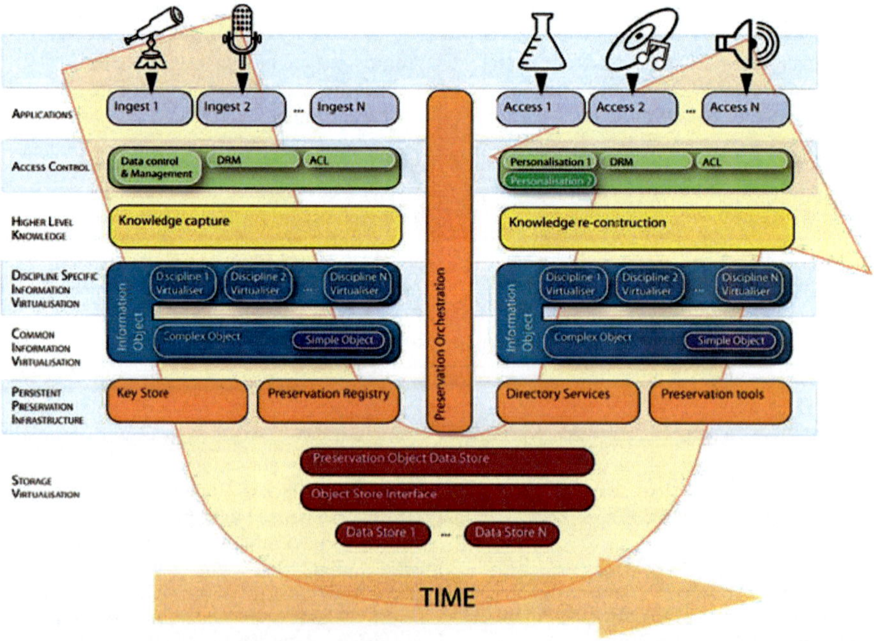

Fig. 16.1 CASPAR information flow architecture

Step in Lifecycle	Function
Create the Information Object – by adding Representation Information to the particular digital data object.	
1. Representation Information – adequate for the Designated Community – must be created. **COMPONENT**: Representation Information Toolbox (see Sect. 17.12)	Guides the user to a number of applications to create adequate Representation Information (RepInfo) – using existing RepInfo from registries where available. Representation Information includes Syntactical and Semantic descriptions and also associated software and standards.
Major components of this toolbox are:	
2. Capture Data Management information **COMPONENT**: Data Access Manager (see Sect. 17.7)	This includes Access Control information such as Access Control Lists. More detailed DRM may also be needed.
3. Capture Digital Rights associated with the data object **COMPONENT**: DRM (see Sect. 17.8)	Digital Rights Management can be an essential part of digital preservation, especially for the short- to medium-term portion of archival storage.
4. Capture Higher level Semantics **COMPONENT**: RepInfo Gap Manager (see Sect. 17.4)	The capture of higher-level, more subtle semantics (knowledge) is closely related to that which the burgeoning Semantic Web research industry is working on. What is needed here is to ensure that what is captured can survive over the long term and over many changes in "knowledge technologies". The RepInfo Gap Manager is applicable at all levels of description, but the most challenging is the more complex, higher-level, semantics.
5. Create Virtualisation description **COMPONENT**: Virtualisation Assistant (see Sect. 17.3)	Virtualisation consists of identifying abstractions – probably many different types of abstractions – to encapsulate important features of the Information Object. This is essentially OAIS Representation Information, but we wish to stress the Virtualisation aspects because of the need to facilitate automated processing.
In the taxonomy of Information Objects, it is useful to distinguish between Simple and Complex Objects, as well as discipline-specific virtualisation, hence the need for:	
6. Describe discipline specific object characteristics **COMPONENT**: Discipline specific Object Virtualiser Manager (see Sect. 17.3)	In order to limit the multiplicity of types of object, it seems reasonable to normalise characteristics, separating those that are discipline specific from those that are common to all objects.

7. Describe Simple Object **COMPONENT**: Simple Object Virtualiser (see Sect. 17.3)	The "simple" in this case refers to the type of Information Object; this is a non-trivial component involving descriptions of the Structure as well as the Semantics of relatively self-contained Objects
8. Describe Complex Object **COMPONENT**: Complex Object Virtualiser (see Sect. 17.3)	A Complex Object is one that can be described in terms of several, possibly a large number of, both Simple Objects and Complex Objects and their inter-relations. In particular, the Complex Object Virtualiser has to cope with multiple partial copies of the datasets forming the referred Object and with the management of the lower-level objects in a fully distributed environment.
9. Some of the Objects are created "on-demand". It may be true to say that most Information is created in this way. **COMPONENT**: On-Demand Object Virtualiser (see Sect. 17.3)	An On-Demand Object is one (Simple or Complex) that can be referred to by the available knowledge and can be instantiated on request.
10. Produce OAIS Preservation Description Information (PDI) **COMPONENT**: Preservation Description Information Toolbox (see Sects. 17.7, 17.8, 17.11, and 17.9)	PDI includes Fixity, Provenance, Reference and Context information. The PDI Toolbox has a number of sub-components that address each of these and guide the user to produce the most complete PDI possible. Knowledge capture techniques should also be applicable here.
Having created the Virtualisation information (which includes and extends the OAIS concept of Representation Information), it must be stored in an accessible location.	
11. Store DRM/Virtualisation Information/Representation Information in Registry **COMPONENT**: Registry	We take the general case that it is stored in an external registry in order to allow the possibility of enhancing the Representation Information etc. to cope with changes in the technologies, Designated Communities etc. The alternative of storing this "metadata" with the data object is possible but would not address long-term preservation because: • the RepInfo cannot be complete; • the RepInfo cannot easily be updated; • the RepInfo has to be repeated for each object or copy of the object and consistency cannot easily be maintained; • the effort of updating the RepInfo cannot easily be shared, in particular when the originator is no longer available.
In addition to Representation Information, there may also be keys, public and private, for encryption etc. that need to be available over the long term.	

12. Store Keys, public and private **COMPONENT**: Key Store	Public keys can be stored in any convenient location that is accessible to users. However, for long-term preservation these keys must be guaranteed to be available, as must the appropriate encryption or digest algorithm. The same applies for private keys, which must be held in "escrow" for some agreed period, with adequate security.
The collection of information adequate for preservation is a key concept in OAIS – the Archival Information Package.	
13. Construct the AIP **COMPONENT**: Archival Information Packager (see Sect. 17.10)	The AIP is a logical construct, and key to preservation in the OAIS Reference Model. The AI Packager logically binds together the information required to preserve the Content Information so that it is suitable for long-term preservation. However, this should not be regarded as a static construct, since, as has been stressed, preservation is a dynamic process. The AI Packager works with the Preservation Orchestration Manager
Having the AIP, this must now be securely stored.	
14. Store the AIP data object securely for the long term. **COMPONENT**: Preservation Data Object (PDO) (see Sect. 17.6)	Digital storage comes in many different forms, and the hardware and software technology is constantly evolving. The PDO virtualises the storage at the level of a data object; in this way, it extends the current virtualised storage, which allows transparent access to distributed data. The PDO hides the details of the storage system, the collection management etc. – all of which can cause a great deal of trouble when migrating, as hardware and software technology changes. One way of looking at this is to view it as an implementation of the OAIS Archival Storage functional element. As such, it allows the development of a market of interchangeable "Archival Storage" elements for a variety of archives.
Now we come to the period when the data object is stored for many years – in principle indefinitely. During this time the originators of the data pass away; hardware and software become obsolete and are replaced; the organisation that hosts the repository evolves, merges, perhaps terminates (but hands on its data holdings); the community of users, their tools, their underlying Knowledge Base change out of all recognition. In the background, something must keep the information alive, in the same way as the body's autonomic nervous system keeps the body alive, namely by triggering breathing, heartbeat etc. Note that the autonomic nervous system does not actually do the breathing etc., but provides the trigger. This is what must be arranged.	

15. Notify the repository when changes must be made **COMPONENTS**: • RepInfo Gap Manager (see Sect. 17.4) • Preservation Orchestration Manager (see Sect. 17.5)	This will provide a number of notification services to alert repositories, which have registered appropriately, of the probable need to take action to ensure the preservation of their holdings. This action could range from the need for migration to new formats to the obsolescence of hardware to the availability of relevant Representation Information. In addition, brokering services and workflow control processes will be available to assist data holders to access services – for example, to transform data or to hand over holdings to longer-lived repositories. Activities include advising on preservation strategies, providing support for Preservation Planning in repositories, and sharing Representation Information. Without this type of background activity, preservation is at risk by neglect. Clearly, larger organisations may not need this, but, even in the largest and best run organisations, individual preservation projects may be funded on a relatively short-term basis. This infrastructure must itself be persistent.

information as it is ingested into an OAIS system and subsequently retrieved for use at some time in the future. The table mentions some components which will be introduced in later sections.

16.2 Discipline Independent Aspects

Building on the previous section we can now look as the OAIS Functional Model (Fig. 16.2) from another viewpoint, and try to make the distinction between the domain dependent and domain independent parts.

The OAIS Functional Entities in the Functional Model (repeated here for convenience from Fig. 6.8) can be used to group the domain independent concepts and components.

16.2.1 Preservation Planning

16.2.1.1 Registries of Representation Information

The Registry/Repository concept was introduced in Sect. 7.1.3 – the term Registry/Repository is used, rather than simply "Registry", in order to stress the fact

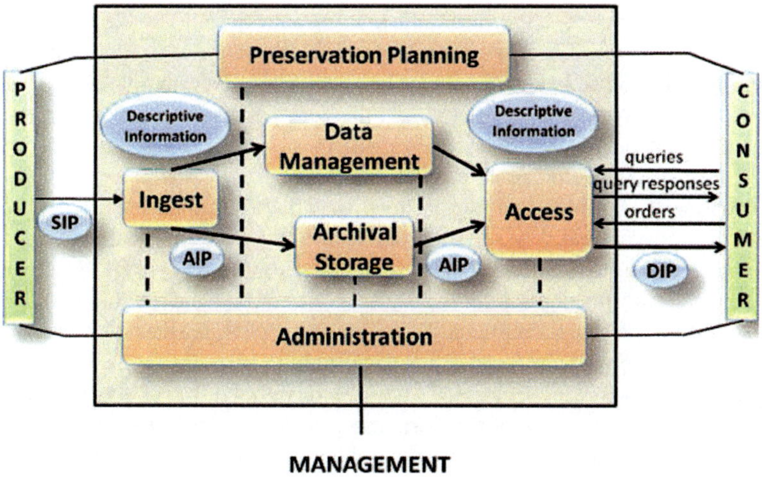

Fig. 16.2 OAIS functional model

that the concept embodies the holding (in the Repository) of a significant amount of digital information – the Representation Information – rather than simply pointers to external resources.

The prime functions of a Registry/Repository are:

- Given an identifier of a piece of Representation Information (RepInfo), return that piece of Representation Information to the requestor. This Representation Information will in general be an opaque binary object as far as the Registry/Repository is concerned.
- Allow searching of the holdings of the Registry in order to enable the re-use of existing RepInfo.
    - To facilitate this searching, each piece of RepInfo should be classified under one or more Classification Schemes, and have a searchable text description of the RepInfo.
- Each piece of RepInfo should itself have a pointer to its own RepInfo, and also details of its PDI.
- The Registry/Repository should itself be an OAIS which can be certified for long-term preservation of information.

> The Registry/Repository functionality is domain independent because pieces of the Representation Information are, as far as the Registry/Repository is concerned, opaque binary objects.

Of course any piece of Representation Information could be domain specific, but that content is not relevant to the Registry/Repository. It is important to note that there may be multiple ways to describe something. For example Structure-type Representation Information may come in the form of an EAST description, or a DRB description or a DFDL description. All these are valid and each of these in turn will have its own Representation Information.

In addition, it is possible that two archives may have identical copies of a piece of data but may provide entirely separate pieces of Representation Information. This is in many ways a duplication of effort. However the Registry/Repository will be entirely unaware of this duplication since (1) it does not have a link back to the data, as this would not be maintainable and (2) the pieces of Representation Information are opaque binary objects as far as it is concerned.

A separate, value added, service may be developed by analysing the links between data and Representation Information, in a way analogous to the ranking algorithm used by Google. Such a service would enable one to say, for example, that 99% of all archives use CPIDYYY as the Representation Information for a certain type of data. Such a statistic may influence others to use that particular piece of Representation Information rather than some other, competing, Representation Information.

New versions of Representation may be created from time to time, to improve usability or accuracy. The versioning must be controlled and it will prove useful to distinguish between a unique identifier for a particular version and a logical identifier for all versions of the Representation Information. Using the logical identifier should return the latest (and presumably the best) version, which will change as new versions are created, whereas using the unique identifier, or, equivalently, providing a specific version number, should always provide that specific piece of Representation Information.

Representation Information may be cached, that is to say copies may, for convenience, be kept, in a variety of locations, including packaged with the Data Object. Caching is a well known optimisation technique and the appropriate steps must be taken to ensure that the cache copies are identical with the original, however the task is made easier because a particular piece of Representation Information is never changed, instead, as discussed above, a new version is created.

16.2.1.2 Orchestration

The Orchestration component has to:

- allow individuals to register their interests and expertise
- collect information from (anonymous or registered) individuals about changes in software, hardware, environment or Knowledge Base of any Designated Community. This information will be passed on to the RepInfo Gap Manager component.
- receive information from the RepInfo Gap Manager component about a gap which has been identified

- send requests to appropriate registered users, based on their interests and expertise, for the creation of required Representation Information

> The Orchestration functionality is domain independent in that it needs no embedded domain specific knowledge in order to match keywords specifying gaps to people, although clearly some domain specific thesauri could help give a wider set of relevant matches.

16.2.1.3 RepInfo Gap Manager

The RepInfo Gap Manager component embodies a small but essential application of Knowledge Management techniques to preservation. Its main purpose is to assist in identifying gaps which have arisen as a result of changes in hardware, software, environment and Knowledge Bases of Designated Communities. This has been discussed extensively in Chap. 8.

The changes are notified by human participants in the preservation process. The RepInfo Gap Manager knows of the existing dependencies between pieces of Representation Information, working closely with one or more instances of the Registry/Repository. The labels in the Registry/Repository capture those dependencies. The changes imply that gaps in the Representation Information network will have arisen, which must be filled. Human participants must be alerted and requested to provide new Representation Information to fill those gaps. The human participation may not always be necessary; the RepInfo Gap Manager may be able to bring in Representation Information from another, existing, source to fill the gap – although this would have to be checked by humans.

As an example of these gaps we can look at the dependencies in the Representation Information about a piece of astronomical data (repeated for convenience from Sect. 6.3.1). FITS is a standard data format that is used in astronomy. To understand a FITS file one needs to understand the FITS standard which is in turn described in a PDF document. To understand the keywords contained in a FITS file one needs to be able to understand the FITS dictionary (that explains the usage of keywords). Figure 16.3 illustrates these dependencies.

At some particular point in time the Dictionary may be part of the Knowledge Base of the Designated Community (i.e. astronomers). However there may come a time when this particular type of Dictionary begins to fall from general use. A gap in the Representation Information net will begin to appear, which must be filled. In most cases some human participant will have to create the additional piece of Representation Information that is required. However it may be the case that in some separate Representation Information Network uses the same Dictionary and provides Representation Information for the Dictionary. The RepInfo Gap Manager may be able to deduce that the latter can be re-used in the astronomical case.

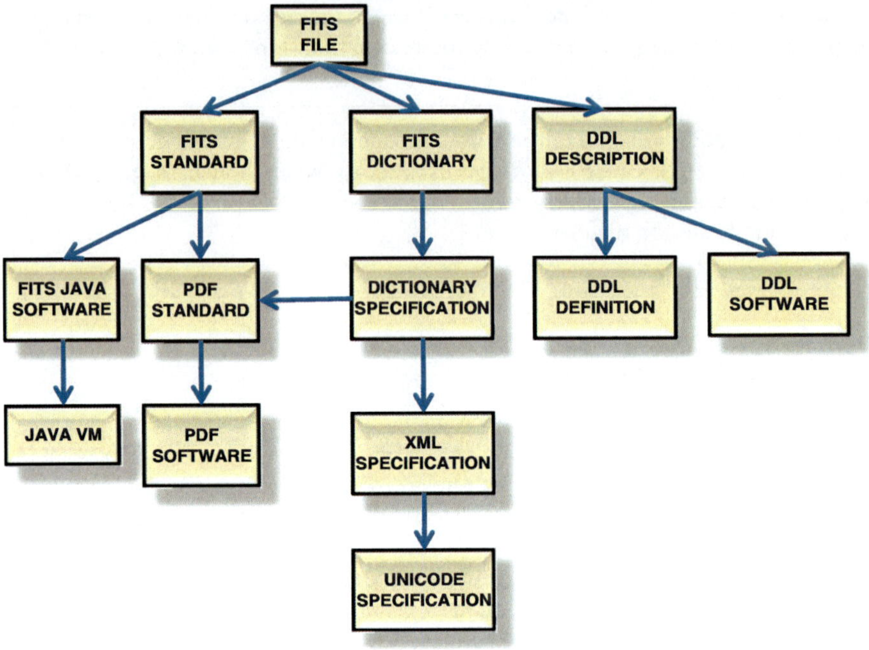

Fig. 16.3 FITS file dependencies

> The RepInfo Gap Manager manipulates symbols and identifiers and does not require embedded domain specific knowledge.

16.2.2 Digital Object Storage

The Digital Object Storage (or sometimes simply "Storage") component takes care of the "Digital Object" and encapsulates:

- The secure preservation of the bits which encode the information of interest. This of course applies to a primary Data Object, Representation Information, Preservation Description Information etc, the latter also being Data Objects. These individual stored objects form the simplest element in the storage system, and each needs only be regarded as opaque binary objects, whose internal structure need not be known or understood by the Storage system, although the structure of the AIP, e.g. how to get the PDI object out of the AIP, will be known to it.
- The association of Representation Information and PDI with the Content Information. This association may include having copies of the Representation

Information or PDI kept within the Storage system. However it is important to recognise that neither of these can be complete. For example the Representation Information Network will change as, for example, the Knowledge Base of the Designated Community changes. Similarly the Provenance information will include not just the technical information about copying but also but also include descriptions of various real-world entities (e.g. persons, organisations and their attributes, roles and actions) whose social context is also associated with the data. Therefore both Representation Information and PDI will have to include a pointer out of the storage system.

- The automatic maintenance of the *technical* provenance information, including details of what are essentially internal events including copying, replication and refreshment and the objects.
- The policies which the archive imposes on the stored objects (and the Representation Information, PDI etc associated with the encoded instances of these policies), for example
  - the number of backup copies, offsite and on-site, on-line and near-line, and replication
  - the access controls
  - the distribution of information among the individual pieces of virtualised storage
  - maintenance of namespaces
  - maintenance of collection level information
- The ability to hand on the stored AIPs, and appropriate collection information, to another OAIS system – either because of technological change or because of organisational change as the preserved information is passed on to the next in the chain of preservation.

The Digital Object Storage concept is intrinsically domain independent.

16.2.3 Ingest

The INGEST functional entity in the OAIS Reference Model provides

> ***the services and functions to accept Submission Information Packages (SIPs) from Producers (or from internal elements under the OAIS Administration control) and prepare the contents for storage and management within the archive. Ingest functions include receiving SIPs, performing quality assurance on SIPs, generating an Archival Information Package (AIP) which complies with the archive's data formatting and documentation standards, extracting Descriptive Information from the AIPs for inclusion in the archive database, and coordinating updates to Archival Storage and Data Management.***

The OAIS Producer-Archive Interface Methodology Abstract Standard (PAIMAS [22]) seeks to identify, define and provide structure for the relationships and interactions between an information Producer and an Archive. It defines the methodology for the structure of actions that are required from the initial time of contact between the Producer and the Archive until the objects of information are received and validated by the Archive. These actions cover the first stage of the Ingest Process. It is expected that a specific standard or "community standard" would be created in order to take into account all of the specific features of the community in question.

The Producer-Archive Interface Specification [23] aims to provide a standard method to formally define the digital information objects to be transferred by an information Producer to an Archive and for effectively transferring these objects in the form of SIPs.

> The general concepts and checklists provided by PAIMAS and PAIS provide domain independent views of the processes that are needed in INGEST.

16.2.4 Access

ACCESS is the OAIS functional entity which provides

> ***the services and functions that support Consumers in determining the existence, description, location and availability of information stored in the OAIS, and allowing Consumers to request and receive information products. Access functions include communicating with Consumers to receive requests, applying controls to limit access to specially protected information, coordinating the execution of requests to successful completion, generating responses (Dissemination Information Packages, result sets, reports) and delivering the responses to Consumers.***

Looking at existing archives one sees a very great variety of ACCESS-type functions. Indeed it is probably true to say that this, the user-facing part of an archive's work, is the area in which the archive will seek to "brand" its services. Clearly the access services have a certain degree of standardisation to allow interoperability, examples of which include provision of Web pages, harvesting, and FTP services. Nevertheless each archive will seek to provide a richer set of "branded" ordering, searching and data provision services, and thus there are limits to the type of domain independent services which might be offered to any archive.

Areas in which we might hope for some discipline independence are Access Control and specialised Finding Aids based on PDI, and these are considered next.

16.2.4.1 Access Control/DRM/Trust

Access Control, Trust and Digital Rights Management must attempt to withstand changes in:

- individuals, and their roles and even their existence
- organisations
- legal systems, including new rights, new types of events and new obligations
- security systems such as certificates and passwords

A digital object may be deposited in an archive with one particular system of Access controls and DRM, but may (in fact certainly will) be used under a completely different access control system.

> While DRM systems could be made specific to domains, the requirement for survivability to change will tend to require a significant independence from domain considerations.

16.2.4.2 Finding Aids Based on PDI

A Finding Aid is defined in OAIS as ***a software program or document that allows Consumers to search for and identify Archival Information Packages of interest.***

> ***If the Consumer does not know a priori what specific holdings of the OAIS are of interest, the Consumer will establish a Search Session with the OAIS. During this Search Session the Consumer will use the OAIS Finding Aids that operate on Descriptive Information, or in some cases on the AIPs themselves, to identify and investigate potential holdings of interest. This may be accomplished by the submission of queries and the return of result sets to the Consumer.***

OAIS provides terminology for the information which is used by the Finding Aids, for example **Descriptive Information, Associated Descriptions and Collection Descriptions.** However further specification of this information is not provided by OAIS, in part because of the great variety of types of information which could be involved.

> A type of Finding Aid which could have some discipline independent aspects is based on standardised PDI components, and in particular discipline independent aspects of Provenance.

16.2.5 Data Management

The DATA MANAGEMENT functional entity in OAIS is the ***entity that contains the services and functions for populating, maintaining, and accessing a wide variety of information. Some examples of this information are catalogs and inventories on what may be retrieved from Archival Storage, processing algorithms that may be run on retrieved data, Consumer access statistics, Consumer billing, Event Based Orders, security controls, and OAIS schedules, policies, and procedures.***

Descriptive Information, mentioned above, is ***the set of information, consisting primarily of Package Descriptions, which is provided to Data Management to support the finding, ordering, and retrieving of OAIS information holdings by Consumers.***

While in general this type of information is extremely diverse, there are some inventory activities which seem particularly basic and which requires relatively straightforward collection of information.

> This domain independent type of Descriptive Information, used by the Data Management entity, is the simple catalogue of which Content Information is in which Archival Information Package.

16.3 Discipline Dependence: Toolboxes/Libraries

As noted in the description of the Registry/Repository, individual pieces of Representation Information are opaque binary objects to it. However the Representation Information must contain specific information about some specific data objects, and must include discipline dependence.

The discipline specificity is captured using a variety of tools and techniques; the umbrella term "toolbox" includes all of these. Chapter 7 provides an overview of the types of Representation Information.

Discipline specificity is also needed for parts of the Preservation Description Information (PDI), and an umbrella toolbox is needed here also. PDI is discussed in more detail in Chap. 10.

The term toolbox should not be interpreted as a Graphical User Interface (GUI), rather is just an umbrella term which could include, for example, many GUIs, software libraries, processes and procedures. There are a number of technologies which appear in many different guises.

16.4 Key Infrastructure Components

Based on the OAIS Reference and Functional Models, CASPAR has defined the basic infrastructure for providing digital preservation services, called the CASPAR

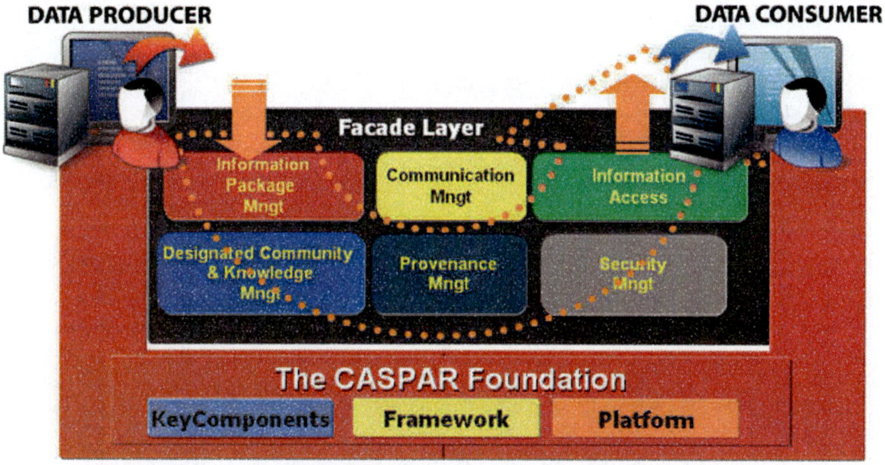

Fig. 16.4 CASPAR key components overview

Foundation which is composed of 11 Key Components built on top of a service oriented Framework. And the CASPAR Framework guarantees portability and interoperability (i.e. compliance to WS-I open standard) with existing systems and platforms.

As shown in Fig. 16.4, the CASPAR Foundation provides a set of fully conformant with the OAIS Information Model by managing key concepts such as:

- Representation Information and Designated Community
- Preservation Description Information
- Information Packaging

The key components identified in the CASPAR Architecture (Fig. 16.5) may be grouped in 6 main facade blocks:

1. Information Package Management
2. Information Access
3. Designated Community and Knowledge Management
4. Communication Management
5. Security Management
6. Provenance Management

16.5 Information Package Management

As shown in Fig. 16.6, the block supports Data Producers in the following main steps:

1. Ingest Content Information
2. Create Information Package, by adding also

   a. Representation Information
   b. Descriptive Information
   c. Preservation Description Information
3. Check Information Package
4. Store Information Package for long term

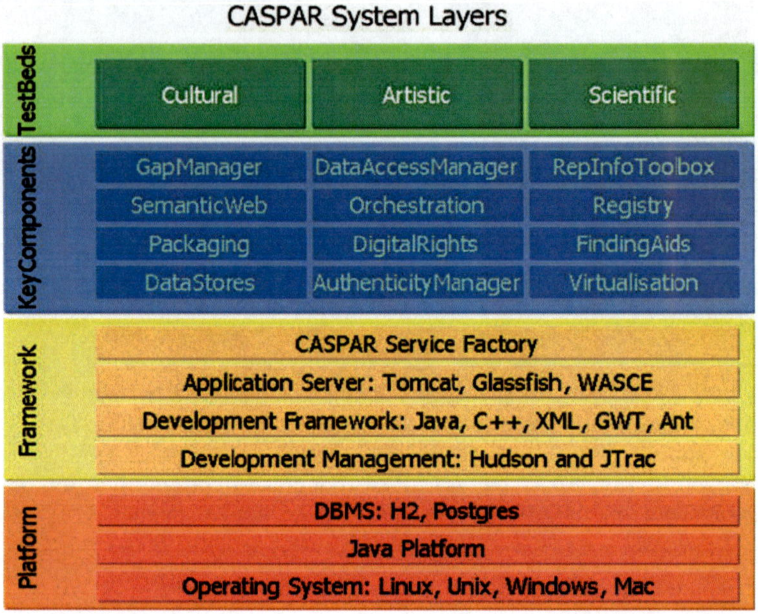

Fig. 16.5 CASPAR architecture layers

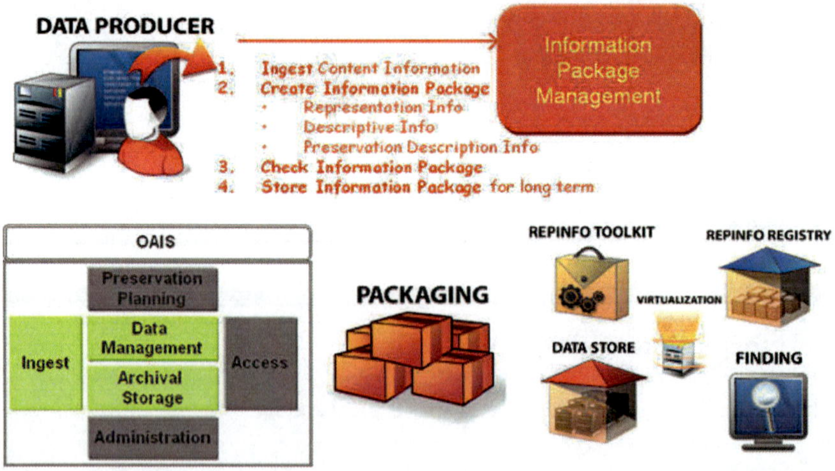

Fig. 16.6 Information package management

Those features are defined in three OAIS functional blocks: Ingest, Data Management and Archival Storage.

The main component of the Information Package Management is the CASPAR Packaging which cooperates together with (i) Representation Information Toolkit, (ii) Representation Information Registry, (iii) Virtualisation, (iv) Preservation DataStores, (v) Finding Manager.

16.6 Information Access

As shown in Fig. 16.7, the block supports Data Consumers in the following main steps:

1. Search Content Information;
2. Obtain Information Package and relative Contents and Descriptions, also by considering the Designated Community Profile of the Consumer.

Those features are defined in three OAIS functional blocks: Access, Data Management and Archival Storage.

The main component of the Information Access is the CASPAR Finding Manager which cooperates together with (i) Knowledge Manager, (ii) Packaging, (iii) Preservation DataStores.

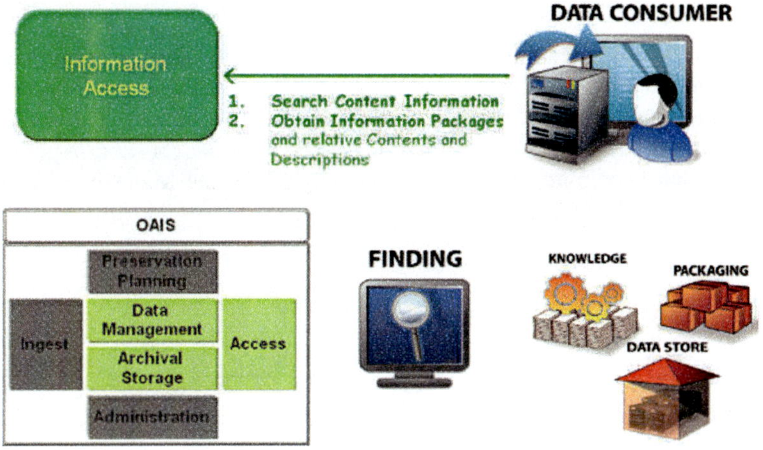

Fig. 16.7 Information access

16.7 Designated Community, Knowledge and Provenance Management

As shown in Fig. 16.8, the blocks support actors in the following main steps:

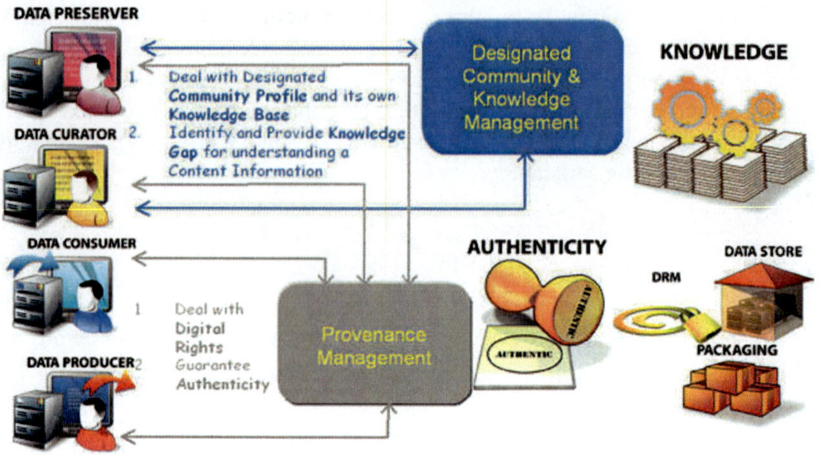

Fig. 16.8 Designated community, knowledge and provenance management

1. Deal with Designated Community Profile and its own Knowledge Base;
2. Identify and Provide Knowledge Gap for understanding a Content Information;
3. Deal with Digital Rights;
4. Guarantee Authenticity.

Those features are defined in three OAIS functional blocks: Preservation Planning, Data Management and Access.

The main components of the Designated Community, Knowledge and Provenance Management are the CASPAR Knowledge Manager and Authenticity Manager which cooperate together with (i) Digital Rights Manager, (ii) Preservation DataStores, (iii) Packaging.

16.8 Communication Management

As shown in Fig. 16.9, the block supports Data Preservers and Curators in the following main steps:

1. Notify and Alert for Change Event impacting long term preservation;
2. Trigger Preservation Process.

Those features are defined in two OAIS functional blocks: Preservation Planning and Administration.

The main component of the Communication Management is the CASPAR Preservation Orchestration Manager which cooperates together with (i) Knowledge Manager, (ii) Authenticity Manager, (iii) Representation Information Registry.

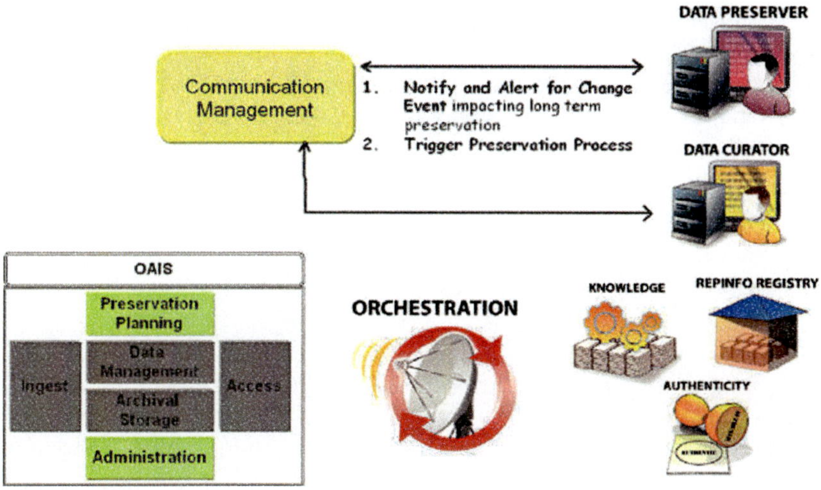

Fig. 16.9 Communication management

16.9 Security Management

As shown in Fig. 16.10, the block supports actors in the following main steps:

1. Deal with User Account, Role and Profile;
2. Deal with Content Access Permissions;
3. Deal with Digital Rights;
4. Guarantee Authenticity.

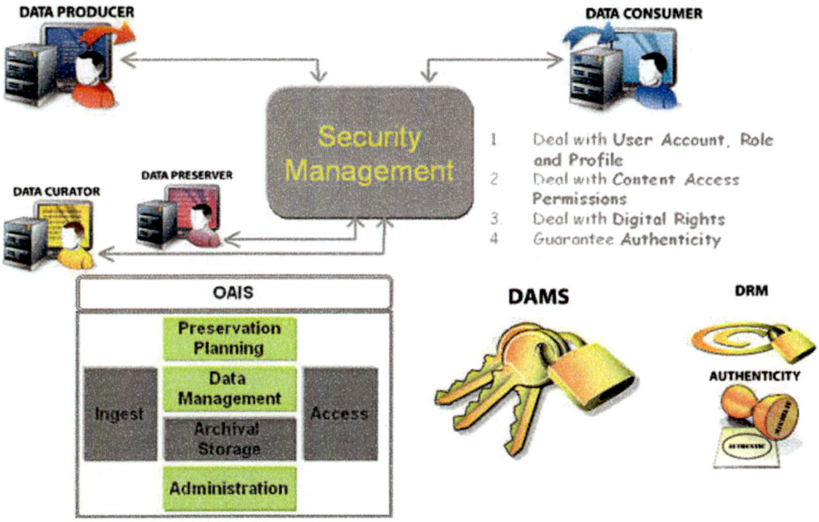

Fig. 16.10 Security management

Those features are defined in three OAIS functional blocks: Preservation Planning, Data Management and Administration.

The main component of the Security Management is the CASPAR Data Access Manager and Security which cooperates together with (i) Digital Rights Manager, (ii) Authenticity Manager.

Chapter 17
The CASPAR Key Components Implementation

This chapter presents the CASPAR Key Components in somewhat greater detail.

Having discussed the various ways of countering the threats to digital preservation, and distinguished the domain dependent from the domain independent, this chapter presents the CASPAR implementation of these components.

17.1 Design Considerations

One important consideration is the preservability of the infrastructure components (Fig. 17.1) themselves. The approach taken by CASPAR was not to use recursion and say that one would use CASPAR to preserve the components. Instead the approach was to make the components relatively easy to re-implement. Thus in the rest of this chapter we provide more details of the components and then give the interface definitions.

- These interfaces have been kept relatively simple in order to make them easier to re-implement.
- it must be possible to integrate these components into existing repositories
- we must not demand that all components are available all the time
- there must not be single points of failure.

17.2 Registry/Repository of Representation Information Details

In terms of access, interpretation and use of the Representation Information, the key concept here is to try to make the access to, and the form of, the initial piece of Representation Information as "standard" as possible. In CASPAR this piece of initial Representation Information is called the "RepInfoLabel" which will be described later. The purpose of this initial piece of RepInfo is to provide a categorisation of the types of RepInfo which are available for the Data Object, using the classification of RepInfo which OAIS provides (Fig. 17.2). Such a breakdown gives

D. Giaretta, *Advanced Digital Preservation*, DOI 10.1007/978-3-642-16809-3_17,

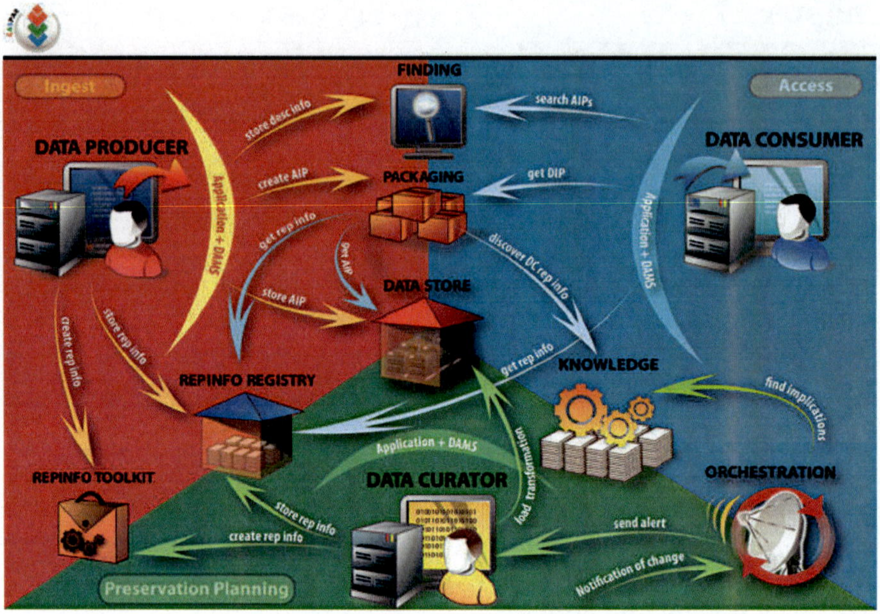

Fig. 17.1 The CASPAR key components

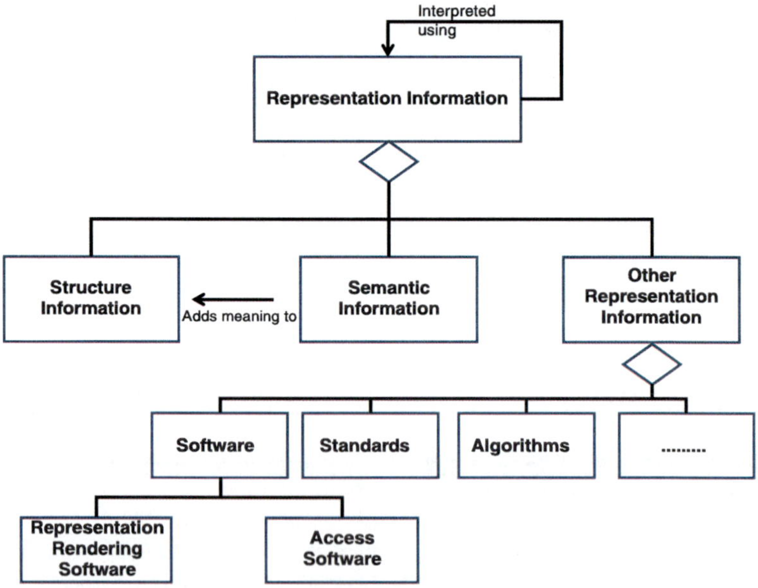

Fig. 17.2 OAIS classification of representation information

users (and applications) a clue as to which piece of RepInfo is of relevance for any particular purpose.

In terms of standardising the access, we propose that identifiers (called here Curation Persistent Identifiers – CPID) are associated with any data object, which point to the appropriate Representation Information, as illustrated in Fig. 17.3. The concepts underlying these Persistent Identifiers are discussed in detail in Sect. 10.3.2.

In this diagram we introduce the idea of a Registry/Repository of Representation Information. However it must be stressed that

this is not intended to indicate a single central registry, which would be a single point of failure in such a preservation system, but rather a network of distributed, perhaps independent, registries and

the arrows are uni-directional, in other words there is a pointer from the "data" to its Representation Information BUT not necessarily vice-versa, because one piece of Representation Information might be applicable to many thousands of data instances.

The registry concept has the advantage that, as will be expanded on later in this book, it facilitates the sharing of the effort in producing Representation Information.

It must also be stressed that this conceptual model does not imply that all Representation Information is kept in Registries; in fact it is perfectly sensible

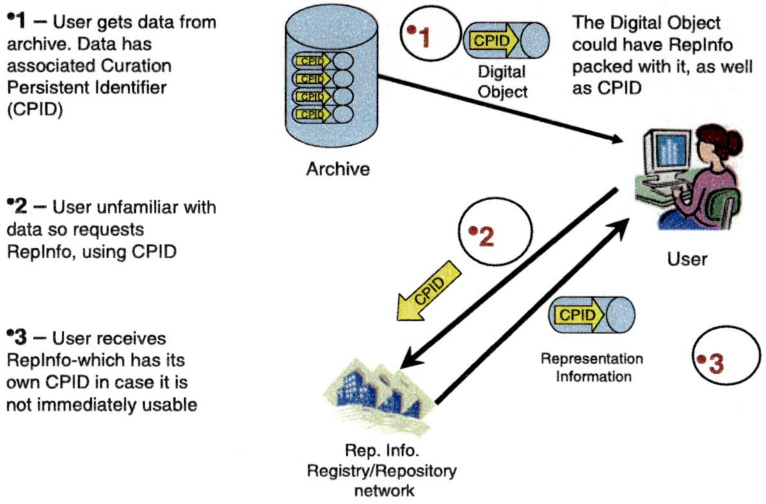

Fig. 17.3 Linking to representation information

to physically package Representation Information with the data content, in the Archival Information Package (AIP). However for any piece of information, changes in the knowledge base of the Designated Community imply that the amount of Representation Information which has been explicitly captured must change, and this is facilitated by being able to point outside of the AIP.

In order to tie this in with the idea of the initial piece of Representation Information, we can expand the first transaction as follows:

The initial RepInfo (a RepInfoLabel) is circled in Fig. 17.4; if the application needs some Semantic RepInfo, then the appropriate CPID is selected and the piece of RepInfo (something to do with Semantics) is obtained from the Registry/Repository and transferred back to the user. This piece of Semantic RepInfo may be understandable by the user; if not then it will itself have a CPID associated with it which points back to the Registry/Repository – to another RepInfoLabel. This iteration continues until the user can understand the RepInfo.

Note that the CASPAR "RepInfoLabel" itself has Representation Information. The RepInfoLabel has been introduced for convenience, but is not in any sense unique or irreplaceable.

Another possible termination point is indicated by the CPID having the special value "MISSING", which indicates that the Representation Information is not available – and this could signal that there is a RepInfo gap.

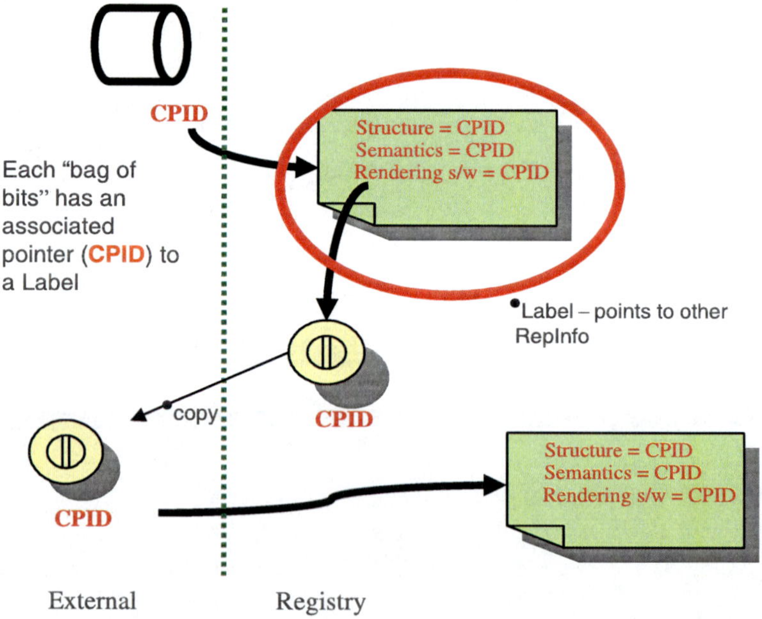

Fig. 17.4 Use of repInfoLabel

Although not indicated, each RepInfoLabel also has a CPID which points to the Representation Information for that RepInfoLabel, which will not be another RepInfoLabel of the same type but instead will be a simple text file – in order to end the recursion.

The above scenario describes the case where all transactions take place with a single Registry/Repository, but of course any CPID may point to any one of what may be a large network of Registry/Repositories. The RepInfo may also be held locally, perhaps a cached copy of something held in a Registry/Repository.

In terms of the getting to the point at which the Representation Information is adequate, this may be a human decision but some automation is possible.

This has been discussed at length in Chap. 8, summarised below. Support for such automation is illustrated in Fig. 17.5 which shows users (*u1, u2. . .*) with user profiles (*p1, p2. . .* – each a description of the user's Knowledge Base) with Representation Information {*m1, m2,. . .*) to understand various digital objects (*o1, o2. . .*).

Take for example user *u1* trying to understand digital object *o1*. To understand *o1*, Representation Information *m1* is needed. The profile *p1* shows that user *u1* understands *m1* (and therefore its dependencies *m2, m3* and *m4*) and therefore has enough Representation Information to understand *o1*.

When user *u2* tries to understand *o2* we see that *o2* needs Representation Information *m3* and *m4*. Profile *p2* shows that *u2* understands *m2* (and therefore *m3*), however there is a gap, namely *m4* which is required for *u2* to understand *o2*.

For *u2* to understand *o1*, we can see that Representation Information *m1* and *m4* need to be supplied.

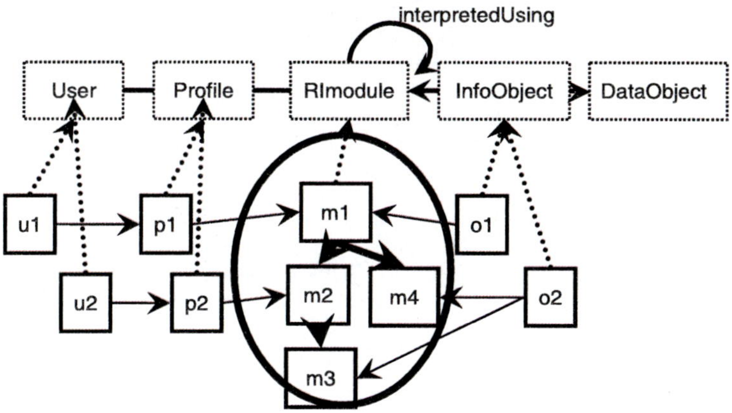

Fig. 17.5 Modelling users, profiles, modules and dependencies

17.2.1 REG – Representation Information Registry Interfaces

Component name	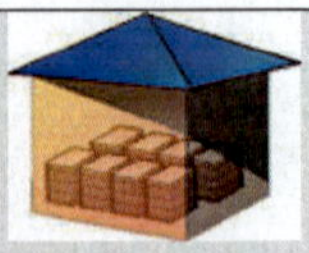 CASPAR Registry
Component acronym	REG
Component description	REG is the component which allows centralised and persistent storage and retrieval of OAIS Representation Information (RepInfo) (including Preservation Description Information (PDI)) in a centralised Registry/Repository. It also contains maintenance tools for user interaction with the Registry for:- • Manual RepInfo ingest • Creation and maintenance of the XML structures (RepInfoLabels) which connect related RepInfo in the Registry into an OAIS network (using the defined categories Semantic, Structure and Other) • Other RepInfo maintenance REG has the following responsibilities • Ingest RepInfo into Registry – with appropriate name, description and classification • Extract RepInfo from Registry reliably. • Search Registry for RepInfo matching appropriate (wild carded) criteria (a combination of name, description or classification)

Component interfaces	• RepInfo Factory
	  o getRepInfoManager() – gets an Ingest/Extract Object
	  o getRegistrySearch() – returns a search Object
	  o getClassificationScheme() – returns the OAIS classification scheme
	• RepInfo Manager
	• RepInfo – Object encapsulating the classification and Repository Item
	• RILabel – Relates RepInfo to other related items
	• RIGUITool – graphical user interface component

Component artefacts	• registry-0.2.jar (or later) – the registry API code • RoRI-install.jar – client izPack installer for Registry API, GUI Tool and freebXML (including Java docs) • omar.war and supporting files – server side setup files
Component UML diagram	☐ REG Interfaces – see Fig. 17.6
Component specification	REGISTRY_-Spec-Ref-v1.1.doc

Component author	STFC – Science and technology facilities council (UK)
License	LGPLv3

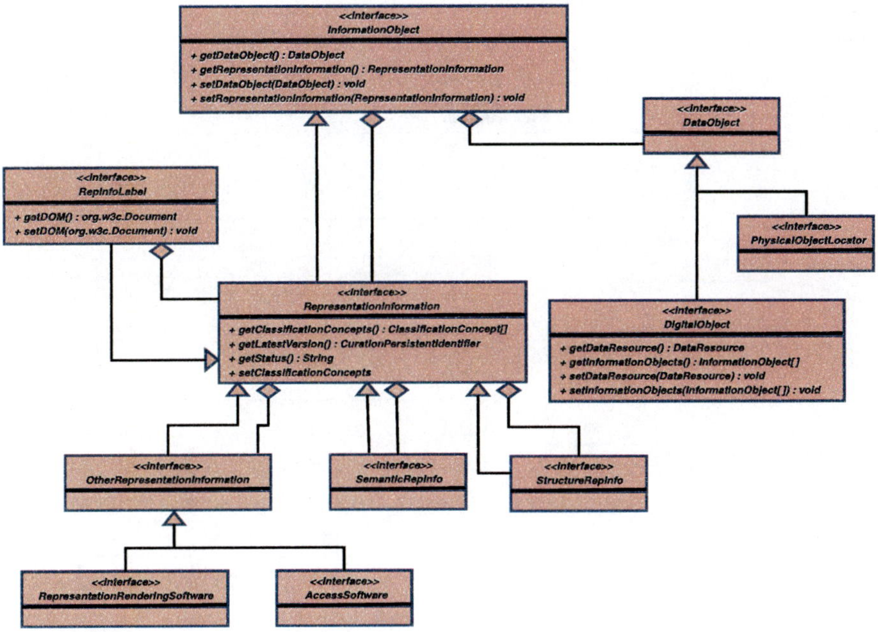

Fig. 17.6 REG Interfaces

17.3 Virtualizer

Component name	CASPAR Virtualiser
Component acronym	VIRT
Component description	The application allows the user to: • understand a file • inspect its content and nested components • tag the whole file or the part of the file he needs It allows one to inspect a simple or a complex object (e.g. zip file) both from the structural and semantic point of view. Produces an xml file containing virtualisation information which integrates the Representation Information.

Component interfaces	• The virtualiser runs as a stand-alone application. It interacts with the registry and knowledge manager.
Component artefacts	
Component UML diagram	VIRT – Logical components see Fig. 17.7
Component specification	
Component author	Advanced computer systems A.C.S.
Licence	LGPL v3

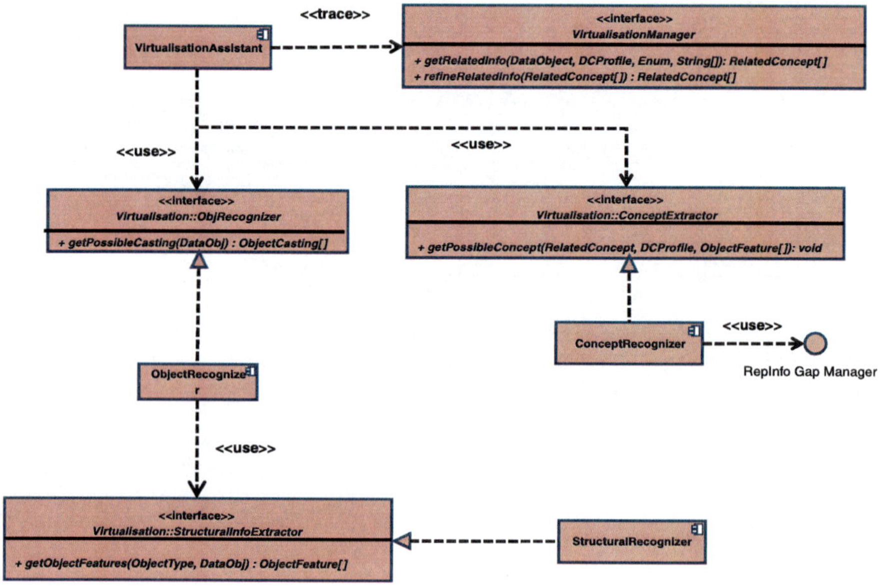

Fig. 17.7 Virtualiser logical components

17.3.1 VIRTUALIZER Logical Components

The virtualiser is based on two main logical components:

- **Virtualisation Assistant** – is responsible for the object type recognition. It extracts structural information from the digital object representation.
- **Virtualisation Manager** – collects information provided by the Assistant characterizing the object under inspection as a simple or a complex. It then builds the object hierarchical and semantic structure, allowing the user to browse and describe the object and its nested components.

17.3.2 VIRTUALISER Main Plugins

Specific plugins have been developed in order to support the following file formats:

- Images: Jpeg, Bmp, Tiff, etc.
- Word documents
- Pdf Documents
- Archives: Zip, Rar, Jar, Tar, TgZip, etc
- XML Files

Channel-Inspection: enable the user to inspect remotely a connection:

- HTTP inspection
- FTP inspection

17.3.3 VIRTUALIZER Main Screenshots

Once the simple or complex object has been loaded into the application user interface (Fig. 17.8), the Virtualiser allows the following set of operations (Figs. 17.9 and 17.10):

- inspect the file as a FileSystem – *Inspect Button*
- view it using a dedicated viewer available on your machine – View Button
- view it using the vrt-plugin – Open Button
- dump the binary content of the file – Dump Button
- Tag with a label the object – Tag Button

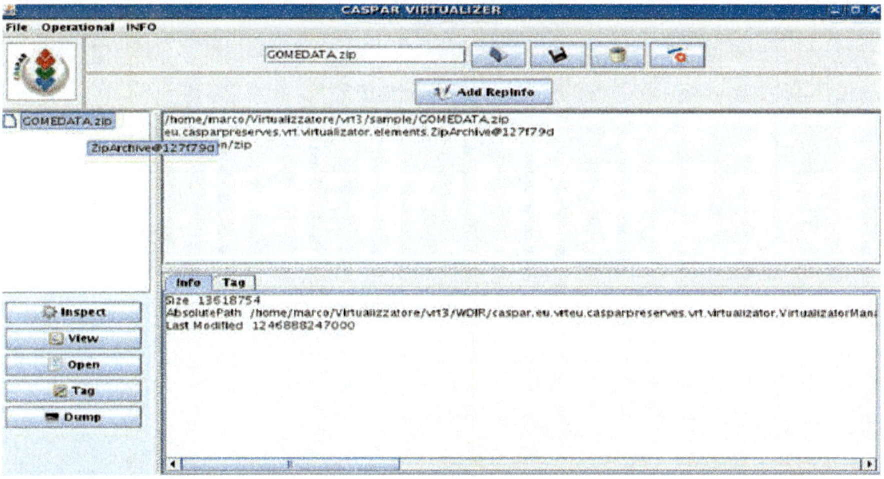

Fig. 17.8 Virtualiser User Interface

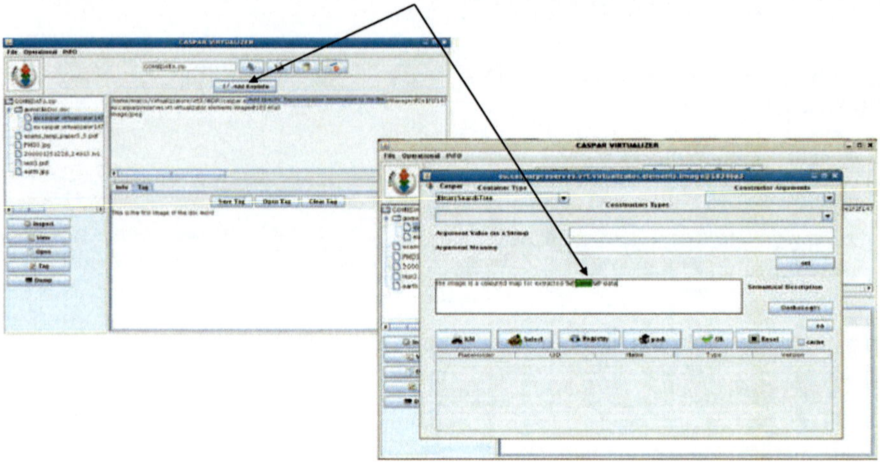

Fig. 17.9 Adding representation information

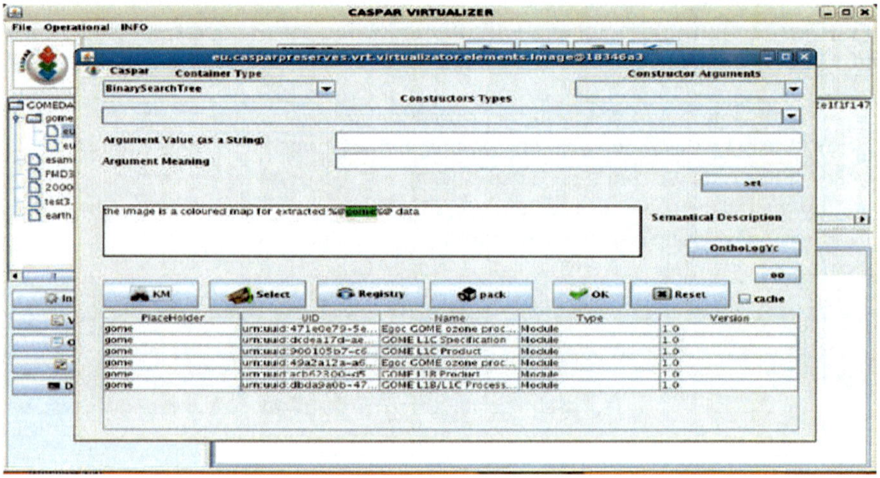

Fig. 17.10 Link to the knowledge manager

17.3.3.1 Simple or Complex Object Semantic Annotation

Each object can be labelled and then be “extended” semantically once viewed and explored. The add RepInfo button allows to organize the semantic information, to add a new Representation to the object under inspection.

Main functions are described as follows

- Connect current Virt-Info to RepInfo modules stored into the Knowledge Manager – KM Button
- Connect current Virt-Info to the RepInfo instances stored into the Registry

17.4 Knowledge Gap Manager

17.4.1 KM – Knowledge Manager Interfaces

Component name	 CASPAR Knowledge Manager
Component acronym	KM
Component description	Knowledge manager comprises two parts: SWKM and GapManager. SWKM offers basic knowledge-related services, as importing and exporting knowledge bases, and performing declarative queries and updates. GapManager manages modules, inter-module dependencies and DC profiles, and can be used to identify the intelligibility gap of a user (or more accurately, a profile which describes the knowledge background of a community) which needs to be filled in order to understand a module.
Component interfaces	• SWKM • GapManager
Component artefacts	• CASPAR_SWKM_WS.war • GapManager.war • GapManager.jar • PreScan
UML diagrams	KM and GapManager Interfaces – see Fig. 17.11
Component specification	• SWKM Web Site [http://athena.ics.forth.gr:9090/SWKM/] • GapManager Web Site [http://athena.ics.forth.gr:9090/ • Applications/GapManager/] • D2102: Prototype of registry-related KM services • PreScan Web Site [http://www.ics.forth.gr/prescan/]

Component author	FORTH – Institute of Computer Science, Foundation for Research and Technology – Hellas (FORTH-ICS) (GR)
License	LGPLv3

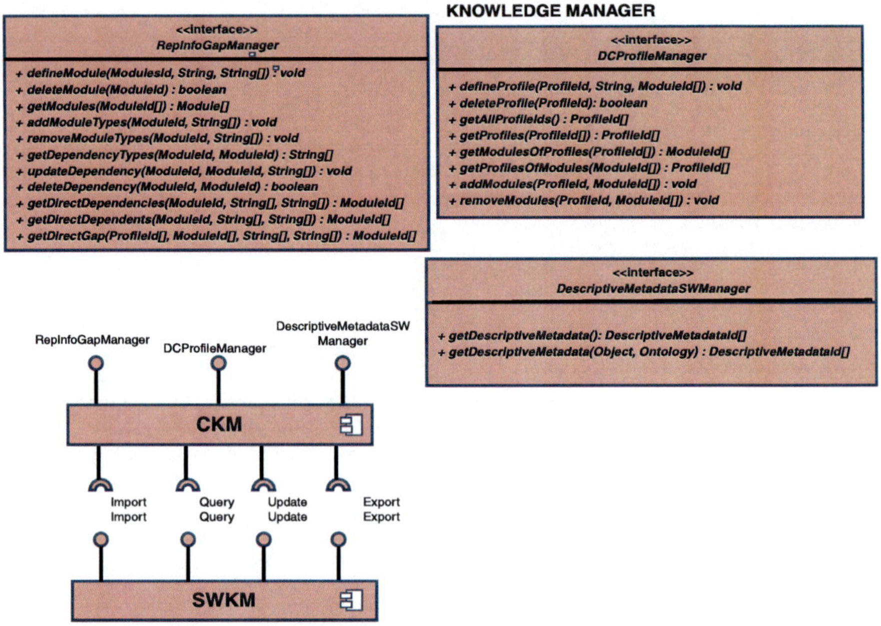

Fig. 17.11 KM and GapManager interfaces

17.4.2 Preservation Scanner Component

PreservationScanner [117, 185] (PreScan for short) is a tool developed by FORTH for automating the ingestion and transformation of "metadata" from file systems. PreScan is quite similar in spirit with the crawlers of Web search engines. In this case the file system is scanned, the embedded "metadata" is extracted and an index built. In contrast to web search engine crawlers one wants to: (a) support more advanced extraction services, (b) allow the manual enrichment of "metadata", (c) use more expressive representation frameworks for keeping and exploiting the "metadata" (i.e. "metadata" schemas expressed in Semantic Web languages), (d) offer

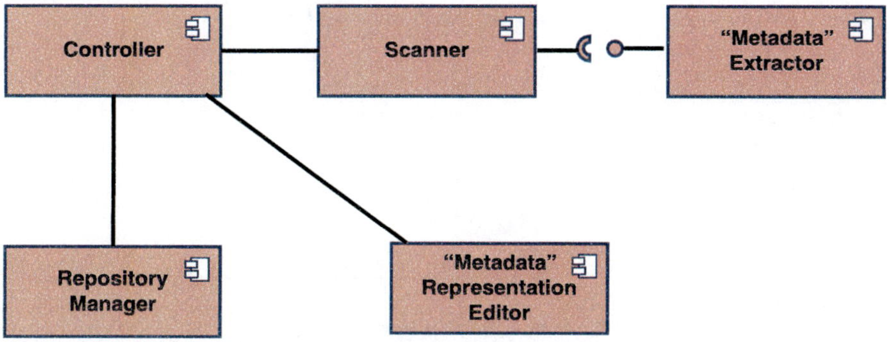

Fig. 17.12 The Component diagram of PreScan

rescanning services that do not start from scratch but exploit the previous status of the index, and (e) associate the extracted "metadata" with other sources of knowledge (i.e. registries of Representation Information). Figure 17.12 shows the overall architecture of PreScan.

17.5 Preservation Orchestration Manager

Preservation is not a static activity, but an evolving process which involves persons and systems. They react in response to evolving conditions (i.e. change events) which could impact on long-term preservation of the digital content information. So, it is important for a digital archive to monitor, notify and alert (in order to synchronise) any evolving condition and entity within the preservation environment.

The CASPAR Preservation Orchestration Management provides notification and alert service within the CASPAR Preservation Infrastructure. The CASPAR Preservation Orchestration Manager (POM) component is an implementation of the Publish-Subscribe pattern. The Publisher-Subscriber design pattern helps to keep the state of cooperating entities synchronized. To achieve this it enables one-way propagation of changes: one publisher notifies any number of subscribers about changes to its state.

In the proposed solution, one component takes the role of the publisher and all components/entities dependent on changes in the publisher are its subscribers. In the CASPAR preservation environment we can say that any information change (such as a gap in the Representation Information, a file format change, etc.) can be viewed as a state change about which the Data Holder can declare an interest to be notified.

The components involved in the role of Data Preserver have the responsibility to publish notification messages in order to alert the interested Data Holder. Both Data Preserver and Data Holder can be humans or software components.

17.5.1 POM – Preservation Orchestration Manager

Component name	 CASPAR Preservation Orchestration Manager
Component acronym	POM
Description	The component is an implementation of the Publish-Subscribe pattern. Mainly, POM receives (event) *notifications* from a Data Preserver (with *publisher* role) for a specific *"topic"*. A Data Holder (with *subscriber* role) is registered to the POM in order to receive *alerts*. POM has the following responsibilities: • Manage Registration – allow Data Holder to subscribe their interests in order to receive alerts; • Manage Notification – allow Data Preserver to create and send notification messages for specific events/topics; • Manager Alert – allow Data Holder to receive alerts, according to their registered interests.
Interfaces	• RegistrationManager – This interface deals with Subscribers and Expertises. • NotificationManager – This interface deals with Messages, Publishers and Topics.
Artefacts	• POM Notification Web Service WSDL • POM Registration Web Service WSDL • POM.war – Web service • POM-stub.jar – Client library to access POM web service • caspar-framework-client-libs.zip – Common CASPAR client library to access any CASPAR key component (includes jax-ws libraries) • POM-client-test.zip – Use case scenario source code
UML diagram	• CASPAR POM component interface – see Fig. 17.13
Specification	POM-Spec-Ref-2.0.1.pdf
Author	ENG – Engineering ingegneria informatica S.p.A. (Italy)
Licence	

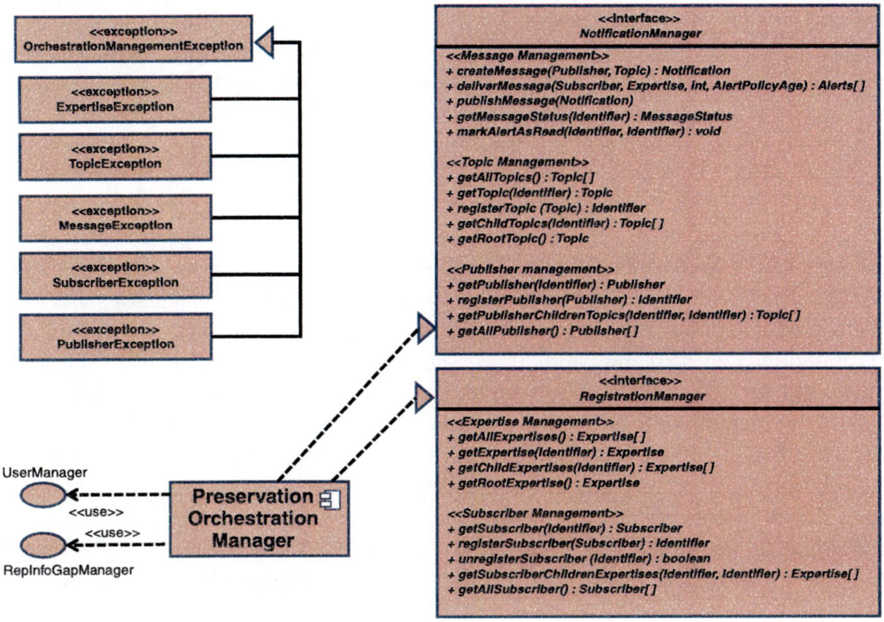

Fig. 17.13 CASPAR POM component interface

17.6 Preservation DataStores

17.6.1 Introduction

Long-Term Digital Preservation (LTDP) systems aim to ensure the use of digital information beyond the lifetime of the technology used to create that information. While data on paper can easily be stored and dispersed for 100 years or more at low cost, in the digital world this task is more challenging and requires carefully planned digital preservation and distribution systems. The preservation challenge is twofold: bit preservation and logical preservation. Bit preservation is the ability to restore the bits in the presence of storage media degradation and obsolescence, or even environmental catastrophes like fire or flooding. Logical preservation includes preserving the understandability and usability of the data in the future when current technologies for computer hardware, operating systems, data management products and applications may no longer exist.

At the heart of any LTDP system, there is a storage component that includes the ultimate place of the data. This storage component needs to store the ever growing data produced by diverse devices in different formats using dispersed delivery vehicles. Traditional archival storage support mostly bit preservation and may include storing multiple copies of the data at separate physical locations, employing data protection mechanisms such as RAID, performing periodic media refresh, etc. However, LTDP systems will be more robust and have less probability for data corruption or loss if their storage component supports also logical preservation. We call such storage components preservation-aware storage.

Preservation DataStores (PDS) are OAIS-based preservation-aware storage [186, 187] that focuses on supporting logical preservation in addition to the traditional bit preservation. PDS is aware of the structure of an archival information package (AIP), and offloads functions traditionally performed by applications to the storage layer. These functions include handling AIP "metadata", calculating and validating fixity, supporting authenticity processes, managing the AIP representation information (RepInfo) and validating referential integrity. A unique and innovative capability of PDS is the support for computation near the data; a paradigm that moves the execution module to the location of the data instead of moving the data to the execution module's location. To achieve this, PDS enables the load and execution of storlets, which are execution modules for performing data intensive functions (e.g., data transformation) close to the data. This saves network traffic and improves performance and robustness. Additionally, this enables optimal scheduling of tasks (e.g., performing data transformation during bit migration saves repeated reading of massive amounts of data).

Tape storage systems and disk storage systems are currently the prominent types of media on which data is preserved. In many cases, the preservation data tends to be cold (inactive) and is seldom accessed over time. Tapes are attractive in these cases as they are more reliable than disks and their expected lifetime is 3–10 times higher than that of disks. Additionally, tapes consume 25 times less power than disks. Thus, overall, tapes are much more cost-effective than disks and are especially attractive for preservation. PDS is flexible, able to use any type of media as well as able to be used for any type of data. It supports placement of the AIPs in containers where each such container is self-describing and self-contained. This capability is especially useful for offline storage media.

PDS serves as the infrastructure storage of CASPAR and was installed and integrated at Europe Space Agency (ESA) where it was tested with scientific data. PDS is integrated in CASPAR graphical user interface and can be used directly or via the PACK component that packages raw data into AIPs and calls PDS to store them. PDS implements and supports the CASPAR OAIS-compliant authenticity model that includes authenticity protocols and steps. PDS interfaces are published in SourceForge. Finally, PDS is available for public download and free evaluation at alphaWorks [188].

17.6.2 PDS Description

In this section we describe PDS architecture, its detailed functionality and the means to ensure this functionality and to extend PDS over time.

17.6.2.1 Architecture

PDS has a flexible architecture where each layer can be reused independently [189]. It includes three layers as shown in Fig. 17.14, each based on an open standard. At the top, the OAIS-based *preservation engine* layer provides an external interface to PDS and implements preservation functionalities. This layer also maps between the OAIS and eXtensible Access Method (XAM) [190] levels of abstraction. XAM serves as the storage mid-layer which provides logical abstraction for objects that include data and large amounts of "metadata". This layer contains the XAM Library, which provides the XAM interface, and a Vendor Interface Module (VIM) to communicate with the underlying storage system.

The bottom layer of PDS (Object layer) may consist of either of two backend storage systems: a standard file system, or an Object-based Storage Device (OSD) [191, 192]. A higher-level API (HL-OSD) on top of OSD provides abstraction and simplification to the Object Store's SCSI-like interface. OSD is preferred when the actual disks are network-attached and there is a requirement to access them securely.

For the case where the mid-layer abstraction is not desired, we have an alternative implementation that maps the preservation engine layer directly to a file system object layer without using XAM.

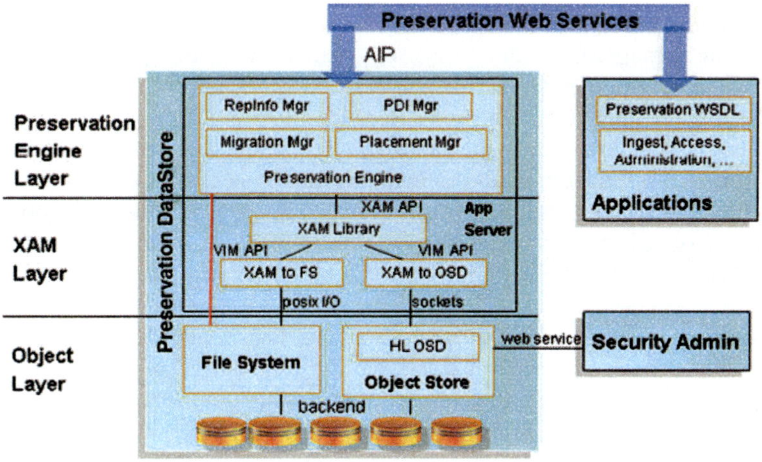

Fig. 17.14 Preservation data stores architecture

17.6.2.2 PDS Functionality

PDS exposes a set of interfaces that form the PDS entry points accompanied with their arguments and return values. The PDS entry points cover some of the functionality PDS exposes to its users including different ways to ingest and access data and "metadata", manipulate previously ingested data and "metadata", retrieve

PDS system information and configure policies. The entry points may be called directly or via web services to enable flexible and platform independent use of PDS. The PDS interfaces aim to be abstract, technology independent and to survive implementation replacements. The entry points may throw different exceptions also defined as PDS interfaces.

The main functions PDS provides are:

1. **Ingest and access:** various methods to ingest and access AIPs packaged in XFDU [193] or SAFE formats. The ingest operation consists of unpacking the AIP, assigning an AIP identifier, validating and computing its fixity, updating its provenance and reference, and storing each section separately for future access and manipulation. Access includes fetching and validating the data and "metadata" of the AIP. Each section of the AIP (content data, RepInfo, fixity, provenance, etc.) may be accessed separately. However, PDS encapsulates data and "metadata" at the storage level and attempts to physically co-locate them on the same media.
2. **AIP generation:** generation of preservation "metadata" and creation of AIPs for the case that the ingestion to PDS includes just bare content data.
3. **"Metadata" enrichment:** automatic extraction of "metadata" from the submitted content data and addition of representation information and/or PDI to the stored AIP. Third party "metadata" extractors for different data types can be easily added via an API that PDS provides.
4. **RepInfo management:** allows sharing, search and categorization of RepInfo [194]. Given the expected vast amount of RepInfo, the RepInfo manager employs a sharing architecture by which the RepInfo are grouped into expandable categories, and the AIPs point to the categories rather than directly to their associated RepInfo. This architecture allows updating and expanding the categories without the necessity to update existing RepInfo. Also, in addition to storing the RepInfo of the content data, PDS stores RepInfo of "metadata" (of fixity, provenance, etc.) so these "metadata" can be interpreted when accessed in the future.
5. **Fixity management:** fixity calculations and its documentation in the AIP ensure that the particular content data object has not been altered in an undocumented manner. PDS enables one to compute and validate fixity (data integrity) within the storage component. This reduces the risk of data loss and frees-up network bandwidth otherwise required for transferring the data. PDS provides an extendible mechanism to compute fixity values based on specified algorithms, and the computations are calculated separately on various parts of the AIP. The resulting fixity values are stored in the fixity section of the AIP in a standard PREMIS (v2) format [139]. Each calculation may be later validated by accessing the given AIP and running a complementary fixity validation routine. New fixity algorithms can be easily added by uploading execution module (storlet) via an API that PDS provides.
6. **Data transformations:** provide the ability to load transformation modules (storlets) and apply them on AIPs at the storage level. When a transformation is

invoked, a new AIP with adequate representation information is created; the new AIP is a new version of the original AIP containing the transformed content data and its provenance documents that it was created via transformation.
7. **Authenticity management:** supporting authenticity protocols composed of steps, as defined in the CASPAR authenticity model (see Chap. 13 and [195]). PDS documents internal AIP changes that impact authenticity (e.g., format transformations) in the PDI section of the AIP. PDS performs some of this work automatically while allowing external authenticity management by providing APIs to manipulate the PDI. PDS provides a secure environment in terms of maintaining the authenticity (i.e., the identity and integrity) of the data objects and aims to preserve the relations of a data object to its environment.
8. **Preservation policies:** AIP preservation policies may be added on ingest or manipulated later on. These policies can be used for example to state the selected fixity algorithms, and more.
9. **Support preservation-aware placement of AIPs:** organizing the AIPs into self-describing self-contained clusters according to different parameters to optimize co-location of AIP sections and related AIPs. Theses clusters may be moved to secondary storage.

17.6.2.3 PDS Continuous Functionality over Time

A preservation system aimed at preserving data for the long term must first of all be able to preserve itself, that is, remain functioning and relevant throughout its entire life span. PDS employs the following means to keep itself up-to-date:

1. **Loading new software modules:** the storlet mechanism facilitates the addition and update of fixity algorithms and transformations.
2. **Flexible data structures:** as technology and knowledge changes, new structures may be used for "metadata" such as PDI records. PDS enables to use different inner structures (accompanied by their relevant RepInfo) to reside in a uniform record set in a transparent manner.
3. A **layered architecture based on open standards** enables simple replacement and reimplementation of layers according to changes in the system environment.
4. **Well-defined abstract interfaces** enable simple replacement of implementation and easy addition of third-party modules (e.g., packaging-format handlers, "metadata" extractors), according to developments in the technology.

17.6.3 Integration with Existing Archives

In many cases, the data subject to long-term digital preservation already resides in existing archives. The enterprises recognize the need to have preservation functionalities in their systems, but are not willing to switch their entire archival system for that. Reasons may include compatibility with other systems, satisfaction with current software and hardware, service contracts, or lack of funding, time, or knowledge necessary for installing an entirely new system. Instead, they seek a solution that allows the addition of long-term preservation capabilities to their existing archives.

The existing archives may be simple file systems or more advanced archives that include enhanced functions: "metadata" advanced query, hierarchical storage management, routine or special error checking, disaster recovery capabilities, bit preservation, etc. Some of these data are generated by applications that are unaware of the OAIS specification and the AIP logical structure, and generally include just the raw content data with minimal "metadata". While these archives are appropriate for short-term data retention, they cannot ensure long-term data interpretation at some arbitrary point in the future when everything can become obsolete including hardware, software, processes, format, people, and so forth.

PDS can be integrated with existing file systems and archives to enhance such systems with support for OAIS-based long-term digital preservation. Figure 17.15 depicts the generic architecture for such integration. We propose the addition of two components to the existing archive: an AIP Generator and a PDS box. The AIP Generator wraps existing content data with an AIP, by creating a manifest file that contains links to these data as well as relevant "metadata", which may or may not already exist in the archive. If some "metadata" is missing (e.g., RepInfo), the AIP Generator will be programmed to add that part either by embedding it into the manifest file or by saving it as a separate file or database entry linked from the manifest file. Sometimes, programming the AIP Generator to generate those manifest files can be quite simple, for example, if there is an existing naming scheme that relates the various AIP parts. Note that data can be entered into the archive using the existing data-generation applications and will, thus, not require writing new applications.

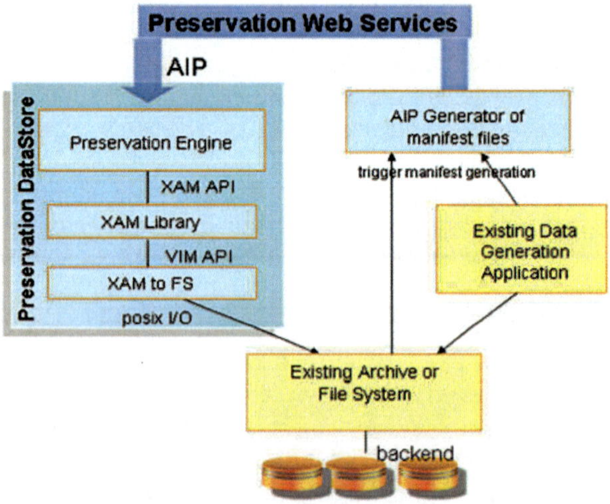

Fig. 17.15 Integrating PDS with an existing archive

The generated AIPs (consisting of a manifest with links to data and "metadata") are ingested into the second component: the PDS box. PDS provides most of its functionality – including awareness of the AIP structure and execution of data-intensive functions such as transformations – within the storage. It handles technical provenance records internally, supports media migration, and maintains referential integrity.

17.6.3.1 Integration with ECM

Enterprise Content Management (ECM) is the technology used to capture, manage, store, preserve, and deliver content and documents related to organizational processes. ECM tools and strategies enable the management of an organization's unstructured information, wherever that information exists. New business needs and legislations require sustaining content stored in an ECM system for decades to come, and hence require defining and storing preservation objects in the ECM. The goal is to leverage existing ECM capabilities and make the storing of objects subject to LTDP as transparent as possible to the user – almost no difference between LTDP objects and non-LTDP objects.

PDS can be integrated with ECM without changing the ECM normal flow [196] by automatic generation of the AIP, and mapping the AIP to the ECM object model. The AIP is mapped to two unique objects and shared RepInfo objects. The unique objects are (1) a Manifest file that is the root of the AIP and includes all the AIP "metadata" as well as references to the CDO and RepInfo of this AIP, (2) the original added object in its native format that will serve as the CDO of this preservation object.

The Content Management Interoperability Services (CMIS) [197] standard provides a uniform means for applications to work with content repositories. PDS can be mapped to ECM using CMIS and then it may be adequate to different ECMs that support the CMIS interface.

17.6.3.2 Integration with iRODS

The Storage Resource Broker (SRB)/Intelligent Rule-Oriented Data management System (iRODS) [198] is a data grid technology developed by the San Diego Supercomputing Center (SDSC). iRODS manages distributed data, enabling the creation of data grids that focus on the sharing of data, and was recently extended to persistent archives that focus on the preservation of data. Data grid technology provides fundamental management mechanisms for distributed data in a scalable manner. This includes support for managing data on remote storage systems, a uniform name space for referencing the data, a catalogue for managing information about the data, and mechanisms for interfacing with the preferred access method. The SRB/iRODS is middleware software, which builds on top of standard file systems, commercial archives, and storage systems.

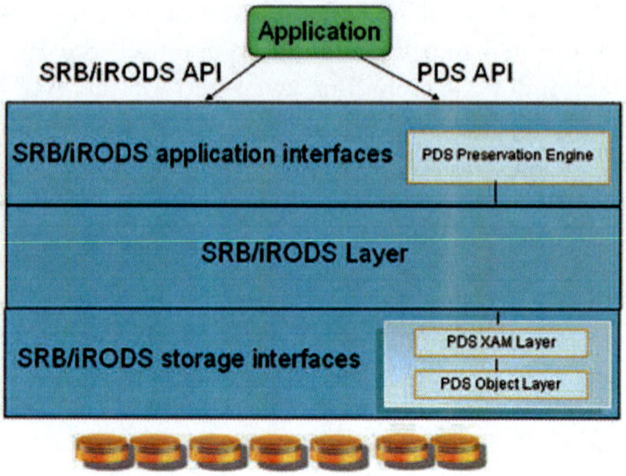

Fig. 17.16 Integrating PDS and SRB/iRODS

When considering the option of integrating PDS with iRODS (see Fig. 17.16), each layer should be referenced separately. Integrating PDS' preservation engine layer into iRODS will add a new OAIS-compliant API dedicated for long term preservation, that offloads OAIS functionality from the client and provides it in the API. The XAM library may be exposed as an application interface (at the top) or as a storage interface (at the bottom). The OSD layer may be placed at the storage interface layer. The utilization of XAM and OSD layers is optional. Instead, a new mapping layer of the preservation engine to iRODS may be developed.

17.6.4 PDS Summary and Future Directions

The long-term digital preservation problem is becoming more real as we find ourselves in the midst of a digital era. Old assumptions regarding information preservation are no longer valid, and it is clear that significant actions are needed to ensure the understandability of data for decades to come. In order to address these changes, new technologies and systems are being developed. Such systems will be able to better address these vital issues if they are equipped with storage technology that is inherently dedicated to preservation and that supports the different aspects of the preservation environment. An appropriate storage system will make any solution more robust and decrease the probability of data corruption or loss.

PDS is an innovative OAIS-based preservation-aware storage component. Awareness of preservation "metadata" facilitates authenticity and referential integrity management, and eventually supports logical preservation. Moreover, many preservation actions are executed within PDS and do not require the involvement of higher application logic as they are best executed close to the data (e.g., periodic fixity checks). Avoiding the transfer of the data to the higher application not only saves network bandwidth, but also simplifies the LTDP system, which in turn results in higher overall system reliability.

Although designed and built as the preservation-aware storage component for the CASPAR project, PDS's flexible layered architecture enables its use as the storage subsystem in other preservation settings as well. PDS variants have been built that integrated with an ECM solution, and over a plain file system. These implementations demonstrate that PDS can extend a preservation-agnostic archival storage to provide LTDP functionality. Since data subject to long-term data preservation may already reside in existing systems and archives, easy integration of PDS with other (existing) systems is important.

The PDS subsystem may be improved and completed in several aspects. To enhance and complete the support for the CASPAR authenticity model, PDS should support authenticity protocols explicitly, e.g., by implementing Authenticity Protocol as an object and preserving each protocol as an AIP. PDS should support the execution of such a protocol object whether it is a pre-defined protocol implemented in PDS or one loaded and executed by external users. This enhancement will provide uniform behaviour to internal (automatic) and external (manual) protocol executions. The authenticity protocol history will be documented transparently for all protocols by preserving them as AIPs in the system.

Another aspect that requires additional research and absorption into the PDS implementation is a placement mechanism that takes into account the different parameters that influence the optimized clustering of AIPs to be moved to secondary storage. These parameters involve understanding the relations between AIPs, prediction of access patterns of AIPs, legal issues and aspects related to the physical secondary storage (e.g., capacity, reliability etc.). In addition, there is a need for a standardized format that will describe the content of each cluster in order to make it self-describing and self-contained and thus interpretable by future systems. Towards that end we are working on Self-contained Information Retention Format (SIRF) standard in SNIA Long Term Retention working group [199].

17.6.5 PDS Component Details

Component name	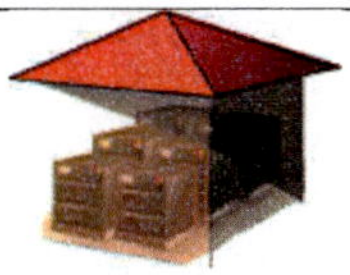 CASPAR Preservation datastores
Component acronym	PDS

Component description	The PDS component provides preservation storage functionality. It is preservation-aware and OAIS compliant. It handles the ingest, access and preservation of AIPs, while supporting the long term readability and understandability of the preserved data. It handles the Fixity calculations on the AIPs and updates the Provenance and Fixity documentations up-to-date. For more details see PDS description. The PDS interfaces and web client source code can be found on CASPAR SVN and SourceForge PDS server deployment package can be found on CASPAR SVN and are published on alphaWorks for public download.
Component interfaces	• PDSManager – defines basic OAIS preservation functions • PDSPdiManager – defines functions that manipulate PDI • PDSRepInfoManager – defines RepInfo management functions • PDSMigrationManager – defines functions to support migration • PDSPackagingManager – defines packaging management functions • PDSIntegratedManager – defines functions to implement when PDS is integrated with existing system See http://www.alliancepermanentaccers.org/caspar/implementation/CASPAR_PDS_INTERFACES_1_1.doc
Component artefacts	See PDSWebServices.wsdl
Component UML diagram	See UML diagrams in http://wiki.casparpreserves.eu/pub/Main/TaskId2201/CASPAR_PDS_INTERFACES_1_1.doc
Component specification	See PDS refined specification in http://wiki.casparpreserves.eu/pub/Main/TaskId2201/CASPAR_PDS_INTERFACES_1_1.doc See PDS Java docs at http://www.alliancepermanentaccess.org/caspar/implementation/CASPAR_PDSJAVADOCS_Dec_10_2008.zip
Component author	IBM (Israel)
License	For PDS interfaces and client code – Apache Public License (APL), that is compatible with GPL3.

17.7 Data Access and Security

Authorization defines whether a given subject is allowed to perform a specific action on a resource and must be proven before the requested action could be executed.

In CASPAR this was done by the Data Access Manager and Security module through the definition and evaluation of access control policies. For each resource, an access control policy can be declared within the security manager, binding users (aggregated into authorized communities) to permissions (rights to execute operations). The DAMS acts effectively both as a Policy Enforcement Point and a Policy Definition Point, as it lets administrator define policies and then assures the enforcement of these policies.

Authorization must be handled at two different levels: a static one that defines basic policies for accessing services and content, and a dynamic one that overrides the static policies if particular conditions are required (e.g. a license is required for getting the content). Thus this functionality is linked to the DRM module. When an actor tries to access a service or content the following procedure must be followed:

- the content or service is checked against the related security policy;
- a check is made to verify if the user has the right to perform the required operation according to the static permissions;
- when content is governed by copyright restrictions, a check is made if the user has a valid license to access/use the content.

CASPAR access control model is mainly based on the Rule Role-based access control (RBAC) approach. RBAC provides user authorization and access control in an elegant way. This model is however modified and extended to encompass allowing the ability to personalize the concept of role and to preserve and re-use the system in the future. In this sense the concept of role, which is the key point of this model, has been modified into that of Authorized Community. In this interpretation an Authorized Community is just an aggregation of any kind of users and does not need to refer to the already registered system users. It can be defined extensionally, namely by listing explicitly the members (e.g. a list of full names) or intentionally, by specifying the membership criteria (e.g. to be a member of an association, relatives of a certain person, citizens of a precise country that have reached a certain age, etc.). Membership evaluation might be complex and require human intervention.

The introduction of this novel concept of Authorised Community allows us to face the main challenge in the preservation of users and access policies: authorisation policies which are defined today must apply to the possible users of tomorrow. CASPAR DAMS implementation addresses this challenge by introducing proper mechanisms to define Authorised Communities, policies and authorisation verification processes. In the definition of an access policy it is possible to associate permissions to Authorized Communities. A user can access services and resources according to the permissions granted in the policies to the Authorized Community (s)he belongs to.

17.7.1 DAMS – Data Access Manager and Security Interfaces

Component name	 CASPAR Data access manager and Security
Component acronym	DAMS
Component description	The component provides basic services to perform data access security. Challenge: access policies which are defined today must apply to possible users of tomorrow. For further details see [200]
Component interfaces	• UserManager – allows to manage users, profiles and *Authorized Communities* • AuthenticationManager – allows the management of credentials and perform user authentication • AuthorizationManager – allows the management of access policies and performance authorization
Component artefacts	• DAMS.war – web service • DAMS-stub.jar – client library to access DAMS web service • caspar-framework-client-libs – common CASPAR client library to access any CASPAR key component (includes jax-ws libraries)
Component UML diagram	• DAMS Interfaces – see Fig. 17.17 • Conceptual Model – see Fig. 17.18
Component specification	DAMS-Spec-Ref-1.1.pdf [201]
Component author	MW – Metaware S.p.A. (Italy)
Licence	LGPLv3

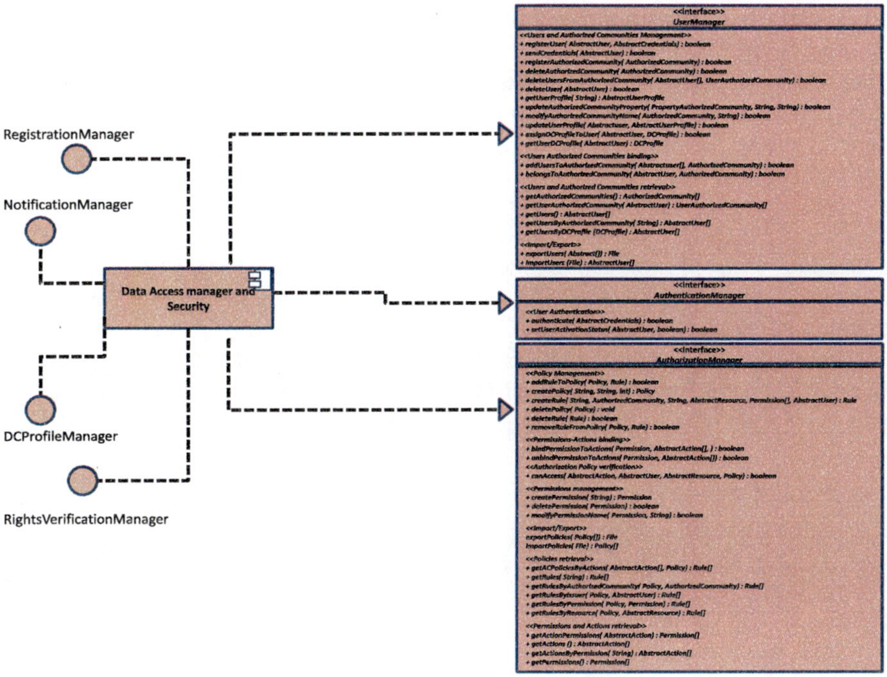

Fig. 17.17 DAMS interfaces

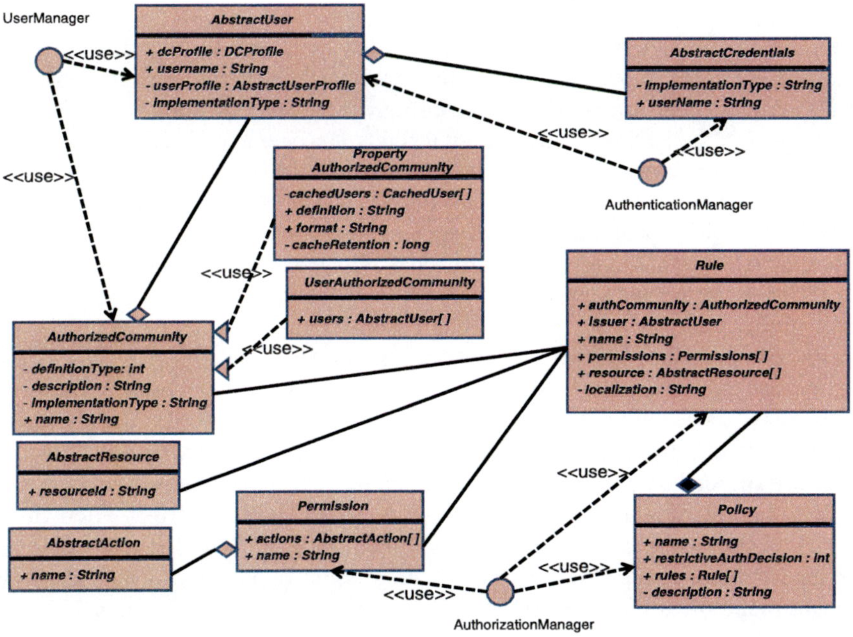

Fig. 17.18 DAMS conceptual model

17.8 Digital Rights Management Details

The role of the Digital Rights Management module inside the CASPAR architecture is basically that of defining and registering provenance information on a digital work to derive and retrieve right holding information and intellectual property rights. Such rights are interpreted differently depending on the country and on the legal framework, i.e. the set of laws and regulations which refer to digital rights. Changes in the legal framework can occur, so the CASPAR system provides services to keep up-to-dated laws and regulations and to handle the consequences of such changes in order to guarantee the preservation of IPR information and of the way to interpret it.

The primary goal is to allow users of tomorrow to access and use the copyrighted works of today, complying with all the actual existing restrictions, as well as to provide to right holders the guarantee of protecting their rights.

The DRM addresses in particular:

- identification and registration of provenance information on digital works;
- derivation and preservation of ownership rights and individual permissions attached to Data Objects, possibly defined a long time before their dissemination;
- management of changes in copyright laws and regulations, which apply to disseminated Data Objects, depending on the distribution country.

CASPAR DRM implementation includes also the definition of a Digital Rights Ontology (DRO), which is aimed at modelling the entities in the Copyright domain and at providing a formal dictionary to describe intellectual property rights ownership.

In the long term, it is quite difficult to identify and clear all the existing rights, because the evolution in legislation and international agreements, as well as relevant events related to the history of single items may influence the status of things. This is what makes the environment for digital rights management particularly difficult for long term preservation. Both the exclusive ownership rights and the permissions to use intellectual property are subject to change in time. Changes in the legislation (either locally or through international agreements) might affect the duration of the copyright, the type of works that are protected, the type of actions that are restricted, etc. But they also impact the permissions, as new rules may be introduced that authorise or disallow certain uses of intellectual property materials. Moreover there are other elements that influence the existing rights, namely those related to each particular work. It is, for instance, possible that the original rights holder transfers some of his exclusive ownership rights to another person, or he could decide to put his creation under Public Domain, or still keep the ownership rights but release the work under a more or less permissive license model. Finally the death of an author is another event that influences the expiration date of the ownership right, after which date no permission is needed to use his/her creation. The DRO also aims at taking into consideration these long term preservation issues by identifying the impact of changes in multi-national legal framework on the rights on digital holdings.

17.8.1 DRM – Digital Rights Manager Interfaces

Component name	CASPAR Digital Right Manager
Component acronym	DRM
Component description	The component provides basic services to deal with digital rights, in particular registering provenance information on a digital work and to derive the existing Intellectual Property Rights from them. Functionalities: 1. Registration of the creation history (part of the Digital Provenance) 2. Derivation of all the existing Intellectual Property Rights from the creation history 3. Export of the Intellectual Property Rights information in terms of the Digital Rights Ontology Challenge: The Intellectual Property Rights should be preserved along with the creative content, and represent one part of the PDI (Preservation Description Information) of a Content Data Object. To that purpose the DRM allows to export rights information in terms of instances of the Digital Rights Ontology. The ontology has been chosen as a suitable way to express information that should be preserved in the long term. For further information see [202]
Component interfaces	• RightsDefinitionManager – allows to register provenance information on digital works and to retrieve right holding information and IPR
Component artefacts	• DRM.war – web service • DRM-stub.jar – client library to access DRM web service caspar-framework-client-libs – common CASPAR client library to access any CASPAR key component (includes jax-ws libraries)
Component UML diagram	• RightsDefinitionManager Interface – see Fig. 17.19 • DRM Conceptual Model – see Fig. 17.20
Component specification	DRM-Spec-Ref-1.1.pdf [203]
Component author	MW – Metaware (Italy)
Licence	LGPLv3

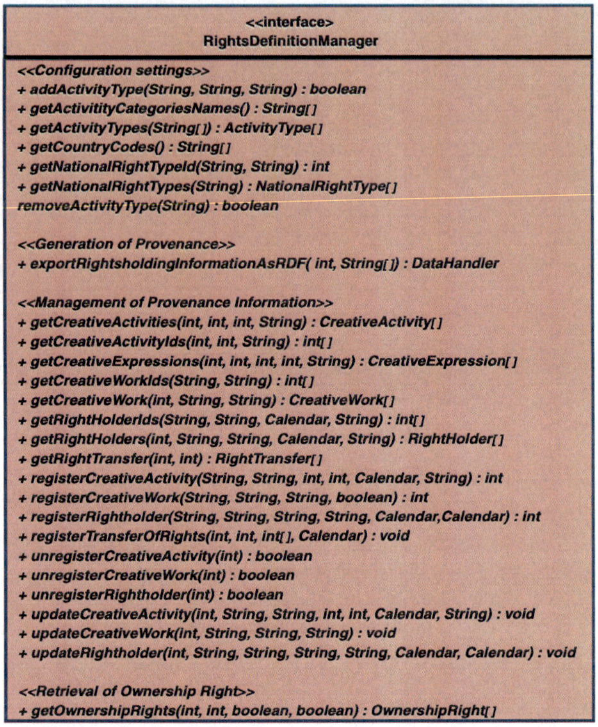

Fig. 17.19 Rights definition manager interface

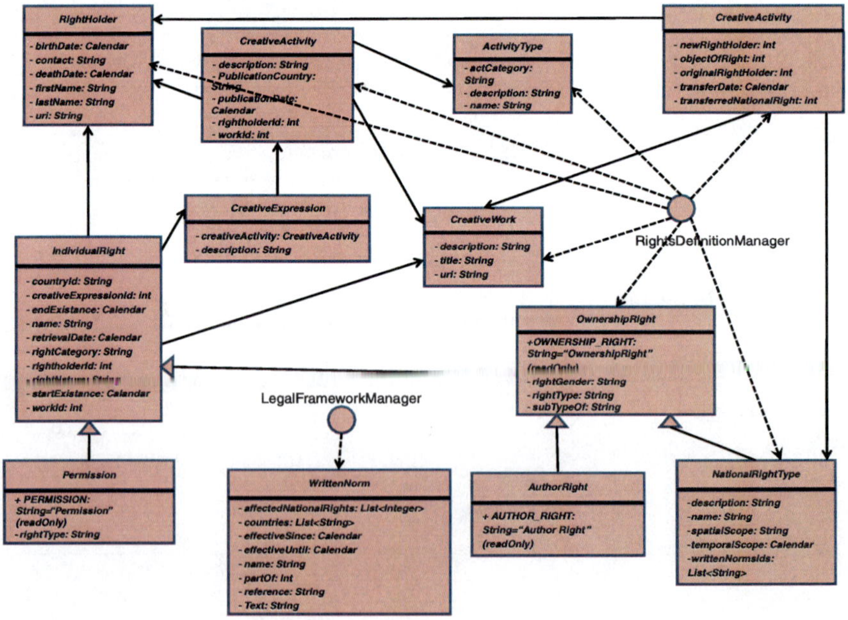

Fig. 17.20 DRM conceptual model

17.9 Find – Finding Manager

Component name	 CASPAR Finding Aids
Component acronym	FIND
Component description	The component provides data retrieval functionality. The main responsibility of the Finding Aids module is to function as the "link" between the end-user (consumer or digital archive) and the rest of the CASPAR system, with respect to the search and retrieval facilities.
Component interfaces	• Finding Manager allows one to: 1) Store Descriptive Information objects and corresponding schemas 2) Associate Descriptive Information objects to AIP objects 3) Discovery Descriptive Information objects and associated AIPs • Finding Registry allows one to: 1) Preserve registered Finding Managers information (DL, QL, etc.) 2) Provides Text-query functionalities over DescInfo objects
Component artefacts	• Finding Manager (FM) Web Service WSDL • FINDMANAGER.war – FM web service archive • FINDMANAGER-stub.jar – FM client library to access FM web service • Finding Register (FR) Web Service WSDL • FINDREGISTRY.war – FR web service archive • FINDREGISTRY-stub.jar – FR client library to access FR web service • caspar-client.jar – common CASPAR client library to access any CASPAR key component (includes jax-ws libraries)
Component UML diagram	• FINDING AIDS overall interface – see Fig. 17.21 • Finding manager model (Class Diagram) – see Fig. 17.22 • Finding Manager model implementation with SWKM – see Fig. 17.23 • Finding registry model (class diagram) – see Fig. 17.24
Component specification	FindingAids-Spec-Ref-1.0.pdf [204]
Component author	National research council (CNR) – institute of information science and technologies (ISTI) (Italy)
Licence	LGPLv3 Free Software

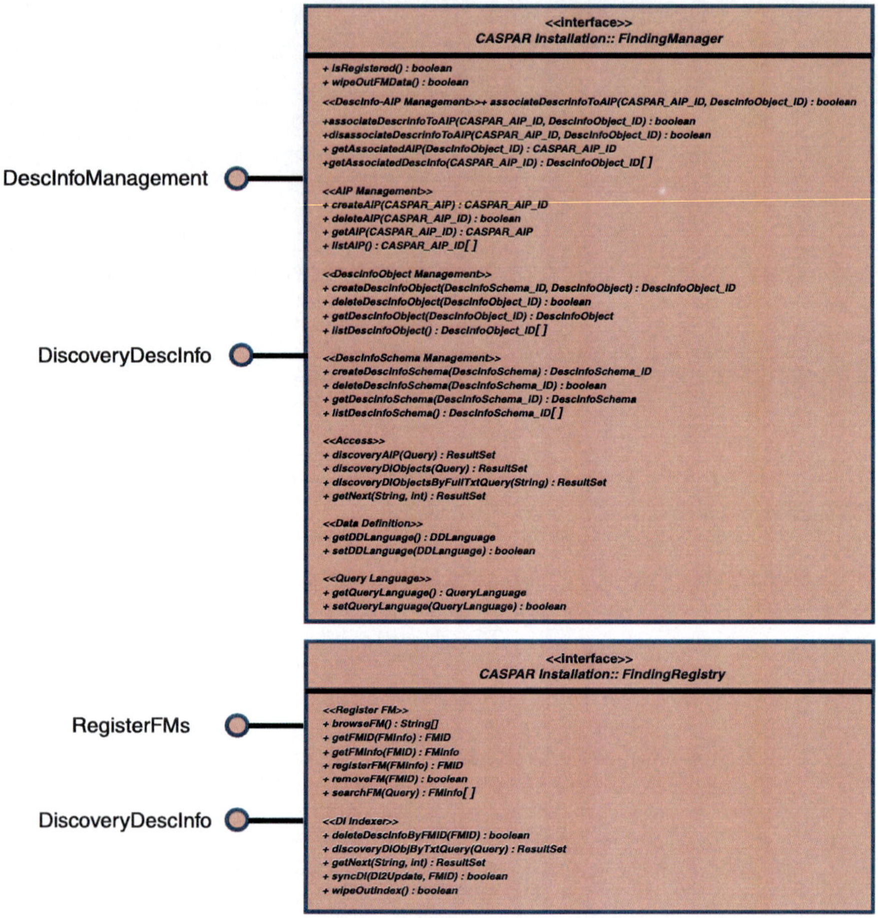

Fig. 17.21 Finding AIDS overall interface

17.10 Information Packaging Details

As shown in the above figure, the block supports Data Producers in the following main steps:

1. Ingest Content Information
2. Create Information Package, by adding also
   a. Representation Information
   b. Descriptive Information
   c. Preservation Description Information
3. Check Information Package
4. Store Information Package for long term

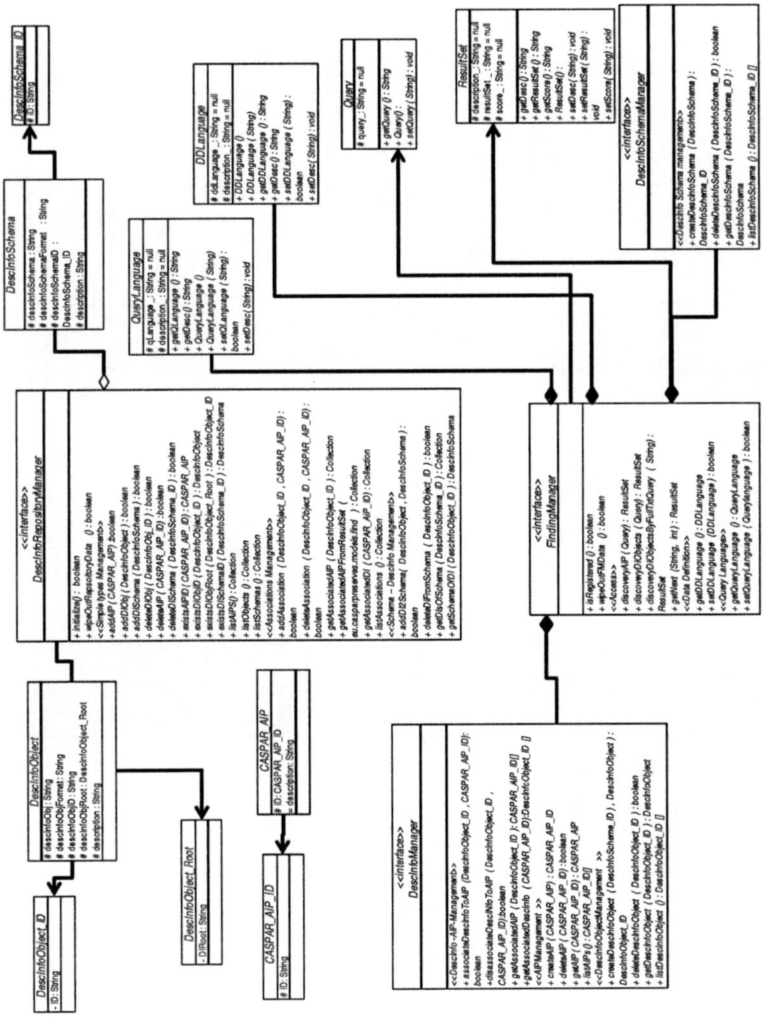

Fig. 17.22 Finding manager model (class diagram)

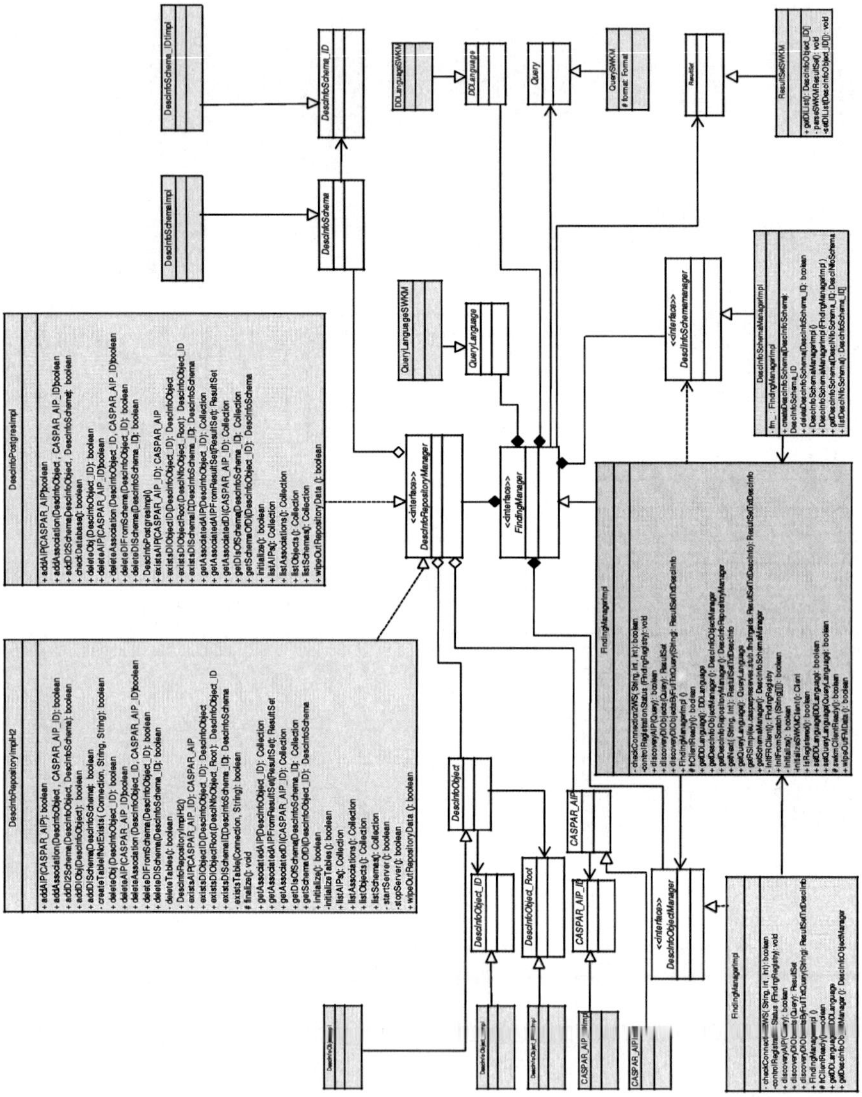

Fig. 17.23 Finding manager model implementation with SWKM

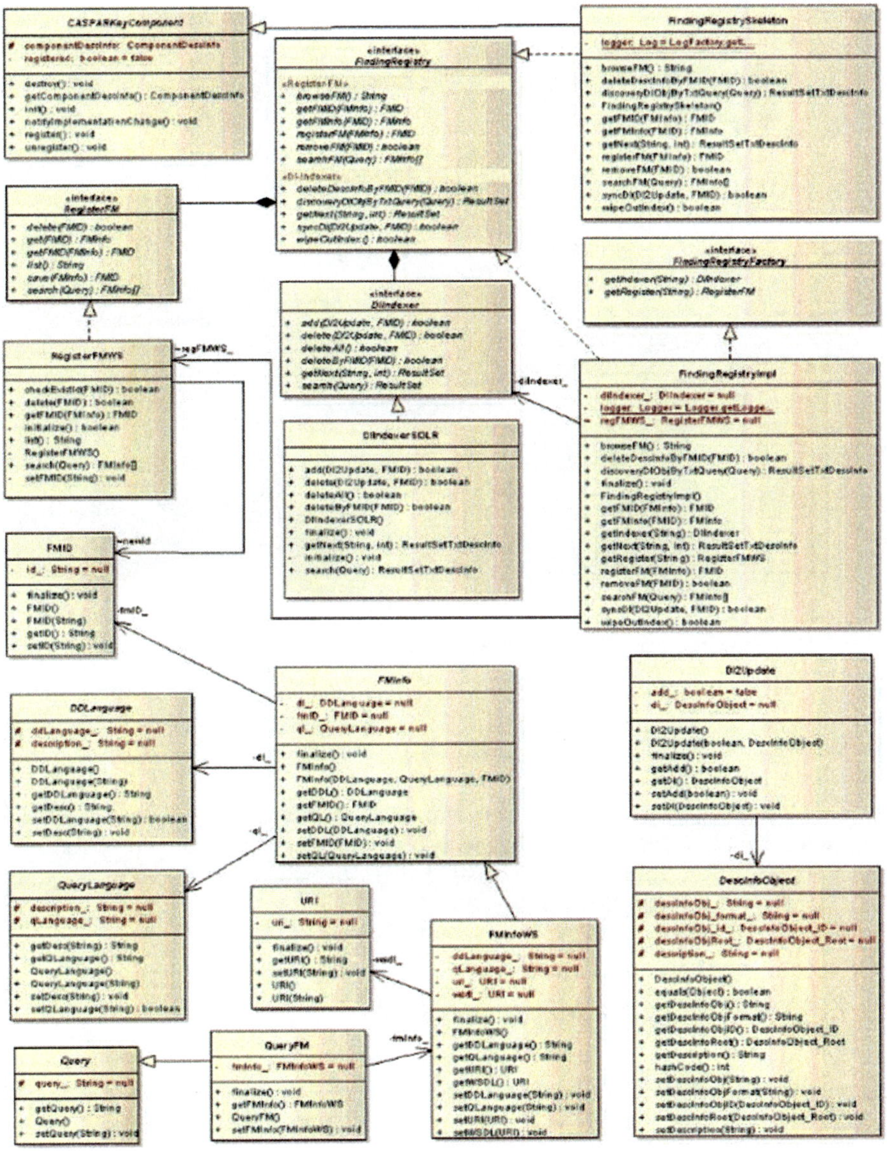

Fig. 17.24 Finding registry model (class diagram)

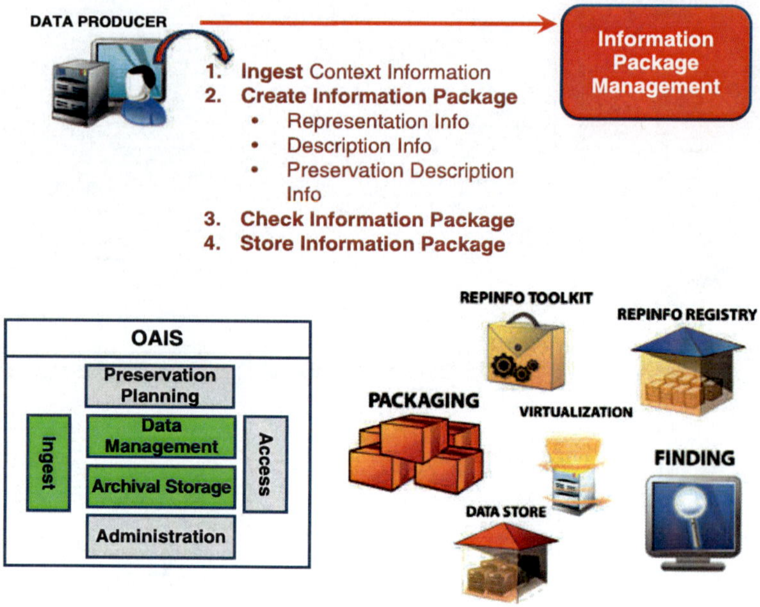

Fig. 17.25 Information package management

Those features are defined in three OAIS functional blocks: Ingest, Data Management and Archival Storage.

The main component of the Information Package Management is the CASPAR Packaging which cooperates together with (i) Representation Information Toolkit, (ii) Representation Information Registry, (iii) Virtualisation, (iv) Preservation DataStores, (v) Finding Manager (Fig. 17.25).

17.10.1 PACK – Packaging Interfaces

Component name	 CASPAR Packaging Manager
Component acronym	PACK
	The Package Manager is an implementation of XFDU packaging and has the main responsibilities of Constructing XFDU Information Packages conforming to the OAIS reference model and Un-packaging XFDU packages into component information objects.

Component description	PACK has the following responsibilities: • Construct Information Packages – allows the construction of SIP/AIP/DIP, Supporting extraction of Information from CASPAR Representation Information Registry • Unpackage Information Packages – allows unpackaging of SIP/AIP/DIP into component Information Objects • Validation of XFDU Information Packages – Validate an XFDU against the XFDU XML schema • Supports a Storage Handler interface which is implemented with IBMs Preservation DataStores, the storage handler provides submission of an IP to the PDS, allows accessing Information Objects within the PDS and supports operations such as transformations on content information objects within the PDS
Component interfaces	• PackageManager • InformationPackage • RepresentationInformation • PreservationDescriptionInformation • DigitalObject ContentInformation • StorageHandler
Component artefacts	packaging0.X.jar – library JAR providing the PackageManager libs.zip – required libraries
Component UML diagram	Packaging interfaces – see Fig. 17.26
Component specification	PACKAGE_-Spec-Ref-v1_5.doc [205]
Component author	STFC – Science and technology facilities council (UK)
License	GPLv3 Free Software

17.10.2 Referencing a RepInfo Network (RIN)

A RIN referenced from an AIP becomes a logical part of it, even though it is physically separate from that AIP; it is therefore important to discuss how this was applied in CASPAR. RepInfo within the CASPAR Registry can be referenced in the XFDU manifest in either of two ways: by referencing the Curation Persistent Identifier (CPID) of a single RepInfo object directly, or by using a RepInfo Label to reference a set of RepInfo objects. Either way, the manifest reference provides an entry point into the RIN and its recursive structure.

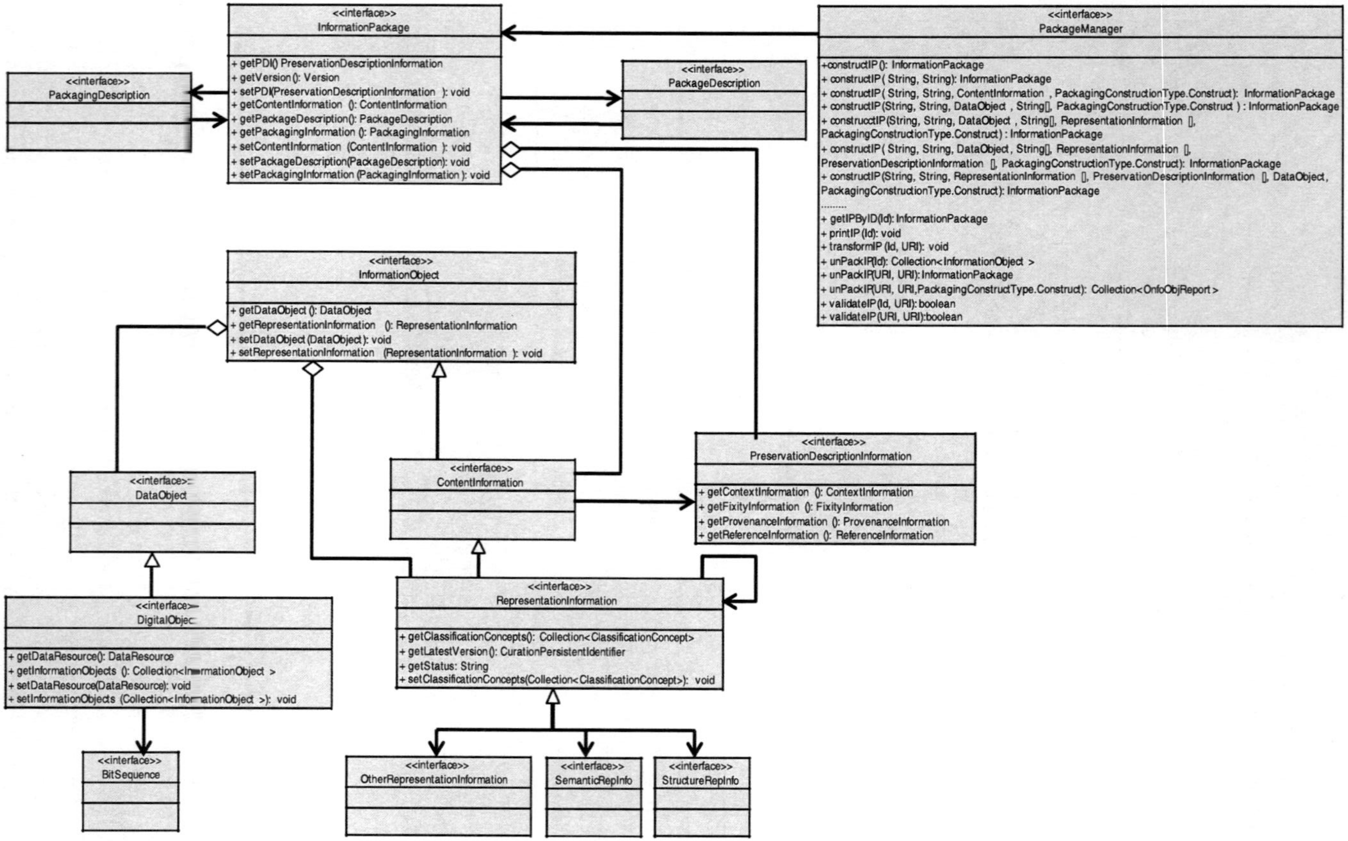

Fig. 17.26 Packaging interfaces

CASPAR XFDU packages are connected to the RIN in the CASPAR Registry using the attributes of the XFDU metadataReference element, as demonstrated in the example below. Using OAIS terminology, the containing metadataObject is classified and categorized as Data Entity Description (DED) RepInfo; we use the vocabularyName attribute to also identify the object as ‘SEMANTIC’. The RepInfo object in the CASPAR/DCC RRORI is referenced by a URI through the href attribute, the otherLocatorType attribute indicating that the URI is a CPID. The id attribute also contains the CPID.

```
<metadataObject category="REP" classification="DED"
ID="REP_DESCRIPTION01">
<metadataReference
 vocabularyName="SEMANTIC" otherLocatorType="CPID"
locatorType="OTHER"

href="http://registry.dcc.ac.uk/omar/registry/http?interface=
QueryManager&amp;
 method=getRepositoryItem&amp;param-id=urn:uuid:40e0c3de-
a405-4759-b116-
 eda15d77df59"
 textInfo="Semantic Information about MST version 3 NetCDF
data files "
 ID="cpid-40e0c3de-a405-4759-b116-eda15d77df59" />
</metadataObject>
```

Given the data to preserve and a CPID, the CASPAR packaging component can pull extra information from the RRORI upon package construction – such as textual descriptions of the RepInfo, which can be inserted into the XFDU manifest. This method provides an entry point into the RIN, a first level dependency. Using the CASPAR Packaging sub-system it is possible to download all further necessary RepInfo in the network for addition into an AIP.

Using the Packaging and Registry APIs for this purpose the Packaging Visualization Tool provides the visual inspection and construction of RIR connected XFDU AIPs. Having been developed over the packaging API, the tool is flexible enough to allow alternative packaging formats to be used, for example a METS toolkit could used in place of the XFDU toolkit allowing the visual construction and visualization of METS based AIPs.

Figure 17.27 shows an example of using the tool to construct an MST package, where the AIPs first level RepInfo dependencies are embedded within the package itself with subsequent levels stored in the Registry.

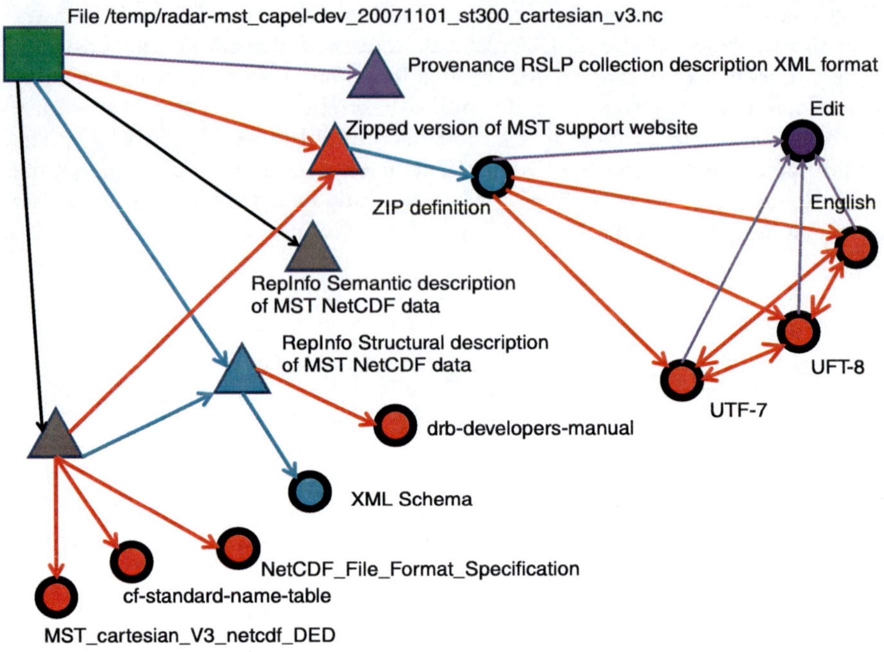

Fig. 17.27 Screenshot of the packaging visualization tool

The square icon represents the data object, the triangles represent RepInfo embedded directly within the AIP, and the circles represent RepInfo stored within the RRORI.

17.10.3 The Packaging Component

The CASPAR Packaging software component is a Java API based closely around OAIS concepts, and exposes operations that provide for the general management of AIPs as identified in the CASPAR User Requirements document [206]. The packaging components main responsibilities are:

- **Construction** – providing operations to build AIPs conforming to OAIS standards.
- **Unpackaging** – providing access to the internal information objects or resolvable references to information objects if they are external to the package
- **Validation** – providing operations to validate the contents and structure of an AIP
- **Transmission** – providing operations to send an AIP to a location for storage
- **Storage** – provides operations to store packages by calling PDS.

As XFDU was chosen as the default AIP format, CASPAR implemented the NASA XFDU Java based toolkit [148] to provide construction, unpackaging and validation of AIPs. Storing AIPs locally or sending them to remote storage is done using the PDS Demo Web Client by IBM. Other clients may also be implemented for this purpose.

17.10.3.1 XFDU Manifest Editor

Packaging an AIP requires tremendous care, as errors made in the present are difficult to detect and correct in the distant future. XFDU manifests, which are extremely detailed and rely heavily on identifiers, are quite prone to errors. This is where the XFDU Manifest Editor (XME) yields an enormous benefit. Developed by the PDS team at IBM, XME – formerly known as XFDU AIP Generator [207] – is an easy-to-use graphical tool for viewing, creating and editing XFDU manifest files (Fig. 17.28). Most graphical XML editors find errors only after they have been made; XME prevents the user from making them in the first place, by limiting one to enter valid values only. For example, XME will decline non-numeral values entered for the *size* attribute, used for recording the content data object's size in bytes; or, upon editing the metadataObject attribute *classification*, will present a drop-down menu listing only the possible values.

By removing irrelevant options, XME reduces the potential for confusion and facilitates the creation of XFDU manifests, thus significantly reducing errors.

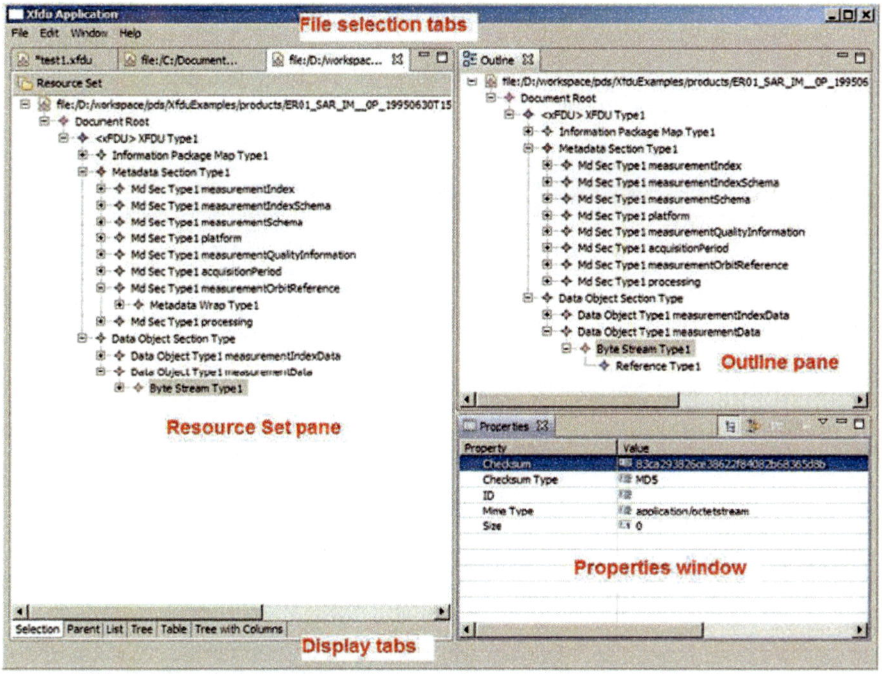

Fig. 17.28 XFDU manifest editor screen capture

17.10.3.2 AIP Roles

While all AIPs are built around a digital asset that needs to be preserved, some fill additional functions in the preservation system, such as transformation modules, fixity modules, or even serving as another AIP's RepInfo. To handle these "special AIPs" properly, a preservation system needs to somehow mark them as such. For this reason, PDS supports various AIP roles, which are indicated upon ingest through the packageType attribute of the XFDU manifest's informationPackageMap element. An AIP that also serves as another AIP's RepInfo should thus be marked as follows:

```
<informationPackageMap packageType="ContentRepInfo">
...
</informationPackageMap>
```

Other roles include FixityModule for AIPs containing ingest modules for fixity calculation, CategoryRepInfo for classifying RepInfo objects, etc. An AIP that is not "special" is indicated by packageType="Standard", or, as the packageType attribute is optional, by not adding the attribute.

17.11 Authenticity Manager Toolkit

Chapter 13 is devoted to Authenticity and some useful tools. Therefore in this section we focus only on the interfaces.

17.11.1 AUTH – Authenticity Manager Interfaces

Component name	 CASPAR Authenticity Manager
Component acronym	AUTH
Component description	Authentication is a process. In order to manage this process, it's necessary to describe: 1. the procedure to be followed (per object type), 2. its outcome (per object), 3. the evolution of the procedure and its outcome over time. In this perspective, the Authenticity Management responsibilities is to manage/monitor Protocol (Procedure) for Authenticity in order to:

	1. Ensure Integrity of Content and Contextual Information 2. Ensure Authenticity of Content and Contextual Information o Ensure Authorship o Identify Provenance o Evaluate Reliability
Component interfaces	• AuthenticityManager
Component artefacts	Authenticity Model Framework Authenticity PACK Authenticity PDS Authenticity DRM
Component UML diagram	• Authenticity Conceptual Model – see Fig. 17.29 • Authenticity Manager Interface – see Fig. 17.30
Component specification	Authenticity and Provenance in Long Term Digital Preservation: Modelling and Implementation in Preservation Aware Storage
Component author	UU – University of Urbino (Italy)

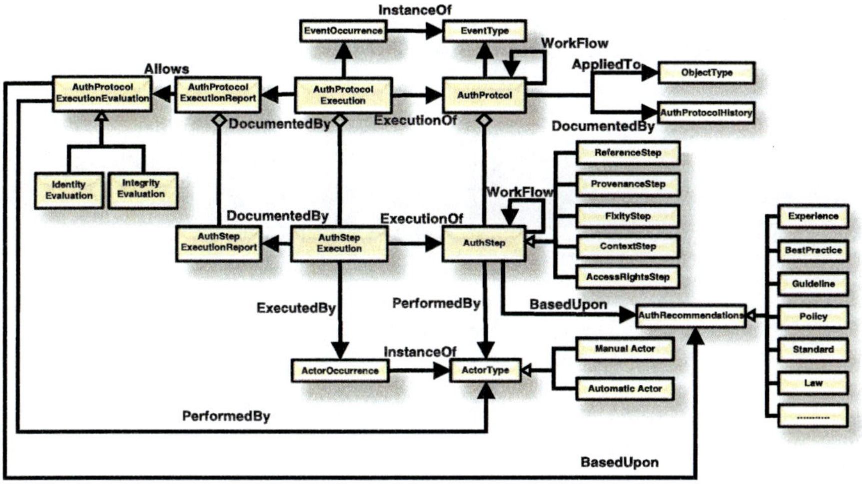

Fig. 17.29 Authenticity conceptual model

17.12 Representation Information Toolkit

Tools for creating Representation Information have been extensively discussed in Chap. 7 therefore this sub-section simply describes the shell which provides a more uniform access to those tools.

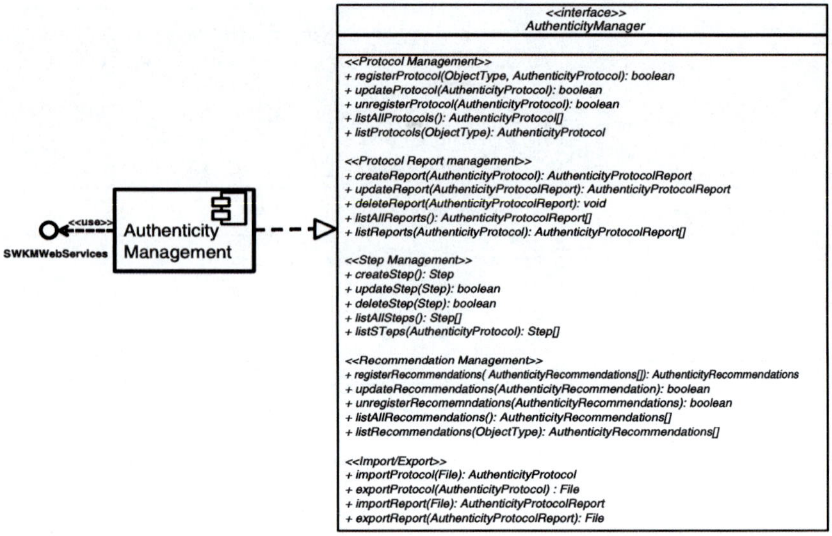

Fig. 17.30 Authenticity manager interface

17.12.1 Representation Information Toolkit

Component name	CASPAR RepInfoToolbox
Component acronym	REPINF
Component description	• An information model and GUI tools for curating OAIS Access and RepInfo Rendering Software. • An information model and GUI tools for curating OAIS Access and RepInfo Rendering Software. • Tools for virtualisation – DSSLI interface for formal structure and semantic description languages. • Tools for virtualisation – JNIEAST a wrapper for EAST C libraries. • Tools for virtualisation – DRB/DEDSL implementation of DSSLI. • Tools for virtualisation – EAST/DEDSL implementation of DSSLI.
Component interfaces	RepInfo Toolbox API DSSLI API

Component artefacts	• repinfotoolbox.jar – Interfaces • DSSLI.jar – Interfaces • repinfotoolbox.jar – Interfaces • dsslidrb.jar – DRB/DEDSL Implementation of DSSLI • dsslieast.jar – EAST/DEDSL Implementation of DSSLI • repinfotoolbox.jar – Implementation of RepInfo Toolbox Interfaces and Swing GUI.
Component UML diagram	
Component specification	
Component author	STFC – Science and Technology Facilities Council (UK)
License	

17.13 Key Components – Summary

REPINFO TOOLKIT

Creation, maintenance and reuse of OAIS Representation Information

---

VIRTUALIZATION

Allow search of an object using either a related measurable parameter or a linkage to remote values

---

PACKAGING

Construction and unpackaging of OAIS Information Packages

REPINFO REGISTRY

Centralised and persistent storage and retrieval of OAIS Representation Information, including PDI

DATA STORE

OAIS-based Preservation Aware Storage, providing built-in support for bit and logical preservation

---

FINDING

Information discovery services

DAMS

Definition and enforcement of access control policies

DRM

Registration of provenance information on digital works and retrieval of right holding information

---

AUTHENTICITY

Maintenance and verification of authenticity in terms of identity and integrity of the digital objects

---

ORCHESTRATION

Reception of notifications from Publishers for a specific "topic" and sending of alerts to Subscribers

---

KNOWLEDGE

Definition of Designated Communities, identification of missing Representation Information

17.14 Integrated tools

After the identification and implementation of the Key Components, the CASPAR development activities were spent in the evaluation of provided functionality and supported scenarios for the Testbed applications. Moreover, the CASPAR Foundation Team has been involved in many training and dissemination activities for presenting its own outcomes, in terms of models and prototypes.

In order to simplify and clarify the explanation of preservation issues and solutions, CASPAR has designed and implemented two integrated tools, built on top of the CASPAR Key Components:

1. The CASPAR Web Desktop
2. The Preservation Scanner (PreScan)

17.14.1 The CASPAR Web Desktop

It has been developed for demonstrating the functionality of each key component with a web based application. That has been useful for suggesting solutions for the Testbeds and for showing the functionality during the training and dissemination events.

Built by adopting the Google Web Toolkit technology, the CASPAR Web Desktop allows the user to:

- Use the DAMS in order to register and access the CASPAR Preservation Web Services through a simple web GUI by any browser;
- Use the DRM for managing the digital rights;
- Use the FIND for retrieving information objects;
- Use the KM for managing designated community knowledge base and evaluating the intelligibility gap;
- Use the POM for notifying and receiving alerts of change events;
- Use the PACK for managing the information packages;
- Use the PDS for storing, maintaining and retrieving information packages;

17.14.2 Preservation Scanner (PreScan)

The preservation of digital objects is a topic of prominent importance for archives and digital libraries. However the creation and maintenance of "metadata" is a laborious task that does not always pay off immediately. For this reason there is a need for tools that automate as much as possible the creation and curation of preservation "metadata". PreScan is a tool for automating the ingestion phase. It can bind together automatically extracted embedded "metadata" with manually provided "metadata", and dependency management services. In addition it offers some features for keeping the "metadata" repository up-to-date. It binds together and exploits several parts of CASPAR work (i.e. GapManager, SWMK, CIDOC CRM Digital, Provenance queries, FIND, Cyclops). Specifically:

It automates parts of the ingestion process so it can be of great value for testbeds;

It links the automatically extracted "metadata" with the dependencies of Gap Manager (so its exploits the recorded registry entries and the dependencies that might exist);

It is now able to express (actually transform) some of the extracted "metadata" in RDF, specifically according to CIDOC CRM Digital. The underlying storage layer can be the file system or a SWMK repository. This means that this approach allows exploiting SWMK, FIND, as well as the Provenance Query Templates. In addition dependencies can be added/changed through the API or the Web App of GapManager.

More CIDOC CRM descriptions could be afterwards added manually (e.g. using the CNRS Cyclops tool).

For further details see [117] and [185] and Sect. 17.4.2.

17.14.3 Summary

Digital preservation is not easy, as should have been made clear by the first part of this book. This chapter has provided a significant amount of details of some practical ways developed by the CASPAR project to address these complexities.

The CASPAR project has addressed important and research issues, many of which are still open, and advanced the state of the art within the Digital Preservation context by:

- Adopting the OAIS ISO:14721:2003 Reference Model as a basis for the CASPAR Conceptual Model;
- Extending the OAIS Information Model and investigating fundamental aspects, such as:
  - Representation Information and Information Packaging;

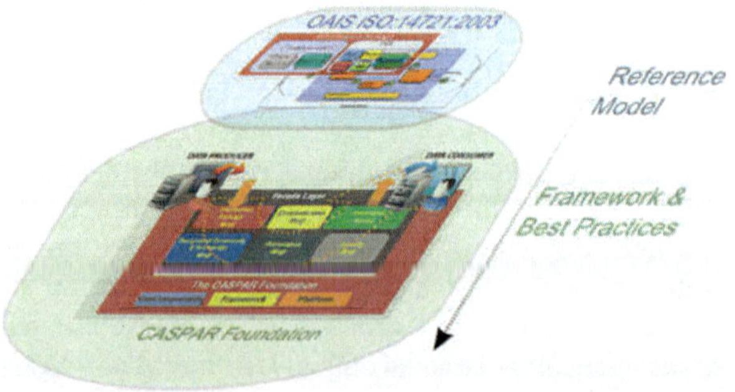

Fig. 17.31 From the reference model to the framework and best practices

  - Characterisation and Management of the Designated Community Knowledge Base and its evolution;
  - Authenticity Protocols;
  - Preservation of Intellectually Property Rights;
- Proposing revisions to OAIS;
- Identifying, Designing and Prototyping Key Components which deal with main concepts of the OAIS Information Model.

For those reasons, the CASPAR outcomes, and in particular the Foundation and its Key Components, may be considered a useful starting point (i.e. Framework in terms of models and prototypes), for adopting and implementing OAIS guidelines as illustrated in Fig. 17.31. Moreover, the CASPAR models and implementations represent Best Practices for many important Digital Preservation issues which could be used in a plethora of projects for Digital Archives.

Chapter 18
Overview of the Testbeds

The bulk of the rest of Part II concerns the testbed reports which provide "accelerated lifetime" tests for a variety of datasets over a number of disciplines.

Further background to these scenarios are available from the CASPAR project deliverable D4101 [208] and related material available from the CASPAR deliverables [209]. This work was undertaken in the summer of 2009.

18.1 Typical Preservation Scenarios

The following illustrates a typical scenario which guides the CASPAR solutions for preservation of any particular digitally encoded piece of information.

General steps occur in each scenario

1. The Designated Community is defined by the repository
2. A variety of information is captured about the object including Access rights and DRM, high level knowledge, various types of Representation Information etc
   a. These artefacts must themselves be preserved i.e. be usable in the future
3. Preservation Aims must be identified
4. A Preservation Analysis must be carried out
5. Preservation workflows to maintain RepInfo, using Orchestration, Knowledge manager, RepInfo toolkit and Registry etc.

In the testbed descriptions we will not repeat these common steps for each scenario, except for detailing the artefacts such as Access Rights or RepInfo which are created.

D. Giaretta, *Advanced Digital Preservation*, DOI 10.1007/978-3-642-16809-3_18,

18.2 Generic Criteria and Method to Organise and to Evaluate the Testbeds

18.2.1 Method

The method to evaluate the success or the compliance of the testbeds is based on an iterative process of tests and feedback reports. Only Designated Community members can really evaluate the preservation results by access and manipulation; Authenticity is also crucial.

Scenarios defined in the D4105 are implemented in the testbed, illustrating:

- the hardware is changing
- the software is changing
- the environment is changing (including legal framework)
- the knowledge bases of the Designated Communities are changing

18.2.2 Preservation Aims

Examples of preservation aims include:

- ability to process a dataset and generate the same data products as previously
- ability to re-perform an artistic performance
- ability to understand a dataset and use it in analysis tools
- ability to render images and documents

Checks on the success of the preservation activity must include confirmation that these aims have been fulfilled and details provided as to how this has been performed and how, and to what extent, this evidence supports the claim that the CASPAR approach is valid.

18.3 Cross References Between Scenarios and Changes

Table 18.1 Summary of scenarios vs. threats countered

Threat	STFC	ESA	UNESCO	IRCAM	UnivLeeds	CIANT	INA
Users may be unable to understand or use the data e.g. the semantics, format, processes or algorithms involved	☑		☑	☑	☑	☑	
Non-maintainability of essential hardware, software or support environment may make the information inaccessible	☑	☑	☑	☑		☑	
The chain of evidence may be lost and there may be lack of certainty of provenance or authenticity	☑			☑			☑
Access and use restrictions may make it difficult to reuse data, or alternatively may not be respected in future							☑
Loss of ability to identify the location of data	Not addressed						
The current custodian of the data, whether an organisation or project, may cease to exist at some point in the future	☑						
The ones we trust to look after the digital holdings may let us down	Covered by Chap. 25						

In their work, each of the testbeds addressed a large number of threats with many sub-scenarios but we highlight in this table, and in this document, only those which we believe illustrate the important points.

The scenarios may be classified in a variety of ways, but for convenience in the following chapters they are presented according to the host organisation. Each is essentially the report from the testbed and therefore is often written in the first person.

Chapter 19
STFC Science Testbed

Background

For the STFC testbeds a methodology was developed in response to the challenge of digital preservation. This challenge lies in the need to preserve not only the dataset itself but also the ability it has to deliver knowledge to a future user community. The preservation objective is defined by the knowledge that a data set is capable of imparting to any future designated user community and has a profound impact on the required preservation actions an archive must carry out.

We sought to incorporate a number of analysis techniques tools and methods into an overall process capable of producing an actionable preservation plan for scientific data archives. The Implementation Plans

19.1 Dataset Selection

Several datasets are used in four scenarios in order to illustrate a number of important points. The datasets come from the archives located in STFC acquired from instruments in other locations, illustrated in Fig. 19.1, and for the study the MST radar in Wales (Fig. 19.2) and Ionosonde data from many stations around the world.

19.2 Challenges Addressed

The challenges addressed are that the physical phenomena about which the data is being collected are complex and specialist knowledge is needed to use the data. Moreover the data is in specialised formats and needs specialised software in order to access it. Therefore the risks to the preservation of this data include

D. Giaretta, *Advanced Digital Preservation*, DOI 10.1007/978-3-642-16809-3_19,

Fig. 19.1 Examples of acquiring scientific data

The MST Radar at Capel Dewi near Aberystwyth is the UK's most powerful and versatile wind-profiling instrument. Data can currently accessed via the British Atmospheric Data Centre. It is a 46.5 MHz pulsed Doppler radar ideally suited for studies of atmospheric winds, waves and turbulence. It is run predominantly in the ST mode (approximately 2–20 km altitude) for which MST radars are unique in their ability to give continuous measurements of the three dimensional wind vector at high resolution (typically 2–3 min in time and 300 m in altitude).

Fig. 19.2 MST radar site

- the risk to the continued ability of users to understand and use it, especially since intimate knowledge of the instruments is needed, and, as we will see, this knowledge is not widespread. Much is contained in Web sites, which are probably ephemeral.
- the likelihood that the software currently used to access and analyse the data will not be supported in the long term
- the provenance of the data depends on the what is in the head of the repository manager
- the funding of the archives is by no means guaranteed and yet, because much knowledge is linked to key personnel, there is a risk that it will not be possible to hand over the data/information holdings fully to another archive.

19.3 Preservation Aims

After discussion with the archive managers and scientists it was agreed that the preservation aims should be to preserve the ability of users to extract from the data and understand in sufficient detail to use in scientific analyses, a number of key measurements.

The knowledge base of the Designated Community will be somewhat lower than the experts, but still include the broad disciplinary understanding of the subject.

In order to be in a position to hand over its holdings, some example AIPs must be constructed. Note that we do not attempt to construct AIPs for the whole archive, nevertheless the Representation Information and PDI we capture are applicable to most of the individual datasets. With the ability to create AIPs, the archive would be in a position to hand over its holdings to the next in the chain of preservation if and when this is necessary.

19.4 Preservation Analysis

We structure the analysis of the detailed work around constructing the AIP.

A number of strategies were considered. Of those eliminated it is worth mentioning that emulation was not regarded as useful by the archive scientists because it restricted the ways in which they could use the data. Similarly transformation of the data might be an option in future but only when other options became too difficult. In order to understand this, a preservation risk analysis was conducted which allows the archive managers to assess when this point is likely to arrive.

19.5 MST RADAR Scenarios

Four scenarios are detailed here, for two different instruments. IN the interests of brevity we list the actions carried out in each scenario, including where appropriate the use of the Key Components and toolkits.

19.5.1 STFC1: Simple Scenario MST

A user from a future designated user community should be able to extract the following information from the data for a given altitude and time

- Horizontal wind speed and direction
- Wind sheer
- Signal Velocity
- Signal Power
- Aspect
- Correlated Spectral Width

MST1.1

An example of data set specific plotting and analysis programs for the MST would be the MST GNU plot software. This software plots Cartesian product of wind profiles from NetCDF data files. This software was developed by the project scientist due to specialised visualization requirements where finer definition of colour and font was needed than that provided by generic tools. Preservation risks are due to the following user skill requirements and technical dependencies.

- UNIX http://www.unix.org/ or Linux distribution
- The user must be able to install python http://www.python.org/ with python-dev module installed with numpy array package and pycdf
- GNU plot to be installed http://www.gnuplot.info/docs/gnuplot.html and a user must be able to set environmental variables
- The ability to run required python scripts through a UNIX command line
- GNU plot template file to format plot output.

A number of preservation strategies presented themselves

Emulation Strategy

One solution is preserving the software through emulation, for example Dioscuri http://dioscuri.sourceforge.net/faq.html. Current work with the PLANETS project http://www.planets-project.eu/news/?id=1190708180 will make Dioscuri capable of running operating systems such as Linux Ubuntu which should satisfy platform dependencies. With the capture of specified software packages/libraries and the provision of all necessary user instructions this would become a viable strategy.

Conversion Strategy

It is additionally possible to convert NetCDF files to another compatible format such as NASA AMES http://badc.nerc.ac.uk/help/formats/NASA-Ames/. We were able to achieve this conversion using the community developed software Nappy http://home.badc.rl.ac.uk/astephens/software/nappy/, CDAT http://www2-pcmdi.llnl.gov/cdat and Python. This is a compatible self describing ASCII format, so the information should still be accessible and easily understood as long as ASCII encoded text can still be read. There would be however reluctance to do this as NASA AMES files are not as easily manipulated making it more cumbersome to analyse data in the desired manner.

Preservation by Addition of Representation Information Strategy

An alternate strategy is to gather the following documentation relating to the NetCDF file format which contains adequate information for future users to extract the required parameters from the NetCDF file. Currently this information can be found in the BADC support pages on NetCDF http://badc.nerc.ac.uk/help/formats/NetCDF/ which can be archived using the HTtrack tool or adequately referenced. These pages suggest some useful generic software a future user may wish to utilize. If these pages or no longer available or the software is unusable a user can consult documents from the NetCDF documentation and libraries from Unidata http://www.unidata.ucar.edu/software/NetCDF/docs/. This means that if future user community still have skills in FORTRAN, C, C++, Python or Java they will be able to easily write software to access the required parameters.

The BADC decided to opt for the following strategies

- Referencing BADC support
- Referencing Unidata support
- Crystallising out RepInfo from UNIDATA doc library to allow developer to write or extend their own software in the following languages
  - JAVA
  - C++
  - FORTRAN 77
  - Python

MST1.2

The GAP manager can be used to identify NetCDF file as at risk when BADC or UNIDATA support goes away either to a variety of technical or organisational reasons. This can now be replaced with other RepInfo from the registry repository which we will take from the NetCDF document library at UNICAR whose longevity is not guaranteed http://www.unidata.ucar.edu/software/netcdf/docs/. We will use this documentation and the real life BADC user survey to create different designated community profile with the GAP manager. This will show how we can satisfy the needs of different communities of C++, Fortran, Python and Java programmers who wish to use the data.

MST1.3

We explored good about NetCDF standardisation and show CASPAR supports it by archiving the CF standard name list monitoring it and using POM to send notification of changes therefore supporting the semantic integrity of the data.

NetCDF (network Common Data Form) is an interface for array-orientated data access and a library that provides an implementation of that interface. NetCDF is used extensively in the atmospheric and oceanic science communities. It is a preferred file format of the British Atmospheric data centre that currently provides access to the data. The NetCDF software was developed at the Unidata Program Center in Boulder Colorado USA http://www.unidata.ucar.edu/. NetCDF facilitates preservation for the following reasons

- NetCDF is a portable, self-describing binary data format so is ideal for capture of provenance, descriptive and semantic information.
- NetCDF is network-transparent, meaning that it can be accessed by computers that store integers, characters and floating-point numbers in different ways. This provides some protection against technology obsolescence.
- NetCDF datasets can be read and written in a number of languages, these include C, C++, FORTRAN, IDL, Python, Perl, and Java. The spread of languages capable of reading these datasets ensures greater longevity of access because as one language becomes obsolete the community can move to another.
- The different language implementations are freely available from the UNIDATA Center, and NetCDF is completely and methodically documented in UNIDATA's NetCDF User's Guide making capture of necessary representation information a relatively easy low cost option.
- Several groups have defined conventions for NetCDF files, to enable the exchange of data. BADC has adopted the Climate and Forecasting (CF) conventions for NetCDF data and have created standard names.

CF conventions are guidelines and recommendations as to where to put information within a NetCDF file, and they provide advice as to what type of information you might want to include. CF conventions allow the creator of the dataset to include information representation and preservation description information in a structured way. Global attributes describe the general properties and origins of the dataset capturing vital provenance and descriptive information, while local attributes are used.

MST1.5

Archive the MST support website and carrying out an assessment of it constituent elements and use the Registry to repository to add basic information on HTML, Word, PDF, JPEG, PNG and PostScript to facilitate preservation of a simple static website Much additional valuable provenance information has also been recorded in the MST radar support website. Selected pages or the entire site could be archived as Preservation Description Information.

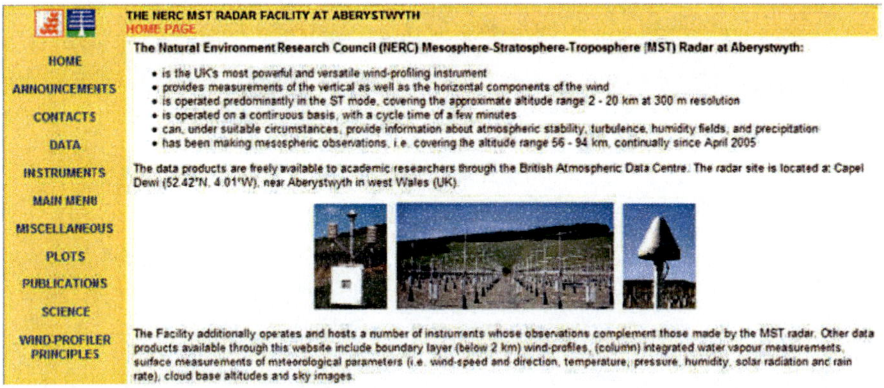

Fig. 19.3 STFC MST website

The MST website is currently located at http://mst.nerc.ac.uk (Fig. 19.3). Due to the sites' simple structure, which consists of a set of static pages and common file types it would be a relatively simple operation to run a web archiving tool such as HTtrack (http://www.httrack.com/) to copy the website and add additional RepInfo on HTML, PDF, MS Word and JPEG from the DCC Registry Repository of Representation Information RRORI. HTtrack is only one of a range of web-archiving tools which are freely available and require minimal skill to operate. However it is worth noting that it is only by virtue of the technical simplicity of the site that it is so relatively easy to archive and preserve.

MST1.6

PACK component was used to create and add checksum to the AIP maintaining the existing directory structure of data files.

MST 1.7

The current directory structure is logical and well thought out. This should be maintained in the AIP package. Details of archiving conventions are recorded in the MST website http://mst.nerc.ac.uk/archiving_conventions.html which will need to be altered by the removal of the BADC from the top of the directory hierarchy structure to avoid confusion.

/badc/dataset-name/data/data-type-name/YYYY/MM/DD/

19.5.1.1 Preservation Information Network Model for MST Simple Solution

A preservation information network model (Fig. 19.4) is a representation of the digital objects, operations and relationships which allow a preservation objective to be met for a future designated community. The model provides a sharable, stable and organized structure for digital objects and their associated requirements. The

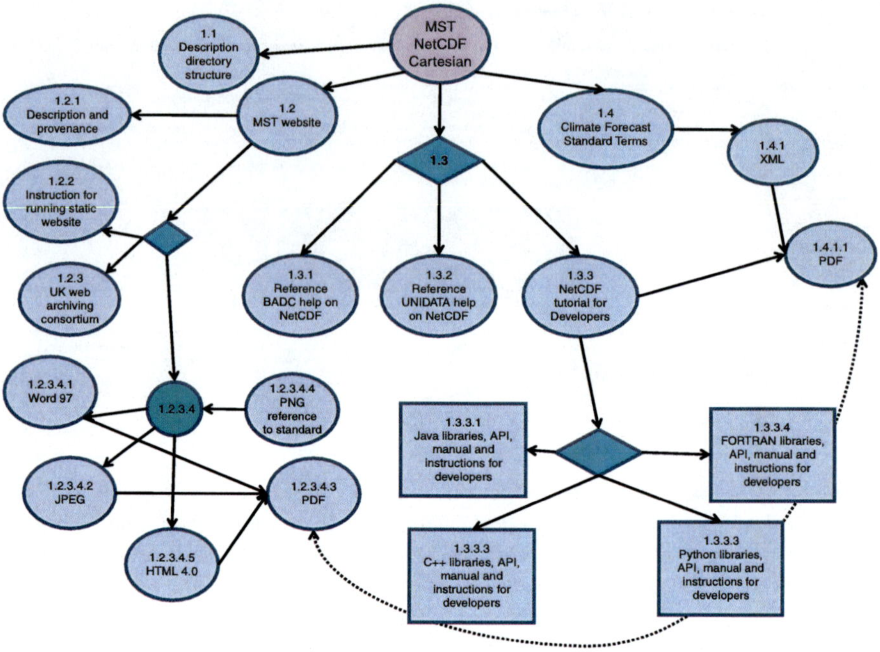

Fig. 19.4 Preservation information network model for MST-simple solution

model also directs the capture and description of digital objects which need to be packaged and stored within an OAIS compliant Archival Information Package.

19.5.1.2 Components of a Preservation Network Models

Preservation network modelling has many similarities to classic conceptual modelling approaches such as Entity-Relationship or Class diagrams, as it is based upon the idea of making statements about resources. The preservation network model consist of two components the digital objects and the relationships between them.

Objects are uniquely identified digital entities capable of an independent existence which possess the following attributes

- **Information** is a description of the key information contained by the digital object. This information should have been identified during preservation analysis as being the information required to satisfy the preservation objective for the designated user community.
- **Location** information is the information required by the end user to physically locate and retrieve the object. AIP's may be logical in construction with key digital object being distributed and managed within different information systems. This tends to be the case when data is in active use with resources evolving in dynamic environment.

- **Physical State** describes the form of the digital object. It should contain sufficient information relating to the version, variant, instance and dependencies.
- **Risks** most digital solutions will have inherent risks and a finite lifespan. Risks such interpretability of information, technical dependencies or loss designated community skill. Risks should be recorded against the appropriate object so they can be monitored and the implication of them being realised assessed.
- **Termination** of network occurs when a user requires no additional information or assistance to achieve, the defined preservation objective given the accepted risks will not be imminently realised.
- **Relationship** captures how two objects are related to one another in order to fulfil the specified preservation objective whilst being utilized by a member of the designated user community.
- **Function**, in order to satisfy the preservation objective a digital object will perform a specific function for example the delivery of textual information or the extraction and graphical visualisation of specific parameters
- **Tolerance,** not every function is critical for the fulfilment of the preservation objective with some digital objects included as they enhance the quality of the solution or ease of use. The loss of this function is denoted in the model as a tolerance.
- **Quality assurance and testing,** The ability of an object to perform the specified function may have been subjected to quality assurance and testing which may be recorded against the relationship.
- **Alternate and Composite relationships** can be thought of as logical "And" (denoted in diagrams by circle) or "Or" (denoted in diagrams by diamond) relationships. Where either all relationships must function in order to fulfil the required objective or in the case of the later only one relationship needs to function in order to fulfil the specified objective.

19.5.1.3 Quality Assurance and Testing of MST Simple Solution

19.5.1.3.1 Overall All Solution Validated By

Curation Manager at the British Atmospheric Data Centre and the NERC Earth Observation Data Centre. His role is to oversee the operations of the data centres ensuring that they are trusted repositories that deliver data efficiently to users. He has a particular interest in data publication issues. He is also the facility manager for the NERC MST radar facility.

NERC MST radar facility project scientist and is part of the committee for the MST radar international workshop. The international workshop on MST radar, held about every 2–3 years, is a major event gathering together experts from all over the world, engaged in research and development of radar techniques to study the mesosphere, stratosphere, troposphere (MST).

19.5.1.3.2 Element of Solution Validated as Follows

MST1.1 Directory Structure – Directory structure validation trivial as very simple structure easy to navigate

MST1.2 MST website Content supplied validated and managed by the project scientist and is subject to community and user group scrutiny

MST1.2.1 MST website provenance validate by the website creator and manager

MST1.2.2 Instructions for running static website – this was tested locally with the group user where able to unzip and use website providing they had Firefox/Internet Explorer, Adobe and Word installed on their laptops/PC

MST1.2.3 – reference testing trivial easily, risk that this reference needs to be monitored is accepted

MST1.2.3.4 – composite strategy elements of MST website have been scrutinised by research team

We confirmed that the site contained jpeg, png, word, pdf and html file (Fig. 19.5). We then established that use of these file types was stable in the user community. Use of file types is monitored by the BADC who carry a regular survey of their user community. We accepted there was a risk that users may at some point in the future not be able to use these file and will use the BADC survey mechanism to monitor the situation. RepInfo for this file type was also added to the AIP so the file type could easily be understood and monitored.

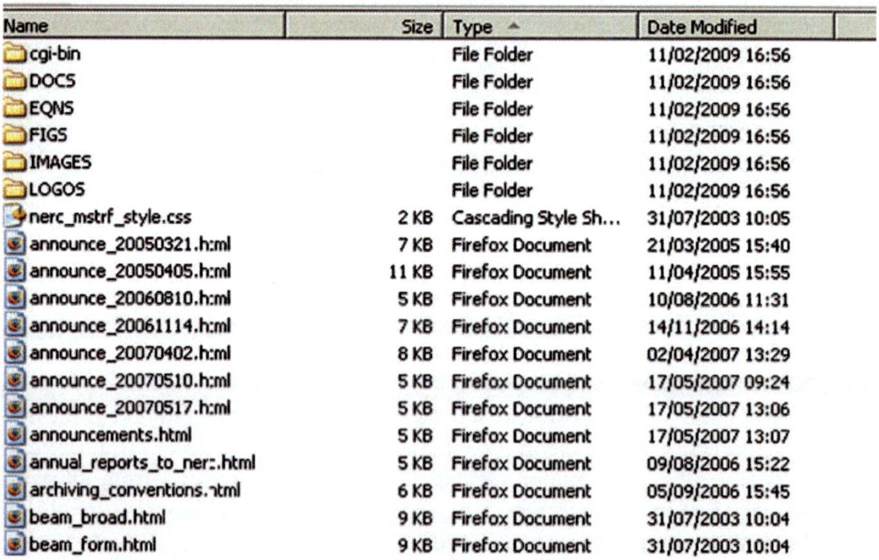

Name	Size	Type	Date Modified
cgi-bin		File Folder	11/02/2009 16:56
DOCS		File Folder	11/02/2009 16:56
EQNS		File Folder	11/02/2009 16:56
FIGS		File Folder	11/02/2009 16:56
IMAGES		File Folder	11/02/2009 16:56
LOGOS		File Folder	11/02/2009 16:56
nerc_mstrf_style.css	2 KB	Cascading Style Sh...	31/07/2003 10:05
announce_20050321.h:ml	7 KB	Firefox Document	21/03/2005 15:40
announce_20050405.h:ml	11 KB	Firefox Document	11/04/2005 15:55
announce_20060810.h:ml	5 KB	Firefox Document	10/08/2006 11:31
announce_20061114.h:ml	7 KB	Firefox Document	14/11/2006 14:14
announce_20070402.h:ml	8 KB	Firefox Document	02/04/2007 13:29
announce_20070510.h:ml	5 KB	Firefox Document	17/05/2007 09:24
announce_20070517.h:ml	5 KB	Firefox Document	17/05/2007 13:06
announcements.html	5 KB	Firefox Document	17/05/2007 13:07
annual_reports_to_ner:.html	5 KB	Firefox Document	09/08/2006 15:22
archiving_conventions.html	6 KB	Firefox Document	05/09/2006 15:45
beam_broad.html	9 KB	Firefox Document	31/07/2003 10:04
beam_form.html	9 KB	Firefox Document	31/07/2003 10:04

Fig. 19.5 MST web site files

MST 1.2.3.4.1 Information on Word 97 supplied by Microsoft

MST 1.2.3.4.2 Reference to British and ISO standards on JPEG

MST 1.2.3.4.3 W3C validated description

MST 1.2.3.4.4 Reference to ISO standard

MST 1.2.3.4.1 Reference to ISO standard

MST1.3.1 Reference to BADC software solutions for NETCDF. Tested by CASPAR STFC and IBM Haifa.

Successfully tested and validated the extraction parameters using software supplied by the BADC InfrastructureManager. He looks after the software that runs the BADC, including the registration system and dataset access control software

and

Met Office Coordinator, who works for the NCAS/British Atmospheric Data Centre (but is located in Hadley Centre for Climate Prediction and Research at the UK Met Office (http://www.metoffice.gov.uk). Main duties involve work with:

- Global model datasets obtained from the European Centre for Medium Range Weather Forecasts (ECMWF).
- Liaison with the Met Office regarding scientific and technical interactions.
- Development of software tools for data extraction, manipulation and delivery (based on Climate Data Analysis Tools (CDAT).
- Development of software for data format conversion such as NAppy.

MST 1.3.2 & 1.3.3.9(1–4); RepInfo has been subjected to community scrutiny and published by UNIDATA

The Unidata mission is to provide the data services, tools, and cyber infrastructure leadership that advance Earth system science, enhance educational opportunities, and broaden participation. Unidata, funded primarily by the National Science Foundation, is one of eight programs in the University Corporation for Atmospheric Research (UCAR) Office of Programs (UOP). UOP units create, conduct, and coordinate projects that strengthen education and research in the atmospheric, oceanic and earth sciences.

Unidata is a diverse community of over 160 institutions vested in the common goal of sharing data, and tools to access and visualize that data. For 20 years Unidata has been providing data, tools, and support to enhance Earth-system education and research. In an era of increasing data complexity, accessibility, and multidisciplinary integration, Unidata provides a rich set of services and tools.

The Unidata Program Center, as the leader of a broad community:

- Explores new technologies
- Evaluates and implements technological standards and tools
- Advocates for the community

- Provides leadership in solving community problems in new and creative ways
- Negotiates for new and valuable data sources
- Facilitates data discovery and use of digital libraries
- Enables student-centred learning in the Earth system sciences by promoting use of data and tools in education
- Values open standards, interoperability, and open-source approaches
- Develops innovative solutions and new capabilities to solve community needs
- Stays abreast of computing trends as they pertain to advancing research and education

MST1.4 CF standard names list. The conventions for climate and forecast (CF) "metadata" are designed to promote the processing and sharing of files created with the NetCDF API. The CF conventions are increasingly gaining acceptance and have been adopted by a number of projects and groups as a primary standard. The conventions define "metadata" that provide a definitive description of what the data in each variable represents, and the spatial and temporal properties of the data. This enables users of data from different sources to decide which quantities are comparable, and facilitates building applications with powerful extraction, re-gridding, and display capabilities. The CF conventions generalize and extend the COARDS conventions.

19.5.1.3.3 Discussion and Validation of CF "metadata" Takes Place in Two Formats

1. CF "metadata" Trac, and
2. cf-"metadata" mailing list.

The list is then published by Alison Pamment CF meta data secretary. Alison is research scientist based at the Rutherford Appleton Laboratory and is responsible for Climate and Forecast (CF) "metadata" support.

MST 1.4.1 W3C validate standard

MST 1.4.1.1 PDF ISO standard

Inputs needed for the creation of the AIP are illustrated in Fig. 19.6.

19.5.2 Scenario2 MST-Complex

A user from a future designated user community should be able to extract the following information from the data for a given altitude and time

- Horizontal wind speed and direction
- Wind sheer
- Signal Velocity
- Signal Power
- Aspect
- Correlated Spectral Width

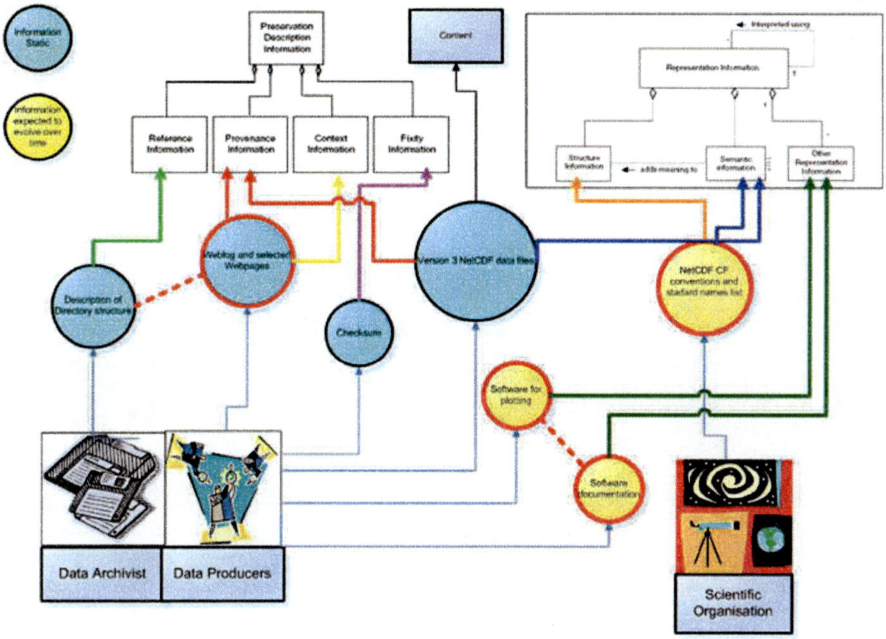

Fig. 19.6 Preservation information flow for scenario 1 - MST-simple

The Preservation Information Network is shown in Fig. 19.7. In addition future users should have access to User group notes, MST conference proceedings and peer reviewed literature published by previous data users.

MST Scenario2 has a higher level preservation objective and can be considered an extension of scenario 1 as the AIP information content is simply extended. The significance of this is that future data users will have access to important information which will help in the studying the following types of phenomena captured within the data

- Precipitation
- Convection
- Gravity Waves
- Rossby Waves
- Mesoscale and Microscale Structures
- Fallstreak Clouds
- Ozone Layering

19.5.2.1 Preservation Objectives for Scenario2 MST-Complex

A user from a future designated user community should be able to extract the following information from the data for a given altitude and time

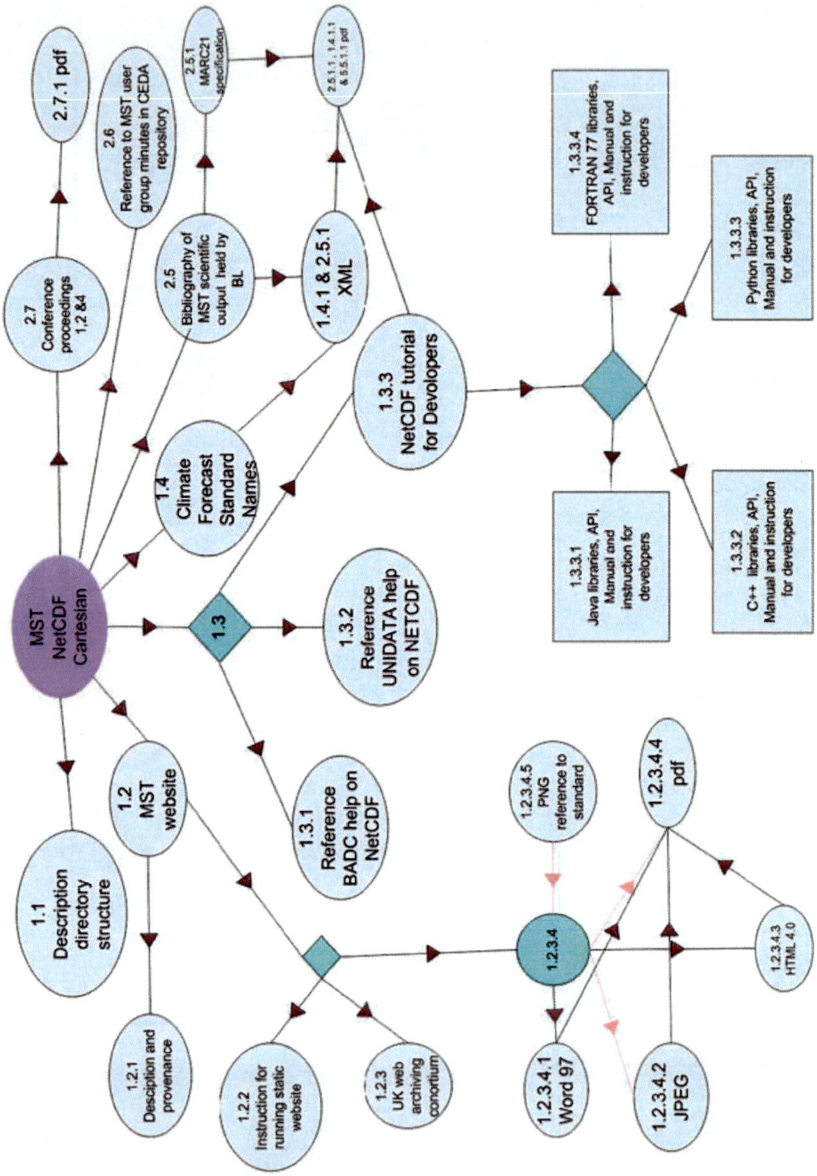

Fig. 19.7 Preservation information network model for MST-complex solution

- Horizontal wind speed and direction
- Wind sheer
- Signal Velocity
- Signal Power
- Aspect
- Correlated Spectral Width

In addition future users should have access to User group notes, MST conference proceedings and peer reviewed literature published by previous data users.

MST Scenario2 has a higher level preservation objective and can be considered an extension of scenario 1 as the AIP information content is simply extended. The significance of this is that future data users will have access to important information which will help in the studying the following types of phenomena captured within the data

- Precipitation
- Convection
- Gravity Waves
- Rossby Waves
- Mesoscale and Microscale Structures
- Fallstreak Clouds
- Ozone Layering

Implementation points based on strategies for scenario1

MST1.7 We reviewed bibliography contained by website and quality of references. Carried out an investigation and review of technical reports which are used heavily at STFC but have not been generated here. Identify clear cases of reports which have correctly cited but have not need been deposited anywhere as they have no natural home and digitise for inclusion within the AIP. The website additionally contains a bibliographic record of publications resulting from use of the data. This record contains good quality citations but there would be concerns regarding permanent access to some of these materials, consider the two examples below

W. Jones and S. P. Kingsley. MST radar observations of meteors. In Proceedings of the Wagstaff (USA) Conference on Astroids, Comets and Meteors. Lunar and Planetary Institute (NASA Houston), July 1991

S. P. Kingsley. Radio-astronomical methods of measuring the MST radar antenna. Technical report to MST radar user community, 1989.

Neither of these two items is current held by either The British Library http://www.bl.uk/ or The Library of Congress http://catalog.loc.gov/ based on searches of their catalogues. Nor do they in exist in the local STFC institutional repository http://epubs.cclrc.ac.uk/. The preservation strategy to deal with this bibliography was to create MARC http://www.loc.gov/marc/ http://www.dcc.ac.uk/diffuse/?s=36 records in XML format for items held by the British Library and to begin the process of obtaining copies of the other items from the current community and digitise them in PDF format for direct inclusion within the AIP.

MST1.8

The international workshop on MST radar is held about every 2–3 years, and is a major event gathering together experts from all over the world, engaged in research and development of radar techniques to study the mesosphere, stratosphere and troposphere (MST). It was additionally attended by young scientists, research students and also new entrants to the field to facilitate close interactions with the experts on all technical and scientific aspects of MST radar techniques. It is this aspect which makes the proceedings an ideal resource for future users who are new to the field.

Permanent access to these proceedings is again at risk. The MST 10 proceedings are available for download from the internet http://jro.igp.gob.pe/mst10/ and from the British Library. Proceedings 3, 5–10 are also available from the British library, meeting 4 is only available from the Library of Congress and unfortunately the proceedings from meetings 1 and 2 have not been deposited in either institution.

A number of strategies present themselves. Copies of proceedings 1, 2 and 4 could be obtained from the still active community, digitised and incorporated into the AIP. The proceedings which are currently held by the British Library can be obtained, digitised and incorporated into the AIP or alternatively the XML MARC record can be obtained and incorporated into the AIP as a reference as there is a high to degree of confidence in the permanence of these holdings.

MST1.9 The project scientist has again been quite diligent in keeping minutes of the user group meetings which are run for data-using scientists several times a year. As result this information is easily captured. It currently resides in the NCAS CEDA repository which provides easy access to current data users however there are no guarantees that this repository will persist in the longer term so a simple reference in the form of URL would not be considered to be sufficient to guarantee permanent access to this material. This leaves two strategies open to the archive. The first involves taking a copy of this material and including it physically within the AIP. The second involves orchestration where the CEDA repository would be required to alert the custodians of the MST data to the demise of the repository or migration of this material, so it may be obtained for direct inclusion in the AIP. We created reference to the MST user group minutes held in the newly created CEDA institutional repository for the Nation Centre for Atmospheric studies http://cedadocs.badc.rl.ac.uk/. We registered the demise of this repository as a risk to monitored and recommended the development of an orchestration strategy for material held. This repository as it is representative of a proliferation of repositories in academia whose longevity is not guaranteed.

19.5.2.2 Quality Assurance and Testing of MST Complex Solution

MST 2.5 Bibliography content supplied and validated by the project scientist
MST 2.5.1 MARC21 specification standard validated by library of congress
MST 2.5.1 XML specification validated by W3C
MST 2.5.1.1 & 2.5.2.1 PDF ISO standard

Inputs needed for the creation of the AIP are illustrated in Fig. 19.8.

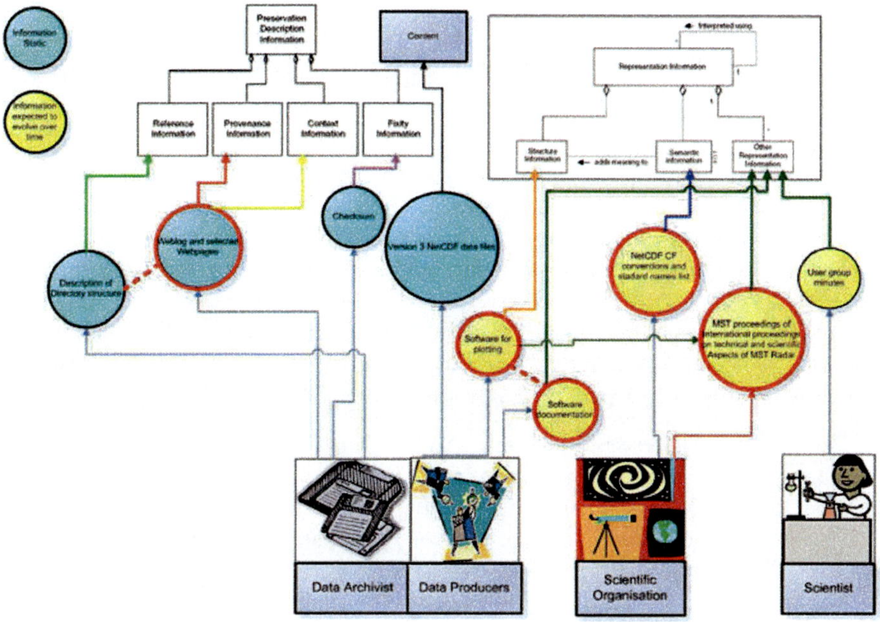

Fig. 19.8 Preservation information flow for scenario 2 - MST-complex

19.6 Ionosonde Data and the WDC Scenarios

The World Data Centre (WDC) system was created to archive and distribute data collected from the observational programmes of the 1957–1958 International Geophysical Year. Originally established in the United States, Europe, Russia, and Japan, the WDC system has since expanded to other countries and to new scientific disciplines. The WDC system now includes 52 Centres in 12 countries. Its holdings include a wide range of solar, geophysical, environmental, and human dimensions data. The WDC for Solar-Terrestrial Physics based at the Rutherford Appleton laboratory holds ionospheric data comprising vertical soundings from over 300 stations, mostly from 1957 onwards, though some stations have data going back to the 1930s.

The Ionosonde is a basic tool for ionospheric research. Ionosondes are "Vertical Incidence" radars which record the time of flight of a radio signal swept through a range of frequencies (1–30 MHz) and reflected from the ionised layers of the upper atmosphere (90–800 km) as an "ionogram". These results are analysed to give the variation of electron density with height up to the peak of the ionosphere. Such electron-density profiles provide most of the Information required for studies of the ionosphere and its effect on radio communications. Only a small fraction of the recorded ionograms are analysed in this way, however, because of the effort required. The traditional input to the WDC has been hourly resolution scaled data, but many stations take soundings at higher resolutions.

The WDC receives data from the many ionosonde stations around the world through a variety of means including ftp, email, CD-ROM. Data is provided in a number of formats: URSI (simple hourly resolution) and IIWG (more complex, time varying) standard formats as well as station specific "bulletins". The WDC stored data in digital formats comprises 2.9 GB of data in IIWG format and 70 GB of raw MMM, SAO, ART files from Lowell digisondes. The WDC also holds about 40,000 rolls of 16/35 mm film ionograms and ~10,000 monthly bulletins of scaled ionospheric data. Some of this data is already in digital from, but much, particularly the ionogram images, is not yet digitised.

- Many stations' data is provided in IIWG or URSI format directly. This data may be automatically or manually scaled.
- selection of European stations provide "raw" format data from Lowell digisondes, a particular make of ionosonde, as part of a COST project. This data is in a proprietary format, but Lowell provides Java based software for analysis. The WDC uses this software to manipulate this data, particularly from the CCLRC's own Ionospheric Monitoring Groups Ionosondes at Chilton, UK and Stanley, Falkland Islands. The autoscaled data from these stations is also stored in a PostgreSQL database.
- Other stations provide a small set of standard parameters in a station specific "bulletin" format which is similar to the paper bulletins traditionally produced from the 1950s onwards. The WDC has some bespoke, configurable software to extract the data from these bulletins and convert it to IIWG format.

It is important to realise that this is a totally voluntary data collection and archive system. The WDCs have no control or means of enforcing a "standard" means of data processing or dissemination, though "weight" of history and ease-of-use tends to make this the preferred option.

19.6.1 STFC3: Implementation Plan for Scenario3 Ionosonde-Simple

The first preservation scenario show us again supporting and integrating with existing preservation practices of the World Data Centre, which means creating a consistent global record from 252 station by extracting a standardise set of parameters from the Ionograms produced around the world. A user from a future designated community should be able to the following fourteen standard Ionospheric parameters from the data for a given station and time. They should also be able to understand what these parameters represent. *F*min, *foE' h_E,foes h_Es,* type of *Es,* *fbEs, foF*1, *M*(3000)*F*1, *h_F, h_F*2, *foF*2, *fx, M*(3000)*F*2. The preservation information flow is shown in Fig. 19.9 and the corresponding information network is shown in Fig. 19.10.

19.6.1.1 Preservation Information Flow for Scenario3 Ionosonde-Simple

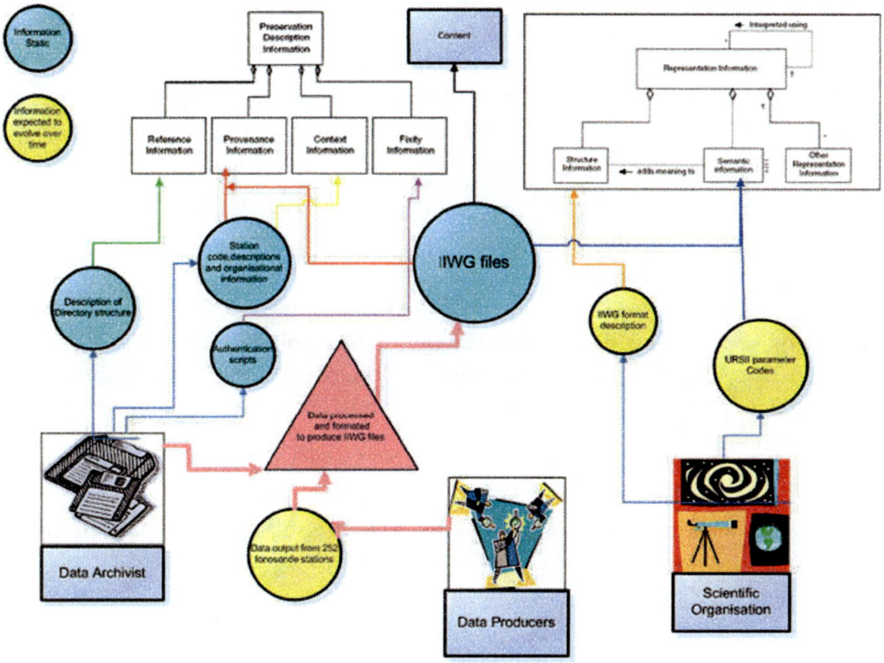

Fig. 19.9 Preservation information flow for scenario 3 – Ionosonde-simple

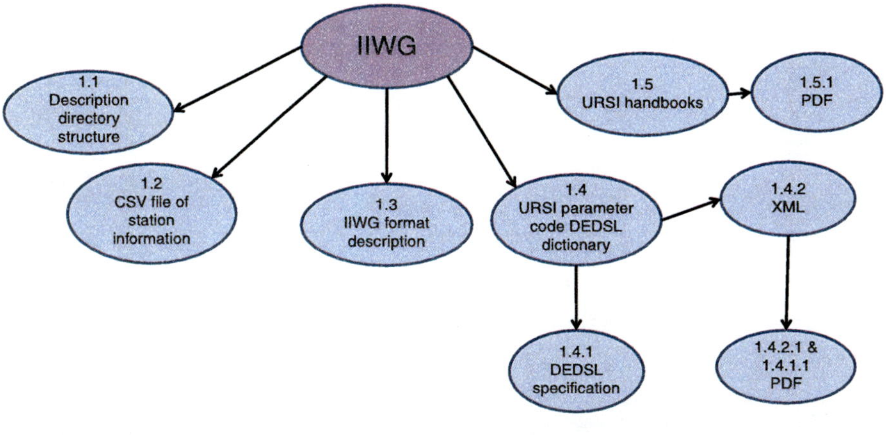

Fig. 19.10 Preservation network model for scenario 3 Ionosonde simple

19.6.1.2 Implementation Points Based on Strategies for Scenario3

IO1.1 New RepInfo based on IIWG format description removing need to understand FORTRAN as is the case with comprehending the current version
IO1.2 Create DEDSL dictionary for 14 standard parameters and add RepInfo from the Registry Repository on the XML DEDSL standard
IO1.3 Authenticity information from the current archivist for the 252 stations and the data transformation/ingest process
IO1.4 Perform CSV dump of station information from Postgres database
IO1.5 A logical description of the directory structure was created
IO1.6 PACK was used to create and add checksum to the AIP maintaining the existing directory file structure

19.6.2 STFC4: Implementation Plan for Scenario4 Ionosonde-Complex

The second preservation scenario for the Ionosonde can only be carried out for 7 European stations but will allow a consistent Ionogram record for the Chilton site which dates back to the 1920s. A user from a future designated community should be able reproduce an Ionogram from the raw mmm/sao data files (see Fig. 19.11) and have access to the Ionospheric Monitoring group's website, the URSI handbooks of interpretation and Lowell technical documentation. Being able to preserve the Ionogram record is significant as it a much richer source of information more accurately able to covey the state of the atmosphere when correctly interpreted. The preservation information flow is shown in Fig. 19.12.

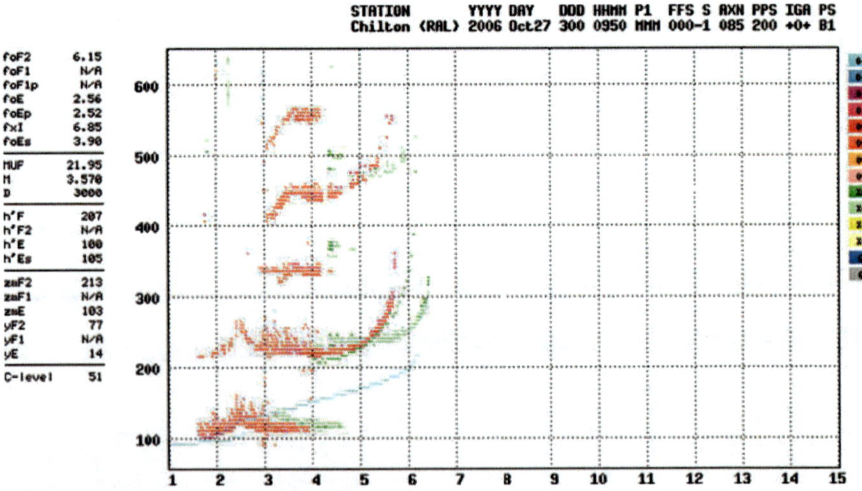

Fig. 19.11 Example plot of output from Ionosonde

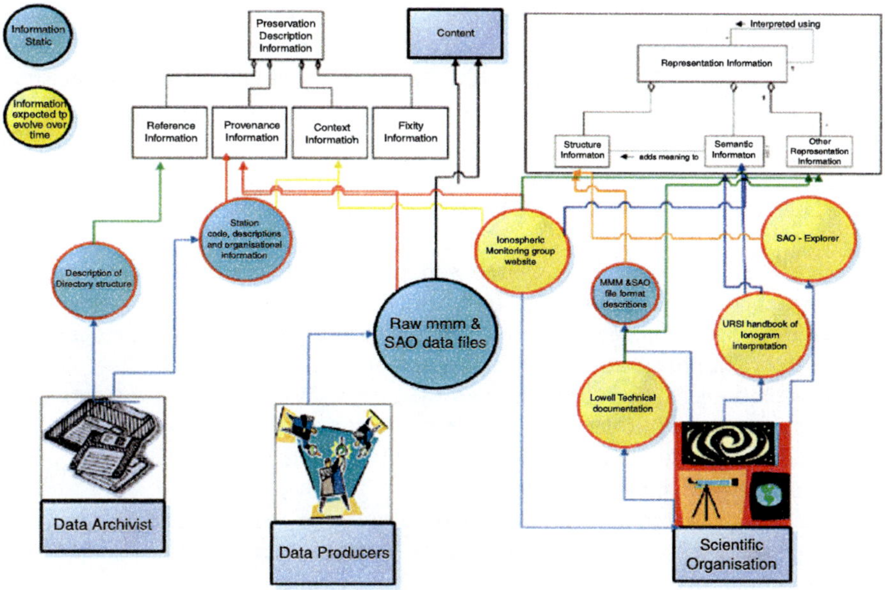

Fig. 19.12 Preservation information flow for scenario 4 Ionosonde-complex

19.6.2.1 Implementation Points Based on Strategies for Scenario4

IO2.1 Archive SAO explorer with RepInfo from registry repository for JAVA 5 software

IO2.2 Digitise and include URSI handbooks of interpretation in the AIP and deposit in Registry Repository for other repository users

IO2.3 Digitise and include Lowell technical documentation in the AIP and deposit in Registry Repository for other repository users

IO2.4 Archive the Ionospheric monitoring group website and carrying out an assessment of its constituent elements and use the Registry to repository to add basic information on HTML, Word, PDF, JPEG, PNG and PostScript to facilitate preservation of a simple static website

IO2.5 Review bibliography contained by website and quality of references. Carry out an investigation and review of technical reports which are used heavily at STFC but have not been generated here. Identify clear cases of reports which have correctly cited but have not need been deposited anywhere as they have no natural home and digitise for inclusion within the AIP.

IO2.6 Perform CSV dump of station information from Postgres database

IO2.7 Create logical description of directory structure

IO2.8 Use PACK to create and add checksum to the AIP maintaining the existing directory structure

IO2.9 Use the GAP manager to identify a GAP based on the demise of the JAVA virtual machine. Use POM to notify us of the gap and update the AIP with a replacement EAST description of the mmm file structure from the registry repository.

19.7 Summary of Testbed Checks

At each of the steps listed above checks were performed to ensure that, for example the Representation Information e.g. IO1.1 the description of the IIWG format was checked by extracting numbers from the data file using generic tools and comparing these to the values obtained using the current tools.

The overall check was to go through the AIP with the archive managers and scientists and ensure that they agreed with the Representation Information and PDI which had been captured – this required several iterations but in the end they were willing to "sign-off" on all the materials.

Users with the appropriate knowledge base have also been successful in extracting and performing the basic analysis tasks with the specified data. Taking this together with the acceptance by the archive managers and scientists of the preservation analysis, risks analysis and the adequacy of the AIP, we believe that the aims of the testbed have been successfully achieved.

Chapter 20
European Space Agency Testbed

Background

ESA-ESRIN, the European Space Agency establishment in Frascati (Italy), is the largest European EO data provider and operates as the reference European centre for EO payload data exploitation.

EO data provide global coverage of the Earth across both a continuum of timescales (from historical measurement to real time assessment to short and long term predictions) and a variety of geographical scales (from global scale to very small scale). In more detail, EO data are generated by many different instruments (passive multi-spectral radiometers working in the visible, infrared, thermal and microwave portion of the electromagnetic spectrum or active instruments in the microwave field) generating multi-sensor data in long time series (time-span from a few years to decades) with a variable geographical coverage (local, regional, global), variable geometrical resolution (from few meters to several hundreds of meters) and variable temporal resolution (from few days up to several months).

EO data acquired from space constitute therefore a powerful scientific tool to enable better understanding and management of the Earth and its resources. More specifically, large international initiatives such as ESA-EU GMES (Global Monitoring for Environment and Security) and the intergovernmental GEO (Group on Earth Observations) focus on coordinating international efforts to environmental monitoring, i.e. to provide political and technical solutions to global issues, such as climate change, global environment monitoring, management of natural resources and humanitarian response.

At present several thousand ESA users worldwide (Earth scientists, researchers, environmentalists, climatologists, etc.) have online access to EO missions' "metadata" (millions of references), data (in the range of 3–5 PB) and derived information for the long term science and the long term environmental monitoring; moreover the requirements for accessing historical archives have been

D. Giaretta, *Advanced Digital Preservation*, DOI 10.1007/978-3-642-16809-3_20,

strongly increased over the last years and the trend is likely to increase and increase. Therefore, the prospect of losing the digital records of science (and with the specific unique data, information and publications managed by ESA) is very alarming. Issues for the near future concern: (1) the identification of the type and amount of data to be preserved; (2) the location of archives and their replication for security reasons; (3) the detailed technical choices (e.g. formats, media); (4) the availability of adequate funds. Of course decisions should be taken in coordination with other data owners and with the support/advice of the user community.

ESA overall strategies

Currently major constraints are that the data volumes are increasing dramatically (the ESA plans of new missions indicate 5–10 times more data to be archived in next 10–15 years), the available financial budgets are inadequate (preservation and access to data of each ESA mission are covered only until 10 years after the end of the mission) and data preservation/access policies are different for each EO mission and each operator or Agency.

To respond to the urgent need for a coordinated and coherent approach for the long term preservation of the existing European EO space data, ESA started consultations with its member States in 2006 in order to develop the European LTDP (Long Term Data Preservation) strategy which was presented at DOSTAG (Data, Operations, Scientific and Technical Advisory Group) in 2007 and also formed a LTDP Working Group (Jan 2008) within the GSCB (Ground Segment Coordination Body) to define European LTDP Common Guidelines (in cooperation with the European EO data stakeholders) and to promote them in CEOS (Committee on Earth Observation Satellites) and GEO.

This group is defining an overall strategy for the long term preservation of all European EO data, ensuring accessibility and usability for an unlimited time-span, through a cooperative and harmonized collective approach among the EO data owners (European LTDP Framework) by the application of European LTDP Common Guidelines. Among these guidelines we should highlight at least the following ones: (1) "Archived data shall contain all the elements necessary to be accessed, used, understood and processed to obtain mission products to be delivered to users"; (2) "Adoption of ISO 14721 – OAIS standard as the reference model and adoption of common archive data formats for AIPs (e.g. SAFE, Standard Archive Format for Europe)".

ESA member states, as part of ESA's mandatory activities, have currently approved a 3 year initial LTDP programme with the aim to establish a full long term data preservation concept and programme by 2011; ESA is now starting the application of the European LTDP Common Guidelines to its own missions.

High priority ESA LTDP activities for the next 3 years are focused on issues such as security improvement, migration to new technologies, increase in the number of datasets to be preserved and enhancement of data access. In addition ESA-ESRIN is participating to a number of international projects partially funded by the European Commission and concerned with technology development and integration in the areas of long term data preservation and distributed data processing and archiving. The scope of ESA participation to such LTDP related projects is: (1) to evaluate new technical solutions and procedures to maintain leadership in using emerging services in EO; (2) to share knowledge with other entities, also outside of the scientific domain; (3) to extend the results/outputs of these cooperative projects in other EO (and ESA) communities.

The ESA role in CASPAR

In CASPAR, ESA plays the role of both user and infrastructure provider for the scientific data testbed. ESA participation to CASPAR (coherently with the above guidelines of the LTDP Working Group) is mainly driven by the interest in: (1) consolidating and extending the validity of the OAIS reference model, already adopted in several internal initiatives (e.g. SAFE, an archiving format developed by ESA in the framework of its Earth Observation ground segment activities); (2) developing preservation techniques/tools covering not only the data but also the knowledge associated with them. In fact locating and accessing historical data is a difficult process and their interpretation can be even more complicated given the fact that scientists may not have (or may not have access to) the right knowledge to interpret these data. Storing such information together with the data and ensuring all remain accessible over time would allow not only for a better interpretation but would also support the process of data discovery, now and in the future.

20.1 Dataset Selection

The selected ESA scientific dataset consists of data from GOME (Global Ozone Monitoring Experiment), a sensor on board ESA ERS-2 (European Remote Sensing) satellite, which has been in operation since 1995.

In particular, the GOME dataset: (1) has a large total amount of information distributed with a high level of complexity; (2) is unique because it provides more than 14 years global coverage; (3) is very important for the scientific community and the Principal Investigators (PI) that on a routine basis receive GOME data (e.g. KNMI and DLR) for their research projects (e.g. concerning ozone depletion or climate change).

Note that GOME is just a demonstration case because similar issues are involved in many other Earth Observation instrument datasets.

The GOME dataset includes different data products, processing levels and associated information. The commonly used names and descriptions of these types of data are as follows:

- Level 0 – raw data as acquired from the satellite, which is processed to:
- Level 1 – providing measures of radiances/reflectances. Further processing of this gives:
- Level 2 – providing geophysical data as trace gas amounts. These can be combined as:
- Level 3 – consisting of a mosaic composed by several level 2 data products with interpolation of data values to fill the satellite gaps.

The figure below illustrates the processing chain to derive GOME Level 3 data from Level 0.

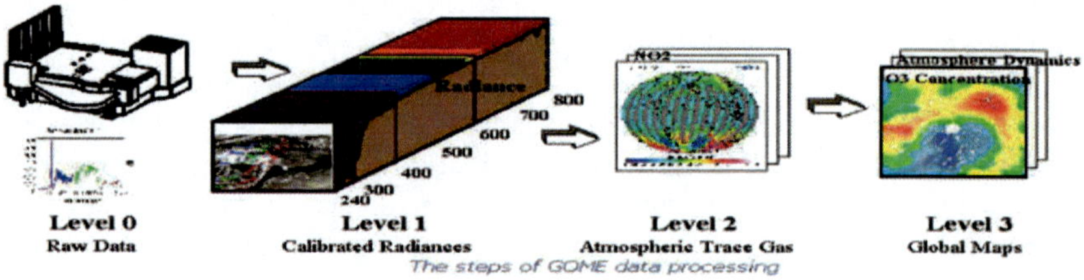

Fig. 20.1 The steps of GOME data processing

Figure 20.1 illustrates in more detail the processing chains to derive GOME Level 2 data from Level 0 and GOME Level 1C data from Level 1B.

As shown in Fig. 20.2 an ad-hoc process generates GOME Level 1C data (fully calibrated data) starting from Level 1 data (raw signals plus calibration data, also called L1B or L1b data. A single Level 1b data can generate (applying different calibration parameters as shown in the figure) several different Level 1C products and so a user asking for GOME Level 1C data will be supplied with L1 data and the processor needed to generate Level 1C data

20.2 Challenge Addressed

The ESA processing pipeline runs on particular hardware and software systems. These systems can change over time. While the project is funded, these changes will be overcome trough porting of software between systems. The challenge is to achieve preservation by supporting software updates after the end of the satellite project.

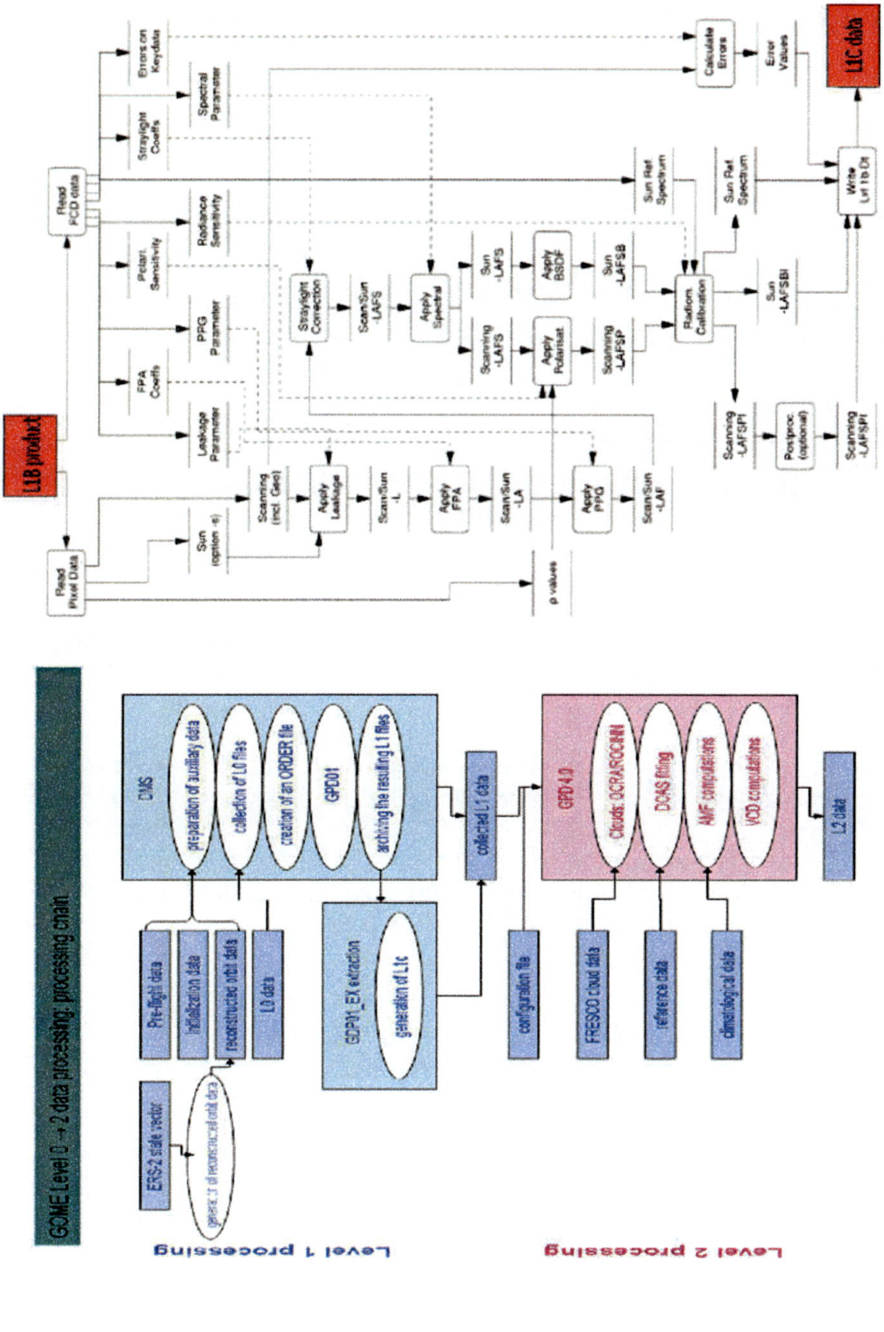

Fig. 20.2 The GOME L0->L2 and L1B->L1C processing chains

20.3 Preservation Aim

The core of the CASPAR dedicated testbed is the preservation of the ability to process data from one level to another, that is the preservation of GOME data and of all components that enable the operational processing for generating products at higher levels.

20.4 Preservation Analysis

A brief analysis involved looking at various possibilities including:

- Preserving the hardware and operating systems on which to run the processing software
- Discarding the software not needed
- Preserving the processing software

This last option is the one chosen and a Designated Community was decided as one which understood how to run software and had knowledge of C.

As first demonstration case, it has been decided to preserve the ability to produce GOME Level 1C data starting from Level 1 data; at this moment the ESA testbed is able to demonstrate the preservation of this GOME processing chain at least against changes of operating system or compilers/libraries/drivers affecting the ability to run the GOME Data Processor.

The Preservation Scenario is the following: after the ingestion in the CASPAR system of a complete and OAIS-compliant GOME L1 processing dataset, something (e.g. OS or gLib version) changes and a new L1->L1C processor has to be developed/ingested to preserve the ability to process data from L1 to L1C.

So we must cope with changes related to the processing by managing a correct information flow through the system, the system administrators and the users, using a framework developed using only the CASPAR components.

20.5 Scenario ESA1 – Operating System Change

The update phase shown in Fig. 20.3, can be summarized as follows:

1. OS Change – an external event affects the processor and an Alert is forwarded to the ESA System Administrator.
2. The System administrator uses the Software Ontology to see which are the modules that need to be recompiled and updated. CIDOC-CRM defines the relationships between the modules.

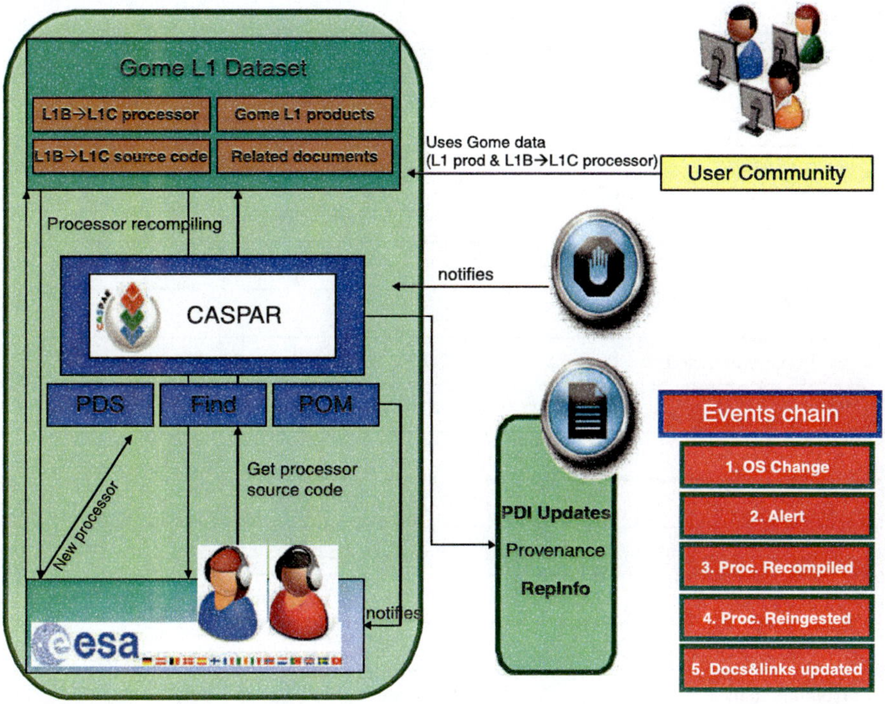

Fig. 20.3 Update scenario

3. By this information he is able to log into the PDS and retrieve the appropriate source code of the processor, to download it and work on it in order to deliver a new version of the processor.
4. The new version, with appropriate Provenance and RepInfo, is re-ingested into the PDS
5. An alert mechanism notifies the users that a new version is available.
6. The new processor can be directly used to generate a new Level 1C product.

20.5.1 AIP Components

20.5.1.1 GOME Data, Its Representation Information and Designated Community

The dataset and its associated knowledge that will be used in the CASPAR ESA Scientific testbed consists of the following items:

Dataset item to be preserved	Associated representation information
Gome L1 B products (*.lv1b)	
• Technical data	ERS – products specification (.pdf)
	L1B – product specification (.pdf)
	Gome sensor specification (.pdf)
• EO general knowledge	ERS 2 – Satellite (.pdf)
	The Gome sensor (.pdf)
• Legal	Disclaimer (.pdf)
	License (.pdf)
Level 1B to Level 1C processor	
• Help manuals	Readme files (.doc and .pdf)
	User manual (.doc)
	How to use (.doc)
L1B → L1C processor source code	
• General specifications	C Language specifications
	Linux OS specifications

20.5.1.1.1 GOME Data Knowledge Ontology and DC Profiles

The ACS-ESA team has developed in cooperation with the FORTH team a CIDOC-Digital based ontology representing the Representation Information relationships and dependencies which are stored on the Knowledge Manager module used for the Testbed.

The Ontology is divided into two logic modules which are connected through the "L1B→L1C processing" event:

- The first module (Fig. 20.4) links the processing event to the management of EO products and it is used to retrieve the DC profile with the adequate knowledge on the data he is searching;

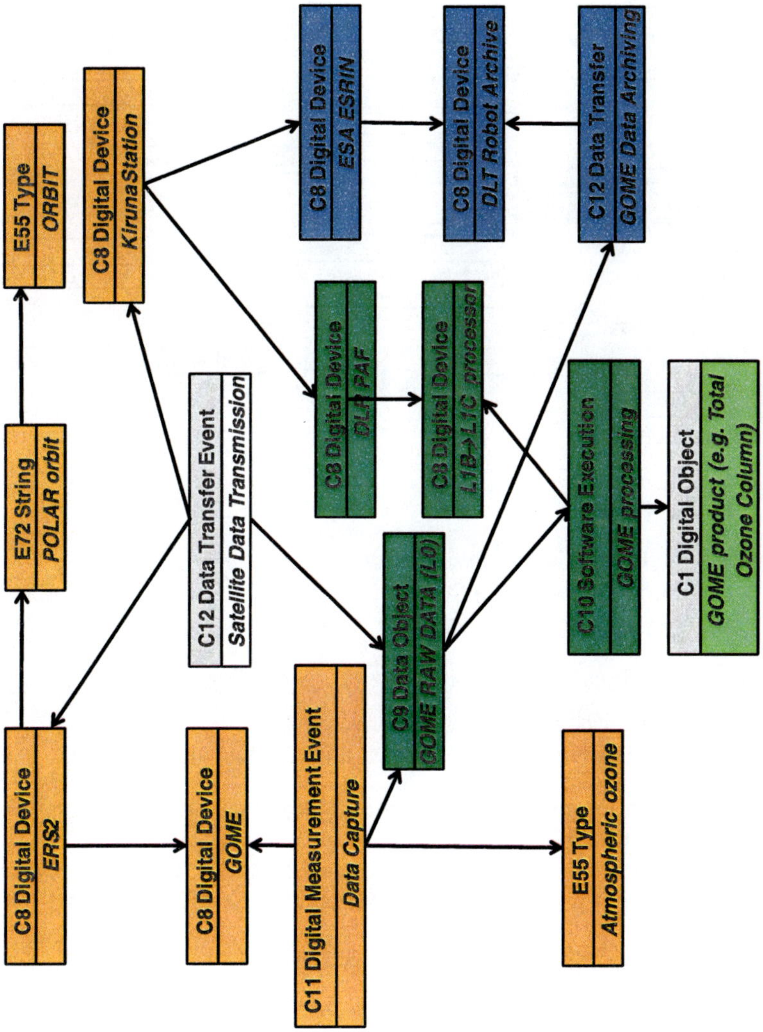

Fig. 20.4 EO based ontology

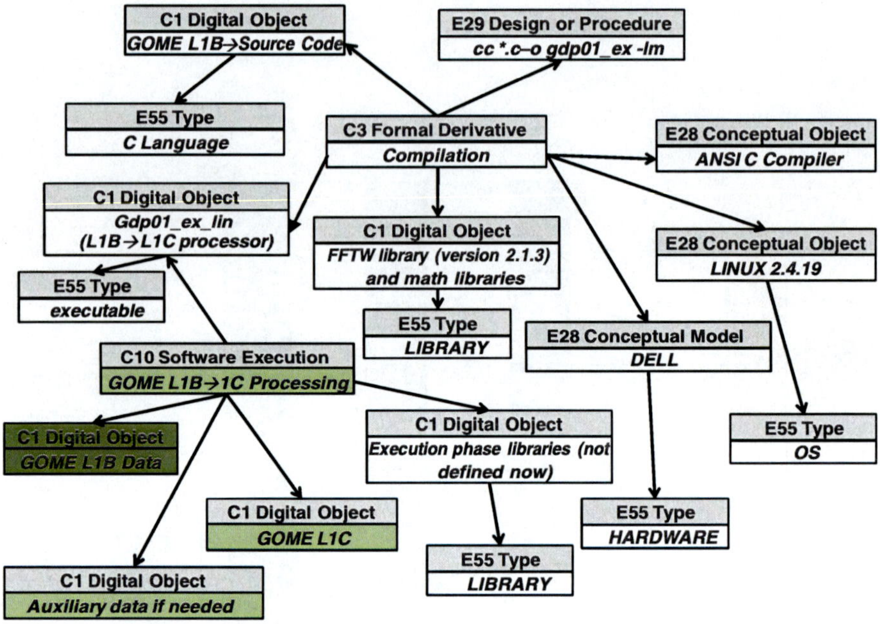

Fig. 20.5 Software based ontology

- The second module (Fig. 20.5) links the processing to those elements (e.g. compiler, OS, programming language) that are needed to have a processor. Software related ontologies are used by the System Administrator when the upgrade is needed.

  The two parts of the schema are shown below:
  The colours used in this ontology summarize different knowledge profiles

  Earth Observation Expertise: left hand side and top row of boxes
  EO archive Expertise: 3 boxes lower right
  GOME Expertise: boxes “C8 Digital Device DLR PAF”, “C8 Digital Device L1b-L1c processor” and “C18 Software Execution GOME processing”

On this basis the Testbed foresees four different DC profiles which are linked to each knowledge profile:

- **GOME User**: user with no particular expertise about Earth Observation, GOME and related EO archives.
- **GOME Expert**: Expert in Earth Observation and GOME data and products, not necessarily on archiving techniques.
- **Archive Expert**: not necessarily expert in EO.
- **System Administrator**: the archive curator with knowledge of all modules.

The System administrator is the only DC Profile that can use the second ontology.

This is used during the upgrade procedure.

20.5.2 Testbed Checks

20.5.2.1 Introduction

The ESA testbed is divided into three logical phases:

- CASPAR system setup – configuration, modules creation, profile creation;
- Access, Ingestion and browsing;
- Software processing preservation – update procedure.

The third part – Software processing preservation – is the testbed focus.

This is the reason for which – while the system setup, the ingestion, the search and retrieve parts of the scenario are validated by performing and then analyzing (and evaluating of) the correct implementation of CASPAR functionalities (e.g. profile creation, data ingestion, search and retrieval, Representation Information, etc.) – the update procedure needed a more specific validation methodology. The present chapter focuses on the testbed checks performed on the Update Procedure.

20.5.2.2 Purpose

Update procedure validation activities have been carried out in order to demonstrate two main scenarios:

1. **Library change**: an object external to the system currently needed by the processor is out of date due to the release of a new version (e.g. a new library).
2. **OS Change**: the processor needs to be run on a new Operating System

In both cases the scenario purpose is to preserve the ability to process a Level 1B product generating a Level 1C. In case of a change the following functionalities have to be granted:

- Allow the CASPAR user to notify an alert concerning the processor;
- Help the System Administrator to create, test and validate, upload and install a new processor version;
- Link the new processor version to the previous ones;
- Notify all users about the change.

20.5.2.3 Environment

The following table reports the testbed validation procedure pre-conditions.

Pre-condition	
HW	x86 Intel like processor, 128 M ram minimum, Disk Space [% 100 M avail]
OS	RedHat Enterprise 5 LIKE (CentoS 5.x, SciLinux DistCern. . . .) 2.6.x Kernel
SW	gcc 3.6 ++ compiler posix; glib 1.2 ++; glibc 2.5 ++; FFTW 3.2.x ++;

The CASPAR testbed acts as a client for the Caspar key components and as a server for the final user accessing via web interface.

Client. The client application is deployed in a Caspar-demo.war file which has to be installed on the client machine, under the ./applications directory of a Tomcat web-server Version 6. Java 6 is also needed to run the testbed.

Server. The client application interacts with the CASPAR Service Components deployment running on the Caspar-NAS machine in ESA ESRIN which hosted the CASPAR preservation system and all the data and processes to be preserved.

20.5.2.4 Level 1C Generation Procedure

The Operation of L1C Data Product is performed as follows:

L1C Data Product is a file that comes out from the data-elaboration made on L1B product data file: carried out by performing on the L1B the <<gdp1_ex>> application.

gdp1_ex is an operator that accepts as

Input >> IN_data_product

Input >> IN_data_parameters

```
            -i [-g] [-q] $IN
      [-b b_filter] [-p p1 p2 | -t t1 t2] [-r lat long lat long]
      [-x  x_filter] [-c c_filter]
      [-a] [-j] [-d] [-w] [-n] [-k]
      [-l slitfunction_filename[:BBBB]]
      [-e degradation_par_filename]
      [-f channel_filter degradation_par_filename | -u channel_filter
                degradation_par_filename]
      [-F channel_filter degradation_par_filename]
   -s [-b b_filter] [-p p1 p2 | -t t1 t2] [-r lat long lat long]
      [-x  x_filter] [-c c_filter]
      [-w] [-n] [-k]
      [-e degradation_par_filename]
      [-f channel_filter degradation_par_filename | -u channel_filter
                degradation_par_filename]
```

-m [-b b_filter] [-p p1 p2 | -t t1 t2] [-r lat long lat long]
[-x x_filter] [-c c_filter]
[-w] [-n] [-k]
[-e degradation_par_filename]
[-f channel_filter degradation_par_filename | -u channel_filter
degradation_par_filename]
[-F channel_filter degradation_par_filename]

Gives results:

Output >> OUT_data_product

Execute DataElaboration:

{[L1C Data Product] == gdp1_ex ([L1B Data Product], {IN_data_parameters});}

PostConditions:

- ESA expert by using ad-hoc viewers validates L1C product-data;
- ESA expert compares result obtained with a L1C obtained using the same CLASS of IN_Parameters
- He bases his test on the set of IN_parameters given to the gdp1_ex application during the data_elaboration.

The current L1->L1C processor is the gdp01_ex.lin (PC LINUX 2.4.19) developed by DLR. The source code is in C language and it can be compiled by an ANSI C compiler. It also needs a FFTW library (for Fast Fourier Transformation) to be run (current version 2.1.3).

20.5.2.5 Testbed Update Procedure Case 1 – New FFT Library Release

FFTW_CasparTest is the new library released. This library differs from the FFTW 2.1.3. by a simple redefinition of the fftw_one signature method. This does not impact with the core business logic of the FFT transformation but actually inhibits the processor to be recompiled and ran. The validation process tested the correct email sending and the correct browsing, searching and retrieval of all those elements needed to rebuild the processor with the new library. By using the knowledge associated to the L1B $\rightarrow$ L1C processor he is able to access and download:

- Processor source code;
- GCC compiler;
- All related how-to's.

Once all the needed material and knowledge was downloaded, the new processor was recompiled, re-ingested and all associated RepInfo were updated to take into account the new version. The validation procedure wants to demonstrate the correct process preservation by generating a new Level 1C product from an ESA certified Level 1B. The processing result is then compared to the correspondent ESA validated Level 1C obtained from a previous processing.

As the whole operation is happening on the same CentOS operating system a special PDS feature is used to produce the new Level 1C product to be tested and compared to the original one.

This procedure is known as the AIP transforming module developed at IBM Haifa and implemented by the ESA-ACS staff. It allows to create and retrieve a Level 1C product on demand overtaking the original approach which was based on the simple ability for the user to download both Level 1B and processor and create locally the Level 1C product.

The on–demand generated data was successfully compared with the original one by the Linux *diff* program.

20.5.2.6 Testbed Update Procedure Case 2 – New Operating System

In order to simulate a change in environment, we have created a demonstration case in which we have supposed that the LINUX operating system is becoming obsolete and so there is the need to migrate to the more used SUN SOLARIS. After the notification of the need to switch to a SUN SOLARIS operating system, CASPAR has to allow the L1C creation on the new platform.

The L1B->L1C processor creation and ingestion for SUN SOLARIS 5.7 was performed by using the same steps used in the previous example, that is retrieving, compiling and ingesting the new executable. For this case, the Representation Information knowledge tree has included an emulation system based on two open source OS emulators. For every emulator both the executable and the source code are available and browsable by means of CASPAR.

The validation tests were successfully performed in the following environments:

- **VMware** Emulator: emulates *Open Solaris* and *Ubuntu*. Characteristics: VMware emulates the OS, including its kernel, libraries and the user interface. The processor architecture is not changed: does not change from 32 to 64 bits and doesn't swap from big-endian to little-endian. The VMware Server can be downloaded from CASPAR as an executable or can be rebuilt from CASPAR through source code in order to be run on another processor.
- **QEMU Emulator**. It emulates a Solaris 5.10 with a T1000 architecture, Sparc. It emulates the OS with external kernel, libraries and is able to emulate the processor architecture. To be underlined that if the processor architecture is emulated the QEMU software is really slow in performances. QEMU is available directly from CASPAR as an executable or can be rebuilt from CASPAR through its source code in order to be run on another processor.
- **SOLARIS T1000 Sparc**. This second workstation was provided in order to perform the validation process on a not emulated Solaris environment.

The validation objective was to assist the system administrator to perform the processor update for all the above mentioned environments. By using the proper

Representation Information, the System Administrator was able to perform the following updates:

GDP1ex was compiled for the followings:

- From Linux 5.3 to Linux Ubuntu – no major changes;
- From Linux 5.3 to Open Solaris – change in OS, libraries;
- From Linux 5.3 to Solaris 5.10 – change in OS (i.e. kernel and environment), libraries and CPU architecture

as shown in Fig. 20.6.

The comparison was successfully performed between the original result and the result obtained on the emulated Operative Systems. Individual data values in the Level 1C products, created by the various paths, were compared as well as bit level differences with no differences.

More in detail, the target of the whole operation is the creation of an Lvl1C product data File. Having several platforms on which this result has been produced, the goal of the Update-Procedure (fulfilled by Administrator/Expert) is the production with the updated processor of a new Level 1C product which has to be equivalent at bit level of the LevelC created by the older processor version. Check is based on

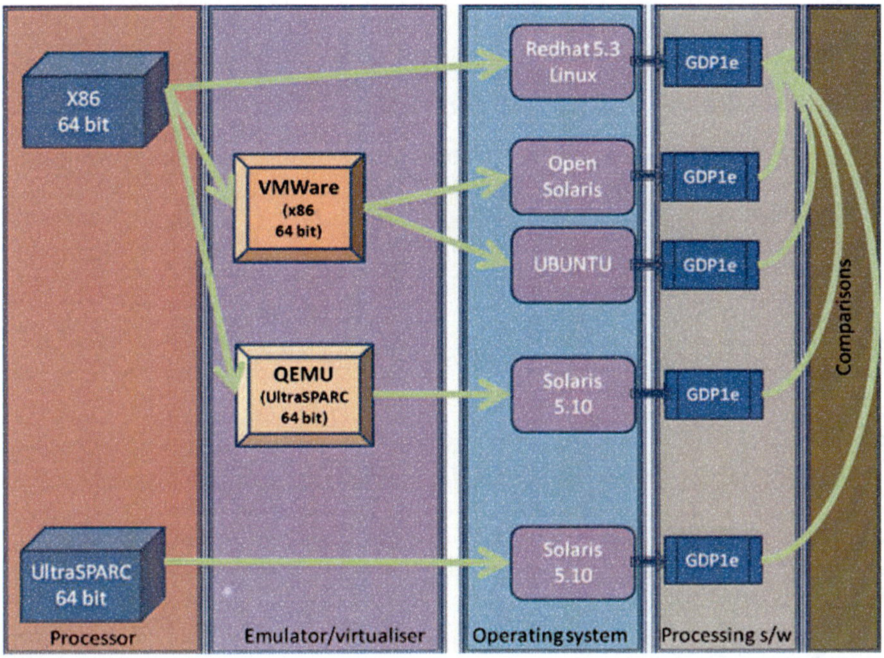

Fig. 20.6 Combinations of hardware, emulator, and software

those results which are generated from the same set of IN_parameters and IN_data through the execution of the following

gdp01_ex {-i -g -b -p} 50714093.lv1* creating the following file *50714093.lv1c

This is a test file Level 1B certified by ESA and the resultant Level 1C product validated by ESA. The method is based either on a comparison between the two files obtained by applying the same parameters and on a absolute SysAdmin/Earth Observation Scientist/expert evaluation based on a personal criteria (inspection by using an appropriate viewer looking at values that the expert knows correctly).

Parameterised and automatic test were performed using the following main test:

Extract the complete Level 1 Data product in one output file and test the two files by the diff function:

gdp01_ex 50714093.lv1 new_50714093

The md5sum algorithm certified that the 2 files have same computed and checked MD5 msg-digest; the diff function states zero differences.

Other subtest procedures were performed and the results compared:

Get the ground pixel geolocation information of the Level 1 Data product:
gdp01_ex -g 50714093.lv1

Extract only channel 2B of a Level 1 data product:
gdp01_ex -b nnnynn 50714093.lv1 myres

Extract the geolocation and PMD data from the 10th to 12th data packets:
gdp01_ex -b nnnnnn -p 10 10 50714093.lv1 myres

Extract ground pixels between pixel number 500 and 510:
gdp01_ex -p 500 510 50714093.lv1 myres

20.5.2.7 All the Performed Tests Returned the Same Results

Conclusions

The two update test performed on the GOME data ingested into CASPAR have been very simple but they are representative of more complex scenarios (e.g. changes in compilers, hardware, etc.). In both cases the System Administrator is able to collect together all that is needed to recompile, update, link, and notify users of the changes. The ability to test the new processor on several operative systems accessible directly through CASPAR and emulated by open source emulators is a significant plus.

By browsing the RepInfo the System Administrator is able to collect the source code, the compilers, the software environment, the emulators and all the related instructions in order to perform the critical steps needed to maintain the ability to process data.

This would improve the ability of the System Administrator to guarantee the processing ability in more critical conditions. The overall impact of this system and its potentials are quite clear to both people that developed it and used it.

Of course we have tested a limited number of possible changes. Most importantly our emulators match existing chips; we argue however that we do have the source code for QEMU which does cross-emulate a whole set of chip processors e.g. emulates an x86 chip on a SPARC64 and vice-versa. We hope that it is plausible argue that, based on QEMU, an emulator could be implemented for some future chip – however this is not guaranteed.

The need to preserve and link tools and data is becoming more and more evident and the ESA team is confident that the CASPAR solutions are going to be increasingly adopted in the years to come; the application is available now and is open to everyone for exploitation and further work.

20.5.3 CASPAR Components Involved

The complete events chain for the scenario of the ESA scientific testbed is described in the following table:

Action	Main CASPAR components involved	Notes
L1 data and L1->L1C processor are ingested in the PDS of the CASPAR system	• PACK • KM • REG • PDS • FIND	Data and processor are OAIS-compliant (SAFE-like format), with appropriate representation information and descriptive information
Data and appropriate Representation Information are returned to users according to their Knowledge Base	• FIND • DAMS • KM • REG	It is also possible to ingest as AIP an appropriate L1 to L1C Transformation Module into the PDS and access directly L1C data (with fixed user-decided calibration parameters) using a processor previously installed on the user machine
The OS or gLib version changes and an alert is sent by informed users to appropriate people	• POM	People interested about changes are POM dedicated topic subscribers
The system administrator retrieve and access the source code of the processor	• FIND • DAMS • PDS • REG	The system administrator is one of the POM dedicated topic subscriber and has the responsibility to take appropriate corrective actions

Action	Main CASPAR components involved	Notes
The system administrator recompiles/upgrades the processor executable and reingest it into the CASPAR system	• PACK • KM • PDS • REG	An appropriate administrator panel showing the semantic dependencies between data will help the system administrator to identify what representation (and descriptive) information have also to be updated
By a notification system all the interested users communities are correctly notified of this change	• POM	People interested about changes are POM dedicated topic subscribers

The scenario above has been implemented in ESA-ESRIN by ESA and ACS (Advanced Computer Systems SpA, technical partner for the testbed implementation) through a web-based interface which allows users to perform and visualize the scenario step by step by rich graphical components.

20.6 Additional Workflow Scenarios

20.6.1 Scenario ESA2.1 – Data Ingestion

The scenario is represented in Fig. 20.7:

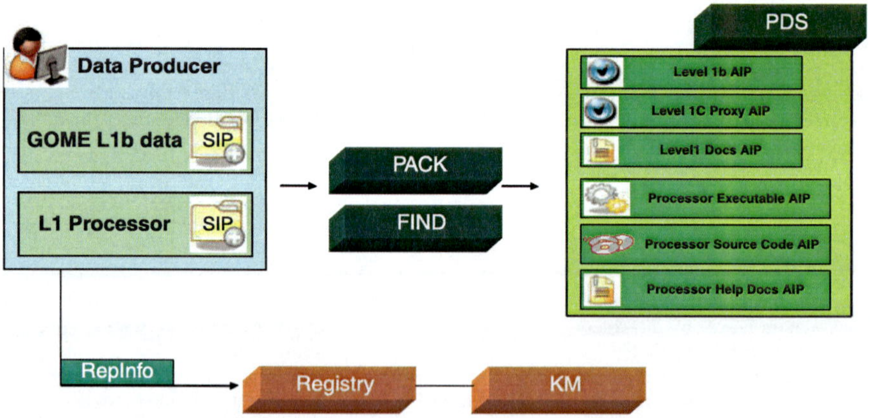

Fig. 20.7 Ingestion phase

The ingestion process allows the Data producer to ingest into the CASPAR system the following type of data:

- GOME Level 1B;
- L1B → L1C Processor;
- Representation Information including all knowledge related to the GOME and L1B->L1C processor data.

While GOME data and Processor are stored/searched/retrieved on the CASPAR PDS component, all RepInfo are stored on the Knowledge Manager and browsed through the Registry.

20.6.2 Scenario ESA2.2 – Data Search and Retrieval

According to the DC Profiles knowledge (see Fig. 20.4: EO based ontology), different knowledge means different RepInfo modules retrieved during the search and retrieve session. The scenario is summarized in the following picture.

More in detail, we want to be able to return to an user asking for L1C data not only the related L1 data plus the processor needed to generate them but also all the information needed to perform this process depending on the user needs and knowledge. So different Representation Information are returned to different users according to their Knowledge Base: after the creation of different profiles (i.e. different Knowledge Base) for different users and the ingestion of appropriate Knowledge Modules (i.e. the competences that you should have to be able to understand the meaning of data) related to data (based on a specialisation of the ISO 21127:2006 CIDOC-CRM), the Knowledge Manager component is able to understand that an

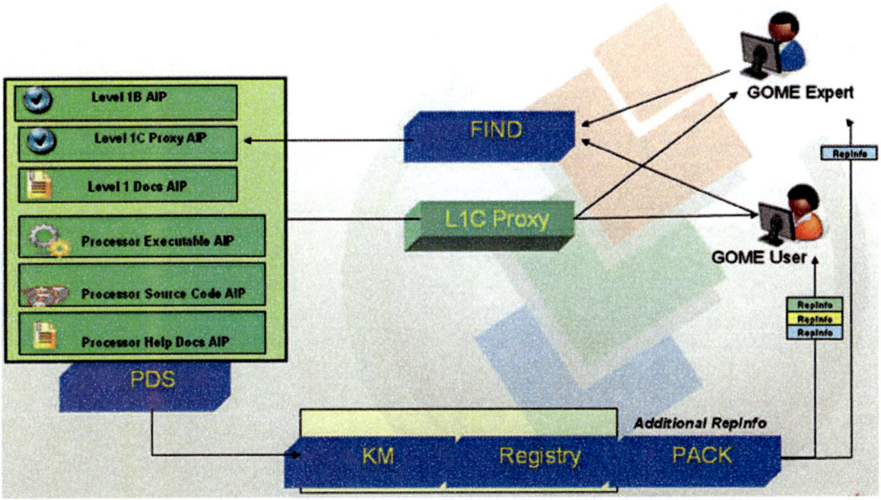

Fig. 20.8 Search and retrieve scenario

user does not need anything to use the data while another user (who is performing the same query) has to be returned with some documents in order to be able to understand the meaning of the data.

20.6.3 Scenario ESA2.3 – Level 1C Creation

As visible on – Fig. 20.8 Search and retrieve Scenario – the user is able to ask to the CASPAR system the Level 1C data. The ESA testbed scenario allows the direct creation of a Level 1C product directly "on demand" starting from the relative Level 1B.

This feature is achieved by using a dedicated PDS functionality which was customized and adopted into the ESA scenario.

20.7 Conclusions

The detailed description of the scientific testbed implemented in ESA-ESRIN provides reasonable evidence of the effectiveness of the CASPAR preservation framework in the Earth Observation domain.

Chapter 21
Cultural Heritage Testbed

Background
The concept of cultural heritage has a wide range of applications: museums, books and libraries, paintings, etc. It also includes monuments, archaeological sites, etc. The CASPAR project we used the definition of Cultural Heritage given in the UNESCO World Heritage Convention (UNESCO, 1972):

"monuments: architectural works, works of monumental sculpture and painting, elements or structures of an archaeological nature, inscriptions, cave dwellings and combinations of features, which are of outstanding universal value from the point of view of history, art or science;

groups of buildings: groups of separate or connected buildings which, because of their architecture, their homogeneity or their place in the landscape, are of outstanding universal value from the point of view of history, art or science;

sites: works of man or the combined works of nature and man, and areas including archaeological sites which are of outstanding universal value from the historical, aesthetic, ethnological or anthropological point of view."

The conservation community has a long tradition of documenting cultural heritage sites. However, the use of digital technology to document such sites is relatively new. Over the last 15 years the techniques used have advanced significantly, particular with the evolution of digital photogrammetry. Today, using relatively simple to use laser scanners, 3D scanning technology has become an outstanding medium for rapidly generating reliable inventory documentation in civil and structural engineering as well as for architectural recordings, especially in the heritage field.

By deploying mid-range and close-range scanners, depending on the complexity of the object, we can ensure a high-resolution 3D recording even when dealing with intricate facade sculptures or ornaments.

These new technologies have enormously increased the amount of digital information being handled in the cultural heritage domain. However, the digital preservation of all this data is still an extremely new concept.

D. Giaretta, *Advanced Digital Preservation*, DOI 10.1007/978-3-642-16809-3_21,

On the other hand, advances in digital information technology are making that all previously cultural heritage data: text, documents, books, maps, etc. are slowly being converted into digital format (example PDF), this again increases the amount of digital cultural heritage data.

Other documentation supports have seen digital advances, with digital images and scanned PDF files supplanting paper photos and documents.

One major problem in the cultural heritage domain is that the community using all the digital data (cultural conservationists, archaeologists, etc.) are by far not information technology experts. The community cares about its digital data but considers that storing the data in a CD or DVD is good enough for its preservation! This has been a major consideration for the CASPAR project where the whole of the testbed was designed to bring into the digital data preservation domain a community that has no expertise in digital data preservation.

Understanding that digital data was at risk of being lost and that its preservation for the benefit of present and future generations was an urgent issue of worldwide concern, UNESCO adopted in 2003 the "Charter on the Preservation of the Digital Heritage".

This Charter proclaims that "The world's digital heritage is at risk of being lost to posterity. Contributing factors include the rapid obsolescence of the hardware and software which brings it to life, uncertainties about resources, responsibility and methods for maintenance and preservation, and the lack of supportive legislation.

UNESCO, by virtue of its mandate and functions, has the responsibility to assist Member States to take the principles set forth in this Charter into account in the functioning of its programmes and promote their implementation within the United Nations system and by intergovernmental and international non-governmental organizations concerned with the preservation of the digital heritage;"

Within the framework of the CASPAR project and following the recommendations of the Charter on the Preservation of the Digital Heritage, the objectives of UNESCO's cultural testbed are as follows:

21.1 Dataset Selection

21.1.1 World Heritage Inscription

All of the documentation and data on World Heritage cultural sites which is held at UNESCO premises represents the justification for the sites' World Heritage status. This is official data which is needed within the context of an International Convention to provide a legal record of a successful inscription, proving that they have met all the requirements for nomination.

When such data is submitted to the World Heritage Committee, there are two possible scenarios:

- The candidate cultural heritage site is not accepted and the inscription is deferred. In this case the file remains alive and the file will receive any updates that the country will send in order to improve the quality of the data so that the cultural heritage site can be re-presented as a candidate.
- The candidate is accepted. In this case, the cultural heritage site changes status from "candidate" to "inscribed site" (i.e. inscribed as a World Heritage site). The file will receive any updates that the country or the Committee wants to add to it e.g. State of Conservation, Periodic Reporting, etc.

21.1.2 Laser Scanning to Produce 3D Models (Ref. **www.helm.org.uk/upload/pdf/publishing-3d-laser-scanning-reprint.pdf***)*

The recording of position, dimensions and/or shape is a necessary part of almost every project related to the documentation and associated conservation of cultural heritage, forming an important element of the analysis process. For example, knowing the size and shape of a topographic feature located in a historic landscape can help archaeologists identify its significance, knowing how quickly a stone carving is eroding helps a conservator to determine the appropriate action for its protection, while simply having access to a clear and accurate record of a building façade helps a project manager to schedule the work for its restoration.

It is common to present such measurements as plans, sections and/or profiles plotted onto hardcopy for direct use on site. However, with the introduction of new methods for three-dimensional measurement and increasing user-friendly software as well as computer literacy among users, there is a growing demand for three-dimensional digital information. 3D digital information is widely used because:

- It is considered to be a non-invasive technology, so that conservation experts can work on the different aspects of the site in virtual form without having to step into the site and eventually damage the site.
- It allows the conservation experts an easier and faster form to do research and assessment of the site without having to be physically on the site

There is a wide variety of techniques for three-dimensional measurement. These techniques can be characterized by the scale at which they might be used (which is related to the size of the object they could be used to measure), and on the number of measurements they might be used to acquire (which is related to the complexity of the object).

While hand measurements can provide dimensions and position over a few meters, it is impractical to extend this to larger objects; and collecting many measurements (for example 1,000 or more) would be a laborious and, therefore, unattractive process.

For objects with too much detail e.g. the façade of a gothic cathedral that has a large amount of small stone carving elements, it is impossible to do the measurements manually.

Photogrammetry and laser scanning can be used to provide a greater number of measurements for similar object sizes, and, therefore, are suitable for more complex objects. Photogrammetry and laser scanning may also be deployed from the air so as to provide survey data covering much larger areas.

While GPS might be used to survey similarly sized areas, the number of points it might be used to collect is limited when compared to airborne or even spaceborne techniques. This advice and guidance is focused closely on laser scanning (from the ground or air), although the reader should always bear in mind that another technique may be able to provide the information required. Laser scanning, from the air or from the ground, is one of those technical developments that enables a large quantity of three-dimensional measurements to be collected in a short space of time.

The term laser scanner applies to a range of instruments that operate on differing principles, in different environments and with different levels of accuracy. A generic definition of a laser scanner, taken from Böhler and Marbs is: "any device that collects 3D co-ordinates of a given region of an object's surface automatically and in a systematic pattern at a high rate (hundreds or thousands of points per second) achieving the results (i.e. three-dimensional co-ordinates) in (near) real time."

The scanning process might be undertaken from a static position or from a moving platform, such as an aircraft. Airborne laser scanning is frequently referred to as LiDAR, although LiDAR is a term that applies to a particular principle of operation, which includes laser scanners used from the ground. Laser scanning is the preferred generic term to refer to ground based and airborne systems.

Laser scanning from any platform generates a point cloud: a collection of XYZ co-ordinates in a common coordinate system that portrays to the viewer an understanding of the spatial distribution of a subject. It may also include additional information, such as pulse amplitude or colour information (RED, GREEN BLUE or RGB values). Generally, a point cloud contains a relatively large number of co-ordinates in comparison with the volume the cloud occupies, rather than a few widely distributed points. Laser scanning is usually combined with colour digital images (RGB) that are then used over the laser structure to provide a virtual texture to the object making that the object becomes a "virtual reality" object.

21.1.2.1 When to Use Laser Scanning

In order for a heritage expert to decide if the use of laser scanning is appropriate depends on various factors about the "What does the heritage object look like?" or "How big is it?" For example, a conservator might want to know how quickly a feature is changing, while an archaeologist might be interested in understanding how one feature in the landscape relates to another. An engineer might simply want to know the size of a structure and where existing services are located. In other terminology, laser scanning might be able to help inform on a particular subject by contributing to the understanding. Scanning may also improve the accessibility of the object.

Once the experts have a clear idea of the heritage site and the ultimate purpose of the task, then whether laser scanning is appropriate or not depends on a range of variables and constraints.

21.1.2.2 Frequent Applications for Laser Scanning

- Contributing to a record prior to renovation of a subject or site which would help in the design process, in addition to contributing to the archive record.
- Contributing to a detailed record where a feature, structure or site might be lost/changed forever, such as in an archaeological excavation or at a site at risk.
- Structural or condition monitoring, such as looking at how the surface of an object changes over time in response to weather, pollution or vandalism.
- Providing a digital geometric model from which a replica model may be generated for display or as a replacement in a restoration scheme.
- Contributing to three-dimensional models, animations and illustrations for presentation in visitor centres, museums and through the media (enhancing accessibility/engagement and helping to improve understanding).
- Aiding the interpretation of archaeological features and their relationship across a landscape, thus contributing to the understanding about the development of a site and its significance to the area.
- Working, at a variety of scales, to uncover previously unnoticed archaeologically significant features such as tool marks on an artefact, or looking at a landscape covered in vegetation or woodland.
- Spatial analysis, not possible without three-dimensional data, such as line of sight or exaggeration of elevation, etc.

However, it is important to recognise that laser scanning is unlikely to be used in isolation to perform these tasks. It is highly recommended that photography should be collected to provide a narrative record of the subject. In addition, on-site drawings, existing mapping and other survey measurements might also be required. The capture of additional data helps to protect a user as it helps to ensure the required questions can be answered as well as possible, even if the a subject has changed or even been destroyed since its survey.

21.1.2.3 Meta Data – RepInfo

One major issue is that all existing data (and meta-data) of UNESCO is not yet compatible with the OAIS model. In this sense UNESCO provides meta-data for the testbed and the new tools developed within CASPAR for the UNESCO testbed convert such a meta-data in order that it matches the RepInfo requirements and associated compatibility with OAIS.

An important component of the data management process is the definition and management of "metadata": data about the data. One major problem is that for the moment the data still remains with the group that implemented the laser scanning and therefore usually meta-data is neglected. In other words there is no need to elaborate meta-data since I was the one doing the laser scanning and I know perfectly how the scanning was done, under which conditions, using what type of equipment, etc.

However, the large amount of data is forcing the experts to submit the final record for archiving in other organizations. It is then that the issue of meta-data becomes urgently needed and necessary.

The very minimum level of information that might be maintained for raw scan data might include the following:

1. file name of the raw data
2. date of capture
3. scanning system used (with manufacturers serial number)
4. company name
5. monument name
6. monument number (if known)
7. survey number (if known)
8. scan number (unique scan number for this survey)
9. total number of points
10. point density on the object (with reference range)
11. weather conditions during scanning (outdoor scanning only)

21.1.2.4 Different File Formats

The laser scanning technology for digital heritage has emerged from a large variety of industrial applications. From cars, boats, aircraft, and buildings to turbine blades, dental implants, and mechanical parts, 3D scanning provides you with high quality digital models – no matter how big or small your part is. Scanning systems today are capable of scanning miniature figurines a mere 4 mm high and can also scan a 240′ long jumbo jet – all with incredible accuracy and resolution.

21.1.2.5 A Simple Illustrative Example

It would be extremely complex for CASPAR software developers to understand the whole laser scanning process of for example all archaeological monuments of Villa Livia: too much data, too many different techniques according to the various monuments and too many different devices (hardware used).

However, the most important for UNESCO testbed developers as well as for UNESCO is to understand the main concept, each step involved and the data resulting out of each step.

For this purpose, UNESCO, in joint coordination with the CASPAR developers as well as in partnership with the Pisa Visual Laboratory from the Italian National Research Centre of Pisa, undertook the laser scanning of a simple handcraft-heritage-object.

By doing this, the CASPAR developers were able to see directly the whole process starting from scratch and they were able to receive back for insertion into CASPAR modules each data set resulting from each individual step of the laser scanning.

This exercise allowed CASPAR to understand completely the laser scanning process and to undertake all the necessary developments in order to ensure the preservation of such a process and the preservation of the resulting data sets.

By doing this, the UNESCO testbed would be completed since by preserving a complete process for this small heritage object, a complete similar process would be necessary to undertake for a more complex heritage monument.

The process allowed also identifying the need to elaborate associated RepInfo for each step and for each resulting data set.

Below is the whole information that was developed in order to support this exercise and to be able to completely include it in to the different CASPAR modules.

21.1.2.5.1 Description of the Object

- Material: wood
- What it represents: Armadillo
- Dimension: 22 cm (length) / 5.5 cm (wide)

21.1.2.5.2 General Information

The object is an alebrije, a brightly-coloured Mexican folk art wooden sculpture of a fantastical creature (in this case an armadillo). The armadillo was wood-carved in Oaxaca, Mexico. Carvers use wood from the Copal tree that is primarily found within the warm regions of Oaxaca. The wood from the female trees has few knots and is soft and easy to carve when it is first cut. Once dried, it becomes light, hard, and easy to sand smooth. The wood is often treated with chemicals before being painted and finished pieces can be frozen for 1–2 weeks to kill any powderpost beetle eggs or larvae that might be present. Some artists now use other woods like cedar or imported hardwoods.

Pieces are carved using machetes and knives. Carvings created from a single piece of wood are normally considered of higher quality than those assembled from multiple pieces, although elements such as ears and horns are frequently carved separately and fitted into holes.

Finished pieces are typically hand-painted with acrylics.

In 1930 Pedro Linares started creating elaborate decorative pieces that represented imaginary creatures he called alebrijes. Inspired by a dream when he fell ill at age 30, these papier mache sculptures were brightly-painted with intricate patterns and frequently featured wings, horns, tails, fierce teeth, and bulgy eyes.

Manuel Jiménez, recognized as the founder of folk art woodcarving in Oaxaca, started in the 1960s to woodcarve alebrijes. Nowadays (2009) there are over 200 woodcarving families concentrated in the villages San Antonio Arrazola, San Martin Tilcajete, La Union Tejalapa, and San Pedro Cajonos.

21.1.2.5.3 Process Flow

- **Laser points acquisition**
  - Task name: Data capture (laser cloud points)
  - Scanning Place: Visual Computing Lab, Information Science and Technologies, National Research Council, Pisa, Italy
  - Scanned by: Marco Callieri
  - Purpose: research (World Heritage preservation)
  - Description: One side or face of the cultural heritage object is scanned.
  - 3D Scanner model (hardware): MINOLTA VI – 900/910 [210]
    - input: original cultural heritage object
    - input digital items: none;
    - output digital items: a range map in PLY format [211], [212] representing the scanned face of the cultural heritage object.
  - Task information:
    - Scanner resolution: 0.1 mm
    - Scanning distance: between 0.6 and 1.2 m
    - Total amount range-map: 11 range maps (laser capture acquisitions, each one corresponding to one side/face of the cultural heritage object) where necessary;
    - Plate rotation angle: none
    - Time for acquisition: 30 min.
- **Geometric registration or alignment of each individual range map so that all can fit together to build the final single range map:**
  - Task name: Alignment Session
  - Description: All the different range-maps (each with its own geometry and/or coordinate system) have to be transformed in order to obtain range-maps with a uniform and common coordinate system. In this task each individual range map is transformed into a new coordinate system (in other words, a matrix transformation).
  - Software: MeshLab [213]
  - Input digital items: original PLY files coming from the laser scanner
  - Output digital items: geometrically corrected/transformed PLY files. Representation Information of the process stored in an ALN file and MA2 file
  - Task information: The user identifies control points on each pair of the range maps and asks software to transform range_map1 to match with the geometry of range_map2. The same process is applied to each individual range map. MA2 file describes each individual step.

- **Combining or fusioning each face of the cloud points to obtain a single set of cloud points for the total object**
  - Task name: Fusion Session
  - Description: All the range-maps, with a uniform coordinate system, are combined to produce a 3D model of the object. In addition any redundant data is eliminated, so that each laser point appears only once and represents one point of the surface of the original cultural heritage object. Before this task all the range-maps represent a collection of different surfaces that may also overlap rather than form a single solid.
  - Software: MeshLab
  - Input digital items: the geometrically corrected set of PLY files and a ALN File
  - Output digital items: a single PLY file that represents the overall 3D model
  - Task information:
    - total amount of range-map used: 11 range-maps
    - precision: 0.25 mm
    - time needed for the overall fusion task: 15 min
- **Data capture for texture** (obtaining digital images for each side/face of the cultural heritage object)
  - Task name: Texture Capture
  - Description: A series of 8 digital images
  - Hardware: Canon EOS 350D (digital camera) [214]
  - Software: none
  - Input: original cultural heritage object
  - Input digital items: none
  - Output digital items: a series of 8 JPG images
  - Task information:
    - total amount of digital images used: 8
    - precision: 72 dpi (resolution)
    - time needed for the overall texture capture task: 10 min
    - photo shoot distance: between 0.4 and 1.0 m
- **Merging or aligning texture with 3D model**
  - Task name: Texture Alignment
  - Description: this task is aimed at geometrically registering the digital images with the 3D PLY. The process requires human intervention where the user identifies control points on the JPG images and their corresponding matching point on the PLY file.
  - Software: TexAlign [215], an application developed by the CNR
  - Input digital items: 8 JPG images
  - Output digital items: A new PLY file that has the previous "wire PLY file" plus the Texture. In addition a XML file describing the alignment of all digital images with the 3D model is elaborated.
  - Task information: The task requires human intervention where the user identifies control points on the JPEG images and their corresponding matching point on the PLY file.

- **Visualizing the 3D model with texture: virtual heritage reconstruction**
  - Task name: Visualization of the 3D model with texture
  - Description: the 3D models are now textured allow enabling interactive visualization and manipulation for the user.
  - Software: Virtual Inspector [216]
  - Input digital items: the single PLY file that represents the overall 3D model
  - Output digital items: a navigable textured 3D model
  - Task information:
    - total amount of file: 1 PLY file
    - time needed for the overall fusion task: 20 min.

21.2 Challenges Addressed

UNESCO has a large volume of data of many different kinds which describes the sites which have been inscribed. This data must be able to be used in future on order that, for example, UNESCO in the future can compare the state of a site with the original state of the site. This has to be achieved despite the certainty that the instruments used to measure the site will be different; the way the data is captured will be different; the way in which the data is encoded will be different; the software used to analyse the data will be different.

21.3 Preservation Aim

Preserve all steps required to create associated digital virtual reconstructions from real tangible cultural heritage objects.

Find possible solutions to assist Member States on the preservation of cultural heritage digital data.

21.4 Preservation Analysis

The variety of data which UNESCO must collect from world heritage sites present a great challenge because of their diversity. Many datasets are used with proprietary applications; complex workflows are used to create the higher level products. UNESCO must be able to compare modern measurements of heritage sites with older measurements in order to see if there has been a degradation in the site. Both the measurements techniques and data encoding change over time, therefore it must be possible to combine data from various sources. The better option is therefore to describe the digital encodings in as great a depth as possible.

21.5 Scenario UNESCO1: Villa LIVIA

The Villa of Livia was a Roman villa with a view down the Tiber towards Rome. The villa was rediscovered in 1596, and in 1867 the Augustus of Prima Porta was retrieved from the site. Modern archaeological excavations of the site have been ongoing since 1970.

The Villa Livia dataset is a collection of files used within the "virtual museum of the ancient Via Flaminia" project: a 3D reconstruction of several archaeological sites along the ancient Via Flaminia, the largest of them being Villa Livia.

A rough estimate of the total dataset size is 500 GB. File types in this set include:

- 3D point clouds (imp, dxf, dwg)
- Elevation grids (agr, bt)
- 3D meshes (mdl, vrml, v3d)
- Textured 3D models (max, pmr, ive, osg)
- Satellite data (ers, ecw)
- GPS data, maps (txt, apm, shp)
- Digital images (targa, jpeg, tiff, png, psd, bmp, gif, dds)

21.5.1 Actors/Designated Communities

The actors in the scenario can be characterised as being in one or more of the following three categories:

- Providers
  - Providers provide the materials to be archived.
- Consumers
  - Consumers access the archived materials.
- Curators
  - Curators manage the preservation of the archived materials.

Five groups of actors have been identified within the context of the scenario, and have been characterised as follows:

- 3D Reconstruction Experts
  - Providers, Consumers
- UNESCO World Heritage experts
  - Curators
- World Heritage site authorities
  - Providers, Consumers
- World Heritage Committee
  - Consumers
- General public
  - Consumers

These will be discussed further in the next section, *Designated Communities*.

21.5.2 Designated Communities

The rationale behind the Designated Communities is the characterisation of group of persons interested in the long-term preservation of digital information within an OAIS compliant archive system.

In this perspective, first of all it's important to identify which are the group of persons.

And within the UNESCO testbed, the following designated communities:

- 3D Reconstruction Experts
- UNESCO World Heritage Experts
- World Heritage Site Responsible people
- World Heritage Committee
- General Public

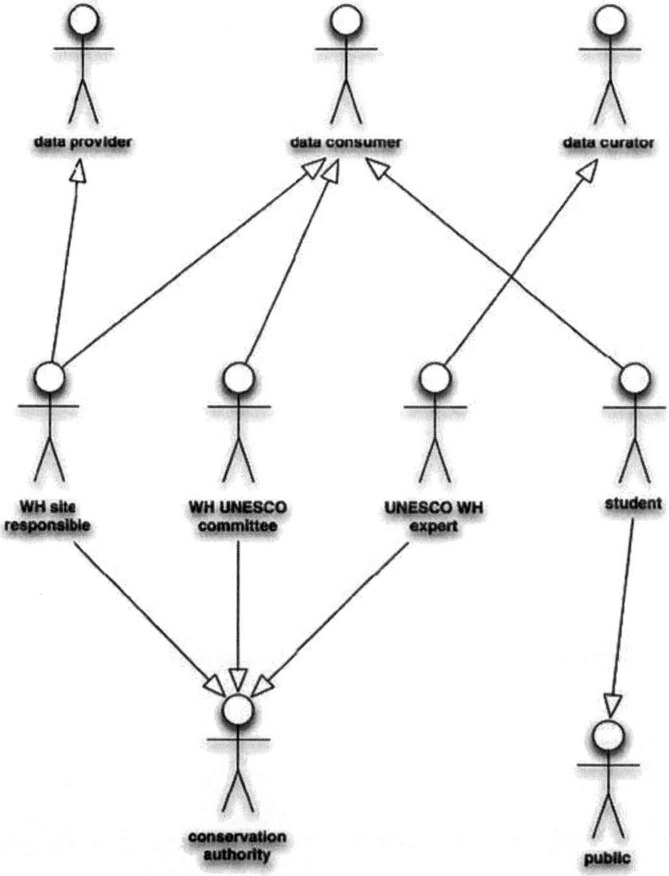

Fig. 21.1 Designated communities taxonomy

Each Designated Community is characterised by its own knowledge base, that is the set of concepts which the community is able to understand.

According to the CASPAR conceptual model, characterisation of Designated Community is done through the Designated Community Profile (i.e. DCProfile) which contains the set of Modules (i.e. RIModules). Both concepts are focus of the research activities and are handled by the Semantic Web Knowledge Middleware (SWKM) and the Gap Manager.

In this section each Designated Community within the UNESCO World Heritage Scenario is characterised.

Figure 21.1 shows the hierarchy of the potential identified users within the UNESCO testbed scenario. According the CASPAR terminology, the four identified actors involved in the CASPAR scenario were classified as data curators, provider and consumer. More specifically:

- World Heritage UNESCO committee member
- World Heritage Site Responsible
- World Heritage UNESCO expert
- Student

Each type of use is a DCProfile: the first three profiles are generically conservation authorities, that, informally, comprise such persons with a common background that allows them to be involved in the UNESCO submission procedures [217]. While,

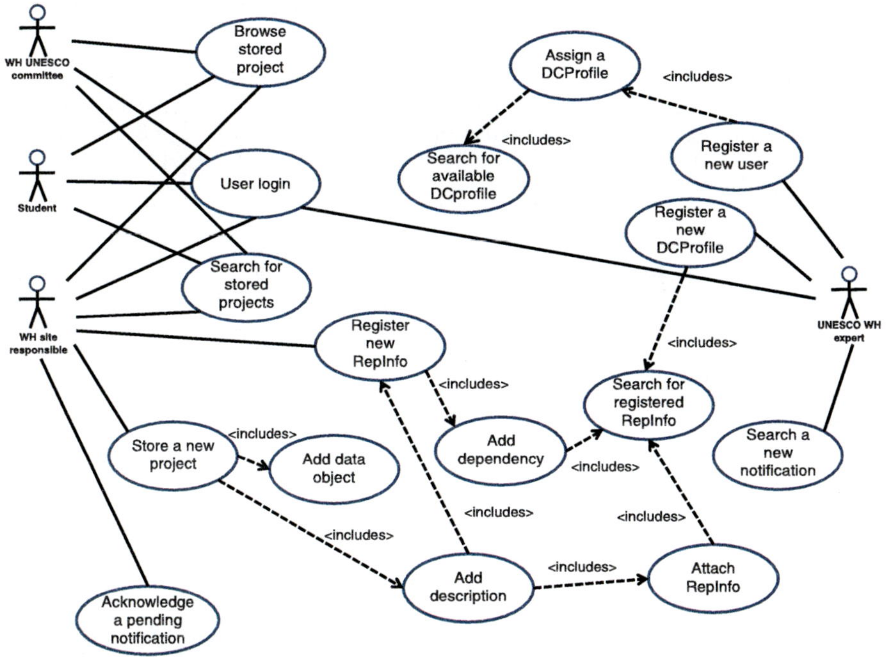

Fig. 21.2 Relationship between UNESCO use cases

the generic Public DCProfile comprises such users without any kind of specific knowledge about the submission processes. Student DCProfile, in fact, meaningfully represents such kind of users. The use cases diagram, depicted in Fig. 21.2, shows the main use cases detailed below.

21.5.3 UNESCO Terminology Applied to OAIS Concepts

UNESCO terminology	Description	Relative OAIS concept	CASPAR functionality
Registration of cultural heritage UNESCO actors	Each actor involved in the UNESCO cultural heritage process needs to be registered for obtaining the right permissions for accessing the data. Each actor has a "role" in the process		User management and access permission: DAMS
Registration of DCProfiles and representation information	Each actor involved in the UNESCO cultural heritage process has a specific "knowledge background" for handling the data. UNESCO identifies the following communities: 1. 3D reconstruction experts 2. UNESCO world heritage experts 3. World heritage site responsibles 4. World heritage committee 5. General public	Designated community	DCProfile: SWKM and GAP
Submission of a cultural heritage site as candidate for world heritage inscription	The world heritage site responsible submits a cultural heritage site as candidate for world heritage inscription. In this perspective, he/she gathers all the required material (i.e. data, content and relative description) for the submission. The minimum set of required material is:	Information package (IP) and collection of IPs	SIP and AIP generation, adding RepInfo and storage: PACK (+ REG and PDS)
Search and browse WH inscriptions based on DCProfile	A "Student" has not the "knowledge background" of a "3D reconstruction experts". The latter has the know-how for "understanding and using" PLY files, but the former is not able, and so he/she needs further details	Designated community, descriptive information and finding aids	Descriptive information, DCProfile: FIND, SWKM, GAP
Notification of change events in the UNESCO scenarios	The preservation is not a static activity, but a process. And within the process any involved actor needs to be informed about any "change event" which potentially may impact on the preservation. And each actor, with his/her own expertise, has to receive the proper "alert" in order to address it, by enacting the adequate preservation activity		Notification of change events: POM

Nomination of submitted candidates	The world heritage committee receives the submission of a candidate site and evaluates it for the WH Site. At the end of the evaluation additional description and content may be added to the "folder" received from the candidate site (at least the nomination file)	Update Information Package	Update of an AIP: PACK, PDS, REG

21.5.4 AIP Components

Collected files have to be intended as an example of digital heritage data obtained as laser range scans, GPS data or traditional archaeological documentation.

The Villa Livia dataset is a collection of files used within the "virtual museum of the ancient Via Flaminia" [218] project: a 3D reconstruction of several archaeological sites along the ancient Via Flaminia, the largest of them being *Villa Livia* shown in Fig. 21.3:

A rough estimate of the total dataset size is 500 GB. File types in this set include:

- 3D point clouds (imp, dxf, dwg)
- Elevation grids (agr, bt)
- 3D meshes (mdl, vrml, v3d)
- Textured 3D models (max, pmr, ive, osg)
- Satellite data (ers, ecw)
- GPS data, maps (txt, apm, shp)
- Digital images (targa, jpeg, tiff, png, psd, bmp, gif, dds)

Currently (as of end of Y2), two file types have been used for testing:

- an elevation grid of the site (agr/grd)
- map of the site contours (shp)

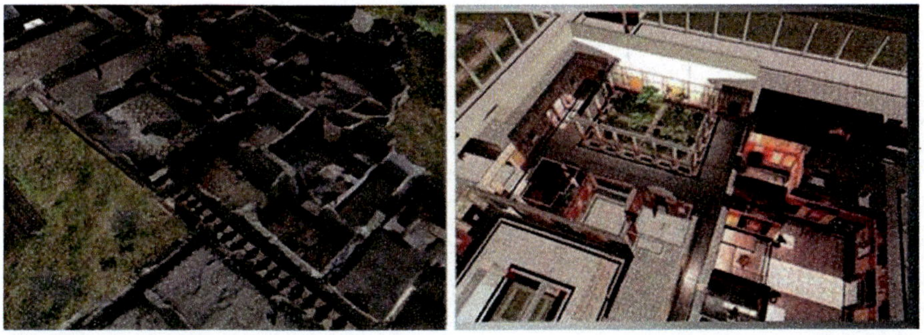

Fig. 21.3 Villa Livia

21.5.4.1 ESRI ASCII GRID File: *dem_LOD3_livia.grd*

Figure 21.4 is an elevation grid (height map) of the area where *Villa Livia* is located. It is an ASCII file in the ESRI GRID file format [219]:

Fig. 21.4 Elevation grid (height map) of the area where Villa Livia is located

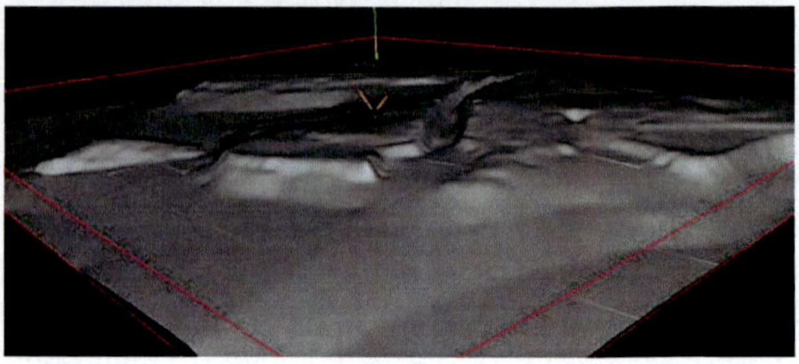

21.5.4.1.1 Structural and Semantic RepInfo for ESRI GRID File Format

DataObject dem_LOD3_livia.grd and related RepInfo relationship is shown in Fig. 21.5:

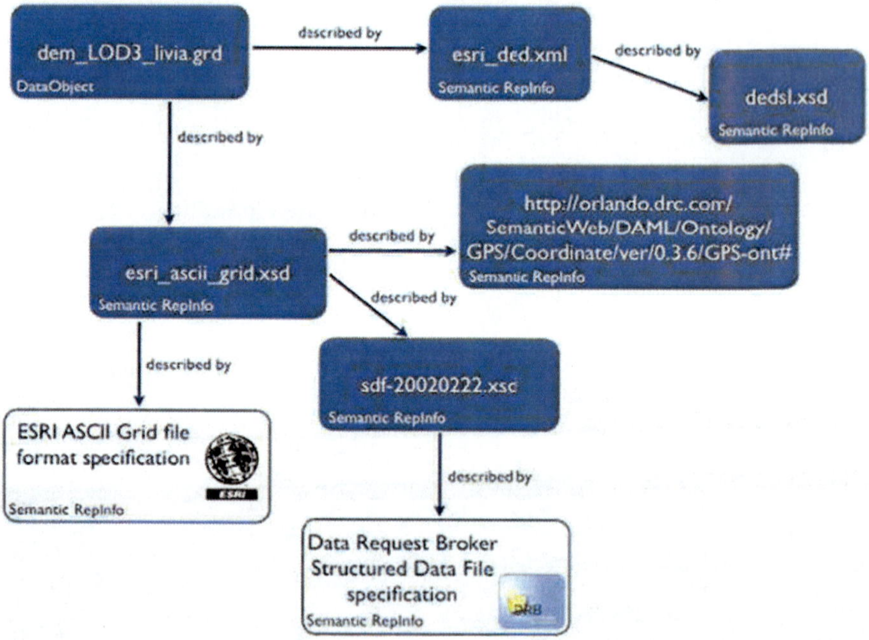

Fig. 21.5 RepInfo relationships

where

- esri_ascii_grid.xsd is the XML schema describing the ESRI ASCII GRID File to be used with the Data Request Broker tool. It provides information about the structure of the DataObject.
- sdf-20020222.xsd is the XML schema of the Structured Data File implementation. It defines XML elements to be used in the esri_ascii_grdi.xsd schema.
- http://orlando.drc.com/SemanticWeb/DAML/Ontology/GPS/Coordinate/ver/0.3.6/GPS-ont# is the XML namespace of the DAML ontology for GPS coordinate values, adding meaning to xllcorner and yllcorner.
- ESRI GRID file format specification
- Data Request Broker: Structured Data File implementation notes. SDF breaks down any binary file into a tree of nodes thanks to an external description. The internal description is an XML Schema with a few additional markups providing the physical description of the binary file. drbdemo_for_ESRI_ASCII_Grid.zip a DRB demo example with Shape file data can be found.
- esria_ded.xml is an instance of the Data Entity Dictionary Specification Language. It allows to add some simple data semantics.
- dedsl.xsd is the XML schema for the Data Entity Dictionary Specification Language. See DEDSL Schema page for more information.

21.5.4.1.2 Preservation Description Information for an ESRI GRID File AIP

Figure 21.6 represents the complete AIP for ESRI GRID files:

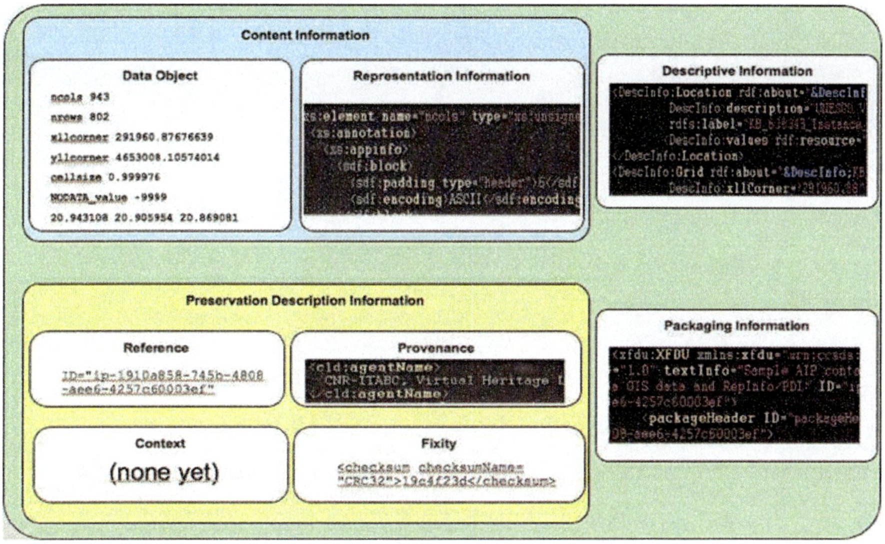

Fig. 21.6 Diagram of AIP for ESRI GRID files

where:

- **Provenance**: villa_livia_dem_LOD3_livia.rdf is the RSLP collection description created with the online tool available at Research Support Libraries Programme (http://www.ukoln.ac.uk/metadata/rslp/tool/). This file describes a collection, its location and associated owner(s), collector(s) and administrator(s).

21.5.4.1.3 Complete AIP for ESRI GRID File

UNESCO_Villa_Livia_20080501_AIP_V1_1.zip First Draft Elevation Grid data AIP built using PACK Component.

21.5.4.2 ESRI SHAPE File: *vincoli_livia.grd*

It is a vector file of site contours. It is a binary file in the ESRI Shape file format [220]. A possible visualisation is shown in Fig. 21.7.

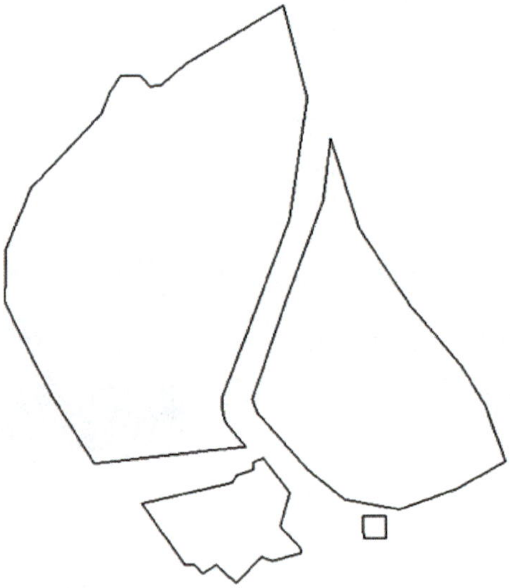

Fig. 21.7 Visualisation of site contours

21.5.4.2.1 Structural and Semantic RepInfo for ESRI Shape File Format

DataObject vincoli_livia.shp and related RepInfo relationship are showed in Fig. 21.8:

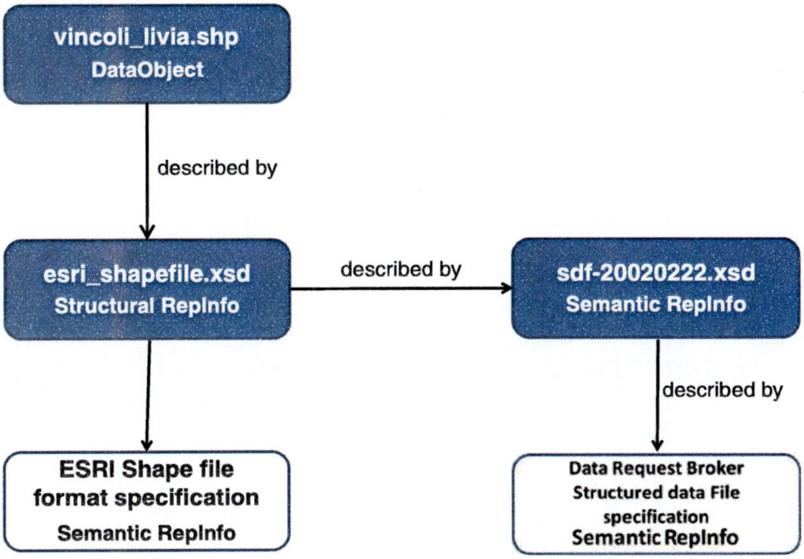

Fig. 21.8 RepInfo relationships

where:

- esri_shapefile.xsd is the XML schema describing the ESRI ASCII GRID File to be used with the Data Request Broker tool. It provides information about the structure of the DataObject.
- sdf-20020222.xsd is the XML schema of the **Structured Data File** implementation. It defines XML elements to be used in the esri_shapefile.xsd schema.
- ESRI Shape file format
- Data Request Broker: Structured Data File implementation notes. SDF breaks down any binary file into a tree of nodes thanks to an external description. The internal description is an XML Schema with a few additional markups providing the physical description of the binary file. drbdemo_for_ESRI_SHAPEFILE_advanced.zip an DRB demo example with Shape file data can be found.

21.5.5 Testbed Checks

The Representation Information which has been created and collected have been used in a number of generic applications which understand, for example DRB or EAST, and plots compared to those produced by the current, proprietary, tools. The UNESCO staff were convinced that the values adequately matched.

21.6 Related Documentation

- UNESCOJune19CASPARreviewJune2008v14.ppt Cultural Testbed presentation on the June 19 2008 EU review
- GRID_AIP.pdf ESRI ASCII AIP Overview

21.7 Other Misc Data with a Brief Description

- ESRI_wikipage.zip: archived Wikipedia page ESRI grid format
- ESRI_wiki_shapefile.zip: ESRI shapefile format archived wiki page
- html40.txt: HTML 4.0 specification in plain text
- ISO-IEC-14772-VRML97.zip: ISO standards for VRML
- msn-dds_format.txt: TEXT file containing link to MSN format support for DDRS
- shapefile.pdf: White paper on shapefiles
- VRML97Am1.zip: ISO extension to VRML standard adds geospatial NURBS

21.8 Glossary

VHRP – Acronym for Virtual Heritage Reconstruction Processes. The class of all the processes aimed at the digital reproduction of physical and existent cultural heritage.

CASPAR-based application – an application that uses of at least one of the components developed within the CASPAR Project in order to achieve some digital preservation needs.

Range-map – A Range Map is a two-dimensional image, where each pixel is the floating point distance from the image plane to the object in the scene. This is especially useful for generating synthetic data sets for use in Computer Vision research, e.g. depth from stereo and shape from shading.

Chapter 22
Contemporary Performing Arts Testbed

22.1 Historical Introduction to the Issue

Since the 1970s, the field of performance arts has quickly evolved thanks to the development of, and innovation in computers, software and electronic devices that have transformed stage practices. Whereas performers used hardware devices for all signal processing required on stage, they progressively moved to software environments enabling them to develop personal interactive modules. This initially applied to music, but quickly expanded to dance, theatre and installations.

22.1.1 The 1950s: The Pioneers

The idea of using computers in order to generate music emerged in the 50s, but was mainly reserved to laboratories. Max Mathews, a pioneer in the domain, writes for instance: "Computer performance of music was born in 1957 when an IBM 704 in NYC played a 17s composition on the Music I program which I wrote. The timbres and notes were not inspiring, but the technical breakthrough is still reverberating."

22.1.2 The 1970s: The Popularization

One major step was the invention of sound synthesis by using frequency modulation in the 1970s. This invention, patented in 1975, was discovered at Stanford University by John Chowning, another pioneer. The technique which consists in applying a frequency modulation in the audio range to a waveform also in the audio range, results in complex sounds that cannot be generated by other means, such as "boings", "clang", "twang" and other complex sounds that everyone can now easily recognize as "sounds from the 1970s or 1980s". This invention was the basis of some of the early generation digital synthesizers like the famous Yamaha DX7.

D. Giaretta, *Advanced Digital Preservation*, DOI 10.1007/978-3-642-16809-3_22,

22.1.3 The 1980s and Later: Mixed Music and Extension to Other Domains

The first interactive works combining performers and real-time electronic modulation of their parts have appeared in the middle of the 1980s. Electronic devices, either hardware or software, have been used with various musical configurations: the instrument-computer duet, for instance in Philippe Manoury's works (*Jupiter*, for flute and computer, 1987–1992 ; *En Echo*, for voice and computer, 1993–1994); the works for ensemble and live electronics, such as *Fragment de lune* (1985–1987) by Philippe Hurel; the works for soloists, ensemble and electronics, such as *Répons* (1981–1988) by Pierre Boulez.

Various digital techniques have been developed since then: from the use of various forms of sound synthesis (additive, granular, by physical modelling...), to the real-time analysis and recognition of inputs (audio as well as video input), based on artificial intelligence (neural networks, hidden Markov models...), passing through various forms of distortion of the input sounds (reverberation, harmonization, filtering...).

Meanwhile, these techniques penetrated into some neighbouring domains, such as opera with live sound transformations (*K*, music and text by Philippe Manoury, 2001), theatre with live sound transformations (*Le Privilège des Chemins*, by Fernando Pessoa, stage direction by Eric Génovèse, sound transformations by Romain Kronenberg, 2004), theatre with image generation (*La traversée de la nuit*, by Geneviève de Gaulle-Anthonioz, stage direction by Christine Zeppenfeld, real-time neural networks and multi-agent systems by Alain Bonardi, 2003), music and video performances (*Sensors Sonic Sights*), music/gestures/images with Atau Tanaka, Laurent Dailleau and Cécile Babiole), or installations (*Elle et la voix*, virtual reality installation by Catherine Ikam and Louis-François Fléri, music by Pierre Charvet, 2000).

22.1.4 And Now...

After nearly 25 years of interactive works, institutions have become aware that this type of music is completely dependent on its hardware and software implementations. Should the operating system or the processor evolve, the work cannot be performed again. This is for instance what nearly happened to *Diadèmes*, a work by composer Marc-André Dalbavie for alto solo, ensemble and electronics. First created in 1986 and honoured by the Ars Electronica Prize, the work was last performed in 1992. In December 2008, its American creation was planned, more than 22 years after its premiere in France. But the Yamaha TX 816 FM synthesizers previously used are no longer available, and the one still present at IRCAM is nearly out of commission. Moreover, composer Dalbavie has tried several software emulators, but none of them was suitable according to him to replace the old hardware synthesizer.

In April 2008, Dalbavie and his musical assistant Serge Lemouton decided to choose another technique: they built a sampler. It is a kind of database of sounds produced by an instrument. The sounds have been recorded from the old TX 816 at various pitches and intensities. This solution enabled to re-perform the piece by means of a kind of photography of the previous sounds. When no sound corresponding to a given pitch exists, the sampler is able to interpolate between existing files in order to give the illusion that the missing note exists.

22.1.5 What Is to Be Preserved?

As for music from the past centuries, we need to preserve the ability to re-perform the works, and not simply to preserve the outputs – audio or video recordings – even if these recordings are clearly part of the objects to be preserved. This implies a careful analysis of the objects that have to be preserved, including the objects that are at the core of the digital part of the work: the *process*. The context of these objects is also to be preserved, from its various dependencies – hardware and software – to the knowledge that is needed in order to install it and run it correctly. The amount of dependencies of the process is immense, from the hardware platform on which it runs, to the almost uncontrollable amount of libraries used by the multiple layers of software: from the underlying operating system with its device controllers, to the libraries included in the course of the software development process. One quickly understands that the maintenance activity needed in order to be able to re-perform a work is a never ending activity that should moreover respect a minimum of authenticity.

Authenticity in this context means that, despite the various migrations, emulations and other transformations that have to be applied to objects, one has also to maintain the information needed in order to allow future actors to answer the very important question: "DOES IT SOUND LIKE IT WAS INTENDED TO?". This is not the most straightforward task, since any judgment on authenticity in this context incorporates a certain amount of fuzziness...

22.2 An Insight into Objects

22.2.1 Complexity

Complexity seems to be inherent to musical creation, at least in the Occidental approach. This is not the right place to expose a musicological treatise on this important question, but on can refer to many examples from the past, from Jean Sebastian Bach to Mahler, Wagner, Stravinsky.... Moreover, some musicologists have shown that even in songs from Africa there is a hidden complexity, see for instance in the CD-ROM by Simha Arom *Pygmées Aka. Peuple et musique*. One can also refer to Claude Levi-Strauss for an approach of the importance of complexity in cultures...

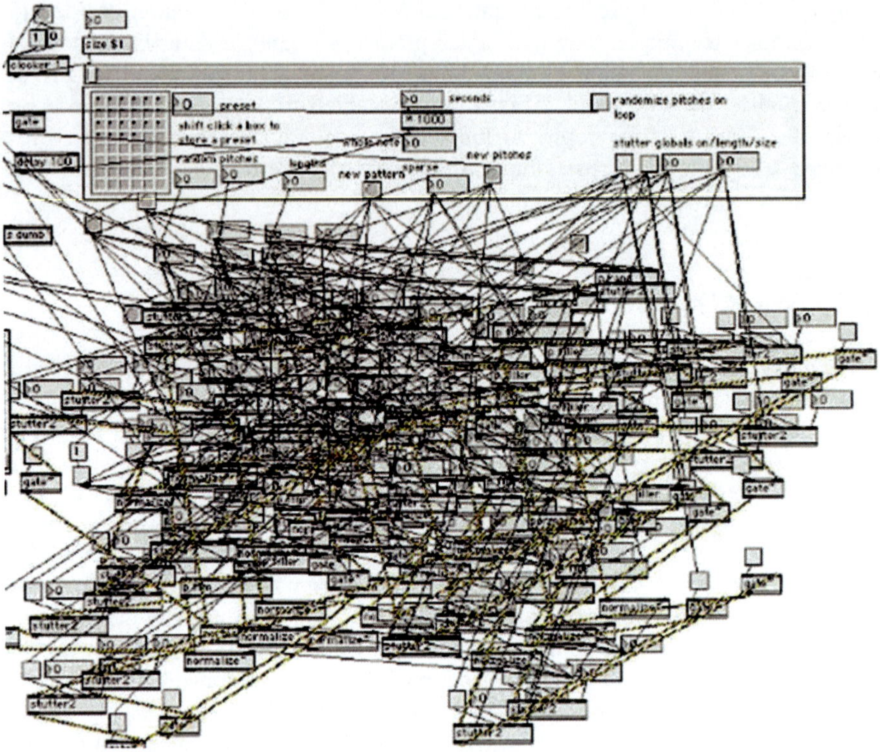

Fig. 22.1 A complex patch by Olivier Pasquet, musical assistant at IRCAM

Modern music does not escape from this law, and works produced by modern composers are very often judged as too complex for our ears. In the technical part, complexity is inevitable, as shown in Fig. 22.1.

One can think of the hidden part of a modern piano for comparison.

22.2.2 Obsolescence and Risk

In our domain, obsolescence is very rapid, and this is a quite new experience for musicians. We are accustomed to objects that last for centuries (scores, musical instruments), and we also benefit from structures that are dedicated to the transmission of knowledge about music (conservatories, music schools, treatises, schools for musical instruments manufacturing. . .). This allows for the long-term preservation of musical works in the future, even in the case where the original instrument which were to be used when a piece was composed have disappeared, such as Schubert's *Sonata* for Arpeggione, or Mozart's works for Glass Harmonica. In this case, the knowledge makes it possible to find a similar instrument, to adapt the musical score or the techniques for the sake of a new performance, assuming a certain degree of authenticity...

But for digital music, things are not so well organized. The dependency on industry is very high, knowledge is not maintained, obsolescence of systems and software is very rapid, thereby increasing the risk.

Consider for example Emmanuel Nunes' *Lichtung II.* This work was first created in 1996 in Paris, using a NeXT workstation extended with a hardware DSP platform developed by IRCAM. The work was then recreated in 2000, using then a Silicon Graphics workstation with a specific piece of software (jMax). The work was recreated again in Lisbon in 2008, using a Macintosh with the Max/MSP software. For each of the subsequent re-performances, a porting of the original process was needed, and was implemented by the original engineer who had developed the first version.

This is only one example, but the amount of works that were originally created for the NeXT/ISPW workstation is huge, and for all of them, the cycle of obsolescence is similar.

The risk is then to completely lose some works: for lost compositions from the past, the musical score is sufficient for any new performance. For the digital part, the score does not give any information.

22.3 Challenges of Preservation

The most important challenge for preservation in performing arts is to be able to re-perform the works. It is not sufficient to preserve the recordings (audio or video), but to preserve all the objects that allow for a new live performance of the work. This implies not only the preservation of all objects that are part of a work, but also preservation of the whole set of logical relationship between these elements.

Objects that have to be preserved are:

- data objects ("midi" files, audio files)
- processes (real-time processes)
- documentation (images, text)
- recordings (audio, video)

Data objects and processes are used during the live performance, while documentation and recordings are used when preparing a new live performance. Recordings can be considered to be a specific kind of documentation which aims at providing a descriptive documentation of the work (how it sounds like...), while documentation as images and text aim to provide a prescriptive documentation on the work (what has to be done). As explained above, recordings are part of the objects to be preserved, but are not sufficient to preserve the ability to re-perform the work.

There can be several objects that are used inside a work. For example, there can be several hundreds of different data objects (audio files, midi files...), several real-time processes (for instance, more than 50 in *En Echo* by Philippe Manoury), several different documentation files (one for speakers installation, one for microphones, one for general setup and installation...). All these documentation files can be grouped together in a single PDF file.

22.3.1 Challenge 1: Preserving the Whole Set of Objects, with Its Logical Meaning

The first important challenge is to preserve the logical relationship between all these objects. That logical relationship is one of the most important part of the challenge, since the preservation strategy applicable to each element can be dependent on the logical relationship an element has with the whole set.

An example of this is a set of audio files used to store parameters. During our analysis of the content of the repository, some problems occurred, one of the most glaring being the case of audio files used to store numerical parameters: instead of storing audio, some audio files are used to store numerical parameters that serve as input to real-time processes in order to change their behaviour. This behaviour seems to be very frequent, since audio files are well known to the community, and their use is thus facilitated.

Due to this fact, migration techniques that are applicable to audio files cannot be applied to these specific parameter files (the reason of this is very evident to any member of the community). Thus, the logical relationship to the whole set of objects has to be maintained in order to achieve preservation.

22.3.2 Challenge 2: Preserving the Processes, and Achieving Authenticity Throughout Migrations

As explained in detail below, the second important challenge is to preserve the real-time process (the so-called "patch"). The obsolescence of the environments able to execute the real-time process is so rapid that processes need to be migrated approximately every 5 years. Moreover, there is a need to achieve a certain form of authenticity throughout the successive migrations that cannot be evidently based on simple provenance and Fixity Information, as defined by the OAIS model.

22.4 Preserving the Real-Time Processes

Briefly speaking, the Representation Information for our real-time processes is:

- Structure: the structure is a block-diagram flow structure.
- Semantics: semantic of each element is (most of the time) already existing in documentation.

A simple example, showing the structure of a (very simple) process, that provides the structure and the semantics of one of these elements is shown in Fig. 22.2.

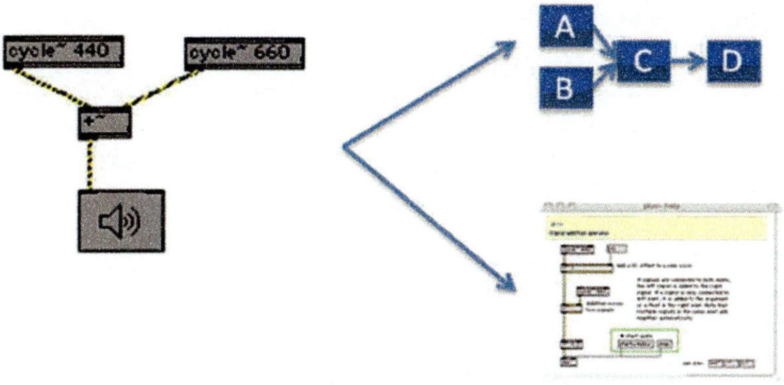

Fig. 22.2 Splitting a process into structure and semantics

Moreover, existing documentation is written according to a template (which can be expressed either in LaTEX or PDF).

The methodology was defined as follows:

- Reduce the block-diagram flow to an algebra (choice of existing « FAUST » language, concise and sufficiently expressive developed by Grame, Lyon, France).
- Store the semantics of the elements, by extracting them from existing documentation

To this end, several tools have been developed, according to the architecture shown in Fig. 22.3.

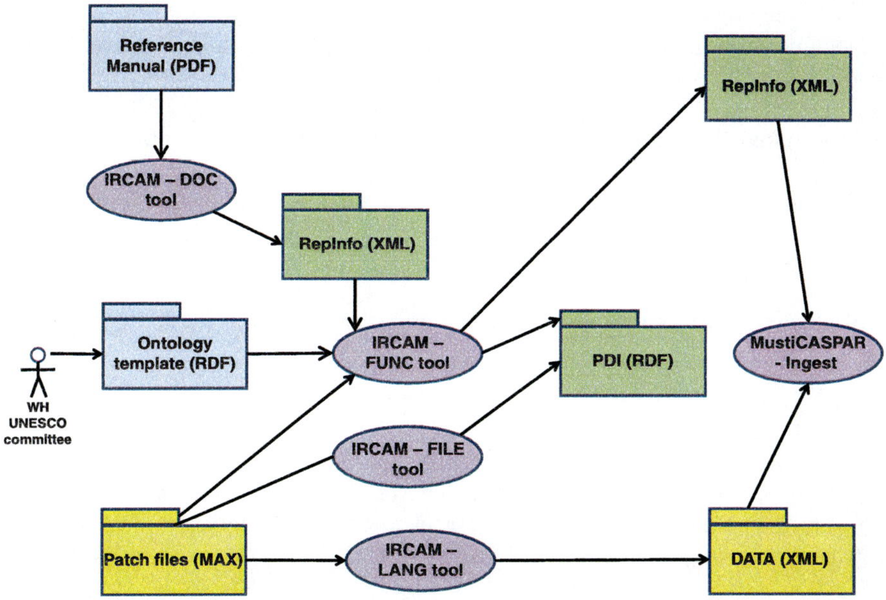

Fig. 22.3 The process for generation of RepInfo and PDI

The role of each of these tools is defined as follows:

- DOC tool: extracts from existing documentation the semantics of elements
- FUNC tool: parses the code of each single process in order to identify elements, verify existence of RepInfo (if RepInfo missing, a warning is generated, see demo below), and provides PDI for the process according to the PATCH ontology template
- FILE tool: analyze the global structure of all provided files, encodes PDI of work according to provided WORK ontology template
- LANG tool: re-encodes the syntax of the original process according to the chosen language (FAUST)

The results of these extractions are stored in the archive, according to the OAIS methodology, during the Ingest phase.

22.4.1 Preserving Logical Relationships

In order to preserve logical relationship, we developed several ontology templates for specific elements of the objects we have to preserve. These ontologies have been expressed using CIDOC-CRM (Conceptual Reference Model), that provides definitions and a formal structure for describing the implicit and explicit concepts and relationships used in cultural heritage documentation. CIDOC CRM is an ISO standard (ISO 21127:2006).

Ontologies have been defined, and expressed in RDF for each element we have to preserve:

- Work
- Real-time process (with subclasses, patch libraries, functions)
- Documents: program notes, Hall program, Biography, Interview, audio sample, Video sample, Score, Recording...

These ontologies provide a template for relationship with other elements of the work to be preserved.

Examples: Ontology for WORK provides a template aimed to express the relationship between all elements composing the work, and particularly documentation files is shown in Fig. 22.4.

The ontology for "patch" (real-time process) is shown in Fig. 22.5.

22.4.2 IRCAM Scenario

In order to test the validity of the provided information (PDI as well as Representation Information), we developed specifically an "accelerated lifetime test", by assuming that one of the main elements in use today (the Max/MSP software) is not available anymore.

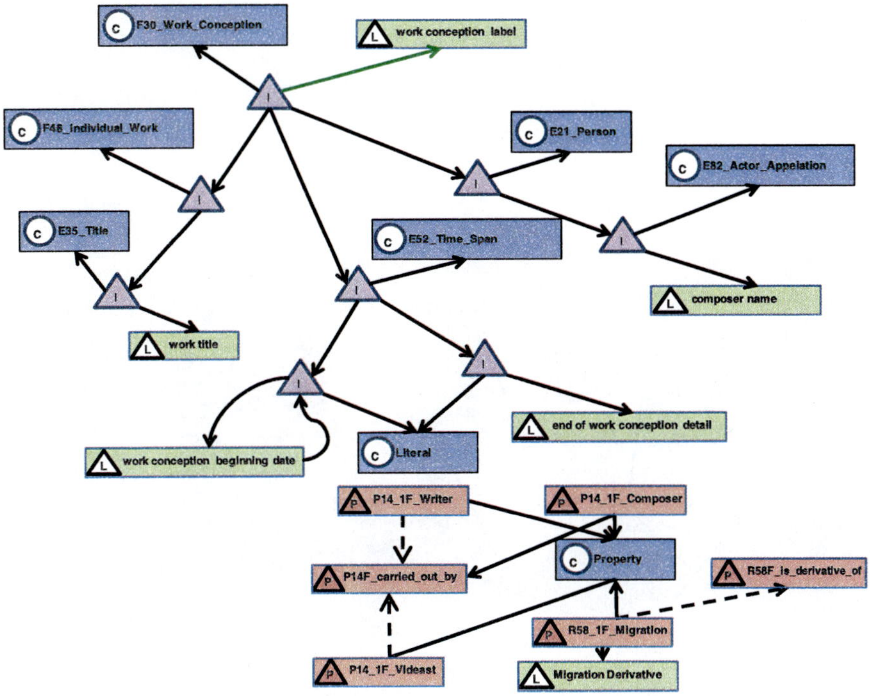

Fig. 22.4 Ontology for work

22.4.3 Scenario Summary

- We (as archivists) ingest of a new WORK into MustiCASPAR,
- We (as registered experts) receive an asynchronous notification of loss of availability for a COMPONENT,
- We (as registered experts) search for equivalent COMPONENTS:
    - o A new version of the COMPONENT becomes available, or:
    - o We apply a migration of the component, on the basis of RepInfo
- We (as archivists) ingest of the new version of the COMPONENT.

Used Packages

- Representation Information Toolbox
- Registry
- Authenticity manager
- Preservation Orchestration Manager
- Packaging
- Knowledge Manager

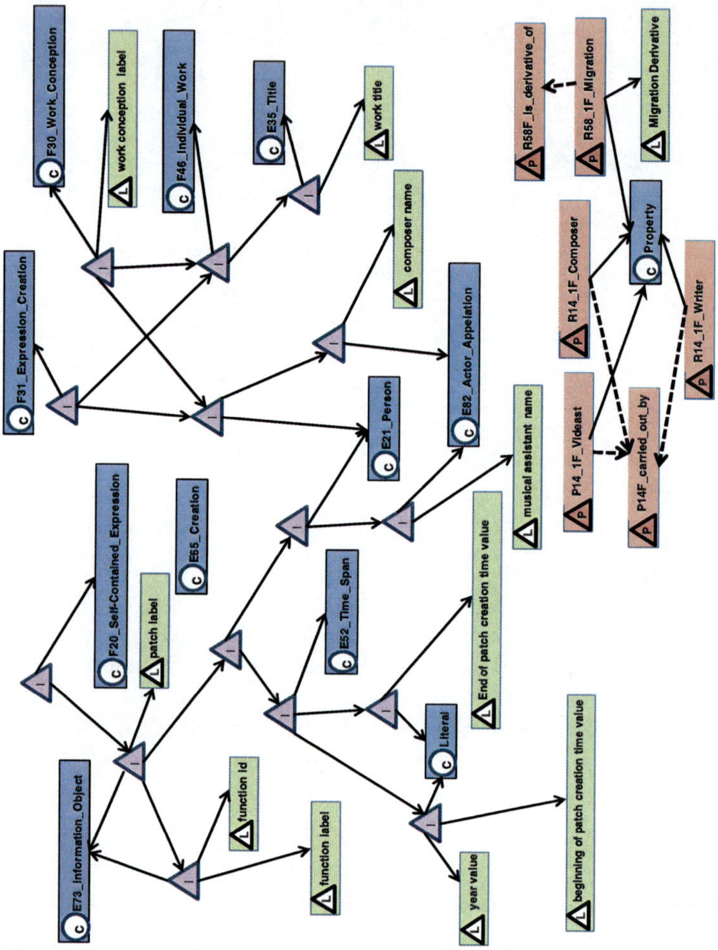

Fig. 22.5 Ontology for real-time process

22.4.4 Validation of Representation Information

The purpose of this checking is to validate the Representation Information extracted from the real-time process (see Fig. 22.6).

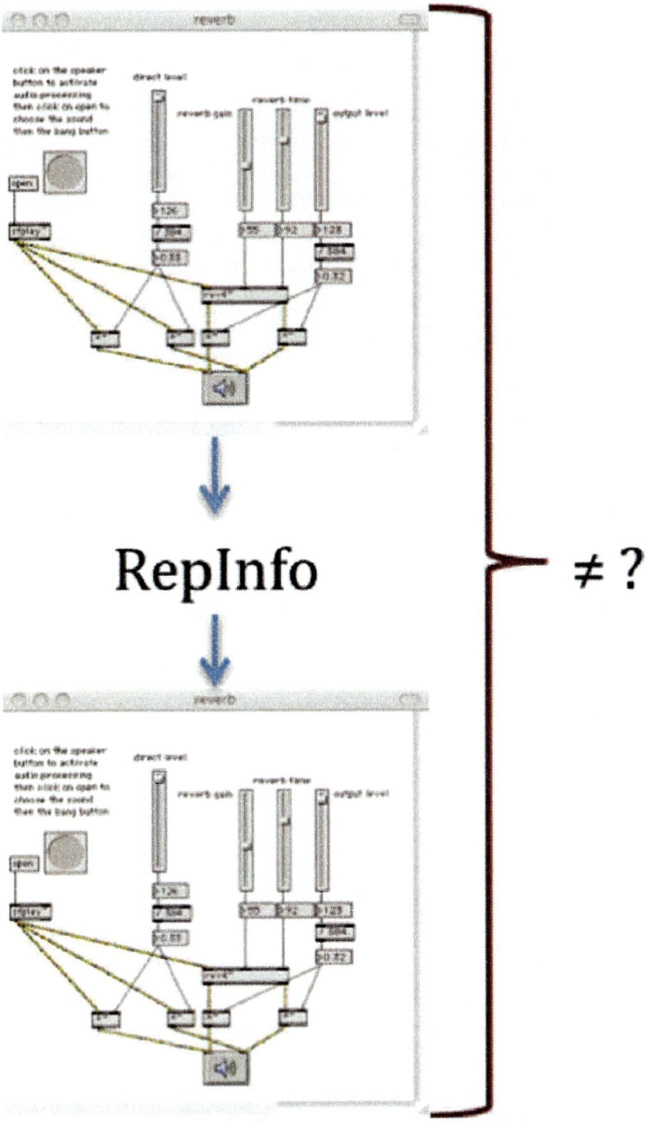

Fig. 22.6 Checking completeness of RepInfo

To this end, Representation Information checking is performed in three steps:

1. Checking completeness of information: reconstruction of original process from extracted Representation Information
2. Checking usefulness: construction of an equivalent process, from extracted RepInfo , but executed from PureData (equivalent to a migration)
3. Authenticity: comparison of audio outputs, according to defined Authenticity protocol

22.4.4.1 Checking Completeness of Information

The purpose of this checking is to check the completeness of Information Representation. To this end, we apply a transformation using the Language Tool (described above) to the original object (process). We then apply the reverse transformation in order to obtain a new process. This process is supposed to be the same as the original one. We can apply a bit-to-bit comparison method to the objects in order to detect any loss of information illustrated in Fig. 22.7.

22.4.4.2 Checking Usefulness of Information

The purpose of this check is to show that a new process, different from the original one, but functional, can be reconstructed from the provided Representation Information as illustrated in Fig. 22.7.

In order to show this, an automatic translation tool is used (based on the Language Tool already described), replacing the original Max/MSP environment by the PureData environment.

It should be noticed that some manual adjustments have to be made in the current version of the tools (due to incompleteness of Representation Information with PureData).

22.4.4.3 Checking Authenticity

In order to check Authenticity, we apply an Authenticity protocol.

Here is a slightly simplified version of the AP:

- At Ingest phase, 3-steps Authenticity Protocol:
  - Choose an input audio file (inputFile1)
  - Apply audio effect on it
  - Record output audio file (outputFile1)
- At Migration phase, 3-steps Authenticity Protocol :
  - After migration, apply new audio effect on inputFile1
  - Record output audio file (outputFile2)
  - Compare outputFile1 and outputFile2 (by ear – audio engineer, or any other method of comparison, for example comparing spectrograms), illustrated in Fig. 22.8

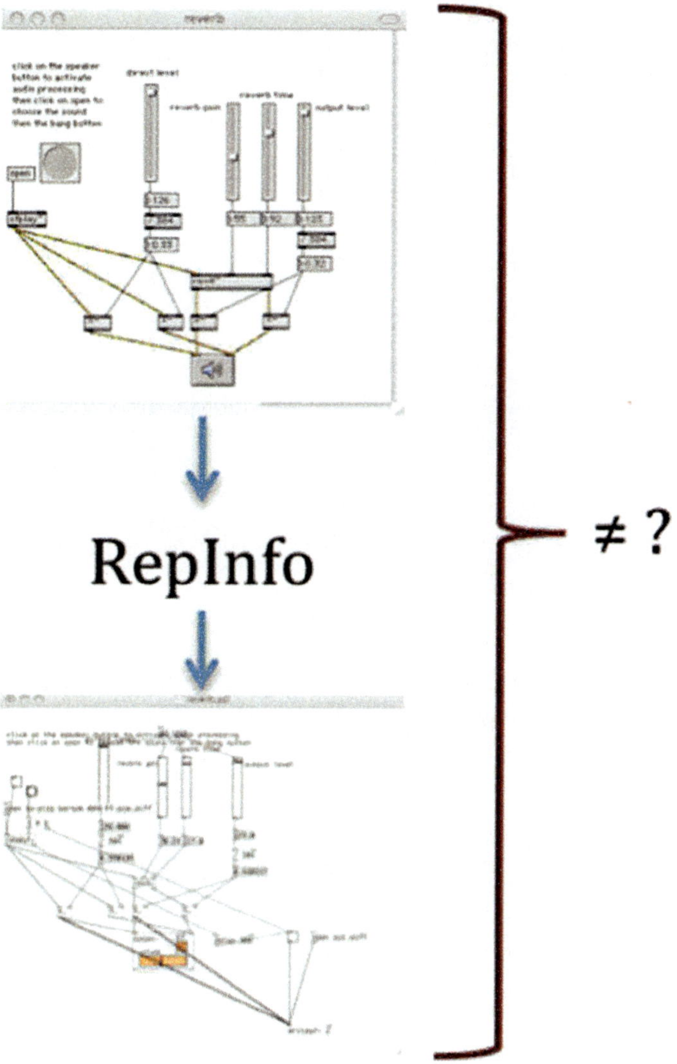

Fig. 22.7 Checking usefulness of RepInfo

As an important remark, it has to be noticed that, when comparing output files, some adjustments have to be made on the object itself in order to achieve authenticity.

22.5 Interactive Multimedia Performance

In this Section, we discuss the motivation, considerations, approaches and results of the CASPAR contemporary arts testbed with a particular attention on Interactive

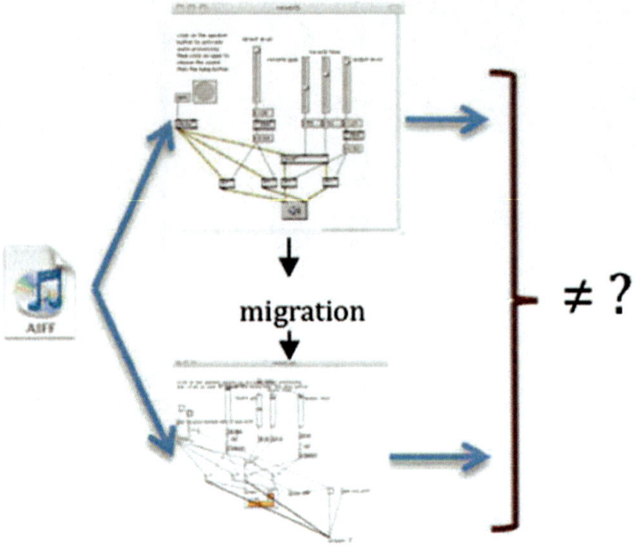

Fig. 22.8 Checking authenticity

Multimedia Performances (IMP) [221]. The section describes several different IMP systems and presents an archival system, which has been designed and implemented based on the CASPAR framework and components for preserving Interactive Multimedia Performances.

22.5.1 Introduction

IMP is chosen as part of the testbeds for its challenges due to the complexity and multiple dependencies and typically involves several difference categories of digital media data. Generally, an IMP involves one or more performers who interact with a computer based multimedia system making use of multimedia contents that may be prepared as well as generated in real-time including music, audio, video, animation, graphics, and many others [222, 223].

The interactions between the performer(s) and the multimedia system [224–226] can be done in a wide range of different approaches, such as body motions (for example, see Music via Motion (MvM) [227, 228]), movements of traditional musical instruments or other interfaces, sounds generated by these instruments, tension of body muscle using bio-feedback [229], heart beats, sensors systems, and many others. These "signals" from performers are captured and processed by multimedia systems. Depending on specific performances, the input can be mapped onto multimedia contents and/or as control parameters to generate live contents/feedback using a mapping strategy.

Traditional music notation as an abstract representation of a performance it is not sufficient to store all the information and data required to reconstruct the performance with all the specific details. In order to keep an IMP performance alive through time, not only its output, but also the whole production process to create the output needs to be preserved.

22.5.2 Interactive Multimedia Performance (IMP) Systems

In this section we describe several different IMP systems and software with different types of interaction and different types of data while the following section explains how the CASPAR framework is used for their preservation.

22.5.3 The 3D Augmented Mirror (AMIR) System

The 3D Augmented Mirror (AMIR) [230, 231] is an example IMP system which has been developed in the context of the i-Maestro project (www.i-maestro.org) [232], for the analysis of gesture and posture in string practice training. Similar to many other performing arts, string players (e.g. violinist, cellists) often use mirrors to observe themselves practicing to understand and improve awareness of their playing gesture and posture. More recently, video has also been used. However, this is generally not effective due to the inherent limitations of 2D perspective views of the media.

The i-Maestro 3D Augmented Mirror is designed to support the teaching and learning of bowing technique, by providing multimodal feedback based on real-time analysis of 3D motion capture data. Figures 22.9 and 22.10 show screenshots of the i-Maestro 3D Augmented Mirror interface which explore visualization and sonification (e.g. 3D bow motion pathway trajectories and patterns) to provide gesture and posture support. It uses many different types of data including 3D motion data (from a 12-camera motion capture system), pressure sensor, audio, video and balance.

The i-Maestro AMIR multimodal recording, which includes 3D motion data, audio, video and other optional sensor data (e.g. balance, etc) can be very useful to provide in-depth information beyond the classical audio visual recording many different purposes including technology-enhanced learning, and in this context for the preservation of playing gesture and style for detailed musicological analysis (now and in the future).

22.5.4 ICSRiM Conducting Interface

The ICSRiM Conducting System is another IMP system example. It has been developed for the tracking and analysis of a conductor's hand movements [233, 234]. The system is aiming at supporting students learning and practicing conducting, and

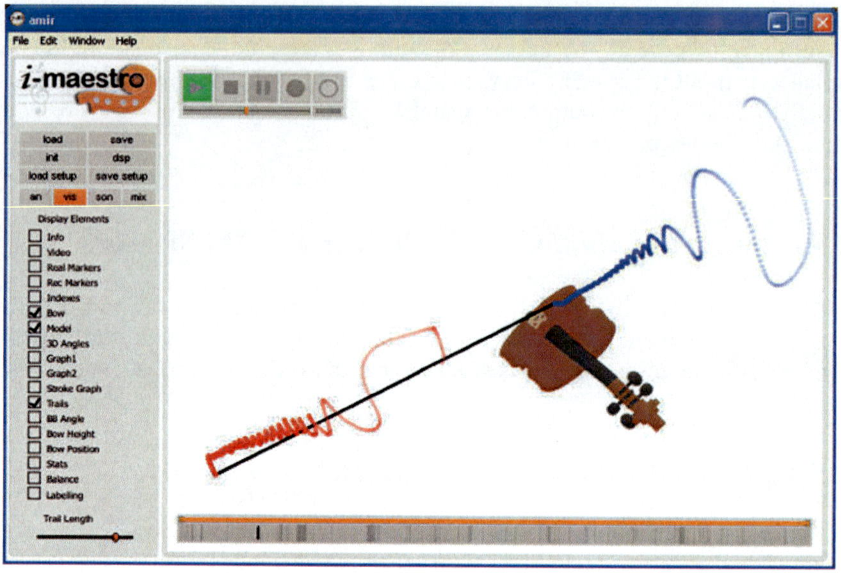

Fig. 22.9 The i-Maestro 3D augmented mirror system showing the motion path visualisation

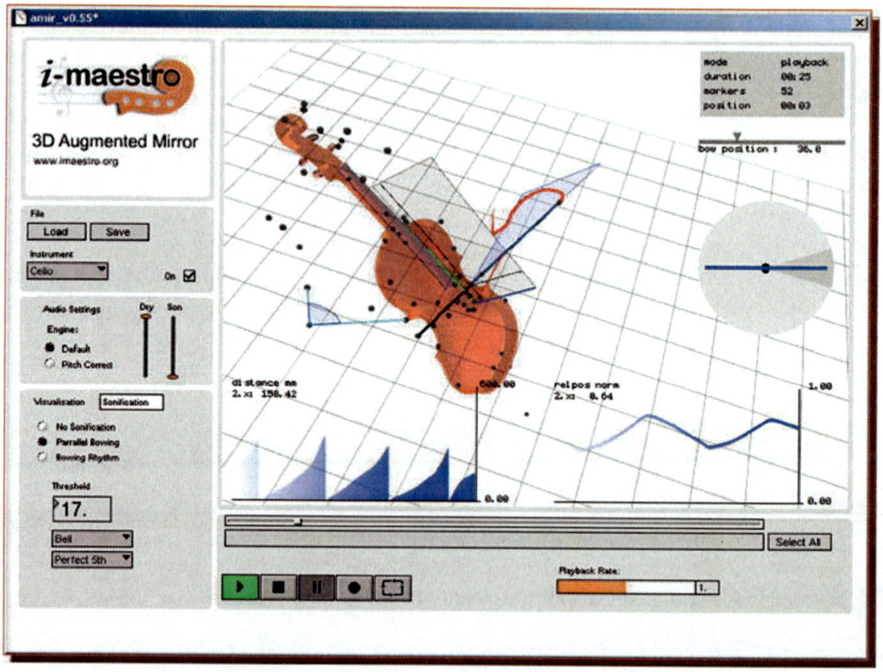

Fig. 22.10 AMIR interface showing 3D motion data, additional visualizations and analysis

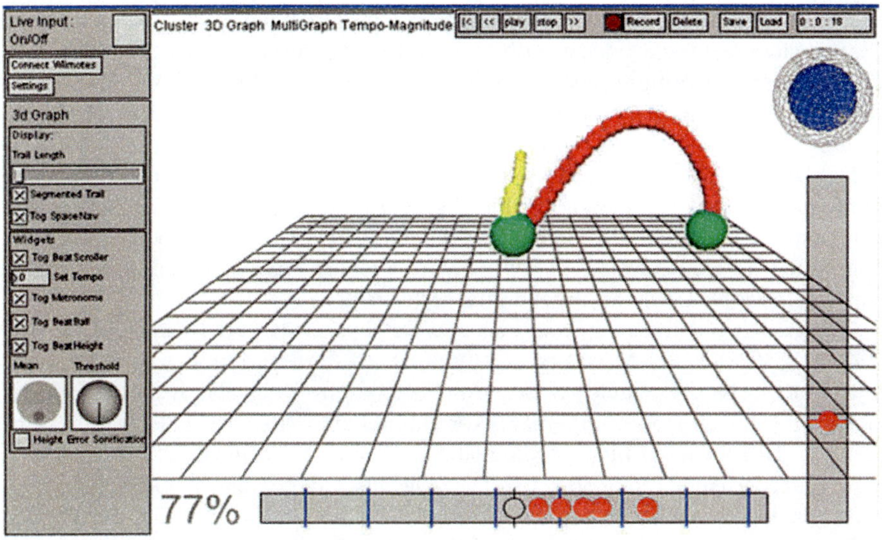

Fig. 22.11 The ICSRiM conducting interface showing a conducting gesture with 3D visualisation

also provides a multimodal recording (and playback) interface to capture/measure detailed conducting gesture in 3D for the preservation of the performance.

A portable motion capture system composed by multiple Nintendo Wiimotes is used to capture the conductor's gesture. The Nintendo Wiimote has several advantages as it combines both optical and sensor based motion tracking capabilities, it is portable, affordable and easily attainable. The captured data are analyzed and presented to the user highlighting important factors and offer helpful and informative monitoring for raising self-awareness that can be used during a lesson or for self-practice. Figure 22.11 shows a screenshot of the Conducting System Interface with one of the four main visualization mode.

22.5.5 Preservation with Ontology Models

The preservation of these IMP systems is of great importance in order to allow future re-performance, understanding and analysis. The multimodal recordings of these systems offer an additional level of detail for the preservation of musical gesture and performance (style, interpretation issues and others) that may be vital for the musicologist of the future.

Preserving an interactive multimedia performance is not easy. Preserving the single digital media object for a longer term is already a challenging issue. However, putting all the necessary digital objects together does not reconstruct the full system to allow a re-performance. For the preservation of IMP, we proposed to preserve the whole production process with all the digital objects involved together with their inter-relationships and additional information considering the reconstruction issues. It is a challenging issue since it is difficult to preserve the knowledge about the logical and temporal components, and all the objects such as the captured 3D motion data, Max/MSP patches, configuration files, etc, in order to be properly connected for the reproduction of a performance [235].

Due to these multiple dependencies, the preservation of an IMP requires robust representation and association of the digital resources. This can be performed using entities and properties defined for CIDOC-CRM and FRBRoo. The CIDOC Conceptual Reference Model (CRM) is being proposed as a standard ontology for enabling interoperability amongst digital archives [236].

CIDOC-CRM defines a core set concepts for physical as well as temporal entities [237, 238]. CIDOC-CRM was originally designed for describing cultural heritage collections in museum archives. A harmonisation effort has also been carried out to align the Functional Requirements for Bibliographic Records (FRBR) [239] to CIDOC-CRM for describing artistic contents. The result is an object oriented version of FRBR, called FRBRoo [240]. The concepts and relations of the FRBRoo are directly mapped to CIDOC-CRM.

Figure 22.12 demonstrates how the CIDOC-CRM and FRBR ontologies are used for the modelling of an IMP.

22.5.6 ICSRiM IMP Archival System

The CASPAR project evaluated a set of preservation scenarios and strategies in order to validate its conceptual model and architectural solutions within the different

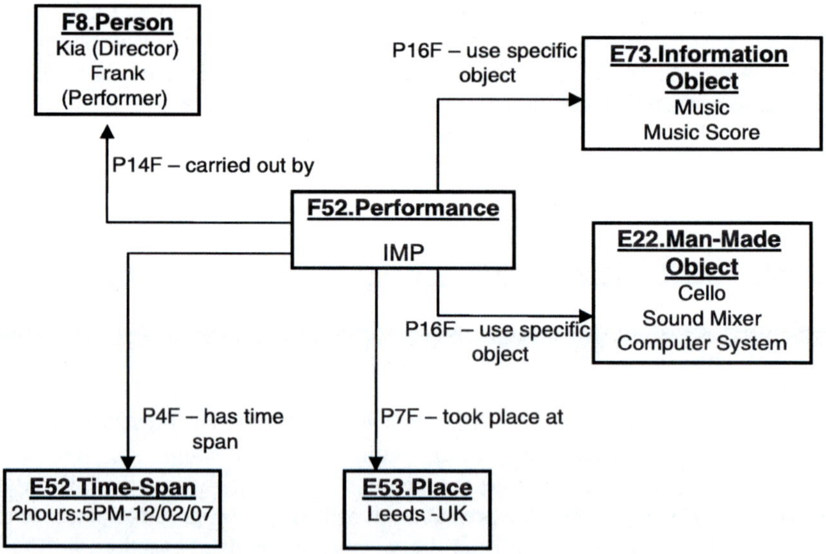

Fig. 22.12 Modelling an IMP with the use of the CIDOC-CRM and FRBR ontologies

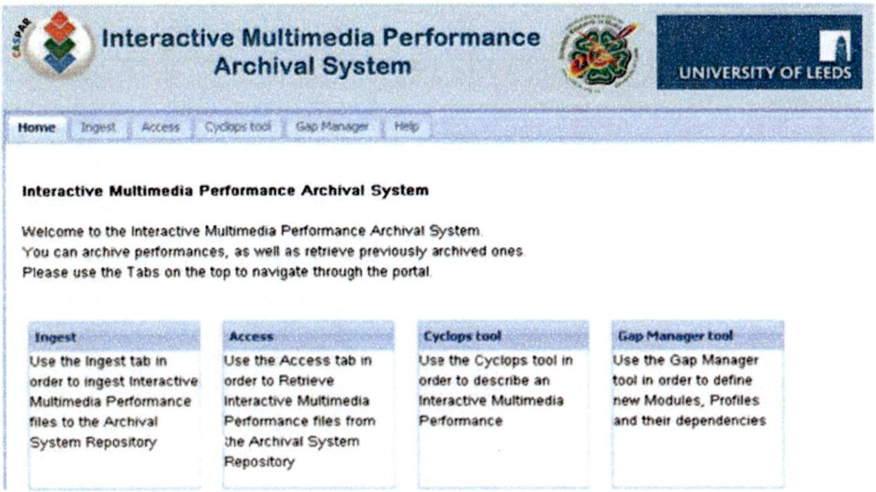

Fig. 22.13 The interface of the Web archival system

testbed domains. In this case, our scenarios are related with the ingestion, retrieval and preservation of IMPs.

The ICSRiM IMP Archival System has been designed and developed with the CASPAR framework integrating a number of selected CASPAR components via web services. The system has been used to implement and validate the preservation scenarios.

The archival system is a web interface, shown in Fig. 22.13, which communicates with a Repository containing the IMPs and the necessary "metadata" for preserving the IMPs. The first step for preserving an IMP is to create its description based on the CIDOC-CRM and FRBRoo ontology. This information is generated in RDF/XML format with the use of the CASPAR Cyclops tool. The Cyclops tool [241] is used to capture appropriate Representation Information to enhance virtualisation and future re-use of the IMP. In particular, this web tool is integrated into the Archival System and it used in order to model various IMPs.

During ingestion, the IMP files and the "metadata" are uploaded and stored in the Repository with the use of the web-based IMP Archival System. For the retrieval of an IMP, queries are performed on the "metadata" and the related objects are returned to the user. The following Figure shows the web interface of the ICSRiM IMP Archival system.

In case a change occurs in the dataset of an IMP, such as the release of a new version of the software, the user has the ability to update the Representation Information and the dataset of the IMP with the new modules (e.g. the version of new software). A future user will be able to understand which one is the latest version of a component and how these components can be reassembled for the reproduction of the Performance by retrieving the Representation Information of the IMP.

22.5.7 Conclusion

This section of the chapter introduces the usages and applications of interactive multimedia for contemporary performing arts as well as its usefulness for capturing/measuring multimedia and multimodal data that are able to better represent the playing gesture and/or interactions. With two example IMP systems, it discusses key requirements and complexities of the preservation considerations and presents a digital preservation framework based on ontologies for Interactive Multimedia Performances.

With the CASPAR framework, standard ontology models were adopted in order to define the relations between the individual components that are used for the re-performance. We also described the development and implementation of a web-based archival system using the CASPAR framework and components.

The ICSRiM IMP Archival System has been successfully validated by users who have created their own IMP systems using their own work for ingestion and using ingested works from others (without any prior knowledge) to reconstruct a performance with only the instruction and information provided by the archival system.

22.6 CIANT Testbed

22.6.1 RepInfo Validation

It is quite difficult to properly demonstrate that all the RepInfo necessary to re-perform the performance has been collected making the information in the archive Independently Understandable. The only ultimate proof would be to grant access to the archive to a group of artists (Designated Community) that would hire a theatre and attempt to re-perform the piece. Since this is not a convenient solution from obvious reasons, we decided to implement a Performance Viewer tool that would facilitate the process of RepInfo validation by providing immediate visual and audio feedback.

The architecture of Performance Viewer tool consists of the following components:

- Ontology loader
- Timeline controller
- Different visualisation profiles

The "Ontology loader" component serves as a bridge between the ontology which is stored in the repository and the rest of the application. It understands the peculiarities of the CIDOC-CRM and the semantics of our CIDOC extensions. It also provides a modular architecture where other components, so called "Visualisation profiles" can register their event handlers. When the loading procedure is initiated, all registered observers would receive data depending on their focus. For instance:

- VRML profile would render the 3D scene in using the 3D geometry-related "metadata"
- Unreal profile would render the same scene in a more advanced environment of the Unreal Engine
- Media player profile would wait for video files in order to interpret the data by playing the video
- Timeline profile would wait for the list of all processes found in the ontology and, based on this information, it would generate the nice-looking timeline widget
- Graph profile would render the RDF graph and would highlight nodes within the graph based on their activity
- Subtitles profile would display subtitles added by the modeller for annotation purposes

At the very end of the loading process, a slider widget (timeline controller) is instantiated and configured. The end-user controls the whole visualisation tool from the control panel of the slider widget synchronising the other components. In our case, the synchronisation is achieved by sending small UDP packets to software applications representing the selected visualisation profiles.

An example could be the synchronisation of multiple video players showing the recorded video of the stage from different angles, at the same time rendering the 3D scene based on the recorded motion capture data (see Figs. 22.14, 22.15 and 22.16).

More details can be found in an article ambitiously titled >>Long-term digital preservation of a new media performance: "Can we re-perform it in 100 years?"<< for May's issue of International Preservation News published by IFLA Core Activity on Preservation and Conservation (PAC) group accessible at http://www.ifla.org/files/pac/IPN_47_web.pdf

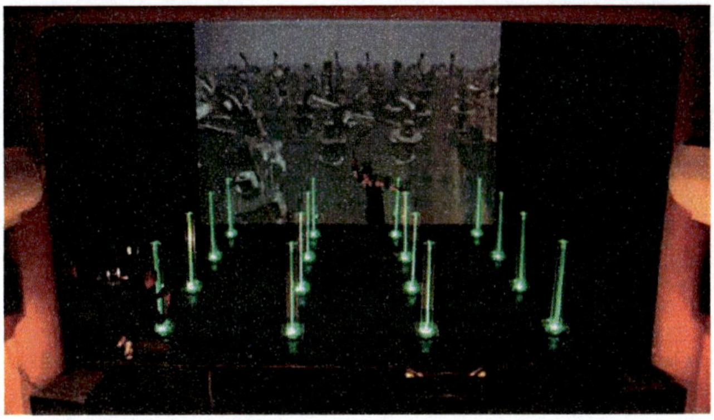

Fig. 22.14 Still image from the original recording of the GOLEM performance

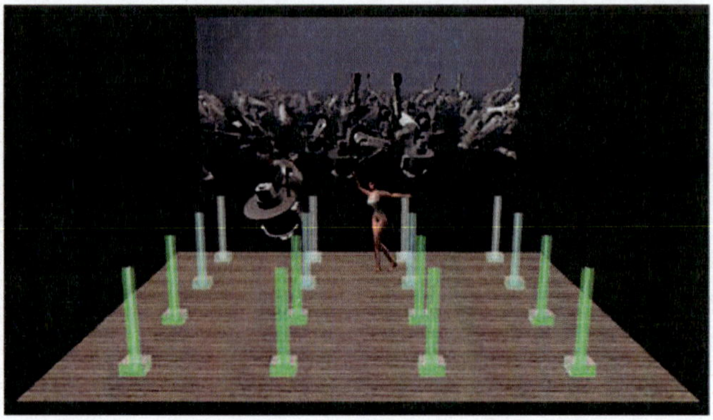

Fig. 22.15 Screenshot of the preview of the GOLEM performance in the performance viewer tool

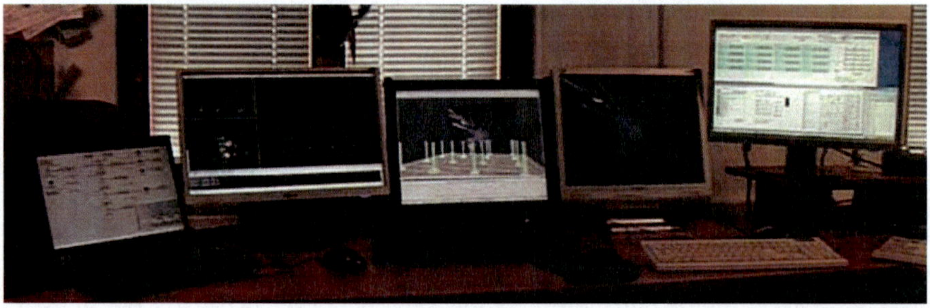

Fig. 22.16 Performance viewer: from left to right, model of the GOLEM performance, timeline slider, three different video recordings of the performance, 3D model of the stage including the virtual dancer, 3D model used for the video projection, audio patch in Max/MSP and pure data

22.7 Summary

This chapter has shown some of the results from the Contemporary Performing Arts testbeds which apply the techniques described in this book to the multitude of digital objects used in this area. The view of preservation as involving re-performance, and the ideas of authenticity, introduce a number of new ways to test our concepts, tools and techniques.

Part III
Is Money Well Spent? Cutting the Cost and Making Sure Money Is Not Wasted

Chapter 23
Sharing the Effort

23.1 Chain of Preservation

The concepts introduced here are aimed at providing an infrastructure which can be shared across the widest range of information. In that way we can spread the cost and effort of preservation and reduce the risk that the infrastructure upon which we would depend might itself disappear by broadening its potential support.

In Chap. 16 those concepts which are discipline independent, and those where the domain dependence occurs, was described in some detail. This chapter builds on that discussion and considers a number of practical implementation issues.

> We further focus on things to do with Representation Information in that can be shared between data archives, whereas the Preservation Description Information (PDI) tends by its nature to be unique to data instances and archives.

Some of the components which we identify, illustrated in Fig. 28.1 could conceivably be large, unique, resources, for example the Registry and the RepInfo Gap Manager (although issues of scalability would naturally arise). Other components make no real sense as single resources – for example the Archival Store (i.e. it would be difficult to advocate keeping all data in a large central data store). Nevertheless it would make more sense to allow multiple instances of any component, in order to provide adequate resilience and scalability. For example it would be perfectly reasonable to have multiple independent Registries, some of which may interoperate or federate.

23.2 Mechanisms for Sharing the Burden of Preservation

The rather generic scenario is as follows:

- A user uses an application to perform some task – this can range from displaying a document to performing some scientific analysis to playing a piece of music.

D. Giaretta, *Advanced Digital Preservation*, DOI 10.1007/978-3-642-16809-3_23,

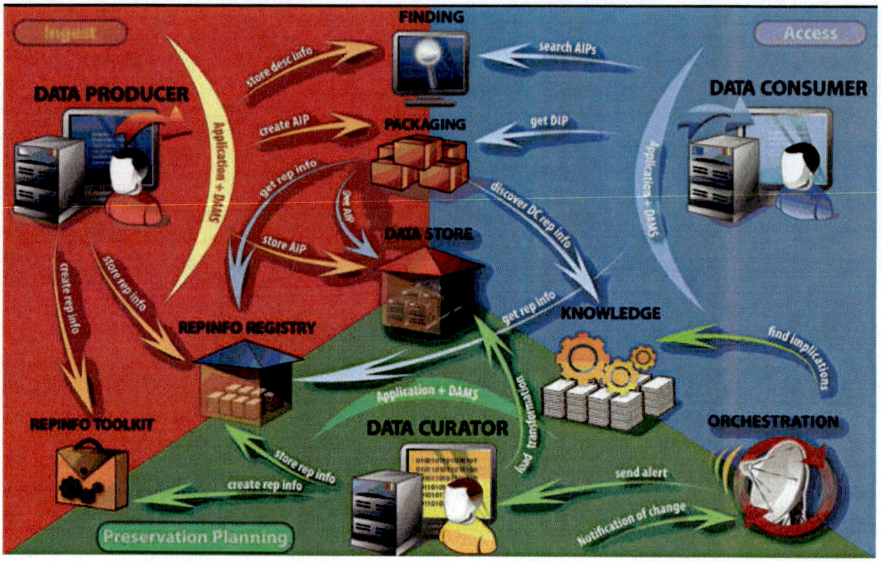

Fig. 23.1 Infrastructure components

- The user must find the appropriate data needed for the task (using Finding Aids), then must obtain the data (from the Archive)
- Either the user knows how to use the application to deal with the data or else, by definition, additional Representation Information is needed.
- Additional Representation Information may be obtained from the Archive, or else from somewhere else (from the Registry). That Representation Information may itself need further Representation Information.

In the future, as time passes, additional Representation Information will be needed, as the Knowledge Base of the Designated Community changes. The question is: how can this Representation Information be identified and generated? The scenario we have in mind, bearing in mind the previous discussion, is the following:

- People know that things have changed – this may be the Data Preservers, or a member of the Designated Community. These people inform something – the RepInfo Gap Manager.
- The RepInfo Gap Manager identifies a gap in some Representation Information net. It is unlikely that the RepInfo Gap Manager itself can fill this gap. In general only people can fill the gap, by generating new Representation Information. The next question is "who should be asked to do this?" Again, the only answer to this has to be provided by the individuals themselves.
- In order to facilitate this network of people we need a component (the Orchestration Manager) where people can register their experience or expertise. The RepInfo Gap Manager informs the Orchestration Manager that some type of

Representation Information is needed. The Orchestration Manager sends requests to those with the appropriate expertise.
- If such a person can be found then they can generate the Representation Information using anything at hand, but some set of tools would be useful (Representation Information Toolkit). The newly created Representation Information is placed somewhere (most likely in a Registry).

The claim is that, apart from the Representation Information toolkit, the other components mentioned above are not discipline dependent, and this is underpinned by the fact that the Representation Information is, as far as those components are concerned, opaque binary objects.

Chapter 24
Infrastructure Roadmap

By the PARSE.Insight team, led by David Giaretta

You and I come by road or rail, but economists travel on infrastructure.

(***Margaret Thatcher***)

This chapter is taken from the PARSE.Insight Roadmap [1]

24.1 Requirements for a Science Data Infrastructure

We base the requirements for the preservation/re-use/access infrastructure on a broad analysis of the threats and an initial set of solutions.

Threat	Requirements for solution
Users may be unable to understand or use the data e.g. the semantics, format, processes or algorithms involved	Ability to create and maintain adequate representation information
Non-maintainability of essential hardware, software or support environment may make the information inaccessible	Ability to share information about the availability of hardware and software and their replacements/substitutes
The chain of evidence may be lost and there may be lack of certainty of provenance or authenticity	Ability to bring together evidence from diverse sources about the authenticity of a digital object
Access and use restrictions may make it difficult to reuse data, or alternatively may not be respected in future	Ability to deal with digital rights correctly in a changing and evolving environment
Loss of ability to identify the location of data	An ID resolver which is really persistent

D. Giaretta, *Advanced Digital Preservation*, DOI 10.1007/978-3-642-16809-3_24,

The current custodian of the data, whether an organisation or project, may cease to exist at some point in the future	Brokering of organisations to hold data and the ability to package together the information needed to transfer information between organisations ready for long term preservation
The ones we trust to look after the digital holdings may let us down	Certification process so that one can have confidence about whom to trust to preserve data holdings over the long term (see Chap. 25)

24.2 Possible Financial Infrastructure Concepts and Components

It seems difficult describe an explicit business model, and indeed there may be different business models at different phases; for example one might distinguish (1) prototype (2) emerging infrastructure for early adopters and (3) a long-lived infrastructure to rely on. Certainly phase (1) would need specific funding and a number of the technical components described below have been prototyped in a variety of EU projects. For phase (2) it is difficult to avoid the conclusion that the short to medium term funding to go from prototype to stable, robust and scalable infrastructure components must be provided by the EU in the first instance, together perhaps with major stakeholders such as the members of the Alliance for Permanent Access. The longer term business model needed for phase (3) must clearly be linked to the business models for the rest of the infrastructure on which the components described here depend, for example the basic network.

It is worth making a number of observations, for example that there is also significant commercial need for digital preservation, although this tends not to be for the indefinite future, there may be options to create a self-funding set of services, especially where the service does not scale with the amount of data needing preservation. The Registry of Representation Information, the Knowledge gap manager, the Authenticity tools, the licence tool dark archive, the brokerage systems and the certification system, to name a few, do not necessarily suffer the problem of scaling with the amount of information being preserved. For example one piece of Representation Information may be used to describe 1 billion data objects.

A Storage Facility on the other hand would grow with data growth, although the declining cost of storage means that this does not imply a simple linear cost relationship. Nevertheless such a facility may be able to supply added value services such as disaster recovery and integrity checking.

Cost/benefit analyses are likely to be very highly instance specific yet some common models are essential if judgments are to be made about what can be afforded.

A common framework for at least collecting the information would be useful if a good understanding of the important parameters is to be gained.

The Blue Ribbon Task Force report provides a number of important considerations including the important idea of buying future options. Here funders put off making a long term commitment, instead funding preservation for a sufficient time that allows future decision makers to be in a position to make that decision.

Another issue concerns the incentives for data producers to make their data available; for example funders could require, perhaps by making part of the funding depend upon it, that steps are taken by researchers that their research outputs are make available for preservation.

There are a number of resource generating value-added services which can be associated with digital preservation. These include services such as Portico (http://www.portico.org/digital-preservation/) used by some libraries for an outsourced preservation service. However funding for such services derives from the usual sources – national research funders, EU or research organisations. New sources of funding may come from advertising revenue where there is wide public interest in the data, for example images of the Earth or the sky.

24.3 Possible Organisational and Social Infrastructure Concepts and Components

It is clear that a number of the infrastructure components described in the previous sections are themselves archives which need to preserve digital information over the long term and which therefore themselves require the support of that very preservation infrastructure. For example, the threat of The current custodian of the data, whether an organisation or project, may cease to exist at some point in the future should be taken into account by securing the handover to another host organisation. Also, Persistent Identifiers must support such a move and resolve correctly.

An initial organisational setup could be supported by a government-level organisation, for example a component of the EU, although commitment to provide a service for an indefinite time tends not to be popular. An alternative approach is to move the responsibility to an arms-length or consortium-based organisational structure, such as the Alliance for Permanent Access. This structure is bringing together key stakeholders in many sectors and may play a key role. Even this may need to be underpinned by governmental guarantee in order to provide real confidence in the infrastructure's longevity.

Aside from the organisational component, social/behavioural aspects must be considered. For example, a science data research infrastructure must facilitate data sharing and data mining. However researchers do have concerns about this; indeed, it has been (jokingly) said that data sharing/mining means either "*this data* is ***mine*** [*and no one else's*]" or else "*my data is mine, and now your data is mine [to use as I like]*"

More light can be shed on this through the survey results conducted by PARSE.insight. While a majority of researchers say they would like to make use of the research data of others, the researcher's survey also shows that a considerable number of researchers foresee problems in making their own research data available for others. No more than 25% make their data available for everyone (against close to 60% who share it within their research group). What are the problems mentioned? Over 40% are afraid of misuse, around 40% foresee legal problems (e.g. breach of privacy, misuse of anonymous surveys, etc), between 25 and 30% mention technical problems (lack of infrastructure, incompatible data, and access restricted, etc).

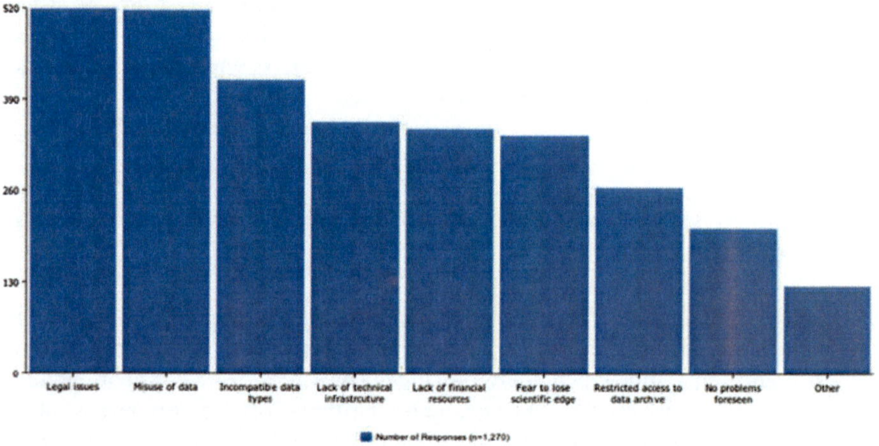

Fig. 24.1 Responses to query "Do you experience or foresee any of the following problems in sharing your data? (multiple answers available)"

This implies that even when a technical infrastructure is in place for the preservation of research data, the current behaviour patterns may prevent people from using it. This observation is enforced by another outcome of the survey regarding additional needs to operate in a digital research environment. Many researchers noted they feel the need for more resources (64%), more digital repositories (63%), more expertise (60%) and training in how to preserve and share your information (54%). In addition, they noted that guidelines/manuals on preservation, workshops, a knowledge platform and user-oriented training sessions are very important.

Although large scale facilities often have archived copies (backups, held for at least a little while) of the data they are used to create, the data created by individual researchers are often treated less well. Institutional repositories have not been great magnets for such data. Instead, most researchers that responded on the survey still use their own computer at work to store their research data (81%).

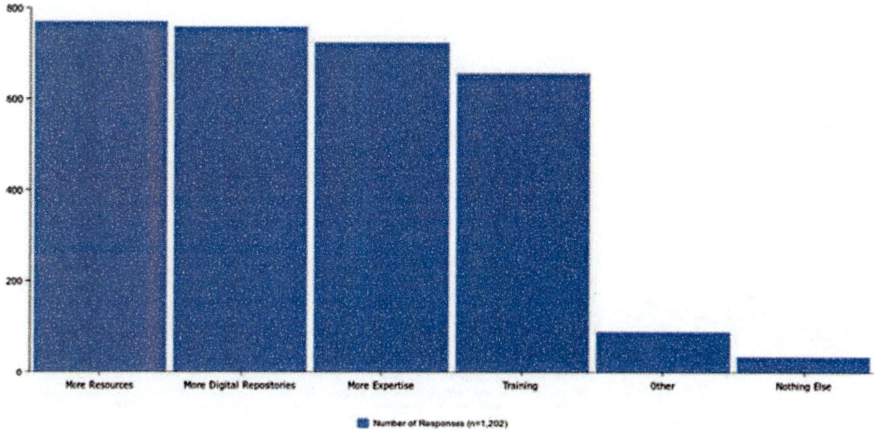

Fig. 24.2 Responses to query "Apart from an infrastructure, what do you think is needed to guarantee that valuable digital research data is preserved for access and use in the future? (multiple answers possible)"

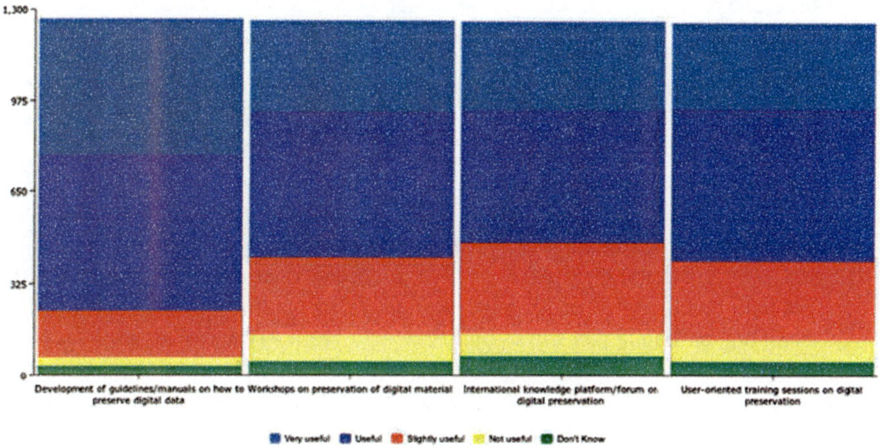

Fig. 24.3 Responses to query "Do you think the following initiatives would be useful for raising the level of knowledge about preservation of digital research data?"

To encourage and facilitate the behavioural changes PARSE.insight identified a number of benefits for researchers to get their data preserved and re-used:

- Safe your data for future research: 53% of the researchers that responded on the survey mentioned that they have experienced data created previously by other researchers was not available (anymore). By offering a guarantee that data deposited in a digital archive is kept for the long term, researchers do not have to worry about taking archiving actions by themselves.

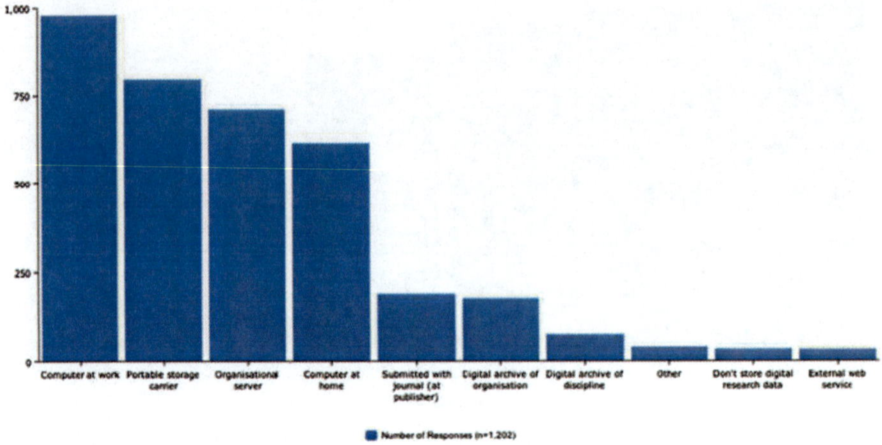

Fig. 24.4 Responses to query "How do you presently store your digital research data for future access and use, it al all? (multiple answers possible)"

- Citability: with persistent identification, preserved data can be found and re-used any time and any place. Based on the science data infrastructure, data sets could be cited as well. This way, a researcher gains extra visibility and can receive credits for publishing the data.

This requires several organisational components to be put in place:

1. Policies: in some countries mandates exist for depositing research data and in some cases funding agencies require so. But clearly, this shall not be enough as certainly not all researchers seem to obey the mandate.
2. Robust and reliable deposit places, where researchers can be sure their data will not get lost, be corrupted or misused. Reliable also means with the right access mechanisms, perhaps even some kind of access permission system for retrieval via the creator of the data. In response to being asked where they would like to store their data, the three best scoring options are: digital archive of their institute (63%), discipline based archive (60%) and at the publisher (47%).
3. Elements that increase comfort levels so that new users will know how to use and interpret the available data. And that new users will not take these data out of context. This could be achieved by a good linking system between the data and all publications that exist for and mention these data. In the survey, some 96% of respondents say they publish about their data in journals of publishers – surely these articles will contain a section on methods and protocols where new users can find how the data were gathered, if there are any restrictions on how to (re)use them and what the context of these research data is.
4. Communication and awareness around these issues.
5. Have publication of data as valued and referenced as is a publication of a paper in a journal.

These incentives can be grouped in soft and hard encouragements. Furthermore, each stakeholder in research can play a specific role in this. Below, a table is depicted which outlines the carrots and sticks that can be applied by a stakeholder.

Stakeholder	Can offer carrots	Can offer sticks	Has dependencies	Has boundary conditions
Data manager	Training support, guarantee trustworthiness	Archiving regulations	Funding, standards and guidelines	Institutional policy, infrastructure
Publisher	Citability, accessibility, high quality papers	Journal rejects if data not supplied and preserved or if DOI for data is lacking	Good infrastructure, persistent identifiers for linking	Editors agree, reviewers can review, agreed standards on how to review data
Funder	Extra funding for preservation of research data in trusted digital archive. Extra funding for sharing data with other researchers and communities	No funding and no payment if data not deposited, require proposal to address preservation aspects	Budgets	Manageable, controllable ? Is infrastructure in place ?
Researcher	Reproducible results, basis for more research, citability and recognition	Embargoes, no access for researchers who do not make data available	Good infrastructure	Part of bigger group
Research institute	High quality research environment, no worry about cost or safe deposit places, easy tools for automatic generation of contextual information for data	Rules of the house, limit budgets if not done restricting budgets	Budgets, good infrastructure	Common standards
Employer	Eternal fame	Labour condition	Common practice elsewhere	Labour laws
Policy makers	More budgets, awareness raising	No budgets	Good infrastructure	Common practice

Research Peers	Help improve results, add citations, crowd sourcing, become part of social network (online collaboratory)	Community pressure, punish by means of oblivion	Infrastructure, common practice	Common practice
Library	Accessibility and retrievability, ensure trustworthiness of digital archive	Oblivion	Persistent identifiers, good linking between publications and data, trusted digital repository, policy, standards and guidelines	Common practice
Data collectors	Preservation requirements integrated into way data is collected	Data will be lost or never found	Persist identifiers, good "metadata" schemes, central registries like TIB and Datacite	Common practice

24.3.1 Scenarios

***SCENARIO**: the researcher*

After several years of hard work and gathering tremendous amounts of raw data, a researcher gets her paper accepted for top-journal AAA – the ground breaking conclusions of her research stem from a new analysis methodology that she developed herself to allow for proper processing of the data. Her paper extensively describes the data set as well as the methodology, in terms of its richness as well as its shortcomings. She decides to make the data available for sharing with other researchers via the subject specific data repository at an international research institute (or at a national data centre) and adds the software code of the analysis methodology to it. But she has the following demands:

- *she wants anyone looking at the data or at the software to first consult her extensive research paper in journal AAA, to avoid misuse of the data or taking conclusions out of context;*
- *she wants any researcher wanting to re-use these data to be aware of the special methodology needed for the proper analysis and how that was applied in the software (hence: to read the paper);*
- *she wants her dataset to be properly cited when re-used, with a pertinent and persistent link to where the dataset resides, idem for the software code and of course with a link to her original research paper in journal AAA;*

- *she wants the data to be available as a separately citable item, counted in all significant citation scores;*
- *she wants to be sure that any reader of her research paper in journal AAA can easily link to the datasets and the related software.*

SCENARIO: *the library*

A National library in Europe has changed its policy to broaden its scope of their digital collection. From now on, data sets and accompanied tools for analysis of that data (software) in the field of Social Science and Humanities are part of their digital collection plan. In conjunction with that, they have adjusted their existing digital archive to also cope with digital material other than electronic scientific papers, book and magazines. To do so, they put in place extra preservation strategies that deal with this new type of content such as an emulation delivery service for running research software. Furthermore, they enriched their catalogue functionality with a linking mechanism for data sets and improved Digital Rights Management to allow several levels of access such as "open access all time", "open access after X period", "restricted access – only after author's approval". However, the descriptive information of the data will always be open.

With the new functionality in place, the National library is technically speaking ready for accepting data and software. To ensure researchers and their institutes are aware of this, they started a audit and certification procedure so that they can proof that their organisation is a trusted place for research output. In parallel, the library contacted several research organisations in their domain to set up archiving agreements. Part of these agreements is that researchers should spent a minimum amount of their valuable time to selection and archiving research data. The library committed themselves to this by building flexible tools for selection and "metadata" capture in cooperation with the research organisations. Furthermore, they will offer training courses of 2 days for each researcher that will start using the archive. In turn, each research institute pays a yearly fee for depositing the research output at the library. Also, the institutes are intended to form an international group of experts that will support the developments of data standards and selection procedures in their domain.

SCENARIO: the funding organization

As part of a significant new research initiative, a national funding organisation in Europe issues a call for research proposals in the area of behavioural social sciences. The theme is about eating habits of adolescents, to be measured and collected and analysed over a period of 25 years, with reporting on trends every 5 years. The call is hugely oversubscribed but the multitude of proposals deliver a wide spectrum with some very interesting different approaches. The aspects to compare and analyse cover many different areas and topics – all of them innovative and promising in their own right. A substantial part of the research costs involve the collection of large amounts of data. Given the size of the grant and without further interference, a maximum of 2 or 3 proposals could be granted.

In order to allow more output for the same research budget, the funding organisation decides to concentrate data collection within one research group and to require them to undertake it in such a way that several other groups who submitted good proposals can use the same data. It means that one group will need more money, but others substantially less, with the positive effect that between 8 and 10 proposals could be granted! The funding organisation starts an inventory of what is required in such a collaborative set up, based on the sharing of data. Enthusiastic about this idea, the Funding Organisation decides to require any data collection under this call to be stored and preserved properly so that also in the future the data can be accessed and re-used for new initiatives.

***SCENARIO**: privacy aspects*

A research group is about to publish a study in the well regarded journal Science&Nature. The study has analysed and compared the data of the first 5 years of 6 million EMR's (electronic medical records) and drawn shocking conclusions about:

- *Indications for many untreated chronic diseases in early stages;*
- *Incorrect diagnoses in more than 20% of cases by 60% of general practitioners;*
- *Prescription of wrong medicines in 32% of cases where medicines were prescribed.*

The journal Science&Nature requires since early 2008 that any research of which the conclusions are based on datasets, make these datasets available for peer review but also for those willing to dig into it. But in this case there is a serious problem with privacy aspects as many data are retrace-able to individual patients. There is also the ethical aspect to the study: the indications for early chronic diseases: should the patients to which this applies be informed or not?

The journal Science&Nature is prepared to limit the requirement for availability of data to the peer reviewers only who shall look at the datasets only from the point of the way the data was gathered and analysed – without entering specific EMR's. With reference to their normal preconditions that data can only be made available to readers if no security, privacy, or other commercial or ethical aspects are in the way, the journal shall drop its requirement to make the data available.

***SCENARIO**: training those who (will) deposit research data*

DataManager Z works at a national research institute that was one of the very first to require from its researchers that all data collected for their research is stored in its datacentre. It took a little while before the practice had found its pattern, but now Mr Z gets inundated by datasets, of any sort, size and shape. On the website of his datacentre a manual was published about the formats to use, the "metadata" to add and the descriptors to use to ensure optimal storage, preservation and re-use of the data. But to no avail. The biggest problem is that hardly any of the researchers have been thinking through what later storage, preservation and re-use implies for the way the data is collected. And after the fact, it is difficult to repair any flaws, if only because many of the researchers have already moved on to their next project.

Z decides that the situation will not get any better if the researchers (most of them young and enthusiastic but relatively inexperienced PhD? 's) do not get any training. So he starts 1-day training sessions, widely announced, but with very few attendants. Then he thinks of e-learning modules. New researchers who join the institute are required to work through the module in their first month and finish it with an online test. Also, any research proposal at the institute requires a separate paragraph about the data collection, preservation and possibilities for re-use.

24.3.2 Next Steps

- Make organisations aware that digital preservation is not only a technical challenge but also requires adjustments to their policies and procedures.
- Define and apply standards for exchange of data sets across research institutes and archives.
- Define and apply standards for openness of data (aka Creative Commons for data).
- Agree on a checklist for digital archives to become "trusted".
- Develop training courses to teach researchers how to cope with digital data (awareness raising).
- Develop e-learning modules for training researchers to work with data sets and how to archive and share them.
- Develop guidelines for researchers and their institutes to come to common practice data formats which are suitable for archiving.
- Build a cross-domain virtual platform for researchers to learn about best practices in sharing and archiving of data.
- Commission expert panels (for each discipline) to support the selection process of what needs to be preserved and what not.

- Develop easy-to-use tools for data selection and archiving preparations (limiting misinterpretation of data and fragility of data formats).
- Demonstrate citability of data sets within and across disciplines.

24.3.3 Final Destination

- Safely deposited data sets at a (perhaps limited) number of trusted digital archives.
- Updated policies and procedures of research institutes taking long-term preservation of their assets into account.
- Data sets (or access copies) that can be cited amongst disciplines and for which researchers can be credited.
- Respected access mechanisms to protect data and researcher from misuse and misinterpretation.
- Trained researchers that are aware of digital fragility and how to cope with that (selection, Representation Information including file formats and data semantics, descriptive information).

24.3.4 Relevant Projects, Policies, Organisations, Activities

- ISO Repository Audit and Certification work [6]
- DANS Data Seal of Approval
- OAIS reference model
- Creative Commons
- Alliance for Permanent Access

24.4 Possible Policy Infrastructure Concepts and Components

There are a number of broad policies or statements of intents about preservation, re-use and (open) access. Although it is not clear when or whether these will converge, it is clear that there will almost certainly be a variety of such policies for the foreseeable future. The preservation infrastructure must be able to operate in this environment. Nevertheless alignment of policies will undoubtedly make the task simpler, for which co-ordination at national, EU and international levels, including EU and transnational consortia of key stakeholders such as the Alliance for Permanent Access, would be essential. Clarity is also needed in policies which not just encourage but also require researchers, perhaps with financial incentives, to deposit their data, and which also indicate practical ways for them to do so.

It is important that policy makers distinguish between open access on one hand and digital preservation on the other. Those whose main interest is open access – if it is to be maintained over the long term – should understand that it is equally dependent on digital preservation, as is non-open access.

24.4.1 Deployment and Adoption

The need for an infrastructure on an international scale is evident. To ensure that such an infrastructure will be supported by all stakeholders across Europe and beyond, a well-defined strategy is needed to stimulate its adoption. This strategy can be considered from two perspectives: a bottom-up view, representing the view of the end-users (researchers, publishers, data managers, etc) and a top-down view which represents the perspective of the initiators of the infrastructure.

The bottom-up perspective currently gives a view on many initiatives taken on sharing data amongst researchers within their research domain as mentioned in the previous section (e.g. GEANT, EGEE). These national or domain-specific solutions (islands of capabilities) are mostly developed to enable interoperability between different science stakeholders. The clustering of information resources is an ongoing process already and will eventually lead to larger networks that allow stakeholders to share information. However cross-domain cooperation will still be limited due to incompatibility of these domain-specific infrastructures. The solutions often do not share a standardised and certified approach, which limits overall sustainability of the infrastructure. While respecting the existing solutions, it is a challenge to achieve a global infrastructure that not only allows researchers to share data, but also to keep the information trusted, reliable and secure.

To achieve better sustainability and interoperability, the top-down approach can help by promoting the foundation of guidelines and recommendations for sustainable data archives. The Repository Audit and Certification work aims in this direction. Moreover, standards should be promoted which are compliant with a trans-national infrastructure, but also are easy to adopt in the already existing networked domains. The EU as well as other international bodies can play an important role in this process.

It is worth noting that Audit and Certification can apply not just to the data holdings but also to most of the other infrastructural components which are mentioned in the next section. These components depend upon their holdings of information, for example Representation Information, which must itself be preserved over the long term. Thus those infrastructure components should themselves be audited and certified if the infrastructure itself – or at least the information on which it depends – is to be usable over the long term.

The benefit of this top-down approach not only ends with better interoperable and sustainable networks, it also draws a clear scenery of the European science landscape, allowing new stakeholders to build a business model on top of the infrastructure. Researchers are assured that their data is compatible and safe because of certification and legislation while new businesses can offer new services on top of this secure layer of the infrastructure.

A good example is the OAIS Reference Model (ISO 14721:2003), which has become a worldwide adopted standard for building a sustainable digital archive. Today, various vendors developed their own archiving solutions and bring them to the market.

24.5 Virtualisation of Policies, Resources and Processes

Virtualisation is a commonly used technique in systems to insulate services from underlying implementations. The science data infrastructure described here is implemented by services including management, trust, workflow, data storage and other resources. In order to insulate the science data infrastructure components from changes it is necessary to try to virtualise access and use of all these. Virtualization would for example facilitate the migration between preservation environments, i.e. enabling policy enforcement across systems.

> ***SCENARIO***
> *Due to its size, a large scientific dataset has to be stored across multiple distributed locations. These storage locations are maintained by different organisations using diverse hardware/software infrastructures. Researchers who wish to access the dataset are provided with a uniform interface, hence they do not need to be aware of the actual physical location of the data. Data managers are provided with a standardized set of actions, which are then mapped to concrete operations and executed by the respective underlying infrastructures. Computing-intensive operations such as format migrations might be scheduled and submitted to external (grid-based) services.*

24.5.1 Next Steps

- Specify standards promoting the interoperability between services, grid operations and existing archive systems.
- Scalable storage abstractions capable of handling increased data volume without impacting the running of the archive
- Support for data replication to geographically disparate storage resources.
- Provision of logical namespaces for resources, data and users.
- Define data virtualisations for common data objects

24.5.2 Final Destination

- Infrastructure independence, collections can be moved across preservation systems without any loss of information.
- Management virtualization, seamless federation of preservation environments while maintaining control over policies, processes and resources.

24.5.3 Relevant Projects, Policies, Organisations, Activities

- SHAMAN (http://www.shaman-ip.eu/), Chronopolis (http://chronopolis.sdsc.edu/mediawiki/index.php/Main_Page), CASPAR (http://www.casparpreserves.eu/), iRODS (http://www.irods.org)

24.6 Technical Science Data Concepts and Components

Each of the solutions is analysed next. For each solution there is a particular need to review the existing digital preservation projects, review the proposals and identify open issues. The Warwick workshop report is also relevant here.

24.6.1 Create and Maintain Representation Information

The information needed to understand and use a digital object is termed, in OAIS, "Representation Information". This is a catch-all term which includes information about a digital object's format, semantics, software, algorithms, processes and indeed anything else needed.

SCENARIO

A dataset created by one researcher may need to be used by a second, either contemporaneously or at some later time. This second researcher may come from a different discipline and use different analysis tools. In order to avoid producing misleading results he/she must be able to understand what the data actually means. For example, given an astronomical image in the current FITS format, with its several variants, the researcher would need to be able to extract the values of the pixels of the image from what may be quite a complex and highly tailored digital object. In order to use an analysis tool one would need to know how to deal with these pixel values, their units, their coordinates on the sky and the way in which the photons have been selected e.g. the bandpass of the filters used. Representation Information is the OAIS term for everything that is needed in order to understand a digital object. A registry would help to ensure that the required Representation Information is available in the future and across disciplines.

24.6.1.1 Next Steps

- Representation Information Registry holding copies of Representation Information of all types which can be shared and enhanced by contributions from many people.
- Virtualisation techniques to facilitate easier integration into contemporary tools

- Preservation features should be embedded in the "creation" environment, automating/facilitating the generation of necessary representation information (data, models, assumptions, configurations, . . .).
- Knowledge Gap Manager which provides a semi-automated way of identifying where additional Representation Information needs to be created, based on information collected by the Orchestrator/Broker
- Processing Context which helps to maintain information about the processing history of a dataset

24.6.1.2 Final Destination

- A set of services, supported over the long term, which make it easier to maintain adequate Representation Information, particularly after active work on the dataset has ceased or slowed. Automated capturing of the creation and processing context.

24.6.1.3 Relevant Projects, Policies, Organisations, Activities

- CASPAR (http://www.casparpreserves.eu/), Planets (http://www.planets-project.eu/), DCC (http://www.dcc.ac.uk/), JISC (http://www.jisc.ac.uk/), OAIS (http://public.ccsds.org/publications/archive/650x0b1.pdf), SHAMAN (http://www.shaman-ip.eu/), nestor (http://www.langzeitarchivierung.de/)

24.6.2 Sharing of Information About Hardware and Software

Ability to share information about the availability of hardware and software and their replacements/substitutes:

> ***SCENARIO***
> *A performing artist finds a masterpiece of (formerly) modern music which requires a signal processing system which used to run on an Apple Macintosh to add a special type of reverberation to the sound. The artist has a number of options including finding the signal processing software together with a working Apple Macintosh, or an emulator running on his/her computer*
>
> *A way to sharing information about hardware and software would facilitate the re-performance of this masterpiece.*

24.6.2.1 Next Steps

- Development and sharing of information about emulation and migration strategies
- Development of orchestrator/broker to share available substitutes

- Acts as (1) a clearing house for demands for Representation Information, (2) for collecting information about changes in availability of hardware, software, environment and changes in the knowledge bases of Designated Communities and, (3) to broker agreements about datasets between the current custodian, which is unable to continue in this role, and an appropriate successor.

24.6.2.2 Final Destination

- A set of services which make it easier to exchange information about obsolescence of hardware and software and techniques for overcoming these.

24.6.2.3 Relevant Projects, Policies, Organisations, Activities

- CASPAR (http://www.casparpreserves.eu/), KEEP (with regard to emulation) (http://www.keep-project.eu), Planets, nestor (http://www.langzeitarchivierung.de/)
- Need for a software archive

24.6.3 Authenticity of a Digital Object

Ability to bring together evidence from diverse sources about the Authenticity of a digital object: Authenticity is not a Boolean concept. It is in general not possible to state that an object is authentic. Instead one can provide evidence on which a judgement may be made about the degree to which a person (or system) may regard an object as what it is purported to be. This evidence will be technical, for example details of what has happened to the object (Provenance) as well as social, for example does one trust the person who was in charge of the system under which the object has been held. In general the provenance information associated with various objects will be encoded according to one of a multitude of different system e.g. CIDOC-CRM (http://cidoc.ics.forth.gr/), OPM (http://openprovenance.org/). There is at minimum a need to be able to interpret and present provenance evidence in a uniform way so that users can make an informed judgment about the degree of belief that a data object is what it is claimed to be. These tools would also facilitate the collection of appropriate evidence.

SCENARIO
A virtual reconstruction of the Taj Mahal created at the start of the twenty first century shows that there has, 50 years later, been subtle damage caused by a local development. The developer disputes this and argues that the digital data on which the virtual reconstruction has been made is not what is claimed. What evidence can and should be provided to support the claims of authenticity and hence save the Taj Mahal? Strong techniques and support tools are needed to allow curators to support claims of authenticity

24.6.3.1 Next Steps

- Develop an authenticity formalism
- Develop international standards and common policies on authenticity and provenance.
- Creation of tools to capture evidence relevant to authenticity
- Develop tools to map provenance to authenticity tools
- Maintain the chain of evidence through (automated) digital audit (provenance) trails by embedding support for capturing knowledge about the actual operations performed

24.6.3.2 Final Destination

- A set of standards and tools through which a user in the future can be provided with evidence on which he/she may judge the degree of Authenticity which may be attributed to a digital object.

24.6.3.3 Relevant Projects, Policies, Organisations, Activities

- CASPAR(http://www.casparpreserves.eu/), SHAMAN (http://www.shaman-ip.eu/), nestor (http://www.langzeitarchivierung.de/)

24.6.4 Digital Rights

Ability to deal with Digital Rights correctly in a changing and evolving environment:

Allow the digital rights associated with an object to be presented in a consistent way, taking into account the changes in legislation. There are several digital rights expression languages in the academic community and commercial world – some are being standardised – the infrastructure must be able to cope with this variety and their evolution and possibly of the underlying rights. An associated problem is the circumstance in which the licence to access the object (or without which the required software is unusable) expires and the originating company no longer exists.

> ***SCENARIO***
> *A piece of software was produced by an inventor and is protected by a user key which must be renewed every year. Several years after the death of the inventor the software is needed by a researcher in another country with a different legal system. What restrictions on usage are there under this rather different system? Even if the software could legally be used, how can the appropriate software key be created?*

A way is needed to be able to handle the link between the rights and restrictions originally associated with the digital object and the legal system under which it is eventually used.

24.6.4.1 Next Steps

- Share information on how constraints, which DRM (Digital Rights Management) systems possibly impose on preservation planning and preservation actions, can be handled under different and changing legal systems
- Develop a dark archive for holding tools to generate licences, which would only be used if and when the commercial supplier is unable to provide this capability

24.6.4.2 Final Destination

- Registry of/Clearinghouse for rights information and dark archive of licensing tools

24.6.4.3 Relevant Policies, Organisations, Activities

- CASPAR (http://www.casparpreserves.eu/), ARROW (Accessible registries of rights information and orphan works towards Europeana) (http://www.arrow-net.eu/), nestor (http://www.langzeitarchivierung.de/), KoLaWiss (http://kolawiss.uni-goettingen.de)

24.6.5 Persistent Identifiers

Need an ID resolver which is really persistent:

There is no shortage of things which are claimed to be Persistent Identifier systems. The issues associated with these are the scalability of the solutions and the longevity of the underlying organisational structure. A name resolving system whose persistence is guaranteed by an international, government based organisation is needed. This could build on one or more existing name resolving systems, strengthening the organisational structures underpinning the resolver.

SCENARIO
A researcher reads a paper in a journal which refers to a dataset which he realises can be re-analysed and combined with some new data he has recently obtained. The paper has an identifier string for the dataset which after some investigation he sees is some sort of a "persistent identifier". Unfortunately the originator of that system is long gone, the DNS entry for the identifier name

resolver system host has lapsed and the database system which was used is not available. A more permanent persistent identifier system is needed which itself has the appropriate longevity with committed long-term financial and social support.

24.6.5.1 Next Steps

- Review the existing persistent identifier systems and their technical, organisation and social underpinnings with respect to longevity and scalability
- Develop or adopt a sufficiently scalable/maintainable identifier system
- Investigate potential organisational underpinnings and the links to, for example, the EU or USA.

24.6.5.2 Final Destination

- An identifier system for locating and cross-referencing digital objects which has adequate organisational, financial and social backing for the very long term which can be used with confidence

24.6.5.3 Relevant Projects Policies, Organisations, Activities:

- DOI (http://www.doi.org/), DNS (Domain Name System), CASPAR (http://www.casparpreserves.eu/), URN (Uniform Resource Name), nestor catalogue of criteria for trusted PI-systems (http://www.langzeitarchivierung.de/), XRI (Extensible Resource Identifier), DPE (http://www.digitalpreservationeurope.eu/)

24.6.6 Transfer of Custody and Brokering Services

Brokering of organisations to hold data and the ability to package together the information needed to transfer information between organisations ready for long term preservation:

Projects and organisations can and do run out of funding for preserving digital holdings, for example projects from Earth Observation (EO) projects are often only funded for 10 years after the closure of the satellite from which the data is derived. There are in the EO case some more or less formal mechanisms for finding a host who could take over responsibility. A brokering/orchestration system is needed to formalise the finding of new hosts.

However even if agreement is reached there is the issue of collecting all the information related to a set of digital objects held, perhaps in a variety of systems, by the original host, and transferring this to the new host, itself with a variety of systems.

OAIS defines in very general terms an Archival Information Package which (logically) contains all the information needed for the long term preservation of a digital object. In addition to the Brokering/Orchestration mentioned above we need to be able to create the AIP so that these can be handed over to the new host.

> ***SCENARIO***
> *An archive finds that its funding agency has been wound-up and the archive must close in 6 months time. Moreover the data holdings are currently in a set of inter-related database tables with embedded binary large objects, and a sophisticated access system with much embedded business logic. How can the archive find someone willing to look after its holdings and how can they be handed over in practice? Although individual repositories tend to have specialised access systems tailored to help their users, attention must also be paid to ensuring that the holdings can be handed over if/when necessary, and appropriate tools and techniques are needed to help do this.*

24.6.6.1 Next Steps

- Create tools for collecting and (logically) packaging information into AIPs using information from a variety of underlying information systems
- Investigate the options for mapping systems from one major system to another.

24.6.6.2 Final Destination

- A system which will allow organisations which are no longer able to fund the preservation of a particular dataset is able to find an organisation willing and able to take over the responsibility. The ultimate fallback could be the Storage Facility (see Sect. 4.8.1.1)

24.6.6.3 Relevant Projects, Policies, Organisations, Activities

- CASPAR (http://www.casparpreserves.eu/), SHAMAN (http://www.shaman-ip.eu/, OAIS http://public.ccsds.org/publications/archive/650x0b1.pdf)

24.6.7 Certified Repositories

Certification process so that one can have confidence about whom to trust to preserve data holdings over the long term:

Although one cannot guarantee anything into the indefinite future there has, for more than a decade, been a demand for an international process for accreditation, auditing and certification of digital repositories, based on an ISO standard.

SCENARIO
A funding agency wishes to instruct its researchers to deposit their data into one or other of the long term archives it will support. This will involve a large and continuing commitment of resources. How can the funder be sure that the archives it wishes to support are up to the job? An internationally recognised certification system would give funders and depositors a way to distinguish and evaluate archives.

24.6.7.1 Next Steps

- Support the development of a set of ISO standards about digital repository audit and certification
- Help set up the organisation and processes to provide accreditation and certification services

24.6.7.2 Final Destination

- An internationally recognised accreditation, audit and certification process with a well defined and long-lived support organisation, with appropriate tools and best practice guides.

24.6.7.3 Relevant Projects, Policies, Organisations, Activities

- Repository Audit and Certification Working Group (http://wiki.digitalrepositoryauditandcertification.org), DCC (http://www.dcc.ac.uk/), DRAMBORA (http://www.repositoryaudit.eu/), OAIS (http://public.ccsds.org/publications/archive/650x0b1.pdf), Alliance for Permanent Access, EU (http://europa.eu/), NSF (http://www.nsf.gov/), JISC (http://www.jisc.ac.uk/), nestor (http://www.langzeitarchivierung.de/)

24.7 Aspects Excluded from This Roadmap

A number of science data related activities have been excluded from this document on the basis that (1) they provide the islands of capabilities and therefore (by definition) are not infrastructure and (2) it is not at all clear that an infrastructure can be created to support these activities, however this must be reviewed. Access methods have not been discussed above because they are expected to be largely provided by GRID-type capabilities, although clearly infrastructure such as persistent identifiers will play an important role in access services.

The list of excluded topics is as follows:

- Specific organisational budgets
- Decisions of what to preserve i.e. appraisal – although clearly some co-ordination would be useful
- Specific domain software
- Specific national legal aspects – although the ability to cope with a variety of these must be built into the infrastructure.

24.7.1 Relevant Documents

- Report on Roadmapping of Large Research Infrastructures, 2008, OECD International Scientific Co-operation (Global Science Forum). Retrieved from http://www.oecd.org/dataoecd/49/36/41929340.pdf
- Understanding Infrastructure: Dynamics, Tensions and Design http://www.si.umich.edu/~pne/PDF/ui.pdf

24.7.2 Implementations

One can see from the above that it is possible to add an extra column to Table 24.1 showing some possible implementations of the solutions.

Many are related to the work reported in this book; others require economic, legal and social aspects to their solution.

24.8 Relationship to Other Infrastructures

Figure 24.5 illustrates one view of the interaction between infrastructure levels.

The model we adopt here is that each organisation (or discipline, or country) forms its own "island of capability", for example a country has its own network connectivity. The infrastructure which we are thinking about is that which connects these "islands". This is consistent with the idea of an infrastructure being something which provides common facilities across for example heterogeneous disciplines.

At the lowest level we have the network layer. Here the infrastructure components are things like interconnects, gateways and internetwork management centres.

The network layer supplies capabilities to the next level up, which consists of "islands of capabilities" of storage and compute power each with its own local authentication and authorisation systems. The infrastructure components are things like resource registries, schedulers, cross-organisation process identifiers and connections between authentication systems.

In turn these supply services to "island of capabilities" of repositories of digitally encoded information which have their own sets of data, users and automated

Table 24.1 Threats and solutions

Threat	Requirements for solution	Example implementations
Users may be unable to understand or use the data e.g. the semantics, format, processes or algorithms involved	Ability to create and maintain adequate representation information	RepInfo toolkit, packager and registry – to create and store representation information. In addition the orchestration manager and knowledge gap manager help to ensure that the RepInfo is adequate
Non-maintainability of essential hardware, software or support environment may make the information inaccessible	Ability to share information about the availability of hardware and software and their replacements/ substitutes	Registry and orchestration manager to exchange information about the obsolescence of hardware and software, amongst other changes. The representation information will include such things as software source code and emulators
The chain of evidence may be lost and there may be lack of certainty of provenance or authenticity	Ability to bring together evidence from diverse sources about the authenticity of a digital object	Authenticity toolkit will allow one to capture evidence from many sources which may be used to judge authenticity
Access and use restrictions may make it difficult to reuse data, or alternatively may not be respected in future	Ability to deal with digital rights correctly in a changing and evolving environment	Digital rights and access rights tools allow one to virtualise and preserve the DRM and access rights information which exist at the time the content information is submitted for preservation
Loss of ability to identify the location of data	An ID resolver which is really persistent	Persistent identifier system: such a system will allow objects to be located over time
The current custodian of the data, whether an organisation or project, may cease to exist at some point in the future	Brokering of organisations to hold data and the ability to package together the information needed to transfer information between organisations ready for long term preservation	Orchestration manager will, amongst other things, allow the exchange of information about datasets which need to be passed from one curator to another
The ones we trust to look after the digital holdings may let us down	Certification process so that one can have confidence about whom to trust to preserve data holdings over the long term (see RAC)	The audit and certification standard to which CASPAR has contributed will allow a certification process to be set up

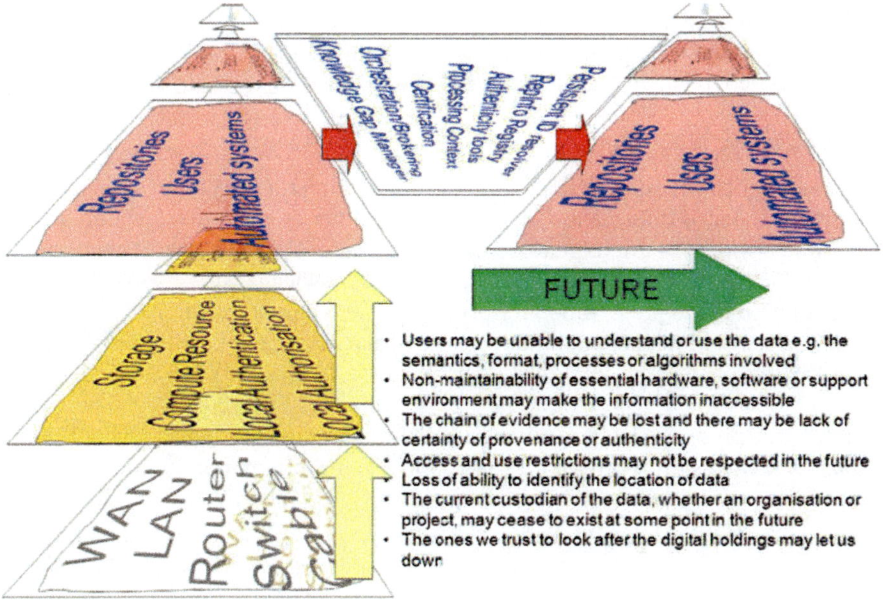

Fig. 24.5 Infrastructure levels

systems. Infrastructure components in this case would be, for example, thesauri, translators and cross-references.

Finally we come to the preservation aspects. Here we imagine there is another stack of levels – much like the current stack but almost certainly implemented in different ways.

By analogy with the other infrastructures we regard the present and future as two "islands of capabilities" which are joined by a number of infrastructure components – which are essentially those described in the previous chapter, with implementations of many described in Chaps. 16 and 17.

24.9 Summary

This short, but important, chapter tries to place the infrastructure needed to support digital preservation in the context of the broader e-science infrastructure (also known as Cyber-infrastructure).

Remember from Sect. 3.4 there are disincentives against digital preservation. Therefore it is beneficial to look not just at controlling costs, which is the focus of Part III, but also to look at increasing the benefits.

In particular it was pointed out in Sect. 3.4.2 that providing benefits for future generations is laudable but insufficient.

Therefore it is pleasing to say that there is a strong argument to support the view that besides being useful for preservation, these components can perform another important function which benefits current users.

The argument is based on the following two observations:

- E-science infrastructure enables users to discover and access a huge amount of digitally encoded information. However the number of resources available must mean that most of these digital resources are unfamiliar to any particular user – in OAIS terms this would be outside the user's Knowledge Base.
- the function of the preservation infrastructures is to ensure that digitally encoded information – which is unfamiliar because of the passage of time and changes in the Knowledge Base.

Therefore the preservation infrastructure makes unfamiliar data understandable and usable – which benefits both future generation and, most importantly, current users also.

Chapter 25
Who Is Doing a Good Job? Audit and Certification

By the CCSDS/ISO RAC working group, led by David Giaretta

Comradeship and trust will emerge naturally when discipline and high standards are enforced.

(***Tao Zhu Gong***)

25.1 Background

The Preserving Digital Information report of the Task Force on Archiving of Digital Information [242] declared,

- a critical component of digital archiving infrastructure is the existence of a sufficient number of trusted organizations capable of storing, migrating, and providing access to digital collections.
- a process of certification for digital archives is needed to create an overall climate of trust about the prospects of preserving digital information.

The issue of certification, and how to evaluate trust into the future, as opposed to a relatively temporary trust which may be more simply tested, has been a recurring request, repeated in many subsequent studies and workshops.

The OAIS Reference Model Open Archival Information System (OAIS) [4], is now adopted as the "de facto" standard for building digital archives [243].

25.1.1 Testability and Key OAIS Concepts

As discussed in Chap. 6 one of the key drivers of OAIS is the need for claims about preservation of digitally encoded information to be testable. These are summarised here and then developed in more detail.

D. Giaretta, *Advanced Digital Preservation*, DOI 10.1007/978-3-642-16809-3_25,

25.1.1.1 Preservation

We need first some methodology by which to test the basic claim that someone is preserving some digitally encoded information; without such a test this is a meaningless claim. OAIS introduces the, quite reasonable, test that the digital object must somehow be useable and understandable in the future. However by itself this is too broad – are we to be forced to ensure that the digitally encoded designs of a battleship are to be understood by everyone, for example a 6 year old child? In order to make this a practical test the obvious next refinement is to describe the type of person – and more particularly their background knowledge – by whom the information should be understandable. Thus OAIS introduces the concept of **Designated Community**, defined as an identified group of potential Consumers who should be able to understand a particular set of information. The Designated Community may be composed of multiple user communities. Note that a Designated Community is defined by the repository and this definition may change/evolve over time.

Bringing these ideas together we can then say, following OAIS, that preserving digitally encoded information means that we must ensure that the information to be preserved is **Independently Understandable** to (and usable by) the Designated Community.

We are clearly concerned about long term preservation, but how long is that? OAIS defines **Long Term** as long enough to be concerned with the impacts of changing technologies, including support for new media and data formats, or with a changing Designated Community. Long Term may extend indefinitely.

25.1.1.2 Definition of the Designated Community

An important clarification is needed here, namely that the definition of the Designated Community is left to the preserver. The same digital object held in different repositories could be being preserved for different Designated Communities, each of which could consist of many disjoint communities.

The quid pro quo is that those funding or entrusting digital objects to the repository can judge whether the definition of the Designated Community is appropriate for their needs.

25.1.1.3 OAIS Conformance

OAIS conformance was discussed in some detail in Sect. 6.1. The standard itself defines conformance in terms of the Information Model and the mandatory responsibilities.

OAIS introduces a number of important concepts and conformance criteria; however this is not enough on which to base a certification scheme. The next section describes some of the factors which must also be taken into consideration.

25.2 TRAC and Related Documents

Section 1.5 of OAIS (the section entitled *Road map for development of related standards*) included an item for accreditation of archives, reflecting the long-standing demand for a standard against which Repositories of digital information may be audited and on which an international accreditation and certification process may be based. It was agreed that RLG and NARA take a lead on this follow-on standard.

A group was gathered by NARA and RLG (the latter subsequently incorporated into OCLC) to form the Task Force on Trusted Digital Repositories. This group produced the Trustworthy Repositories Audit and Certification: Criteria and Checklist [244]. The work combined concepts from OAIS and the Trusted Digital Repositories: Attributes and Responsibilities [245]. The latter allowed the group to supplement OAIS with considerations of financial stability and training of personnel.

The document has a number of metrics grouped into

- Organisational Infrastructure
- Digital Object Management and Technologies
- Technical Infrastructure
- Security.

Accompanying each of the metrics is extensive additional explanatory text and examples of the types of evidence which might be used as proof of fulfilling the metrics. The document has being used as the basis for internal and test audits in a number of repositories, however it is not part of a formal audit and certification process.

Other work in this area includes:

- the German preservation consortium, nestor, has produced a Catalogue of Criteria for Trusted Digital Repositories [246]
- in early 2007 representatives from the Digital Curation Center [3], DigitalPreservationEurope (DPE, http://www.digitalpreservationeurope.eu/), NESTOR (Germany) and the Center for Research Libraries (North America) met and produced a list of 10 core criteria for digital preservation repositories, to guide further international efforts on auditing and certifying repositories [247]. A comparison of this list with the OAIS responsibilities was produced [248].
- Ross et al. [249] produced comments on the TRAC document
- a cross-walk between the TRAC, nestor and Ross documents was produced [250]
- the DCC and DPE projects produced the Digital Repository Audit Method Based on Risk Assessment (DRAMBORA) toolkit. This toolkit is intended to facilitate internal audit by providing repository administrators with a means to assess their capabilities, identify their weaknesses, and recognise their strengths.

All this work has been helpful in providing information and experience in assessing digital repositories, and some provide a local or project-backed certificate of quality. However none provide an ISO based accreditation and certification system of the kind which is available in other areas, such as the one concerning Information Security, based on ISO 27001 series. Without this we cannot expect to have a mark of quality and trustability for digital repositories which is recognised world-wide. Efforts to produce such a system are described next.

25.3 Development of an ISO Accreditation and Certification Process

The development of OAIS was hosted by the Consultative Committee for Space Data Systems [5] and approved by ISO as ISO 14721. OAIS contained a roadmap which listed a number of possible follow-on standards, some of which e.g. the Producer-archive interface – Methodology abstract standard (ISO 20652:2008), have already become ISO standards, after development within CCSDS.

The need for a standard for certification of archives was included in that list and the RLG/NARA work which produced TRAC was the first step in that process. The next step was to bring the output of the RLG/NARA working group back into CCSDS. This has been done and the Digital Repository Audit and Certification (RAC) Working Group [6] has been created, the CCSDS details are available from http://cwe.ccsds.org/moims/default.aspx#_MOIMS-RAC, while the working documents are available from http://wiki.digitalrepositoryauditandcertification.org. Both may be read by anybody but, in order to avoid hackers, only authorised users may add to them. The openness of the development process is particularly important and the latter site contains the notes from the weekly virtual meetings as well as the live working version of the draft standards.

Besides developing the metrics, which started from the TRAC document, the working group also has been working on the strategy for creating the accreditation and certification process. Review of existing systems which have accreditation and certification standard processes it became clear that there was a need for two documents

1. Audit and Certification of Trustworthy Digital Repositories [251]
2. Requirements for bodies providing audit and certification of candidate trustworthy digital repositories. [252]

The first document lists the metrics against which a digital repository may be judged. It is anticipated that this list will be used for internal metrics or peer-review of repositories, as well as for the formal ISO audit process. In addition tools such as DRAMBORA could use these metrics as guidance for its risk assessments.

25.4 Understanding the ISO Trusted Digital Repository Metrics

It is clear that one cannot cover all possible situations in the metrics, nor can one prescribe exactly what each repository must do. This is the case with all types of audits. Instead one must leave a lot to the judgement of the auditors.

To understand the way in which the metrics in *Audit and Certification of Trustworthy Digital Repositories* [251] (referred to below as the "metrics document") were written it is helpful to think about the document in the following way, building it up in the same way that the authors of that document.

A very important thing to understand is that in judging a repository one could look at many types of issues. For example is the restaurant good, is the lighting adequate, is wheelchair access, does the repository respond to requests within 3 min, is it easy to find what one is looking for and so on. However these are not the things against which the repository is to be judged here. Instead we are concerned about how well a repository preserves the digitally encoded information with which it has been entrusted.

With this in mind, one could say that since the audit and certification depends on the judgement of the auditors, the metrics document could have one metric, namely "*Make sure the repository does a good job in preserving its holdings*".

Of course this would not be adequate. We need to provide more guidance for the auditors. Therefore we start by saying "Well at least look at the organisation – make sure it cannot suddenly go out of business, and also make sure that they know how to preserve the digital objects." This one can say that there are two guidelines for auditors:

- Look at the organisation and its finances
- Look at the way it takes care of the digital stuff

In fact there is a third area, which one could argue is part of the second one, namely:

- Make sure that the digital holdings cannot be stolen or otherwise lost.

The reason this third bullet is added is that the repository could undergo a security audit separately (ISO 27000) so that it seemed sensible to provide a separate group which could essentially be replaced by ISO 27000 certification – but such additional certification is definitely not required.

Therefore we have three main headings:

- Organisational Infrastructure
- Digital Object Management
- Infrastructure and Security Risk Management

Continuing this process we can specify the topics where the auditor really needs to be sure to look. The metrics document has the following breakdown:

- Organisational Infrastructure
  - GOVERNANCE & ORGANIZATIONAL VIABILITY
  - ORGANIZATIONAL STRUCTURE & STAFFING
  - PROCEDURAL ACCOUNTABILITY & PRESERVATION POLICY FRAMEWORK
  - FINANCIAL SUSTAINABILITY
  - CONTRACTS, LICENSES, & LIABILITIES
- Digital Object Management
  - INGEST: ACQUISITION OF CONTENT
  - INGEST: CREATION OF THE AIP
  - PRESERVATION PLANNING
  - AIP PRESERVATION
  - INFORMATION MANAGEMENT
  - ACCESS MANAGEMENT
- Infrastructure and Security Risk Management
  - TECHNICAL INFRASTRUCTURE RISK MANAGEMENT
  - SECURITY RISK MANAGEMENT

This breakdown into topics is not unique and indeed several different breakdowns have been tried; this one seemed to fit best.

Looking in even more detail the guidance for the auditors is further split out into metrics. Some of these metrics are broken into sub-metrics indicating that the auditor needs to check these even more specific points; a few of these sub-metrics have some even more specific sub-sub-metrics specified. Even these sub-sub-metrics are not hugely specific – it is still a matter for the judgement of the auditor. Indeed the metrics themselves are a matter of judgement; in this case of course it is the judgement of the working group which produced the metrics.

The following table shows the metrics at the time of writing, showing clearly the metrics and sub-metrics, with number of comments which should be helpful.

Each metric has one or more of the following informative pieces of text associated with it

- Supporting text: giving an explanation of why the metric is important
- Examples of Ways the Repository can Demonstrate it is Meeting this Requirement: providing examples of the evidence which might be examined to test whether the repository satisfies the metric
- Discussion: clarifications about the intent of the metric

Table 25.1 Audit and certification metrics

Comments	Metric
Must have organisational commitment	3 Organizational Infrastructure
	3.1 Governance and Organizational Viability
	3.1.1 The repository shall have a mission statement that reflects a commitment to the preservation of, long term retention of, management of, and access to digital information.
	3.1.2 The repository shall have a Preservation Strategic Plan that defines the approach the repository will take in the long-term support of its mission.
These two are some specific things which are essential parts of such an approach – have a plan and know when to put in into effect.	3.1.2.1 The repository shall have an appropriate, formal succession plan, contingency plans, and/or escrow arrangements in place in case the repository ceases to operate or the governing or funding institution substantially changes its scope.
	3.1.2.2 The repository shall monitor its organizational environment to determine when to execute its formal succession plan, contingency plans, and/or escrow arrangements.
	3.1.3 The repository shall have a Collection Policy or other document that specifies the type of information it will preserve, retain, manage and provide access to.
Must have appropriate organisation and staff	**3.2 Organizational Structure and Staffing**
	3.2.1 The repository shall have identified and established the duties that it needs to perform and shall have appointed staff with adequate skills and experience to fulfil these duties.
These are the essential components of the metric – know what the duties are and have people capable of carrying them out.	3.2.1.1 The repository shall have identified and established the duties that it needs to perform.

Table 25.1 (continued)

	3.2.1.2 The repository shall have the appropriate number of staff to support all functions and services.
	3.2.1.3 The repository shall have in place an active professional development program that provides staff with skills and expertise development opportunities.
These are the policy level requirements – details come later.	**3.3 Procedural Accountability and Preservation Policy Framework**
To have a Designated Community defined is a fundamental requirement	3.3.1 The repository shall have defined its designated community and associated knowledge base(s) and shall have these definitions appropriately accessible.
	3.3.2 The repository shall have Preservation Policies in place to ensure its Preservation Strategic Plan will be met.
The policies must not be static – they must be reviewed	3.3.2.1 The repository shall have mechanisms for review, update, and ongoing development of its Preservation Policies as the repository grows and as technology and community practice evolve
	3.3.3 The repository shall have a documented history of the changes to its operations, procedures, software, and hardware.
	3.3.4 The repository shall commit to transparency and accountability in all actions supporting the operation and management of the repository that affect the preservation of digital content over time.
	3.3.5 The repository shall define, collect, track, and appropriately provide its information integrity measurements.
	3.3.6 The repository shall commit to a regular schedule of self-assessment and external certification.

Table 25.1 (continued)

Money is fundamental – one cannot ask for guarantees about funding for ever, but one can make sure that the repository cannot suddenly go out of business.	**3.4 Financial Sustainability**
	3.4.1 The repository shall have short- and long-term business planning processes in place to sustain the repository over time.
	3.4.2 The repository shall have financial practices and procedures which are transparent, compliant with relevant accounting standards and practices, and audited by third parties in accordance with territorial legal requirements.
	3.4.3 The repository shall have an ongoing commitment to analyze and report on risk, benefit, investment, and expenditure (including assets, licenses, and liabilities).
The repository must ensure that it has appropriate legal authority.	**3.5 Contracts, Licenses, and Liabilities**
	3.5.1 The repository shall have and maintain appropriate contracts or deposit agreements for digital materials that it manages, preserves, and/or to which it provides access.
These are some of the key aspects to the legal authority needed.	3.5.1.1 The repository shall have contracts or deposit agreements which specify and transfer all necessary preservation rights, and those rights transferred shall be documented.
	3.5.1.2 The repository shall have specified all appropriate aspects of acquisition, maintenance, access, and withdrawal in written agreements with depositors and other relevant parties.
	3.5.1.3 The repository shall have written policies that indicate when it accepts preservation responsibility for contents of each set of submitted data objects.
	3.5.1.4 The repository shall have policies in place to address liability and challenges to ownership/rights.
Legal rights and IPR etc change over time and this must be tracked and responded to.	3.5.2 The repository shall track and manage intellectual property rights and restrictions on use of repository content as required by deposit agreement, contract, or license.

Table 25.1 (continued)

This collection of metrics is about the digital objects themselves.	**4 Digital Object Management**
First one must ingest the objects. There are a number of checks which must be made. In addition a number of pieces of information ("metadata") must be captured.	**4.1 Ingest: Acquisition of Content**
The "Information Properties" will be the Transformational Information Properties discussed in Sect. 13.6.	4.1.1 The repository shall identify the Content Information and the Information Properties that the repository will preserve.
	4.1.1.1 The repository shall have a procedure(s) for identifying those Information Properties that it will preserve.
	4.1.1.2 The repository shall have a record of the Content Information and the Information Properties that it will preserve.
This includes such things as Provenance.	4.1.2 The repository shall clearly specify the information that needs to be associated with specific Content Information at the time of its deposit.
Of course the information comes in as SIPs	4.1.3 The repository shall have adequate specifications enabling recognition and parsing of the SIPs.
The producers are a key part of Provenance and the start of the evidence about Authenticity. The repository must be sure of the source of the information.	4.1.4 The repository shall have mechanisms to appropriately verify the identity of the Producer of all materials.
	4.1.5 The repository shall have an ingest process which verifies each SIP for completeness and correctness.

Table 25.1 (continued)

	4.1.6 The repository shall obtain sufficient control over the Digital Objects to preserve them.
	4.1.7 The repository shall provide the producer/depositor with appropriate responses at agreed points during the ingest processes.
There must be records of what happens – part of the Provenance.	4.1.8 The repository shall have contemporaneous records of actions and administration processes that are relevant to content acquisition.
The AIP must be created.	**4.2 Ingest: Creation of the AIP**
There should be some pre-planning for the AIPs	4.2.1 The repository shall have for each AIP or class of AIPs preserved by the repository an associated definition that is adequate for parsing the AIP and fit for long-term preservation needs.
	4.2.1.1 The repository shall be able to identify which definition applies to which AIP.
	4.2.1.2 The repository shall have a definition of each AIP that is adequate for long-term preservation, enabling the identification and parsing of all the required components within that AIP.
	4.2.2 The repository shall have a description of how AIPs are constructed from SIPs.
The repository must be able to show that it has not lost any of the input information (SIPs).	4.2.3 The repository shall document the final disposition of all SIPs.
Of particular concern is to be sure that any SIPs that are not used in AIPs are accounted for.	4.2.3.1 The repository shall follow documented procedures if a SIP is not incorporated into an AIP or discarded and shall indicate why the SIP was not incorporated or discarded.
	4.2.4 The repository shall have and use a convention that generates persistent, unique identifiers for all AIPs.
	4.2.4.1 The repository shall uniquely identify each AIP within the repository.

Table 25.1 (continued)

Persistent Identifiers are quite tricky, as discussed in Sect. 10.3.2. It seems worthwhile to make sure a number of points are checked..	4.2.4.1.1 The repository shall have unique identifiers.
	4.2.4.1.2 The repository shall assign and maintain persistent identifiers of the AIP and its components so as to be unique within the context of the repository.
	4.2.4.1.3 Documentation shall describe any processes used for changes to such identifiers.
	4.2.4.1.4 The repository shall be able to provide a complete list of all such identifiers and do spot checks for duplications.
	4.2.4.1.5 The system of identifiers shall be adequate to fit the repository's current and foreseeable future requirements such as numbers of objects.
	4.2.4.2 The repository shall have a system of reliable linking/resolution services in order to find the uniquely identified object, regardless of its physical location.
Representation Information is key for preservation.	4.2.5 The repository shall have access to necessary tools and resources to provide authoritative Representation Information for all of the digital objects it contains.
There are a number of ways to obtain enough Representation Information. These sub-metrics about at least these aspects of Representation Information.	4.2.5.1 The repository shall have tools or methods to identify the file type of all submitted Data Objects.
	4.2.5.2 The repository shall have tools or methods to determine what Representation Information is necessary to make each Data Object understandable to the Designated Community.
	4.2.5.3 The repository shall have access to the requisite Representation Information.
	4.2.5.4 The repository shall have tools or methods to ensure that the requisite Representation Information is persistently associated with the relevant Data Objects.

Table 25.1 (continued)

PDI is the other key part of the AIP.	4.2.6 The repository shall have documented processes for acquiring Preservation Description Information (PDI) for its associated Content Information and acquire PDI in accordance with the documented processes.
	4.2.6.1 The repository shall have documented processes for acquiring PDI.
	4.2.6.2 The repository shall execute its documented processes for acquiring PDI.
	4.2.6.3 The repository shall ensure that the PDI is persistently associated with the relevant content information.
This is a very important metric – this is where the repository can prove it has done enough in creating the AIP.	4.2.7 The repository shall ensure that the content information of the AIPs is understandable for their designated community at the time of creation of the AIP.
	4.2.7.1 Repository shall have a documented process for testing understandability for their designated communities of the content information of the AIPs at their creation.
	4.2.7.2 The repository shall execute the testing process for each class of content information of the AIPs.
	4.2.7.3 The repository shall bring the content information of the AIP up to the required level of understandability if it fails the understandability testing.
	4.2.8 The repository shall verify each AIP for completeness and correctness at the point it is created.
	4.2.9 The repository shall provide an independent mechanism for verifying the integrity of the repository collection/content.
As before, enough evidence must be collected.	4.2.10 The repository shall have contemporaneous records of actions and administration processes that are relevant to AIP creation.

Table 25.1 (continued)

Having created the AIP, the repository must ensure their preservation.	**4.3 Preservation Planning**
There should be some pre-planning.	4.3.1 The repository shall have documented preservation strategies relevant to its holdings.
Things change and these changes can threaten preservation; the repository must be sure it knows what changes have happened to that it can counter them.	4.3.2 The repository shall have mechanisms in place for monitoring its preservation environment.
	4.3.2.1 The repository shall have mechanisms in place for monitoring and notification when representation information is inadequate for the designated community to understand the data holdings.
The plans which have been made earlier may have to be changed.	4.3.3 The repository shall have mechanisms to change its preservation plans as a result of its monitoring activities.
	4.3.3.1 The repository shall have mechanisms for creating, identifying or gathering any extra representation information required.
This is an absolutely vital metric because here the repository must show that its plans actually work – showing the designated community can understand the digitally encoded information. The discussion associated with this metric says:	4.3.4 The repository shall provide evidence of the effectiveness of its preservation activities.

Table 25.1 (continued)

The repository should be able to demonstrate the continued preservation, including understandability, of its holdings. This could be evaluated at a number of degrees and depends on the specificity of the designated community. If a designated community is fairly broad, an auditor could represent the test subject in the evaluation. More specific designated communities could require significant efforts.	
AIP preservation is a special case of preservation.	**4.4 AIP Preservation**
	4.4.1 The repository shall have specifications for how the AIPs are stored down to the bit level.
	4.4.1.1 The repository shall preserve the content information of AIPs.
	4.4.1.2 The repository shall actively monitor the integrity of AIPs.
	4.4.2 The repository shall have contemporaneous records of actions and administration processes that are relevant to storage and preservation of the AIPs.
	4.4.2.1 The repository shall have procedures for all actions taken on AIPs.
	4.4.2.2 The repository shall be able to demonstrate that any actions taken on AIPs were compliant with the specification of those actions.

Table 25.1 (continued)

Here we want to make sure that the content information can be found.	**4.5 Information Management**
	4.5.1 The repository shall specify minimum information requirements to enable the designated community to discover and identify material of interest.
	4.5.2 The repository shall capture or create minimum descriptive information for each AIP.
	4.5.3 The repository shall create bi-directional linkages between each AIP and its descriptive information.
	4.5.3.1 The repository shall maintain the bi-directional associations between its AIPs and their descriptive information over time.
Access needs to be controlled.	**4.6 Access Management**
	4.6.1 The repository shall comply with access policies.
	4.6.1.1 The repository shall log and review all access management failures and anomalies.
	4.6.2 The repository shall follow policies and procedures that enable the dissemination of digital objects that are traceable to the originals, with evidence supporting their authenticity.
	4.6.2.1 The repository shall record and act upon problem reports about errors in data or responses from users.
In this section the auditor should look at the hardware and software is used. In addition clearly security is vital. One option would be to duplicate the ISO 27000 metrics. However this seems excessive so a minimal set of metrics is specified.	**5 Infrastructure and Security Risk Management**

Table 25.1 (continued)

This sub-section is to ensure the hardware and software is checked by the auditor.	**5.1 Technical Infrastructure Risk Management**
	5.1.1 The repository shall identify and manage the risks to its preservation operations and goals associated with system infrastructure.
	5.1.1.1 The repository shall employ technology watches or other technology monitoring notification systems.
	5.1.1.1.1 The repository shall have hardware technologies appropriate to the services it provides to its designated communities.
	5.1.1.1.2 The repository shall have procedures in place to monitor and receive notifications when hardware technology changes are needed.
	5.1.1.1.3 The repository shall have procedures in place to evaluate when changes are needed to current hardware.
	5.1.1.1.4 The repository shall have procedures, commitment and funding to replace hardware when evaluation indicates the need to do so.
	5.1.1.1.5 The repository shall have software technologies appropriate to the services it provides to its designated communities.
	5.1.1.1.6 The repository shall have procedures in place to monitor and receive notifications when software changes are needed.
	5.1.1.1.7 The repository shall have procedures in place to evaluate when changes are needed to current software.
	5.1.1.1.8 The repository shall have procedures, commitment and funding to replace software when evaluation indicates the need to do so.
	5.1.1.2 The repository shall have adequate hardware and software support for backup functionality sufficient for preserving the repository content and tracking repository functions.
	5.1.1.3 The repository shall have effective mechanisms to detect bit corruption or loss.

Table 25.1 (continued)

	5.1.1.3.1 The repository shall record and report to its administration all incidents of data corruption or loss, and steps shall be taken to repair/replace corrupt or lost data.
	5.1.1.4 The repository shall have a process to record and react to the availability of new security updates based on a risk-benefit assessment.
	5.1.1.5 The repository shall have defined processes for storage media and/or hardware change (e.g., refreshing, migration).
	5.1.1.6 The repository shall have identified and documented critical processes that affect its ability to comply with its mandatory responsibilities.
	5.1.1.6.1 The repository shall have a documented change management process that identifies changes to critical processes that potentially affect the repository's ability to comply with its mandatory responsibilities.
	5.1.1.6.2 The repository shall have a process for testing and evaluating the effect of changes to the repository's critical processes.
	5.1.2 The repository shall manage the number and location of copies of all digital objects.
	5.1.2.1 The repository shall have mechanisms in place to ensure any/multiple copies of digital objects are synchronized.
	5.2 Security Risk Management
	5.2.1 The repository shall maintain a systematic analysis of security risk factors associated with data, systems, personnel, and physical plant.
	5.2.2 The repository shall have implemented controls to adequately address each of the defined security risks.
	5.2.3 The repository staff shall have delineated roles, responsibilities, and authorizations related to implementing changes within the system.
	5.2.4 The repository shall have suitable written disaster preparedness and recovery plan(s), including at least one off-site backup of all preserved information together with an offsite copy of the recovery plan(s).

An example metric with its informative text is:

The repository shall have mechanisms in place for monitoring and notification when Representation Information is inadequate for the Designated Community to understand the data holdings.

Supporting Text

This is necessary in order to ensure that the preserved information remains understandable and usable by the Designated Community.

Examples of Ways the Repository can Demonstrate it is Meeting this Requirement

Subscription to a Representation Information registry service; subscription to a technology watch service, surveys amongst its designated community members, relevant working processes to deal with this information.

Discussion

The repository must show that it has some active mechanism to warn of impending obsolescence. Obsolescence is determined largely in terms of the knowledge base of the Designated Community.

It must be recognised that the audit process cannot be specified in very fine, rigid, detail. An audit process must depend upon the experience and expertise of the auditors. For this reason the second document sets out the system under which the audit process is carried out; in particular the expertise of the auditors and the qualification which they should have is specified. In this way the document specifies how auditors are accredited and thereby helps to guarantee the consistency of the audit and certification process.

There is a hierarchy of ISO standards concerned with good auditing practice [253–256]. The second standard [252] is positioned within this hierarchy in order to ensure that these good practices can be applied to the evaluation of TDRs.

ISO/IEC 17021 [255] is an International Standard which sets out criteria for bodies operating audit and certification of organizations′ management systems. If such bodies are to be accredited as complying with ISO/IEC 17021 with the objective of auditing and certifying Trusted Digital Repositories (TDR) in accordance with [251], some additional requirements and guidance to ISO/IEC 17021 are necessary.

For this reason the RAC Working Group refers to accreditation and certification processes.

The second standard [252] addresses issues arising from applying good audit practice to auditing and certifying whether to what extent digital repositories can be trusted to look after digitally encoded information for the long-term, or at least for the period of their custodianship of that digitally encoded information.

It covers principles needed to inspire confidence that third party certification of the management of the digital repository has been performed with

- impartiality,
- competence,
- responsibility,
- openness,
- confidentiality, and
- responsiveness to complaints

At the time of writing both documents are in an advanced state of preparation; the first of these documents has been submitted for ISO review and the second should be submitted soon. While the reviews are underway further preparations for the accreditation and certification processes will be undertaken. It should be noted that the OAIS reference Model has also been undergoing revision and the new version has been submitted for ISO review. Because of the close links between the metrics and OAIS concepts and terminology it is important that the two remain consistent, and cross-membership of the working groups will ensure this.

In addition to the "central" accreditation body there will be an eventual need for a network of local accreditation and certification bodies.

25.5 Summary

It has been recognised for a long time that there is a need for a way to judge the extent to which an archive can be trusted to preserve digitally encoded information. On the one hand funders of such archives need some formal certification process to provide assurance that their funding is well spent and that their important digital holdings will continue to be usable and understandable into the future. On the other hand it is probably also true that many who manage such archives would want some less formal process.

Considerable work has been carried out on the second of these aims, namely peer or informal certification. The RAC Working Group seems, at the time of writing, to be close to take important steps towards the first aim (formal ISO certification). Difficult organisational issues still need to be addressed but there is a clear roadmap for doing this. Even if all this is put in place the take-up of the process and its impact on, for example, determining the funding of digital repositories is far from guaranteed. However in order to make progress the RAC Working Group believes that the effort must be made.

Chapter 26
Final Thoughts

After reading Part I of this book the reader should have a better idea of the variety of types of digital objects which may need to be preserved, and some of the challenges which will need to be addressed. In particular the reader should be armed with most of the key questions which need to be asked about the digital object to be preserved and the key concepts needed to answer them.

The OAIS Reference Model is quite fundamental to any serious attempts at digital preservation and the reader should now appreciate the important concepts and models of OAIS, and should also appreciate why these are what they are – the hows and whys of OAIS.

While Part II of this book does not provide details of all possible preservation strategies, it should, we hope, provide enough to give the reader the ability to make his or her own judgement about the type of information which must be captured. Perhaps most importantly the reader should be able to use the term "metadata" with a real understanding of the plethora of things which this covers, and even more importantly will be able to avoid being misled when others misuse that term.

In Part III the reader should have gained an insight into how the international audit and certification process will work and the kinds of evidence one needs to present, and the infrastructure required to share the effort needed to preserve digitally encoded information.

Taken as a whole this book should provide the reader with the intellectual tools to ask, and answer, sensible, fundamental questions relevant to the preservation of his/her digital objects.

It may be disconcerting to realise that there are no absolutes: preservation is defined in terms of the Designated Community – which is up to the preserver; authenticity is evaluated according to the evidence and there is not a simple yes/no answer. Nevertheless there is the comfort that everything can be evidence based and that preservation techniques can be tested. Moreover it is possible to identify and counter the things which can change over the course of time.

This book was entitled "Advance Digital Preservation" to distinguish it from the simpler, more limited, approaches. We hope the reader will agree that this title is justified and has fulfilled its aims.

D. Giaretta, *Advanced Digital Preservation*, DOI 10.1007/978-3-642-16809-3_26,

References

1. PARSE. Insight project http://www.parse-insight.eu
2. CASPAR (Cultural, Artistic and Scientific knowledge for Preservation, Access and Retrieval) project, part funded by the EU under contract 033572. Web site http://www.casparpreserves.eu
3. Digital Curation Centre (DCC), part funded by JISC. Web site http://www.dcc.ac.uk
4. Reference Model for an Open Archival System (ISO 14721:2002) http://public.ccsds.org/publications/archive/650x0b1.pdf or later version. At the time of writing the revised version is available at http://public.ccsds.org/sites/cwe/rids/Lists/CCSDS%206500P11/Attachments/650x0p11.pdf or elsewhere on the CCSDS web site http://www.ccsds.org
5. CCSDS (Consultative Committee for Space Data Systems) web site www.ccsds.org
6. Repository Audit and Certification Working Group http://wiki.digitalrepositoryauditandcertification.org
7. Masanès J (ed) (2006) Web Archiving, ISBN-13 978-3-540-23338-5, Springer
8. Gladney HM (2007) Preserving Digital Information, ISBN 978-3-540-37886-0, Springer
9. Deegan M, Tanner S (eds) (2006) Digital Preservation, ISBN-13 978-1-85604-485-1, Facet publishing
10. Brown A (2006) Archiving Websites, ISBN-13 978-1-85604-553-7, Facet publishing
11. Banat-Berger F, Duplouy L, Huc C (2009) L'archivage numérique à long terme, ISBN 978-2-11-006942-9, La documentation Française.
12. Borghoff UM, Rodig P, Scheffczyk J, Schmitz L (2003) Long-Term Preservation of Digital Documents, ISBN-13 978-3-540-33639-6, Springer
13. Aoki K, Fujii N, Kageyama H, Yoshimura K, Ohuchi J, Tusboya T (2008) Durable Media for Long-Term Preservation of Geological Repository Records. Available from http://www.wmsym.org/archives/2008/pdfs/8320.pdf
14. National Science Foundation Cyberinfrastructure Council (2007) Cyberinfrastructure Vision for 21st Century Discovery. Available from http://www.nsf.gov/pubs/2007/nsf0728/nsf0728.pdf
15. Digital digests http://en.wikipedia.org/wiki/Message_digest
16. Vajcner M (2008) The Importance of Context for Digitized Archival Collections. Available from http://mcel.pacificu.edu/jahc/2008/issue1/vajcner.php
17. PADI web site with collection of information about costs of digital preservation http://www.nla.gov.au/padi/topics/5.html
18. Fontaine K, Hunolt G, Booth A, Banks M (2007) Observations on Cost Modelling and Performance Measurement of Long-Term Archives. Presented at PV 2007, Germany. Available from http://www.pv2007.dlr.de/Papers/Fontaine_CostModelObservations.pdf
19. NSF Blue Ribbon Task Force on Sustainable Digital Preservation and Access. Web site http://brtf.sdsc.edu/

D. Giaretta, *Advanced Digital Preservation*, DOI 10.1007/978-3-642-16809-3,

20. Folk M, Sawyer D, Reich L (2000) Thoughts about levels of complexity and specialization in data types and structures for storing scientific data. Available from http://nssdc.gsfc.nasa.gov/nost/fep/levels-layers16.doc
21. GOME (Global Ozone Monitoring Experiment) see http://earth.esa.int/ers/gome/
22. PAIMAS (Producer-Archive Interface Methodology Abstract Standard). Available free from http://public.ccsds.org/publications/archive/651x0b1.pdf
23. PAIS (Producer-Archive Interface Specification). Available from the CCSDS web site (http://www.ccsds.org)
24. International Study on the Impact of Copyright Law on Digital Preservation (2008) http://www.digitalpreservation.gov/library/resources/pubs/docs/digital_preservation_final_report2008.pdf
25. It is Interesting to Note that the Vatican Library has adopted the FITS image data format for digitisation of its 80,000 manuscripts [276] Report of Vatican use of FITS format – see http://www.dariah.eu/index.php?option=com_wordpress&p=27&Itemid=198
26. CEDARS http://www.leeds.ac.uk/cedars/guideto/cdap/guidetocdap.pdf
27. Corney DR, De Vere, M, Folkes, T, Giaretta, D, Kleese van Dam K, Lawrence BN, Pepler SJ, Strong B (2004) Applying the OAIS standard to CCLRC's British Atmospheric Data Centre and the Atlas Petabyte Storage Service. Available from http://home.badc.rl.ac.uk/lawrence/papers/ahm04/CorEA04.pdf
28. American Standard Code for Information Interchange (ASCII) see http://en.wikipedia.org/wiki/ASCII (accessed 2010-01-01)
29. ISO/IEC 8859 see http://en.wikipedia.org/wiki/ISO/IEC_8859 (accessed 2010-0101)
30. The UNICODE Consortium see http://unicode.org/ (accessed 2010-01-01)
31. EISCAT (European Incoherent Scatter) see http://www.eiscat.rl.ac.uk/intro/step-by-step/s13 (accessed 2010-01-01)
32. IEEE 754 see http://en.wikipedia.org/wiki/IEEE_754-2008 (accesses 2010-01-01)
33. CCSDS Data Description Language EAST – List of Conventions, CCSDS 646.0-G-1 (1997). See http://public.ccsds.org/publications/archive/646x0g1.pdf (accessed 2010-01-01)
34. SITOOLS web site http://vds.cnes.fr/sitools/index.html
35. UTF-8 (8-bit UCS/Unicode Transformation Format) http://en.wikipedia.org/wiki/UTF-8 (accessed 2010-01-01)
36. Backus Naur Form (BNF) http://en.wikipedia.org/wiki/Backus%E2%80%93Naur_Form (accessed 2010-01-01)
37. Extended Backus Naur Form (BNF) http://en.wikipedia.org/wiki/Extended_Backus%E2%80%93Naur_Form (accessed 2010-01-01)
38. Extensible Markup Language (XML) http://www.w3.org/XML/ (accessed 2010-01-01)
39. Yacc Yet Another Compiler-Compiler http://dinosaur.compilertools.net/yacc/ (accessed 2010-01-01)
40. Java Compiler Compiler https://javacc.dev.java.net/ (accessed 2010-01-01)
41. ISO/IEC 9899 – Programming languages – C http://www.open-std.org/jtc1/sc22/wg14/www/standards (accessed 2010-01-01)
42. The Perl Programming Language http://www.perl.org/ (accessed 2010-01-01)
43. POSIX (Portable Operating System Interface [for Unix]) http://en.wikipedia.org/wiki/POSIX (accessed 2010-01-01)
44. TIFF (Tagged Image File Format) http://partners.adobe.com/public/developer/tiff
45. NetCDF (network Common Data Form) http://www.unidata.ucar.edu/software/netcdf/
46. FITS (Flexible Image Transport System) http://fits.gsfc.nasa.gov/
47. EAST support web site http://east.cnes.fr/
48. Development of EAST Based Access Tools – the BEST toolkit http://debat.c-s.fr/
49. CDPP (Centre de Données de Physique des Plasmas) http://cdpp.cesr.fr/
50. Data Request Broker – DRB http://www.gael.fr/drb/
51. XML Schema – http://www.w3.org/XML/Schema
52. XQuery 1.0 An XML Query Language W3C Recommendation 23 January 2007 – http://www.w3.org/TR/xquery/

53. XML Path Language (XPath) Version 1.0 – http://www.w3.org/TR/xpath
54. PRONOM web site http://www.nationalarchives.gov.uk/PRONOM/Default.aspx
55. MIME type (Multipurpose Internet Mail Extensions) http://www.iana.org/assignments/media-types/
56. Magic numbers http://en.wikipedia.org/wiki/Magic_number_%28programming%29
57. MAGIC file format http://linux.die.net/man/5/magic
58. Dunckley M, Rankin S (2007). The Use of File Description Languages for File Format Identification and Validation. Paper presented at PV 2007. Available from http://www.pv2007.dlr.de/Papers/Dunckley_fileFormatIdentification.pdf
59. DROID web site http://droid.sourceforge.net/
60. JHOVE – JSTOR/Harvard Object Validation Environment web site http://hul.harvard.edu/jhove/
61. Data Entity Dictionary Specification Language (DEDSL) Abstract specification http://public.ccsds.org/publications/archive/647x1b1.pdf
62. DEDSL XML/DTD syntax http://public.ccsds.org/publications/archive/647x3b1.pdf
63. ISO 11179 http://*"metadata"*-stds.org/11179/ and http://en.wikipedia.org/wiki/ISO/IEC_11179
64. DCC/CASPAR registry http://registry.casparpreserves.eu
65. JPEG – length standard/ Specification. http://www.w3.org/Graphics/JPEG/itu-t81.pdf INFORMATION TECHNOLOGY – DIGITAL COMPRESSION AND CODING OF CONTINUOUS-TONE STILL IMAGES – REQUIREMENTS AND GUIDELINES – Includes structural description and methods for working with JPEG images
66. W3C HTML 4.01 Specification page http://www.w3.org/TR/html4/ and XHTML2 Working Group Home Page http://www.w3.org/MarkUp/
67. Buneman OP, Khanna S, Tan W-C. On the Propagation of Deletions and Annotations through Views. Proceedings of 21st ACM Symposium on Principles of Database Systems.
68. http://www.dlib.org/dlib/october00/granger/10granger.html
69. Giaretta D, Weaver H (eds) (2005) Warwick workshop report. Available from http://www.dcc.ac.uk/events/warwick_2005/Warwick_Workshop_report.pdf
70. Java AWT Image Class documentation http://java.sun.com/j2se/1.4.2/docs/api/java/awt/Image.html
71. JTable interface documentation http://java.sun.com/j2se/1.4.2/docs/api/javax/swing/JTable.html
72. TOPCAT application web site http://www.star.bris.ac.uk/~mbt/topcat/
73. CSV (Comma-separated value) format http://en.wikipedia.org/wiki/Comma-separated_values
74. VOTable definition http://www.ivoa.net/Documents/VOTable/
75. Java TreeModel interface http://java.sun.com/javase/7/docs/api/javax/swing/tree/TreeModel.html
76. Multivalent browser http://multivalent.sourceforge.net/
77. W3C Document Object Model http://www.w3.org/DOM/
78. W3C DOM Java interface http://java.sun.com/j2se/1.4.2/docs/api/org/w3c/dom/package-summary.html
79. Wikipedia. Accessed July 24 2010 http://en.wikipedia.org/wiki/Emulator
80. SIMH is a highly portable, multi-system simulator – http://simh.trailing-edge.com/
81. IBM 709 Computer Mainframe – http://www-03.ibm.com/ibm/history/exhibits/mainframe/mainframe_PP709.html
82. See http://www.clir.org/pubs/reports/rothenberg/pub77.pdf or http://www.kb.nl/pr/publ/usingemulation.pdf and http://iwaw.europarchive.org/05/papers/iwaw05-hoeven.pdf
83. Burnet M, Supnik R (1996) Preserving Computing's Past: Restoration and Simulation. Digital Technical Journal, 8 (3)
84. Digital Simulator – http://web.mit.edu/ara/www/ds.html
85. An overview of Electronic Design Automation (EDA) -http://en.wikipedia.org/wiki/Electronic_design_automation

86. Intel® 64 and IA-32 Architectures Software Developer's Manuals – http://www.intel.com/products/processor/manuals/index.htm
87. VMware virtualisation products – http://www.vmware.com/
88. Xen virtualisation products – http://www.xen.org/
89. UVC (Universal Virtual Computer) http://www.nla.gov.au/padi/topics/492.html
90. Java Virtual Machine Specification http://java.sun.com/docs/books/jvms/
91. The UVC: a method for preserving digital documents, proof of concept. Available from http://www.kb.nl/hrd/dd/dd_onderzoek/reports/4-uvc.pdf
92. Digital Asset Preservation Tools – based on UVC – http://www.alphaworks.ibm.com/tech/uvc
93. QEMU – a generic and open source machine emulator and virtualiser. -http://www.nongnu.org/qemu/
94. Bochs – is a highly portable open source IA-32 (x86) PC emulator written in C++, that runs on most popular platforms. – http://bochs.sourceforge.net/
95. JPC – is a pure Java emulation of an x86 PC hardware in software -http://www-jpc.physics.ox.ac.uk/home_home.html
96. Dioscuri – the modular emulator – http://dioscuri.sourceforge.net/
97. van der Hoeven J, van Wijngaarden H, Verdegem R, Slats J (2005) Emulation – a viable preservation strategy. Available from http://www.kb.nl/hrd/dd/dd_projecten/Emulation_research_KB_NA_2005.pdf
98. van der Hoeven J, van Wijngaarden H (2005) Modular emulation as a long-term preservation strategy for digital objects. Paper presented at the International Web Archiving Workshop (IWAW'05), Vienna, Austria, 2005. Available from http://www.iwaw.net/05/papers/iwaw05-hoeven.pdf
99. Java Virtual Machine specification – http://java.sun.com/docs/books/jvms/
100. The Java Language Specification, Third Edition – http://java.sun.com/docs/books/jls/third_edition/html/j3TOC.html
101. Java 1.6 API – http://java.sun.com/javase/6/docs/api/
102. J2SE Compatibility Test Sources Released, Graham Hamilton's Blog – http://weblogs.java.net/blog/kgh/archive/2004/12/j2se_compatibil.html
103. OpenJDK Community TCK License Agreement V 1.1. Available from http://openjdk.java.net/legal/openjdk-tck-license.pdf
104. OpenJDK, see http://en.wikipedia.org/wiki/OpenJDK
105. Common Language Infrastructure (CLI), ECMA 335 and ISO/IEC 23271:2006 -http://www.ecma-international.org/publications/standards/Ecma-335.htm
106. List of CLI languages – Wikipedia article http://en.wikipedia.org/wiki/List_of_CLI_Languages
107. Mono – http://www.mono-project.com/Main_Page
108. Davidson SB, Freire J (2008) Provenance and scientific workflows: challenges and opportunities. In: Procs of the 2008 ACM SIGMOD International Conference on Management of Data, pages 1345–1350. ACM.
109. Sunagawa E, Kozaki K, Kitamura Y, Mizoguchi R (2003) An Environment for Distributed Ontology Development Based on Dependency Management. In: Procs of the 2nd International Semantic Web Conference (ISWC'03), pages 453–468.
110. Fox MS, Huang J (2003) Knowledge provenance: An approach to modelling and maintaining the evolution and validity of knowledge. EIL Technical Report, University of Toronto. Available from http://www.eil.utoronto.ca/km/papers/fox-kp1.pdf
111. Bobb N, Brandt SA, Hiatt A, Maltzahn C, Miller EL, Neeman A, Tuteja D (2005). Richer file system metadata using links and attributes. In: Procs of the 22nd IEEE/13th NASA Goddard Conference on Mass Storage Systems and Technologies (MSST'05), Monterey, California, April 2005.
112. Belguidoum M, Dagnat F (2007) Dependency Management in Software Component Deployment. In: Electronic Notes in Theoretical Computer Science, 182:17–32.

113. Franch X, Maiden NAM (2003) Modelling Component Dependencies to Inform their Selection. In :Procs of the 2nd International Conference on COTS-Based Software Systems, Springer.
114. Vieira M, Dias M, Richardson DJ (2001) Describing Dependencies in Component Access Points. In: Procs of the 23rd International Conference on Software Engineering (ICSE'01), Toronto, Canada, pages 115–118.
115. Vieira M, Richardson D (2002) Analyzing dependencies in large component-based systems. In: Procs of the 17th IEEE International Conference on Automated Service Engineering, ASE'02. Los Alamitos, CA, USA, 2002. IEEE Computer Society.
116. Walter M, Trinitis M, Karl W (2001) OpenSESAME: an intuitive dependability modelling environment supporting inter-component dependencies. In: Procs of Pacific Rim International Symposium on Dependable Computing, 76–83.
117. Tzitzikas Y, Marketakis Y, Antoniou G (2010) Task-based Dependency Managemt for the Preservation of Digital Objects using Rules. In: Procs of the 6th Hellenic Conference on Artificial Intelligence (SETN'10), Athens, Greece, May, 2010
118. Wikipedia Article About Datalog http://en.wikipedia.org/wiki/Datalog
119. Tzitzikas Y, Flouris G (2007) Mind the (Intelligibily) Gap. In: Procs of the 11th European Conference on Research and Advanced Technology for Digital Libraries, (ECDL'07), Budapest, Hungary, September 2007. Springer-Verlag.
120. Kakas AC, Kowalski RA, Toni F (1998) The Role of Abduction in Logic Programming. In: Handbook of Logic in Artificial Intelligence and Logic Programming: Logic programming, page 235
121. Console L, Dupre DT, Torasso P (1991). On the relationship between abduction and deduction. In: Journal of Logic and Computation. 1(5):661
122. Eiter T, Gottlob G (1995) The complexity of logic-based abduction. In: Journal of the ACM (JACM), 42(1):3–42.
123. PreScan Tool web site http://www.ics.forth.gr/prescan
124. Open Provenance Model (OPM) see http://openprovenance.org/
125. Moreau L, Freire J, Myers J, Furelle J, Paulson P (2007) The Open Provenance Model, University of Southampton.
126. Theodoridou M, Tzitzikas Y, Doerr M, Marketakis Y, Melessanakis V (2010) Modelling and Querying Provenance by Extending CIDOC CRM. Journal of Distributed and Parallel Databases, 27:169–210.
127. Christiansen H, Dahl V (2004) Assumptions and abduction in Prolog. In: 3rd International Workshop on Multiparadigm Constraint Programming Languages, MultiCPL, Saint-Malo, France, September 2004
128. Christiansen H, Dahl V (2005) HYPROLOG: A new logic programming language with assumptions and abduction. In: Lecture Notes in Computer Science, 3668:159–173, 2005.
129. Horrocks I, Patel-Schneider PF, Boley H, Tabet S, Grosof B, Dean M (2004) SWRL: A Semantic Web Rule Language Combining OWL and RuleML, May 2004. Available from http://www.w3.org/Submission/SWRL/.
130. Arecibo Message http://en.wikipedia.org/wiki/Arecibo_message
131. Song S, JaJa J (2007) ACE: a Novel Software Platform to Ensure the Long Term Integrity of Digital Archives. Available from http://www.umiacs.umd.edu/~joseph/ace-archiving07.pdf
132. DCC Workshop on Persistent Identifiers. Available at http://www.dcc.ac.uk/events/pi-2005/
133. Archival Resource Key (ARK) http://www.ietf.org/internet-drafts/draft-kunze-ark-09.txt
134. N2T (Name-To-Thing resolver) http://n2t.info/
135. PURL (Persistent Uniform Resource Locators) http://purl.org
136. Handle System web site http://www.handle.net/
137. DOI (Digital Object Identifier system) http://www.doi.org/
138. UUID (Universally Unique IDentifier) http://www.ietf.org/rfc/rfc4122.txt

139. PREMIS – http://www.loc.gov/standards/premis/
140. Foster I, Vöckler J, Wilde M, Zhao Y (2002) Chimera: A Virtual Data System for Representing, Querying, and Automating Data Derivation. Available from http://citeseerx.ist.psu.edu/viewdoc/summary?doi=10.1.1.19.9995
141. Barkstrom B (2010) Earth Science Informatics: A mathematical framework for earth science data provenance tracing. Available from http://www.springerlink.com/content/v5642126m57322q5/)
142. ZIP file format http://en.wikipedia.org/wiki/ZIP_(file_format)
143. IMS content packaging http://www.imsglobal.org/content/packaging/
144. SOAP (Simple Object Access Protocol) http://xml.coverpages.org/soap.html
145. METS -Metadata Encoding and Transmission Standard http://www.loc.gov/standards/mets/
146. XFDU (XML Formatted Data Unit) Structure and Construction Rules (2008). Available from http://public.ccsds.org/publications/archive/661x0b1.pdf
147. Standard Archive Format for Europe (SAFE) – details available from http://earth.esa.int/SAFE/
148. XFDU web site http://sindbad.gsfc.nasa.gov/xfdu/
149. GAEL XFDU web site http://www.gael.fr/xfdu/site/
150. InterPARES Project http://www.interpares.org
151. InterPARES Project, Authenticity Task Force, Requirements for Assessing and Maintaining the Authenticity of Electronic Records, March 2002 (http://www.interpares.org)
152. Cedars project, http://www.leeds.ac.uk/cedars/
153. Sergeant D (2002) Interpretation of the OAIS Model. Available from http://www.erpanet.org/events/2002/copenhagen/presentations/dmserpanet.ppt
154. OCLC/RLG Working Group on Preservation *"metadata"*, 2002, Preservation *"metadata"* and the OAIS Information Model, A *"metadata"* Framework to Support the Preservation of Digital Objects. Retrieved from http://www.oclc.org/research/projects/pmwg/pm_framework.pdf
155. Hedstrom M, Lee CA (2002) Significant properties of digital objects: definitions, applications, implications. Proceedings of the DLM-Forum. Available from http://ec.europa.eu/transparency/archival_policy/dlm_forum/doc/dlm-proceed2002.pdf
156. Wilson A (2007) Significant Properties Report. Available from http://www.significantproperties.org.uk/documents/wp22_significant_properties.pdf
157. Coyne M, Duce D, Hopgood B, Mallen G, Stapleton M (2007) The Significant Properties of Vector Images. JISC report, 27 November 2007. Available from http://www.jisc.ac.uk/media/documents/programmes/preservation/vector_images.pdf
158. Coyne M, Stapleton M (2008) The Significant Properties of Moving Images. JISC report, 26 March 2008. Available from http://www.jisc.ac.uk/media/documents/programmes/preservation/spmovimages_report.pdf
159. Matthews B, McIlwrath B, Giaretta D, Conway E (2008) The Significant Properties of Software: A Study. JISC report, March 2008. Available from http://www.jisc.ac.uk/media/documents/programmes/preservation/spsoftware_report_redacted.pdf
160. Ashley K, Davis R, Pinsent E (2008) Significant Properties of E-learning Objects. JISC report, March 2008. Available from http://www.jisc.ac.uk/media/documents/programmes/preservation/spelos_report.pdf
161. PARADIGM project, Workbook on Digital Private Papers. http://www.paradigm.ac.uk/workbook/preservation-strategies/file-properties.html
162. Knight G (2008) Framework for the definition of significant properties. Available from http://www.significantproperties.org.uk/documents/wp33-propertiesreport-v1.pdf
163. Rothenberg J, Bikson T (1999) Carrying Authentic, Understandable and Usable Digital Records Through Time. Report to the Dutch National Archives and Ministry of the Interior. Available from http://www.digitaleduurzaamheid.nl/bibliotheek/docs/final-report_4.pdf
164. Wilson A (2008) Significant Properties of Digital Objects. Presented at "What to preserve? Significant Properties of Digital Objects". Available from http://www.dpconline.org/docs/events/080407sigpropsWilson.pdf

165. DELOS Digital Preservation Testbed. Retrieved from http://www.ifs.tuwien.ac.at/dp/testbed.html
166. Digital Curation Centre SCARP project http://www.dcc.ac.uk/scarp/
167. Science and Technology Facilities Council http://www.stfc.ac.uk/
168. British Atmospheric Data Centre http://badc.nerc.ac.uk/home/index.html
169. World Data Centre for Solar Terrestrial Physics www.ukssdc.ac.uk/wdcc1/wdc_menu.html
170. European Incoherent Scatter Radar http://www.eiscat.rl.ac.uk
171. Drambora http://www.repositoryaudit.eu/
172. PLATTER http://www.digitalpreservationeurope.eu/platter/
173. Planets http://www.planets-project.eu/
174. Plato http://www.ifs.tuwien.ac.at/dp/plato/intro.html
175. CASPAR Questionnaire http://www.casparpreserves.eu/Members/cclrc/ReferenceDocuments/caspar-test-case-questionnaire/
176. CASPAR Ionosonde Case Study http://www.casparpreserves.eu/other-caspar-products/other-caspar-products/ionosonde-case-study.pdf
177. The Natural Environment Research Council (NERC) Mesosphere-Stratosphere-Troposphere (MST) Radar at Aberystwyth http://mst.nerc.ac.uk/
178. Dioscuri on Sourceforge http://dioscuri.sourceforge.net/
179. NASA Ames http://badc.nerc.ac.uk/help/formats/NASA-Ames/
180. NetCDF Document Library http://www.unidata.ucar.edu/software/NetCDF/docs/
181. Conway E (2009) Curating Atmospheric Data for long term use: Infrastructure and Preservation Issues for the Atmospheric Sciences community. Digital Curation Centre Scarp project case study
182. Conway E, Dunckley M (2009) Preservation Network Models: Creating Stable Networks of Information to Ensure the Long Term use of Scientific Data. In: Proceeding Ensuring Long-Term Preservation and Adding Value to Scientific and Technical Data (PV 2009), Villafranca del Castillo, Madrid, Spain, 01–03 Dec 2009
183. Conway E, Giaretta D, Dunckley M (2009) Curating scientific research data for the long term: A preservation analysis method in context. In: Proceeding 6th International Conference on Preservation of Digital Objects (iPres 2009) San Francisco
184. Matthews B, Shaon A, Bicarregui J, Jones C, Woodcock J, Conway E (2009) Towards a methodology for software preservation In proceedings of iPres 2009, The 6th International Conference on Preservation of Digital Objects
185. Marketakis Y, Tzanakis M, Tzitzikas Y (2009) PreScan: Towards Automating the Preservation of Digital Objects. In: Procs of the International ACM Conference on Management of Emergent EcoSystems (MEDES'09), pp 404–411, Lyon, France, October, 2009.
186. Factor M, Naor D, Rabinovici-Cohen S, Ramati L, Reshef P, Satran J (2007) The Need for Preservation Aware Storage – A Position Paper. ACM SIGOPS Operating Systems Review. Special Issue on File and Storage Systems, 41(1): pages 19–23, (Jan 2007).
187. Factor M, Naor D, Rabinovici-Cohen S, Ramati L, Reshef P, Ronen S, Satran J, Giaretta D (2008) Preservation DataStores: New storage paradigm for preservation environments. IBM Journal of Research and Development on Storage Technologies and Systems, 52, Number 4/5).
188. PDS on alphaWorks – http://www.alphaworks.ibm.com/tech/pds
189. Factor M, Naor D, Rabinovici-Cohen S, Ramati L, Reshef P, Satran J, Giaretta D (2007) Preservation DataStores: Architecture for Preservation Aware Storage. Proceedings of the IEEE Conference on Mass Storage Systems and Technologies (MSST), September 24–27, 2007, San Diego, USA.
190. XAM, the eXtensible Access Method – see http://www.snia.org/forums/xam/
191. International Committee for Information Technology Standards (formerly NCITS), SCSI Object-Based Storage Device Commands (OSD). Document Number: ANSI/INCITS 400–2004.

192. Factor M, Meth K, Naor D, Rodeh O, Satran J (2005) Object storage: The future building block for storage systems – a position paper. Paper presented at Local to Global Data Interoperability – Challenges and Technologies, Sardinia Italy
193. Dunckley M, Ronen S, Henis E, Rabinovici-Cohen S, Reshef P, Giaretta D, Conway E (2010) Using XFDU for CASPAR Information Packaging. Accepted to OCLC Systems & Services: International Digital Library Perspectives.
194. Henis E, Rabinovici-Cohen S, Reshef P, Ronen S (2009) A System and Method for Managing Representation Information in a Preservation Data System. Available from http://www.priorartdatabase.com/IPCOM/000183331/
195. Factor M, Henis E, Naor D, Rabinovici-Cohen S, Reshef P, Ronen S, Michetti G, Guercio M (2009) Authenticity and Provenance in Long Term Digital Preservation: Modelling and Implementation in Preservation Aware Storage. Paper presented at TaPP '09. First Workshop on the Theory and Practice of Provenance. San Francisco, 23 February 2009, http://www.usenix.org/event/tapp09/tech/full_papers/factor/factor.pdf
196. Babich A, Henis E, Rabinovici-Cohen S, Ronen S (2009) A Method for Storing of Preservation Objects in an Enterprise Content Management (ECM) System. Available from http://priorartdatabase.com/IPCOM/000188067
197. Content Management Interoperability Services v 1.0 OASIS standard see http://docs.oasis-open.org/cmis/CMIS/v1.0/os/cmis-spec-v1.0.pdf
198. iRODS: Intelligent Rule-Oriented Data System, San Diego Supercomputer Center (SDSC); see http://irods.sdsc.edu/index.php/Main_Page.
199. SNIA Long Term Retention (LTR) technical working group. See https://www.snia.org/apps/org/workgroup/ltrtwg/
200. DAMS Leaflet. Available from http://developers.casparpreserves.eu/DAMS/res/DAMS&DRMleaflet.pdf
201. DAMS Specification. Available from http://developers.casparpreserves.eu/DAMS/res/DAMS-Spec-Ref-1.1.pdf
202. DRM Leaflet. Available from http://developers.casparpreserves.eu/DRM/res/DAMS&DRMleaflet.pdf
203. CASPAR DRM Specification. Available at http://developers.casparpreserves.eu/DRM/res/DRM-Spec-Ref-1.1.pdf
204. CASPAR FIND Component Specification. Available from http://www.alliancepermanentaccess.org/caspar/implementation/FindingAids-Spec-Ref-1.0.pdf
205. CASPAR PACK Specification. Available from http://www.alliancepermanentaccess.org/caspar/implementation/PACKAGE_-Spec-Ref-v1_5.doc
206. CASPAR D4101: User requirements and scenario specifications (CASPAR-D4101-SCEN-0101-1_0). Available from www.casparpreserves.eu/Members/metaware/Deliverables/user-requirements-and-scenario-specifications/at_download/file
207. CASPAR D2201: Preservation DataStore Interface (CASPAR-D2201-TN-0101-1_0). Available from www.casparpreserves.eu/Members/cclrc/Deliverables/preservation-datastore-interface/at_download/file
208. CASPAR D4101 User requirements and scenario specifications http://www.casparpreserves.eu/Members/metaware/Deliverables/integrated-report-of-r-d-activities-on-the-cultural-performing-arts-and-science-data-preservation-activities/at_download/file
209. CASPAR deliverables http://www.casparpreserves.eu/caspar-project/deliverables
210. Minolta VI scanner http://www.konicaminolta.com/sensingusa/products/3d/non-contact/vivid910/index.html
211. PLY file format http://en.wikipedia.org/wiki/PLY_%28file_format%29
212. PLY File Format http://local.wasp.uwa.edu.au/~pbourke/dataformats/ply/
213. Meshlab http://meshlab.sourceforge.net
214. Canon EOS 350D camera http://www.canon.co.uk/for_home/product_finder/cameras/digital_slr/eos_350d/index.asp?specs=1
215. TexAlign http://vcg.isti.cnr.it/joomla/index.php?option=com_content&task=view&id=221&Itemid=48

216. Virtual Inspector http://vcg.isti.cnr.it/Publications/2008/CPCS08/Inspector_IEEECGA_07.pdf
217. UNESCO, *Convention concerning the protection of the world cultural and natural heritage*, 17th Session General Conference, 16 November 1972, Paris
218. http://vcg.isti.cnr.it/ Visual Computing Lab informal *"metadata"* for the scanning archiving
219. ESRI Grid file format http://en.wikipedia.org/wiki/ESRI_grid
220. ESRI SHP file format http://www.esri.com/library/whitepapers/pdfs/shapefile.pdf
221. www.leeds.ac.uk/icsrim/caspar/
222. Ng K (ed) (2006) Proceedings of the COST287-ConGAS 2nd International Symposium on Gesture Interface for Multimedia Systems (GIMS2006), 9-10 May 2006, Leeds, UK. Available from http://www.i-maestro.org/documenti/view_documenti.php?doc_id=1052
223. Ng K, Nasi P (eds) (2008) Interactive Multimedia Music Technologies IGI Global, Information Science Reference, Library of Congress 2007023452, 2008.
224. Young D, Nunn P, Vassiliev A.(2006) Composing for Hyperbow: A Collaboration between MIT and the Royal Academy of Music. In: Proceeding of the New Interfaces for Musical Expression International Conference (NIME). Paris, France
225. Overholt D (2005) The Overtone Violin. In: Proceeding of the International Conference on New Interfaces for Musical Expression. Vancouver, BC, Canada
226. Lévy B, Ng K (2008) Audio-driven Augmentations for the Cello. In: Proceeding of the 4th i-Maestro Workshop on Technology-Enhanced Music Education, co-located with the 8th International Conference on New Interfaces for Musical Expression (NIME 2008), Genova, Italy, ISBN: 978 0 85316 269 8, pages. 15–20, 4 June 2008
227. MvM. Music via Motion, http://www.kcng.org/mvm or http://www.leeds.ac.uk/icsrim/mvm
228. Ng K (2004) Music via Motion: Transdomain Mapping of Motion and Sound for Interactive Performances. In: Proceedings of the IEEE, vol. 92, 2004.
229. Nagashima Y (2003) Bio-Sensing Systems and Bio-Feedback Systems for Interactive Media Arts. In: Proceeding of the New Interfaces for Musical Expression Inter-national Conference (NIME-03). Montreal, Canada
230. Ng K, Weyde T, Larkin O, Neubarth K, Koerselman T, Ong B (2007) 3D Augmented Mirror: A Multimodal Interface for String In-strument Learning and Teaching with Gesture Support. In: Proceeding of the 9th International Conference on Multimodal Interfaces, Nagoya, Japan, pages. 339–345, ISBN: 978-1-59593-817-6, ACM, SIGCHI, DOI: http://doi.acm.org/10.1145/1322192.1322252
231. Ng K, Ong B, Weyde T, Neubarth K (2008) Interactive Multimedia Technology-Enhanced Learning for Music with i-Maestro. In: Proceeding of ED-MEDIA 2008 World Conference on Education Multimedia, Hypermedia & Telecommunications, Vienna, Austria, 30 June – 4 July 2008.
232. Ng K (ed) (2008) Proceedings of the 4th i-Maestro Workshop on Technology-Enhanced Music Education, co-located with the 8th International Conference on New Interfaces for Musical Expression (NIME 2008), Genova, Italy, ISBN: 978 0 85316 269 8, 4 June 2008. Available from http://www.i-maestro.org/workshop/
233. Bradshaw D, Ng K (2008) Tracking Conductors Hand Movements Using Multiple Wiimotes. In: Proceeding of the International Conference on Automated Solutions for Cross Media Content and Multi-channel Distribution (AXMEDIS 2008), Florence, Italy, pages. 93–99, Digital Object Identifier 10.1109/AXMEDIS.2008.40, IEEE Computer Society Press, ISBN: 978-0-7695-3406-0. 4. 17–19 Nov. 2008.
234. Bradshaw D, Ng K (2008). Analyzing a Conductor's Gestures with the Wii-mote. In: Proceeding of EVA London 2008: the International Conference of Electronic Visualisation and the Arts, British Computer Society, 5 Southampton Street, London WC2E 7HA, UK, 22-24 July 2008.
235. Ng K, Pham TV, Ong B, Mikroyannidis A, Giaretta D (2008) Preservation of interactive multimedia performances, International Journal of Metadata Semanticssemantics and Ontologies, 3(3) 183–196. doiDOI: 10.1504/IJMSO.2008.023567. 2009.

236. Ng K, Mikroyannidis A, Ong B, Bonardi A, Barthélemy J, Ciavarella R, Boutard G (2008) Ontology Management for Preservation of Interactive Multimedia Performances. In: Proceeding of the International Computer Music Conference (ICMC), Belfast, 24–29 August 2008.
237. Gill T (2004) Building semantic bridges between museums, libraries and archives: The CIDOC Conceptual Reference Model. First Monday, 9
238. Doerr M (2003) The CIDOC CRM – an Ontological Approach to Semantic Interoperability of metadata. AI Magazine, 24
239. FRBR. Functional Requirements for Bibliographic Records – Final Report (1997) Frankfurt am Main, Germany, International Federation of Library Associations and Institutions (IFLA)
240. Doerr M, Leboeuf P (2006) FRBRoo Introduction. http://cidoc.ics.forth.gr/frbr_inro.html
241. CYCLOPS prototype http://www.utc.fr/caspar/wiki/pmwiki.php?n=Main.Proto
242. Garrett J, Waters D (eds) (1996). Preserving Digital Information, Report of the Task Force on Archiving of Digital Information commissioned by The Commission on Preservation and Access and The Research Libraries Group. Available from http://www.ifla.org/documents/libraries/net/tfadi-fr.pdf
243. National Science Foundation Cyberinfrastructure Council (NSF, 2007), Cyberinfrastructure Vision for 21st Century Discovery. Retrieved from http://www.nsf.gov/pubs/2007/nsf0728/nsf0728.pdf
244. TRAC (2007), Trustworthy Repositories Audit & Certification: Criteria and Checklist. Available from http://www.crl.edu/PDF/trac.pdf
245. RLG-OCLC (2002) Report on Trusted Digital Repositories: Attributes and Responsibilities. Available from http://www.oclc.org/programs/ourwork/past/trustedrep/repositories.pdf
246. nestor Working Group Trusted Repositories – Certification, (2006), Catalogue of Criteria for Trusted Digital Repositories. English version retrieved from http://edoc.hu-berlin.de/series/nestor-materialien/8en/PDF/8en.pdf
247. CRL, (2007) Retrieved from http://www.crl.edu/content.asp?l1=13&l2=58&l3=162&l4=92
248. Giaretta D (2008) Comparison of OAIS and the Chicago Meeting 10 points. Available from http://wiki.digitalrepositoryauditandcertification.org/bin/view/Main/ComparisonOaisAndChicago10Points
249. Ross S., Bütikofer N, McHugh A (2006), DCC Comments on RLG/NARA Audit and Certification Checklist. Available from http://wiki.digitalrepositoryauditandcertification.org/pub/Main/ReferenceInputDocuments/Ross_McHugh_Buetikofer_comments_RLGNARA_AUDIT_ver2.pdf
250. Dale R (2007) Mapping of Audit & Certification Criteria for CRL Meeting (15-16 January 2007). Available from http://wiki.digitalrepositoryauditandcertification.org/pub/Main/ReferenceInputDocuments/TRAC-Nestor-DCC-criteria_mapping.doc
251. Audit and Certification of Trustworthy Digital Repositories – review copy. Available from http://public.ccsds.org/sites/cwe/rids/Lists/CCSDS%206520R1/Attachments/652x0r1.pdf. Final version should be available free from the CCSDS site http://www.ccsds.org
252. Requirements for bodies providing audit and certification of trustworthy digital repositories http://wiki.digitalrepositoryauditandcertification.org or from the CCSDS web site http://www.ccsds.org
253. ISO 9000:2005, Quality management systems – Fundamentals and vocabulary
254. ISO 19011:2002, Guidelines for quality and/or environmental management systems auditing1)
255. ISO/IEC 17021:2006, Conformity assessment – Requirements for bodies providing audit and certification of management systems
256. ISO/IEC 17000:2004, Conformity assessment – Vocabulary and general principles
257. Unified Modelling Language (UML) http://www.uml.org/
258. Unified Digital Format Registry (UDFR) http://www.udfr.org/
259. Presidential Electronic Records Project Operational System (PERPOS) http://perpos.gtri.gatech.edu/

260. FILE command http://darwinsys.com/file/
261. DFDL – being developed by the Data Format Description Language WG (DFDL-WG) – web site http://forge.gridforum.org/projects/dfdl-wg
262. Fortran see http://en.wikipedia.org/wiki/Fortran (accessed 2010-01-01)
263. DFDL Working group http://forge.gridforum.org/projects/dfdl-wg
264. Mylopoulos J, Borgida A, Jarke M, Koubarakis M (1990): Telos: Representing Knowledge about Information Systems, ACM Transactions on Information Systems, 8(4)
265. Cost Estimation Models in Software Engineering http://en.wikipedia.org/wiki/Estimation_in_software_engineering
266. On provenance in the eScience/grid-environment http://www.sigmod.org/sigmod/record/issues/0509/p31-special-sw-section-5.pdf
267. On provenance in OAI-PMH http://www.openarchives.org/OAI/2.0/guidelines-provenance.htm
268. On provenance OAI-ORE (referred to as ore:lineage) http://www.openarchives.org/ore/meetings/Soton/ore_beyond_basics.pdf (general) and http://www.openarchives.org/ore/1.0/vocabulary (definition)
269. Named Graphs, Provenance and Trust (Caroll et al.) http://www4.wiwiss.fu-berlin.de/bizer/SWTSGuide/carroll-ISWC2004.pdf
270. W3C: On provenance in RDF http://www.w3.org/2001/12/attributions/
271. Open Provenance Model http://eprints.ecs.soton.ac.uk/14979/1/opm.pdf
272. Investigating the Significant Properties of Electronic Content over time (InSPECT) http://www.significantproperties.org.uk/
273. The InterPARES project, http://www.interpares.org/
274. CASPAR Access Model, http://www.casparpreserves.eu/Members/cclrc/Deliverables/report-on-oais-access-model/at_download/file especially section 2.
275. CASPAR Conceptual Model, http://www.casparpreserves.eu/Members/cclrc/Deliverables/caspar-conceptual-model-phase-1-1/at_download/file
276. Giaretta D (2007) The CASPAR Approach to Digital Preservation, The International Journal of Digital Curation 1(2). Available from http://www.ijdc.net/index.php/ijdc/article/viewFile/29/18
277. CASPAR – Cultural, Artistic and Scientific knowledge for Preservation, Access and Retrieval. See http://www.casparpreserves.eu
278. Open Archival Information System (OAIS) – Reference Model, ISO 14721:2003, (2003). Available from http://public.ccsds.org/publications/archive/650x0b1.pdf or later version
279. Report on Roadmapping of Large Research Infrastructures (2008) OECD International Scientific Co-operation (Global Science Forum). Available from http://www.oecd.org/dataoecd/49/36/41929340.pdf
280. Understanding Infrastructure: Dynamics, Tensions and Design (2006) Available from http://www.si.umich.edu/~pne/PDF/ui.pdf
281. PADI web site with collection of information about Authenticity http://www.nla.gov.au/padi/topics/4.html
282. Tzitzikas Y (2007) Dependency Management for the Preservation of Digital Information. Presented at 18th International Conference on Database and Expert Systems Applications, DEXA'2007, Regensburg, Germany, September 2007. Available from http://www.ics.forth.gr/~tzitzik/publications/Tzitzikas_2007_DEXA.pdf
283. CASPAR D1101: Review of State of the Art (CASPAR-D1101-TN-0101-1_0). Available from www.casparpreserves.eu/Members/cclrc/Deliverables/review-of-state-of-the-art-1/at_download/file
284. DIFF format http://en.wikipedia.org/wiki/Diff
285. Dean M, Connolly D, van Harmelen F, Hendler J, Horrocks I, McGuinness DL, Patel-Schneider PF, Stein LA (2002) OWL Web Ontology Language 1.0 Reference. Available from http://www.w3c.org/TR/owl-ref

286. Tzitzikas Y, Marketakis Y (2010) Automating the Ingestion and Transformation of Embedded Metadata. ERCIM News 2010(80).
287. Patel M, Ball A (2008) Challenges and Issues Relating to the User of Representation Information for the Digital Curation of Crystallography and Engineering Data. In: International Journal of Digital Curation, Vol. 3 No. 1, pages. 76–88. Available from www.ijdc.net/index.php/ijdc/article/download/64/43
288. Alliance for Permanent Access to the Records of Science http://www.alliancepermanentaccess.org

Contributors

The following table provides details of some, although not all, of the contributors to this book.

	**Dr David Giaretta** the editor and main author of the book, received his MA, MSc and DPhil from Oxford University. He has had extensive experience in planning, developing and running scientific archives and providing and managing a variety of services to large numbers of users. In 2003 he was awarded an MBE for services to Space Science. As chair of CCSDS Panel 2 he made fundamental contributions to the OAIS Reference Model (ISO 14721) and continues to contribute to developing the follow on standards and updates to OAIS. He has been Associate Director for Development in the DCC; he also led the CASPAR project which addressed fundamental issues of digital preservation. In addition he led the PARSE.Insight EU project. He also chairs the CCSDS Repository Audit and Certification Working Group which is developing the standards on which the ISO audit and certification of digital repositories will be based. He currently splits his time between working on European projects at STFC and as the Director of the Alliance for Permanent Access to the Records of Science.

Mr **Sergio Albani** received a Masters in "Journalism and Scientific & Institutional Communication" from the University of Ferrara (Italy) in 2005. He then worked in industry as System and Software Engineer for the processing of EO data from 2006 to 2009. He was employed at ESA as Project Manager of the CASPAR project at ESRIN. He currently contributes to several European initiatives on long term preservation, discovery, access and exploitation of Earth Science data. He has published several papers in international conferences.

Pasquale Andriani has a Bachelor degree in Computer Science from the U. of Tor Vergata (Rome) in 2005. He then joined Engineering. His research interests include development process, distributed systems, web development, SOA, REST, Internet of Things. In CASPAR, he was the responsible for the development of the Preservation Orchestration Manager. He was also involved in leading the development framework activities.

Jerome Barthelemy is a musician, having received degrees from the Conservatoire National Supérieur de Musique de Paris. For more than 20 years, he has been active in the sector of software engineering for dissemination of culture, and particularly music. He joined Ircam in 2000 where he manages several European and National research projects. He is currently head of the On-line Services team in Ircam.

Luigi Briguglio received a degree in Electronic Engineering at University of Padua in 1996. In 2001 he joined Engineering, where he is a Project Manager at the Engineering R&D Laboratory. He is involved as technical expert in IST European R&D Projects, providing his experience in software architecture and development processes. He is a tutor of degree theses and stage two. Recent research activities include: leader of the architecture and integration in the CASPAR Project; Technical Director in the BeAware Project.

	**Vassilis Christophides** has a DEA in CS from the U. PARIS VI and Ph.D. from the Conservatoire National des Arts et Metiers of Paris. He is an Assoc. Professor at the Dept. of CS, U. of Crete, and researcher at the Information Systems and Software Technology Laboratory of FORTH-ICS. His main research interests include Semantic Web and Peer-to-Peer information management systems, semi-structured and XML/RDF data models and query languages as well as description and composition languages for e-services. He has published over 80 articles in international conferences and journals
	**Esther Conway** is a technical analyst working on digital preservation projects at STFC. Esther trained in Physics at Imperial College London after which she worked as a professional librarian specializing in scientific information. She has a Masters in Information Systems and Technology from City University. Esther worked for several years in the area of commercial publishing as a Solutions Consultant for Thomson Learning Digital Archives. For the last 4 years she has played a major role in the CASPAR and DCC projects, working with repositories in STFC, analysing their preservation requirements and strategies.
	**Alessio D'Innocenti** is a software analyst/programmer. From 2001 he works for ACS (Advanced Computer Systems S.p.A., Rome) as computer adviser, taking part in several Java/J2EE projects concerning EO (Earth Observation) and CASPAR
	**Matt Dunckley** is an Information Systems Developer, holding a BEng degree in Electronic Engineering and Computer Science from Aston University UK. He worked on the CASPAR project and the UK Digital Curation Centre at STFC. He now works in the private sector.

Marco Fulcoli is an astrophysicist. He designed a calibration system for the COBE ref. Black Body optimized for the frequencies of CMBR. Having designed the GridEngine system to optimize resolution techniques for jobs on distributed systems, he now focuses on multi-platform and distributed systems (operating systems, distributed and parallel computing techniques) and Cluster of computers. He also has experience in the processing of satellite data. In CASPAR he was involved in the development of the ESA testbed and designed the virtualization SW tool.

Luigi Fusco has worked in ESA since 1974 in the Earth Observation (EO) system and application domain. He is involved in the planning and management of projects dealing with different aspects of EO payload data systems, EO applications and related innovation technologies. He now leads the ESA participation in the development and use of GRID, Open GIS, emerging Web-based and e-collaboration technologies for EO and environmental applications throughout ESA, EC and Italian (Lazio Region) funded projects. He is the coordinator of the GRID-based Research Infrastructure Project GENESI-DR (Ground European Network for Earth Science Interoperations – Digital Repositories).

John Garrett is a Principal Analyst in the NASA/Science Office of Standards and Technology at NSSDC. He holds a B.Sc. in Electrical Eng. from the U of Missouri-Rolla, a B.Sc. in Technology and Management from the U of Maryland and an M.Sc. in Comp. Sci. from Johns Hopkins Univ. He has extensive experience of standards and applications programming. He helped to develop the OAIS Reference Model (ISO 14721) and is an active participant in the CCSDS RAC Group. He chairs the CCSDS Data Archives Ingest Working Group, which works on additional international archiving and format standards.

Yann Geslin is currently a Research Project Manager at INA. More recently he has worked on sound description, representations and information retrieval researches as well as long term preservation of artistic works in projects including GAMELAN, CASPAR, Mustica and Écrins. He studied classical music at the French "Conservatoire National Supérieur de Musique de Paris", where he has taught "New Technologies applied to Composition Cursus" since 1987, as an associated professor. He has written scientific and dictionary articles and played and composed computer and electroacoustic music.

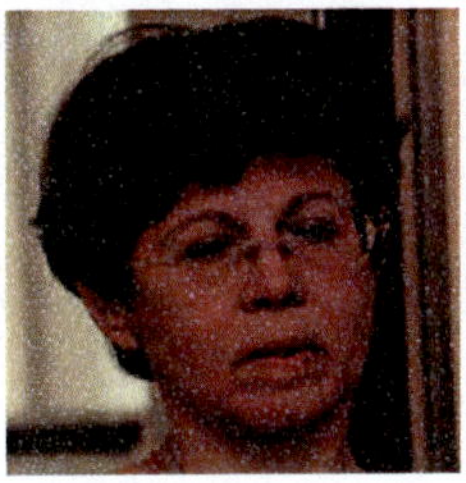	**Maria Guercio** has been a full professor in archival science and ERM at the U of Urbino since 2000. She works with the State Authority to define the Italian legislation for ERMS. She has worked in European projects including ERPANET (as co-director), DELOS and CASPAR. She is member of the European working group for defining a master profile for digital curation and director of the Italian team of the InterPARES project. Since 2002, she has been the director of the journal Archivi & Computer. She has chaired Masters in archival sectors for the University and for Italian Scuola superiore della pubblica amministrazione where now she is responsible of all the education and advanced training programmes for digital curation. She has published many articles, a manual on archival science (as co-author with Paola Carucci) and a manual on electronic records.
	**Ealan A. Henis** received a Ph.D. in CS at the Weizmann Institute of Science, Israel in 1991. After a postdoc at U of Pennsylvania, Ealan joined AT&T's Bell Labs in Murray Hill (1993) where he worked on mapping natural language to robotic manipulatory actions. He joined the IBM research labs, Haifa, in 1997, where his work included compiler and post-link code optimization, object storage and system/service performance management. He managed the Storage Management group in IBM Haifa Research, and he is now focusing on long term digital preservation.
	**Mario Hernandez** is responsible for the UNESCO space partnerships initiative on the use of space technologies to support World Heritage sites. He was in charge of the cultural heritage testbed work in CASPAR.
	**Michal Máša** graduated with his PhD in Computer Science at Czech Technical University in Prague in 2007. He is currently researching the area of new media art preservation with special focus on multimedia performances based on motion tracking devices and interactive 3D projections. Over the past several years, he has been working with Polhemus electromagnetic motion capture systems in CIANT – International Centre for Art and New Technologies (http://www.ciant.cz). He has published several papers at various international conferences including Eurographics.

	**Brian McIlwrath** has a degree in Physics and has undertaken research in Radio Astronomy at Jodrell Bank. He worked in the Digital Curation Centre from 2004 –with a technical and tools perspective. He implemented a practical Registry Repository of Representation Information based on concepts from the DCC and CASPAR.
	**Carlo Meghini** played a leading role in CASPAR. As a researcher, he has been active in the field of knowledge modelling and information discovery for more than 2 decades. He is the author of the Model of Multimedia Information Retrieval entry of the Encyclopedia of Database Systems, co-author of the DELOS Reference Model on Digital Libraries and has authored more than 50 papers in major journals and conferences in the information system area. He has contributed to many European initiatives in the area of digital libraries including DELOS, BRICKS and more recently Europeana.
	**Giovanni Michetti** is professor of Archival science at the U of Rome "La Sapienza" and visiting professor at the U of British Columbia. His work is focused on digital archives, recordkeeping systems, and applications of new technologies to archives. He worked on InterPARES3 and CASPAR. President of SC DIAM/SC11 "Archives & Records Management" of UNI and vice-president of TC DIAM focused on documentation and information, he is the Italian representative in WGs of ISO TC46/SC11. He is author of articles for Italian reviews, co-author of a manual on municipal archives.
	**Dalit Naor** holds M.S. and Ph.D. degrees from the University of California Davis, and a B.S. degree from the Technion, Israel Inst. of Technology, all in CS. She works at the IBM Haifa Research Lab as a manager of the Storage Systems group. She works on developing advanced functions for storage systems, with a focus on cloud storage and long term digital preservation. She contributed to the object storage T10 OSD standard, a new object-based storage interface and is a co-author of the IEEE 1619 standard for "Cryptographic Protection of Data on Block-Oriented Storage Devices".

	**Dr. Kia Ng** is director of the ICSRM at the U of Leeds. He has worked in a range of large research projects, including i-Maestro (Coordinator), CASPAR, and AXMEDIS (Principle Investigator). Kia has more than 150 publications and presented talks in over 30 countries. He has appeared on TV and radio and has been featured in the New York Times, Guardian, Financial Times, and others. Kia is a chartered scientist, a fellow of the Royal Society of Arts and a fellow of the Institute of Directors. Web: www.kcng.org
	**Dr Claudio Prandoni** worked as Project Manager at Metaware. He has a Masters in Applied Mathematics and had been involved in several projects of the European Commission where he managed and developed trusted web applications based on smart card and XML technologies. His skills include security, DRM and IPR protection, database management, object oriented programming and web services development. He was responsible for the Security and Digital Rights Management aspects for CASPAR.
	**Simona Rabinovici-Cohen** holds B.Sc. and M.Sc. degrees in CS, both from the Technion, Israel Institute of Technology. Since 1993, she has been a Research Staff Member at the IBM Haifa Research Laboratory. She worked on projects in the area of information integration and knowledge management systems, including data integration for performance management, integrated medical records, de-identification, and biomedical information integration. Currently, she focuses on technology to support long-term digital preservation and co-chairs the SNIA Long Term Retention (LTR) technical working group.
	**Stephen Rankin** has been working in the area of scientific software development and digital preservation for a number of years and currently works on the DCC and CASPAR projects as a data research scientist and software developer. His particular interests include the long-term archiving and reuse of scientific data. Prior to this Stephen studied for a Ph.D. in Physics at Manchester University (UK).

	**Louis Reich** received a B.S degree in CS from MIT in 1971 and has over 35 years of experience in systems software engineering. For the last 23 years Mr. Reich has worked with Goddard Space Flight Center in his role as a CSC Senior Consulting Engineer. He is a leader in emerging digital information preservation technologies and co-authored the OAIS RM. He is chair of the Information Packaging and Registries WG in CCSDS and the Principal Systems Engineer in a NARA sponsored NASA research project. He was the co-chair of the GML and Cataloging Working Groups of the OpenGIS Consortium. He acted the lead of the CASPAR External Review Committee.
	**Petra Reshef** is a Research Staff Member at the IBM Haifa Research Laboratory. She holds a B.S. degree in computer science from the University of Haifa. Her work has focused on storage and network technologies: SCSI, Internet SCSI (iSCSI), Fibre Channel Protocol, and OSD. Since 2006, she has been working on technology to support long-term digital preservation, developing a prototype for the storage component within a preservation system.
	**Shahar Ronen** is a research staff member at IBM Research Haifa. Since joining IBM in 2006, he is focusing on storage technologies, including long-term digital preservation and storage cloud solutions. Shahar holds a B.Sc. degree in computer science from the University of Haifa and is now concluding his M.A. studies in ancient history.
	**Don Sawyer** retired from NASA in 2008 after 20 years of service that included the establishment of the NASA/Science Office of Standards and Technology at the NSSDC, and interim Head of the NSSDC. He chaired the Archive Ingest Working Group within the CCSDS, a co-editor of OAIS, and an active participant in the development of the related Audit and Certification work. He is now a consultant under VIE, Inc. and continues to do research work on standards use and application – including development of the CCSDS/ISO "Producer-Archive Interface Specification" and the recent update of the OAIS reference model.

Yannis Tzitzikas is Assistant Professor in the CS at U of Crete (Greece) and Associate Researcher in Information Systems Lab at FORTH-ICS. His research interests fall in the intersection of: Information Systems, Information Indexing and Retrieval, Conceptual Modelling, Knowledge Representation and Reasoning, and Collaborative Distributed Applications. His current research revolves around faceted "metadata" and semantics, the P2P paradigm and flexible interaction schemes for information bases. He has published more than 40 papers in refereed international conferences and journals, and has received two best paper awards (at CIA'2003 and ISWC'07).

We would also like to thank

- colleagues at STFC: David Hooper, Sam Pepler, Matthew Wild, Steve Crothers, Chris Davis, Rita Blake, Ruth Bamford, Simon Lambert and Juan Bicarregui.
- Roberto Scopigno and Marco Callieri from CNR-ISTI Visual Computing Lab for their support with the UNESCO testbed.
- the entire RAC Working Group who deserve credit for the vision and effort which they are putting into the work on Audit and Certification.

Part of the research presented here has also been supported in part by the European Commission under Contracts

- IST-2006-033572 CASPAR (www.casparpreserves.eu)
- FP7-2007-223758 PARSE.Insight (www.parse-insight.eu)
- IST-026883 I-MAESTRO (www.i-maestro.org),

and we need to express gratitude to all these projects' partners and participants, for their interest, contributions and collaboration.

Index